See the Difference with LearningCurve!

LearningCurve
macmillan learning

learningcurveworks.com

LearningCurve is a winning solution for everyone: students come to class better prepared and instructors have more flexibility to go beyond the basic facts and concepts in class. LearningCurve's game-like quizzes are book-specific and link back to the textbook in LaunchPad so that students can brush up on the reading when they get stumped by a question. The reporting features help instructors track overall class trends and spot topics that are giving students trouble so that they can adjust lectures and class activities.

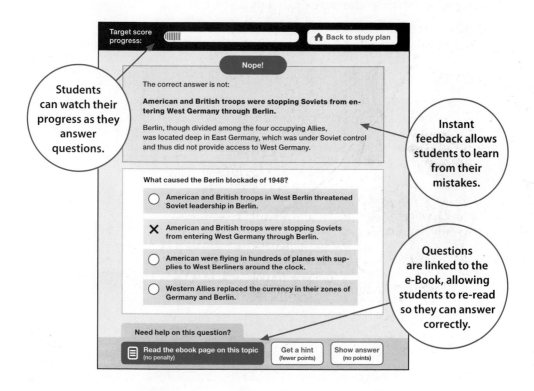

LearningCurve is easy to assign, easy to customize, and easy to complete. See the difference LearningCurve makes in teaching and learning history.

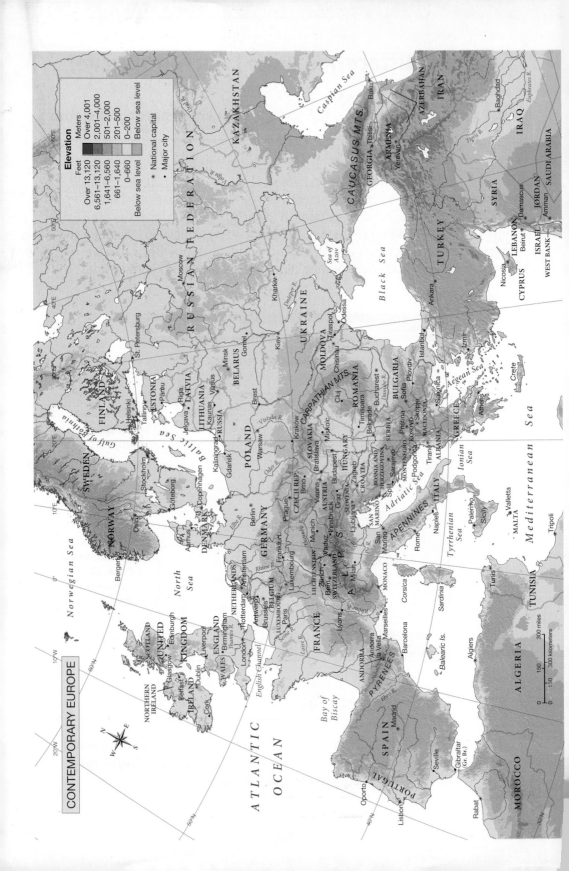

VALUE EDITION

The Making of the West

PEOPLES AND CULTURES

Fifth Edition

Volume II: Since 1500

Lynn Hunt
University of California, Los Angeles

Thomas R. Martin
College of the Holy Cross

Barbara H. Rosenwein
Loyola University Chicago

Bonnie G. Smith
Rutgers University

 bedford/st.martin's
Macmillan Learning

Boston | New York

FOR BEDFORD/ST. MARTIN'S

Vice President, Editorial, Macmillan Learning Humanities: Edwin Hill
Publisher for History: Michael Rosenberg
Acquiring Editor for History: Laura Arcari
Director of Development for History: Jane Knetzger
Developmental Editor: Melanie McFayden
Production Editor: Louis C. Bruno Jr.
Publishing Services Manager: Andrea Cava
Production Manager, Humanities: Joe Ford
History Marketing Manager: Melissa Famiglietti
Project Management: Jouve
Cartography: Mapping Specialists, Limited
Photo Researcher: Bruce Carson
Permissions Manager: Kalina Ingham
Senior Art Director: Anna Palchik
Text Design: Jonathon Nix
Cover Design: William Boardman
Cover Art: Arrival of a Seaplane in Ulyanovsk in 1927 (oil on canvas), Guryev, Ivan Petrovich
    (1875–1943) / Regional Art Museum, Simbirsk / Bridgeman Images
Composition: Jouve
Printing and Binding: RR Donnelley and Sons

Manufactured in the United States of America.

1   0   9   8   7   6
f   e   d   c   b   a

For information, write: Bedford/St. Martin's, 75 Arlington Street, Boston, MA 02116
    (617-399-4000)

ISBN 978-1-319-06546-1 (Combined Edition)
ISBN 978-1-319-06559-1 (Volume I)
ISBN 978-1-319-06561-4 (Loose-leaf Edition, Volume I)
ISBN 978-1-319-06562-1 (Volume II)
ISBN 978-1-319-06564-5 (Loose-leaf Edition, Volume II)

ACKNOWLEDGMENTS

Preface
Why This Book This Way

We are pleased to introduce the first Value Edition of our popular textbook, *The Making of the West: Peoples and Cultures*. The Value Edition provides our signature synthetic approach to history, linking the history of the West to wider developments in the world, in a two-color, trade-sized format at a low price. Featuring the full narrative of the parent text and select images, maps, and pedagogical tools, the Value Edition continues to incorporate the latest and best scholarship in the field in an accessible, student-friendly manner. As an additional value, all of the color as well as an extensive primary source and feature program are available to students in LaunchPad, Macmillan's premier learning platform.

A Book for the Digital Age

We know that many students today are on a budget and that instructors want greater flexibility and more digital options in their choice of course materials. Accordingly, *The Making of the West* is offered in **LaunchPad**, an intuitive, interactive e-book and course space. Free when packaged with the print text or available at a low price when used as a stand alone, LaunchPad grants students and teachers access to a wealth of online tools and resources built specifically for our text to enhance reading comprehension and promote in-depth study. Developed with extensive feedback from history instructors and students, **LaunchPad** includes the complete narrative of the print book, the **companion reader** *Sources of the Making of the West*, by Katherine J. Lualdi, **LearningCurve** adaptive quizzing, and a **full suite of skill-building features**.

The adaptive learning tool known as **LearningCurve** is designed to get students to read before they come to class. With LearningCurve, students move through questions based on the narrative text at their own pace and accumulate points as they go in a game-like fashion. Feedback for incorrect responses explains why the answer is incorrect and directs students back to the text to review. The end result is a better understanding of the key elements of the text.

The LaunchPad e-book features five unique skill-building features. Four of these features appear in every chapter in LaunchPad. They extend the narrative by revealing the process of interpretation, providing a solid introduction to historical argument and critical thinking, and capturing the excitement of historical investigation.

- **Primary Sources** — at least two per chapter — give students a more direct experience of the past through original voices. Whether it is Frederick Barbaraossa replying to the Romans when they offer him the emperor's crown, Marie de Sévigne's description of the French court, or an ordinary person's account of the outbreak of the Russian Revolution, primary documents offer a window into the thoughts and actions of the past. Each document is accompanied by a short, auto-graded multiple-choice quiz.

- **Contrasting Views** compares two or more often conflicting primary sources focused on a central event, person, or development—such as Roman attitudes toward Cleopatra, the Mongols, the consumer revolution of the eighteenth century, and decolonization in Africa—enabling students to understand history from a variety of contemporaneous perspectives. Each feature contains analytical questions along with an auto-graded multiple-choice quiz.
- **Seeing History** guides students through the process of reading images as historical evidence. Each one provides either a single image or paired images for comparison and contrast, with background information, and questions that encourage visual analysis. It also has an auto-graded multiple-choice quiz.
- **Taking Measure** introduces students to quantitative analysis in every chapter. Each highlights a chart, table, graph, or map of historical statistics that illuminates an important political, social, or cultural development. Topics include the distances covered by Alexander the Great's army, the expansion of the printing press to 1500, and wartime production of the major powers during the Second World War. Each comes with a question for analysis and an auto-graded multiple-choice quiz.
- **Terms of History** appears in 11 of the chapters and looks not only at the origin of a term—such as *civilization, renaissance, progress,* and *globalization*—but also at the changing meaning of the term over time, which further underscores historical skill building. The feature comes with an auto-graded multiple-choice quiz.

About *The Making of the West*

Even with all the exciting digital changes, our primary goal remains the same: to demonstrate that the history of the West is the story of an ongoing process, not a finished result with one fixed meaning. No one Western people or culture has existed from the beginning until now. Instead, the history of the West includes many different peoples and cultures. To convey these ideas, we have written a sustained story of the West's development in a broad, global context that reveals the cross-cultural interactions fundamental to the shaping of Western politics, societies, cultures, and economies. Indeed, the first chapter opens with a section on the origins and contested meaning of the term *Western civilization*.

Chronological Framework

We know from our own teaching that introductory students need a solid chronological framework, one with enough familiar benchmarks to make the material easy to grasp. Each chapter is organized around the main events, people, and themes of a period in which the West significantly changed; thus, students learn about political and military events and social and cultural developments as they unfolded. This **chronological integration** also makes it possible for students to see the **interconnections among varieties of historical experience**—between politics and cultures, between public events and private experiences, between wars and diplomacy and everyday life. For teachers, our chronological approach ensures a balanced account and provides the opportunity to present themes within their greater context. But perhaps best of all, this approach provides a text that reveals history as a process that is constantly alive, subject to pressures, and able to surprise us.

An Expanded Vision of the West

Cultural borrowing between the peoples of Europe and their neighbors has characterized Western civilization from the beginning. Thus, we have insisted on an **expanded vision of the West** that includes the United States and fully incorporates Scandinavia, eastern Europe, and the Ottoman Empire. Now this vision encompasses **an even wider global context** than before, as Latin America, Africa, China, Japan, and India also come into the story. We have been able to offer sustained treatment of crucial topics such as Islam and to provide a more thorough examination of globalization than any competing text. Study of Western history provides essential background to today's events, from debates over immigration to conflicts in the Middle East. Instructors have found this synthesis essential for helping students understand the West amid today's globalization.

The Latest Scholarship

As always, we have also incorporated the latest scholarly findings throughout the book so that students and instructors alike have a text on which they can confidently rely. In this edition, we have included **new and updated** discussions of topics such as fresh archaeological evidence for the possible role of religion in stimulating the major changes of the Neolithic Revolution; the dating of the Great Sphinx in Egypt, the scholarly debate that could radically change our ideas of the earliest Egyptian history; the newest thinking on the origins of Islam; the crucial issues in the Investiture Conflict between pope and emperor; the impact of the Great Famine of the fourteenth century; the slave trade, especially its continuation into the nineteenth century; and the ways in which scholars are considering recent events within the context of the new digital world.

Study Aids to Support Active Reading and Learning

We know from our own teaching that students need all the help they can get in absorbing and making sense of information, thinking analytically, and understanding that history itself is often debated and constantly revised. With these goals in mind, we retained the class-tested learning and teaching aids that worked well in the previous editions, but we have also done more to help students distill the central story of each age.

Focused Reading

Each chapter begins with a vivid **anecdote** that draws readers into the atmosphere of the period and introduces the chapter's main themes. The **Chapter Focus** poses an overarching question at the start of the narrative to help guide students' reading. Strategically placed at the end of each major section, a **Review Question** helps students assimilate core points in digestible increments. **Key Terms** and names that appear in boldface in the text have been updated to concentrate on likely test items; these terms are defined in the **Glossary of Key Terms and People** at the end of the book.

Reviewing the Chapter

At the end of each chapter, the **Conclusion** further reinforces the central developments covered in the chapter. The **Chapter Review** begins by asking students to revisit the key terms, identifying each and explaining its significance. **Review Questions** are also presented again so that students can revisit the chapter's core points. **Making Connections** questions then follow and prompt students to think across the sections of a given chapter. A chronology of **Important Events** enables students to see the sequence and overlap of important events in a given period.

Geographic Literacy

The map program of *The Making of the West* has been praised by reviewers for its comprehensiveness. In each chapter, we offer two types of maps: **full-size maps** show major developments, and *Mapping the West* **summary maps** at the end of each chapter provide a snapshot of the West at the close of a transformative period and help students visualize the West's changing contours over time. All of these maps—plus up to four "spot" maps per chapter that are positioned within the discussion right where students need them—appear in full color in LaunchPad.

Images and Illustrations

Over **100 images and illustrations** were carefully chosen to reflect this edition's broad topical coverage and geographic inclusion, reinforce the text, and show the varieties of visual sources from which historians build their narratives and interpretations. All artifacts, illustrations, paintings, and photographs are contemporaneous with the chapter; there are no anachronistic illustrations. The captions for the maps and art help students learn how to read visuals, and we have frequently included specific questions or suggestions for comparisons that might be developed. In addition, all of the 240 full-color images from the parent text appear in LaunchPad.

Acknowledgments

In the vital process of revision, the authors have benefited from repeated critical readings by many talented scholars and teachers. Our sincere thanks go to the following instructors, whose comments on the fourth edition often challenged us to rethink or justify our interpretations and who always provided a check on accuracy down to the smallest detail:

Stephen Andrews, *Central New Mexico Community College*; David Bachrach, *University of New Hampshire*; Curtis Bostick, *Southern Utah University*; Fedja Buric, *Bellarmine University*; Marie Therese Champagne, *University of West Florida*; Sviatoslav Dmitriev, *Ball State University*; Gabrielle Everett, *Jefferson College*; William Grose, *Wytheville Community College*; Elizabeth Heath, *Baruch College-CUNY*; Kevin Herlihy,

University of Central Florida; Renzo Honores, *High Point University*; Chris Laney, *Berkshire Community College*; Christina Bosco Langert, *Suffolk Community College*; Elizabeth Lehfeldt, *Cleveland State University*; James Martin, *Campbell University*; Walter Miszczenko, *College of Western Idaho*; Yvonne Rivera, *Montgomery County Community College*; David Pizzo, *Murray State University*; Kevin Robbins, *Indiana University/ Purdue University*; James Robertson, *College of San Mateo*; Brian Rutishauser, *Fresno City College*; Charles Levine, *Mesa Community College*; Lisa Ossian, *Des Moines Area Community College*; Ruma Salhi, *Northern Virginia Community College*; Christopher Sleeper, *Mira Costa College*; Allison Stein, *Pellissippi State Community College*; Pamela Stewart, *Arizona State University*; Nancy Vavra, *University of Colorado at Boulder*; K. Steven Vincent, *North Carolina State University*; and Joanna Vitiello, *Rockhurst University*.

Many colleagues, friends, and family members have made contributions to this work. They know how grateful we are. We also wish to acknowledge and thank the publishing team at Bedford/St. Martin's who brought this new Value Edition to completion: editorial director Edwin Hill; publisher for history Michael Rosenberg; acquiring editor Laura Arcari; director of development for history Jane Knetzger; developmental editor Melanie McFadyen; history marketing manager Melissa Famiglietti; senior production editor Louis Bruno; art researcher Bruce Carson; and cover designer William Boardman.

Our students' questions and concerns have shaped much of this work, and we welcome all our readers' suggestions, queries, and criticisms. Please contact us at our respective institutions or via **history@macmillan.com**.

Versions and Supplements

Adopters of *The Making of the West: Peoples and Cultures* and their students have access to abundant print and digital resources and tools, the acclaimed Bedford Series in History and Culture volumes, and much more. The LaunchPad course space for *The Making of the West* provides access to the narrative as well as a wealth of primary sources and other features, along with assignment and assessment opportunities at the ready. Available in both LaunchPad and in print, the companion reader, *Sources of the Making of the West*, Fourth Edition, by Katharine J. Lualdi, provides additional options for working with written and visual sources. See below for more information, visit the book's catalog site at **macmillanlearning.com**, or contact your local Bedford/St. Martin's sales representative.

Get the Right Version for Your Class

To accommodate different course coverage and course budgets, *The Making of the West*, Value Edition, is available in several different formats, including loose-leaf versions and low-priced PDF e-books. And for the best value of all, package a new print book with LaunchPad at no additional charge to get the best each format offers—a print version for easy portability with a LaunchPad interactive e-book and course space with LearningCurve and loads of additional assignment and assessment options.

- **Combined Volume** (Chapters 1–29): available in paperback, loose-leaf, and e-book formats and in LaunchPad
- **Volume I: To 1750** (Chapters 1–17): available in paperback, loose-leaf, and e-book formats and in LaunchPad
- **Volume II: Since 1500** (Chapters 14–29): available in paperback, loose-leaf, and e-book formats and in LaunchPad

As noted below, any of these volumes can be packaged with additional titles for a discount. To get ISBNs for discount packages, visit **macmillanlearning.com** or contact your Bedford/St. Martin's representative.

◣ LaunchPad macmillan learning Assign LaunchPad—an Assessment-Ready Interactive e-book and Course Space.

Available for discount purchase on its own or for packaging with new books at no additional charge, LaunchPad is a breakthrough solution for today's courses. Intuitive and easy-to-use for students and instructors alike, LaunchPad is ready to use as is, and can be edited, customized with your own material, and assigned in seconds. *LaunchPad* for *The Making of the West* includes Bedford/St. Martin's high-quality content all in one place, including the full interactive e-book with all of the full-color maps and images of the fifth edition and the companion reader *Sources of The Making of the West*, by Katharine Lualdi, plus LearningCurve formative quizzing, guided reading activities designed to help students read actively for key concepts, additional primary sources, including auto-graded source-based questions to build skill development, chapter summative quizzes, and more.

Through a wealth of formative and summative assessments, including the adaptive learning program of LearningCurve (see the full description below), students gain confidence and get into their reading before class. In addition to LearningCurve, we are delighted to offer a full skill-building feature program to accompany the print book. Each chapter in LaunchPad has at least two primary source documents, a "Contrasting Views" feature that compares two or more primary sources, a "Seeing History" visual analysis of one or more images, and "Taking Measure" focuses on quantitative analysis. Each of these features is accompanied by analytical questions and auto-graded quizzes. These LaunchPad features do for skill development what LearningCurve does for content mastery and reading comprehension.

LaunchPad easily integrates with course management systems, and with fast ways to build assignments, rearrange chapters, and add new pages, sections, or links, it lets teachers build the courses they want to teach and hold students accountable. For more information, visit **launchpadworks.com** or to arrange a demo, contact us at **history@ macmillan.com**.

LearningCurve macmillan learning Assign LearningCurve So Your Students Come to Class Prepared

Students using LaunchPad receive access to LearningCurve for *The Making of the West*. Assigning LearningCurve in place of reading quizzes is easy for instructors, and the reporting features help instructors track overall class trends and spot topics that are giving students trouble so they can adjust their lectures and class activities. This online learning tool is popular with students because it was designed to help them rehearse content at their own pace in a nonthreatening, game-like environment. The feedback for wrong answers provides instructional coaching and sends students back to the book for review. Students answer as many questions as necessary to reach a target score, with repeated chances to revisit material they haven't mastered. When LearningCurve is assigned, students come to class better prepared.

Take Advantage of Instructor Resources

Bedford/St. Martin's has developed a rich array of teaching resources for this book and for this course. They range from lecture and presentation materials and assessment tools to course management options. Most can be found in LaunchPad or can be downloaded or ordered from the Instructor's Resources tab of the book's catalog site at **macmillanlearning.com**.

Bedford Coursepack for Blackboard, Canvas, D2L, or Moodle. We can help you integrate our rich content into your course management system. Registered instructors can download coursepacks that include our popular free resources and book-specific content for *The Making of the West*.

Instructor's Resource Manual. The instructor's manual offers both experienced and first-time instructors tools for presenting textbook material in engaging ways. It includes content learning objectives, annotated chapter outlines, and strategies for teaching with the textbook, plus suggestions on how to get the most out of LearningCurve, and a survival guide for first-time teaching assistants.

Online Test Bank. The test bank includes a mix of fresh, carefully crafted multiple-choice, short-answer, and essay questions for each chapter. All questions appear in easy-to-use test bank software that allows instructors to add, edit, re-sequence, and print questions and answers. Instructors can also export questions into a variety of course management systems.

The Bedford Lecture Kit: **Lecture Outlines, Maps, and Images.** Look good and save time with *The Bedford Lecture Kit*. These presentation materials include fully customizable multimedia presentations built around chapter outlines that are embedded with maps, figures, and images from the textbook and are supplemented by more detailed instructor notes on key points and concepts.

Print, Digital, and Custom Options for More Choice and Value

For information on free packages and discounts up to 50%, visit **macmillanlearning .com**, or contact your local Bedford/St. Martin's sales representative.

Sources of The Making of the West, **Fourth Edition.** This companion sourcebook provides written and visual sources to accompany each chapter of *The Making of the West*. Political, social, and cultural documents offer a variety of perspectives that complement the textbook and encourage students to make connections between narrative history and primary sources. To aid students in approaching and interpreting documents, each chapter contains an introduction, document headnotes, and questions for discussion. Available free when packaged with the print book and included in the LaunchPad e-book. Also available on its own as a downloadable PDF e-book.

Bedford Custom Tutorials for History. Designed to customize textbooks with resources relevant to individual courses, this collection of brief units—each 16 pages long and loaded with examples—guides students through basic skills such as using historical evidence effectively, working with primary sources, taking effective notes, avoiding plagiarism and citing sources, and more. Up to two tutorials can be added to a Bedford/St. Martin's history survey title at no additional charge, freeing you to spend your class time focusing on content and interpretation. For more information, visit **macmillanlearning.com/historytutorials.**

The Bedford Series in History and Culture. More than 100 titles in this highly praised series combine first-rate scholarship, historical narrative, and important primary documents for undergraduate courses. Each book is brief, inexpensive, and focused on a specific topic or period. Revisions of several best-selling titles, such as *The Black*

Death: A Brief History with Documents by John Aberth; *The Prince,* edited by William J. Connell; and *The French Revolution and Human Rights: A Brief History with Documents* by Lynn Hunt, are now available. For a complete list of titles, visit **macmillanlearning.com**. Package discounts are available.

Rand McNally Atlas of Western Civilization. This collection of almost seventy full-color maps illustrates the eras and civilizations in world history from the emergence of human societies to the present. Free when packaged.

Trade Books. Titles published by sister companies Hill and Wang; Farrar, Straus and Giroux; Henry Holt and Company; St. Martin's Press; Picador; and Palgrave Macmillan are available at a 50% discount when packaged with Bedford/St. Martin's textbooks. For more information, visit **macmillanhighered.com/tradeup**.

A Pocket Guide to Writing in History. This portable and affordable reference tool by Mary Lynn Rampolla provides reading, writing, and research advice useful to students in all history courses. Concise yet comprehensive advice on approaching typical history assignments, developing critical reading skills, writing effective history papers, conducting research, using and documenting sources, and avoiding plagiarism — enhanced with practical tips and examples throughout — have made this slim reference a best-seller. Available at a 50% discount when packaged with Bedford/St. Martin's textbooks.

A Student's Guide to History. This complete guide to success in any history course provides the practical help students need to be successful. In addition to introducing students to the nature of the discipline, author Jules Benjamin teaches a wide range of skills from preparing for exams to approaching common writing assignments, and explains the research and documentation process with plentiful examples. Available at a 50% discount when packaged with Bedford/St. Martin's textbooks.

Brief Contents

Contents

CHAPTER 14

Global Encounters and the Shock of the Reformation, 1492–1560   397

CHAPTER 15

Wars of Religion and the Clash of Worldviews, 1560–1648   426

CHAPTER 16

Absolutism, Constitutionalism, and the Search for Order, 1640–1700   457

CHAPTER 17

The Atlantic System and Its Consequences, 1700–1750   490

Maps

Figures

Authors' Note
The B.C.E./C.E. Dating System

When Were You Born? What year is it? We customarily answer questions like these with a number, such as "1991" or "2008." Our replies are usually automatic, taking for granted the numerous assumptions Westerners make about how dates indicate chronology. But to what do numbers such as 1991 and 2008 actually refer? In this book, the numbers used to specify dates follow a recent revision of the system most common in the Western secular world. This system reckons the dates of solar years by counting backward and forward from the traditional date of the birth of Jesus Christ, over two thousand years ago.

Using this method, numbers followed by the abbreviation B.C.E., standing for "before the common era" (or, as some would say, "before the Christian era"), indicate the number of years counting backward from the assumed date of the birth of Jesus Christ. B.C.E. therefore indicates the same chronology marked by the traditional abbreviation B.C. ("before Christ"). The larger the number preceding B.C.E. (or B.C.), the earlier in history is the year to which it refers. The date 431 B.C.E., for example, refers to a year 431 years before the birth of Jesus and, therefore, comes earlier in time than the dates 430 B.C.E., 429 B.C.E., and so on. The same calculation applies to numbering other time intervals calculated on the decimal system: those of ten years (a decade), of one hundred years (a century), and of one thousand years (a millennium). For example, the decade of the 440s B.C.E. (449 B.C.E. to 440 B.C.E.) is earlier than the decade of the 430s B.C.E. (439 B.C.E. to 430 B.C.E.). "Fifth century B.C.E." refers to the fifth period of 100 years reckoning backward from the birth of Jesus and covers the years 500 B.C.E. to 401 B.C.E. It is earlier in history than the fourth century B.C.E. (400 B.C.E. to 301 B.C.E.), which followed the fifth century B.C.E. Because this system has no year "zero," the first century B.C.E. covers the years 100 B.C.E. to 1 B.C.E. Dating millennia works similarly: the second millennium B.C.E. refers to the years 2000 B.C.E. to 1001 B.C.E., the third millennium to the years 3000 B.C.E. to 2001 B.C.E., and so on.

To indicate years counted forward from the traditional date of Jesus's birth, numbers are followed by the abbreviation C.E., standing for "of the common era" (or "of the Christian era"). C.E. therefore indicates the same chronology marked by the traditional abbreviation A.D., which stands for the Latin phrase *anno Domini* ("in the year of the Lord"). A.D. properly comes before the date being marked. The date A.D. 1492, for example, translates as "in the year of the Lord 1492," meaning 1492 years after the birth of Jesus. Under the B.C.E./C.E. system, this date would be written as 1492 C.E. For dating centuries, the term "first century C.E." refers to the period from 1 C.E. to 100 C.E. (which is the same period as A.D. 1 to A.D. 100). For dates C.E, the smaller the number, the earlier the date in history. The fourth century C.E. (301 C.E. to 400 C.E.) comes before the fifth century C.E. (401 C.E. to 500 C.E.). The year 312 C.E. is a date in the early fourth century C.E., while 395 C.E. is a date late in the same century. When numbers are given without either B.C.E. or C.E., they are presumed to be dates C.E. For example, the term *eighteenth century* with no abbreviation accompanying it refers to the years 1701 C.E. to 1800 C.E.

No standard system of numbering years, such as B.C.E./C.E., existed in antiquity. Different people in different places identified years with varying names and numbers. Consequently, it was difficult to match up the years in any particular local system with those in a different system. Each city of ancient Greece, for example, had its own method for keeping track of the years. The ancient Greek historian Thucydides, therefore, faced a problem in presenting a chronology for the famous Peloponnesian War between Athens and Sparta, which began (by our reckoning) in 431 B.C.E. To try to explain to as many of his readers as possible the date the war had begun, he described its first year by three different local systems: "the year when Chrysis was in the forty-eighth year of her priesthood at Argos, and Aenesias was overseer at Sparta, and Pythodorus was magistrate at Athens."

A Catholic monk named Dionysius, who lived in Rome in the sixth century C.E., invented the system of reckoning dates forward from the birth of Jesus. Calling himself *Exiguus* (Latin for "the little" or "the small") as a mark of humility, he placed Jesus's birth 754 years after the foundation of ancient Rome. Others then and now believe his date for Jesus's birth was in fact several years too late. Many scholars today calculate that Jesus was born in what would be 4 B.C.E. according to Dionysius's system, although a date a year or so earlier also seems possible.

Counting backward from the supposed date of Jesus's birth to indicate dates earlier than that event represented a natural complement to reckoning forward for dates after it. The English historian and theologian Bede in the early eighth century was the first to use both forward and backward reckoning from the birth of Jesus in a historical work, and this system gradually gained wider acceptance because it provided a basis for standardizing the many local calendars used in the Western Christian world. Nevertheless, B.C. and A.D. were not used regularly until the end of the eighteenth century. B.C.E. and C.E. became common in the late twentieth century.

The system of numbering years from the birth of Jesus is far from the only one in use today. The Jewish calendar of years, for example, counts forward from the date given to the creation of the world, which would be calculated as 3761 B.C.E. under the B.C.E./C.E. system. Under this system, years are designated A.M., an abbreviation of the Latin *anno mundi*, "in the year of the world." The Islamic calendar counts forward from the date of the Prophet Muhammad's flight from Mecca, called the *Hijra*, in what is the year 622 C.E. The abbreviation A.H. (standing for the Latin phrase *anno Hegirae*, "in the year of the Hijra") indicates dates calculated by this system. Anthropology commonly reckons distant dates as "before the present" (abbreviated B.P.).

History is often defined as the study of change over time; hence the importance of dates for the historian. But just as historians argue over which dates are most significant, they disagree over which dating system to follow. Their debate reveals perhaps the most enduring fact about history—its vitality.

14

Global Encounters and the Shock of the Reformation

1492–1560

CHAPTER FOCUS

How did the conquest of the New World and the Protestant Reformation transform European governments and societies in this era?

IN 1539 IN TLAXCALA, NEW SPAIN (present-day Mexico), Indians newly converted to Christianity performed a pageant organized by Catholic missionaries. It featured a combined Spanish and Indian army fighting to protect the pope, defeat the Muslims, and win control of the holy city of Jerusalem. In the play, after a miracle saves the Christian soldiers, the Muslims give up and convert to Christianity. Although it is hard to imagine what the Indians made of this celebration of places and people far away, the event reveals a great deal about the Europeans: the Catholic missionaries hoped that their success in converting Indians in the New World signaled God's favor for Catholicism the world over.

Led first by the Portuguese and then Spanish explorers, Europeans sailed into contact with peoples and cultures previously unknown to them. European voyagers subjugated native peoples, declared their control over vast new lands, and established a new system of slavery linking Africa and the New World. Millions of Indians died of diseases unknowingly imported by the Europeans. The discovery of new crops—corn, potatoes, tobacco, and cocoa—and of gold and silver mines brought new patterns of consumption, and new objects of conflict, to Europe. Historians now call this momentous spiral of changes in ecology, agriculture, and social patterns the Columbian exchange, after Christopher Columbus, who started the process.

While the Spanish were converting Indians in the New World, a different kind of challenge confronted the Catholic church in central and western Europe. Religious reformers attacked the leadership of the pope in Rome and formed competing groups of Protestants (so-called because they protested against some beliefs of the Catholic church). The movement began when the German Catholic monk Martin Luther criticized the sale of indulgences in 1517. Other reformers raised their voices, too, but did not agree with the Lutherans. Before long, religious division engulfed the German states and reached into Switzerland, France, and England. In response, Catholics undertook their own renewal, which strengthened the Catholic church. Catholic missionaries continued to dominate efforts to convert indigenous peoples for a century or more.

These two new factors—the development of overseas colonies and divisions between Catholics and Protestants within Europe—reshaped the long-standing rivalries between princes and determined the course of European history for several generations.

The Discovery of New Worlds

Portugal's and Spain's maritime explorations brought Europe to the attention of the rest of the world. Inspired by a crusading spirit against Islam and by riches to be won through trade in spices and gold, the Portuguese and Spanish sailed across the Atlantic, Indian, and Pacific Oceans. The English, French, and Dutch followed later in the sixteenth century, creating a new global exchange of people, crops, and diseases. As a result of these European expeditions, the people of the Americas for the first time confronted forces that threatened to destroy not only their culture but even their existence.

Portuguese Explorations

The first phase of European overseas expansion began in 1434 with Portuguese exploration of the West African coast. The Portuguese hoped to find a sea route to the spice-producing lands of South and Southeast Asia in order to bypass the Ottoman Turks, who controlled the traditional land routes between Europe and Asia. Prince Henry the Navigator of Portugal (1394–1460) personally financed many voyages with revenues from a noble crusading order. The first triumphs of the Portuguese attracted a host of Christian, Jewish, and even Arab sailors, astronomers, and cartographers to the service of Prince Henry and King John II (r. 1481–1495). They compiled better tide calendars and books of sailing directions for pilots that enabled sailors to venture farther into the oceans and reduced—though did not eliminate—the dangers of sea travel. Success in the voyages of exploration depended on the development in the late 1400s of the caravel, a 65-foot, easily maneuvered three-masted ship that used triangular lateen sails adapted from the Arabs. (The sails permitted a ship to tack against headwinds and therefore rely less on currents.)

Searching for gold and then slaves, the Portuguese gradually established forts down the West African coast. In 1487–1488, they reached the Cape of Good Hope at the tip of Africa; ten years later, Vasco da Gama led a Portuguese fleet around the cape and reached as far as Calicut, India, the center of the spice trade. His return to Lisbon with twelve pieces of Chinese porcelain for the Portuguese king set off two centuries of porcelain mania. Until the early eighteenth century, only the Chinese knew how to produce porcelain. Over the next two hundred years, Western merchants would import no fewer than seventy million pieces of porcelain, still known today as "china." By 1517, a chain of Portuguese forts dotted the Indian Ocean (Map 14.1). In 1519, Ferdinand Magellan, a Portuguese sailor in Spanish service, led the first expedition to circumnavigate the globe.

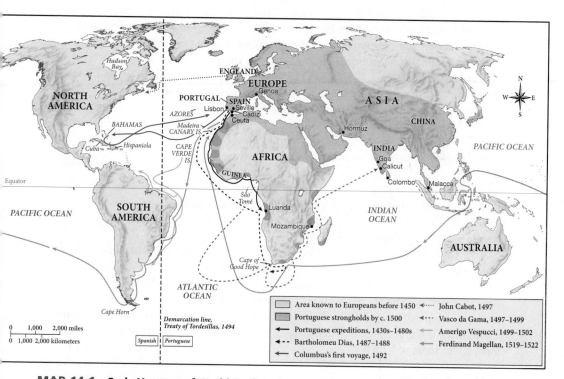

MAP 14.1 Early Voyages of World Exploration Over the course of the fifteenth and early sixteenth centuries, European shipping dominated the Atlantic Ocean after the pioneering voyages of the Portuguese, who also first sailed around the Cape of Good Hope to the Indian Ocean and Cape Horn to the Pacific. The search for spices and the need to circumnavigate the Ottoman Empire inspired these voyages.

The Voyages of Columbus

One of many sailors inspired by the Portuguese explorations, **Christopher Columbus** (1451–1506) opened an entirely new direction for discovery. Most likely born in Genoa of Italian parents, Columbus sailed the West African coast in Portuguese service between 1476 and 1485. Fifteenth-century Europeans already knew that the world was round. Columbus wanted to sail west to reach "the lands of the Great Khan" because he hoped to find a new route to the East's gold and spices. After the Portuguese refused to fund his plan, Columbus turned to the Spanish monarchs Isabella of Castile and Ferdinand of Aragon, who agreed to finance his venture.

On August 3, 1492, with ninety men on board two caravels and one larger merchant ship for carrying supplies, Columbus set sail westward. His contract stipulated that he would claim Castilian sovereignty over any new land and inhabitants, and share any profits with the crown. Reaching what is today the Bahamas on October 12, Columbus mistook the islands to be part of the East Indies, not far from Japan. As the Spaniards explored the Caribbean islands, they encountered communities of peaceful Indians, the Arawaks, who were awed by the Europeans' military technology, not to mention their appearance. Although many positive entries in the ship's log testified to Columbus's personal goodwill toward the Indians, the Europeans' objectives were clear: find gold, subjugate the Indians, and propagate Christianity. Excited by the prospect of easy riches, many flocked to join Columbus's second voyage. When Columbus departed the Spanish port of Cádiz in September 1493, he commanded a fleet of seventeen ships carrying some fifteen hundred men. Failing to find the imagined gold mines and spices, Columbus and his crew began capturing Caribs, enemies of the Arawaks, with the intention of bringing them back as slaves. The Spaniards exported enslaved Indians to Spain, and slave traders sold them in Seville. When the Spanish monarchs realized the vast potential for material gain from their new dominions, they asserted direct royal authority by sending officials and priests to the Americas, which were named after the Italian navigator Amerigo Vespucci, who led a voyage across the Atlantic in 1499 to 1502.

To head off looming conflicts between the Spanish and the Portuguese, Pope Alexander VI helped negotiate the Treaty of Tordesillas of 1494. It divided the Atlantic world between the two maritime powers, reserving for Portugal the West African coast and the route to India, and giving Spain the oceans and lands to the west (see Map 14.1, page 399). The agreement allowed Portugal to claim Brazil in 1500, when it was accidentally "discovered" by Pedro Alvares Cabral (1467–1520) on a voyage to India.

A New Era in Slavery

The European voyages of discovery initiated a new era in slavery. Slavery had existed since antiquity and flourished in many parts of the world. Some slaves were captured in war or by piracy; others—Africans—were sold by other Africans and Bedouin traders to Christian buyers; in western Asia, parents sold their children out of poverty into servitude; and many in the Balkans became slaves when their land was devastated by Ottoman invasions. Slaves could be Greek, Slav, European, African, or Turkish. Many served as domestics in European cities of the Mediterranean such as Barcelona or Venice. Others sweated as galley slaves in Ottoman and Christian fleets. In the Ottoman army, slaves even formed an important elite contingent.

From the fifteenth century onward, Africans increasingly filled the ranks of slaves. Exploiting warfare between groups within West Africa, the Portuguese traded in gold and "pieces," as African slaves were called, a practice condemned at home by some conscientious clergy. Critical voices, however, could not deny the potential for profits that the slave trade brought to Portugal. Most slaves toiled in the sugar plantations that the Portuguese established on the Atlantic islands and in Brazil. African freedmen and slaves—some thirty-five thousand in the early sixteenth century— constituted almost 3 percent of the population of Portugal, a percentage that was much higher than in other European countries.

In the Americas, slavery would expand enormously in the following centuries. Even outspoken critics of colonial brutality toward indigenous peoples defended the development of African slavery. The Spanish Dominican Bartolomé de Las Casas (1474–1566), for example, argued that Africans were constitutionally more suitable for labor than native Americans and should therefore be imported to the plantations in the Americas to relieve the indigenous peoples, who were being worked to death.

Conquering the New World

The native peoples of the Americas lived in a great diversity of social and political arrangements. Some were nomads roaming large, sparsely inhabited territories; others practiced agriculture in complexly organized states. Among the settled peoples, the largest groupings could be found in the Mexican and Peruvian highlands. Combining an elaborate religious culture with a strict social and political hierarchy, the Aztecs in Mexico and the Incas in Peru ruled over subjugated Indian populations in their respective empires. From their large urban capitals, the Aztecs and Incas controlled large swaths of land and could be ruthless as conquerors.

The Spanish explorers organized their expeditions to the mainland of the Americas from a base in the Caribbean. Two prominent commanders, **Hernán Cortés** (1485–1547) and Francisco Pizarro (c. 1475–1541), gathered men and arms and set off in search of gold. With them came Catholic priests intending to bring Christianity to supposedly uncivilized peoples. When Cortés first landed on the Mexican coast in 1519, the natives greeted him with gifts, thinking that he might be an ancient god returning to reclaim his kingdom. Some natives who resented their subjugation by the Aztecs joined Cortés and his soldiers. With a band of fewer than three hundred Spanish soldiers and a few thousand native allies, Cortés captured the Aztec capital, Tenochtitlán (present-day Mexico City), in 1519. With 200,000 inhabitants, Tenochtitlán was bigger than any European capital. Two years later, Mexico, then named New Spain, was added to the empire of the new ruler of Spain, Charles V, grandson of Ferdinand and Isabella. To the south, Pizarro conquered the Peruvian highlands in 1532 to 1533. The Spanish Empire was now the largest in the world, stretching from Mexico to Chile.

The gold and silver mines in Mexico proved a treasure trove for the Spanish crown, but the real prize was the discovery of vast silver deposits in Potosí (today in Bolivia). When the Spaniards began importing the gold and silver they found in the New World, inflation soared in a fashion never before witnessed in Europe.

Not to be outdone by the Spaniards, other European powers joined the scramble for gold in the New World. In North America, the French went in search of a "northwest passage" to China. The French wanted to establish settlements in what became Canada, but permanent European settlements in Canada and the present-day United States would succeed only in the seventeenth century. By then the English and Dutch had also entered the contest for world mastery.

The Columbian Exchange

The movement of peoples, animals, plants, manufactured goods, precious metals, and diseases between Europe, the New World, and Africa—the Columbian exchange—was one of the most dramatic transformations of ecology, agriculture, and ways of life in all of human history. Columbus started the process when he brought with him firearms, unknown in the Americas, and on his second voyage, horses, which had become extinct in the Americas, as well as pigs, chickens, goats, sheep, cattle, and various plants including wheat, melons, and sugarcane. Enslaved Africans, first brought to the Caribbean in 1503 to 1505, worked on sugarcane plantations, foreshadowing the development of a massive slave economy in the seventeenth and eighteenth centuries (see Chapter 17).

The Europeans also brought with them diseases. Amerindians died in catastrophic numbers because they lacked natural immunity from previous exposure. Smallpox first appeared in the New World in 1518; it and other epidemic diseases killed as many as 90 percent of natives in some places (though the precise numbers are unknown). Syphilis, or a genetic predecessor to it, came back with the explorers to Europe.

The Spanish also brought back tobacco, cacao (chocolate), sweet potatoes, maize, and tomato seeds, changing consumption patterns in Europe. (Their native American wives, concubines, and domestics taught them to drink chocolate in the native fashion: frothy, red in color, and flavored with peppers.) At the same time, Spanish and Portuguese slave traders brought these crops and others—such as manioc, capsicum peppers, pineapples, cashew nuts, and peanuts—from the Americas to West Africa, where their cultivation altered local agriculture and diets. The slavers bought African yams, sorghum, millet, and especially rice to feed the slaves in transit, and the slaves then grew those crops in the Americas. Thus the exchange went in every conceivable direction.

REVIEW   Which European countries led the way in maritime exploration, and what were their motives?

The Protestant Reformation

When Columbus's patrons Ferdinand and Isabella expelled all Jews from Spain in 1492 and chased the last Muslims from Granada in 1502, it appeared as if the triumph of the Catholic church had been assured. Only fifteen years later, however, Martin Luther started a movement for religious reform that would fracture the unity of Western Christianity. Instead of one Catholic church, there would be many different kinds of Christians. The invention of printing with movable type helped spread the Protestant message, which grew in part out of waves of popular piety that washed over Europe in the closing decades of the 1400s. Reformers had also been influenced by Christian humanists who focused attention on clerical abuses.

The Invention of Printing

Printing with movable type, first developed in Europe in the 1440s by Johannes Gutenberg, a German goldsmith, marked a revolutionary departure from the old practice of copying works by hand or stamping pages with individually carved woodblocks. The Chinese invented movable type in the eleventh century, but they preferred woodblock printing because it was more suitable to the Chinese language, with its thousands of different characters. In Europe, with only twenty-six letters to the

Printing Press　This illustration from a French manuscript of 1537 depicts typical printing equipment of the sixteenth century. An artisan is using the screw press to apply the inked type to the paper. Also shown are the composed type secured in a chase, the printed sheet (four pages of text printed on one sheet) held by the seated proofreader, and the bound volume. When two pages of text were printed on one standard-sized sheet, the bound book was called a folio. A bound book with four pages of text on one sheet was called a quarto ("in four"), and a book with eight pages of text on one sheet was called an octavo ("in eight"). The octavo was a pocket-size book, smaller than today's paperback.

alphabet, movable type allowed entire manuscripts to be printed more quickly than ever before. Single letters, made in metal molds, could be emptied out of a frame and new ones inserted to print each new page.

In 1467, two German printers established the first press in Rome; within five years, they had produced twelve thousand volumes, a feat that in the past would have required a thousand scribes working full-time. Printing also depended on the large-scale production of paper. Papermaking came to Europe from China via Arab intermediaries. By the fourteenth century, paper mills in Italy were producing paper that was more fragile but also much cheaper than parchment or vellum, the animal skins that Europeans had previously used for writing. Early printed books attracted an elite audience. Their expense made them inaccessible to most literate people, who comprised a minority of the population in any case. Gutenberg's famous two-volume Latin Bible was a luxury item, and only 185 copies were printed. Gutenberg Bibles remain today a treasure that only the greatest libraries possess.

The invention of mechanical printing dramatically increased the speed at which people could transmit knowledge, and it freed individuals from having to memorize everything they learned. Printed books and pamphlets, even one-page flyers, would create a wide community of scholars no longer dependent on personal patronage or church sponsorship for texts. Printing thus encouraged the free expression and exchange of ideas, and its disruptive potential did not go unnoticed by political and religious authorities. Rulers and bishops in the German states, the birthplace of the printing industry, moved quickly to issue censorship regulations, but their efforts could not prevent the outbreak of the Protestant Reformation.

Popular Piety and Christian Humanism

The Christianizing of Europe had taken many centuries to complete, but by 1500 most people in Europe believed devoutly. However, the vast majority of them had little knowledge of Catholic doctrine. More popular forms of piety—such as processions, festivals, and marvelous tales of saints' miracles—captivated ordinary believers.

Urban merchants and artisans, more likely than the general population to be literate and critical of their local priests, yearned for a faith more meaningful to their daily lives and for a clergy more responsive to their needs. They generously donated money to establish new preaching positions for university-trained clerics. The merchants resented the funneling of the Catholic church's rich endowments to the younger children of the nobility who took up religious callings to protect the wealth of their families. The young, educated clerics funded by the merchants often came from cities themselves. They formed the backbone of **Christian humanism** and sometimes became reformers, too.

Humanism had originated during the Renaissance in Italy among highly educated individuals attached to the personal households of prominent rulers. North of the Alps, however, humanists focused more on religious revival and the inculcation of Christian piety, especially through the schools of the Brethren of the Common Life. The Brethren preached religious self-discipline, specialized in the copying of manuscripts, and were among the first to print the ancient classics. Their most influential pupil was the Dutch

Christian humanist Desiderius Erasmus (c. 1466–1536). The illegitimate son of a man who became a priest, Erasmus joined the Augustinian Order of monks, but the pope allowed him to leave the monastery and pursue the life of an independent scholar. An intimate friend of kings and popes, he became known across Europe. He devoted years to preparing a critical edition of the New Testament in Greek with a translation into Latin, which was finally published in 1516.

Erasmus strove for a unified, peaceful Christendom in which charity and good works, not empty ceremonies, would mark true religion and in which learning and piety would dispel the darkness of ignorance. He elaborated many of these ideas in his *Handbook of the Militant Christian* (1503), an eloquent plea for a simple religion devoid of greed and the lust for power. In *The Praise of Folly* (1509), Erasmus used satire to show that modesty, humility, and poverty represented the true Christian virtues in a world that worshipped pomposity, power, and wealth. The wise appeared foolish, he concluded, for their wisdom and values were not of this world.

Erasmus instructed the young future emperor Charles V to rule as a just Christian prince. A man of peace and moderation, Erasmus soon found himself challenged

Albrecht Dürer, *The Knight, Death, and the Devil* Dürer's 1513 engraving of the knight depicts a grim and determined warrior advancing past death (wearing a crown entwined with a serpent and holding out an hourglass) and the devil (the pig-snouted horned figure wielding a menacing pike). An illustration for Erasmus's *The Handbook of the Militant Christian*, this scene is often interpreted as portraying a Christian clad in the armor of righteousness on a path through life beset by death and demonic temptations. Yet the knight in early-sixteenth-century Germany had become a mercenary, selling his martial skills to princes. Some knights waylaid merchants, robbed rich clerics, and held citizens for ransom. The most notorious of these robber-knights, Franz von Sickingen, was declared an outlaw by the emperor and murdered in 1522. (Hungarian National Gallery, Budapest, Hungary/Bridgeman Images.)

by angry younger men and radical ideas once the Reformation took hold; he eventually chose Christian unity over reform and schism. His dream of Christian pacifism crushed, he lived to see dissenters executed — by Catholics and Protestants alike — for speaking their conscience. Erasmus spent his last years in Freiburg and Basel, isolated from the Protestant community, his writings condemned by many in the Catholic church. After the Protestant Reformation had been secured, the saying arose that "Erasmus laid the egg that Luther hatched." Some blamed the humanists for the emergence of Luther and Protestantism, despite the humanists' decision to remain in the Catholic church.

Martin Luther's Challenge

The crisis of faith of one man, **Martin Luther** (1483–1546), started the international movement known as the Protestant Reformation. The son of a miner and a deeply pious mother, Luther abandoned his studies in the law and, like Erasmus, entered the Augustinian Order. There he experienced his religious crisis: despite fervent prayers, fasting, intense reading of the Bible, a personal pilgrimage to Rome (on foot), and study that led to a doctorate in theology, Luther did not feel saved.

Luther found peace inside himself when he became convinced that sinners were saved only through faith and that faith was a gift freely given by God. Shortly before his death, Luther recalled his crisis:

> Though I lived as a monk without reproach, I felt that I was a sinner before God with an extremely disturbed conscience. Secretly . . . I was angry with God. . . . At last, by the mercy of God, meditating day and night, I gave heed to the context of the words, namely, "In [the gospel] the righteousness of God is revealed, as it is written, 'He who through faith is righteous shall live.'" There I began to understand that the righteousness of God is that by which the righteous live by a gift of God, namely by faith.

No amount of good works, Luther believed, could produce the faith on which salvation depended.

Just as Luther was working out his own personal search for salvation, a priest named Johann Tetzel arrived in Wittenberg, where Luther was a university professor, to sell indulgences. In the sacrament of penance, according to Catholic church doctrine, the sinner confessed his or her sin to a priest, who offered absolution and imposed a penance. Penance normally consisted of spiritual duties (prayers, pilgrimages), but the church also sold the monetary substitutions known as indulgences. A person could even buy indulgences for a deceased relative to reduce that person's time in purgatory and release his or her soul for heaven.

In ninety-five theses that he proposed for academic debate in 1517, Luther denounced the sale of indulgences as a corrupt practice. Printed, the theses became public and unleashed a torrent of pent-up resentment and frustration among the laypeople. What began as a theological debate in a provincial university soon engulfed the Holy Roman Empire. Luther's earliest supporters included younger Christian humanists and clerics who shared his critical attitude toward the church establishment. None of these Evangelicals, as they called themselves, came from the upper echelons of the church; many were from urban middle-class backgrounds, and most were university trained. But illiterate artisans and peasants also rallied to Luther, sometimes with an almost fanatical zeal. They and he believed they were living in the last days of the world, and that Luther and his cause might be a sign of the approaching Last Judgment. In 1520, Luther burned his bridges with the publication of three fiery treatises. In *Freedom of a Christian*, Luther argued that faith, not good works, saved sinners from damnation, and he sharply distinguished between true Gospel teachings and invented church doctrines. Luther advocated "the priesthood of all believers," insisting that the Bible provided all the teachings necessary for Christian living and that a professional caste of clerics should not hold sway over laypeople. These principles — "by faith alone," "by Scripture alone," and "the priesthood of all believers" — became central features of the reform movement.

In his second treatise, *To the Nobility of the German Nation*, Luther denounced the corrupt Italians in Rome and called on the German princes to defend their nation and reform the church. Luther's third treatise, *On the Babylonian Captivity of the Church*, condemned the papacy as the embodiment of the Antichrist.

From Rome's perspective, the Luther Affair, as church officials called it, concerned only one unruly monk. When the pope ordered him to obey his superiors and keep quiet, Luther tore up the decree. Spread by the printing press, Luther's ideas circulated widely, letting loose forces that neither the church nor Luther could control. Social, nationalist, and religious protests fused with lower-class resentments, much as in the Czech movement that the priest and professor Jan Hus had inspired a century earlier. Like Hus, Luther appeared before an emperor: in 1521, he defended his faith at the Imperial Diet of Worms before **Charles V** (r. 1519–1556), the newly elected Holy Roman Emperor who, at the age of nineteen, ruled over the Low Countries, Spain, Spain's Italian and New World dominions, and the Austrian Habsburg lands. Luther shocked Germans by declaring his admiration for the Czech heretic. But unlike Hus, Luther enjoyed the protection of his lord, Frederick the Wise, the elector of Saxony (called an elector because he was one of seven princes charged with electing the Holy Roman Emperor). To become Holy Roman Emperor, Charles V had bribed Frederick and therefore had to treat him with respect.

Lutheran propaganda flooded German towns and villages. Sometimes only a few pages in length, these broadsheets were often illustrated with crude satirical cartoons. Magistrates began to curtail clerical privileges and subordinate the clergy to municipal authority. From Wittenberg, the reform movement quickly swelled and threatened to swamp all before it. Lutheranism spread northward to Scandinavia when reformers who studied in Germany brought back the faith and converted the kings from Catholic to Protestant beliefs.

Protestantism Spreads and Divides

Other Protestant reformers soon challenged Luther's doctrines even while applauding his break from the Catholic church. In 1520, just three years after Luther's initial rupture with Rome, the chief preacher of Zurich, Huldrych Zwingli (1484–1531), openly declared himself a reformer. Like Luther, Zwingli attacked corruption in the Catholic church hierarchy, and he also questioned fasting and clerical celibacy. Zwingli disagreed with Luther on the question of the Eucharist, the central Christian sacrament that Christians partook of in communion. The Catholic doctrine of transubstantiation held that when the priest consecrated them, the bread and wine of communion actually turned into the body and blood of Christ. Luther insisted that the bread and wine did not change their nature: they were simultaneously bread and wine and the body and blood of Christ. Zwingli, however, viewed the Eucharistic bread and wine as symbols of Christ's union with believers, not the real blood and body of Christ. This issue aroused such strong feelings because it concerned the role of the priest and the church in shaping the relationship between God and the believer.

In 1529, troubled by these differences and other disagreements, Protestant princes and magistrates assembled the major reformers in the Colloquy of Marburg, in central Germany. After several days of intense discussions, the reformers managed to resolve some differences over doctrine, but Luther and Zwingli failed to agree on the meaning of the Eucharist. The issue of the Eucharist would soon divide Lutherans and Calvinists as well.

Under the leadership of **John Calvin** (1509–1564), another wave of reform challenged Catholic authority. Born in Picardy, in northern France, Calvin studied in Paris and Orléans, where he took a law degree. Experiencing a crisis of faith, like Luther, Calvin sought salvation through intense theological study. Gradually, he, too, came to question fundamental Catholic teachings.

On Sunday, October 18, 1534, Parisians found church doors posted with crude broadsheets denouncing the Catholic Mass. Smuggled into France from the Protestant and French-speaking parts of Switzerland, the broadsheets provoked a wave of royal repression in the capital. In response to this so-called Affair of the Placards, the government arrested hundreds of French Protestants, executed some of them, and forced many more, including Calvin, to flee abroad.

Calvin made his way to Geneva, the French-speaking Swiss city-state where he would find his life's work. Genevans had renounced their allegiance to the Catholic bishop, and local supporters of reform begged Calvin to stay and labor there. Although it took some time for Calvin to solidify his position in the city, his supporters eventually triumphed and he remained in Geneva until his death in 1564.

Under Calvin's leadership, Geneva became a Christian republic on the model set out in his *Institutes of the Christian Religion*, first published in 1536. No reformer prior to Calvin had expounded on the doctrines, organization, history, and practices of Christianity in such a systematic, logical, and coherent manner. Calvin followed Luther's doctrine of salvation to its ultimate logical conclusion: if God is almighty and humans cannot earn their salvation by good works, then no Christian can be certain of salvation. Developing the doctrine of **predestination**, Calvin argued that God had ordained every man, woman, and child to salvation or damnation — even before the creation of the world. Thus, in Calvin's theology, God saved only the "elect" (a small group).

Predestination could terrify, but it could also embolden. For Calvinists, a righteous life might be a sign that a person had been chosen for salvation. Thus, Calvinist doctrine demanded rigorous discipline. Fusing church and society into what followers named the Reformed church, Geneva became a theocratic city-state dominated by Calvin and the elders of the Reformed church. Its people were rigorously monitored; detractors said that they were bullied. From its base in Geneva, the Calvinist movement spread to France, the Low Countries, England, Scotland, the German states, Poland, Hungary, and eventually New England.

In Geneva, Calvin tolerated no dissent. While passing through the city in 1553, the Spanish physician Michael Servetus was arrested because he had published books attacking Calvin and questioning the doctrine of the Trinity, the belief that there are three persons in one God — the Father, the Son (Jesus), and the Holy Spirit. Upon Calvin's advice, the authorities executed Servetus. Calvin was not alone in persecuting dissenters. Each religious group believed that its doctrine was absolutely true and grounded in the Bible and that therefore violence in its defense was not only justified but required. Catholic and Protestant polemicists alike castigated their critics in the harshest terms, but they often saved their cruelest words for the Jews. Calvin, for example, called the Jews "profane, unholy, sacrilegious dogs," but Luther went even further and advocated burning down their houses and their synagogues. Religious toleration was still far in the future.

The Contested Church of England

England followed yet another path, with reform led by the king rather than by men trained as Catholic clergy. Despite a tradition of religious dissent that went back to the fourteenth-century theologian John Wycliffe, Protestantism gained few English adherents in the 1520s. King **Henry VIII** (r. 1509–1547) changed that when he broke with the Roman Catholic church. The resulting Church of England retained many aspects of Catholic worship but nonetheless aligned itself in the Protestant camp.

At first, Henry opposed the Protestant Reformation, even receiving the title Defender of the Faith from Pope Leo X for a treatise he wrote against Luther. With the aid of his chancellors Cardinal Thomas Wolsey and Thomas More, Henry vigorously suppressed Protestantism and executed its leaders. More had made a reputation as a Christian humanist, publishing a controversial novel about an imaginary island called Utopia (1516), the source of the modern word for an ideal community. Unlike his friend Erasmus, More chose to serve the state directly and became personal secretary to Henry VIII, Speaker of the House of Commons, and finally Lord Chancellor.

By 1527, the king wanted to annul his marriage to Catherine of Aragon (d. 1536), the daughter of Ferdinand and Isabella of Spain and the aunt of Charles

V. The eighteen-year marriage had produced a daughter, Mary (known as Mary Tudor), but Henry desperately needed a male heir to consolidate the rule of the still-new Tudor dynasty. Moreover, he had fallen in love with Anne Boleyn, a lady at court and a supporter of the Reformation. Henry claimed that his marriage to Catherine had never been valid because she was the widow of his older brother, Arthur. Arthur and Catherine's marriage, which apparently was never consummated, had been annulled by Pope Julius II to allow the marriage between Henry and Catherine to take place. Now Henry asked the reigning pope, Clement VII, to declare his marriage to Catherine invalid.

Around "the king's great matter" unfolded a struggle for political and religious control. When Cardinal Wolsey failed to secure papal approval of the annulment, Henry dismissed him and had him arrested. Wolsey died before he could be tried, and More took his place as Lord Chancellor. However, More resigned in 1532 because he opposed Henry's new direction; Henry then had him executed as a traitor in 1535. Henry now turned to two Protestants, Thomas Cromwell (1485–1540) as chancellor and Thomas Cranmer (1489–1556) as archbishop of Canterbury. Under their leadership, the English Parliament passed a number of acts that severed ties between the English church and Rome. The most important of these, the Act of Supremacy of 1534, made Henry the head of the Church of England. Other legislation invalidated the claims of Mary Tudor to the throne, recognized Henry's marriage to Anne Boleyn, and allowed the English crown to embark on the dissolution of the monasteries. In an effort to consolidate support behind his version of the Reformation, Henry sold off monastic lands to the local gentry and aristocracy. His actions prompted an uprising in 1536 in the north of the country called the Pilgrimage of Grace. Though suppressed, it revealed that many people remained deeply Catholic in their sympathies.

Henry grew tired of Anne Boleyn, who had given birth to a daughter, the future Queen Elizabeth I, but had produced no sons. He ordered Anne beheaded in 1536 on the charge of adultery. The king would go on to marry four other wives but father only one son, Edward. When Henry died in 1547, much would now depend on who held the crown. Henry himself held ambiguous views on religion: he considered himself Catholic but would not accept the supremacy of the pope; he closed the monasteries and removed shrines but kept the Mass and believed in clerical celibacy.

REVIEW   How did Luther, Zwingli, Calvin, and Henry VIII each challenge the Roman Catholic church?

Reshaping Society through Religion

The religious reformers and their followers challenged political authority and the social order, yet in reaction to any extreme manifestation of disorder, they underlined the need for discipline in worship and social behavior. Some Protestants took the phrase "priesthood of all believers" quite literally and sided with the poor and the downtrodden. Like Catholics, Protestant authorities then became alarmed by the subversive potential of religious reforms. They viewed the Reformation as a way of instilling greater discipline in individual worship and church organization. At the same time, the Roman Catholic church undertook reforms of its own and launched an offensive against the Protestant Reformation that is sometimes called the Counter-Reformation.

Protestant Challenges to the Social Order

When Luther described the freedom of the Christian, he meant an entirely spiritual freedom. But others interpreted his call for freedom in social and political terms. In the spring of 1525, peasants in southern and central Germany rose in a rebellion known as the Peasants' War and attacked nobles' castles, convents, and monasteries (Map 14.2). Urban workers joined them, and together they looted church properties in the towns. In Thuringia (central/eastern Germany), the rebels followed an ex-priest, Thomas Müntzer (1468?–1525), who promised to chastise the wicked and thus clear the way for the Last Judgment.

The Peasants' War split the reform movement. Princes and city officials, ultimately supported by Luther, turned against the rebels. Catholic and Protestant princes joined forces to crush Müntzer and his supporters. All over the empire, princes trounced peasant armies and hunted down their leaders. By the end of the year, more than 100,000 rebels had been killed. Initially, Luther had tried to mediate the conflict, but he believed that God ordained rulers, who must therefore be obeyed even if they were tyrants. Luther considered Müntzer's mixing of religion and politics the greatest danger to the Reformation, nothing less than "the devil's work." Fundamentally conservative in its political philosophy, the Lutheran church henceforth depended on established political authority for its protection.

Some followers of Zwingli also wanted to pursue their own path to reform. They believed that true faith came only to those with reason and free will. How could a baby knowingly choose Christ? Only adults could believe and accept baptism; hence, the **Anabaptists** ("rebaptizers") rejected the validity of infant baptism and called for adult rebaptism. Many were pacifists who also refused to acknowledge the authority of law courts. The Anabaptist movement drew its leadership primarily from the artisan class and its members from the middle and lower classes — men and women attracted by a simple but radical message of peace and salvation.

Zwingli immediately attacked the Anabaptists for their refusal to bear arms and swear oaths of allegiance, sensing accurately that they were repudiating his theocratic (church-directed) order. When persuasion failed to convince the Anabaptists, Zwingli urged Zurich magistrates to impose the death sentence. Thus, the Evangelical reformers themselves created the Reformation's first martyrs of conscience.

Despite the Holy Roman Emperor's condemnation of the movement in 1529, Anabaptism spread rapidly from Zurich to many cities in southern Germany. In 1534, one Anabaptist group, believing the end of the world was imminent, seized control of the city of Münster. Proclaiming themselves a community of saints, the

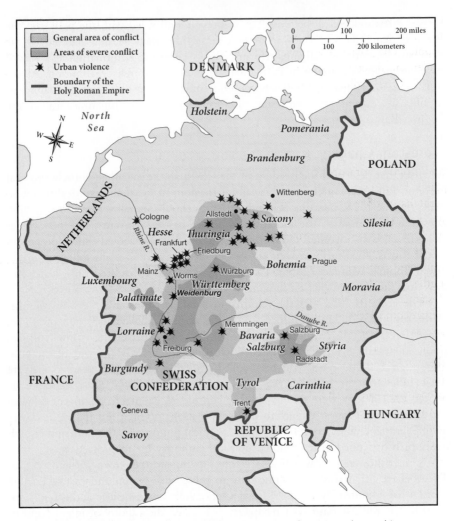

MAP 14.2 The Peasants' War of 1525 The centers of uprisings clustered in southern and central Germany, where the density of cities encouraged the spread of discontent and allowed for alliances between urban masses and rural rebels. The proximity to the Swiss Confederation, a stronghold of the Reformation movement, also inspired antiestablishment uprisings.

Münster Anabaptists abolished private property in imitation of the early Christians and dissolved traditional marriages, allowing men, like Old Testament patriarchs, to have multiple wives, to the consternation of many women. Besieged by a combined Protestant and Catholic army, the city fell in June 1535. The Anabaptist leaders died in battle or were executed, their bodies hung in cages affixed to the church tower. Their punishment was intended as a warning to all who might want to take the Reformation away from the Protestant authorities and hand it to the people. The Anabaptist movement in northwestern Europe nonetheless survived under the determined pacifist leadership of the Dutch reformer Menno Simons (1469–1561), whose followers were eventually named Mennonites.

New Forms of Discipline

Faced with the social firestorms ignited by religious reform, the middle-class urban-ites who supported the Protestant Reformation urged greater religious conformity and stricter moral behavior. Protestants did not have monasteries or convents or saints' lives to set examples; they sought moral examples in their own homes, in the sermons of their preachers, and in their own reading of the Bible. Some of these attitudes had medieval roots, yet the Protestant Reformation fostered their spread and Catholics soon began to embrace them.

Although the Bible had been translated into German before, Luther's translations (of the New Testament in 1522 and of the Old Testament in 1534) quickly became authoritative. A new Bible-centered culture began to take root, as more than 200,000 copies of Luther's New Testament were printed over twelve years, an immense number for the time. Peppered with witty phrases and colloquial expressions, Luther's Bible not only made the sacred writings more accessible to ordinary people but also helped standardize the German language.

Torture and Execution of an Anabaptist Leader Not long after their capture in 1535, the Anabaptist leaders of Münster were tortured with hot tongs before being killed. Their bodies were placed in cages and hung from a church steeple. This print shows the cage with the body of John of Leiden. He was a tailor's apprentice from the Dutch town of Leiden. (16th-century Dutch engraving / Private Collection / Roger-Viollet, Paris, France / Bridgeman Images.)

Bible reading became a common pastime undertaken in solitude or at family and church gatherings. To counter Protestant success, Catholic German Bibles soon appeared, thus sanctioning Bible reading by the Catholic laity, a sharp departure from medieval church practice.

The new emphasis on self-discipline led to growing impatience with the poor. Between 1500 and 1560, rapid economic and population growth created prosperity for some and stress—heightened by increased inflation—for many. Wanderers and urban beggars were by no means novel, but now moralists, both Catholic and Protestant, denounced vagabonds as lazy and potentially criminal.

The Reformation provided an opportunity to restructure relief for the poor. Instead of decentralized, private initiatives often overseen by religious orders, Protestant magistrates appointed officials to head urban agencies that would certify the genuine poor and distribute welfare funds to them. Catholic authorities did the same. In 1531, Henry VIII asked justices of the peace (unpaid local magistrates) to license the poor in England and to differentiate between those who could work and those who could not. In 1540, Charles V imposed a welfare tax in Spain to augment that country's inadequate system of private charity.

In their effort to establish order and discipline, Protestant reformers denounced sexual immorality and glorified the family. The early Protestant reformers like Luther championed the end of clerical celibacy and embraced marriage. Luther, once a celibate priest himself, married a former nun. Protestant magistrates closed brothels and established marriage courts to handle disputes over marriage promises, child support, and divorce (allowed by Protestants in some rare situations). The magistrates also levied fines or ordered imprisonment for violent behavior, fornication, and adultery.

Prior to the Reformation, despite the legislation of church councils, marriages had largely been private affairs between families; some couples never even registered with the church. The Catholic church recognized any promise made between two consenting adults (with the legal age of twelve for females, fourteen for males) in the presence of two witnesses as a valid marriage. As the Reformation took hold, Protestants asserted government control over marriage, and Catholic governments followed suit. A marriage was legitimate only if registered by both a government official and a member of the clergy.

Catholic Renewal

The Catholic church decided in the 1540s to undertake drastic action to fend off the Protestant threat. Pope Paul III convened a general council of the church in 1545 at Trent, a town on the border between the Holy Roman Empire and Italy. Meeting sporadically over eighteen years (1545–1563), the **Council of Trent** effectively set the course of Catholicism until the 1960s. Catholic leaders sought renewal of religious devotion and reform of clerical morality (some priests had had sexual relationships and fathered children) as well as clarification of church doctrine. New religious orders set out to win converts overseas or to reconvert Catholics who had turned to Protestantism. At the same time, the church did not hesitate to root out dissent by giving greater powers to the Inquisition, including the power to censor books. The papal Index, or list of prohibited books, was established in 1557 and not abolished until 1966.

Italian and Spanish clergy predominated among the 255 bishops, archbishops, and cardinals attending the Council of Trent, which condemned all the central doctrines of Protestantism. According to the council, salvation depended on faith and good works, not faith alone. On the sacrament of the Eucharist, the council reaffirmed that the bread of communion "really, truly" becomes Christ's body. It reasserted the supremacy of clerical authority over the laity; the church's interpretation of the Bible could not be challenged, and the Latin Vulgate was the only authoritative version. The council rejected divorce and reaffirmed the legitimacy of indulgences. It also called for reform from within, however, insisting that bishops henceforth reside in their dioceses and decreeing that seminaries for the training of priests be established in every diocese. Henceforth, the schism between Protestant and Catholic remained permanent, and all hopes of reconciliation faded.

The renewed energy of Catholicism expressed itself most vigorously in the founding of new religious orders such as the Society of Jesus, or **Jesuits**, founded by a Spanish nobleman, Ignatius of Loyola (1491–1556). In 1521, while recovering from an injury suffered as a soldier in the Spanish army, Ignatius read lives (biographies) of the saints; once he recovered, he abandoned his quest for military glory in favor of serving the church. In 1540, the pope recognized his small band of followers.

With Ignatius as its first general, the Jesuits became the most vigorous defenders of papal authority. The society quickly expanded; by the time of Ignatius's death in 1556, Europe had one thousand Jesuits. They established hundreds of colleges throughout the Catholic world, educating future generations of Catholic leaders. Jesuit missionaries played a key role in the Spanish and Portuguese empires and brought Roman Catholicism to Africans, Asians, and native Americans. They saw their effort as proof of the truth of Roman Catholicism and the success of their missions as a sign of divine favor, both particularly important in the face of Protestant challenge.

Catholic missionary zeal brought conflicting messages to indigenous peoples: for some, the message of a repressive and coercive alien religion; for others, a sweet sign of reason and faith. Frustrated in his efforts to convert Brazilian Indians, a Jesuit missionary wrote to his superior in Rome in 1563, "For this kind of people it is better to be preaching with the sword and rod of iron."

Catholic missionaries focused initially on winning over local elites. They learned the local languages and set up schools for the sons of conquered nobles. After an initial period of relatively little racial discrimination, the Catholic church in the Americas and Africa adopted strict rules based on color. For example, the first Mexican Ecclesiastical Provincial Council in 1555 declared that holy orders were not to be conferred on Indians, mestizos (people of mixed European-Indian parentage), or mulattoes (people of mixed European-African heritage); along with descendants of Muslims, Jews, and persons who had been sentenced by the Spanish Inquisition, these groups were deemed "inherently unworthy of the sacerdotal [priestly] office."

European missionaries in Asia greatly admired Chinese and Japanese civilization, and thus used the sermon rather than the sword to win converts. The Jesuit Francis Xavier preached in India and Japan, his work greatly assisted by a network of Portuguese trading stations. Overall the efforts of the Catholic missionaries seemed highly successful: vast multitudes of native Americans had become nominal Christians by the second half of the sixteenth century, and thirty years after Francis Xavier's 1549 landing in Japan, the Jesuits could claim more than 100,000 Japanese converts.

REVIEW	How did the forces for radical change unleashed by the Protestant Reformation interact with the urge for social order and stability?

Striving for Mastery

Although the riches of the New World and the conflicts generated by the Reformation raised the stakes of international politics, life at court did not change all at once. Princes and popes continued to sponsor the arts and literature of the Renaissance. Henry VIII, for example, hired the German artist Hans Holbein as king's painter. While Protestantism was taking root, Catholic monarchs still fought one another and battled the powerful Ottoman Empire. Holy Roman Emperor Charles V dominated the political scene with his central position in Europe and his rising supply of gold and silver from the New World. Yet even his wealth proved insufficient to subdue all his challengers. Religious difference led to violence in every country, even Spain, where there were almost no Protestants but many Muslims who were forced to convert by Charles V in 1526. For the most part, violence failed to settle religious differences. By 1560, an exhausted Europe had achieved a provisional peace, but one sowed with the seeds of future conflict.

Courtiers and Princes

Kings, princes, and popes alike used their courts to keep an eye on their leading courtiers (cardinals in the case of popes) and impress their other subjects. Briefly defined, the court was the ruler's household. Around the prince gathered a community of household servants, noble attendants, councilors, officials, artists, and soldiers. Renaissance culture had been promoted by this political elite, and that culture now entered its "high," or most sophisticated, phase. Its acclaimed representative was Michelangelo Buonarroti (1475–1564), an immensely talented Italian artist who sculpted the gigantic nude *David* for officials in Florence and then painted the ceiling of the Sistine Chapel for the recently elected Pope Julius II.

Italian artists also flocked to the French court of Francis I (r. 1515–1547), which swelled to the largest in Europe. In addition to royal officials and guards, physicians, librarians, musicians, dwarfs, animal trainers, and a multitude of hangers-on bloated its size to more than sixteen hundred members. Although Francis built a magnificent Renaissance palace at Fontainebleau, where he hired Italian artists to produce paintings and sculpture, the French court often moved from palace to palace. It took no fewer than eighteen thousand horses to transport the people, furniture, documents, dogs, and falcons for the royal hunt. Hunting represented a form of mock combat, essential in the training of a military elite. Francis almost lost his own life when, storming a house during one mock battle, he was hit on the head by a burning log.

Two Italian writers helped define the new culture of courtesy, or proper court behavior: Ludovico Ariosto (1474–1533), in service at the Este court in Ferrara, and Baldassare Castiglione (1478–1529), a servant of the duke of Urbino and the pope. Ariosto composed an epic poem, *Orlando Furioso*, which represented court culture as the highest synthesis of Christian and classical values. The poem's captivating tales of combat, valor, love, and magic ranged across Europe, Africa, Asia, and even the moon. In *The Courtier*, Castiglione's characters debate the qualities of an ideal courtier in a series of eloquent dialogues. The true courtier, Castiglione asserts, is a gentleman who carries himself with nobility and dignity in the service of his prince and his lady.

Courtesy was recommended to courtiers, but not always to princes. The Italian politician and writer Niccolò Machiavelli (1469–1527) helped found modern political science by treating the maintenance of power as an end in itself. In his provocative essay *The Prince*, he underlined the need for pragmatic, even cold calculation. Was it better, he asked, for a prince to be feared by his people or loved? "It may be answered that one should wish to be both, but, because it is difficult to unite them in one person, [it] is much safer to be feared than loved." Machiavelli insisted that princes could benefit their subjects only by keeping a firm grip on power, if necessary through deceit and manipulation. *Machiavellian* has remained ever since a term for using cunning and duplicity to achieve one's ends.

Dynastic Wars

Even as the Renaissance developed in the princely courts and the Reformation began in the German states, the Habsburgs (the ruling family in Spain and then the Holy Roman Empire) and the Valois (the ruling family in France) fought each other for domination of Europe. French claims provoked the Italian Wars in 1494, which soon escalated into a general conflict that involved the major Christian monarchs and the Muslim Ottoman sultan as well. From 1494 to 1559, the Valois and Habsburg dynasties, both Catholic, remained implacable enemies. The fighting raged in Italy and the Low Countries. In 1525, the troops of Charles V crushed the French army at Pavia, Italy, counting among their captives the French king himself, Francis I. Forced to renounce all claims to Italian territory to gain his freedom, Francis furiously repudiated the treaty the moment he reached France, reigniting the conflict.

In 1527, Charles's troops captured and sacked Rome because the pope had allied with the French. Many of the imperial troops were German Protestant mercenaries, who pillaged Catholic churches and brutalized the Catholic clergy. Protestants and Catholics alike interpreted the sack of Rome by imperial forces as a punishment of God; even the Catholic church read it as a sign that reform was necessary. Finally, in 1559, the French gave up their claims in Italy and signed the Treaty of Cateau-Cambrésis, ending the conflict. To seal the peace the French king Henry II married his sister to the duke of Savoy, an ally of the Habsburgs, and his daughter to the Habsburg king of Spain, Philip II, who had succeeded his father Charles V in 1556.

Charles V and Francis I Make Peace   This fresco from the Palazzo Farnese in the town of Caprarola, north of Rome, shows French king Francis I and Holy Roman Emperor Charles V (shown pointing his finger) agreeing to the Truce of Nice in 1538, one of many peace agreements made and then broken during the wars between the Habsburgs and the Valois. Pope Paul III, who negotiated the truce, stands behind and between them. Charles is on the right pointing to Francis. The truce is the one celebrated in the Tlaxcala pageant described at the start of this chapter. (From the fresco *Sala del Consiglio Trento*, by Taddeo Zuccaro [1529–1566] and Federico Zuccaro [1542–1609]/Palazzo Farnese, Rome, Italy/Bridgeman Images.)

The dynastic struggle (Valois versus Habsburg) had drawn in many other belligerents, who fought on one side or the other for their own benefit. Some acted purely out of power considerations, such as England, first siding with the Valois and then with the Habsburgs. Others fought for their independence, such as the papacy and the Italian states, which did not want any one power to dominate Italy. Still others chose sides for religious reasons, such as the Protestant princes in Germany, who exploited the Valois-Habsburg conflict to extract religious concessions from the emperor in 1555. The Ottoman Turks saw in this fight an opportunity to expand their territory.

The Ottoman Empire reached its height of power under Sultan Suleiman I, known as **Suleiman the Magnificent** (r. 1520–1566). In 1526, a Turkish expedition destroyed the Hungarian army at Mohács. Three years later, the Ottomans laid siege to Vienna; though unsuccessful, the attack sent shock waves throughout Christian Europe. In 1535, Charles V led a campaign to capture Tunis, the lair of North African pirates loyal to the Ottomans. Desperate to overcome Charles's superior Habsburg forces, the French king Francis I forged an alliance with the Turkish sultan. The Turkish fleet besieged the Habsburg troops holding Nice, on the southern coast of France. Francis even ordered all inhabitants of nearby Toulon to vacate the town so that he could turn it into a Muslim colony for eight months, complete with a mosque and a slave market.

The French alliance with the Turks reflected the spirit of the times: the age-old idea of the Christian crusade against Islam now had to compete with a new political strategy that considered religion only one factor among many in power politics. Religion could be sacrificed, if need be, on the altar of state building. Constantly distracted by the challenges of the Ottomans to the east and the German Protestants at home, Charles V could not crush the French with one swift blow.

Financing War

The sixteenth century marked the beginning of superior Western military technology. All armies grew in size and their firepower became ever more deadly, increasing the cost of war. Heavier artillery pieces meant that the rectangular walls of medieval cities had to be transformed into fortresses with jutting ramparts and gun emplacements. Royal revenues could not keep up with war expenditures. To pay their bills, governments routinely devalued their coinage (the sixteenth-century equivalent of printing more paper money), causing prices to rise rapidly.

Charles V boasted the largest army in Europe, supported by the gold and silver coming in from the New World. Immediately after conquest, the Spanish looted gold and silver objects, melted them down, and sent the precious metals to Spain. Mining began with forced Indian labor in the 1520s, and the amount of silver extracted in Mexico and sent to Spain increased twentyfold in the 1530s and 1540s. Nevertheless, Charles could never make ends meet because of his extravagant war costs: the debt of 37 million ducats accumulated during his forty years in power exceeded by 2 million ducats all the gold and silver brought from the Americas. His opponents fared even worse. On his death in 1547, Francis I owed the bankers of Lyon almost 7 million French pounds—approximately the entire royal income for that year. Foremost among the financiers of war debts was the Fugger bank, based in the southern German imperial city of Augsburg. The enterprise began with Jakob Fugger (1459–1525), who became personal banker to Charles V's grandfather Maximilian I. By the end of his life, Maximilian was so deeply in debt to Jakob Fugger that he had to pawn the royal jewels. In 1519, Fugger assembled a consortium of German and Italian bankers to secure the election of Charles V as Holy Roman Emperor. For the next three decades, the alliance between Europe's biggest international bank and its largest empire remained very close. Charles stayed barely one step ahead of his creditors; in 1531, for example, he had to grant to the Fuggers eight years of mining rights in Spanish lands south of Peru (present-day Bolivia and Chile).

Divided Realms

European rulers viewed religious division as a dangerous challenge to the unity and stability of their rule. Subjects who considered their rulers heretics or blasphemers could only cause trouble, and religious differences encouraged the formation of competing noble factions, which easily led to violence when weak monarchs or children ruled.

In France, King Francis I tolerated Protestants until the Affair of the Placards in 1534. Even then, the government could not stop many French noble families— including some of the most powerful—from converting to Calvinism, especially in southern and western France. Francis and his successor, Henry II (r. 1547–1559), succeeded in maintaining a balance of power between Catholics and Calvinists, but after Henry's death the weakened monarchy could no longer hold together the fragile realm. The real drama of the Reformation in France took place after 1560, when the country plunged into four decades of religious wars, whose savagery was unparalleled elsewhere in Europe (see Chapter 15).

In England and Scotland religious divisions at the very top threatened the control of the rulers. Before his death in 1547, Henry VIII had succeeded in making himself head of the Church of England, but the nature of that church remained ambiguous. The advisers of the boy king Edward VI (r. 1547–1553) furthered the Protestant cause by welcoming prominent religious refugees who had been deeply influenced by Calvinism and wanted to see England move in that austere direction. But Edward died at age fifteen, opening the way to his Catholic half sister, Mary Tudor, who had been restored to the line of succession by an act of Parliament under Henry VIII in 1544.

When Mary (r. 1553–1558) came to the throne, she restored Catholicism and persecuted Protestants. Nearly three hundred Protestants perished at the stake, and more than eight hundred fled to the Protestant German states and Switzerland. Finally, when Anne Boleyn's daughter, Elizabeth, succeeded her half sister Mary, becoming Queen Elizabeth I (r. 1558–1603), the English Protestant cause gained lasting momentum. Under Elizabeth's leadership, Protestantism came to define the character of the English nation, though the influence of Calvinism within it was still a cause for dispute. Catholics were tolerated only if they kept their opinions on religion and politics to themselves. A tentative but nonetheless real peace returned to England.

Still another pattern of religious politics unfolded in Scotland, where Protestants formed a small minority until the 1550s. At the center of Scotland's conflict over religion stood Mary of Guise, a French native and Catholic married to the king of Scotland, James V. After James died in 1542, Mary surrounded herself and her daughter Mary Stuart, also a Catholic and heir to the throne, with French advisers. When, in 1558, Mary Stuart married Francis, the son of Henry II and the heir to the French throne, many Scottish noblemen, alienated by this pro-French atmosphere, joined the pro-English, anti-French Protestant cause. They gained control of the Scottish Parliament in 1560 and dethroned the regent, Mary of Guise. Eventually they forced her daughter—by then known as Mary, queen of Scots—to flee to England, and installed Mary's infant son, James, as king. Scotland would turn toward the Calvinist version of the Reformation and thus establish the potential for conflict with England.

In the German states, the Protestant princes and cities formed the Schmalkaldic League in 1531. Opposing the league were Emperor Charles V, the bishops, and the few remaining Catholic princes. Although Charles had to concentrate on fighting the French and the Turks during the 1530s, he eventually secured the western Mediterranean and then turned his attention back home to central Europe to try to resolve the growing religious differences in his lands.

After efforts to mediate between Protestants and Catholics broke down, Charles prepared to fight the Protestant Schmalkaldic League. War broke out in 1547, the year after Martin Luther's death. Using seasoned Spanish veterans and German allies, Charles occupied the German imperial cities in the south, restoring Catholic elites and suppressing the Reformation. When Protestant commanders could not agree on a joint strategy, Charles crushed the Schmalkaldic League's armies at Mühlberg in Saxony and captured the leading Lutheran princes. Jubilant, Charles restored Catholics' right to worship in Protestant lands while permitting Lutherans to keep their own rites. Protestant resistance to the declaration was deep and widespread: many pastors went into exile, and riots broke out in many cities. Charles's success did not last long. The Protestant princes regrouped, declared war in 1552, and chased a surprised, unprepared, and practically bankrupt emperor back to Italy.

Forced to compromise, Charles V agreed to the **Peace of Augsburg** in 1555. The settlement recognized the Lutheran church in the empire; accepted the secularization of church lands but "reserved" the remaining ecclesiastical territories for Catholics; and, most important, established the principle that all princes, whether Catholic or Lutheran, enjoyed the sole right to determine the religion of their lands and subjects. Calvinist, Anabaptist, and other dissenting groups were excluded from the settlement. Ironically, the religious revolt of the common people had culminated in a princes' reformation. The Augsburg settlement preserved a fragile peace in central Europe until 1618, but the exclusion of Calvinists would prompt future conflict.

Exhausted by decades of war and dismayed by the disunity in Christian Europe, Emperor Charles V resigned his many thrones in 1555 and 1556, leaving his Netherlandish-Burgundian and Spanish dominions to his son, Philip II, and his Austrian lands to his brother, Ferdinand (who was also elected Holy Roman Emperor to succeed Charles). Retiring to a monastery in southern Spain, the most powerful of the Christian monarchs spent his last years quietly seeking salvation.

REVIEW　　How did religious divisions complicate the efforts of rulers to maintain political stability and build stronger states?

Conclusion

Charles V's decision to divide his empire reflected the tensions pulling Europe in different directions. Even as Charles's kingdom of Spain joined Portugal as a global power with new conquests overseas, Luther, Calvin, and a host of others sought converts to competing branches of Protestantism within the Holy Roman Empire. The reformers disagreed on many points of doctrine and church organization, but they all broke definitively from the Roman Catholic church. The pieces were never put together again. Portugal and Spain, the leaders in global exploration and conquest, remained resolutely Catholic, but as ruler of the Holy Roman Empire, where the Reformation began, Charles could not stifle the growing religious ferment. In the decades to come, Protestantism would spread, religious conflict would turn even more deadly, and emerging Protestant powers would begin to contest the global reach of Spain and Portugal.

MAPPING THE WEST **Reformation Europe, c. 1560**   The fortunes of Roman Catholicism were at their lowest point around 1560. Northern Germany and Scandinavia owed allegiance to the Lutheran church; England broke away under a national church headed by its monarchs; and the Calvinist Reformation extended across large areas of western, central, and eastern Europe. Southern Europe remained solidly Catholic.

Chapter Review

KEY TERMS AND PEOPLE

Be sure that you can identify the term or person and explain its historical significance.

Christopher Columbus (p. 400)
Hernán Cortés (p. 401)
Christian humanism (p. 404)
Martin Luther (p. 406)
Charles V (p. 407)
John Calvin (p. 408)
predestination (p. 409)

Henry VIII (p. 409)
Anabaptists (p. 411)
Council of Trent (p. 414)
Jesuits (p. 415)
Suleiman the Magnificent (p. 419)
Peace of Augsburg (p. 421)

REVIEW QUESTIONS

1. Which European countries led the way in maritime exploration, and what were their motives?
2. How did Luther, Zwingli, Calvin, and Henry VIII each challenge the Roman Catholic church?
3. How did the forces for radical change unleashed by the Protestant Reformation interact with the urge for social order and stability?
4. How did religious divisions complicate the efforts of rulers to maintain political stability and build stronger states?

MAKING CONNECTIONS

1. In what ways did the discovery of the Americas affect Europe?
2. Why was Charles V ultimately unable to prevent religious division in his lands?
3. How did the different religious groups respond to the opportunity presented by the printing press?
4. What motives besides religious differences caused war in this period?

IMPORTANT EVENTS

1492	• Columbus reaches the Americas
1494	• Italian Wars begin; Treaty of Tordesillas divides Atlantic world between Portugal and Spain
1516	• Erasmus publishes Greek edition of the New Testament
1517	• Luther composes ninety-five theses to challenge Catholic church
1519	• Cortés captures Aztec capital of Tenochtitlán
1520	• Luther publishes three treatises; Zwingli breaks from Rome
1525	• German Peasants' War
1527	• Charles V's imperial troops sack Rome
1529	• Colloquy of Marburg addresses disagreements between German and Swiss church reformers
1534	• Henry VIII breaks with Rome; Affair of the Placards in France
1536	• Calvin publishes *Institutes of the Christian Religion*
1540	• Jesuits established as new Catholic order
1545–1563	• Catholic Council of Trent condemns Protestant beliefs, confirms Catholic doctrine
1547	• Charles V defeats Protestants at Mühlberg
1555	• Peace of Augsburg ends religious wars and recognizes Lutheran church in German states
1559	• Treaty of Cateau-Cambrésis ends wars between Habsburg and Valois rulers

15

Wars of Religion and the Clash of Worldviews

1560–1648

CHAPTER FOCUS

What were the long-term political, economic, and intellectual consequences of the conflicts over religious belief in this era?

IN NOVEMBER 1576, SPAIN'S SOLDIERS sacked Antwerp, Europe's wealthiest city. In eleven days of horror known as the Spanish Fury, the troops slaughtered seven to eight thousand people and burned down a thousand buildings, including the city hall. The king of Spain had sent an army of ten thousand men in 1566 to occupy his rebellious northern domains and punish Calvinists, who had smashed stained-glass windows and statues in Catholic churches. By 1575, however, the king had run out of funds, and his men rioted after being unpaid for months. The Spanish Fury was far from an isolated incident in this time of religious upheaval. It showed, moreover, that violence often exploded from a dangerous mixture of religious, political, and economic motives.

The first two generations of battles over the Protestant Reformation had ended with the Peace of Augsburg in 1555. That agreement helped maintain a relative calm in the lands of the Holy Roman Empire, but in western Europe religious strife multiplied after 1560 as Calvinists made inroads in France, the Netherlands, and England. In 1618, fighting broke out again in the Holy Roman Empire—and before it ended in 1648, the Thirty Years' War involved most of the European powers and desolated lands and peoples across central

Europe. All in all, nearly constant warfare marked the century between 1560 and 1648. Like the Spanish Fury, these struggles began as religious disputes but soon revealed other motives: political ambitions, long-standing rivalries between the leading powers, and greed—all of which raised the stakes of conflict.

Suffering only increased when a major economic downturn in the early seventeenth century led to food shortages, famine, and disease in much of Europe. These catastrophes hit especially hard in the central European lands devastated by the fighting of the Thirty Years' War. In intellectual life a new understanding of the motion of the planets in the heavens and of mechanics on Earth developed among experimenters in "natural philosophy," that is, what came to be called science. This scientific revolution ultimately reshaped Western attitudes in virtually every field of knowledge, but at its beginnings it still had to compete with traditional religious views and popular beliefs in magic and witchcraft.

Religious Conflicts Threaten State Power, 1560–1618

The Peace of Augsburg made Lutheranism a legal religion in the predominantly Catholic Holy Roman Empire, but it did not extend recognition to Calvinists. The rapid expansion of Calvinism after 1560 threatened to alter the religious balance of power as Calvinists challenged Catholic dominance in France, the Spanish-ruled Netherlands, Scotland, and Poland-Lithuania. In England, they sought to influence the new Protestant monarch, Elizabeth I. Calvinists were not the only source of religious contention, however. Philip II of Spain fought the Muslim Ottoman Turks in the Mediterranean and expelled the remnants of the Muslim population in Spain. To the east, the Russian tsar Ivan IV fought to establish an empire based on Russian Orthodox Christianity.

French Wars of Religion, 1562–1598

Calvinism spread in France after 1555, when the Genevan Company of Pastors sent missionaries supplied with false passports and often disguised as merchants. By the end of the 1560s, nearly one-third of the nobles had joined the Huguenots (French Calvinists), and they raised their own armies. Conversion to Calvinism in French noble families often began with the noblewomen, who protected pastors, provided money and advice, and helped found schools and establish relief for the poor.

A series of family tragedies prevented the French kings from acting decisively to prevent the spread of Calvinism. King Henry II was accidentally killed during a jousting tournament in 1559, and his fifteen-year-old son, Francis, died soon after.

Ten-year-old Charles IX (r. 1560–1574) became king, with his mother, **Catherine de Médicis**, as regent, or acting ruler. The Huguenots followed the lead of the Bourbon family, who stood first in line to inherit the throne if the Valois kings failed to produce a male heir. The most militantly Catholic nobles took their cues from the Guise family. Catherine tried to play the Bourbon and Guise factions against each other, but civil war erupted in 1562. Both sides committed terrible atrocities. Priests and pastors were murdered, and massacres of whole congregations became frighteningly commonplace.

Although a Catholic herself, Catherine feared the rise of Guise influence, so she arranged the marriage of the king's Catholic sister, Marguerite de Valois, to Henry of Navarre, a Huguenot and Bourbon. Just four days after the wedding, in August 1572, an assassin tried but failed to kill one of the Huguenot leaders. Violence against Calvinists spiraled out of control. On St. Bartholomew's Day, August 24, a bloodbath began, fueled by years of growing animosity between Catholics and Protestants. In three days, Catholic mobs murdered some two thousand Huguenots in Paris. Three thousand Huguenots died in the provinces over the next six weeks. The pope joyfully ordered the church bells rung throughout Catholic Europe.

Huguenot pamphleteers now proclaimed their right to resist a tyrant who worshipped idols (a practice that Calvinists equated with Catholicism). This right of resistance was linked to a political notion of contract; upholding the true religion was part of the contract binding the ruler to his subjects. Both the right of resistance and the idea of a contract fed into the larger doctrine of constitutionalism — that a government's legitimacy rested on its upholding a constitution, or contract between ruler and ruled. The religious division in France grew even more dangerous when Charles IX died and his brother Henry III (r. 1574–1589) became king. Like his brothers before him, Henry III failed to produce an heir. Convinced that Henry III lacked the will to root out Protestantism, the Guises formed the Catholic League, which requested help from Spanish king Philip II. Henry III responded in 1588 by having his men kill two Guise leaders. A few months later, a fanatical Catholic monk stabbed Henry III to death, and Henry of Navarre became Henry IV (r. 1589–1610), despite Philip II's military intervention.

With the Catholic League threatening to declare his succession invalid, Henry IV publicly embraced Catholicism, reputedly explaining, "Paris is worth a Mass." Within a few years he defeated the ultra-Catholic opposition and drove out the Spanish. In 1598, he issued the **Edict of Nantes**, in which he granted the Huguenots a large measure of religious toleration. The approximately 1.25 million Huguenots became a legally protected minority within an officially Catholic kingdom of some 20 million people. Protestants were free to worship in specified towns and were allowed their own troops, fortresses, and even courts.

Few believed in religious toleration as an ideal, but Henry IV followed the advice of those moderate Catholics and Calvinists — together called *politiques* — who urged him to give priority to the development of a durable state. The politiques believed that religious disputes could be resolved only in the peace provided by strong government. The French Catholic writer Michel de Montaigne (1533–1592) went even further than this pragmatic position and revived the ancient doctrine of skepticism, which held that total certainty is never attainable. On the beams of his study he painted the statement "All that is certain is that nothing is certain." Like toleration of religious differences, such skepticism was repugnant to Protestants and Catholics alike, both of whom were certain that their religion was the right one.

The Edict of Nantes ended the French Wars of Religion, but Henry still needed to reestablish monarchical authority and hold the fractious nobles in check. He allowed rich merchants and lawyers to buy offices and, in exchange for an annual payment, pass their positions on to their heirs or sell them to someone else. This new social elite was known as the "nobility of the robe" (named after the robes that magistrates wore, much like the ones judges wear today). Income raised by the increased sale of offices reduced the state debt and also helped Henry strengthen the monarchy. His efforts did not, however, prevent his enemies from assassinating him in 1610 after nineteen unsuccessful attempts.

Dutch Revolt against Spain

Although he failed to prevent Henry IV from taking the French throne in 1589, **Philip II** of Spain (r. 1556–1598) was the most powerful ruler in Europe (Map 15.1). In addition to the western Habsburg lands in Spain and the Netherlands, Philip had inherited from his father, Charles V, all the Spanish colonies recently settled in the New World of the Americas. Gold and silver funneled from the colonies supported his campaigns against the Ottoman Turks and the French and the English Protestants. But all the money of the New World could not prevent Philip's eventual defeat in the Netherlands, where Calvinist rebels established the independent Dutch Republic, which soon vied with Spain, France, and England for commercial supremacy.

A deeply devout Catholic, Philip II came to the Spanish throne at age twenty-eight determined to restore Catholic unity in Europe and lead the Christian defense against the Muslims. His brief marriage to Mary Tudor (Mary I of England) did not produce an heir, but it and his subsequent marriage to Elisabeth de Valois, the sister of Charles IX and Henry III of France, gave him reason enough for involvement in English and French affairs. In 1578, the king of Portugal died fighting Muslims in Morocco, and two years later Philip took over this neighboring realm with its rich empire in Africa, India, and the Americas.

Philip insisted on Catholic unity in the lands under his control and worked to forge an international Catholic alliance against the Ottoman Turks. In 1571, he achieved the single greatest military victory of his reign when he joined with Venice and the papacy to defeat the Turks in a great sea battle off the Greek coast at **Lepanto**. Seventy thousand sailors and soldiers fought on the allied side, and eight thousand died. The Turks lost twenty thousand men.

Spain now controlled the western Mediterranean but could not pursue its advantage because of threats elsewhere. Between 1568 and 1570, the Moriscos — Muslim converts to Christianity who remained secretly faithful to Islam — had revolted in the south of Spain, killing ninety priests and fifteen hundred Christians. Philip retaliated

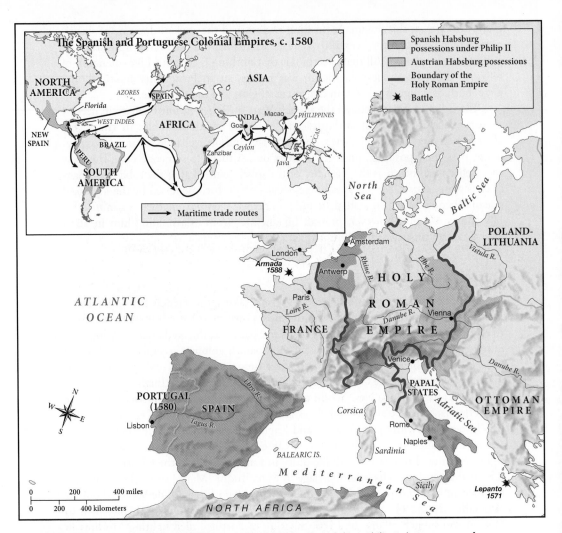

MAP 15.1   The Empire of Philip II, r. 1556–1598   Spanish king Philip II drew revenues from a truly worldwide empire. In 1580, he was the richest European ruler, but the demands of governing and defending his control of such far-flung territories eventually drained his resources.

by forcing fifty thousand Moriscos to leave their villages and resettle in other regions. In 1609, his successor, Philip III, ordered their expulsion from Spanish territory, and by 1614 some 300,000 Moriscos had been forced to relocate to North Africa.

The Calvinists of the Netherlands were less easily intimidated: they were far from Spain and accustomed to being left alone. After the Spanish Fury of 1576 outraged

The Battle of Lepanto   The Greek artist Antonio Vassilacchi painted this mural in 1600 to celebrate the Christian victory at the battle of Lepanto. Vassilacchi was working in Venice, which was one of the main Christian allies in the campaign against the Turks. The victory was considered so important that it was celebrated in writings, medals, paintings, and sculptures. The mural captures the violence and confusion of the battle. (Villa Barbarigo, Noventa Vicentina, Italy / Giraudon / Bridgeman Images.)

Calvinists and Catholics alike, Prince William of Orange (whose name came from the lands he owned in southern France) led the Netherlands' seven predominantly Protestant northern provinces into a military alliance with the ten mostly Catholic southern provinces and drove out the Spaniards. The Catholic southern provinces returned to the Spanish fold in 1579. Despite the assassination in 1584 of William of Orange, Spanish troops never regained control in the north. Spain would not formally recognize Dutch independence until 1648, but by the end of the sixteenth century the Dutch Republic (sometimes called Holland after the most populous of its seven provinces) was a self-governing state sheltering a variety of religious groups.

Religious toleration in the Dutch Republic developed for pragmatic reasons: the central government did not have the power to enforce religious orthodoxy. Each province governed itself and sent delegates to the one common institution, the States General. Although the princes of Orange resembled a ruling family, their powers paled next to those of local elites, known as regents. One-third of the Dutch population remained Catholic, and local authorities allowed them to worship as they chose in private. The Dutch Republic also had a relatively large Jewish population because many Jews had settled there after being driven out of Spain and Portugal. From 1597, Jews could worship openly in their synagogues. This openness to various religions would help make the Dutch Republic one of Europe's chief intellectual and scientific centers in the seventeenth and eighteenth centuries.

Well situated for maritime commerce, the Dutch Republic developed a thriving economy based on shipping and shipbuilding. Dutch merchants favored free trade in Europe because they could compete at an advantage. After the Dutch gained independence, Amsterdam became the main European money market for two centuries. The Dutch controlled many overseas markets thanks to their preeminence in seaborne commerce: by 1670, the Dutch commercial fleet was larger than the English, French, Spanish, Portuguese, and Austrian fleets combined.

Elizabeth I's Defense of English Protestantism

As the Dutch revolt unfolded, Philip II became increasingly infuriated with **Elizabeth I** (r. 1558–1603), who had succeeded her half sister Mary Tudor as queen of England. Philip had been married to Mary and had enthusiastically seconded Mary's efforts to return England to Catholicism. When Mary died in 1558, Elizabeth rejected Philip's proposal of marriage and promptly brought Protestantism back to England. She had to squash uprisings by Catholics in the north and at least two serious plots against her life. In the long run, however, her greatest challenges came from the Calvinist Puritans and Philip II.

The **Puritans** were strict Calvinists who opposed all vestiges of Catholic ritual in the Church of England. After Elizabeth became queen, many Puritans returned from exile abroad, but Elizabeth resisted their demands for drastic changes in church ritual and governance. The Church of England's Thirty-Nine Articles of Religion, issued under her authority in 1563, incorporated elements of Catholic ritual along with Calvinist doctrines. Puritans tried to undercut the crown-appointed bishops' authority by placing control of church administration in the hands of a local presbytery, that is, a group made up of the minister and the elders of the congregation. Elizabeth rejected this Calvinist presbyterianism.

The Puritans nonetheless steadily gained influence. Known for their emphasis on strict moral lives, the Puritans tried to close England's theaters and Sunday fairs. Every Puritan father—with the help of his wife—was to "make his house a little church" by teaching the children to read the Bible. Believing themselves God's elect—those whom God has chosen for mercy and salvation—and England an "elect nation," the Puritans also pushed Elizabeth to help Protestants on the continent. After Philip II annexed Portugal and began to interfere in French affairs, Elizabeth dispatched seven thousand soldiers in 1585 to help the Dutch rebels.

Philip II bided his time as long as Elizabeth remained unmarried and her Catholic cousin Mary Stuart, better known as Mary, queen of Scots, stood next in line to inherit the English throne. In 1568, Scottish Calvinists forced Mary to abdicate the throne of Scotland in favor of her one-year-old son James (eventually James I of England), who was then raised as a Protestant. After her abdication, Mary spent nearly twenty years under house arrest in England. In 1587, when a letter from Mary offering her succession rights to Philip was discovered, Elizabeth overcame her reluctance to execute a fellow monarch and ordered Mary's beheading.

Now determined to act, Philip II sent his armada (Spanish for "fleet") of 130 ships from Lisbon toward the English Channel in May 1588. The English scattered the Spanish Armada by sending blazing fire ships into its midst. A great gale then forced the Spanish to flee around Scotland. When the armada limped home in September, half the ships had been lost and thousands of sailors were dead or starving. Protestants throughout Europe rejoiced.

By the time Philip II died in 1598, the costs of fighting the Ottomans, Dutch, English, and French had finally bankrupted the treasury. In his novel *Don Quixote* (1605), the Spanish writer Miguel de Cervantes captured the disappointment of thwarted Spanish ambitions. Cervantes himself had been wounded at Lepanto. His novel's hero, a minor nobleman, reads so many romances and books of chivalry that he loses his sense of proportion and wanders the countryside futilely trying to mimic the heroic deeds he has come across in his reading.

Elizabeth made the most of her limited means and consolidated England's position as a Protestant power. In her early years, she held out the prospect of marriage to many political suitors; but in order to maintain her—and England's—independence, she never married. Her successor, James I (r. 1603–1625), came to the throne as king of both Scotland and England. Shakespeare's tragedies *Hamlet* (1601), *King Lear* (1605), and *Macbeth* (1606), written around the time of James's succession, might all be read as commentaries on the uncertainties faced by Elizabeth and James. But Elizabeth's story, unlike Shakespeare's tragedies, had a happy ending: she left James secure in a kingdom of growing weight in world politics.

The Clash of Faiths and Empires in Eastern Europe

In the east, the most contentious border divided Christian Europe from the Islamic realm of the Ottoman Turks. Recovering quickly from their defeat at Lepanto in 1571, the Ottomans continued their attacks, seizing Venetian-held Cyprus in 1573. In the Balkans, rather than forcibly converting their Christian subjects to Islam, the Turks allowed them to cling to the Greek Orthodox faith. They welcomed Jews expelled from Spain, and Jews soon made up 10 percent of the population of Istanbul.

The Muscovite tsars officially protected the Russian Orthodox church, which faced no competition within Russian lands. Building on the base laid by his grandfather Ivan III, Tsar Ivan IV (r. 1533–1584) stopped at nothing in his endeavor to make Muscovy (the grand duchy centered on Moscow) the heart of a mighty Russian empire. Given to unpredictable fits of rage, Ivan murdered his own son with an iron rod during a quarrel. His epithet "the Terrible" reflects not only the terror he unleashed but also the awesome impression he evoked. Cunning and cruel, Ivan came to embody barbarism in the eyes of Westerners.

Ivan initiated Russian expansion eastward into Siberia, but two formidable foes blocked his plans for expansion westward: Sweden (which then included much of present-day Finland) and Poland-Lithuania. Poland and the grand duchy of Lithuania united into a single commonwealth in 1569 and controlled an extensive territory. After Ivan IV died in 1584, a terrible period of chaos known as the Time of Troubles ensued, during which the king of Poland-Lithuania tried to put his son on the Russian throne. In 1613, an army of nobles, townspeople, and peasants finally expelled the intruders and put on the throne a nobleman, Michael Romanov (r. 1613–1645), who established an enduring new dynasty.

> **REVIEW**   How did state power depend on religious unity at the end of the sixteenth century and start of the seventeenth?

The Thirty Years' War, 1618–1648

Although the eastern states managed to avoid civil wars over religion in the early seventeenth century, the rest of Europe was drawn into the final and most deadly of the wars of religion, the Thirty Years' War. It began in 1618 with conflicts between Catholics and Protestants within the Holy Roman Empire and eventually involved most European states. By its end in 1648, many central European lands lay in ruins and the balance of power had shifted away from the Habsburg powers—Spain and Austria—toward France, England, and the Dutch Republic. Prolonged warfare created turmoil and suffering, but it also fostered the growth of armies and bureaucracies; out of the carnage would emerge centralized and powerful states that made increasing demands on ordinary people.

Origins and Course of the War

The fighting that devastated central Europe had its origins in a combination of religious disputes, ethnic competition, and political weakness. The Austrian Habsburgs officially ruled over the huge Holy Roman Empire, which comprised eight major ethnic groups. The emperor and four of the seven electors who chose him were Catholic; the other three electors were Protestants. The Peace of Augsburg of 1555 (see page 421) maintained the balance between Catholics and Lutherans, but it had no mechanism for resolving conflicts; tensions rose as Calvinism, unrecognized under the peace, made inroads into Lutheran areas. By 1613, two of the three Protestant electors had become Calvinists.

These conflicts came to a head when the Catholic Habsburg heir Archduke Ferdinand was crowned king of Bohemia (present-day Czech Republic) in 1617. The Austrian Habsburgs held not only the imperial crown of the Holy Roman Empire but also a collection of separately administered royal crowns, of which Bohemia was one. Once crowned, Ferdinand began to curtail the religious freedom previously granted to Czech Protestants. When Ferdinand was elected emperor (as Ferdinand II, r. 1619–1637), the rebellious Czechs deposed him and chose in his place the young Calvinist Frederick V of the Palatinate (r. 1616–1623). A quick series of clashes ended in 1620 when the imperial armies defeated the outmanned Czechs at the battle of White Mountain, near Prague. The Czechs would not gain their independence until 1918.

The battle of White Mountain did not end the war, which soon spread to the German lands of the empire. Private mercenary armies (armies for hire) began to form during the fighting, and the emperor had little control over them. Albrecht von Wallenstein (1583–1634), a Czech Protestant by birth, offered in 1625 to raise an army for Ferdinand II and soon had in his employ 125,000 soldiers, who plundered much of Protestant Germany with the emperor's approval. The Lutheran king of Denmark, Christian IV (r. 1596–1648), responded by invading northern Germany. General Wallenstein's forces defeated him. Emboldened by his general's victories, Emperor Ferdinand issued the Edict of Restitution in 1629, which outlawed Calvinism in the empire and reclaimed Catholic church properties confiscated by the Lutherans.

With Protestant interests in serious jeopardy, Gustavus Adolphus (r. 1611–1632) of Sweden marched into Germany in 1630 with a highly trained army of 100,000 soldiers. Hoping to block Spanish intervention in the war, the French monarchy's chief minister, Cardinal Richelieu (1585–1642), offered to subsidize the Lutheran Gustavus. This agreement between the Swedish Lutheran and French Catholic powers to fight the Catholic Habsburgs showed that state interests could outweigh religious considerations.

Gustavus defeated the imperial army and occupied the Catholic parts of southern Germany before he was killed at the battle of Lützen in 1632. Once again the tide turned, but this time it swept Wallenstein with it. Because Wallenstein was rumored to be negotiating with Protestant powers, Ferdinand had him assassinated.

France openly joined the fray in 1635 by declaring war on Spain. The two Catholic powers pummeled each other. The French king Louis XIII (r. 1610–1643) hoped to profit from the troubles of Spain in the Netherlands and from the conflicts between the Austrian emperor and his Protestant subjects. A series of internal revolts shook the perennially cash-strapped Spanish crown. In 1640, peasants in the rich northeastern province of Catalonia rebelled, overrunning Barcelona and killing the viceroy of the province. The Portuguese also revolted in 1640 and proclaimed independence like the Dutch. In 1643, the Spanish suffered their first major defeat at French hands. Although the Spanish were forced to concede independence to Portugal (annexed to Spain only since 1580), they eventually suppressed the Catalan revolt.

France, too, faced exhaustion after years of rising taxes and recurrent revolts. Richelieu died in 1642. Louis XIII followed him a few months later and was succeeded by his five-year-old son, Louis XIV. With yet another foreign queen mother — she was the daughter of the Spanish king — serving as regent and an Italian cardinal, Mazarin, providing advice, French politics once again moved into a period of instability, rumor, and crisis. All sides were ready for peace.

The Effects of Constant Fighting

When peace negotiations began in the 1640s, they did not come a moment too soon. Some towns had faced several prolonged sieges during the decades of fighting. Even worse suffering took place in the countryside. Peasants fled their villages, which were often burned down. At times, desperate peasants revolted and attacked nearby castles and monasteries. War and intermittent outbreaks of plague cost some German towns one-third or more of their population. One-third of the inhabitants of Bohemia also perished.

Soldiers did not fare all that much better. An Englishman who fought for the Dutch army in 1633 described how he slept on the wet ground, got his boots full of water, and "at peep of day looked like a drowned ratt." Governments increasingly short of funds often failed to pay the troops, and frequent mutinies, looting, and pillaging resulted. Armies attracted all sorts of displaced people desperately in need of provisions. In the last year of the Thirty Years' War, the Imperial-Bavarian Army had 40,000 men entitled to draw rations—and more than 100,000 wives, prostitutes, servants, children, and other camp followers forced to scrounge for their own food.

The Peace of Westphalia, 1648

The comprehensive settlement provided by the **Peace of Westphalia**—named after the German province where negotiations took place—would serve as a model for resolving future conflicts among warring European states. For the first time, a diplomatic congress convened to address international disputes, and those signing the treaties guaranteed the resulting settlement. A method still in use, the congress was the first to bring *all* parties together, rather than two or three at a time.

France and Sweden gained most from the Peace of Westphalia. France acquired parts of Alsace and replaced Spain as the prevailing power on the continent. Sweden took several northern territories from the Holy Roman Empire (Map 15.2). The Habsburgs lost the most. The Spanish Habsburgs recognized Dutch independence after eighty years of war. Each German prince in the Holy Roman Empire gained the right to establish Lutheranism, Catholicism, or Calvinism in his state, a right denied to Calvinist rulers by the Peace of Augsburg in 1555. The independence ceded to German princes sustained political divisions that prepared the way for the emergence of a new power, the Hohenzollern Elector of Brandenburg, who increased his territories and developed a small but effective standing army. After losing considerable territory in the west, the Austrian Habsburgs turned eastward to concentrate on restoring Catholicism to Bohemia and wresting Hungary from the Turks.

The Peace of Westphalia settled the distribution of the main religions in the Holy Roman Empire: Lutheranism would dominate in the north, Calvinism in the area of the Rhine River, and Catholicism in the south. Most of the territorial changes in Europe remained intact until the nineteenth century. In the future, international warfare would be undertaken for reasons of national security, commercial ambition, or dynastic pride rather than to enforce religious uniformity. As the politiques of the

MAP 15.2　The Thirty Years' War and the Peace of Westphalia, 1648　The Thirty Years' War involved many of the major continental European powers. The arrows marking invasion routes show that most of the fighting took place in central Europe in the lands of the Holy Roman Empire. The German states and Bohemia sustained the greatest damage during the fighting. None of the combatants emerged unscathed because even ultimate winners such as Sweden and France depleted their resources of men and money.

late sixteenth century had hoped, state interests now outweighed motivations of faith in political affairs.

The nearly constant warfare that preceded the peace had one surprising result: despite the death and destruction, warfare had increased state authority. As armies grew to bolster the war effort, governments needed more money and more supervisory officials. The rate of land tax paid by French peasants doubled in the eight years after France joined the war. In addition to raising taxes, governments deliberately depreciated the value of the currency, which often resulted in soaring prices. When all else failed, rulers declared bankruptcy. The Spanish government, for example, did so three times in the first half of the seventeenth century. From Portugal to Muscovy, ordinary people resisted new taxes by forming makeshift armies and battling royal forces. With their colorful banners, unlikely leaders, strange names (the Nu-Pieds, or "Barefooted," in France, for instance), and crude weapons, the rebels usually proved no match for state armies, but they did keep troops occupied.

To meet these new demands, monarchs relied on advisers who took on the role of modern prime ministers. Louis XIII's chief minister, Cardinal Richelieu, proclaimed the priority of *raison d'état* ("reason of state"), that is, the state's interest

The Arts and State Power   In this enigmatic painting from 1656 called *Las Meninas* ("Maids of Honor"), the Spanish artist Diego Velázquez depicts the Spanish king Philip IV's five-year-old daughter, Margarita, with her maids of honor, chaperone, bodyguard, two dwarves, and a large dog. The painter himself is working at a large canvas on the viewer's left side of the room. In the background on the left, a mirror reflects the upper bodies of the king and queen, who are presumably watching the scene. Which of these many figures is the real center of the painting? Like most monarchs of the time, Philip employed court painters like Velázquez to paint their portraits and contribute to their prestige. Ten years later Margarita would marry Holy Roman Emperor Leopold I, who was her uncle. (Detail, *Las Meninas*, by Diego Velázquez [1599–1660]. Prado, Madrid, Spain / Giraudon / Bridgeman Images.)

above all else. He silenced Protestants within France because they had become too independent, and he crushed noble and popular resistance to Louis's policies. He set up intendants—delegates from the king's council dispatched to the provinces—to oversee police, army, and financial affairs.

To justify the growth of state authority and the expansion of government bureaucracies, rulers carefully cultivated their royal images. James I of England argued that he ruled by divine right and was accountable only to God: "The state of monarchy is the supremest thing on Earth; for kings are not only God's lieutenant on Earth, but even by God himself they are called gods." He advised his son to maintain a manly appearance even as some courtiers complained of his behavior toward certain male favorites. Appearance counted for so much that most rulers regulated who could wear which kinds of cloth and decoration, reserving the richest and rarest, such as ermine and gold, for themselves.

> **REVIEW**   Why did a war fought over religious differences result in stronger states?

Economic Crisis and Realignment

The devastation caused by the Thirty Years' War deepened an economic crisis that was already under way. After a century of rising prices, caused partly by massive transfers of gold and silver from the New World and partly by population growth, in the early 1600s prices began to level off and even to drop, and in most places population growth slowed. International trade fell into recession. Agricultural yields also declined, and peasants and townspeople alike were less able to pay the escalating taxes needed to finance the wars. Famine and disease trailed grimly behind economic crisis and war, in some areas causing large-scale uprisings and revolts. Behind the scenes, the economic balance of power gradually shifted as northwestern Europe began to dominate international trade and broke the stranglehold of Spain and Portugal in the New World.

From Growth to Recession

Population grew and prices rose in the second half of the sixteenth century. England's population grew by 70 percent and in parts of Spain the population grew by 100 percent (that is, it doubled). The supply of precious metals from the New World reached its height in the 1590s. This flood of precious metals combined with population growth to fuel an astounding inflation in food prices in western Europe—400 percent in the sixteenth century—and a more moderate rise in the cost of manufactured goods. Wages rose much more slowly, at about half the rate of the increase in food prices.

Recession did not strike everywhere at the same time, but the warning signs were unmistakable. Foreign trade slumped as war and an uncertain money supply made business riskier. Imports of gold and silver declined, in part because so many of the native Americans who worked in Spanish colonial mines died from disease. Textile production fell in many countries, largely because of decreased demand and a shrinking labor force. The trade in African slaves grew steadily between 1580 and 1630 and then it, too, declined by a third, though its growth would resume after 1650 and skyrocket after 1700. African slaves were first transported to the new colony of Virginia in 1619, foreshadowing a major transformation of economic life in the New World colonies.

Demographic slowdown also signaled economic trouble. In the Mediterranean, growth had already stopped in the 1570s. The most sudden reversal occurred in central Europe as a result of the Thirty Years' War: one-fourth of the inhabitants of the Holy Roman Empire perished in the 1630s and 1640s. Population growth continued only in England, the Dutch Republic, the Spanish Netherlands, and Scandinavia.

Where the population stagnated or declined, agricultural prices dropped because of less demand, and farmers who produced for the market suffered. The price of grain fell most precipitously, causing many farmers to convert grain-growing land to pasture or vineyards. The only country that emerged unscathed from this downturn was the Dutch Republic, thanks to a growing population and a tradition of agricultural innovation. Inhabiting Europe's most densely populated area, the Dutch developed systems of field drainage, crop rotation, and animal husbandry that provided high yields of grain for both people and animals. Their foreign trade, textile industry, crop production, and population all grew. After the Dutch, the English fared best; unlike the Spanish, the English never depended on infusions of New World gold and silver to shore up their economy, and unlike most continental European countries, England escaped the direct impact of the Thirty Years' War.

Historians have long disagreed about the causes of the early-seventeenth-century recession. Some cite the inability of agriculture to support a growing population by the end of the sixteenth century; others blame the Thirty Years' War, the states' demands for more taxes, or the waste caused by middle-class expenditures in the desire to emulate the nobility. To this list of causes, recent researchers have added climatic changes. Cold winters and wet summers meant bad harvests, and these natural disasters ushered in a host of social catastrophes. When the harvest was bad, prices shot back up and many could not afford to feed themselves.

Consequences for Daily Life

The recession of the early 1600s had both short-term and long-term effects. In the short term, it aggravated the threat of food shortages, increased the outbreaks of famine and disease, and caused people to leave their families and homes. In the long term, it deepened the division between prosperous and poor peasants and fostered the development of a new pattern of late marriages and smaller families.

When grain harvests fell short, peasants immediately suffered because, outside of England and the Dutch Republic, grain had replaced more expensive meat as the essential staple of most Europeans' diets. By the end of the sixteenth century, the average adult European ate more than four hundred pounds of grain per year. Peasants

The Life of the Poor This mid-seventeenth-century painting by the Dutch artist Adriaen Pietersz van de Venne depicts the poor peasant weighed down by his wife and child. An empty food bowl signifies their hunger. In reality, many poor men abandoned their homes in search of work, leaving their wives behind to cope with hungry children and what remained of the family farm. What did the artist intend to convey about women? (*Allegory of Poverty*, 1630s [oil on panel] by Adriaen Pietersz van de Venne [1589–1662]/Allen Memorial Art Museum, Oberlin College, Ohio, USA/Mrs. F. F. Prentiss Fund, Bridgeman Images.)

lived on bread, soup with a little fat or oil, peas or lentils, garden vegetables in season, and only occasionally a piece of meat or fish.

When faced with famine, most people simply left their huts and hovels and took to the road in search of food and charity. Men left their families to search for better conditions elsewhere. Those left behind might be reduced to eating chestnuts, roots, bark, and grass. In eastern France in 1637, a witness reported, "The roads were paved with people. . . . Finally it came to cannibalism." Compassion sometimes gave way to fear when hungry vagabonds became more aggressive, occasionally threatening to burn a barn if they were not given food.

Successive bad harvests led to malnutrition, which weakened people and made them more susceptible to such epidemic diseases as the plague, typhoid fever, typhus, dysentery, smallpox, and influenza. The plague was feared most: in one year it could cause the death of up to half of a town's or village's population, and it struck with no discernible pattern. Nearly 5 percent of France's entire population died just in the plague of 1628–1632.

Economic crisis widened the gap between rich and poor. Peasants paid rent to their landlords as well as fees for inheriting or selling land and tolls for using mills, wine presses, or ovens. States collected direct taxes on land and sales taxes on consumer goods such as salt, an essential preservative. Protestant and Catholic churches alike exacted a tithe (a tax equivalent to one-tenth of the parishioner's annual income); often the clergy took their tithe in the form of crops and collected it directly during the harvest. Any reversal of fortune could force peasants into the homeless world of vagrants and beggars, who numbered as much as 2 percent of the total population.

In England, the Dutch Republic, northern France, and northwestern Germany, improvements gave some peasants the means to become farmers who rented substantial holdings, produced for the market, and in good times enjoyed relative comfort and higher status. Those who could not afford to plant new crops such as maize (American corn) or to use techniques that ensured higher yields became simple laborers with little or no land of their own. One-half to four-fifths of the peasants did not have enough land to support a family. They descended deeper into debt during difficult times and often lost their land to wealthier farmers or to city officials intent on developing rural estates.

As the recession deepened, women lost some of their economic opportunities. Widows who had been able to take over their late husbands' trade now found themselves excluded by the urban guilds or limited to short tenures. Many women went into domestic service until they married, some for their entire lives. Town governments carefully regulated the work of female servants, requiring women to stay in their positions unless they could prove mistreatment by a master.

European families reacted to economic downturn by postponing marriage and having fewer children. When hard times passed, more people married and had more children. But even in the best of times, one-fifth to one-quarter of all children died in their first year, and half died before age twenty. Childbirth still carried great risks for women, about 10 percent of whom died in the process. Midwives delivered most babies; physicians were scarce, and even those who did attend births were generally less helpful than midwives. The Englishwoman Alice Thornton described in her diary how a doctor bled her to prevent a miscarriage after a fall (bloodletting, often by the application of leeches, was a common medical treatment); her son died anyway in a breech birth that almost killed her, too.

Beginning in the early seventeenth century and continuing until the end of the eighteenth, families in all ranks of society started to limit the number of children. Because methods of contraception were not widely known, they did this for the most part by marrying later; the average age at marriage during the seventeenth century rose from the early twenties to the late twenties. The average family had about four children. Poorer families seem to have had fewer children, wealthier ones more. Because Protestant and Catholic clergy alike stressed sexual fidelity and abstinence before marriage, the number of births out of wedlock was relatively small (2–5 percent of births); premarital intercourse was generally tolerated only after a couple had announced their engagement.

The Economic Balance of Power

Just as the recession of the early seventeenth century produced winners and losers among ordinary people, it also created winners and losers among the competing states of Europe. The economies of southern Europe declined during this period, whereas those of the northwest emerged stronger. Competition in the New World reflected and reinforced this shift as the English, Dutch, and French rushed to establish trading outposts and permanent settlements to compete with the Spanish and Portuguese.

The new powers of northwestern Europe, with their growing Atlantic trade, gradually displaced the Mediterranean economies, which had dominated European commerce since the time of the Greeks and Romans. England and the Dutch Republic vied with France to become the leading mercantile and slave-trading powers. Northern Italian industries were eclipsed; Spanish commerce with the New World dropped. Even the plague contributed to the new disparity in trading power. Whereas central Europe and the Mediterranean countries took generations to recover from its ravages, northwestern Europe quickly replaced its lost population, no doubt because this area's people had suffered less from the effects of the Thirty Years' War and from the malnutrition related to the economic crisis.

All but the remnants of serfdom had disappeared in western Europe, yet in eastern Europe nobles reinforced their dominance over peasants, and the burden of serfdom increased. The rise in the cost of grain in the sixteenth century prompted Polish and eastern German nobles to increase their holdings and step up their production of grain for western markets. In the economic downturn of the first half of the seventeenth century, peasants who were already dependent became serfs—completely tied to the land. Although enserfment produced short-term profits for landlords, in the long run it retarded economic development in eastern Europe and kept most of the population in a stranglehold of illiteracy and hardship.

Economic realignment also took place across the Atlantic Ocean. Because Spain and Portugal had divided between themselves the rich spoils of South America, other prospective colonizers had to carve niches in seemingly less hospitable places, especially North America and the Caribbean (Map 15.3). Eventually, the English, French, and Dutch would dominate commerce with these colonies. Many European states, including Sweden and Denmark, chartered private joint-stock companies to enrich investors by importing fish, furs, tobacco, and precious metals (if they could be found), and to develop new markets for European products. British, French, Dutch, and Danish companies also began trading slaves.

In establishing permanent colonies, the Europeans created whole new communities across the Atlantic. Careful plans could not always surmount the hazards of transatlantic shipping, however. In 1620 the *Mayflower*, which had sailed for Virginia with Pilgrim emigrants, landed off-course far to the north in Massachusetts, where the settlers founded New Plymouth Colony. By the 1640s, the British North American colonies had more than fifty thousand people, of whom perhaps a thousand were Africans. The Indians native to the area had been decimated in epidemics and wars.

In contrast, French Canada had only about three thousand European inhabitants by 1640. Though thin in numbers, the French rapidly moved into the Great Lakes region. Fur traders sought beaver pelts to make the hats that had taken Paris fashion by storm. Jesuit missionaries lived with native American groups, learning their languages and describing their ways of life.

Both England and France turned some attention as well to the Caribbean in the 1620s and 1630s when they occupied the islands of the West Indies after driving off the

MAP 15.3   European Colonization of the Americas, c. 1640   Europeans coming to the Americas established themselves first in coastal areas. The English, French, and Dutch set up most of their colonies in the Caribbean and North America because the Spanish and Portuguese had already colonized the easily accessible regions in South America. Vast inland areas still remained unexplored and uncolonized in 1640.

native Caribs. These islands would prove ideal for a plantation economy of African slaves tending sugarcane and tobacco crops under the supervision of European settlers.

Even as the British and French moved into North America and the Caribbean, Spanish explorers traveled the Pacific coast up to what is now northern California and pushed into New Mexico. On the other side of the world, in the Philippines, the Spanish competed with local Muslim rulers and indigenous tribal leaders to extend their control. Spanish officials worked closely with Catholic missionaries to rule over a colony composed of indigenous peoples, Spaniards, and some Chinese merchants.

REVIEW   What were the consequences of economic recession in the early 1600s?

The Rise of Science and a Scientific Worldview

The countries that moved ahead economically in the first half of the seventeenth century—England, the Dutch Republic, and to some extent France—turned out to be the most receptive to the rise of science and a scientific worldview. In the long-term process known as **secularization**, religion gradually became a matter of private conscience rather than public policy. Secularization did not entail a loss of religious faith, but it did prompt a search for nonreligious explanations for political authority and natural phenomena. During the late sixteenth and early seventeenth centuries, science, political theory, and even art began to break their long-standing bonds with religion. Scientists and scholars sought laws in nature to explain politics as well as movements in the heavens and on Earth. The visual arts more frequently depicted secular subjects. A scientific revolution was in the making. Yet traditional attitudes did not disappear. Belief in magic and witchcraft pervaded every level of society. People of all classes believed that the laws of nature reflected a divine plan for the universe. They accepted supernatural explanations for natural phenomena, a view only gradually and partially undermined by new ideas.

The Scientific Revolution

Although the Catholic and Protestant churches encouraged the study of science and many prominent scientists were themselves clerics, the search for a secular, scientific method of determining the laws of nature undermined traditional accounts of natural phenomena. Christian doctrine had incorporated the scientific teachings of ancient philosophers, especially Ptolemy and Aristotle; now these came into question. A revolution in astronomy contested the Ptolemaic view, endorsed by the Catholic church, which held that the sun revolved around the Earth. Startling breakthroughs took place in medicine, too. Supporters of these new developments argued for the **scientific method**, which combined experimental observation and mathematical deduction. The use of the scientific method culminated in the astounding breakthroughs of Isaac Newton at the end of the seventeenth century. Newton's ability to explain the motion of the planets, as well as everyday objects on Earth, gave science enormous new prestige.

The traditional account of the movement of the heavens derived from the second-century Greek astronomer Ptolemy, who put the Earth at the center of the cosmos. Above the Earth were fixed the moon, the stars, and the planets in concentric crystalline spheres; beyond these fixed spheres dwelt God and the angels. In this view, the sun revolved around the Earth, the heavens were perfect and unchanging, and the Earth was "corrupted." Ptolemy insisted that the planets revolved in circular orbits (because circles were more "perfect" than other figures). To account for the actual elliptical paths that could be observed and calculated, he posited orbits within orbits, or epicycles.

In 1543, the Polish clergyman Nicolaus Copernicus (1473–1543) began the revolution in astronomy by publishing his treatise *On the Revolution of the Celestial Spheres*. Copernicus attacked the Ptolemaic account, arguing that the Earth and other planets revolved around the sun, a view known as **heliocentrism** (a sun-centered universe). He discovered that by placing the sun instead of the Earth at the center of the system of spheres, he could eliminate many epicycles from the calculations and thus simplify the mathematics. Copernicus died soon after publishing his theories, but when the Italian monk Giordano Bruno (1548–1600) taught heliocentrism, the Catholic Inquisition (set up to seek out heretics) arrested him and burned him at the stake.

Copernicus's views began to attract widespread attention in the early 1600s. When the Danish astronomer Tycho Brahe (1546–1601) observed a new star in 1572 and a comet in 1577, the traditional view that the universe was unchanging came into question. Brahe still rejected heliocentrism, but the assistant he employed when he moved to Prague in 1599, Johannes Kepler (1571–1630), was won over to the Copernican view. Kepler developed three laws of planetary motion, published between 1609 and 1619, that provided mathematical backing for heliocentrism and directly challenged the claim long held, even by Copernicus, that planetary motion was circular. Kepler's first law stated that the orbits of the planets are ellipses, with the sun always at one focus of the ellipse.

The Italian astronomer Galileo Galilei (1564–1642) provided more evidence to support the heliocentric view and also challenged the doctrine that the heavens were perfect and unchanging. After learning in 1609 that two Dutch astronomers had built a telescope, Galileo built a better one and observed the Earth's moon, four satellites of Jupiter, the phases of Venus (a cycle of changing physical appearances), and sunspots. The moon, the planets, and the sun were no more perfect than the Earth, he insisted, and the shadows he could see on the moon could only be the product of hills and valleys like those on Earth. Galileo portrayed the Earth as a moving part of a larger system, only one of many planets revolving around the sun, not as the fixed center of a single, closed universe.

In 1616, the Catholic church forbade Galileo to teach that the Earth moves; then, in 1633, it accused him of not obeying the earlier order. Forced to appear before the Inquisition, he agreed to publicly recant his assertion about the movement

The Trial of Galileo In this anonymous painting of the trial held in 1633, Galileo appears seated on a chair in the center facing the church officials who accused him of heresy for insisting that the sun, not the Earth, was the center of the universe (heliocentrism). Catholic officials forced him to recant or suffer the death penalty. Undated, the painting probably comes from a later time because contemporary paintings rarely included so many different figures each occupied in their own fashion. (Private Collection/Bridgeman Images.)

of the Earth to save himself from torture and death. Afterward, Galileo lived under house arrest and could publish his work only in the Dutch Republic, which had become a haven for scientists and thinkers who challenged conventional ideas.

In the same year that Copernicus challenged the traditional account in astronomy (1543), the Flemish scientist Andreas Vesalius (1514–1564) did the same for anatomy. Until then, medical knowledge in Europe was based on the writings of the second-century Greek physician Galen, Ptolemy's contemporary. Drawing on public dissections (which had been condemned by the Catholic church since 1300) he performed himself, Vesalius refuted Galen's work in his illustrated anatomical text, *On the Construction of the Human Body*. The English physician William Harvey (1578–1657) used dissection to examine the circulation of blood within the body, demonstrating how the heart worked as a pump. The heart and its valves were "a piece of machinery," Harvey insisted, and they obeyed mechanical laws. Nature, he said, could be understood by experiment and rational deduction, not by following traditional authorities.

In the 1630s, the European intellectual elite began to accept the new scientific views. Ancient learning, the churches and their theologians, and long-standing popular beliefs all seemed to be undercut by the scientific method. Two men were chiefly responsible for spreading the reputation of the scientific method in the first half of the seventeenth century: the English Protestant politician Sir Francis Bacon (1561–1626) and the French Catholic mathematician and philosopher René Descartes (1596–1650). They represented the two essential halves of the scientific method: inductive reasoning through observation and experimental research, and deductive reasoning from self-evident principles.

In *The Advancement of Learning* (1605), Bacon attacked reliance on ancient writers and optimistically predicted that the scientific method would lead to social progress. The minds of the medieval scholars, he said, had been "shut up in the cells of a few authors (chiefly Aristotle, their dictator) as their persons were shut up in the cells of monasteries and colleges," and they could therefore produce only "cobwebs of learning" that were "of no substance or profit." Knowledge, in Bacon's view, must be empirically based (that is, gained by observation and experiment).

Although Descartes agreed with Bacon's denunciation of traditional learning, he was concerned that the attack on tradition might only replace the dogmatism of the churches with the skepticism of Montaigne—that nothing at all was certain. Descartes aimed to establish the new science on more secure philosophical foundations, those of mathematics and logic. In his *Discourse on Method* (1637), he argued that mathematical and mechanical principles provided the key to understanding all of nature, including the actions of people and states. All prior assumptions must be repudiated in favor of one elementary principle: "I think, therefore I am." Everything else could—and should—be doubted, but even doubt showed the certain existence of someone thinking. Descartes insisted that human reason could not only unravel the secrets of nature but also prove the existence of God. Although he hoped to secure the authority of both church and state, his reliance on human reason rather than faith irritated authorities, and his books were banned in many places. He moved to the Dutch Republic to work in peace. Scientific research, like economic growth, became centered in the northern, Protestant countries, where it was less constrained by church control than in the Catholic south.

The power of the new scientific method was dramatically confirmed in the grand synthesis of the laws of motion developed by the English natural philosopher Isaac Newton (1642–1727). Born five years after the publication of Descartes's *Discourse on Method* and educated at Cambridge University, where he later became a professor, Newton brought his most significant mathematical and mechanical discoveries together in his masterwork, *Principia Mathematica* (1687). In it, he developed his law of universal gravitation, which explained both movement on Earth and the motion of the planets. His law held that every body in the universe exerts over every other body an attractive force directly proportional to the product of their masses and inversely proportional to the square of the distance between them. This law of universal gravitation explained Kepler's elliptical planetary orbits just as it accounted for the way an apple fell to the ground.

Newtonian physics combined mass, inertia, force, velocity, and acceleration— all key concepts in modern science—and made them quantifiable. Once set in motion, in Newton's view, the universe operated like a masterpiece made possible by the ingenuity of God. Newton saw no conflict between faith and science. He believed that by demonstrating that the physical universe followed rational principles, natural philosophers could prove the existence of God and so liberate humans from doubt and the fear of chaos. Even while laying the foundation for modern physics, optics, and mechanics, Newton spent long hours trying to calculate the date of the beginning of the world and its end with the second coming of Jesus. Others, less devout than Newton, envisioned a clockwork universe that had no need for God's continuing intervention.

The Natural Laws of Politics

In reaction to the religious wars, writers not only began to defend the primacy of state interests over those of religious conformity but also insisted on secular explanations for politics. The Italian political theorist Machiavelli had pointed in this direction with his advice to Renaissance princes in the early sixteenth century, but this secular intellectual movement gathered steam in the aftermath of the religious violence unleashed by the Reformation.

The French Catholic lawyer and politique Jean Bodin (1530–1596) sought systematic secular answers to the problem of disorder in *The Six Books of the Commonwealth* (1576). Comparing the different forms of government throughout history, he concluded that there were three basic types of sovereignty: monarchy, aristocracy, and democracy. Only strong monarchical power offered hope for maintaining order, he insisted, and so he rejected any doctrine of the right to resist tyrannical authority. While Bodin's ideas helped lay the foundation for absolutism — the idea that the monarch should be the sole and uncontested source of power — his systematic discussion of types of governments implied that they might be subject to choice and undercut the notion that monarchies were ordained by God, as most rulers maintained.

During the Dutch revolt against Spain, the legal scholar Hugo Grotius (1583–1645) furthered secular thinking by attempting to systematize the notion of "natural law" — laws of nature that give legitimacy to government and stand above the actions of any particular ruler or religious group. Grotius argued that natural law stood beyond the reach of either secular or divine authority; natural law would be valid even if God did not exist (though Grotius himself believed in God). By this account, natural law — not scripture, religious authority, or tradition — should govern politics. Such ideas got Grotius into trouble with both Catholics and Protestants. His work *The Laws of War and Peace* (1625) was condemned by the Catholic church, while the Dutch Protestant government arrested him for taking part in religious controversies. Grotius's wife helped him escape prison by hiding him in a chest of books. Grotius was one of the first to argue that international conventions should govern the treatment of prisoners of war and the making of peace treaties.

Grotius's conception of natural law also challenged the widespread use of torture. Most states and the courts of the Catholic church used torture when a serious crime had been committed and the evidence seemed to point to a particular defendant but no definitive proof had been established. The judges ordered torture—hanging the accused by the hands with a rope thrown over a beam or pressing the legs in a leg screw—to extract a confession, which had to be given with a medical expert and notary present and had to be repeated without torture.

To be in accord with natural law, Grotius argued, governments had to defend natural rights, which he defined as life, body, freedom, and honor. Grotius did not encourage rebellion in the name of natural law or rights, but did hope that someday all governments would adhere to these principles and stop killing their own and one another's subjects in the name of religion. Natural law and natural rights would play an important role in the founding of constitutional governments from the 1640s forward and in the establishment of various charters of human rights in our own time.

The Arts in an Age of Crisis

Two new forms of artistic expression—professional theater and opera—provided an outlet for secular values in an age of conflict over religious beliefs. Religion still played an important role in painting, however, even though many rulers also commissioned paintings on secular subjects.

The first professional acting companies performed before paying audiences in London, Seville, and Madrid in the 1570s. A huge outpouring of playwriting followed upon the formation of permanent professional theater companies. The Spanish playwright Lope de Vega (1562–1635) alone wrote more than fifteen hundred plays. Theaters were extremely popular despite Puritan opposition in England and Catholic objections in Spain. Shopkeepers, apprentices, lawyers, and court nobles crowded into open-air theaters to see everything from bawdy farces to profound tragedies.

The most enduring and influential playwright of the time—in fact, the man considered the greatest playwright of the English language—was William Shakespeare (1564–1616), who wrote three dozen plays (including histories, comedies, and tragedies) and was a member of a chief acting troupe. Although none of Shakespeare's plays were set in contemporary England, they reflected the concerns of his age: the nature of power and the crisis of authority. His tragedies in particular show the uncertainty and even chaos that result when power is misappropriated or misused. In *Hamlet* (1601), for example, the Danish prince Hamlet's mother marries the man who murdered his royal father and usurped the crown. In the end, Hamlet, his mother, and the usurper all die. Like many real-life people, Shakespeare's tragic characters found little peace in the turmoil of their times.

Although painting did not always touch broad popular audiences in the ways that theater could, new styles in art and especially church architecture helped shape ordinary people's experience of religion. In the late sixteenth century, the artistic style known as mannerism emerged in the Italian states and soon spread across Europe. Mannerism was an almost theatrical style that allowed painters to distort perspective to convey a message or emphasize a theme. The most famous mannerist painter, called El Greco because he was of Greek origin, trained in Venice and Rome before he moved to Spain in the 1570s. The religious intensity of El Greco's pictures found a ready audience in Catholic Spain, which had proved immune to the Protestant suspicion of ritual and religious imagery.

The most important new style was the **baroque**, which, like mannerism, originated in the Italian states. In place of the Renaissance emphasis on harmonious design, unity, and clarity, the baroque featured curves, exaggerated lighting, intense emotions, release from restraint, and even a kind of artistic sensationalism. Like many other historical designations, the word *baroque* ("irregularly shaped") was not used as a label by people living at the time; art critics in the eighteenth century coined the word to mean shockingly bizarre, confused, and extravagant, and art historians and collectors largely disdained the baroque until the late nineteenth century.

Closely tied to Catholic resurgence after the Reformation, the baroque melodramatically reaffirmed the emotional depths of the Catholic faith and glorified both church and monarchy. The style spread from Rome to other Italian states and then into central Europe. The Spanish built baroque churches in their American colonies as part of their massive conversion campaign.

A new secular musical form, the opera, grew up parallel to the baroque style in the visual arts. First influential in the Italian states, opera combined music, drama, dance, and scenery in a grand sensual display, often with themes chosen to please the ruler and the aristocracy. Composers could base operas on typically baroque sacred subjects or on traditional stories. Like many playwrights, including Shakespeare, opera composers often turned to familiar stories their audiences would recognize and readily follow. One of the most innovative composers of opera was Claudio Monteverdi (1567–1643), whose earliest operatic production, *Orfeo* (1607), was based on Greek mythology.

Magic and Witchcraft

Although artists, political thinkers, and scientific experimenters increasingly pursued secular goals, most remained as devout in their religious beliefs as ordinary people. Many scholars, including Newton, studied alchemy alongside their scientific pursuits. Alchemists aimed to discover techniques for turning lead and copper into gold. The astronomer Tycho Brahe defended his studies of alchemy and astrology as part of "natural magic," as opposed to demonic "black magic."

Learned and ordinary people alike also firmly believed in witchcraft, that is, the exercise of magical powers gained by a pact with the devil. The same Jean Bodin who argued against religious fanaticism insisted on death for witches—and for those magistrates who would not prosecute them. Trials of witches peaked in Europe between 1560 and 1640, the very time of the celebrated breakthroughs of the new science. Montaigne was one of the few to speak out against executing accused witches: "It is taking one's conjectures rather seriously to roast someone alive for them," he wrote in 1580.

Witches had long been blamed for destroying crops and causing personal catastrophes ranging from miscarriage to madness, but never before had they been officially persecuted in such numbers. Denunciation and persecution of witches coincided with the spread of reform, both Protestant and Catholic. Witch trials concentrated especially in the German lands of the Holy Roman Empire, the boiling cauldron of the Thirty Years' War.

The victims of the persecution were overwhelmingly female: women accounted for 80 percent of the accused witches in about 100,000 trials in Europe and North America during the sixteenth and seventeenth centuries. About one-third were sentenced to death. Before 1400, when witchcraft trials were rare, nearly half of those accused had been men. Why did attention now shift to women? Some official descriptions of witchcraft oozed lurid details of sexual orgies, in which women acted as the devil's sexual slaves. Social factors help explain the prominence of women among the accused. Accusers were almost always better off than those they accused. The poorest and most socially marginal people in most communities were elderly spinsters and widows. Because they were thought likely to hanker after revenge on those more fortunate, they were singled out as witches.

The tide turned against witchcraft trials when physicians, lawyers, judges, and even clergy came to suspect that accusations were based on superstition and fear. In 1682, a French royal decree treated witchcraft as fraud and imposture, meaning that the law did not recognize anyone as a witch. In 1693, the jurors who had convicted twenty people of witchcraft in Salem, Massachusetts, recanted, claiming: "We justly fear that we were sadly deluded and mistaken." The Salem jurors had not stopped believing in witches; they had simply lost confidence in their ability to identify them. When physicians and judges had believed in witches and carried out official persecutions, with torture, those accused of witchcraft had gone to their deaths in record numbers. But when the same groups distanced themselves from popular beliefs, the trials and the executions stopped.

> **REVIEW** How could belief in witchcraft and the rising prestige of the scientific method coexist?

Conclusion

The witchcraft persecutions reflected the traumas of these times of religious war, economic decline, and crises of political and intellectual authority. Deep differences over religion came to a head in the Thirty Years' War (1618–1648), which cut a path of destruction through central Europe and involved most of the European powers. Repulsed by the effects of religious violence, European rulers agreed to a peace that effectively removed disputes between Catholics and Protestants from the international arena. Almost everywhere rulers emerged from these decades of war with expanded powers that they would seek to extend further in the second half of the seventeenth century. The constant extension of state power is one of the defining themes of modern history; religious warfare gave it a jump-start.

For all their strength, however, rulers could not control economic, social, or intellectual trends. The economic downturn of the seventeenth century shifted economic

MAPPING THE WEST   The Religious Divisions of Europe, c. 1648   The Peace of Westphalia recognized major religious divisions within Europe that have endured for the most part to the present day. Catholicism dominated in southern Europe, Lutheranism had its stronghold in northern Europe, and Calvinism flourished along the Rhine River. In southeastern Europe, the Islamic Ottoman Turks accommodated the Greek Orthodox Christians under their rule but bitterly fought the Catholic Austrian Habsburgs for control of Hungary.

power from the Mediterranean world to northwestern Europe because England, France, and the Dutch Republic suffered less from the fighting of the Thirty Years' War and recovered more quickly from bad times. They would become even more powerful in the decades to come.

An underlying shift in cultural attitudes and intellectual expectations accompanied these changes. Secularization encompassed the establishment of the scientific method as the standard of truth, the search for nonreligious foundations of political authority, and the growing popularity of nonreligious forms of art, such as theater and opera. Proponents of these changes did not renounce their religious beliefs, and it would be foolish to claim that everyone's mental universe changed. The significance of secularization would only emerge over the long term.

Chapter Review

KEY TERMS AND PEOPLE

Be sure that you can identify the term or person and explain its historical significance.

Catherine de Médicis (p. 428)
Edict of Nantes (p. 428)
politiques (p. 428)
Philip II (p. 429)
Lepanto (p. 429)
Elizabeth I (p. 432)
Puritans (p. 432)

Peace of Westphalia (p. 436)
raison d'état (p. 438)
secularization (p. 445)
scientific method (p. 445)
heliocentrism (p. 446)
baroque (p. 451)

REVIEW QUESTIONS

1. How did state power depend on religious unity at the end of the sixteenth century and start of the seventeenth?
2. Why did a war fought over religious differences result in stronger states?
3. What were the consequences of economic recession in the early 1600s?
4. How could belief in witchcraft and the rising prestige of the scientific method coexist?

MAKING CONNECTIONS

1. How did the balance of power shift in Europe between 1560 and 1648? What were the main reasons for the shift?
2. What were the limits to the growth of secularization?
3. What was the influence of New World colonies on Europe from 1560 to 1648?
4. How did religious conflict mix with political concerns in this period?

IMPORTANT EVENTS

1562 • French Wars of Religion begin

1566 • Revolt of Calvinists against Spain begins in Netherlands

1569 • Formation of commonwealth of Poland-Lithuania

1571 • Battle of Lepanto marks victory of West over Ottomans at sea

1572 • St. Bartholomew's Day Massacre of French Protestants

1576 • Spanish Fury erupts in Antwerp

1588 • English defeat of Spanish Armada

1598 • French Wars of Religion end with Edict of Nantes

1601 • William Shakespeare, *Hamlet*

1618 • Thirty Years' War begins

1625 • Hugo Grotius publishes *The Laws of War and Peace*

1633 • Galileo Galilei forced to recant his support of heliocentrism

1635 • French join the Thirty Years' War by declaring war on Spain

1648 • Peace of Westphalia ends Thirty Years' War

16

Absolutism, Constitutionalism, and the Search for Order

1640–1700

CHAPTER FOCUS

What were the most important differences between absolutism and constitutionalism, and how did each system establish order?

IN MAY 1664, KING LOUIS XIV of France organized the first of many spectacular entertainments for his court at Versailles, where he had recently begun construction of a magnificent new palace. More than six hundred members of his court attended the weeklong series of parades, races, ballets, plays, and fireworks. In the opening parade, Louis was accompanied by an eighteen-foot-high float in the form of a chariot dedicated to Apollo, Greek god of the sun and Louis's personally chosen emblem. The king's favorite writers and musicians presented works specially prepared for the occasion, and each evening ended with a candlelit banquet served by masked and costumed servants.

Louis XIV designed his pageants to awe those most dangerous to him, the leading nobles of his kingdom. To make his authority and glory concrete, the king relentlessly increased the power of his bureaucracy, expanded his army, and insisted on Catholic orthodoxy. This model of state building was known as **absolutism**, a system of government in which the ruler claims sole and uncontestable power. Other mid-seventeenth-century rulers followed Louis XIV's example or explicitly rejected it, but they could not afford to ignore it.

Although absolutism exerted great influence beginning in the mid-1600s, it faced competition from **constitutionalism**, a system in which the ruler shares power with an assembly of elected representatives. Constitutionalism provided a strong foundation for state power in England, the Dutch Republic, and the British North American colonies, while absolutism dominated in central and eastern Europe. Constitutionalism triumphed in England, however, only after one king had been executed as a traitor and another had been deposed. The English conflicts over the nature of authority found their most enduring expression in the writings of Thomas Hobbes and John Locke, which laid the foundations of modern political science.

The search for order took place not only in government and politics but also in intellectual, cultural, and social life. Artists sought means of glorifying power and expressing order and symmetry in new ways. As states consolidated their power, elites endeavored to distinguish themselves more clearly from the lower orders. Officials, clergy, and laypeople worked to reform the poor, now seen as a major source of disorder. Whether absolutist or constitutionalist, seventeenth-century states all aimed to extend control over their subjects' lives.

Louis XIV: Absolutism and Its Limits

French king **Louis XIV** (r. 1643–1715) personified the absolutist ruler, who in theory shared his power with no one. In 1655, he reputedly told the Paris high court of justice, *"L'état, c'est moi"* ("I am the state"), emphasizing that state authority rested in him personally. Louis cleverly manipulated the affections and ambitions of his courtiers, chose as his ministers middle-class men who owed everything to him, built up Europe's largest army, and snuffed out every hint of religious or political opposition. Yet the absoluteness of his power should not be exaggerated. Like all other rulers of his time, Louis depended on the cooperation of many people: local officials who enforced his decrees, peasants and artisans who joined his armies and paid his taxes, clergy who preached his notion of Catholicism, and nobles who joined court festivities rather than causing trouble.

The Fronde, 1648–1653

Louis XIV's absolutism built on a long French tradition of increasing centralization of state authority, but before he could establish his preeminence he had to weather a series of revolts known as the Fronde. Louis was only five when he came to the throne in 1643 upon the death of his father, Louis XIII, who with his chief minister, Cardinal Richelieu, had steered France through increasing involvement in the Thirty Years' War, rapidly climbing taxes, and innumerable tax revolts. Louis XIV's mother, Anne of Austria, and her Italian-born adviser and rumored lover, Cardinal Mazarin (1602–1661), ruled in the young monarch's name.

To meet the financial pressure of fighting the Thirty Years' War, Mazarin sold new offices, raised taxes, and forced creditors to extend loans to the government. In 1648, a coalition of his opponents presented him with a charter of demands that, if granted, would have given the parlements (high courts) a form of constitutional power with the right to approve new taxes. Mazarin responded by arresting the leaders of the parlements. He soon faced a series of revolts.

Fearing for the young king's safety, his mother took Louis and fled Paris. With civil war threatening, Mazarin and Anne agreed to compromise with the parlements. The nobles saw an opportunity to reassert their claims to power against the weakened monarchy and demanded greater local control. Leading noblewomen often played key roles in the opposition to Mazarin, carrying messages and forging alliances, especially when male family members were in prison. While the nobles sought to regain power and local influence, the middle and lower classes chafed at the repeated tax increases. Conflicts erupted throughout the kingdom as nobles, parlements, and city councils all raised their own armies to fight either the crown or one another. The urban poor, such as those in the southwestern city of Bordeaux, sometimes revolted as well.

Mazarin and Anne eventually got the upper hand because their opponents failed to maintain unity in fighting the king's forces. But Louis XIV never forgot the humiliation and uncertainty that marred his childhood. His own policies as ruler would be designed to prevent the recurrence of any such revolts. Yet, for all his success, peasants would revolt against the introduction of new taxes on at least five more occasions in the 1660s and 1670s, requiring tens of thousands of soldiers to reestablish order.

Louis XIV, Conqueror of the Fronde In this painting of 1654, Louis XIV is depicted as the Roman god Jupiter, who crushes the discord of the Fronde (represented on the shield by the Medusa's head, made up of snakes). When the Fronde began, Louis was only ten years old; at the time of this painting, he was sixteen. The propaganda about his divine qualities had already begun. (By Charles Poerson [1609–1667], Château de Versailles, France/Bridgeman Images.)

Court Culture as an Element of Absolutism

When Cardinal Mazarin died in 1661, Louis XIV, then twenty-two years old, decided to rule without a first minister. He described the dangers of his situation in memoirs he wrote later for his son's instruction: "Everywhere was disorder. My Court as a whole was still very far removed from the sentiments in which I trust you will find it." Louis listed many other problems in the kingdom, but none occupied him more than his attempts to control France's leading nobles, some of whom came from families that had opposed him militarily during the Fronde.

The French nobles had long exercised local authority by maintaining their own fighting forces, meting out justice on their estates, arranging jobs for underlings, and resolving their own conflicts through dueling. Louis set out to domesticate the warrior nobles by replacing violence with court ritual, such as the festivities at Versailles described at the beginning of this chapter. Using a systematic policy of bestowing pensions, offices, honors, gifts, and the threat of disfavor or punishment, Louis induced the nobles to cooperate with him. The aristocracy increasingly vied for his favor and in the process became his clients, dependent on him for advancement. Great nobles competed for the honor of holding his shirt when he dressed, foreign ambassadors squabbled for places near him, and royal mistresses basked in the glow of his personal favor. Far from the court, however, nobles could still make considerable trouble for the king, and royal officials learned to compromise with them.

Those who did come to the king's court were kept on their toes. The preferred styles of behavior changed without notice, and the tiniest lapse in attention to etiquette could lead to ruin. Marie-Madeleine Pioche de La Vergne, known as Madame de Lafayette, described the court in her novel *The Princess of Clèves* (1678): "The Court gravitated around ambition. . . . Everybody was busily trying to better his or her position by pleasing, by helping, or by hindering somebody else."

Louis XIV appreciated the political uses of every form of art. Calling himself the Sun King, after Apollo, Louis stopped at nothing to burnish this radiant image. He played Apollo in ballets performed at court; posed for portraits with the emblems of Apollo (laurel, lyre, and tripod); and adorned his palaces with statues of the god. He also emulated the style and methods of ancient Roman emperors. At a celebration for the birth of his first son in 1662, Louis dressed in Roman attire, and many engravings and paintings showed him as a Roman emperor.

The king gave pensions to artists who worked for him and sometimes protected writers from clerical critics. The most famous of these writers was the playwright Molière (the pen name of Jean-Baptiste Poquelin, 1622–1673), whose comedy *Tartuffe* (1664) made fun of religious hypocrites and was loudly condemned by church leaders. Louis forced Molière to delay public performances of the play after its premiere at the festivities of May 1664 but resisted calls for his dismissal. Louis's ministers set up royal academies of dance, painting, architecture, music, and science. The government regulated the number and locations of theaters and closely censored all forms of publication.

Louis commissioned operas to celebrate royal marriages and military victories. His favorite composer, Jean-Baptiste Lully, wrote sixteen operas for court performances as well as many ballets. Playwrights often presented their new plays first to the court. Pierre Corneille and Jean Racine wrote tragedies set in Greece or Rome that celebrated the new aristocratic virtues that Louis aimed to inculcate: a reverence for order and self-control. All the characters were regal or noble, all the language lofty, all the behavior aristocratic.

Louis glorified his image as well through massive public works projects. Veterans' hospitals and new fortified towns on the frontiers represented his military might. Urban improvements, such as the reconstruction of the Louvre palace in Paris, proved his wealth. But his most ambitious project was the construction of a new palace at Versailles, twelve miles from the turbulent capital.

Building began in the 1660s. By 1685, the frenzied effort had engaged thirty-six thousand workers, not including the thousands of troops who diverted a local river to supply water for pools and fountains. The gardens designed by landscape architect André Le Nôtre reflected the spirit of Louis XIV's rule: their geometrical arrangements and clear lines showed that art and design could tame nature and that order and control defined the exercise of power. Versailles symbolized Louis's success at reining in the nobility and dominating Europe, and other monarchs eagerly mimicked French fashion and often conducted their business in French.

Yet for all its apparent luxury and frivolity, life at Versailles was often cramped and cold. Fifteen thousand people crowded into the palace's apartments, including all the highest military officers, the ministers of state, and the separate households of each member of the royal family. Refuse collected in the corridors during the incessant building, and thieves and prostitutes overran the grounds. By the time Louis actually moved from the Louvre to Versailles in 1682, he had reigned as monarch for thirty-nine years. After his wife's death in 1683, he secretly married his mistress, Françoise d'Aubigné, marquise de Maintenon, and conducted most state affairs from her apartments at the palace. She inspired Louis XIV to increase his devotion to Catholicism.

Enforcing Religious Orthodoxy

Louis believed that he reigned by divine right. As Bishop Jacques-Bénigne Bossuet (1627–1704) explained, "We have seen that kings take the place of God, who is the true father of the human species. We have also seen that the first idea of power which exists among men is that of the paternal power; and that kings are modeled on fathers." The king, like a father, should instruct his subjects in the true religion, or at least make sure that others did so.

Louis's campaign for religious conformity first focused on the Jansenists, Catholics whose doctrines and practices resembled some aspects of Protestantism. Following the posthumous publication of the book *Augustinus* (1640) by the Flemish theologian Cornelius Jansen (1585–1638), the Jansenists stressed the need for God's grace in achieving salvation. They emphasized the importance of original sin and resembled the English Puritans in their austere religious practice. Prominent among the Jansenists was Blaise Pascal (1623–1662), a mathematician of genius, who wrote his *Provincial Letters* (1656–1657) to defend Jansenism against charges of heresy. Many judges in the parlements likewise endorsed Jansenist doctrine. Louis rejected any doctrine that gave priority to considerations of individual conscience over the demands of the official church hierarchy. Therefore, in 1660 he began enforcing various papal bulls (decrees) against Jansenism and closed down Jansenist theological centers.

Protestants posed an even greater obstacle to religious conformity. After many years of escalating pressure on the Calvinist Huguenots, Louis decided to eliminate all of the Calvinists' rights. Louis considered the Edict of Nantes (1598), by which his grandfather Henry IV granted the Protestants religious freedom and a degree of political independence, a temporary measure, and he fervently hoped to reconvert the Huguenots to Catholicism. In 1685, his **revocation of the Edict of Nantes** closed Calvinist churches and schools, forced all pastors to leave the country, and ordered the conversion of all Calvinists. Children of Calvinists could be taken away from their parents and raised Catholic. Tens of thousands of Huguenots responded by illegally fleeing to England, Brandenburg-Prussia, the Dutch Republic, or North America. Protestant European countries were shocked by this crackdown on religious dissent and would cite it in justification of their wars against Louis.

Extending State Authority at Home and Abroad

Louis XIV could not have enforced his religious policies without the services of a nationwide bureaucracy. **Bureaucracy**—a network of state officials carrying out orders according to a regular and routine line of authority—comes from the French word *bureau*, for "desk," which came to mean "office," both in the sense of a physical space and a position of authority. Louis personally supervised the activities of his bureaucrats and worked to ensure his supremacy in all matters. But he always had to negotiate with nobles and local officials who sometimes thwarted his will.

Louis extended the bureaucratic forms his predecessors had developed, especially the use of intendants. He handpicked an intendant for each region to represent his rule against entrenched local interests such as the parlements, provincial estates, and noble governors. The intendants supervised the collection of taxes, the financing of public works, and the provisioning of the army. In 1673, Louis decreed that the parlements could no longer vote against his proposed laws or even speak against them.

To keep tabs on all the issues before him, Louis relied on a series of talented ministers, usually of modest origins, who gained fame, fortune, and even noble status from serving the king. Most important among them was Jean-Baptiste Colbert (1619–1683), a wool merchant's son turned royal official. Colbert had managed Mazarin's personal finances and worked his way up under Louis XIV to become head of royal finances, public works, and the navy.

Colbert used the bureaucracy to establish a new economic doctrine, **mercantilism**. According to mercantilist policy, governments must intervene to increase national wealth by whatever means possible. Such government intervention inevitably increased the number of bureaucrats needed. Under Colbert, the French government established overseas trading companies and granted manufacturing monopolies. A government inspection system regulated the quality of finished goods and compelled all craftsmen to organize into guilds, in which masters could supervise the work of the journeymen and apprentices. To protect French production, Colbert rescinded many internal customs fees but enacted high foreign tariffs, which cut imports of competing goods. To compete more effectively with England and the Dutch Republic, Colbert also subsidized shipbuilding, a policy that dramatically expanded the number of seaworthy French vessels. Such mercantilist measures aimed to ensure France's prominence in world markets and to provide the resources needed to fight wars against the nation's increasingly long list of enemies. Although later economists questioned the value of mercantilism, virtually every government in Europe embraced it.

Colbert's mercantilist projects shaped life in the French colonies, too. He forbade colonial businesses from manufacturing anything already produced in mainland France. In 1663, he took control of the trading company that had founded New France (Canada). With the goal of establishing permanent settlements like those in the British North American colonies, he transplanted several thousand peasants from western France to the present-day province of Quebec, which France had claimed since 1608. He also tried to limit expansion westward, without success.

Despite the Iroquois' initial interruption of French fur-trading convoys, fur trader Louis Jolliet and Jesuit missionary Jacques Marquette reached the upper Mississippi River in 1672 and traveled downstream as far as Arkansas. In 1684, French explorer Sieur de La Salle went all the way down to the Gulf of Mexico, claiming a vast territory for Louis XIV and calling it Louisiana after him. Colbert's successors embraced the expansion he had resisted, thinking it crucial to competing successfully with the English and the Dutch in the New World.

Colonial settlement occupied only a portion of Louis XIV's attention, however, for his main foreign policy goal was to extend French power in Europe. To expand the army, Louis's minister of war centralized the organization of French troops. Barracks built in major towns received supplies—among which were uniforms to reinforce discipline—from a central distribution system. Louis's wartime army could field a force as large as that of all his enemies combined.

Absolutist governments always tried to increase their territorial holdings, and as Louis extended his reach, he gained new enemies. In 1667–1668, in the War of Devolution (so called because Louis claimed that lands in the Spanish Netherlands should devolve to him since the Spanish king had failed to pay the dowry of Louis's Spanish bride), Louis defeated the Spanish armies but had to make peace when England, Sweden, and the Dutch Republic joined the war. In the Treaty of Aix-la-Chapelle in 1668, he gained control of a few towns on the border of the Spanish Netherlands.

In 1672, Louis XIV opened hostilities against the Dutch because they stood in the way of his acquisition of more territory in the Spanish Netherlands. He declared war again on Spain in 1673. By now the Dutch had allied themselves with their former Spanish masters to hold off the French. Louis also marched his troops into territories of the Holy Roman Empire, provoking many of the German princes to join with the emperor, the Spanish, and the Dutch in an alliance against

Louis, whom they now denounced as a "Christian Turk" for his imperialist ambitions. Faced with bloody but inconclusive results on the battlefield, the parties agreed to the Treaty of Nijmegen of 1678–1679, which ceded several Flemish towns and the Franche-Comté region to Louis, linking Alsace to the rest of France. French government deficits soared, and in 1675 increases in taxes touched off the most serious antitax revolt of Louis's reign.

Louis had no intention of standing still. Heartened by the Habsburgs' seeming weakness, he pushed eastward, seizing the city of Strasbourg in 1681 and invading the province of Lorraine in 1684. In 1688, he attacked some of the small German cities of the Holy Roman Empire. So obsessed was Louis with his military standing that he had miniature battle scenes painted on his high heels and commissioned tapestries showing his military processions into conquered cities, even those he did not take by force. It took a large coalition known as the League of Augsburg—made up of England, Spain, Sweden, the Dutch Republic, the Austrian emperor, and various German princes—to hold back the French king. When hostilities between Louis and the League of Augsburg ended in the Peace of Rijswijk in 1697, Louis returned many of his conquests made since 1678, with the exception of Strasbourg (Map 16.1).

Four years later, Louis embarked on his last and most damaging war, the War of the Spanish Succession (1701–1713). It was caused by disagreement over who would inherit the throne of Spain. Before he died, Spanish king Charles II (r. 1665–1700) named Louis XIV's second grandson—Philip, duke of Anjou—as his heir, but the Austrian emperor Leopold I refused to agree and the British and the Dutch supported his refusal. In the ensuing war, the French lost several major battles and had to accept disadvantageous terms in the Peace of Utrecht of 1713–1714. France ceded possessions in North America (Newfoundland, the Hudson Bay area, and most of Nova Scotia) to Britain. Although Philip was recognized as king of Spain, he had to renounce any future claim to the French crown, thus barring unification of the two kingdoms. Spain surrendered its territories in Italy and the Netherlands to the Austrians, and Gibraltar to the British. Lying on his deathbed in 1715, the seventy-six-year-old Louis XIV watched helplessly as his accomplishments began to unravel.

Louis XIV's policy of absolutism fomented bitter hostility among his own subjects. Critics complained about the secrecy of Louis's government, and nobles resented his promotions of commoners to high office. The duke of Saint-Simon complained that "falseness, servility, admiring glances, combined with a dependent and cringing attitude, above all, an appearance of being nothing without him, were the only ways of pleasing him." Ordinary people suffered the most for Louis's ambitions. By the end of the Sun King's reign, one in six Frenchmen had served in the military. In addition to the higher taxes paid by everyone, those who lived on the routes leading to the battlefields had to house and feed soldiers; only nobles were exempt from this requirement.

REVIEW   How "absolute" was the power of Louis XIV?

MAP 16.1 Louis XIV's Acquisitions, 1668–1697 Every ruler in Europe hoped to extend his or her territorial control, and war was often the result. Louis XIV steadily encroached on the Spanish Netherlands to the north and the lands of the Holy Roman Empire to the east. Although coalitions of European powers reined in Louis's grander ambitions, he nonetheless incorporated many neighboring territories into the French crown.

Constitutionalism in England

Of the two models of state building—absolutism and constitutionalism—the first seemed unquestionably more powerful because Louis XIV could raise such large armies and tax his subjects without much consultation. In the end, however, Louis could not defeat the coalition led by England's constitutional monarch. Constitutionalism had its own distinctive strengths, which came from the ruler sharing power through a representative assembly such as the English houses of Parliament. But the English rulers themselves hoped to follow Louis XIV's lead and install their own absolutist policies. Two revolutions, in 1642–1660 and 1688–1689, overturned two kings and confirmed the constitutional powers of an elected parliament, laying the foundation for the idea that government must guarantee certain rights to the people under the law.

England Turned Upside Down, 1642–1660

Disputes about the right to levy taxes and the nature of authority in the Church of England had long troubled the relationship between the English crown and Parliament. For more than a hundred years, wealthy English landowners had been accustomed to participating in government through Parliament and expected to be consulted on royal policy. Although England had no single constitutional document, it did have a variety of laws, judicial decisions, customary procedures, and charters and petitions granted by the king that all regulated relations between king and Parliament. When Charles I tried to assert his authority over Parliament, a civil war broke out. Some historians view the English civil war of 1642–1646 as the last great war of religion because it pitted Puritans against those trying to push the Church of England toward Catholicism; others see in it the first modern revolution because it gave birth to democratic political and religious movements.

When Charles I (r. 1625–1649) succeeded his father, James I, he faced an increasingly aggressive Parliament that resisted efforts to extend his personal control. In 1628, Parliament forced Charles to agree to the Petition of Right, by which he promised not to levy taxes without Parliament's consent. Charles hoped to avoid further interference with his plans by simply refusing to call Parliament into session between 1629 and 1640. Without it, the king's ministers had to find every loophole possible to raise revenues. They tried to turn "ship money," a levy on seaports in times of emergency, into an annual tax collected everywhere in the country. The crown won the ensuing court case, but many subjects still refused to pay what they considered to be an illegal tax.

Religious tensions brought conflicts over the king's authority to a head. With Charles's encouragement, the archbishop of Canterbury, William Laud (1573–1645), imposed increasingly elaborate ceremonies on the Church of England. Angered by these moves toward "popery," the Puritans responded with pamphlets and sermons filled with fiery denunciations. Laud then hauled them before the feared Court of Star Chamber, which the king personally controlled. The court ordered harsh sentences for Laud's Puritan critics; they were whipped, pilloried, branded, and even had their ears cut off and their noses split. When Laud tried to apply his policies to Scotland, however, they backfired completely: the stubborn Presbyterian Scots invaded the north of England in 1640. To raise money to fight the war, Charles called Parliament into session and unwittingly opened the door to a constitutional and religious crisis.

The Parliament of 1640 did not intend revolution, but reformers in the House of Commons (the lower house of Parliament) wanted to undo what they saw as the royal tyranny of the 1630s. Parliament removed Laud from office, ordered the execution of an unpopular royal commander, abolished the Court of Star Chamber, repealed recently levied taxes, and provided for a parliamentary assembly at least once every three years, thus establishing a constitutional check on royal authority. Moderate reformers expected to stop there and resisted Puritan pressure to abolish bishops and eliminate the Church of England prayer book. The reformers also faced a rebellion in Ireland by native Catholics against the English and Scottish settlers who had taken over their lands. The reformers in Parliament feared that the Irish Catholics would make common cause with Charles to reestablish Catholicism as the religion of England and Scotland. Their hand was forced in January 1642, when Charles and his soldiers invaded Parliament and tried unsuccessfully to arrest those leaders who had moved to curb his power. Faced with mounting opposition within London, Charles quickly withdrew from the city and organized an army.

The ensuing civil war between king and Parliament lasted four years (1642–1646) and divided the country. The king's army of royalists, known as Cavaliers, enjoyed the most support in northern and western England. The parliamentary forces, called Roundheads because they cut their hair short, had their stronghold in the southeast, including London. Although Puritans dominated on the parliamentary side, they were divided among themselves about the proper form of church government: the Presbyterians wanted a Calvinist church with some central authority, whereas the Independents favored entirely autonomous congregations free from other church government (hence the term *congregationalism*, often associated with the Independents). The Puritans put aside their differences for the sake of military unity and united under an obscure member of the House of Commons, the country gentleman Oliver Cromwell (1599–1658), who sympathized with the Independents. After Cromwell skillfully reorganized the parliamentary troops, his New Model Army defeated the Cavaliers at the battle of Naseby in 1645. Charles surrendered in 1646.

Although the civil war between king and Parliament had ended in victory for Parliament, divisions within the Puritan ranks now came to the fore: the Presbyterians dominated Parliament, but the Independents controlled the army. The disputes between the leaders drew lower-class groups into the debate. When Parliament tried to disband the New Model Army in 1647, disgruntled soldiers protested. Called **Levellers** because of their insistence on leveling social differences, the soldiers took on their officers in a series of debates about the nature of political authority. The Levellers demanded that Parliament meet annually, that members be paid so as to allow common people to participate, and that all male heads of households be allowed to vote. Their ideal of political participation excluded servants, the propertyless, and women but offered access to artisans, shopkeepers, and modest farmers. Cromwell and other army leaders rejected the Levellers' demands as threatening to property owners. Speaking to his advisers, Cromwell insisted, "You have no other way to deal with these men but to break them in pieces."

While political differences between Presbyterians and Independents helped spark new political movements, their conflicts over church organization fostered the emergence of new religious sects that emphasized the "inner light" of individual religious inspiration and a disdain for hierarchical authority. The Baptists, for example, insisted on adult baptism because they believed that Christians should choose their own church and that children should not automatically become members of the Church of England. The Religious Society of Friends, who came to be called Quakers, demonstrated their beliefs in equality and the inner light by refusing to doff their hats to men in authority. Manifesting their religious experience by trembling, or "quaking," the Quakers believed that anyone—man or woman—inspired by a direct experience of God could preach. In keeping with their notions of equality and individual inspiration, many of the new sects provided opportunities for women to become preachers and prophets.

Parliamentary leaders feared that the new sects would overturn the whole social hierarchy. Some sects did advocate sweeping change. The Diggers promoted rural communism—collective ownership of all property. Seekers and Ranters questioned just about everything. One notorious Ranter, John Robins, even claimed to be God. A few men advocated free love. The political elite decided that tolerating the new sects would lead to skepticism, anarchism, and debauchery, and they therefore took measures to suppress the most radical ones.

The king tried to negotiate with the Presbyterians in Parliament, but Independents in the army purged the Presbyterians from Parliament in late 1648, leaving a "rump" of about seventy members. This Rump Parliament then created a high court to try Charles I. The court found him guilty of attempting to establish "an unlimited and tyrannical power" and pronounced a death sentence. On January 30, 1649, Charles was beheaded before an enormous crowd, which reportedly groaned as one when the ax fell. Although many had objected to Charles's autocratic rule, few had wanted him killed. For royalists, Charles immediately became a martyr, and reports of miracles, such as the curing of blindness by the touch of a handkerchief soaked in his blood, soon circulated.

The Rump Parliament abolished the monarchy and the House of Lords (the upper house of Parliament) and set up a Puritan republic with Oliver Cromwell as chairman of the Council of State. Cromwell did not tolerate dissent from his policies. When his agents discovered plans for mutiny within the army, they executed the perpetrators; new decrees silenced the Levellers. Although under Cromwell the various Puritan sects could worship rather freely and Jews with needed skills were permitted to return to England for the first time since the thirteenth century, Catholics could not worship publicly, nor could adherents of the Church of England use the Book of Common Prayer, thought to be too Catholic. The elites were troubled by Cromwell's religious policies but pleased to see some social order reestablished.

The new regime aimed to extend state power just as Charles I had before. Cromwell laid the foundation for a Great Britain—made up of England, Ireland, and Scotland—by reconquering Scotland and brutally subduing Ireland. When his position was secured in 1649, Cromwell went to Ireland with a large force and easily defeated the rebels, massacring whole garrisons and their priests. He encouraged expropriating more lands of the Irish "barbarous wretches," and Scottish immigrants resettled the northern county of Ulster. This seventeenth-century English conquest left a legacy of bitterness that the Irish even today call "the curse of Cromwell."

In 1651, Parliament turned its attention overseas, putting mercantilist ideas into practice in the first Navigation Act, which allowed imports only if they were carried on English ships or came directly from the producers of goods. The Navigation Act was aimed at the Dutch, who dominated world trade; Cromwell tried to carry the policy further by waging naval war on the Dutch from 1652 to 1654.

At home, however, Cromwell faced growing resistance. His wars required a budget twice the size of Charles I's, and his increases in property taxes and customs duties alienated landowners and merchants. The conflict reached a crisis in 1653: Parliament considered disbanding the army, whereupon Cromwell abolished the Rump Parliament in a military coup and made himself Lord Protector. He now silenced his critics by banning newspapers and using networks of spies to read mail and keep tabs on his enemies. Cromwell intended that his son should succeed him, but his death in 1658 only revived the prospect of civil war and political chaos. In 1660, a newly elected Parliament invited Charles II, the son of the executed king, to return from exile.

Restoration and Revolution Again

England's traditional monarchical form of government was restored in 1660 under Charles II (r. 1660–1685). More than a thousand Puritan ministers lost their positions, and attending a service other than one conforming with the Book of Common Prayer was illegal after 1664. Two natural disasters in quick succession posed new challenges. The plague struck in 1665, claiming more than thirty thousand victims in just a few months and forcing Charles and Parliament to flee from London. Then in 1666, the Great Fire swept the city. Some saw these disasters as punishment for the sins of the Cromwell era, others as an ill omen for Charles's reign.

Many in Parliament feared that Charles II wanted to emulate Louis XIV. In 1670, Charles made a secret agreement, soon leaked, with Louis in which he promised to announce his conversion to Catholicism in exchange for money for a war against the Dutch. Charles never proclaimed himself a Catholic, but in his Declaration of Indulgence (1673) he did suspend all laws against Catholics and Protestant dissenters. Parliament refused to continue funding the Dutch war unless Charles rescinded his Declaration of Indulgence. Asserting its authority further, Parliament passed the Test Act in 1673, requiring all government officials to profess allegiance to the Church of England and in effect disavow Catholic doctrine. Then in 1678, Parliament precipitated the so-called Exclusion Crisis by explicitly denying the throne to a Roman Catholic. This action was aimed at the king's brother and heir, James, an open convert to Catholicism. Charles refused to allow it to become law.

The dynastic crisis over the succession of a Catholic gave rise to two distinct factions in Parliament: the Tories, who supported a strong, hereditary monarchy and the restored ceremony of the Church of England, and the Whigs, who advocated parliamentary supremacy and toleration of Protestant dissenters such as Presbyterians. Both labels were originally derogatory: *Tory* meant an Irish Catholic bandit; *Whig* was the Irish Catholic designation for a Presbyterian Scot. The Tories favored James's succession despite his Catholicism, whereas the Whigs opposed a Catholic monarch.

When James II (r. 1685–1688) succeeded his brother, he seemed determined to force Catholicism on his subjects. Tories and Whigs joined together when a male heir—who would take precedence over James's two adult Protestant daughters—was

Great Fire of London, 1666   This view of London shows the three-day fire at its height. The writer John Evelyn described the scene in his diary: "All the sky was of a fiery aspect, like the top of a burning oven, and the light seen above 40 miles round about for many nights. God grant mine eyes may never behold the like, who now saw above 10,000 houses all in one flame; the noise and cracking and thunder of people, the fall of towers, houses, and churches, was like an hideous storm." Everyone in London at the time felt overwhelmed by the catastrophe, and many deemed it God's punishment for the upheavals of the 1640s and 1650s. (© Museum of London, UK/ Bridgeman Images.)

born to James's second wife, an Italian Catholic, in 1688. They invited the Dutch ruler **William, prince of Orange**, and his wife, James's older daughter, Mary, to invade England. Mary was brought up as a Protestant and was willing to act with her husband against her father's pro-Catholic policies. James fled to France, and Parliament offered the throne jointly to William (r. 1689–1702) and Mary (r. 1689–1694) on the condition that they accept a bill of rights guaranteeing Parliament's full partnership in a constitutional government.

In the Bill of Rights (1689), William and Mary agreed not to raise a standing army or to levy taxes without Parliament's consent. They also agreed to call meetings of Parliament at least every three years, to guarantee free elections to parliamentary seats, and to abide by Parliament's decisions. The agreement gave England's constitutional government a written, legal basis by formally recognizing Parliament as a self-contained, independent body that shared power with the rulers. Victorious supporters of the coup declared it the **Glorious Revolution** because it was achieved with so little bloodshed (at least in England).

The propertied classes who controlled Parliament prevented any resurgence of the popular turmoil of the 1640s. The Toleration Act of 1689 granted all Protestants freedom of worship, though non-Anglicans (those not in the Church of England) were still excluded from the universities; Catholics got no rights but were more often left alone to worship privately. When the Catholics in Ireland rose to defend James II, William and Mary's troops savagely suppressed them.

Social Contract Theory: Hobbes and Locke

Out of the turmoil of the English revolutions came a major rethinking of the foundations of all political authority. Although Thomas Hobbes and John Locke wrote in response to the upheavals of their times, they offered opposing arguments that were applicable to any place and any time, not just England of the seventeenth century. Hobbes justified absolute authority; Locke provided the rationale for constitutionalism. Yet both argued that all authority came not from divine right but from a **social contract** among citizens.

Thomas Hobbes (1588–1679) was a royalist who sat out the English civil war of the 1640s in France, where he tutored the future king Charles II. Returning to England in 1651, Hobbes published his masterpiece, *Leviathan*, in which he argued for unlimited authority in a ruler. Absolute authority could be vested in either a king or a parliament; it had to be absolute, Hobbes insisted, in order to overcome the defects of human nature. Believing that people are essentially self-centered and driven by the "right to self-preservation," Hobbes made his case by referring to science, not religion. To Hobbes, human life in a state of nature—that is, any situation without firm authority—was "solitary, poor, nasty, brutish, and short." Only the assurance of social order could make people secure enough to act according to law; consequently, giving up personal liberty, he maintained, was the price of collective security. Rulers derived their power, he concluded, from a contract in which absolute authority protects people's rights.

Hobbes's notion of rule by an absolute authority left no room for political dissent or nonconformity, and it infuriated both royalists and supporters of Parliament. He enraged his fellow royalists by arguing that authority came not from divine right but from the social contract. Parliamentary supporters resisted Hobbes's claim that rulers must possess absolute authority to prevent the greater evil of anarchy. Like Machiavelli before him, Hobbes became associated with a cynical, pessimistic view of human nature, and future political theorists often began their arguments by refuting Hobbes.

Rejecting both Hobbes and the more traditional royalist defenses of absolute authority, John Locke (1632–1704) used the notion of a social contract to provide a foundation for constitutionalism. Locke experienced political life firsthand as physician, secretary, and intellectual companion to the earl of Shaftesbury, a leading English Whig. In 1683, during the Exclusion Crisis, Locke fled with Shaftesbury to the Dutch Republic. There he continued work on his *Two Treatises of Government*, which, when published in 1690, served to justify the revolution of 1688. Locke's position was thoroughly anti-absolutist. He denied the divine right of kings and ridiculed the common royalist idea that political power in the state mirrored the father's authority in the family. Like Hobbes, he posited a state of nature that applied to all people. Unlike Hobbes, however, he thought people were reasonable and the state of nature peaceful.

Locke insisted that government's only purpose was to protect life, liberty, and property, a notion that linked economic and political freedom. Ultimate authority rested in the will of a majority of men who owned property, and government should be limited to its basic purpose of protection. A ruler who failed to uphold his part of the social contract between the ruler and the populace could be justifiably resisted, an idea that would become crucial for the leaders of the American Revolution a century later. For England's seventeenth-century landowners, however, Locke helped validate a revolution that consolidated their interests and ensured their privileges in the social hierarchy.

Locke defended his optimistic view of human nature in the immensely influential *Essay Concerning Human Understanding* (1690). He denied the existence of any innate ideas and asserted instead that each human is born with a mind that is a tabula rasa (blank slate). Not surprisingly, Locke devoted considerable energy to rethinking educational practices; he believed that education shaped the human personality by channeling all sensory experience. Everything humans know, he claimed, comes from sensory experience, not from anything inherent in human nature. Although Locke himself owned shares in the Royal African Company and justified slavery, his writings were later used by abolitionists in their campaign against slavery.

> **REVIEW**   What differences over religion and politics caused the conflict between king and Parliament in England?

Outposts of Constitutionalism

When William and Mary came to the throne in England in 1689, the Dutch and the English put aside the rivalries that had brought them to war against each other in 1652–1654, 1665–1667, and 1672–1674. The English and Dutch had much in common: oriented toward commerce, especially overseas, they both had developed representative forms of government. Also among the few outposts of constitutionalism in the seventeenth century were the British North American colonies, which developed representative government while the English were preoccupied with their revolutions at home. Constitutionalism was not the only factor shaping this Atlantic world; as constitutionalism developed in the colonies, so, too, did the enslavement of black Africans as a new labor force.

The Dutch Republic

When the Dutch Republic gained formal independence from Spain in 1648, it had already established a decentralized, constitutional state. Rich merchants called regents effectively controlled the internal affairs of each province and (through the Estates

General) chose the *stadholder*, the executive officer responsible for defense and for representing the state at all ceremonial occasions. They almost always picked one of the princes of the house of Orange, but the stadholder resembled a president more than a king.

The Dutch Republic soon became Europe's financial capital. Praised for their industriousness, thrift, and cleanliness—and maligned as greedy, dull, and fat—the Dutch dominated overseas commerce with their shipping (Map 16.2). They imported products from all over the world: spices, tea, and silk from Asia; sugar and tobacco from the Americas; wool from England and Spain; timber and furs from Scandinavia; grain from eastern Europe. A widely reprinted history of Amsterdam that appeared in 1662 described the city as "risen through the hand of God to the peak of prosperity

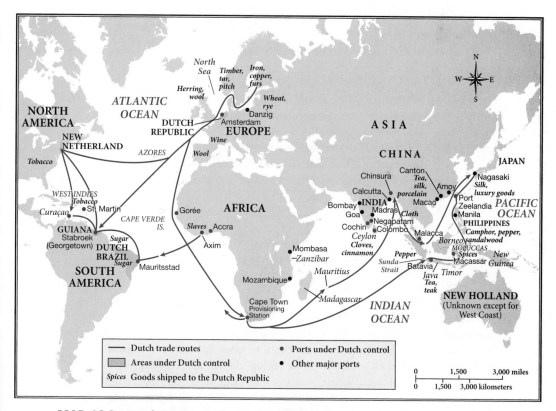

MAP 16.2 Dutch Commerce in the Seventeenth Century   Even before gaining formal independence from the Spanish in 1648, the Dutch had begun to compete with the Spanish and Portuguese all over the world. In 1602, a group of merchants established the Dutch East India Company, which soon offered investors an annual rate of return of 35 percent on the trade in spices with countries located on the Indian Ocean. Global commerce gave the Dutch the highest standard of living in Europe and soon attracted the envy of the French and the English.

and greatness. . . . The whole world stands amazed at its riches and from east and west, north and south they come to behold it."

The Dutch rapidly became the most prosperous and best-educated people in Europe. Whereas in other countries kings, nobles, and churches bought art, in the Dutch Republic art buyers were merchants, artisans, and shopkeepers. One foreigner commented that "pictures are very common here, there being scarce an ordinary tradesman whose house is not decorated with them." Relative prosperity decreased the need for married women to work, so Dutch society developed the clear contrast between middle-class male and female roles that would become prevalent elsewhere in Europe and in America more than a century later.

Extraordinarily high levels of urbanization and literacy created a large reading public. Dutch presses printed books censored elsewhere, and the University of Leiden attracted students and professors from all over Europe. Dutch tolerance extended to the works of Benedict Spinoza (1633–1677), a Jewish philosopher and biblical scholar who was expelled by his synagogue for alleged atheism but left alone by the Dutch authorities. Spinoza strove to reconcile religion with science and mathematics, but his work scandalized many Christians and Jews because he seemed to equate God and nature. Like nature, Spinoza's God followed unchangeable laws and could not be influenced by human actions, prayers, or faith.

The Dutch lived, however, in a world of international rivalries in which strong central authority gave their enemies an advantage. The naval wars with England between 1652 and 1674 and the land wars with France, which lasted until 1713, drained the state's revenues. The Dutch survived these direct military challenges but began to lose their position in international trade as both the British and French limited commerce with their own colonies to merchants from their own nations. At the end of the seventeenth century, as the Dutch elites became more preoccupied with ostentation, the Dutch "golden age" came to an end.

Freedom and Slavery in the New World

The Dutch Republic competed with England, France, and other European nations for its share of the burgeoning slave trade, but it lost its only settler colony in North America, New Netherland (present-day New York, New Jersey, Delaware, and Connecticut), to England in 1674. After the Spanish and Portuguese had shown that African slaves could be transported and forced to labor in South and Central America, the English and French endeavored to set up similar labor systems in their new Caribbean island colonies. White planters with large tracts of land bought African slaves to work fields of sugarcane; and as they gradually built up their holdings, the planters displaced most of the original white settlers.

By the end of the seventeenth century, slavery had become codified as an inherited status that applied only to blacks. In 1661, Barbados instituted a slave code that stripped all Africans of rights under English law. Louis XIV promulgated a "black code" in 1685 to regulate the legal status of slaves in the French colonies and to prevent non-Catholics from owning slaves. The code supposedly set limits on the violence planters could exercise and required them to house, feed, and clothe their slaves. But white planters simply ignored provisions of the code that did not suit them, and in any case, because the code defined slaves as property, slaves could not themselves bring suit in court to demand better treatment.

The highest church and government authorities in Catholic and Protestant countries alike condoned the gradually expanding slave trade. In 1600, seventy-six hundred Africans were exported annually from Africa to the New World; by 1700, this number had increased more than fourfold, to thirty-three thousand. Historians advance several different ideas about which factors increased the slave trade: some claim that improvements in muskets made European slavers more effective; others cite the rising price for slaves, which made their sale more attractive for the Africans who sold them; still others focus on factors internal to Africa such as the increasing size of African armies and their use of muskets in fighting and capturing other Africans for sale as slaves. What is clear is that a combination of factors prepared the way for the development of an Atlantic economy based on slavery.

While blacks were being subjected to the most degrading forms of bondage, whites in the colonies enjoyed more freedom than ever before. Virtually left to themselves during the upheavals in England, the fledgling English colonies in North America developed representative government on their own. Almost every colony had a two-house legislature. William and Mary reluctantly allowed emerging colonial elites even more control over local affairs. The social and political elite among the settlers hoped to impose an English social hierarchy dominated by rich landowners. Ordinary immigrants to the colonies, however, took advantage of plentiful land to carve out their own farms using white servants and, later, in some colonies, African slaves.

For native Americans, the expanding European presence meant something else altogether. They faced death through disease, warfare, and the accelerating loss of their homelands. Many native Americans believed that land was a divine gift provided for their collective use and not subject to individual ownership. Europeans' claims that they owned exclusive land rights consequently resulted in frequent skirmishes. In 1675–1676, for instance, three tribes allied under Metacomet (called King Philip by the English) threatened the survival of New England settlers, who savagely repulsed the attacks and sold their captives as slaves. The benefits of constitutionalism were reserved for Europeans.

REVIEW   Why did constitutionalism thrive in the Dutch Republic and the British North American colonies, even as their participation in the slave trade grew?

Absolutism in Central and Eastern Europe

Constitutionalism had an outpost in central and eastern Europe, too, but there it collapsed in failure. A long crisis in Poland-Lithuania virtually destroyed central state authority and pulled much of eastern Europe into its turbulent wake. Most central and eastern European rulers followed Louis XIV's model of absolutist state building, though they did not blindly emulate him, in part because they confronted conditions peculiar to their regions. Everywhere in eastern Europe, nobles lorded over their serfs but owed almost slavish obedience in turn to their rulers.

Poland-Lithuania Overwhelmed

In the version of constitutionalism adopted in Poland-Lithuania, the great nobles dominated the Sejm (parliament). To maintain an equilibrium among themselves, these nobles each wielded an absolute veto power. This "free veto" constitutional system deadlocked parliamentary government. The monarchy lost its room to maneuver and, with it, much of its remaining power.

Ukrainian Cossack warriors revolted against the king of Poland-Lithuania in 1648, inaugurating two decades of tumult known as the Deluge. *Cossack* was the name given to runaway serfs and poor nobles who formed outlaw bands in the no-man's-land of southern Russia and Ukraine. In 1654, the Cossacks offered Ukraine to Russian rule, provoking a Russo-Polish war that ended in 1667 when the tsar annexed eastern Ukraine and Kiev.

Many towns were destroyed in the fighting, and as much as a third of the Polish population perished. The once prosperous Jewish and Protestant minorities suffered greatly: some fifty-six thousand Jews were killed by the Cossacks, the Polish peasants, or the Russian troops. Surviving Jews moved from towns to shtetls (Jewish villages), where they took up petty trading, moneylending, tax gathering, and tavern leasing—activities that fanned peasant anti-Semitism. Desperate for protection amid the war, most Polish Protestants backed the violently anti-Catholic Swedes, who tried to intervene militarily, and the victorious Catholic majority branded the Protestants as traitors. In Poland-Lithuania people came to assume that a good Pole was a Catholic. The commonwealth had ceased to be an outpost of toleration.

The commonwealth revived briefly when a man of ability and ambition, Jan Sobieski (r. 1674–1696), was elected king. Sobieski gained a reputation throughout Europe when he led twenty-five thousand Polish cavalrymen into battle in the siege of Vienna in 1683. His cavalry helped rout the Turks and turned the tide against the Ottomans. Despite his efforts to rebuild the monarchy, Sobieski could not halt Poland-Lithuania's decline into powerlessness. The Polish version of constitutionalism fatally weakened the state and made it prey to neighboring powers.

Brandenburg-Prussia: Militaristic Absolutism

The contrast between Poland-Lithuania and Brandenburg-Prussia could not have been more extreme. The first was huge in territory and constitutional in government but in the end failed as a state. The second was puny and made up of disparate far-flung territories moving toward absolutism but in the nineteenth century would unify the different German states into modern-day Germany.

The ruler of Brandenburg was an elector, one of the seven German princes entitled to select the Holy Roman Emperor. Since the sixteenth century, the ruler of Brandenburg had also controlled the duchy of East Prussia; after 1618, the state was called Brandenburg-Prussia. Despite meager resources, **Frederick William of Hohenzollern**, who was the Great Elector of Brandenburg-Prussia (r. 1640–1688), succeeded in welding his scattered lands into an absolutist state.

Frederick William was determined to force his territories' estates (representative assemblies) to grant him a dependable income. The Great Elector struck a deal with the Junkers (nobles) of each province: in exchange for allowing him to collect taxes, he gave them complete control over their enserfed peasants and exempted them from taxation. By the end of his reign, the estates met only on ceremonial occasions. Frederick William was able to expand his army from eight thousand to thirty thousand men. Peasants filled the ranks, and Junkers became officers.

As a Calvinist ruler, Frederick William avoided the ostentation of the French court, even while following the absolutist model of centralizing state power. He boldly rebuffed Louis XIV by welcoming twenty thousand French Huguenot refugees after Louis's revocation of the Edict of Nantes. In pursuing foreign and domestic policies that promoted state power and prestige, Frederick William adroitly switched sides in Louis's wars and would stop at almost nothing to crush resistance at home. In 1701, his son Frederick I (r. 1688–1713) persuaded Holy Roman Emperor Leopold I to grant him the title "king in Prussia" in exchange for support in the War of the Spanish Succession. Until then, there was only one kingdom in the Holy Roman Empire, the kingdom of Bohemia. Prussia had arrived as an important power.

An Uneasy Balance: Austrian Habsburgs and Ottoman Turks

Holy Roman Emperor Leopold I (r. 1658–1705) ruled over a variety of territories of different ethnicities, languages, and religions, yet in ways similar to his French and Prussian counterparts, he gradually consolidated his power. Like all other Holy Roman Emperors since 1438, Leopold was an Austrian Habsburg. He was simultaneously duke of Upper and Lower Silesia, count of Tyrol, archduke of Upper and Lower Austria, king of Bohemia, king of Hungary and Croatia, and ruler of Styria and Moravia (Map 16.3). Some of these territories were provinces in the Holy Roman Empire; others were simply ruled from Vienna as Habsburg family holdings.

In response to the weakening of the Holy Roman Empire by the ravages of the Thirty Years' War, the emperor and his closest officials took control over recruiting, provisioning, and strategic planning and worked to replace the mercenaries hired during the war with a permanent standing army that promoted professional discipline. Intent on replacing Bohemian nobles who had supported the 1618 revolt against Austrian authority, the Habsburgs promoted a new nobility made up of Czechs, Germans, Italians, Spaniards, and even Irish who used German as their common tongue, professed Catholicism, and loyally served the Austrian dynasty. Bohemia became a virtual Austrian colony. In addition to holding Louis XIV in check on his western frontiers, Leopold confronted the ever-present challenge of the Ottoman Turks to the east. Austria had fought the Turks for control of Hungary for more than 150 years. In 1682, war broke out again. As they had in 1529, the Turks in 1683 pushed all the way to the gates of Vienna and laid siege to the Austrian capital. With the help of Polish cavalry, the Austrians finally broke the siege and

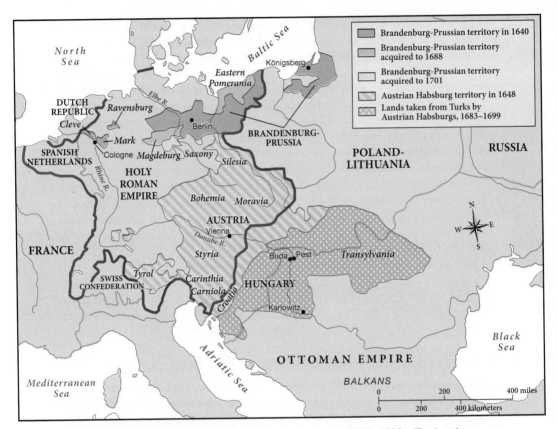

MAP 16.3 State Building in Central and Eastern Europe, 1648–1699 The Austrian Habsburgs had long contested the Ottoman Turks for dominance of eastern Europe, and by 1699 they had pushed the Turks out of Hungary. In central Europe, the Austrian Habsburgs confronted the growing power of Brandenburg-Prussia, which had emerged from relative obscurity after the Thirty Years' War to begin an aggressive program of expanding its military and its territorial base. As emperor of the Holy Roman Empire, the Austrian Habsburg ruler governed a huge expanse of territory, but the emperor's control was in fact only partial because of guarantees of local autonomy.

turned the tide in a major counteroffensive. By the Treaty of Karlowitz of 1699, the Ottoman Turks surrendered almost all of Hungary to the Austrians, marking the beginning of the decline of Ottoman power.

Once the Turks had been beaten back, Austrian rule over Hungary tightened. In 1687, the Habsburg dynasty's hereditary right to the Hungarian crown was acknowledged by the Hungarian diet, a parliament revived by Leopold in 1681 to gain the cooperation of Hungarian nobles. The diet was dominated by a core of pro-Habsburg Hungarian aristocrats, who would support the dynasty until it fell in 1918. To root out remaining Turkish influence and assert Austrian superiority, Leopold systematically destroyed Turkish buildings and rebuilt Catholic churches, monasteries, roadside shrines, and monuments in the flamboyant Austrian baroque style.

The Ottoman Turks pursued their state consolidation in a different fashion. Hundreds of thousands of Turkish families had moved with Turkish soldiers into the Balkan peninsula in the 1400s and 1500s. As locals converted to Islam, administration passed gradually into their hands. The Ottoman state, ultimately, would last longer than the French absolutist monarchy, even though the Ottoman rulers, the sultans, were often challenged by mutinous army officers. Despite frequent palace coups and assassinations of sultans, the Ottoman state continued to pose a massive military threat on Europe's southeastern borders.

Russia: Setting the Foundations of Bureaucratic Absolutism

Seventeenth-century Russia seemed a world apart from the Europe of Leopold I and Louis XIV. Straddling Europe and Asia, the Russian lands stretched across Siberia to the Pacific Ocean. Western visitors either sneered or shuddered at the "barbarism" of Russian life, and Russians reciprocated by nursing deep suspicions of everything foreign. But under the surface, Russia was evolving as an absolutist state; the tsars wanted to claim unlimited autocratic power, but like their European counterparts they had to surmount internal disorder and come to an accommodation with noble landlords.

In 1649, the Russian tsar Alexei (r. 1645–1676) convened the Assembly of the Land (consisting of noble delegates from the provinces) to consult on a sweeping law code to organize Russian society in a strict social hierarchy. The code of 1649 — which held for nearly two centuries — assigned all subjects to a hereditary class according to their current occupation or state needs. Slaves and free peasants were merged into a serf class. As serfs, they could not change occupations or move; they were tightly tied to the soil and to their noble masters. To prevent tax evasion, the code also forbade townspeople to move from the community where they resided. Nobles owed absolute obedience to the tsar and were required to serve in the army, but in return no other group could own estates worked by serfs. Serfs became the chattel of their lord, who could sell them like horses or land. Their lives differed little from those of the slaves on the plantations in the Americas.

Some peasants resisted enserfment. In 1667, **Stenka Razin** (1630–1671), the head of a powerful band of pirates and outlaws in southern Russia, led a rebellion that promised liberation from the great noble landowners. Captured four years later by the tsar's army, Razin was taken to Moscow, where he was dismembered in front of the public and his body thrown to the dogs. Thousands of his followers also suffered grisly deaths, but Razin's memory lived on in folk songs and legends.

Like his Western rivals, Tsar Alexei wanted a bigger army, exclusive control over state policy, and a greater say in religious matters. The size of the army increased dramatically from 35,000 in the 1630s to 220,000 by the end of the century. The Assembly of the Land, once an important source of consultation for the nobles, never met again after 1653. Alexei also imposed firm control over the Russian Orthodox church. The state-dominated church took action against a religious group called the Old Believers, who rejected church efforts to bring Russian worship in

Stenka Razin in Captivity   After leading a revolt of thousands of serfs, peasants, and members of non-Russian tribes of the middle and lower Volga region, Stenka Razin was captured by Russian forces and led off to Moscow, as shown here, where he was executed in 1671. He has been the subject of songs, legends, and poems ever since. (© Imagno / ullstein bild / The Image Works.)

line with Byzantine tradition. Whole communities of Old Believers starved or burned themselves to death rather than submit to the crown.

Nevertheless, modernizing trends prevailed. Tsar Alexei set up the first Western-style theater in the Kremlin, and his daughter Sophia translated French plays. The most adventurous nobles began to wear German-style clothing. Some even argued that service, not just birth, should determine rank. Russia's long struggle over Western influences had begun.

REVIEW   Why did absolutism flourish everywhere in eastern Europe except Poland-Lithuania?

The Search for Order in Elite and Popular Culture

In the period of state building from 1640 to 1715, questions about obedience, order, and the limits of state power occupied poets, painters, architects, and men of science as much as they did rulers and their ministers. How much freedom of expression could be allowed? How did the individual's needs and aspirations fit with the requirements of state authority? The greatest thinkers and writers wrestled with these issues and helped frame debates for generations to come. At the same time, elites worked to distinguish themselves from the lower classes by developing new codes of correct behavior and teaching order and discipline to their social inferiors. Their repeated efforts show, however, that popular culture had its own dynamics that resisted control from above.

Freedom and Constraint in the Arts and Sciences

Most Europeans feared disorder above all else. The French mathematician Blaise Pascal vividly captured their worries in his *Pensées* (Thoughts) of 1660: "I look on all sides, and I see only darkness everywhere." Reason could not determine whether God existed or not, Pascal concluded. Poets, painters, and architects all grappled with similar issues of faith, reason, and authority, but most of them came to more positive conclusions than Pascal about human capacities.

The English Puritan poet John Milton (1608–1674) wrestled with the inevitable limitations on individual liberty. In 1643, in the midst of the civil war between king and Parliament, he published writings in favor of allowing married couples to divorce. When Parliament enacted a censorship law aimed at such literature, Milton responded in 1644 with one of the first defenses of freedom of the press, *Areopagitica*. In it, he argued that even controversial books about religion should be allowed. Forced into retirement after the restoration of the monarchy, Milton published his epic poem *Paradise Lost* in 1667. He used the biblical Adam and Eve's fall from grace to meditate on human freedom and the tragedies of rebellion. His Satan, the proud angel who challenges God and is cast out of heaven, is so compelling as to be heroic. In the end, Adam and Eve learn the limits to their freedom, yet personal liberty remains essential to their humanity.

The dominant artistic styles of the time—the baroque and the classical—both submerged the ordinary individual in a grander design. The combination of religious and political purposes in baroque art is best exemplified in the architecture and sculpture of Gian Lorenzo Bernini (1598–1680), the papacy's official artist. His architectural masterpiece was the gigantic square facing St. Peter's Basilica in Rome. Bernini's use of freestanding colonnades and a huge open space was meant to impress the individual observer with the power of the popes and the Catholic religion.

Although France was a Catholic country, French artists, like their patron Louis XIV, preferred the standards of **classicism** to those of the baroque. As its name suggests, classicism reflected the ideals of the art of antiquity: geometric shapes, order, and harmony of lines took precedence over the sensuous, exuberant, and emotional forms of the baroque. Rather than being overshadowed by the sheer power of emotional display, in classicism the individual could be found at the intersection of converging, symmetrical, straight lines. These influences were apparent in the work of the leading French painters of the period, Nicolas Poussin (1594–1665) and Claude Lorrain (1600–1682), both of whom tried to re-create classical Roman values in their mythological scenes and Roman landscapes.

Art could also serve the interests of science. One of the most skilled illustrators of insects and flowers was Maria Sibylla Merian (1646–1717), a German-born painter-scholar whose engravings were widely celebrated for their brilliant realism and microscopic clarity. Merian separated from her husband and accompanied missionaries to the Dutch colony of Surinam, in South America. She painted watercolors of the exotic flowers, birds, and insects she found in the jungle around the cocoa and sugarcane plantations.

Despite the initial religious controversies associated with the scientific revolution, absolutist rulers quickly saw the potential of the new science for enhancing their prestige and glory. Various German princes supported the work of Gottfried Wilhelm Leibniz (1646–1716), who claimed that he, and not Isaac Newton, had invented modern calculus. A lawyer, mathematician, and philosopher who wrote about

French Classicism   This painting by Nicolas Poussin, *Discovery of Achilles on Skyros* (1649–1650), shows the French interest in classical themes and ideals. In the Greek story, Thetis dresses her son Achilles as a young woman and hides him on the island of Skyros so he would not have to fight in the Trojan War. When a chest of treasures is offered to the women, Achilles reveals himself (he is the figure on the far right) because he cannot resist the sword. In telling the story, Poussin emphasizes harmony and almost a sedateness of composition, avoiding the exuberance and emotionalism of the baroque style. (Museum of Fine Arts, Boston, Massachusetts, USA / Juliana Cheney Edwards Collection / Bridgeman Images.)

metaphysics, cosmology, and history, Leibniz also helped establish scientific societies in the German states. Government involvement in science was greatest in France. In 1666, Jean-Baptiste Colbert founded the Royal Academy of Sciences, which supplied fifteen scientists with government stipends. In contrast, the Royal Society of London grew out of informal meetings of scientists at London and Oxford. It received a royal charter in 1662 but maintained complete independence.

Because of their exclusion from most universities, women only rarely participated in the new scientific discoveries. In 1667, nonetheless, the Royal Society of London invited the writer Margaret Cavendish to watch the exhibition of experiments. Labeled "mad" by her critics, she attacked the use of telescopes and microscopes because she detected in the new experimentalism a mechanistic view of the world that exalted masculine prowess and challenged the Christian belief in freedom of the will. Yet she urged the formal education of women, complaining that "we are kept like birds in cages to hop up and down in our houses."

Women and Manners

Although excluded from the universities and the professions, women played important roles not only in the home but also in more formal spheres of social interaction, such as the courts of rulers. Under the tutelage of their mothers and wives, nobles learned manners, or the fine points of social etiquette. In some ways, aristocratic men were expected to act more like women; just as women had long been expected to please men, now aristocratic men had to please their monarch or patron by displaying proper manners and conversing with elegance and wit.

The upper classes began to reject popular festivals and fairs in favor of private theaters, where seats were relatively expensive and behavior was formal. Clowns and buffoons now seemed vulgar; the last king of England to keep a court fool was Charles I. Some tastes spread downward from the upper classes, however. Chivalric romances that had long entranced the nobility, such as Ariosto's *Orlando Furioso*, now appeared in simplified form in cheap booklets printed for lower-class readers.

Molière, the greatest French playwright of the seventeenth century, wrote sparkling comedies of manners that revealed much about the new aristocratic behavior. His play *The Middle-Class Gentleman*, first performed for Louis XIV in 1670, revolves around the yearning of a rich middle-class Frenchman, Monsieur Jourdain, to learn to act like a *gentilhomme* (both "gentleman" and "nobleman"). Monsieur Jourdain buys fancy clothes; hires private instructors in dancing, music, fencing, and philosophy; and lends money to a debt-ridden noble in hopes that the noble will marry his daughter. Only his sensible wife and his daughter's love for a worthier commoner stand in his way. The message for the king's courtiers seemed to be a reassuring one: only born nobles can hope to act like nobles. But the play also showed how the middle classes were learning to emulate the nobility: If one could learn to act nobly through self-discipline, could not anyone with some education and money pass himself off as noble?

As Molière's play demonstrated, new attention to manners trickled down from the court to the middle class. A French treatise on manners written in 1672 explained proper behavior:

> Formerly one was permitted . . . to dip one's bread into the sauce, provided only that one had not already bitten it. Nowadays that would be a kind of rusticity. Formerly one was allowed to take from one's mouth what one could not eat and drop it on the floor, provided it was done skillfully. Now that would be very disgusting.

The key words *rusticity* and *disgusting* reveal the association of unacceptable social behavior with the peasantry, dirt, and repulsion. Similar rules governed spitting and blowing one's nose in public.

Courtly manners often permeated the upper reaches of society by means of the **salon**, an informal gathering held regularly in a private home and presided over by a socially eminent woman. The French government occasionally worried that these gatherings might challenge its authority, but the three main topics of salon conversation were love, literature, and philosophy. Before publishing a manuscript, many authors, including court favorites like Pierre Corneille and Jean Racine, would read their compositions to a salon gathering.

Some women went beyond encouraging male authors and began to write their own works, but they faced many obstacles. Madame de Lafayette wrote several short novels that were published anonymously because it was considered inappropriate for aristocratic women to appear in print. Following the publication of *The Princess of Clèves* in 1678, she denied having written it. Despite these limitations, French women began to turn out best sellers of that new type of literary form, the novel. Their success prompted the philosopher Pierre Bayle to remark in 1697 that "our best French novels for a long time have been written by women."

The new importance of women in the world of manners and letters did not sit well with everyone. Although the French writer François Poulain de la Barre, in a series of works published in the 1670s, used the new science to assert the equality of women's minds, most men resisted the idea. Clergymen, lawyers, scholars, and playwrights attacked women's growing public influence. Women, they complained, were corrupting forces and needed restraint. Molière wrote plays denouncing women's pretension to judge literary merit. English playwrights derided learned women by creating characters with names such as Lady Knowall, Lady Meanwell, and Mrs. Lovewit.

A real-life target of the English playwrights was Aphra Behn (1640–1689), one of the first professional woman authors. Her short novel *Oroonoko* (1688) told the story of an African prince mistakenly sold into slavery. The story was so successful that it was adapted by playwrights and performed repeatedly in England and France for the next hundred years.

Reforming Popular Culture

Controversies over female influence had little effect on the unschooled peasants who made up most of Europe's population. Peasant culture had three main elements: religion, which shaped every aspect of life and death; knowledge needed to work at farming or in a trade; and popular forms of entertainment such as village fairs and dances. What changed most noticeably in the seventeenth century was the social elites' attitude toward lower-class culture.

In the seventeenth century, Protestant and Catholic churches alike pushed hard to change popular religious practices. Their campaigns against popular "paganism" began during the sixteenth-century Protestant Reformation and Catholic Counter-Reformation but reached much of rural Europe only in the seventeenth century. Puritans in England tried to root out maypole dances, Sunday village fairs, gambling, taverns, and bawdy ballads. In Lutheran Norway, pastors denounced a widespread belief in the miracle-working powers of St. Olaf. The word *superstition* previously meant "false religion" (Protestantism was a superstition for Catholics, Catholicism for Protestants); in the seventeenth century it took on its modern meaning of irrational fears, beliefs, and practices that anyone educated or refined would avoid.

Catholic bishops in the French provinces trained parish priests to reform their flocks by using catechisms in local dialects and insisting that parishioners attend Mass. The church faced a formidable challenge. One bishop in France complained in 1671, "Can you believe that there are in this diocese entire villages where no one has even heard of Jesus Christ?" In some places, believers sacrificed animals to the Virgin; prayed to the new moon; and, as in pre-Christian times, worshipped at the sources of streams.

Like its Protestant counterpart, the Catholic campaign against ignorance and superstition helped extend state power. Clergy, officials, and local police worked together to limit carnival celebrations, to regulate pilgrimages to shrines, and to replace "indecent" images of saints with more restrained and decorous ones. In Catholicism, the cult of the Virgin Mary and devotions closely connected with Jesus, such as the Holy Sacrament and the Sacred Heart, took precedence over the celebration of popular saints who seemed to have pagan origins or were credited with unverified miracles.

The campaign for more disciplined religious practices helped generate a new attitude toward the poor. In the sixteenth and seventeenth centuries, the upper classes, the church, and the state increasingly regarded the poor as dangerous, deceitful, and lacking in character. The courts had previously expelled beggars from cities; now local leaders, both Catholic and Protestant, tried to reform their character. Municipal magistrates and local notables worked together to transform hospitals into houses of confinement for beggars. In Catholic France, upper-class women's religious associations, known as confraternities, set up asylums that confined prostitutes (by arrest if necessary) and rehabilitated them. Such groups advocated harsh discipline as the cure for poverty.

Even as reformers from church and state tried to regulate popular activities, villagers and townspeople pushed back with reassertions of their own values. For hundreds of years, peasants had maintained their own forms of village justice— called variously "rough music," "charivari," or in North America, "shivaree." If a young man married a much older woman for her money, for example, villagers would serenade the couple by playing crude flutes, banging pots and pans, and shooting muskets. If a man was rumored to have been physically assaulted by his wife, a reversal of the usual sex roles, he (or effigies of him and his wife) might be ridden on a donkey facing backward (to signify the role reversal) and pelted with dung before being ducked in a nearby pond or river. Others directed their mockery at tax officials, gamekeepers on big estates who tried to keep villagers from hunting, or unpopular preachers.

No matter how much care went into controlling religious festivals, such events almost invariably opened the door to popular reinterpretation and sometimes drunken celebration. When the Spanish introduced Corpus Christi processions to their colony in Peru in the seventeenth century, elite Incas dressed in royal costumes to carry the banners of their parishes. Their clothing and ornaments combined

Christian symbols with their own indigenous ones. They thus signaled their conversion to Catholicism but also reasserted their own prior identities. The Corpus Christi festival, held in late May or early June, conveniently took place about the same time as Inca festivals from the pre-Spanish era. Carnival, the days preceding Lent on the Christian calendar—of which Mardi Gras ("Fat Tuesday") is the last—offered the occasion for public revelry of all sorts. Although Catholic clergy worked hard to clamp down on the more riotous aspects of Carnival, many towns and villages still held parades, like those of present-day New Orleans or Rio de Janeiro, that included companies of local men dressed in special costumes and gigantic stuffed figures, sometimes with animal skins, animal heads, or elaborate masks.

REVIEW   How did elite and popular culture become more separate in the seventeenth century?

Conclusion

The search for order took place on various levels, from the reform of the disorderly poor to the establishment of bureaucratic routines in government. The absolutist government of Louis XIV served as a model for all those who aimed to increase the power of the central state. Even Louis's rivals—such as the Holy Roman Emperor Leopold I and Frederick William, the Great Elector of Brandenburg-Prussia—followed his lead in centralizing authority and building up their armies. Whether absolutist or constitutionalist in form, seventeenth-century states aimed to penetrate more deeply into the lives of their subjects. They wanted more men for their armed forces; higher taxes to support their projects; and more control over foreign trade, religious dissent, and society's unwanted.

Some tears had begun to appear, however, in the seamless fabric of state power. The civil war between Charles I and Parliament in England in the 1640s opened the way to new demands for political participation. When Parliament overthrew James II in 1688, it also insisted that the new king and queen, William and Mary, agree to the Bill of Rights. In the eighteenth century, new levels of economic growth and the appearance of new social groups would exert pressures on the European state system. The success of seventeenth-century rulers created the political and economic conditions in which their critics would flourish.

MAPPING THE WEST **Europe at the End of the Seventeenth Century** Size was not necessarily an advantage in the late 1600s. Poland-Lithuania, a large country on the map, had been fatally weakened by internal conflicts. In the next century it would disappear entirely. While the Ottoman Empire still controlled an extensive territory, outside of Anatolia its rule depended on intermediaries. The Austrian Habsburgs had pushed the Turks out of Hungary and back into the Balkans. The tiny Dutch Republic, meanwhile, had become very rich through international commerce and was the envy of far larger nations.

Chapter Review

KEY TERMS AND PEOPLE

Be sure that you can identify the term or person and explain its historical significance.

absolutism (p. 457)
constitutionalism (p. 458)
Louis XIV (p. 458)
revocation of the Edict of Nantes
  (p. 462)
bureaucracy (p. 462)
mercantilism (p. 462)
Levellers (p. 467)

William, prince of Orange (p. 470)
Glorious Revolution (p. 470)
social contract (p. 471)
Frederick William of Hohenzollern
  (p. 477)
Stenka Razin (p. 479)
classicism (p. 481)
salon (p. 483)

REVIEW QUESTIONS

1. How "absolute" was the power of Louis XIV?
2. What differences over religion and politics caused the conflict between king and Parliament in England?
3. Why did constitutionalism thrive in the Dutch Republic and the British North American colonies, even as their participation in the slave trade grew?
4. Why did absolutism flourish everywhere in eastern Europe except Poland-Lithuania?
5. How did elite and popular culture become more separate in the seventeenth century?

MAKING CONNECTIONS

1. What accounts for the success of absolutism in some parts of Europe and its failure in others?
2. How did religious differences in the late seventeenth century still cause political conflict?
3. What were the chief differences between eastern and western Europe in this period?
4. Why was the search for order a major theme in science, politics, and the arts during this period?

IMPORTANT EVENTS

1642–1646 • English civil war between Charles I and Parliament

1648 • Peace of Westphalia ends Thirty Years' War; Fronde revolt challenges royal authority in France; Ukrainian Cossack warriors rebel against king of Poland-Lithuania; Spain formally recognizes independence of Dutch Republic

1649 • Charles I of England executed; new Russian legal code assigns all to hereditary class

1651 • Thomas Hobbes publishes *Leviathan*

1660 • Monarchy restored in England

1661 • Slave code set up in Barbados

1667 • Louis XIV begins first of many wars that continue throughout his reign

1678 • Madame de Lafayette anonymously publishes *The Princess of Clèves*

1683 • Austrian Habsburgs break Turkish siege of Vienna

1685 • Louis XIV revokes Edict of Nantes

1688 • Parliament deposes James II; William, prince of Orange, and Mary take the throne

1690 • John Locke publishes *Two Treatises of Government* and *Essay Concerning Human Understanding*

17

The Atlantic System and Its Consequences

1700–1750

CHAPTER FOCUS

What were the most important consequences of the growth of the Atlantic system?

IN 1699, A FEW COFFEE PLANTS changed the history of the world. European travelers at the end of the sixteenth century noticed Middle Eastern people drinking a "black drink" called *kavah*, but the Arab monopoly on its production kept prices high. This all changed in 1699, when Dutch traders brought a few coffee plants from the east coast of India to their colony of Java (now Indonesia), which proved ideal for growing the beans. Within two decades, the trickle of beans going from Java to Europe became a flood of 200,000 pounds a year. After a shoot from a Dutch plant made its way to the Caribbean island of Martinique in 1721, coffee plants quickly spread throughout the Caribbean, where African slaves provided the plantation labor.

European consumption of coffee, tea, sugar, and other novelties increased dramatically as European nations forged worldwide economic links. At the center of this new global economy was the **Atlantic system**, the web of trade routes that bound together western Europe, Africa, and the Americas. Europeans bought slaves in western Africa, transported them to be sold in the colonies in North and South America and the Caribbean, bought raw commodities such as coffee and sugar that were produced by the new colonial plantations, and then sold those commodities in European ports for refining and reshipment. This Atlantic system, which first took clear shape in the early eighteenth century, became the hub of European expansion throughout the world.

Coffee drinking is just one example of the many new social and cultural patterns that took root between 1700 and 1750. Improvements in agricultural production at home reinforced the effects of trade overseas; Europeans now had more disposable income for extras, and they spent their money not only in the new coffeehouses and cafés that sprang up all over Europe but also on newspapers, musical concerts, paintings, and novels. A new middle-class public began to make its presence felt in every domain of culture and social life.

Although the rise of the Atlantic system gave Europe new prominence in the global context, European rulers still focused most of their political, diplomatic, and military energies on their rivalries within Europe. A coalition of countries had succeeded in containing French aggression under Louis XIV, and a more balanced diplomatic system emerged. The more evenly matched competition among the great powers encouraged the development of diplomatic skills and drew attention to public health as a way of encouraging population growth.

In the aftermath of Louis XIV's revocation of the Edict of Nantes in 1685, a new intellectual movement known as the Enlightenment began to germinate. An initial impetus came from French Protestant refugees who published works critical of absolutism in politics and religion. Fed by the popularization of science and the growing interest in travel literature, the early Enlightenment encouraged greater skepticism about religious and state authority. Eventually, the movement would question almost every aspect of social and political life in Europe. The Enlightenment, which began in western Europe in those countries most affected by the new Atlantic system—Britain, France, and the Dutch Republic—can be considered a product of the age of coffee.

The Atlantic System and the World Economy

Although their ships had been circling the globe since the early 1500s, Europeans did not draw most of the world into their economic orbit until the 1700s. Western European nations sent ships loaded with goods to buy slaves from local rulers on the western coast of Africa; the slaves were then transported to the colonies in North and South America and the Caribbean and sold to the owners of plantations producing coffee, sugar, cotton, and tobacco. Money from the slave trade was used to buy the raw commodities produced in the colonies and ship them back to Europe, where they were refined or processed and then sold within Europe and around the world. The Atlantic system and the growth of international trade thus helped create a new consumer society.

Slavery and the Atlantic System

In the eighteenth century, European trade in the Atlantic rapidly expanded and became more systematically interconnected (Map 17.1). By 1650, Portugal had already sent forty thousand African slaves to Brazil to work on the new plantations, which were producing some fifteen thousand tons of sugar a year. A **plantation** was a large tract of land that produced a staple crop such as sugar, coffee, or tobacco; was farmed by slave labor; and was owned by a colonial settler from western Europe.

Realizing that plantations producing staples for Europeans could bring fabulous wealth, the European powers grew less interested in the dwindling trade in precious metals and more eager to colonize. In the 1700s, large-scale planters of sugar,

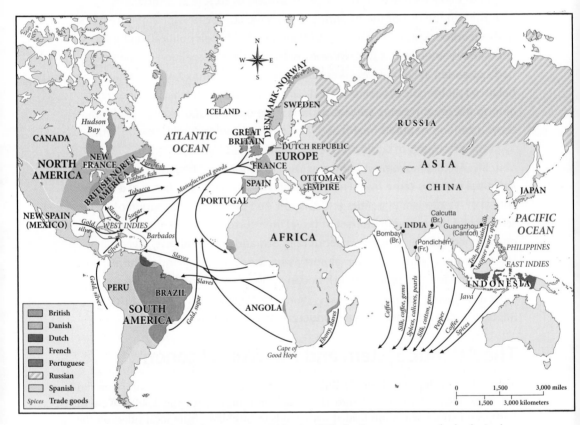

MAP 17.1   European Trade Patterns, c. 1740   By 1740, the European powers had colonized much of North and South America and incorporated their colonies there into a worldwide system of commerce centered on the slave trade and plantation production of staple crops. Europeans still sought spices and luxury goods in China and the East Indies, but few Europeans had settled permanently in these areas (with the exception of Java). How did control over colonies determine dominance in international trade in this period?

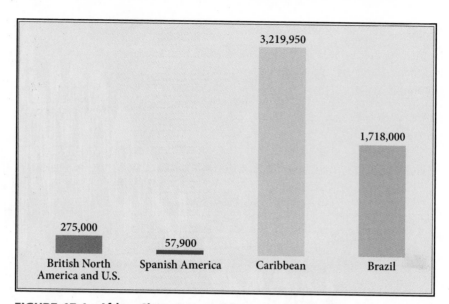

FIGURE 17.1 **African Slaves Imported into American Territories,**
1701–1810 During the eighteenth century, planters in the newly established Caribbean colonies imported millions of African slaves to work the new plantations that produced sugar, coffee, indigo, and cotton for the European market. The vast majority of African slaves transported to the Americas ended up in either the Caribbean or Brazil. Why were so many slaves transported to the Caribbean islands, which are relatively small compared to Spanish America or British North America? (Adapted from http://www.slavevoyages.org/.)

tobacco, and coffee began displacing small farmers who relied on one or two indentured servants (men and women who gained passage to the Americas in exchange for several years of work). Planters and their plantations won out because even cheaper slave labor allowed them to produce mass quantities of commodities at low prices.

State-chartered private companies from Portugal, France, Britain, the Dutch Republic, Prussia, and even Denmark exploited the 3,500-mile coastline of West Africa for slaves. Before 1675, most blacks taken from Africa had been sent to Brazil or Spanish America on Portuguese or Dutch ships, but by 1725 more than 60 percent of African slaves landed in the Caribbean (Figure 17.1), and more and more of them were carried on British or French ships.

After 1700, the plantation economy also began to expand on the North American mainland. The numbers stagger the imagination (Figure 17.2). In all, more than ten million Africans, not counting those who were captured but died before or during the sea voyage, were transported to the Americas before 1850, after which the slave trade finally began to wind down. Europeans traded textiles, cowries (shells from the Indian Ocean), and firearms for slaves, altering local African power structures and creating political instability. Population declined in West Africa, and

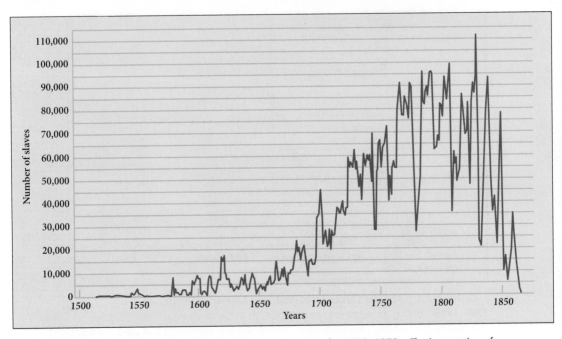

FIGURE 17.2   Annual Imports in the Atlantic Slave Trade, 1500–1870   The importation of slaves to the American territories increased overall from 1650 until 1800 and did not finally collapse until after 1850.

because two-thirds of those enslaved were men, husbands were in short supply and men increasingly took two or more wives in a practice known as polygyny.

The enslaved women and men suffered terribly. Most had been sold to European traders by Africans from the west coast who acquired them through warfare or kidnapping. The vast majority were between fourteen and thirty-five years old. Before cramming them onto the ships for the three-month trip, slavers shaved their heads and stripped them naked; they also branded some with red-hot irons. They separated men and women, and shackled men with leg irons. Sailors and officers raped the women at will. In the cramped and appalling conditions of the voyage, as many as one-fourth of the slaves died.

Those who survived the transit were sold and given new names, often only first names. Slaves had no social identities of their own; they were expected to learn their master's language and to do any job assigned. Slaves worked fifteen- to seventeen-hour days and were fed only enough to keep them on their feet. The death rate among slaves was high, especially on the sugar plantations, where slaves had to cut and haul sugarcane to the grinders and boilers before it spoiled. During the harvest, grinding and boiling went on around the clock. Because so many slaves died in the sugar-growing regions, more and more slaves, especially strong males, had to be imported. In North America, in contrast, where sugar was a minor crop, the slave population increased tenfold by 1863 through natural growth.

Not surprisingly, despite the threat of torture or death on recapture, slaves sometimes ran away. Outright revolt was uncommon, but slaveholders' fears about conspiracy and revolt lurked beneath the surface of every slave-based society. In 1710, the royal governor of Virginia reminded the colonial legislature of the need for unceasing vigilance: "We are not to Depend on Either Their Stupidity, or that Babel of Languages among 'em; freedom Wears a Cap which Can Without a Tongue, Call Togather all Those who Long to Shake off the fetters of Slavery." Masters defended whipping and other forms of physical punishment as essential to maintaining discipline. Laws called for the castration of a slave who struck a white person.

The balance of white and black populations in the New World colonies varied greatly. Because they did not own plantations, New England merchants and farmers bought few slaves. Blacks—both slave and free—made up only 3 percent of the population in eighteenth-century New England, compared with 60 percent in South Carolina. The imbalance of whites and blacks was even more extreme in the Caribbean, where most indigenous people had already died fighting Europeans or the diseases brought by them. By 1713, the French Caribbean colony of St. Domingue (on the western part of Hispaniola, present-day Haiti) had four times as many black slaves as whites; by 1754, slaves there outnumbered whites more than ten to one.

Plantation owners often left their colonial possessions in the care of agents and merely collected the revenue so that they could live as wealthy landowners back home, where they built opulent mansions and gained influence in local and national politics. William Beckford, for example, left his inherited sugar plantations in Jamaica and moved the headquarters of the family business to London in the 1730s to be close to the government and financial markets. His holdings formed the single most powerful economic interest in Jamaica, but he preferred to live in England, where he held political office (he was lord mayor of London and a member of Parliament) and even loaned money to the government.

The slave trade permanently altered consumption patterns for ordinary people. Sugar had been prescribed as a medicine before the end of the sixteenth century, but the development of plantations in Brazil and the Caribbean made it a standard food item. By 1700, the British were sending home fifty million pounds of sugar a year, a figure that doubled by 1730. Equally pervasive was the spread of tobacco; by the 1720s, men of every country and class smoked pipes or took snuff.

Even though the traffic in slaves disturbed some Europeans, in the 1700s slaveholders began to justify their actions by demeaning the mental and spiritual qualities of the enslaved Africans. White Europeans and colonists sometimes described black slaves as animal-like, akin to apes. A leading New England Puritan asserted about the slaves: "Indeed their *Stupidity* is a *Discouragement*. It may seem, unto as little purpose, to *Teach*, as to *wash an Aethiopian* [Ethiopian]." One of the great paradoxes of this time was that talk of liberty and rights, especially prevalent in

Britain and its North American colonies, coexisted with the belief that some people were meant to be slaves. The churches often defended or at least did not oppose the inequities of slavery.

World Trade and Settlement

The Atlantic system helped extend European trade relations across the globe. The textiles that Atlantic shippers exchanged for slaves on the west coast of Africa, for example, were manufactured in India and exported by the British and French East India Companies. As much as one-quarter of the British exports to Africa in the eighteenth century were actually re-exports from India. To expand their trade in the rest of the world, Europeans seized territories and tried to establish permanent settlements. The eighteenth-century extension of European power prepared the way for Western global domination in the nineteenth and twentieth centuries.

In contrast to the sparsely inhabited European trading outposts in Asia and Africa, the colonies in the Americas bulged with settlers. The British North American colonies contained about 1.5 million nonnative (that is, white settler and black slave) residents by 1750. While the Spanish competed with the Portuguese for control of South America, the French competed with the British for control of North America.

Local economies shaped colonial social relations; men in French trapper communities in Canada, for example, had little in common with the men and women of the plantation societies in Barbados or Brazil. Racial attitudes also differed from place to place. Unlike the French and English, the Spanish and Portuguese tolerated intermarriage with the native populations in both America and Asia. By 1800, **mestizos**, people born to a Spanish father and an Indian mother, accounted for more than a quarter of the population in the Spanish colonies. Where intermarriage between colonizers and natives was common, conversion to Christianity proved most successful. However, greater racial diversity seems not to have improved the treatment of slaves.

In the early years of American colonization, many more men than women emigrated from Europe. Although the sex imbalance began to decline at the end of the seventeenth century, it remained substantial; two and a half times more men than women were among the immigrants leaving Liverpool, England, between 1697 and 1707, for example. Women who emigrated as indentured servants ran great risks: many died of disease during the voyage, and at least one in five gave birth to an illegitimate child.

However, the uncertainties of life in the American colonies provided new opportunities for European women and men willing to live outside the law. In the 1500s and 1600s, the English and Dutch governments had routinely authorized pirates to prey on the ships of their rivals, the Spanish and Portuguese. Then, in the late 1600s, English, French, and Dutch bands made up of deserters and crews from wrecked vessels began to form their own associations of pirates, especially in the Caribbean. Called **buccaneers** from their custom of curing strips of beef, called *boucan* by the native Caribs of the islands, the pirates governed themselves and preyed on everyone's shipments without regard to national origin. After 1700, the colonial governments tried to stamp out piracy.

In comparison to those in the Americas, white settlements in Africa and Asia remained small. A handful of Portuguese trading posts in Angola and a few Dutch farms on the Cape of Good Hope provided the only toeholds in Africa for future expansion. In China, the emperors had welcomed Catholic missionaries at court in the seventeenth century, but the priests' credibility diminished as they squabbled among themselves and associated with European merchants, whom the Chinese considered pirates. In 1720, only one thousand Europeans resided in Guangzhou (Canton), the sole place where foreigners could legally trade for spices, tea, and silk (see Map 17.1, page 492).

Europeans exercised more influence in Java (in what was then called the East Indies) and in India. Many Dutch settled in Java to oversee coffee production and Asian trade. Dutch, English, French, Portuguese, and Danish companies competed in India for spices, cotton, and silk; by the 1740s, the English and French had become the leading rivals in India, just as they were in North America. Both countries extended their power as India's Muslim rulers lost control to local Hindu princes, rebellious Sikhs, invading Persians, and their own provincial governors. A few thousand Europeans lived in India, though many thousand more soldiers were stationed there to protect them. The staple of trade with India in the early 1700s was calico—lightweight, brightly colored cotton cloth that caught on as a fashion in Europe. English and French slave traders sold calico to the Africans in exchange for slaves.

The Birth of Consumer Society

As worldwide colonization produced new supplies of goods, from coffee to calico, population growth in Europe fueled demand for them. Beginning in Britain, then in France and the Italian states, and finally in eastern Europe, population surged, growing by about 20 percent between 1700 and 1750. The gap between a fast-growing northwest and a more stagnant south and central Europe now diminished as regions that had lost population during the seventeenth-century downturn recovered. Cities, in particular, grew. Between 1600 and 1750, Paris's population more than doubled and London's more than tripled.

Although contemporaries could not have realized it then, this was the start of the modern population explosion. It appears that a decline in the death rate, rather than a rise in the birthrate, explains the turnaround. Three main factors contributed to increased longevity: better weather and hence more bountiful harvests, improved agricultural techniques, and the plague's disappearance after 1720.

By the early eighteenth century, the effects of economic expansion and population growth brought about a **consumer revolution**. For example, at Nantes, the center of the French sugar trade, imports quadrupled between 1698 and 1733. Tea, chocolate, and coffee became virtual necessities. In 1700, England had two thousand coffeehouses; by 1740, every English country town had at least two. Paris got its first cafés at the end of the seventeenth century, and Berlin opened its first coffeehouse in 1714.

The Exotic as Consumer Item   This painting by the Venetian artist Rosalba Carriera (1675–1757) is titled *Africa*. The young black girl wearing a turban represents the African continent. Carriera was known for her use of pastels. In 1720, she journeyed to Paris, where she became an associate of Antoine Watteau and helped inaugurate the rococo style in painting. Why might the artist have chosen to paint an African girl? (bpk, Berlin / Gemaldegalerie Alte Meister, Staaliche Kunstsammlungen Dresden, Germany / Photo: Elke Estel / Hans-Peter Klut / Art Resource, NY.)

A new economic dynamic steadily took shape that has influenced all of subsequent history. More and more people escaped the confines of a sub-sistence economy, in which peasants produced barely enough to support themselves from year to year. As ordinary people gained more disposable income, demand for nonessential consumer goods rose. These included not only the new colonial products such as coffee and tea but also tables, chairs, sheets, chamber pots, lamps, and mirrors—and for the better off still, coffee- and teapots, china, cutlery, chests of drawers, desks, clocks, and pictures for the walls.

Rising demand created more jobs and more income and yet more purchasing power in a mutually reinforcing cycle. In the English economic literature of the 1690s and early 1700s, writers reacted to these developments by expressing a new view of humans as consuming animals with boundless appetites. Change did not occur all at once, however. The consumer revolution spread from the cities to the countryside, from England to the continent, and from western Europe to eastern Europe only over the long run.

Europe was not the only region experiencing such changes. China's population grew even faster—it may have tripled during the 1700s—and there, too, consump-tion of cloth, furniture, tea, sugar, and tobacco all increased. In China, these goods could be locally produced, and China did not pursue colonization of far-flung lands. Still, foreign trade also increased, especially with lands on China's borders.

REVIEW   How was consumerism related to slavery in the early eighteenth century?

New Social and Cultural Patterns

The rise of consumption in Europe was fueled in part by a revolution in agricultural techniques that made it possible to produce larger quantities of food with a smaller agricultural workforce. As population increased, more people moved to the cities, where they found themselves caught up in innovative urban customs such as attending musical concerts and reading novels. Along with a general increase in literacy, these activities helped create a public that responded to new writers and artists. As always, people's experiences varied depending on whether they lived in wealth or poverty, in urban or rural areas, or in eastern or western Europe.

Agricultural Revolution

Although Britain, France, and the Dutch Republic shared the enthusiasm for consumer goods, Britain's domestic market grew most quickly. In Britain, as agricultural output increased by 43 percent over the course of the 1700s, the population increased by 70 percent. The British imported grain to feed the growing population, but they also benefited from the development of techniques that together constituted an **agricultural revolution**. It was not new machinery but rather increasingly aggressive attitudes toward investment and management that propelled this revolution. The Dutch and the Flemish had pioneered many agricultural management techniques in the 1600s, but the British took them further.

Four major changes occurred in British agriculture that eventually spread to other countries. First, farmers increased the amount of land under cultivation by draining wetlands and by growing crops on previously uncultivated common lands (acreage maintained by the community for grazing). Second, those farmers who could afford it consolidated small, scattered plots into larger, more efficient units. Third, livestock raising became more closely linked to crop growing, and the yields of each increased. For centuries, most farmers had rotated their fields in and out of production to replenish the soil. Now farmers planted carefully chosen fodder crops such as clover and turnips that added nutrients to the soil, thereby eliminating the need to leave a field fallow (unplanted) every two or three years. With more fodder available, farmers could raise more livestock, which in turn produced more manure to fertilize grain fields. Fourth, selective breeding of animals combined with the increase in fodder to improve the quality and size of herds. By the 1730s and 1740s, agricultural output had increased dramatically, and prices for food had fallen because of these interconnected innovations.

Changes in agricultural practices did not benefit all landowners equally. The biggest British landowners consolidated their holdings in the "enclosure movement." They put pressure on small farmers and villagers to sell their land or give up their common lands. The big landlords then fenced off (enclosed) their property. Because enclosure eliminated community grazing rights, it frequently sparked a struggle between the big landlords and villagers, and in Britain it normally required an act of Parliament. Such acts became increasingly common in the second half of the eighteenth century, and by the century's end six million acres of common lands had been enclosed and developed. In this way the English peasantry largely disappeared, replaced by a more hierarchical society of big landlords, enterprising tenant farmers, and poor agricultural laborers.

The new agricultural techniques spread slowly from Britain and the Low Countries (the Dutch Republic and the Austrian Netherlands) to the rest of western Europe. Outside a few pockets, however, subsistence agriculture (producing just enough to get by rather than surpluses for the market) continued to dominate farming in western Europe and Scandinavia. Unlike the populations of the highly urbanized Low Countries (where half the people lived in towns and cities), most Europeans, western and eastern, eked out their existence in the countryside and could barely participate in the new markets for consumer goods.

In eastern Europe, the condition of peasants worsened in the areas where landlords tried hardest to improve crop yields. To produce more for the Baltic grain market, aristocratic landholders in Prussia, Poland, and parts of Russia drained wetlands, cultivated moors, and built dikes. They also forced peasants off lands that the peasants had worked for themselves, and they increased compulsory labor services (the critical element in serfdom). Some eastern landowners grew fabulously wealthy. The Potocki family in the Polish Ukraine, for example, owned three million acres of land and had 130,000 serfs.

Social Life in the Cities

Because of emigration from the countryside, cities grew in population and consequently exercised a growing influence on culture and social life. Between 1650 and 1750, cities with at least ten thousand inhabitants increased in population by 44 percent. From the eighteenth century onward, urban growth has been continuous. Along with the general growth of cities, an important south-to-north shift occurred in the pattern of urbanization. Around 1500, half of the people in cities of at least ten thousand residents could be found in the Italian states, Spain, or Portugal; by 1700, the urbanization of northwestern and southern Europe was roughly equal. Eastern Europe, despite the huge cities of Istanbul and Moscow, was still less urban than western Europe. With 675,000 inhabitants, London was by far the most populous European city in 1750; Berlin had 90,000 people, Warsaw only 23,000.

Many landowners kept a residence in town, so the separation between rural and city life was not as extreme as might be imagined, at least not for the very rich. At the top of the ladder in the big cities were the landed nobles. Some of them filled their lives only with conspicuous consumption of fine food, extravagant clothing, carriages, books, and opera; others held key political, administrative, or judicial offices. However they spent their time, these rich families employed thousands of artisans, shopkeepers, and domestic servants. Many English peers (highest-ranking nobles) had thirty or forty servants at each of their homes.

The middle classes of officials, merchants, professionals, and landowners occupied the next rung down on the social ladder. London's population, for example, included about twenty thousand middle-class families (constituting, at most, one-sixth of the city's population). In this period the middle classes began to develop distinctive ways of life that set them apart from both the rich noble landowners and the lower classes. Unlike the rich nobles, the middle classes lived primarily in the cities and towns, even if they owned small country estates.

Below the middle classes came the artisans and shopkeepers (most of whom were organized in professional guilds), then the journeymen, apprentices, servants, and laborers. At the bottom of the social scale were the unemployed poor, who survived by intermittent work and charity. Women married to artisans and shopkeepers often kept the accounts, supervised employees, and ran the household as well. Every middle-class and upper-class family employed servants; artisans and shopkeepers frequently hired them, too. Women from poorer families usually worked as domestic servants until they married. Four out of five domestic servants in the city were female. In large cities such as London, the servant population grew faster than the population of the city as a whole.

Social status in the cities was readily visible. Wide, spacious streets graced rich districts; the houses had gardens, and the air was relatively fresh. In poor districts, the streets were narrow, dirty, dark, humid, and smelly, and the houses were damp and crowded. The poorest people were homeless, sleeping under bridges or in abandoned buildings. A Neapolitan prince described his homeless neighbors as "lying like filthy animals, with no distinction of age or sex."

Like shelter, clothing was a reliable social indicator. The poorest workingwomen in Paris wore woolen skirts and blouses of dark colors over petticoats, a bodice, and a corset. They also donned caps of various sorts, cotton stockings, and shoes (probably their only pair). Workingmen dressed even more drably. Many occupations could be recognized by their dress: no one could confuse lawyers in their dark robes with masons or butchers in their special aprons, for example. People higher on the social ladder were more likely to sport a variety of fabrics, colors, and unusual designs in their clothing and to own many different outfits. Social status was not an abstract idea; it permeated every detail of daily life.

The ability to read and write also reflected social differences. People in the upper classes were more literate than those in the lower classes; city people were more literate than peasants. Protestant countries appear to have been more successful at promoting education and literacy than Catholic countries, perhaps because of the Protestant emphasis on Bible reading. Widespread literacy among the lower classes was first achieved in the Protestant areas of Switzerland and in Presbyterian Scotland. In France, literacy doubled in the eighteenth century thanks to the spread of parish schools, but still only one in two men and one in four women could read and write. Most peasants remained illiterate. Few schools existed, teachers received low wages, and no country had yet established a national system of education.

A new literate public nonetheless arose among the middle classes of the cities. More books and periodicals were published than ever before, another aspect of the consumer revolution. The trend began in the 1690s in Britain and the Dutch Republic and gradually accelerated. In 1695, new newspapers and magazines proliferated when the British government stopped demanding that each publication have a government-approved license. The first London daily newspaper came out in 1702, and in 1709 Joseph Addison and Richard Steele published the first literary magazine, *The Spectator*. They devoted their magazine to the cultural improvement of the increasingly influential middle class. By the 1720s, twenty-four provincial newspapers were published in England. In the London coffeehouses, an edition of a single newspaper might reach ten thousand male readers. Women did their reading at home. Except in the Dutch Republic, newspapers on the continent lagged behind and often consisted mainly of advertising with little critical commentary. France, for example, had no daily paper until 1777.

New Tastes in the Arts

The new literate public did not just read newspapers; its members now pursued an interest in painting, attended concerts, and besieged booksellers in search of popular novels. Because increased trade and prosperity put money into the hands of the growing middle classes, a new urban audience began to compete with the churches, rulers, and courtiers as chief patrons for new work.

Developments in painting reflected the tastes of the new public, as the **rococo** style challenged the hold of the baroque and classical schools, especially in France. *Rococo*, like *baroque*, was an invented word (from the French word *rocaille*, "shell-work") and originally a derogatory label, meaning "frivolous decoration." Many rococo paintings depicted scenes of intimate sensuality rather than the monumental, emotional grandeur favored by classical and baroque painters. Personal portraits and pastoral paintings took the place of heroic landscapes and grand, ceremonial canvases. Rococo paintings adorned homes as well as palaces and served as a form of interior decoration rather than as a statement of piety. Its decorative quality made rococo art an ideal complement to newly discovered materials such as stucco and porcelain, especially the porcelain vases now imported from China.

Public music concerts were first performed in England in the 1670s and became much more regular and frequent in the 1690s. On the continent, Frankfurt organized the first regular public concerts in 1712; Hamburg and Paris began holding them within a few years. Opera continued to spread in the eighteenth century; Venice had sixteen public opera houses by 1700, and the Covent Garden opera house opened in London in 1732.

The growth of a public that appreciated and supported music had much the same effect as the extension of the reading public: like authors, composers could now begin to liberate themselves from court patronage and work for a paying audience. The composer George Frideric Handel (1685–1759) was among the first to grasp the new directions in music. A German by birth, Handel wrote operas in Italy and then moved in 1710 to Britain, where he wrote music for the court and began composing oratorios. The oratorio, a form Handel introduced in Britain, combined the drama of opera with the majesty of religious and ceremonial music and featured the chorus over the soloists. The "Hallelujah Chorus" from Handel's oratorio *Messiah* (1741) is perhaps the single best-known piece of Western classical music. It reflected the composer's personal, deeply felt piety but also his willingness to combine musical materials into a dramatic form that captured the enthusiasm of the new public.

Nothing captured the imagination of the new public more than the novel, the literary genre whose very name underscored the eighteenth-century taste for novelty. More than three hundred French novels appeared between 1700 and 1730. During this unprecedented explosion, the novel took on its modern form and became more concerned with individual psychology and social description than with the adventure tales popular earlier (such as Miguel de Cervantes's *Don Quixote*). The novel's popularity was closely tied to the expansion of the reading public, and novels were available in serial form in periodicals or from the many booksellers who served the new market.

Women figured prominently in novels as characters, and women writers abounded. The English author Eliza Haywood (1693?–1756) earned her living turning out a stream of novels with titles such as *Persecuted Virtue*, *Constancy Rewarded*, and *The History of Betsy Thoughtless*—all showing a concern for the proper place of women as models of virtue in a changing world. Haywood's male counterpart was Daniel Defoe (1660–1731), a merchant's son who had a diverse and colorful career as a manufacturer, political spy, novelist, and social commentator. Defoe is best known for his novel *Robinson Crusoe* (1719). The story of the adventures of a shipwrecked sailor, *Robinson Crusoe* portrayed the new values of the time: to survive, Crusoe had to employ fearless entrepreneurial ingenuity. He had to be ready for the unexpected and be able to improvise in every situation. He was, in short, the model for the new man in an expanding economy. Crusoe's patronizing attitude toward the black man Friday now draws much critical attention, but his discovery of Friday shows how the fate of blacks and whites had become intertwined in the new colonial environment.

Religious Revivals

Despite the novel's growing popularity, religious books and pamphlets still sold in huge numbers, and most Europeans remained devout, even as their religions were changing. In this period, a Protestant revivalist movement known as **Pietism** rocked the complacency of the established churches in northern Europe. Pietists believed in a mystical religion of the heart; they wanted a deeply emotional, even ecstatic religion. They urged intense Bible study, which in turn promoted popular education and contributed to the increase in literacy. Many Pietists attended catechism instruction every day and also went to morning and evening prayer meetings in addition to regular Sunday services. Although Pietism appealed to both Lutherans and Calvinists, it had the greatest impact in Lutheran Prussia, where it taught the virtues of hard work, obedience, and devotion to duty.

Catholicism also had its versions of religious revival, especially in France. A Frenchwoman, Jeanne Marie Guyon (1648–1717), attracted many noblewomen and a few leading clergymen to her own Catholic brand of Pietism, known as Quietism. Claiming miraculous visions and astounding prophecies, she urged a mystical union with God through prayer and simple devotion. Despite papal condemnation and intense controversy within Catholic circles in France, Guyon had followers all over Europe.

Even more influential were the Jansenists, who gained many new adherents to their austere form of Catholicism despite Louis XIV's harassment and repeated condemnation by the papacy. Under the pressure of religious and political persecution, Jansenism took a revivalist turn in the 1720s. At the funeral of a Jansenist priest in Paris in 1727, the crowd who flocked to the grave claimed to witness a series of miraculous healings. Some believers fell into frenzied convulsions, claiming to be inspired by the Holy Spirit through the intercession of the dead priest. After midcentury, Jansenism became even more politically active as its adherents joined in opposition to the crown's policies on religion.

> **REVIEW**   How were new social trends reflected in cultural life in the early 1700s?

Consolidation of the European State System

The spread of Pietism and Jansenism reflected the emergence of a middle-class public that now participated in every new development, including religion. The middle classes could pursue these interests because the European state system gradually stabilized despite the increasing competition for wealth in the Atlantic system. Warfare settled three main issues between 1700 and 1750: a coalition of powers held France in check on the continent, Great Britain emerged from the wars against France as the preeminent maritime power, and Russia defeated Sweden in the contest for supremacy in the Baltic. After Louis XIV's death in 1715, Europe enjoyed the fruits of a more balanced diplomatic system, in which warfare became less frequent and less widespread. States could then spend their resources establishing and expanding control over their own populations, both at home and in their colonies.

A New Power Alignment

The peace treaties that ended the War of the Spanish Succession (1701–1713) signaled a new alignment of power in western Europe (see Chapter 16). Spain began a long decline, French ambitions for dominance were thwarted, and Great Britain emerged as the new center in the balance of power. A coalition led by Britain and joined by most of the European powers had confronted Louis XIV's French forces across Europe. The conflict extended to the Caribbean and North and South America as well. The casualties mounted inexorably: in the battle of Blenheim in southern Germany in 1704, 108,000 soldiers fought and 33,000 were killed or wounded—in just one day. At Malplaquet, near the northern French border, a great battle in 1709 engaged 166,000 soldiers and cavalrymen, and 36,000 of them were killed or wounded. Those allied against Louis won at Malplaquet, but they lost twice as many men as the French did and could not pursue their advantage. Everyone rejoiced when peace came (Map 17.2).

By the terms of the peace, French king Louis XIV's grandson was confirmed as King Philip V of Spain (r. 1700–1746) but only on the condition that he renounce any claim to the French throne. None of the other powers could countenance

MAP 17.2 Europe, c. 1715 Although Louis XIV succeeded in putting his grandson Philip on the Spanish throne, France emerged considerably weakened from the War of the Spanish Succession. France ceded large territories in Canada to Britain, which also gained key Mediterranean outposts from Spain as well as a monopoly on providing slaves to the Spanish colonies. Spanish losses were catastrophic. Philip had to renounce any future claim to the French crown and give up considerable territories in the Netherlands and Italy to the Austrians. How did the competing English and French claims in North America around 1715 create potential conflicts for the future?

a joint French-Spanish monarchy. Philip opened Spain further to the rest of Europe and stabilized the currency, but he could not revive Spain's military prestige or commercial position. Spain consistently imported more from Britain and France than it exported to them. As a country that had been created by a campaign against Muslims within its boundaries, Spain remained firmly in the grip of the Catholic clergy, which insisted on the censorship of dissident or heretical ideas. Although the capital city, Madrid, had 200,000 inhabitants, laws prohibited people from smoking, reading newspapers, or talking politics in the cafés and inns of the city—precisely the activities flourishing in England, France, and the Dutch Republic.

When Louis XIV died in 1715, his five-year-old great-grandson succeeded him as Louis XV (r. 1715–1774), with the duke of Orléans (1674–1723), nephew of the dead king, serving as regent for the young boy. To raise much-needed funds, in 1719 the regent encouraged the Scottish financier John Law to set up an official trading company for North America and a state bank that issued paper money and stock (without which trade depended on the available supply of gold and silver). The bank was supposed to offer lower interest rates to the state, thus cutting the cost of financing the government's debts. The value of the stock rose rapidly in a frenzy of speculation, only to crash a few months later. France finally achieved a measure of financial stability under the leadership of Cardinal Hercule de Fleury (1653–1743), the most powerful member of the government after the death of the regent. Colonial trade boomed. Peace and the acceptance of limits on territorial expansion inaugurated a century of French prosperity.

British Rise and Dutch Decline

The British and the Dutch had formed a coalition against Louis XIV under their joint ruler, William III, who was simultaneously *stadholder* (elected head) of the Dutch Republic and, with his English wife, Mary (d. 1694), ruler of England, Wales, and Scotland. After William's death in 1702, the British and Dutch went their separate ways. Over the next decades, England incorporated Scotland and subjugated Ireland, becoming "Great Britain" in 1707. At the same time, Dutch imperial power declined; by 1700, the British dominated the seas, and the Dutch, with their small population of less than two million, came to depend on alliances with bigger powers.

English relations with Scotland and Ireland were complicated by the problem of succession: William and Mary had no children. To ensure a Protestant succession, Parliament ruled that Mary's sister, Anne, would succeed William and Mary and that the Protestant house of Hanover in Germany would succeed Anne if she had no surviving heirs. Catholics were excluded. When Queen Anne (r. 1702–1714) died leaving no children, the elector of Hanover, a Protestant great-grandson of James I, consequently became King George I (r. 1714–1727). The house of Hanover—renamed the house of Windsor during World War I—still occupies the British throne today.

Support from the Scots and Irish for this solution did not come easily because many in Scotland and Ireland supported the claims to the throne of the deposed Catholic king, James II, and, after his death in 1701, his son James Edward. Out of fear of this Jacobitism (from the Latin *Jacobus*, for "James"), Scottish Protestant leaders agreed to the Act of Union of 1707, which abolished the Scottish Parliament and affirmed the Scots' recognition of the Protestant Hanoverian succession. The Scots agreed to obey the Parliament of Great Britain, which would include Scottish members in the House of Commons and the House of Lords. A Jacobite rebellion in Scotland in 1715, aiming to restore the Stuart line, was suppressed (see Map 17.2, page 505). The threat of Jacobitism nonetheless continued into the 1740s.

The Irish—90 percent of whom were Catholic—proved even more difficult to subdue. William III had to take command of the joint English and Dutch forces to defeat the Irish supporters of James II, and after that defeat Catholics in Ireland faced yet more confiscation and legal restrictions. By 1700, Irish Catholics, who in 1640 had owned 60 percent of the land in Ireland, owned just 14 percent. The Protestant-controlled Irish Parliament passed a series of laws limiting the rights of the Catholic majority: Catholics could not marry Protestants, send children abroad for education, or establish Catholic schools at home. Moreover, Catholics could not sit in Parliament, nor could they vote for its members unless they took an oath renouncing Catholic doctrine. These and a host of other laws reduced Catholic Ireland to the status of a colony.

In Britain's constitutional system, the monarch ruled with Parliament. The crown chose ministers, directed policy, and supervised administration, while Parliament raised revenue, passed laws, and represented the interests of the people to the crown. The powers of Parliament were reaffirmed by the Triennial Act in 1694, which provided that Parliaments meet at least once every three years (this was extended to seven years in 1716, after the Whigs had established their ascendancy). Only 200,000 propertied men could vote, out of a population of more than 5 million, and a few hundred families controlled all the important political offices.

George I and George II (r. 1727–1760) relied on one man, Sir **Robert Walpole** (1676–1745), to help them manage their relations with Parliament. From his position as First Lord of the Treasury, Walpole made himself into the first, or "prime," minister, leading the House of Commons from 1721 to 1742. Although appointed initially by the king, Walpole established an enduring pattern of parliamentary government in which a prime minister from the leading party guided legislation through the House of Commons. Walpole also built a vast patronage machine that dispensed government jobs to win support for the crown's policies.

The partisan division between the Whigs, who supported the Hanoverian succession and the rights of dissenting Protestants, and the Tories, who had backed the Stuart line and the Church of England, did not hamper Great Britain's pursuit of economic, military, and colonial power. In this period, Great Britain became a great power on the world stage by virtue of its navy and its ability to finance major military involvement in wars. The founding in 1694 of the Bank of England—which, unlike the French bank, endured—enabled the government to raise money at low interest for foreign wars. By the 1740s, the government could borrow more than four times what it could in the 1690s.

When William of Orange (William III of England) died in 1702, he left no heirs, and for forty-five years the Dutch lived without a stadholder. The merchant ruling class of some two thousand families dominated the Dutch Republic more than ever, but they presided over a country that counted for less in international power politics. The Dutch population was not growing as fast as others, and the Dutch share of the Baltic trade decreased from 50 percent in 1720 to less than 30 percent by the 1770s. The output of Leiden textiles dropped to one-third of its 1700 level by 1740. Shipbuilding, paper manufacturing, tobacco processing, salt refining, and pottery production all dwindled as well. The biggest exception to the downward trend was trade with the New World, which increased with escalating demands for sugar and tobacco. The Dutch shifted their interest away from great-power rivalries and toward those areas of international trade and finance where they could establish an enduring presence.

Russia's Emergence as a European Power

The commerce and shipbuilding of the Dutch and British so impressed Russian tsar Peter I (r. 1689–1725) that he traveled incognito to their shipyards in 1697 to learn their methods firsthand. Known to history as **Peter the Great**, he dragged Russia kicking and screaming all the way to great-power status. Although he came to the throne while still a minor (on the eve of his tenth birthday), grew up under the threat of a palace coup, and enjoyed little formal education, his accomplishments soon matched his seven-foot-tall stature. Peter transformed public life in Russia and established an absolutist state based on the Western model. His attempts to create a society patterned after western Europe, known as **Westernization**, ignited an enduring controversy: Did Peter set Russia on a course of inevitable Westernization required to compete with the West? Or did he forever and fatally disrupt Russia's natural evolution into a distinctive Slavic society?

To pursue his goal of Westernizing Russian culture, Peter set up the first laboratories and technical schools and founded the Russian Academy of Sciences. He ordered translations of Western classics and hired a German theater company to perform the French plays of Molière. He replaced the traditional Russian calendar with the Western one,* introduced Arabic numerals, and brought out the first public newspaper. He ordered his officials and the nobles to shave their beards and dress in Western fashion.

---

*Peter introduced the Julian calendar, then still used in Protestant but not Catholic countries. Later in the eighteenth century, Protestant Europe abandoned the Julian for the Gregorian calendar. Not until 1918 was the Gregorian calendar adopted in Russia, at which point Russia's calendar had fallen thirteen days behind Europe's.

Peter the Great Modernizes Russia In this popular print, a barber forces a protesting noble to conform to Western fashions. Peter the Great ordered all nobles, merchants, and middle-class professionals to cut off their beards or pay a huge tax to keep them. An early biographer of Peter claimed that those who lost their beards saved them to put in their coffins, in fear that they would not enter heaven without them. Most western Europeans applauded these attempts to modernize Russia, but many Russians deeply resented the attack on traditional ways. Why was everyday appearance such a contested issue in Russia? (Universal History Archive / UIG / Bridgeman Images.)

Peter encouraged foreigners to move to Russia to offer their advice and skills, especially for building the capital city. Named St. Petersburg after the tsar, the new capital symbolized Russia's opening to the West. Construction began in 1703 in a Baltic province that had been recently conquered from Sweden. By the end of 1709, thirty thousand laborers had been enlisted in the construction. Peter ordered skilled workers to move to the new city and commanded all landowners possessing more than forty serf households to build houses there. In the 1720s, a German minister described St. Petersburg "as a wonder of the world, considering its magnificent palaces, . . . and the short time that was employed in the building of it." At Peter's death in 1725, the new city had forty thousand residents.

Peter aimed to set Russia on a new course. At his new capital he tried to improve the traditionally denigrated, secluded status of women by ordering them to dress in European styles and appear publicly at his dinners for diplomatic representatives. A foreigner headed every one of Peter's new technical and vocational schools, and for its first eight years the new Academy of Sciences included no Russians. Every ministry was assigned a foreign adviser. Upper-class Russians learned French or German, which they spoke even at home. Such changes affected only the very top of Russian society, however; the mass of the population had no contact with the new ideas and ended up paying for the innovations either in ruinous new taxation or by building St. Petersburg, a project that cost the lives of thousands of workers. Serfs remained tied to the land, completely dominated by their noble lords.

Peter also reorganized government and finance on Western models and, like other absolute rulers, strengthened his army. With ruthless recruiting methods, which included branding a cross on every recruit's left hand to prevent desertion, he forged an army of 200,000 men and equipped it with modern weapons. He not only built the first navy in Russian history but also created schools for artillery, engineering, and military medicine. Not surprisingly, taxes tripled.

The tsar allowed nothing to stand in his way. He did not hesitate to use torture, and he executed thousands. He gave a special guard regiment unprecedented power to expedite cases against those suspected of rebellion, espionage, pretensions to the throne, or just "unseemly utterances" against him. Because his only son, Alexei, had allied himself with Peter's critics, the tsar threw him into prison, where the young man mysteriously died.

To control the often restive nobility, Peter insisted that all noblemen engage in state service. The Table of Ranks (1722) classified them into military, administrative, and court categories, a codification of social and legal relationships in Russia that would last for nearly two centuries. Because the nobles lacked a secure independent status, Peter could command them to a degree that was unimaginable in western Europe. State service was not only compulsory but also permanent. Moreover, the male children of those in service had to be registered by the age of ten and begin serving at fifteen. To increase his authority over the Russian Orthodox church, Peter allowed the office of patriarch (supreme head) to remain vacant, and in 1721 he replaced it with the Holy Synod, a bureaucracy of laymen under his supervision.

Peter the Great's success in building up state authority changed the balance of power in eastern Europe. First he took on Sweden, which had dominated the Baltic region since the Thirty Years' War (1618–1648). Peter joined an anti-Swedish coalition in 1700 with Denmark, Saxony, and Poland, but the ensuing Great Northern War (1700–1721) went badly for the allies at first. The Swedes defeated Denmark, quickly marched into Poland and Saxony, and then invaded Russia. Peter's rebuilt army finally defeated the Swedes at the battle of Poltava (1709), taking twenty-three thousand Swedish soldiers prisoner and marking the end of Swedish imperial ambitions in the Baltic (Map 17.3). Russia could then begin to compete with the great powers Prussia, Austria, and France.

When the tide turned in the Great Northern War, King Frederick William I of Prussia (r. 1713–1740) joined the Russian side and gained new territories. Prussia had to make the most of every military opportunity because it was much smaller in size and population than the other powers. Frederick William doubled the size of the Prussian army; though still smaller than those of his rivals, it was the best-trained and most up-to-date force in Europe. The army so dominated life in Prussia that the country earned the label "a large army with a small state attached." One of the first rulers to wear a military uniform as his everyday dress, Frederick William subordinated the entire domestic administration to the army's needs. He financed the army's growth by subjecting all the provinces to an excise tax on food, drink, and manufactured goods and by increasing rents on crown lands.

MAP 17.3 Russia and Sweden after the Great Northern War, 1721
After the Great Northern War, Russia supplanted Sweden as the major power in the north. Although Russia had a much larger population from which to draw its armies, Sweden made the most of its advantages and gave way only after a great military struggle.

Continuing Dynastic Struggles

War broke out again in 1733 when the king of Poland-Lithuania died. France, Spain, and Sardinia joined in the War of the Polish Succession (1733–1735) against Austria and Russia, each side supporting rival claimants to the Polish throne. Prussia chose to sit on the sidelines. Although Peter the Great had been followed by a series of weak rulers, Russian forces were still strong enough to drive the French candidate out of Poland-Lithuania, prompting France to accept the Austrian candidate. In exchange, Austria gave the province of Lorraine to the French candidate, the father-in-law of Louis XV, with the promise that the province would pass to France on his death. France and Britain went back to pursuing their colonial rivalries. Prussia and Russia concentrated on shoring up their influence within Poland-Lithuania.

Because its armies still faced the Turks on its southeastern border, Austria did not want to become mired in a long struggle in Poland-Lithuania. Even though the Austrians had forced the Turks to recognize their rule over all of Hungary and Transylvania in 1699 and had occupied Belgrade in 1717, the Turks did not stop fighting. In the 1730s, the Turks retook Belgrade, and Russia now claimed a role in the struggle against the Turks. Moreover, Hungary proved less than enthusiastic about submitting to Austria. In 1703, the wealthiest Hungarian noble landlord, Ferenc Rákóczi (1676–1735), raised an army of seventy thousand men who fought for "God, Fatherland, and Liberty" until 1711. They forced the Austrians to recognize local Hungarian institutions, grant amnesty, and restore confiscated estates in exchange for confirming hereditary Austrian rule.

When Holy Roman Emperor Charles VI died without a male heir in 1740, another war of succession, the **War of the Austrian Succession** (1740–1748), began. Most European rulers recognized the emperor's chosen heiress, his daughter Maria Theresa, because Charles's Pragmatic Sanction of 1713 had given a woman the right to inherit the Habsburg crown lands. The new king of Prussia, Frederick II, who had just succeeded his father a few months earlier in 1740, saw his chance to grab territory and immediately invaded the rich Austrian province of Silesia. France joined Prussia in an attempt to further humiliate its traditional enemy Austria, and Great Britain allied with Austria to prevent the French from taking the Austrian Netherlands. The war soon expanded to the overseas colonies of Great Britain and France. French and British colonials in North America fought each other all along their boundaries, enlisting native American auxiliaries. Hostilities broke out in India, too.

Maria Theresa (r. 1740–1780) survived only by conceding Silesia to Prussia in order to split the Prussians off from France. The Peace of Aix-la-Chapelle (1748) recognized Maria Theresa as the heiress to the Austrian lands; her husband, Francis I, became Holy Roman Emperor, thus reasserting the integrity of the Austrian Empire. The peace of 1748 failed to resolve the colonial conflicts between Britain and France, however, and fighting for domination continued unofficially.

The Power of Diplomacy and the Importance of Population

No single power emerged from the wars of the first half of the eighteenth century clearly superior to the others, and the Peace of Utrecht explicitly declared that maintaining a balance of power was crucial to keeping peace in Europe. Diplomacy helped preserve that balance, and to meet the new demands placed on it, the diplomatic service, like the military and financial bureaucracies before it, had to develop regular procedures. The French set a pattern that the other European states soon imitated. By 1685, France had embassies in all the important capitals. Nobles of ancient families served as ambassadors to Rome, Madrid, Vienna, and London, whereas royal officials were chosen for Switzerland, the Dutch Republic, and Venice. The ambassador selected and paid for his own staff, which might be as large as eighty people. The diplomatic system ensured a continuation of the principles of the Peace of Westphalia (1648); in the midst of every crisis and war, the great powers would convene and hammer out a written agreement detailing the requirements for peace.

Adroit diplomacy could smooth the road toward peace, but success in war still depended on sheer numbers—of men and of muskets. Because each state's strength depended largely on the size of its army, the growth and health of the population increasingly entered into government calculations. William Petty's *Political Arithmetick* (1690) offered statistical estimates of human capital—that is, of population and wages—to determine Britain's national wealth. Government officials devoted increased effort to the statistical estimation of total population and rates of births, deaths, and marriages.

Physicians used the new population statistics to explain the environmental causes of disease, another new preoccupation in this period. Petty, trained as a physician himself, devised a quantitative scale that distinguished healthy from unhealthy places largely on the basis of air quality, an early precursor of modern environmental studies. Cities were the unhealthiest places because garbage and excrement (animal and human) accumulated where people lived densely packed together. The Irish writer Jonathan Swift described what happened in London after a big rainstorm: "Filths of all hues and colors . . . sweepings from butchers' stalls, dung, guts and blood . . . dead cats and turniptops come tumbling down the flood." Reacting to newly collected data on climate, disease, and population, local governments undertook such measures as draining low-lying areas, burying refuse, and cleaning wells.

Not all changes came from direct government intervention. Hospitals, founded originally as charities concerned foremost with the moral worthiness of the poor, gradually evolved into medical institutions that defined patients by their diseases. Physicians began to rely on postmortem dissections in the hospital to gain better knowledge, a practice most patients' families resented. Press reports of body snatching and grave robbing by surgeons and their apprentices outraged the public well into the 1800s.

Despite the change in hospitals, a medical profession with nationwide organizations and licensing had not yet emerged, and no clear line separated trained physicians from quacks. Patients in a hospital were as likely to catch a deadly disease as to be cured there. Antiseptics were virtually unknown. Because doctors believed that most insanity was caused by disorders in the system of bodily "humors," their prescribed treatments included blood transfusions; ingestion of bitter substances such as coffee, quinine, and soap; immersion in water; various forms of exercise; and burning or cauterizing the body to allow "black vapors" to escape.

Hardly any infectious diseases could be cured, though inoculation against smallpox spread from the Middle East to Europe in the early eighteenth century, thanks largely to the efforts of Lady Mary Wortley Montagu (1689–1762). Wife of the British ambassador to the Ottoman Empire, Montagu witnessed firsthand the Turkish use of inoculation. When a new smallpox epidemic threatened England in 1721, she called on her physician to inoculate her daughter. Inoculation against smallpox spread more widely only after 1796, when the English physician Edward Jenner developed a serum based on cowpox, a milder disease.

Public bathhouses had disappeared from cities in the sixteenth and seventeenth centuries because they seemed to be a source of disorderly behavior and epidemic illness. In the eighteenth century, even private bathing came into disfavor because people feared the effects of contact with water. Bathing was hazardous, physicians insisted, because it opened the body to disease. The upper classes associated cleanliness not with baths but with frequently changed linens, powdered hair, and perfume, which was thought to strengthen the body and refresh the brain by counteracting corrupt and foul air.

> **REVIEW** What events and developments led to greater stability and more limited warfare within Europe?

The Birth of the Enlightenment

Economic expansion, the emergence of a new consumer society, and the stabilization of the European state system all generated optimism about the future. The intellectual corollary was the **Enlightenment**, a term used later in the eighteenth century to describe the movement begun by a loosely knit group of writers and scholars who believed that human beings could apply a critical, reasoning spirit to every problem they encountered in this world. The new secular, scientific, and critical attitude first emerged in the 1690s, scrutinizing everything from the absolutism of Louis XIV to the traditional role of women in society. After 1750, criticism took a more systematic turn as writers provided new theories for the organization of society and politics; but as early as the 1720s, established authorities realized they faced a new set of challenges. Even while slavery expanded in the Atlantic system, Enlightenment writers began to insist on the need for new freedoms in Europe.

Popularization of Science and Challenges to Religion

The writers of the Enlightenment glorified the geniuses of the new science and championed the scientific method as the solution for all social problems. By 1700, mathematics and science had become fashionable topics in high society, and the public flocked to lectures explaining scientific discoveries.

As the prestige of science increased, some developed a skeptical attitude toward attempts to enforce religious conformity. Pierre Bayle (1647–1706), a French Huguenot refugee from Louis XIV's persecutions, launched an internationally influential campaign against religious intolerance from his safe haven in the Dutch Republic. His *News from the Republic of Letters* (first published in 1684) bitterly criticized the policies of Louis XIV and was quickly banned in Paris and condemned in Rome. After attacking Louis XIV's anti-Protestant policies, Bayle took a more general stand in favor of religious toleration. No state in Europe officially offered complete tolerance, though the Dutch Republic came closest with its tacit acceptance of Catholics, dissident Protestant groups, and open Jewish communities. In 1697, Bayle published his *Historical and Critical Dictionary*, which cited all the errors and delusions that he could find in past and present writers of all religions. Even religion must meet the test of reasonableness: "Any particular dogma, whatever it may be, whether it is advanced on the authority of the Scriptures, or whatever else may be its origins, is to be regarded as false if it clashes with the clear and definite conclusions of the natural understanding [reason]."

Bayle's insistence on rational investigation seemed to challenge the authority of faith. Other scholars challenged the authority of the Bible by subjecting it to historical criticism. Discoveries in geology in the early eighteenth century showed that marine fossils dated immensely further back than the biblical flood story suggested. Investigations of miracles, comets, and oracles—like the growing literature against belief in witchcraft—urged the use of reason to combat superstition and prejudice. Defenders of church and state published books warning of the new skepticism's dangers. The spokesman for Louis XIV's absolutism, the bishop Jacques-Bénigne Bossuet, warned that "reason is the guide of their choice, but reason only brings them face to face with vague conjectures and baffling perplexities." Human beings, the traditionalists held, were simply incapable of subjecting everything to reason, especially in the realm of religion.

State authorities found religious skepticism equally unsettling because it threatened to undermine state power, too. The extensive literature of criticism was not limited to France, but much of it was published in French, and the French government took the lead in suppressing the more outspoken works. Forbidden books were then often published in the Dutch Republic, Britain, or Switzerland and smuggled back across the border to a public whose appetite was only whetted by censorship.

The most influential writer of the early Enlightenment was a Frenchman born into the upper middle class, François-Marie Arouet, known by his pen name, **Voltaire** (1694–1778). Voltaire took inspiration from Bayle, once giving him the following tongue-in-cheek description: "He gives facts with such odious fidelity, he exposes the arguments for and against with such dastardly impartiality, he is so intolerably intelligible, that he leads people of only ordinary common sense to judge and even to doubt." Voltaire's tangles with church and state began in the early 1730s, when he published his *Letters Concerning the English Nation* (the English version appeared in 1733), in which he devoted several chapters to scientist Isaac Newton and philosopher John Locke and used the virtues of the British as a way to attack Catholic bigotry and government rigidity in France. He spent two years in exile in Britain when the French state responded to his book with an order for his arrest.

Voltaire also popularized Newton's scientific discoveries in his *Elements of the Philosophy of Newton* (1738). The French state and many European theologians considered Newtonianism threatening because it glorified the human mind and seemed to reduce God to an abstract, external, rationalistic force. So sensational was the success of Voltaire's book on Newton that a hostile Jesuit reported that "all Paris resounds with Newton, all Paris stammers Newton, all Paris studies and learns Newton." Before long, Voltaire was elected a fellow of the Royal Society in London and in Edinburgh as well as being admitted to twenty other scientific academies. Voltaire's fame continued to grow, reaching truly astounding proportions in the 1750s and 1760s.

Travel Literature and the Challenge to Custom and Tradition

Just as scientific method could be used to question religious and even state authority, a more general skepticism also emerged from the expanding knowledge about the world outside of Europe. During the seventeenth and eighteenth centuries, the number of travel accounts dramatically increased as travel writers used the contrast between their home societies and other cultures to criticize the customs of European society.

Travelers to the Americas found "noble savages" (native peoples) who appeared to live in conditions of great freedom and equality; they were "naturally good" and "happy" without taxes, lawsuits, or much organized government. In China, in contrast, travelers found a people who enjoyed prosperity and an ancient civilization. Christian missionaries made little headway in China, and visitors had to admit that

Comparisons of Religions and the Rise of Skepticism   These two engravings come from *Religious Customs and Ceremonies of the All the Peoples of the World*, an influential encyclopedia published in French between 1723 and 1743 in Amsterdam. The artist Bernard Picart depicts a Brahmin who wears an iron collar to raise funds for a hospital and a Brahmin suspended over a fire in devotion. Picart and his fellow French Protestant refugee Jean Frédéric Bernard, the author and publisher, wanted to put Christianity and especially Catholicism in a comparative light; they emphasized the similarities in religious customs across the globe and in this way cast doubt on claims for the absolute truth of any one religion. Their book helped inspire the early Enlightenment. (From Religious Ceremonies and Customs, c. 1724/ Private Collection/The Stapleton Collection/Bridgeman Images.)

China's religious systems had flourished for four or five thousand years with no input from Europe or from Christianity. The basic lesson of travel literature in the 1700s, then, was that customs varied: justice, freedom, property, good government, religion, and morality all were relative to the place. One critic complained that travel encouraged the destruction of religion: "Some complete their demoralization by extensive travel, and lose whatever shreds of religion remained to them. Every day they see a new religion, new customs, new rites."

Travel literature turned explicitly political in Montesquieu's *Persian Letters* (1721). Charles-Louis de Secondat, baron of Montesquieu (1689–1755), the son of an eminent judicial family, was a high-ranking judge in a French court. He published *Persian Letters* anonymously in the Dutch Republic, and the book went into ten printings in just one year—a best seller for the times. Montesquieu tells the fictional story of two Persians, Rica and Usbek, who visit France in the last years of Louis XIV's reign and write home with their impressions. By imagining an outsider's perspective, Montesquieu could satirize French customs and politics without taking them on directly. Montesquieu chose Persians for his travelers because they came from what was widely considered the most despotic of all governments, in which rulers had life-and-death powers over their subjects. In the book, the Persians constantly compare France to Persia, suggesting that the French monarchy might verge on despotism.

Montesquieu's anonymity did not last long, and in the late 1720s, he sold his judgeship and traveled extensively in Europe, staying eighteen months in Britain. In 1748, he published a widely influential work on comparative government, *The Spirit of Laws*. Like the politique Jean Bodin before him (see page 449), Montesquieu examined the various types of government, but unlike Bodin he did not favor absolute power in a monarchy. His time in Britain made him much more favorable to constitutional forms of government. The Catholic church soon listed both *Persian Letters* and *The Spirit of Laws* on its Index (its list of forbidden books).

Raising the Woman Question

Many of the letters exchanged in *Persian Letters* focused on women because Montesquieu considered the position of women a sure indicator of the nature of government and morality. Although Montesquieu was not a feminist, his depiction of Roxana, the favorite wife in Usbek's harem, struck a chord with many women. Roxana revolts against the authority of Usbek's eunuchs and writes a final letter to her husband announcing her impending suicide: "I may have lived in servitude, but I have always been free, I have amended your laws according to the laws of nature, and my mind has always remained independent." Women writers used the same language of tyranny and freedom to argue for concrete changes in their status. Feminist ideas were not entirely new, but they were presented systematically for the first time during the Enlightenment and represented a fundamental challenge to the ways of traditional societies.

The most systematic and successful of these women writers was the English author Mary Astell (1666–1731). In 1694, she published *A Serious Proposal to the Ladies*, in which she advocated founding a private women's college to remedy women's lack of education. Addressing women, she asked, "How can you be content to be in the World like Tulips in a Garden, to make a fine *shew* [show] and be good for nothing?" In later works such as *Reflections upon Marriage* (1706), Astell criticized the relationship between the sexes within marriage: "If absolute sovereignty be not necessary in a state, how comes it to be so in a family? . . . *If all men are born free*, how is it that all women are born slaves?"

Most male writers held that women were less capable of reasoning than men and therefore did not need systematic education. Such opinions often rested on biological suppositions. The long-dominant Aristotelian view of reproduction held that only the male seed carried spirit and individuality. At the beginning of the eighteenth century, however, scientists began to undermine this belief. Physicians and surgeons began to champion the doctrine of *ovism*—that the female egg was essential in making new humans. During the decades that followed, male Enlightenment writers would continue to debate women's nature and appropriate social roles.

REVIEW   What were the major issues in the early decades of the Enlightenment?

Conclusion

Expansion of colonies overseas and economic development at home created greater wealth, longer life spans, and higher expectations for Europeans in the first half of the eighteenth century. In these better times for many, a spirit of optimism prevailed. People could now spend money on newspapers, novels, travel literature, and music as well as on coffee, tea, and cotton cloth. Not everyone shared equally in the benefits, however: slaves toiled in misery for their masters in the Americas, eastern European serfs found themselves ever more closely bound to their noble lords, and rural folk almost everywhere tasted few fruits of consumer society.

Politics changed, too, as experts urged government intervention to improve public health, and states found it in their interest to settle many international disputes by diplomacy, which itself became more regular and routine. The consolidation of the European state system allowed a tide of criticism and new thinking about society to swell in Great Britain and France and begin to spill throughout Europe. Ultimately, the combination of the Atlantic system and the Enlightenment would give rise to a series of Atlantic revolutions.

MAPPING THE WEST   **Europe in 1750**   By 1750, Europe had achieved a kind of diplomatic equilibrium in which no one power predominated despite repeated wars over dynastic succession. Spain, the Dutch Republic, Poland-Lithuania, and Sweden had all declined in power and influence while Great Britain, Russia, and Prussia gained prominence. France's ambitions to dominate had been thwarted, but its combination of a big army and rich overseas possessions made it a major player for a long time to come. In the War of the Austrian Succession, Austria lost its rich province of Silesia to Prussia.

Chapter Review

KEY TERMS AND PEOPLE

Be sure that you can identify the term or person and explain its historical significance.

Atlantic system (p. 490)
plantation (p. 492)
mestizo (p. 496)
buccaneers (p. 496)
consumer revolution (p. 497)
agricultural revolution (p. 499)
rococo (p. 502)

Pietism (p. 503)
Robert Walpole (p. 507)
Peter the Great (p. 508)
Westernization (p. 508)
War of the Austrian Succession (p. 512)
Enlightenment (p. 514)
Voltaire (p. 515)

REVIEW QUESTIONS

1. How was consumerism related to slavery in the early eighteenth century?
2. How were new social trends reflected in cultural life in the early 1700s?
3. What events and developments led to greater stability and more limited warfare within Europe?
4. What were the major issues in the early decades of the Enlightenment?

MAKING CONNECTIONS

1. How did the rise of slavery and the plantation system change European politics and society?
2. Why was the Enlightenment born just at the moment that the Atlantic system took shape?
3. What were the major differences between the wars of the first half of the eighteenth century and those of the seventeenth century? (Refer to Chapters 15 and 16.)
4. During the first half of the eighteenth century, what were the major issues affecting peasants in France and serfs in Poland and Russia?

IMPORTANT EVENTS

1700s	• Beginning of rapid development of plantations in Caribbean
1703	• Peter the Great begins construction of St. Petersburg, founds first Russian newspaper
1713–1714	• Peace of Utrecht treaties end War of Spanish Succession
1714	• Elector of Hanover becomes King George I of England
1715	• Death of Louis XIV
1719	• Daniel Defoe publishes *Robinson Crusoe*
1720	• Last outbreak of bubonic plague in western Europe
1721	• Great Northern War ends; Montesquieu publishes *Persian Letters* anonymously in the Dutch Republic
1733	• War of the Polish Succession; Voltaire's *Letters Concerning the English Nation* attacks French intolerance and narrow-mindedness
1740–1748	• War of the Austrian Succession
1741	• George Frideric Handel composes *Messiah*
1748	• Montesquieu publishes *The Spirit of Laws*

18

The Promise of Enlightenment

1750–1789

CHAPTER FOCUS

How did the Enlightenment influence Western politics, culture, and society?

IN THE SUMMER OF 1766, Empress Catherine II of Russia (known as Catherine the Great) wrote to Voltaire, one of the leaders of the Enlightenment, praising him for entering "into combat against the enemies of mankind" and for fighting superstition, fanaticism, ignorance, and "evil judges." Catherine corresponded regularly with Voltaire, a writer who, at home in France, found himself in constant conflict with authorities of church and state. Her admiring letter shows how influential Enlightenment ideas had become by the middle of the eighteenth century. Even an absolutist ruler such as Catherine endorsed many aspects of the Enlightenment call for reform.

Enlightenment writers such as Voltaire used every means at their disposal—including personal interaction with rulers—to argue for reform. Everything had to be examined in the cold light of reason, and anything that did not promote the improvement of humanity was to be jettisoned. As a result, Enlightenment writers supported religious toleration, attacked the legal use of torture to extract confessions, and criticized censorship by state or church. The book trade and new places for urban socializing, such as coffeehouses and learned societies, spread these ideas within a new elite of middle- and upper-class men and women. In contrast, the lower classes had little contact with Enlightenment ideas. Their lives were shaped more profoundly by an increasing population, rising food prices, and ongoing wars among the great powers.

Rulers pursued Enlightenment reforms that they believed might enhance state power, but they feared changes that might unleash popular discontent. All reform-minded rulers faced potential challenges to their authority. They were right to be concerned, for Enlightenment ideas paved the way for something much more radical and unexpected. The American Declaration of Independence in 1776 showed how Enlightenment ideas could be translated into democratic political practice. After 1789, democracy would come to Europe as well.

The Enlightenment at Its Height

The Enlightenment emerged as an intellectual movement before 1750 but reached its peak in the second half of the eighteenth century. The writers of the Enlightenment called themselves **philosophes**; the word is French for "philosophers," but that definition is somewhat misleading. Whereas philosophers concern themselves with abstract theories, the philosophes were public intellectuals dedicated to solving the real problems of the world. They wrote on subjects ranging from current affairs to art criticism, and they wrote in every conceivable format. Between 1750 and 1789, the Enlightenment acquired its name and, despite heated conflicts between the philosophes and state and religious authorities, gained support in the highest reaches of government.

Men and Women of the Republic of Letters

Although *philosophe* is a French word, the Enlightenment was distinctly cosmopolitan; philosophes could be found from Philadelphia to St. Petersburg. The philosophes considered themselves part of a grand "republic of letters" that transcended national political boundaries. They were not republicans in the usual sense, that is, people who supported representative government and opposed monarchy. What united them were the ideals of reason, reform, and freedom. In 1784, the German philosopher Immanuel Kant summed up the program of the Enlightenment in two Latin words: *sapere aude* ("dare to know") — have the courage to think for yourself.

The philosophes used reason to attack superstition, bigotry, and religious fanaticism, which they considered the chief obstacles to free thought and social reform. Voltaire took religious fanaticism as his chief target: "Once fanaticism has corrupted a mind, the malady is almost incurable. . . . The only remedy for this epidemic malady is the philosophical spirit." Enlightenment writers did not necessarily oppose organized religion, but they strenuously objected to religious intolerance. They believed that the systematic application of reason could do what religious belief could not: improve the human condition by pointing to needed reforms. Reason meant critical, informed, scientific thinking about social issues and problems.

Science in Action   In September 1783, the Montgolfier brothers demonstrated their newly invented hot air balloon at Versailles with the royal family in attendance. The flight reached an altitude of 1,500 feet, covered two miles, and lasted eight minutes. The passengers—a sheep, a duck, and a rooster—landed safely. Hydrogen balloons were developed at the same time and quickly replaced the hot air versions because they could fly higher and longer. Thousands of people flocked to see the launches. Etchings such as the one shown here helped increase public interest. (Private Collection / Bridgeman Images.)

Many Enlightenment writers collaborated on the multivolume *Encyclopedia* (published 1751–1772), which aimed to gather together knowledge about science, religion, industry, and society. The ancestor of all modern encyclopedias from the *Encyclopædia Britannica* to Wikipedia online, the Enlightenment version differed by using knowledge to criticize defects in society. The chief editor of the *Encyclopedia*, Denis Diderot (1713–1784), explained the goal: "All things must be examined, debated, investigated without exception and without regard for anyone's feelings."

The philosophes believed that the spread of knowledge would encourage reform in every aspect of life, from the grain trade to the penal system. Chief among their desired reforms was intellectual freedom—the freedom to use one's own reason to conduct studies and to publish the results. The philosophes wanted freedom of the press and freedom of religion, which they considered "natural rights" guaranteed by "natural law." In their view, progress depended on these freedoms.

Most philosophes, like Voltaire, came from the upper classes, yet the Swiss philosophe Jean-Jacques Rousseau had been born to a modest watchmaker in Geneva, and Diderot was the son of a cutlery maker. Rarely were women philosophes; one, however, was the French noblewoman Émilie du Châtelet (1706–1749), who wrote extensively about the mathematics and physics of Gottfried Wilhelm Leibniz and Isaac Newton. (Châtelet's lover Voltaire learned much of his science from her.)

Madame Geoffrin's Salon in 1755 This 1812 painting by Anicet Charles Lemonnier claims to depict the best-known Parisian salon of the 1750s. Lemonnier was only twelve years old in 1755 and so could not have based his rendition on firsthand knowledge. Madame Geoffrin is the figure on the right facing the viewer. The bust is of Voltaire. Rousseau is the fifth person to the left of the bust (facing right), and behind him (facing left) is Raynal. (De Agostini Picture Library/Gianni Dagli Orti/Bridgeman Images.)

Few of the leading writers held university positions. Enlightenment ideas developed instead through printed books and pamphlets, through hand-copied letters that were circulated and sometimes published, and through informal readings of manuscripts. Salons—informal gatherings, usually sponsored by middle-class or aristocratic women—gave intellectual life an anchor outside the royal court and the church-controlled universities (see page 483). In the Parisian salons of the eighteenth century, the philosophes could discuss ideas they might hesitate to put into print. Best known was the salon of Madame Marie-Thérèse Geoffrin (1699–1777), a wealthy middle-class widow. She corresponded extensively with influential people across Europe, including Catherine the Great. Women's salons helped galvanize intellectual life and reform movements all over Europe. Wealthy Jewish women created nine of the fourteen salons in Berlin at the end of the eighteenth century, and Princess Zofia Czartoryska gathered around her in Warsaw the reform leaders of Poland-Lithuania.

Conflicts with Church and State

Madame Geoffrin did not approve of discussions that attacked the Catholic church, but elsewhere voices against organized religion could be heard. Criticisms of religion required daring because the church, whatever its denomination, wielded enormous power in society, and most influential people considered religion an essential foundation of good society and government. Defying such opinion, the Scottish philosopher David Hume (1711–1776) boldly argued in *The Natural History of Religion* (1755) that belief in God rested on superstition and fear rather than on reason.

At the time, most Europeans believed in God. After Newton, however, and despite Newton's own deep religiosity, people could conceive of the universe as an eternally existing, self-perpetuating machine, in which God's intervention was unnecessary. In short, such people could become either atheists (people who do not believe in God) or **deists** (people who believe in God but give him no active role in earthly affairs). For the first time, writers claimed the label *atheist* and disputed the common view that atheism led inevitably to immorality.

Deists continued to believe in a benevolent, all-knowing God who had designed the universe and set it in motion. But they usually rejected the idea that God directly intercedes in the functioning of the universe, and they often criticized the churches for their dogmatic intolerance of dissenters. Voltaire was a deist, and in his influential *Philosophical Dictionary* (1764) he attacked most of the claims of organized Christianity, both Catholic and Protestant. Christianity, he argued, had been the prime source of fanaticism and brutality among humans. Throughout his life, Voltaire's motto was *Écrasez l'infâme*—"Crush the infamous thing" (the "thing" being bigotry and intolerance). French authorities publicly burned his *Philosophical Dictionary*.

Criticism of religious intolerance involved more than simply attacking the church. Critics also had to confront the states to which churches were closely tied. In 1762, a judicial case in Toulouse provoked an outcry throughout France that Voltaire soon joined. When the son of a local Calvinist was found hanged (he had probably committed suicide), magistrates accused the father, Jean Calas, of murdering him to prevent his conversion to Catholicism. (Since Louis XIV's revocation of the Edict of Nantes in 1685, it had been illegal to practice Calvinism publicly in France.) The all-Catholic parlement of Toulouse tried to extract the names of accomplices through torture—using a rope to pull up Calas's arm while weighing down his feet and then pouring water down his throat—but Calas refused to confess. The torturers then executed him by breaking every bone in his body with an iron rod. Voltaire launched a successful crusade to rehabilitate Calas's good name and to restore the family's properties, which had been confiscated after his death. Voltaire's efforts eventually helped bring about the extension of civil rights to French Protestants and encouraged campaigns to abolish the judicial use of torture.

Critics also assailed state and church support for European colonization and slavery. One of the most popular books of the time was the *Philosophical and Political History of European Colonies and Commerce in the Two Indies*, published in 1770 by the abbé Guillaume Raynal (1713–1796), a French Catholic clergyman. Raynal and his collaborators described in excruciating detail the destruction of native populations by Europeans and denounced the slave trade. Despite the criticism, the slave trade continued. So did European exploration. British explorer James Cook (1728–1779) charted the coasts of New Zealand and Australia, discovered New Caledonia, and visited the ice fields of Antarctica.

The Enlightenment belief in natural rights helped fuel the antislavery movement, which began to organize political campaigns against slavery in Britain, France, and the new United States in the 1780s. Advocates of the abolition of slavery encouraged freed slaves to write the story of their enslavement. One such freed slave, Olaudah Equiano, wrote of his kidnapping and enslavement in Africa and his long effort to free himself. *The Interesting Narrative of the Life of Olaudah Equiano*, published in 1788, became an international best seller. Armed with such firsthand accounts of slavery, **abolitionists** began to petition their governments for the abolition of the slave trade and then of slavery itself.

Enlightenment critics of church and state usually advocated reform, not revolution. For example, though he resided near the French-Swiss border in case he had to flee, Voltaire made a fortune in financial speculations and ended up being celebrated in his last years as a national hero even by many former foes. Other philosophes also believed that published criticism, rather than violent action, would bring about necessary reforms. The philosophes generally regarded the lower classes — "the people" — as ignorant, violent, and prone to superstition; as a result, they pinned their hopes on educated elites and enlightened rulers.

The Individual and Society

The controversy created by the conflicts between the philosophes and the various churches and states of Europe drew attention away from a subtle but profound transformation in worldviews. In previous centuries, questions of theological doctrine and church organization had been the main focus of intellectual and even political interest. The Enlightenment writers shifted attention away from religious questions and toward the secular (nonreligious) study of society and the individual's role in it. Religion did not drop out of sight, but the philosophes tended to make religion a private affair of individual conscience, even while rulers and churches still considered religion very much a public concern.

The Enlightenment interest in secular society produced two major results: it advanced the secularization of European political life that had begun after the French Wars of Religion of the sixteenth and seventeenth centuries, and it laid the foundations for the social sciences of the modern era. Not surprisingly, then, many historians and philosophers consider the Enlightenment to be the origin of modernity, which they define as the belief that human reason, rather than theological doctrine, should set the patterns of social and political life. This belief in reason as the sole foundation for secular authority has often been contested, but it has also proved to be a powerful force for change.

Although most of the philosophes believed that humans could use reason to understand and even remake society and politics, they disagreed about what reason revealed. Among the many different approaches were two that proved enduringly influential, those of the Scottish philosopher Adam Smith and the Swiss writer Jean-Jacques Rousseau. Smith provided a theory of modern capitalist society and devoted much of his energy to defending free markets as the best way to make the most of individual efforts. The modern discipline of economics took shape around the questions raised by Smith. Rousseau, by contrast, emphasized the needs of the community over those of the individual. His work, which led both toward democracy and toward communism, continues to inspire heated debate in political science and sociology.

Adam Smith (1723–1790) optimistically believed that individual interests naturally harmonized with those of the whole society. To explain how this natural harmonization worked, he published *An Inquiry into the Nature and Causes of the Wealth of Nations* in 1776. In this work, commonly known as *The Wealth of Nations*, Smith insisted that individual self-interest, even greed, was quite compatible with society's best interest: the laws of supply and demand served as an "invisible hand" ensuring that individual interests would be synchronized with those of the whole society. Market forces naturally brought individual and social interests in line.

Smith rejected the prevailing mercantilist views that the general welfare would be served by accumulating national wealth through agriculture or the hoarding of gold and silver. Instead, he argued that the division of labor in manufacturing increased productivity and generated more wealth for society and well-being for the individual. Using the example of the ordinary pin, Smith showed that when the manufacturing process was broken down into separate operations—one man to draw out the wire, another to straighten it, a third to cut it, a fourth to point it, and so on—workers who could make only one pin a day on their own could make thousands by pooling their labor.

To maximize the effects of market forces and the division of labor, Smith endorsed a concept called **laissez-faire** ("to leave alone"), in which the government neither controls nor intervenes in the economy. He insisted that governments eliminate all restrictions on the sale of land, remove restraints on the grain trade, and abandon duties on imports. Free international trade, he argued, would stimulate production everywhere and thus ensure the growth of national wealth. Governments, he insisted, should restrict themselves to providing "security," that is, national defense, internal order, and public works.

Much more pessimistic about the relation between individual self-interest and the good of society was **Jean-Jacques Rousseau** (1712–1778). In Rousseau's view, society itself threatened natural rights or freedoms: "Man is born free, and everywhere he is in chains." Rousseau first gained fame by writing a prize-winning essay in 1749 in which he argued that the revival of science and the arts had corrupted social morals, not improved them. This startling conclusion seemed to oppose some of the Enlightenment's most cherished beliefs. Rather than improving society, he claimed, science and art raised artificial barriers between people and their natural state. Rousseau's works extolled the simplicity of rural life over urban society.

Whereas earlier Rousseau had argued that society corrupted the individual by taking him out of nature, in *The Social Contract* (1762) he aimed to show that the right kind of political order could make people truly moral and free. Individual moral freedom could be achieved only by learning to subject one's individual interests to "the general will," that is, the good of the community. Individuals did this by entering into a social contract not with their rulers, but with one another. If everyone followed the general will, then all would be equally free and equally moral because they lived under a law to which they had all consented.

Like Thomas Hobbes (1588–1679) and John Locke (1632–1704) in the seventeenth century, Rousseau derived his social contract from human nature, not from history, tradition, or the Bible. He went much further than Hobbes or Locke, however, when he implied that people would be most free and moral under a republican form of government with direct democracy. Neither Hobbes nor Locke favored republics. Moreover, Rousseau roundly condemned slavery. Authorities in both Geneva and Paris banned *The Social Contract* for undermining political authority. Rousseau's works would become a kind of political bible for the French revolutionaries of 1789, and his attacks on private property inspired the communists of the nineteenth century such as Karl Marx. Rousseau's rather mystical concept of the general will remains controversial because he insisted that the individual could be "forced to be free." Rousseau's version of democracy did not preserve the individual freedoms so important to Adam Smith.

Spreading the Enlightenment

The Enlightenment flourished in places where an educated middle class provided an eager audience for ideas of constitutionalism and reform. It therefore found its epicenter in the triangle formed by London, Amsterdam, and Paris and diffused outward to eastern and southern Europe and North America. Where constitutionalism and guarantees of individual freedoms were most advanced, as in Great Britain and the Dutch Republic, the movement had less of an edge because there was, in a sense, less need for it. As a result, Scottish and English writers concentrated on economics, philosophy, and history rather than on politics or social relations. The English historian Edward Gibbon, for example, portrayed Christianity in a negative light in his immensely influential work *The History of the Decline and Fall of the Roman Empire* (1776–1788), but when he served as a member of Parliament he never even gave a speech. At the other extreme, in places with small middle classes, such as Spain and Russia, Enlightenment ideas did not get much traction because governments immediately suppressed them. France was the Enlightenment hot spot because the French monarchy alternated between encouraging ideas for reform and harshly censuring criticisms it found too threatening.

French writers published the most daring critiques of church and state, and they often suffered harassment and persecution as a result. Voltaire, Diderot, and Rousseau all faced arrest, exile, or even imprisonment. The Catholic church and royal authorities routinely forbade the publication of their books, and the police arrested booksellers who ignored the warnings. Yet the French monarchy was far from the most autocratic in Europe, and Voltaire, Diderot, and Rousseau all ended their lives as cultural heroes. France seems to have been curiously caught in the middle during the Enlightenment: with fewer constitutional guarantees of individual freedom than Great Britain, it still enjoyed much higher levels of prosperity and cultural development than most other European countries. In short, French elites had reason to complain, the means to make their complaints known, and a government torn between the desire to censor dissident ideas and the desire to appear open to modernity and progress.

By the 1760s, the French government regularly ignored the publication of many works once thought offensive or subversive. In addition, a growing flood of works printed abroad poured into France and circulated underground. Private companies in Dutch and Swiss cities made fortunes smuggling illegal books into France over mountain passes and back roads. Foreign printers provided secret catalogs of their offerings and sold their products through booksellers who were willing to market forbidden books for a high price—among them not only philosophical treatises of the Enlightenment but also pornographic books and pamphlets (some by Diderot) lampooning the Catholic clergy and leading members of the royal court. In the 1770s and 1780s, lurid descriptions of sexual promiscuity at the French court helped undermine the popularity of the throne.

Whereas the French philosophes often took a violently anticlerical and combative tone, their German counterparts avoided direct political confrontations with authorities. Gotthold Lessing (1729–1781) complained in 1769 that Prussia was still "the most slavish society in Europe" in its lack of freedom to criticize government policies. Lessing promoted religious toleration for the Jews and spiritual emancipation of Germans from foreign, especially French, models of culture, which still dominated. Lessing also introduced the German Jewish writer Moses Mendelssohn (1729–1786) into Berlin salon society. Mendelssohn labored to build bridges between German and Jewish culture by arguing that Judaism was a rational and undogmatic religion. He believed that persecution and discrimination against the Jews would end as reason triumphed.

Reason was also the chief focus of the most influential German thinker of the Enlightenment, Immanuel Kant (1724–1804). A university professor who lectured on everything from economics to astronomy, Kant wrote one of the most important works in the history of Western philosophy, *The Critique of Pure Reason* (1781). Kant admired Smith and especially Rousseau, whose portrait he displayed proudly in his study. Kant established the doctrine of idealism, the belief that true understanding can come only from examining the ways in which ideas are formed in the mind. Ideas are shaped, Kant argued, not just by sensory information (a position central to empiricism, a philosophy based on John Locke's writings) but also by the operation on that information of mental categories such as space and time. In Kant's philosophy, these "categories of understanding" were neither sensory nor supernatural; they were entirely ideal and abstract and located in the human mind.

The Limits of Reason: Roots of Romanticism and Religious Revival

In reaction to what some saw as the Enlightenment's excessive reliance on the authority of human reason, a new artistic movement called **romanticism** took root. Although it would not fully flower until the early nineteenth century, romanticism traced its emphasis on individual genius, deep emotion, and the joys of nature to thinkers like

Rousseau who had scolded the philosophes for ignoring those aspects of life that escaped and even conflicted with the power of reason.

A novel by the young German writer Johann Wolfgang von Goethe (1749–1832) captured the early romantic spirit with its glorification of emotion. *The Sorrows of Young Werther* (1774) told of a young man who loves nature and rural life and is unhappy in love. When the woman he loves marries someone else, he falls into deep melancholy and eventually kills himself. Reason cannot save him. The book spurred a veritable Werther craze: in addition to Werther costumes, engravings, embroidery, and medallions, there was even a perfume called Eau de Werther. The young Napoleon Bonaparte, who was to build an empire for France, claimed to have read Goethe's novel seven times.

Religious revivals sought to underline the limits of reason by emphasizing a direct emotional connection with God. Much of the Protestant world experienced an "awakening" in the 1740s. In the German states, Pietist groups founded new communities; and in the British North American colonies, revivalist Protestant preachers drew thousands of fervent believers in a movement called the Great Awakening. In North America, bitter conflicts between revivalists and their opponents in the established churches prompted the leaders on both sides to set up new colleges to support their

George Whitefield   This etching depicts one of the most prominent preachers of the Great Awakening, the English Methodist George Whitefield, preaching in the British North American colonies. Whitefield visited the colonies seven times, sometimes for long periods, and drew tens of thousands of people to his dramatic and emotional open-air sermons, which moved many listeners to tears of repentance. Whitefield was a celebrity in his time and is considered by many to be the founder of the Evangelical movement. (The Granger Collection, NYC—All rights reserved.)

beliefs. These included Princeton, Columbia, Brown, and Dartmouth, all founded between 1746 and 1769 by either revivalists or antirevivalists.

Revivalism also stirred eastern European Jews at about the same time. Israel ben Eliezer (1698–1760) laid the foundation for Hasidism in the 1740s and 1750s. He traveled the Polish countryside offering miraculous cures and became known as the Ba'al Shem Tov ("Master of the Good Name") because he used divine names to effect healing and bring believers into closer personal contact with God. He emphasized mystical contemplation of the divine, rather than study of Jewish law, and his followers, the Hasidim (Hebrew for "most pious" Jews), often expressed their devotion through music, dance, and fervent prayer. Their practices soon spread all over Poland-Lithuania.

Most of the waves of Protestant revivalism ebbed after the 1750s, but in Great Britain one movement continued to grow through the end of the century. John Wesley (1703–1791), the Oxford-educated son of a cleric in the Church of England, founded **Methodism**, a term evoked by Wesley's insistence on strict self-discipline and a methodical approach to religious study and observance. In 1738, Wesley began preaching his new brand of Protestantism, which emphasized an intense personal experience of salvation and a life of thrift, abstinence, and hard work. Traveling all over the British Isles, Wesley preached forty thousand sermons in fifty years, an average of fifteen a week. The Church of England refused to let him preach in the churches. In response, Wesley began to ordain his own clergy. While considered radical in religious views, the Methodist leadership remained politically conservative during Wesley's lifetime; Wesley himself wrote many pamphlets urging order, loyalty, and submission to higher authorities.

REVIEW   What were the major differences between the Enlightenment in France, Great Britain, and the German states?

Society and Culture in an Age of Enlightenment

Religious revivals and the first stirrings of romanticism show that not all intellectual currents of the eighteenth century were flowing in the same channel. Some social and cultural developments manifested the influence of Enlightenment ideas, but others did not. The traditional leaders of European societies — the nobles — responded to Enlightenment ideas in contradictory fashion: many simply reasserted their privileges and resisted the influence of the Enlightenment, but an important minority embraced change and actively participated in reform efforts. The expanding middle classes saw in the Enlightenment a chance to make their claim for joining society's governing elite. They bought Enlightenment books, joined Masonic lodges, and patronized new styles in art, music, and literature. The lower classes were more affected by economic growth than by ideas. Trade boomed and the population grew, but people did not benefit equally. The ranks of the poor swelled, too, and with greater mobility, births to unmarried mothers also increased.

The Nobility's Reassertion of Privilege

Nobles made up about 3 percent of the European population, but their numbers and ways of life varied greatly from country to country. At least 10 percent of the population in Poland and 7 to 8 percent in Spain was noble, in contrast to only 2 percent in Russia and between 1 and 2 percent in the rest of western Europe. Many Polish and Spanish nobles lived in poverty, but the wealthiest European nobles luxuriated in almost unimaginable opulence. Many of the English peers, for example, owned more than ten thousand acres of land; invested widely in government bonds and trading companies; kept several country residences with scores of servants as well as houses in London; and occasionally even had their own private orchestras to complement libraries of expensive books, greenhouses for exotic plants, kennels of pedigreed dogs, and collections of antiques, firearms, and scientific instruments.

To support an increasingly expensive lifestyle in a period of inflation, European aristocrats sought to cash in on their remaining legal rights, called seigneurial dues (from the French *seigneur*, "lord"). Peasants felt the squeeze as a result. French landlords required their peasants to pay dues to grind grain at the lord's mill, bake bread in his oven, press grapes at his winepress, or even pass on their own land as inheritance. In addition, peasants had to work without compensation for a specified number of days every year on the public roads. They also paid taxes to the government on salt, an essential preservative, and on the value of their land; customs duties if they sold produce or wine in town; and the tithe on their grain (one-tenth of the crop) to the church.

In Britain, the landed gentry could not claim these same onerous dues from their tenants, but they tenaciously defended their exclusive right to hunt game. The game laws kept the poor from eating meat and helped protect the social status of the rich. The gentry enforced the game laws themselves by hiring gamekeepers who hunted down poachers and even set traps for them in the forests. According to the law, anyone who poached deer or rabbits while armed or disguised could be sentenced to death. In most other countries, too, hunting was the special right of the nobility, a cause of deep popular resentment.

Even though Enlightenment writers sharply criticized nobles' insistence on special privileges, most aristocrats maintained their marks of distinction. The male court nobility continued to sport swords, plumed hats, makeup, and elaborate wigs, while middle-class men wore simpler and more somber clothing. Aristocrats had their own seats in church and their own quarters in the universities. Frederick II of Prussia (r. 1740–1786), who came to be known as Frederick the Great, made sure that nobles dominated both the army officer corps and the civil bureaucracy. Russia's Catherine the Great (r. 1762–1796) granted the nobility vast tracts of land, the exclusive right to own serfs, and exemption from personal taxes and corporal punishment. Her Charter of the Nobility of 1785 codified these privileges in exchange for the nobles' political subservience to the state. In Austria, Spain, the Italian states, Poland-Lithuania, and Russia, most nobles consequently cared little about Enlightenment ideas; they did not read the books of the philosophes and feared reforms that might challenge their dominance of rural society.

In France, Britain, and the western German states, however, the nobility proved more open to the new ideas. Half of Rousseau's correspondents, for example, were nobles. The nobles of western Europe sometimes married into middle-class families and formed with them a new mixed elite, united by common interests in reform and new cultural tastes.

The Middle Class and the Making of a New Elite

The Enlightenment offered middle-class people an intellectual and cultural route to social improvement. The term *middle class* referred to the middle position on the social ladder; middle-class families did not have legal titles like the nobility above them, but neither did they work with their hands like the peasants, artisans, or laborers below them. Most middle-class people lived in towns or cities and earned their living in the professions — as doctors, lawyers, or lower-level officials — or through investment in land, trade, or manufacturing. In the eighteenth century, the ranks of the middle class — also known as the bourgeoisie (from *bourgeois*, French for "city dweller") — grew steadily in western Europe as a result of economic expansion. In France, for example, the overall population grew by about one-third in the 1700s, but the bourgeoisie nearly tripled in size.

Nobles and middle-class professionals mingled in Enlightenment salons and joined the new Masonic lodges and local learned societies. The Masonic lodges began as social clubs organized around elaborate secret rituals of stonemasons' guilds. They called their members **Freemasons** because that was the term given to apprentice masons when they were deemed "free" to practice as masters of their guild. Although the Freemasons were not explicitly political in aim, their members wrote constitutions for their lodges and elected their own officers, thus promoting a direct experience of constitutional government.

Freemasonry arose in Great Britain and spread eastward: the first French and Italian lodges opened in 1726; Prussia's Frederick the Great founded a lodge in 1740; and after 1750, Freemasonry spread in Poland, Russia, and British North America. In France, women set up their own Masonic lodges. Despite the papacy's condemnation of Freemasonry in 1738 as subversive of religious and civil authority, lodges continued to multiply throughout the eighteenth century. After 1789 and the outbreak of the French Revolution, conservatives would blame the lodges for every kind of political upheaval, but in the 1700s many high-ranking nobles became active members and saw no conflict with their privileged status.

Nobles and middle-class professionals also met in local learned societies, whose numbers greatly increased in this period. The societies, sometimes called academies, brought the Enlightenment down from the realm of books and ideas to the level of concrete reforms. They sponsored essay contests, such as the one won by Rousseau in 1749 and the one set by the society in Metz in 1785 on the question "Are there means for making the Jews happier and more useful in France?" The Metz society approved essays that argued for granting civil rights to Jews.

Shared tastes in travel, architecture, the arts, and even reading helped strengthen the links between nobles and members of the middle class. "Grand tours" of Europe often led upper-class youths to recently discovered Greek and Roman ruins at Pompeii, Herculaneum, and Paestum in Italy. These excavations aroused enthusiasm for the neoclassical style in architecture and painting, which began pushing aside the rococo and the long-dominant baroque. Urban residences, government buildings, furniture, fabrics, wallpaper, and even pottery soon reflected the neoclassical emphasis on purity and clarity of forms. Employing neoclassical motifs, the English potter Josiah Wedgwood (1730–1795) almost single-handedly created a mass market for domestic crockery and appealed to middle-class desires to emulate the rich and royal. His designs of special tea sets for the British queen, for Catherine the Great of Russia, and for leading aristocrats allowed him to advertise his wares as fashionable. His pottery was marketed in France, Russia, Venice, the Ottoman Empire, and British North America.

This period also supported artistic styles other than neoclassicism. Frederick the Great built himself a palace outside of Berlin in the earlier rococo style, gave it the French name of Sanssouci ("worry-free"), and filled it with the works of French masters of the rococo. A growing taste for moralistic family scenes in painting reflected the same middle-class preoccupation with the emotions of ordinary private life that could be seen in novels. The middle-class public now attended the official painting exhibitions in France that were held regularly every other year after 1737. Court painting (works commissioned by rulers and nobles) nonetheless remained much in demand.

Although wealthy nobles still patronized Europe's leading musicians, music, too, began to reflect the broadening of the elite and the spread of Enlightenment ideals as classical forms replaced the baroque style. Large sections of string instruments became the backbone of professional orchestras, which now played to large audiences of well-to-do listeners in sizable concert halls. A new attitude toward "the classics" developed: for the first time in the 1770s and 1780s, concert groups began to play older music rather than simply playing the latest commissioned works.

The two supreme masters of the new musical style of the eighteenth century show that the transition from noble patronage to classical concerts was far from complete. Franz Joseph Haydn (1732–1809) and his fellow Austrian Wolfgang Amadeus Mozart (1756–1791) both wrote for noble patrons, but by the early 1800s their compositions had been incorporated into the canon of concert classics all over Europe. Incredibly prolific, both excelled in combining lightness, clarity, and profound emotion. Both also wrote numerous Italian operas, a genre whose popularity continued to grow: in the 1780s, the Papal States alone boasted forty opera houses. Haydn spent most of his career working for a Hungarian noble family, the Eszterházys. Asked once why he had written no string quintets (at which Mozart excelled), he responded simply: "No one has ordered any."

Interest in reading, like attending public concerts, took hold of the middle classes and fed a frenzied increase in publication. By the end of the eighteenth century, six times as many books were being published in the German states, for instance, as at the beginning. Local newspapers, lending libraries, and book clubs multiplied. Despite the limits of women's education, women benefited as much as men from the spread of print. As one Englishman observed, "By far the greatest part of ladies now have a taste for books." Women also wrote them. Catherine Macaulay (1731–1791) published best-selling histories of Britain, and in France Stéphanie de Genlis (1746–1830) wrote children's books—a genre that was growing in importance as middle-class parents became more interested in education.

Life on the Margins

Booming foreign trade fueled a dramatic economic expansion—French colonial trade increased tenfold in the 1700s—but the results did not necessarily trickle all the way down the social scale. The population of Europe grew by nearly 30 percent. Even though food production increased, shortages and crises still occurred periodically. Prices went up in many countries after the 1730s and continued to rise gradually until the early nineteenth century; wages in many trades rose as well, but less quickly than prices. Some people prospered, but those at the bottom of the social ladder—day laborers in the cities and peasants with small holdings—lived on the edge of dire poverty, and when they lost their land or work, they either migrated to the cities or wandered the roads in search of food and work. In France alone, 200,000 workers left their homes every year in search of seasonal employment elsewhere. At least 10 percent of Europe's urban population depended on some form of charity.

The growing numbers of poor people overwhelmed local governments. In some countries, beggars and vagabonds had been locked up in workhouses since the mid-1600s. The expenses for running these overcrowded institutions increased by 60 percent in England between 1760 and 1785. After 1740, most German towns created workhouses that were part workshop, part hospital, and part prison. Such institutions also appeared for the first time in Boston, New York, and Philadelphia. The French government created *dépôts de mendicité* ("beggar houses") in 1767. The government sent people to these new workhouses to labor in manufacturing, but most were too weak or sick to work, and 20 percent of them died within a few months of incarceration.

Those who were able to work or keep their land fared better: an increase in literacy, especially in the cities, allowed some lower-class people to participate in new tastes and ideas. One French observer insisted, "These days, you see a waiting-maid in her backroom, a lackey in an ante-room reading pamphlets. People can read in almost all classes of society." In France, only 50 percent of men and 27 percent of women could read and write in the 1780s, but that was twice the rate of a century earlier. Literacy rates were higher in England and the Dutch Republic, much lower in eastern Europe.

Whereas the new elite might attend salons, concerts, or art exhibitions, peasants enjoyed their traditional forms of popular entertainment, such as fairs and festivals, and the urban lower classes relaxed in cabarets and taverns. Sometimes pleasures were cruel to animals. In Britain, bullbaiting, bearbaiting, dogfighting, and cockfighting were all common forms of entertainment that provided opportunities for organized gambling.

As population increased and villagers began to move to cities to better their prospects, the rates of births out of wedlock soared, from less than 5 percent of all births in the seventeenth century to nearly 20 percent at the end of the eighteenth. Some detect in this change a sign of sexual liberation and the beginnings of a modern sexual revolution: as women moved out of the control of their families, they began to seek their own sexual fulfillment. Others view this change more bleakly, as a story of seduction and betrayal: family and community pressure had once forced a man to marry a woman pregnant with his child, but now a man could abandon a pregnant lover by simply moving away.

Women who came to the city as domestic servants had little recourse against masters or fellow servants who seduced or raped them. The result was a startling rise in abandoned babies. Most European cities established foundling hospitals in the 1700s, but infant and child mortality was 50 percent higher in such institutions than for children brought up at home.

European states had long tried to regulate sexual behavior; every country had laws against prostitution, adultery, fornication, sodomy, and infanticide. Reformers criticized the harshness of laws against infanticide, but they showed no mercy for "sodomites" (as male homosexuals were called), who in some places, in particular the Dutch Republic, were systematically persecuted and imprisoned or even executed. Male homosexuals attracted the attention of authorities because they had begun to develop networks and special meeting places. The stereotype of the effeminate,

Jean-Baptiste Greuze, *Broken Eggs* (1756)   Greuze made his reputation as a painter of moralistic family scenes. In this one, an old woman (perhaps the mother) confronts the lover of a young girl and points to the eggs that have fallen out of a basket, a symbol of lost virginity. Denis Diderot praised Greuze's work as "morality in paint," but the paintings often had an erotic subtext. (© Francis G. Mayer / Corbis.)

exclusively homosexual male seems to have appeared for the first time in the eighteenth century, perhaps as part of a growing emphasis on separate roles for men and women.

The Enlightenment's emphasis on reason, self-control, and childhood innocence made parents increasingly anxious about their children's sexuality. Moralists and physicians wrote books about the evils of masturbation, "proving" that it led to physical and mental degeneration and even madness.

While the Enlightenment thus encouraged excessive concern about children being left to their own devices, it nevertheless taught the middle and upper classes to value their children and to expect their improvement through education. Writers such as de Genlis and Rousseau drew attention to children, who were no longer viewed only as little sinners in need of harsh discipline. Toys, jigsaw puzzles, and clothing designed for children all appeared for the first time in the 1700s. Children were no longer considered miniature adults.

> **REVIEW**   What were the major differences in the impact of the Enlightenment on the nobility, the middle classes, and the lower classes?

State Power in an Era of Reform

Rulers turned to Enlightenment-inspired reforms to improve life for their subjects and to gain commercial or military advantage over rival states. Historians label many of the sovereigns of this time **enlightened despots** or enlightened absolutists, for they aimed to promote Enlightenment reforms without giving up their absolutist powers. Catherine the Great's admiring relationship with Voltaire showed how even the most absolutist rulers championed reform when it suited their own goals. Foremost among those goals was the expansion of a ruler's territory.

War and Diplomacy

Europeans no longer fought devastating wars over religion that killed hundreds of thousands of civilians; instead, professional armies and navies battled for control of overseas empires and for dominance on the European continent. Rulers continued to expand their armies: the Prussian army, for example, nearly tripled in size between 1740 and 1789. Widespread use of flintlock muskets required deployment in long lines, usually three men deep, with each line in turn loading and firing on command. Military strategy became cautious and calculating, but this did not prevent the outbreak of hostilities. Between 1750 and 1775, the instability of the European balance of power resulted in a diplomatic reversal of alliances, a major international conflict, and the partition of Poland-Lithuania among Russia, Austria, and Prussia.

In 1756, a set of events that historians call the Diplomatic Revolution reshaped relations among the great powers. Prussia and Great Britain signed a defensive alliance, prompting Austria to overlook two centuries of hostility and ally with France.

Russia and Sweden soon joined the Franco-Austrian alliance. When Frederick the Great invaded Austria's ally Saxony with his large, well-disciplined army, the long-simmering hostilities between Great Britain and France over colonial boundaries flared into a general war that became known as the **Seven Years' War** (1756–1763).

Fighting soon raged around the world (Map 18.1). The French and British battled on land and sea in North America (where the conflict was called the French and

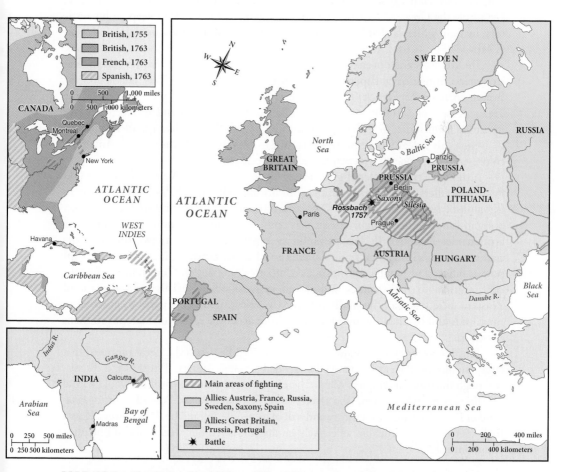

MAP 18.1 The Seven Years' War, 1756–1763 In what might justly be called the first worldwide war, the French and British fought each other in Europe, the West Indies, North America, and India. Skirmishing in North America helped precipitate the war, which became more general when Austria, France, and Russia allied to check Prussian influence in central Europe. The peace treaty between Austria and Prussia simply restored the status quo in Europe, but the changes overseas were much more dramatic. Britain gained control over Canada and India but gave back to France the West Indian islands of Guadeloupe and Martinique. Britain was now the dominant power of the seas.

Indian War), the West Indies, and India. The two coalitions also fought each other in central Europe. At first, in 1757, Frederick the Great surprised Europe with a spectacular victory at Rossbach in Saxony over a much larger Franco-Austrian army. But in time, Russian and Austrian armies encircled his troops. A fluke of history saved him. Empress Elizabeth of Russia (r. 1741–1762) died and was succeeded by the mentally unstable Peter III, a fanatical admirer of Frederick and all things Prussian. Peter withdrew Russia from the war. (This was practically his only accomplishment as tsar. He was soon mysteriously murdered, probably at the instigation of his wife, Catherine the Great.) A separate peace treaty allowed Frederick to keep all his territory, including Silesia, that had been conquered in the War of the Austrian Succession (1740–1748).

The Anglo-French overseas conflicts ended more decisively than the continental land wars. British naval superiority, fully achieved only in the 1750s, enabled Great Britain to rout the French in North America, India, and the West Indies. In the Treaty of Paris of 1763, France ceded Canada to Great Britain and agreed to remove its armies from India, in exchange for keeping its rich West Indian islands. Eagerness to avenge this defeat would motivate France to support the British North American colonists in their War of Independence just fifteen years later.

Although Prussia suffered great losses in the Seven Years' War — some 160,000 Prussian soldiers died either in action or of disease — its army helped vault Prussia to the rank of leading powers. By 1740, the Prussians had the third or fourth largest army in Europe even though Prussia was tenth in population and thirteenth in land area. Under Frederick II, Prussia's military expenditures rose to two-thirds of the state's revenue. Virtually every nobleman served in the army, paying for his own support as officer and buying a position as company commander. Once retired, the officers returned to their estates and served as local officials. This militarization of Prussian society had a profoundly conservative effect: it kept the peasants enserfed to their lords and blocked the middle classes from access to estates or high government positions.

Prussia's power grew so dramatically that in 1772 Frederick the Great proposed that large chunks of Poland-Lithuania be divided among Austria, Prussia, and Russia. Although the Austrian empress Maria Theresa protested that the partition would spread "a stain over my whole reign," she agreed to the first **partition of Poland**, splitting one-third of Poland-Lithuania's territory and half of its people among the three powers. Russia took over most of Lithuania, effectively ending the large but weak Polish-Lithuanian commonwealth.

State-Sponsored Reform

In the aftermath of the Seven Years' War, all the belligerents faced pressing needs for more money. To make tax increases more palatable to public opinion, rulers appointed reform-minded ministers and gave them a mandate to modernize government. Such reforms always threatened the interests of traditional groups, however, and the spread of Enlightenment ideas aroused sometimes unpredictable desires for more change.

Monarchs dedicated to reform insisted on greater attention to merit, hard work, and professionalism. In this view, the ruler should be a benevolent, enlightened administrator who worked for the general well-being of his or her people. Frederick the Great, who drove himself as hard as he drove his officials, boasted, "I am the first servant of the state." A Freemason and supporter of religious toleration, Frederick abolished torture, reorganized taxation, and hosted leading French philosophes at his court. The Prussian king also composed more than a hundred original pieces of music.

Legal reform, both of the judicial system and of the often disorganized and irregular law codes, was central to the work of many reform-minded monarchs. Like Frederick the Great, Joseph II of Austria (r. 1780–1790) ordered the compilation of a unified law code, a project that required many years for completion. Catherine the Great began such an undertaking even more ambitiously. In 1767, she called together a legislative commission of 564 deputies and asked them to consider a long document called the *Instruction*, which represented her hopes for legal reform based on the ideas of Montesquieu and the Italian jurist Cesare Beccaria. Montesquieu had insisted that punishment should fit the crime; he criticized the use of torture and brutal corporal punishment. In his influential book *On Crimes and Punishments* (1764), Beccaria argued that justice should be administered in public, that judicial torture should be abolished as inhumane, and that the accused should be presumed innocent until proven guilty. Despite much discussion and hundreds of petitions and documents about local problems, little came of Catherine's commission.

Rulers everywhere wanted more control over church affairs, and they used Enlightenment criticisms of the organized churches to get their way. In Catholic countries, many government officials resented the influence of the Jesuits, the major Catholic teaching order. Critics mounted campaigns against the Jesuits in many countries, and in 1773, Pope Clement XIV (r. 1769–1774) agreed under pressure to disband the order, an edict that held until a reinvigorated papacy restored the society in 1814. Joseph II of Austria not only applauded the suppression of the Jesuits but also required Austrian bishops to swear fidelity and submission to him. Joseph had become Holy Roman Emperor and co-regent with his mother, Maria Theresa, in 1765. After her death in 1780, he initiated a wide-ranging program of reform. Under him, the Austrian state supervised Catholic seminaries, abolished contemplative monastic orders, and confiscated monastic property to pay for education and poor relief.

Joseph II launched the most ambitious educational reforms of the period. In 1774, once the Jesuits had been disbanded, the General School Ordinance in Austria ordered state subsidies for local schools, which the state would regulate. By 1789, one-quarter of the school-age children attended school. In Prussia, the school code of 1763 required all children between the ages of five and thirteen to attend school. Although not enforced uniformly, the Prussian law demonstrated Frederick the Great's belief that modernization depended on education.

No ruler pushed the principle of religious toleration as far as Joseph II of Austria, who in 1781 granted freedom of religious worship to Protestants, Orthodox Christians, and Jews. For the first time, these groups were allowed to own property, build schools, enter the professions, and hold political and military offices. Louis XVI signed an edict in 1787 restoring French Protestants' civil rights—but still, Protestants could not hold political office. Great Britain continued to deny Catholics freedom of open worship and the right to sit in Parliament. Most European states limited the rights and opportunities available to Jews. Even in Austria, where Joseph encouraged toleration, the laws forced Jews to take German-sounding names. The leading philosophes in theory opposed persecution of the Jews but often in practice treated them with undisguised contempt. Diderot's comment was all too typical: the Jews, he said, bore "all the defects peculiar to an ignorant and superstitious nation."

Limits of Reform

When enlightened absolutist leaders introduced reforms, they often ran into resistance from groups threatened by the proposed changes. Joseph II tried to remove the burdens of serfdom in the Habsburg lands. After 1781, serfs could move freely, enter trades, or marry without their lords' permission. Joseph also abolished the tithe to the church, shifted more of the tax burden to the nobility, and converted peasants' labor services into cash payments.

The Austrian nobility furiously resisted these far-reaching reforms. When Joseph died in 1790, his brother Leopold II (r. 1790–1792) had to revoke most reforms to appease the nobles. Prussia's Frederick the Great, like Joseph, encouraged such agricultural innovations as planting potatoes and turnips (new crops that could help feed a growing population), but Prussia's noble landlords, called Junkers, continued to expand their estates at the expense of poorer peasants and thwarted Frederick's attempts to improve the status of serfs.

In France, a group of economists called the physiocrats urged the government to deregulate the grain trade and make the tax system more equitable to encourage agricultural productivity. In the interest of establishing a free market, they also insisted that urban guilds be abolished because the guilds prevented free entry into the trades. The French government heeded some of this advice and gave up its system of price controls on grain in 1763, but it had to reverse the decision in 1770 when grain shortages caused a famine.

A conflict with the parlements (the thirteen high courts of law) prompted French king Louis XV (r. 1715–1774) to go even further in 1771. He replaced the parlements with courts in which the judges no longer owned their offices and thus could not sell them or pass them on as an inheritance. Justice, he hoped, would then be more impartial. The displaced judges of the parlements succeeded in arousing widespread opposition to what they portrayed as tyrannical royal policy. The furor calmed down only when Louis XV died in 1774 and his successor, Louis XVI (r. 1774–1792), yielded to aristocratic demands and restored the old parlements.

Louis XVI tried to carry out part of the program suggested by the physiocrats, and he chose one of their disciples, Jacques Turgot (1727–1781), as his chief minister. A contributor to the *Encyclopedia*, Turgot pushed through several edicts that again freed the grain trade, suppressed guilds, converted the peasants' forced labor on roads into a money tax payable by all landowners, and reduced court expenses. He also began making plans to introduce a system of elected local assemblies, which would have increased representation in the government. Faced with broad-based resistance led by the parlements and his own courtiers as well as with riots against rising grain prices, Louis XVI dismissed Turgot, and one of the last possibilities to overhaul France's government collapsed.

The failure of reform in France paradoxically reflected the power of Enlightenment thinkers; everyone now endorsed Enlightenment ideas but used them for different ends. The nobles in the parlements blocked the French monarchy's reform efforts using the very same Enlightenment language spoken by the crown's ministers. Where Frederick the Great, Catherine the Great, and even Joseph II used reform to bolster the efficiency of absolutist government, attempts at change in France backfired. French kings found that their ambitious programs for reform succeeded only in arousing unrealistic hopes.

> **REVIEW** What prompted enlightened absolutists to undertake reforms in the second half of the eighteenth century?

Rebellions against State Power

Although traditional forms of popular discontent had not disappeared, Enlightenment ideals and reforms changed the rules of the game in politics. Governments had become accountable for their actions to a much wider range of people than ever before. In Britain and France, ordinary people rioted when they perceived government as failing to protect them against food shortages. The growth of informed public opinion had its most dramatic consequences in the North American colonies, where a struggle over the British Parliament's right to tax turned into a full-scale war for independence. The American War of Independence showed that, once put into practice, Enlightenment ideals could have revolutionary implications.

Food Riots and Peasant Uprisings

Population growth, inflation, and the extension of the market system put added pressure on the already beleaguered poor. In the last half of the eighteenth century, the food supply became the focus of political and social conflict. Poor people in Europe's villages and towns believed that it was the government's responsibility to ensure they had enough food, and many governments did stockpile grain to make up for the occasional bad harvest. At the same time, in keeping with Adam Smith's and the French physiocrats' free-market proposals, governments wanted to allow grain prices to rise with market demand because higher profits would motivate producers to increase the overall supply of food.

Free trade in grain meant selling to the highest bidder, even if that bidder was a foreign merchant. In the short run, in times of scarcity, big landowners and farmers could make huge profits by selling grain outside their hometowns. This practice enraged poor farmers, agricultural workers, and urban wageworkers, who could not afford the higher prices. Lacking the political means to affect policy, the poor could enforce their desire for old-fashioned price regulation only by rioting. Most did not pillage or steal grain but rather forced the sale of grain or flour at a "just" price and blocked the shipment of grain out of their villages to other markets. Women often led these "popular price fixings," as they were called in France, in desperate attempts to protect the food supply for their children.

Such food riots occurred regularly in Britain and France in the last half of the eighteenth century. One of the most turbulent was the so-called Flour War in France in 1775. Turgot's deregulation of the grain trade in 1774 caused prices to rise in several provincial cities. Rioting spread from there to the Paris region, where villagers attacked grain convoys heading to the capital city. Local officials often ordered merchants and bakers to sell at the price the rioters demanded, only to find themselves arrested by the central government for overriding free trade. The government brought in troops to restore order and introduced the death penalty for rioting.

Frustrations with serfdom and hopes for a miraculous transformation provoked the **Pugachev rebellion** in Russia beginning in 1773. An army deserter from the southeast frontier region, Emelian Pugachev (1742–1775) claimed to be Tsar Peter III, the dead husband of Catherine the Great. Pugachev's appearance seemed to confirm peasant hopes for a "redeemer tsar" who would save the people from oppression. He rallied around him Cossacks like himself who resented the loss of their old tribal independence. Nearly three million people eventually participated, making this the largest single rebellion in the history of tsarist Russia. When Pugachev urged the peasants to attack the nobility and seize their estates, hundreds of noble families perished. Finally, the army captured the rebel leader and brought him in an iron cage to Moscow, where he was tortured and executed. In the aftermath, Catherine tightened the nobles' control over their serfs with the Charter of the Nobility and harshly punished those who dared to criticize serfdom.

Public Opinion and Political Opposition

Peasant uprisings might have briefly shaken even a powerful monarchy, but the rise of public opinion as a force independent of court society caused more enduring changes in European politics. Across much of Europe and in the North American colonies, demands for broader political participation reflected Enlightenment notions about individual rights. Aristocratic bodies such as the French parlements, which had no legislative role like that of the British Parliament, insisted that the monarch consult them on the nation's affairs, and the new educated elite wanted more influence, too. Newspapers began to cover daily political affairs, and the public learned the basics of political life, despite the strict limits on political participation in most countries.

The Wilkes affair in Great Britain showed that public opinion could be mobilized to challenge a government. In 1763, during the reign of George III (r. 1760–1820), John Wilkes, a member of Parliament, attacked the government in his newspaper, *North Briton*, and sued the crown when he was arrested. He won his release as well as damages. When he was reelected, Parliament denied him his seat, not once but three times.

The Wilkes episode soon escalated into a major campaign against the corruption and social exclusiveness of Parliament, complaints the Levellers had first raised during the English Revolution of the late 1640s. In one incident eleven people died when soldiers broke up a huge gathering of Wilkes's supporters. The slogan "Wilkes and Liberty" appeared on walls all over London. Middle-class voters formed the Society of Supporters of the Bill of Rights, which circulated petitions for Wilkes; they gained the support of about one-fourth of all the voters. The more determined Wilkesites proposed sweeping reforms of Parliament, including more frequent elections, more representation for the counties, elimination of "rotten boroughs" (election districts so small that they could be controlled by one big patron), and restrictions of pensions used by the crown to gain support. These demands would be at the heart of agitation for parliamentary reform in Britain for decades to come.

Popular demonstrations did not always support reforms. In 1780, the Gordon riots devastated London. They were named after the fanatical anti-Catholic crusader Lord George Gordon, who helped organize huge marches and petition campaigns against a bill the House of Commons passed to grant limited toleration to Catholics. The demonstrations culminated in a seven-day riot that left fifty buildings destroyed and three hundred people dead. Despite the continuing limitation on voting rights in Great Britain, British politicians were learning that they could ignore public opinion only at their peril.

Political opposition also took artistic forms, particularly in countries where governments restricted organized political activity. A striking example of a play with a political message was *The Marriage of Figaro* (1784) by Pierre-Augustin Caron de Beaumarchais (1732–1799). When finally performed publicly, the play caused a sensation. The chief character, Figaro, is a clever servant who gets the better of his noble employer, a count. When speaking of the count, Figaro cries, "What have you done to deserve so many rewards? You went to the trouble of being born, and nothing more." Looking back, Napoleon would say that the play was the "revolution in action."

Revolution in North America

Oppositional forms of public opinion came to a head in Great Britain's North American colonies, where the result was American independence and the establishment of a republican constitution that stood in stark contrast to most European regimes. Many Europeans saw the American War of Independence, or the American Revolution, as a triumph for Enlightenment ideas. As one German writer exclaimed in 1777, American victory would give "greater scope to the Enlightenment, new keenness to the thinking of peoples and new life to the spirit of liberty."

The American revolutionary leaders had participated in the Enlightenment and shared political ideas with the opposition Whigs in Britain. In the 1760s and 1770s, American opposition leaders became convinced that the British government was growing increasingly corrupt and despotic. The colonies had no representatives in Parliament, and colonists claimed that "no taxation without representation" should be allowed.

Indeed, they denied that Parliament had any jurisdiction over the colonies, insisting that the king govern them through colonial legislatures and recognize their traditional British liberties. The failure of the "Wilkes and Liberty" campaign to produce concrete results convinced many Americans that Parliament was hopelessly tainted.

Parliament's encroachment on the autonomy of the colonies transformed colonial attitudes. With the British clamoring for lower taxes at the end of the Seven Years' War and the colonists paying only a fraction of the tax rate paid by the Britons at home, Parliament passed new taxes on the colonies, including the Stamp Act in 1765, which required a special tax stamp on all legal documents and publications. After violent rioting in the colonies, the British repealed the tax, but in 1773 the new Tea Act revived colonial resistance, which culminated in the so-called Boston Tea Party of 1773. Colonists dressed as Indians boarded British ships and dumped the imported tea (by this time an enormously popular beverage) into Boston's harbor.

Political opposition in the American colonies turned belligerent when Britain threatened to use force to maintain control. After actual fighting had begun, in 1776, the Second Continental Congress issued the Declaration of Independence. An eloquent statement of the American cause drafted by the Virginia planter and lawyer Thomas Jefferson, the Declaration of Independence was couched in the language of universal human rights, which enlightened Europeans could be expected to understand. In 1778, France boosted the American cause by entering on the colonists' side. Spain declared war on Britain in 1779; in 1780, Great Britain declared war on the

Resistance to British Rule   To demonstrate their resistance to the 1765 Stamp Act, Boston citizens tar and feather a tax collector. The Stamp Act is nailed upside down to a tree. (Private Collection / Peter Newark Archives / Bridgeman Images.)

Dutch Republic in retaliation for Dutch support of the rebels. The worldwide conflict that resulted was more than Britain could handle. The American colonies achieved their independence in the peace treaty of 1783.

The newly independent states still faced the challenge of republican self-government. The Articles of Confederation, drawn up in 1777 as a provisional constitution, proved weak because they gave the central government few powers. In 1787, a constitutional convention met in Philadelphia to draft a new constitution, which was ratified the following year. It established a two-house legislature, an indirectly elected president, and an independent judiciary. The U.S. Constitution's preamble insisted explicitly, for the first time in history, that government derived its power solely from the people and did not depend on divine right or on the tradition of royalty or aristocracy. The new educated elite of the eighteenth century had now created government based on a "social contract" among male, property-owning, white citizens. It was by no means a complete democracy (women and slaves were excluded from political participation), but the new government represented a radical departure from European models. Appended to the Constitution in 1791, the Bill of Rights outlined the essential rights (such as freedom of speech) that the government could never overturn. Although slavery continued in the American republic, the new emphasis on rights helped fuel the movement for its abolition in both Britain and the United States.

Interest in the new republic was greatest in France. The U.S. Constitution and various state constitutions were published in French with commentary by leading thinkers. Even more important in the long run were the effects of the American war. Dutch losses to Great Britain aroused a widespread movement for political reform in the Dutch Republic, and debts incurred by France in supporting the American colonies would soon force the French monarchy to the edge of bankruptcy and then to revolution. Ultimately, the entire European system of royal rule would be challenged.

REVIEW   Why did public opinion become a new factor in politics in the second half of the eighteenth century?

Conclusion

What began as a cosmopolitan movement of a few intellectuals in the first half of the eighteenth century had reached a relatively wide audience among the educated elite of men and women by the 1770s and 1780s. The spirit of Enlightenment swept from the salons, coffeehouses, and Masonic lodges into the halls of government from Philadelphia to Vienna. Scientific inquiry into the causes of social misery and laws defending individual rights and freedoms gained adherents even among the rulers and ministers responsible for censoring Enlightenment works.

For most Europeans, however, the promise of the Enlightenment did not become a reality. Rulers such as Catherine the Great had every intention of retaining their

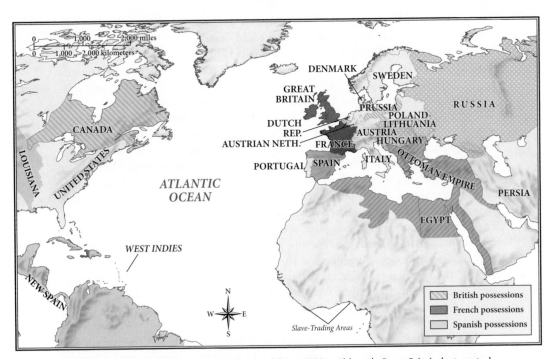

MAPPING THE WEST **Europe and the World, c. 1780**   Although Great Britain lost control over part of its North American colonies, which became the new United States, European influence on the rest of the world grew dramatically in the eighteenth century. The slave trade linked European ports to African slave-trading outposts and to plantations in the Caribbean, South America, and North America. The European countries on the Atlantic Ocean benefited most from this trade. Yet almost all of Africa, China, Japan, and large parts of India still resisted European incursion, and the Ottoman Empire, with its massive territories, still presented Europe with a formidable military challenge.

full, often unchecked powers even as they corresponded with leading philosophes and entertained them at their courts. Yet even the failure of reform contributed to the ferment in Europe after 1770. Peasant rebellions in eastern Europe, the "Wilkes and Liberty" campaign in Great Britain, the struggle over reform in France, and the revolution in America all occurred around the same time, and their conjunction convinced many Europeans that change was brewing. Just how much could change, and whether change made life better or worse, would come into question in the next ten years.

Chapter Review

KEY TERMS AND PEOPLE

Be sure that you can identify the term or person and explain its historical significance.

philosophes (p. 523)

deists (p. 526)

abolitionists (p. 527)

laissez-faire (p. 528)

Jean-Jacques Rousseau (p. 528)

romanticism (p. 530)

Methodism (p. 532)

Freemasons (p. 534)

enlightened despots (p. 538)

Seven Years' War (p. 539)

partition of Poland (p. 540)

Pugachev rebellion (p. 544)

REVIEW QUESTIONS

1. What were the major differences between the Enlightenment in France, Great Britain, and the German states?

2. What were the major differences in the impact of the Enlightenment on the nobility, the middle classes, and the lower classes?

3. What prompted enlightened absolutists to undertake reforms in the second half of the eighteenth century?

4. Why did public opinion become a new factor in politics in the second half of the eighteenth century?

MAKING CONNECTIONS

1. Why might rulers have felt ambivalent about the Enlightenment, supporting reform on the one hand while clamping down on political dissidents on the other hand?

2. Which major developments in this period ran counter to the influence of the Enlightenment?

3. In what ways had politics changed, and in what ways did they remain the same during the Enlightenment?

4. Explain how Catherine the Great of Russia could be taken as a symbol of both the promise and the limits of the Enlightenment.

IMPORTANT EVENTS

1751–1772	• *Encyclopedia* is published in France
1756–1763	• Seven Years' War is fought in Europe, India, and the American colonies
1762	• Jean-Jacques Rousseau, *The Social Contract*
1763	• Wilkes affair begins in Great Britain
1764	• Voltaire, *Philosophical Dictionary*
1771	• Louis XV of France fails to break power of French law courts
1772	• First partition of Poland
1773	• Pugachev rebellion of Russian peasants
1775	• Flour War in France
1776	• American Declaration of Independence from Great Britain; Adam Smith, *The Wealth of Nations*
1780	• Joseph II of Austria undertakes a wide-reaching reform program
1781	• Immanuel Kant, *The Critique of Pure Reason*
1784	• Pierre-Augustin Caron de Beaumarchais, *The Marriage of Figaro*
1785	• Catherine the Great's Charter of the Nobility grants nobles exclusive control over their serfs in exchange for subservience to the state
1787	• Delegates from the states draft the U.S. Constitution

19

The Cataclysm of Revolution

1789–1799

CHAPTER FOCUS

What was so revolutionary about the French Revolution?

ON OCTOBER 5, 1789, a crowd of several thousand women marched in a drenching rain from the center of Paris to Versailles, a distance of twelve miles. They demanded the king's help in securing more grain for the hungry and his reassurance that he did not intend to resist the emerging revolutionary movement. Joined the next morning by thousands of men who came from Paris to reinforce them, they broke into the royal family's private apartments, killing two of the royal bodyguards. To prevent further bloodshed, the king agreed to move his family and his government to Paris. A dramatic procession of the royal family guarded by throngs of ordinary men and women made its slow way back to the capital. The people's proud display of cannons and pikes underlined the fundamental transformation that was occurring. Ordinary people had forced the king of France to respond to their grievances. The French monarchy was in danger, and if such a powerful and long-lasting institution could come under fire, then could any monarch of Europe rest easy?

The French Revolution first grabbed the attention of the entire world because it seemed to promise human rights and broad-based political participation. Its most famous slogan pledged "Liberty, Equality, and Fraternity" for all. Even as the Revolution promised democracy, however, it also inaugurated a cycle of violence and intimidation, seen already in October

1789. When the revolutionaries encountered resistance to their programs, they tried to compel obedience. Some historians therefore see in the French Revolution the origins of modern totalitarianism—that is, a government that tries to control every aspect of life, including daily activities, while limiting all forms of political dissent. As events unfolded after 1789, the French Revolution became the model of modern revolution. Republicanism, democracy, terrorism, nationalism, and military dictatorship all took their modern forms during the French Revolution.

The Revolution might have remained a strictly French affair if war had not involved the rest of Europe. After 1792, huge French republican armies, fueled by patriotic nationalism, marched across Europe, promising liberation from traditional monarchies but often delivering old-fashioned conquest and annexation. French victories spread revolutionary ideas far and wide, from Poland to the colonies in the Caribbean, where the first successful slave revolt established the republic of Haiti.

The Revolutionary Wave, 1787–1789

Between 1787 and 1789, revolts in the name of liberty broke out in the Dutch Republic, the Austrian Netherlands (present-day Belgium and Luxembourg), and Poland as well as in France. At the same time, the newly independent United States of America was preparing a new federal constitution. Historians have sometimes referred to these revolts as the Atlantic revolutions because so many protest movements arose in countries on both shores of the North Atlantic. The French Revolution nonetheless differed greatly from the others. Not only was France the richest, most powerful, and most populous state in Europe, but its revolution was also more violent, more long-lasting, and ultimately more influential.

Protesters in the Low Countries and Poland

Political protests in the Dutch Republic attracted European attention because Dutch banks still controlled a hefty portion of the world's capital at the end of the eighteenth century. The Dutch Patriots, as they chose to call themselves, wanted to reduce the powers of the prince of Orange, the kinglike stadholder who favored close ties with Great Britain. Government-sponsored Dutch banks owned 40 percent of the British national debt, and by 1796 they held the entire foreign debt of the United States. Relations with the British deteriorated during the American War of Independence, however, and by the middle of the 1780s, agitation in favor of the Americans had boiled over into an attack on the stadholder.

Building on support among middle-class bankers and merchants, the Dutch Patriots soon gained a more popular audience by demanding political reforms and organizing armed citizen militias of men, called Free Corps. Before long, the Free

Corps took on the troops of the prince of Orange and got the upper hand. In response, Frederick William II of Prussia, whose sister had married the stadholder, intervened in 1787 with tacit British support. Thousands of Prussian troops soon occupied Utrecht and Amsterdam, and the house of Orange regained its former position. The Orangists got their revenge: lower-class mobs pillaged the houses of prosperous Dutch Patriot leaders, forcing many to flee to the United States, France, or the Austrian Netherlands. Those Patriots who remained nursed their grievances until the French republican armies invaded in 1795.

If Austrian emperor Joseph II had not tried to introduce Enlightenment-inspired reforms, the Belgians of the ten provinces of the Austrian Netherlands might have remained tranquil. Just as he had done previously in his own crown lands (see page 541), Joseph abolished torture, decreed toleration for Jews and Protestants (in this resolutely Catholic area), and suppressed monasteries. His reorganization of the administrative and judicial systems eliminated many offices that belonged to nobles and lawyers, sparking resistance among the upper classes in 1788.

Upper-class protesters intended only to defend historic local liberties against an overbearing government. Nonetheless, their resistance galvanized democrats, who wanted a more representative government and organized clubs to give voice to their demands. At the end of 1788, a secret society formed armed companies to prepare an uprising. By late 1789, each province had separately declared its independence, and the Austrian administration had collapsed. Delegates from the various provinces declared themselves the United States of Belgium, a clear reference to the American precedent.

Once again, however, social divisions doomed the rebels. When the democrats began to challenge noble authority, aristocratic leaders drew to their side the Catholic clergy and peasants, who had little sympathy for the democrats of the cities. Every Sunday in May and June 1790, thousands of peasant men and women, led by their priests, streamed into Brussels carrying crucifixes, nooses, and pitchforks to intimidate the democrats and defend the church. Faced with the choice between the Austrian emperor and "our current tyrants," the democrats chose to support the return of the Austrians under Emperor Leopold II (r. 1790–1792), who had succeeded his brother.

A reform party calling itself the Patriots also emerged in Poland, which had been shocked by the loss of a third of its territory in the first partition of 1772. The Patriots sought to overhaul the weak commonwealth along modern western European lines and looked to King Stanislaw August Poniatowski (r. 1764–1795) to lead them.

In 1788, the Patriots got their golden chance. Bogged down in war with the Ottoman Turks, Catherine the Great of Russia could not block the summoning of a reform-minded parliament, which eventually enacted the constitution of May 3, 1791. It ended the veto power that each aristocrat had over legislation, granted townspeople limited political rights, and vaguely promised future Jewish emancipation. Abolishing serfdom was hardly mentioned. Within a year, however, Catherine had turned her attention to Poland and engineered the downfall of the Patriots.

Origins of the French Revolution, 1787–1789

Many French enthusiastically greeted the American experiment in republican government and supported the Dutch, Belgian, and Polish Patriots. After suffering humiliation at the hands of the British in the Seven Years' War (1756–1763), the French had regained international prestige by supporting the victorious Americans. Yet by the late 1780s, the French monarchy was facing a serious fiscal crisis caused by a mounting deficit. The fiscal crisis soon provoked a constitutional crisis of epic proportions.

About half of the French national budget went to paying interest on the debt that had ballooned because of the American war. In contrast to the British government, which had a national bank to help raise loans, the French government lived off relatively short-term, high-interest loans from private sources, including Swiss banks, government annuities, and advances from tax collectors.

For years the French government had been trying unsuccessfully to modernize the tax system to make it more equitable. The peasants bore the greatest tax burden, whereas the nobles and clergy were largely exempt. Tax collection was also far from systematic: private contractors collected many taxes and pocketed a large share of the proceeds. With the growing support of public opinion, the bond and annuity holders from the middle and upper classes now demanded a clearer system of fiscal accountability.

In a monarchy, the ruler's character is always crucial. Many complained that **Louis XVI** (r. 1774–1792) showed more interest in hunting and in his hobby of making locks than in the problems of government. His wife, **Marie-Antoinette**, was blond, beautiful, and much criticized for her extravagant taste in clothes, elaborate hairdos, and supposed indifference to popular

Queen Marie-Antoinette (detail) Marie-Louise-Élizabeth Vigée-Lebrun painted this portrait of the French queen Marie-Antoinette and her children in 1788. The queen appears in the most stylish and lavish fashions of the day. When her eldest son (not shown in this detail) died in 1789, her second son (on her lap here) became heir to the throne. Known to supporters of the monarch as Louis XVII, the child died in prison in 1795 and never ruled. Vigée-Lebrun fled France in 1789 and returned only in 1805. (Château de Versailles, France / Giraudon / Bridgeman Images.)

misery. It was reported that, when told the poor had no bread, the queen gave a reply that has come to epitomize oblivious cold-heartedness: "Let them eat cake." The queen, whom underground writers called the "Austrian bitch," had been the target of an increasingly nasty pamphlet campaign in the 1780s. By 1789, Marie-Antoinette had become an object of popular hatred. The king's ineffectiveness and the queen's growing unpopularity helped undermine the monarchy as an institution.

Faced with a mounting deficit, in 1787 Louis submitted a package of reforms first to the Assembly of Notables and then to his old rival the parlement of Paris. Both refused to consider the reforms. Louis finally gave in to demands that he call a meeting of the Estates General, which had last met 175 years before.

The calling of the Estates General electrified public opinion. The **Estates General** was a body of deputies from the three estates, or orders, of France. The deputies in the First Estate represented some 170,000 priests, monks, and nuns of the Catholic church, which owned about 10 percent of the land in France and collected a 10 percent tax (the tithe) on peasants. The deputies of the Second Estate represented the nobility, about 140,000 men and women who owned about one-third of the land, enjoyed many tax exemptions, and collected seigneurial dues and rents from their peasant tenants. The deputies of the Third Estate represented everyone else, at least 95 percent of the nation. Included in the Third Estate were the vast mass of peasants, some 75 percent of the population, and the *sans-culottes* ("without breeches") and middle classes of the cities. The sans-culottes were those who worked with their hands and wore long trousers rather than the knee breeches of the upper classes.

Before the elections to the Estates General in 1789, the king agreed to double the number of deputies from the Third Estate (making those deputies equal in number to the other two orders combined), but he refused to mandate voting by individual head rather than by order. Voting by order, allowing each order to have one vote, would conserve the traditional powers of the clergy and nobility; voting by head, allowing each deputy one vote, would give the Third Estate an advantage since many clergymen and even some nobles sympathized with the Third Estate.

As the state's censorship apparatus broke down, pamphleteers by the hundreds denounced the traditional privileges of the nobility and clergy and called for voting by head rather than by order. In the most vitriolic of all the pamphlets, *What Is the Third Estate?*, the middle-class abbé ("abbot") Emmanuel-Joseph Sieyès charged that the nobility contributed nothing at all to the nation's well-being; they were, he said, "a malignant disease which preys upon and tortures the body of a sick man." In the winter and spring of 1789, villagers and townspeople alike held meetings to elect deputies and write down their grievances. The effect was immediate. Although lawyers dominated the meetings at the regional level, the humblest peasants voted in their villages and burst forth with complaints, especially about taxes. One village meeting summed up the frustration: "misery is so great in the country that we cannot make enough complaints." The long series of meetings raised expectations that the Estates General would help the king solve all the nation's ills.

These new hopes soared just at the moment France experienced a food shortage, an increasingly rare but always dangerous situation. Bad weather had damaged the harvest of 1788, causing bread prices to rise dramatically in many places in the spring and summer of 1789 and threatening starvation for the poorest people. In addition, a serious slump in textile production had been causing massive unemployment since 1786. Hundreds of thousands of textile workers were out of work and hungry, adding another volatile element to an already tense situation.

When some twelve hundred deputies journeyed to the king's palace of Versailles for the opening of the Estates General in May 1789, many readers avidly followed the developments in newspapers that sprouted overnight. Although most nobles insisted on voting by order, the deputies of the Third Estate refused to proceed on that basis. After six weeks of stalemate, the deputies of the Third Estate took unilateral action on June 17 and declared themselves and whoever would join them the National Assembly, in which each deputy would vote as an individual. Two days later, the clergy voted by a narrow margin to join them. Suddenly denied access

Fall of the Bastille   A central moment from the storming of the Bastille prison on July 14, 1789, is depicted in this print of a 1793 painting by Charles Thévenin. The insurgents have won the battle and are arresting the governor of the prison; in the next moments, they will cut off his head and parade it on a pike. The artist expresses his ambivalence about the violence by showing an insurgent in the right foreground brutally killing one of the defenders even though the battle is over. (Musée de la Ville de Paris, Musée Carnavalet, Paris, France/© RMN-Grand Palais/Art Resource, NY.)

to their meeting hall on June 20, the deputies met on a nearby tennis court and swore an oath not to disband until they had given France a constitution that reflected their newly declared authority. This "tennis court oath" expressed the determination of the Third Estate to carry through a constitutional revolution.

At first, Louis XVI appeared to agree to the new National Assembly, but he also ordered thousands of soldiers to march to Paris. The deputies who supported the Assembly feared a plot to arrest them and disperse the Assembly. Their fears were confirmed when, on July 11, the king fired Jacques Necker, the Swiss Protestant finance minister and the one high official regarded as sympathetic to the deputies' cause.

The popular reaction in Paris changed the course of the French Revolution. When the news spread, the sans-culottes in Paris began to arm themselves and

REVEIL DU TIERS ETAT.

The Third Estate Awakens   This etching, produced after the fall of the Bastille (note the heads on pikes outside the prison), shows a clergyman (First Estate) and a noble (Second Estate) alarmed by the awakening of the commoners (Third Estate). The Third Estate breaks the chains of oppression and arms itself. In what ways does this print draw attention to the social conflicts that lay behind the political struggles in the Estates General? (The Awakening of the Third Estate, July 1789 [engraving] [see also 266297], French School, [18th century]/Musée de la Ville de Paris, Musée Carnavalet, Paris, France/Bridgeman Images.)

attack places where either grain or arms were thought to be stored. A deputy in Versailles reported home: "Today all of the evils overwhelm France, and we are between despotism, carnage, and famine." On July 14, an armed crowd marched on the Bastille, a huge fortified prison that symbolized royal authority (even though only a few prisoners were actually incarcerated there). After a chaotic battle in which a hundred armed citizens died, the prison officials surrendered.

The fall of the Bastille (an event now commemorated each July 14 as the French national holiday) set an important precedent. The common people showed themselves willing to intervene violently at a crucial political moment. All over France, local governments were forced out of power and replaced by committees of "patriots." To restore order, the patriots relied on newly formed National Guard units composed of civilians. In Paris, the Marquis de Lafayette, a hero of the American War of Independence and a noble deputy in the National Assembly, became commander of the new National Guard. One of Louis XVI's brothers and many other leading aristocrats fled into exile. The Revolution thus had its first heroes, its first victims, and its first enemies.

> **REVIEW** How did the beginning of the French Revolution resemble the other revolutions of 1787–1789?

From Monarchy to Republic, 1789–1793

Until July 1789, the French Revolution had followed a course much like that of the protest movements in the Low Countries. After that point, however, events in France escalated at a pace never before seen in history, leaving witnesses breathless with anticipation, anxiety, even shock. The French revolutionaries first tried to establish a constitutional monarchy based on the Enlightenment principles of human rights and rational government. This effort failed when the king attempted to flee and raise a counterrevolutionary army. When war broke out in 1792 and foreign soldiers invaded, a popular uprising on August 10 led to the arrest of the king and, for the first time in French history, the establishment of a republic.

The Revolution of Rights and Reason

Before drafting a constitution in 1789, the deputies of the National Assembly had to confront growing violence in the countryside. As food shortages spread, peasants feared that the beggars and vagrants crowding the roads might be part of an aristocratic plot to starve the French people by burning crops or barns. In many places, the **Great Fear** (the term used by historians to describe this rural panic) turned into peasant attacks on aristocrats or on the records of peasants' seigneurial dues kept in lords' castles.

Alarmed by peasant unrest, the National Assembly decided to make sweeping changes. On the night of August 4, 1789, noble deputies announced their willingness to give up their tax exemptions and seigneurial dues. The National Assembly decreed the abolition of what it called the feudal regime—that is, it freed the few remaining serfs and eliminated all special privileges in matters of taxation, including all seigneurial dues on land. (A few days later the deputies insisted on financial compensation for some of these dues, but most peasants refused to pay.) The Assembly also mandated equality of opportunity in access to government positions. Talent, rather than birth, was to be the key to success. Enlightenment principles were beginning to become law.

Three weeks later, the deputies drew up the **Declaration of the Rights of Man and Citizen** as the preamble to a new constitution. In words reminiscent of the American Declaration of Independence, whose author, Thomas Jefferson, was in Paris at the time, it proclaimed, "Men are born and remain free and equal in rights." The Declaration granted freedom of religion, freedom of the press, equality of taxation, and equality before the law. It established the principle of national sovereignty: the king derived his authority henceforth from the nation rather than from tradition or divine right.

By pronouncing all *men* free and equal, the Declaration immediately created new dilemmas. Did women have equal rights with men? What about free blacks in the colonies? How could slavery be justified if all men were born free? Did religious toleration of Protestants and Jews include equal political rights? Women never received the right to vote during the French Revolution, though Protestant and Jewish men did.

Some women did not accept their exclusion. In addition to joining demonstrations, such as the march to Versailles in October 1789, women wrote petitions, published tracts, and organized political clubs to demand more participation. In her Declaration of the Rights of Woman of 1791, writer and political activist Olympe de Gouges (1748–1793) played on the language of the official Declaration to make the point that women should also be included: "Woman is born free and lives equal to man in her rights." De Gouges linked her complaints to a program of social reform in which women would have equal rights to property and public office and equal responsibilities in taxes and criminal punishment.

Unresponsive to calls for women's equality, the National Assembly turned to preparing France's first written constitution. The deputies gave voting rights only to white men who passed a test of wealth. Despite these limitations, France became a constitutional monarchy in which the king served as the leading state functionary. A one-house legislature was responsible for making laws. The king could postpone enactment of laws but not veto them. The deputies abolished all the old administrative divisions of the provinces and replaced them with a national system of eighty-three departments with identical administrative and legal structures (Map 19.1). All officials were elected; no offices could be bought or sold. The deputies also abolished the old taxes and replaced them with new ones that were supposed to be uniformly levied. The National Assembly had difficulty collecting taxes, however, because many people had expected a substantial cut in the tax rate. The new administrative system survived nonetheless, and the departments are still the basic units of the French state today.

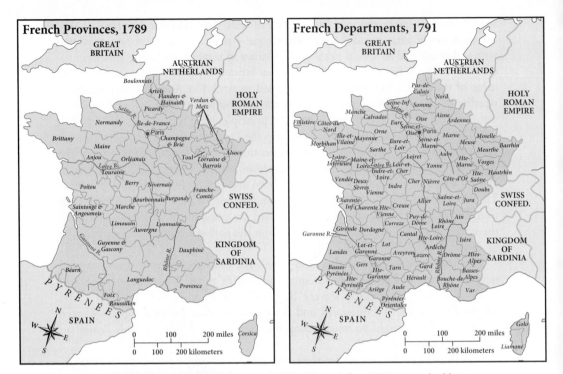

MAP 19.1   Redrawing the Map of France, 1789–1791   Before 1789, France had been divided into provinces named after the territories owned by dukes and counts in the Middle Ages. Many provinces had their own law codes and separate systems of taxation. As it began its deliberations, the new National Assembly determined to install uniform administrations and laws for the entire country. Discussion of the administrative reforms began in October 1789 and became law on February 15, 1790, when the Assembly voted to divide the provinces into eighty-three departments, with names based on their geographical characteristics: Basses-Pyrénées, Haute-Pyrénées, and Pyrénées-Orientales for regions containing the Pyrénées Mountains; Marne and Haute-Marne for areas containing the Marne River; and so on. How did this redrawing of the administrative map reflect the deputies' emphasis on reason over history?

When the deputies to the National Assembly turned to reforming the Catholic church, however, they created enduring conflicts. Convinced that monastic life encouraged idleness and a decline in the nation's population, the deputies outlawed any future monastic vows and encouraged monks and nuns to return to private life by offering state pensions. Motivated partly by the ongoing financial crisis, the National Assembly confiscated all the church's property and promised to pay clerical salaries in return. The Civil Constitution of the Clergy, passed in July 1790, provided that the voters elect their own parish priests and bishops just as they elected other officials. The impounded property served as a guarantee for the new paper money, called assignats, issued by the government. The assignats soon became subject to inflation because the government printed more and more money even as it sold the church lands to the highest bidders in state auctions.

Faced with resistance to these changes, the National Assembly in November 1790 required all clergy to swear an oath of loyalty to the Civil Constitution of the Clergy. Pope Pius VI in Rome condemned the constitution, and half of the French clergy refused to take the oath. The oath of allegiance permanently divided the Catholic population. The revolutionary government lost many supporters by passing laws against the clergy who refused the oath and by sending them into exile, deporting them forcibly, or executing them as traitors.

The End of Monarchy

The reorganization of the Catholic church offended Louis XVI and gave added weight to those pushing him to organize resistance. On June 20, 1791, the royal family escaped in disguise from Paris and fled toward the eastern border of France, where they hoped to gather support from Austrian emperor Leopold II, the brother of Marie-Antoinette. The plans went awry when a postmaster recognized the king from his portrait on the new French money, and the royal family was arrested at Varennes, forty miles from the Austrian Netherlands border. The "flight to Varennes" touched off demonstrations in Paris against the royal family. Cartoons circulated depicting the royal family as animals being returned "to the stable."

The constitution, finally completed in 1791, provided for the immediate election of a new legislature. The status of the king might have remained uncertain if war had not intervened, but by early 1792 everyone seemed intent on war with Austria. Louis and Marie-Antoinette hoped that such a war would lead to the defeat of the Revolution, whereas the deputies who favored a republic believed that war would lead to the king's downfall. On April 21, 1792, Louis declared war on Austria. Prussia immediately entered on the Austrian side. Thousands of French aristocrats, including both of the king's brothers and two-thirds of the army officer corps, had already emigrated and were gathering along France's eastern border in expectation of joining a counterrevolutionary army.

When the fighting broke out, all the powers expected a short, relatively contained war. Instead, it would continue despite brief interruptions for the next twenty-three years. War had an immediate radicalizing effect on French politics. When the French armies proved woefully unprepared for battle, the authority of the new legislature came under fire. In June 1792, an angry crowd invaded the hall of the legislature in Paris and threatened the royal family. The Prussian commander, the duke of Brunswick, issued a manifesto announcing that Paris would be totally destroyed if the royal family suffered any violence.

The sans-culottes of Paris did not passively await their fate. Faced with the threat of military retaliation and frustrated with the inaction of the deputies, on August 10 the sans-culottes organized an insurrection and attacked the Tuileries palace, the residence of the king. The king and his family had to seek refuge in the meeting room of the legislature, where the frightened deputies ordered elections for a constitutional convention. By abolishing the property qualifications for voting, the deputies instituted universal male suffrage for the first time.

Violence soon exploded again when early in September 1792 the Prussians approached Paris. Hastily gathered mobs stormed the overflowing prisons to seek out traitors, and eleven hundred inmates were killed, including many ordinary and completely innocent people. The princess of Lamballe, one of the queen's favorites, was hacked to pieces and her mutilated body displayed beneath the windows where the royal family was kept under guard. These "September massacres" showed the dark side of popular revolution, in which the common people demanded retribution against supposed enemies and conspirators.

When it met, the National Convention abolished the monarchy and on September 22 established the first republic in French history. The republic would answer only to the people, not to any royal authority. Many of the deputies in the Convention belonged to the devotedly republican (and therefore left-wing) **Jacobin Club**, named after the former monastery in Paris where the club had first met in 1789. The Jacobin Club in Paris headed a national political network of clubs that linked all the major towns and cities. Lafayette and other liberal aristocrats who had supported the constitutional monarchy fled into exile.

The National Convention faced a dire situation. It needed to write a new constitution for the republic while fighting a war with external enemies and confronting increasing resistance at home. The French people had never known any government other than monarchy. Only half the population could read and write at even a basic level. In this situation, symbolic actions became very important. Revolutionaries soon pulled down statues of kings and burned reminders of the former regime.

The fate of Louis XVI and the direction of the republic divided the deputies elected to the National Convention. Most of the deputies were middle-class lawyers and professionals who had developed their ardent republican beliefs in the network of Jacobin Clubs. After the fall of the monarchy in August 1792, however, the Jacobins had divided into two factions. The Girondins (named after a department in southwestern France, the Gironde, which provided some of its leading orators) met regularly at the salon of Jeanne Roland, the wife of a minister. They resented the growing power of Parisian militants and tried to appeal to the departments outside of Paris. The Mountain (so called because its deputies sat in the highest seats of the National Convention), in contrast, was closely allied with the Paris militants.

The first showdown between the Girondins and the Mountain was the trial of the king in December 1792. Although the Girondins agreed that the king was guilty of treason, many of them argued for clemency, exile, or a popular referendum on his fate. After a long and difficult debate, the National Convention supported the Mountain and voted by a very narrow majority to execute the king. Louis XVI went to the guillotine on January 21, 1793, sharing the fate of Charles I of England in 1649.

REVIEW   Why did the French Revolution turn in an increasingly radical direction after 1789?

Terror and Resistance

The execution of the king did not solve the new regime's problems. The continuing war required even more men and money, and the introduction of a national draft provoked massive resistance. In response to growing pressures, the National Convention named a Committee of Public Safety to supervise food distribution, direct the war effort, and root out counterrevolutionaries. The leader of the committee, **Maximilien Robespierre** (1758–1794), wanted to go beyond these stopgap measures and create a "republic of virtue," in which the government would teach, or force, citizens to become virtuous republicans through a massive program of political reeducation. Thus began the **Terror**, in which the guillotine became the most terrifying instrument of a government that suppressed almost every form of dissent.

Robespierre and the Committee of Public Safety

The conflict between the more moderate Girondins and the more radical Mountain came to a head in spring 1793. Militants in Paris agitated for the removal of the deputies who had proposed a referendum on the king, and in retaliation the Girondins engineered the arrest of Jean-Paul Marat, a deputy allied with the Mountain who in his newspaper had been calling for more and more executions. Marat was acquitted, and Parisian militants marched into the National Convention on June 2, forcing the deputies to decree the arrest of their twenty-nine Girondin colleagues. The Convention consented to the establishment of paramilitary bands called revolutionary armies to hunt down political suspects and hoarders of grain. The deputies also agreed to speed up the operation of special revolutionary courts.

Setting the course for government and the war increasingly fell to the twelve-member Committee of Public Safety. When Robespierre was elected to the committee in July 1793, he became the chief spokesman. A lawyer from northern France known as "the incorruptible" for his stern honesty and fierce dedication to democratic ideals, Robespierre remains one of the most controversial figures in world history because of his association with the Terror. Although he originally opposed the death penalty and the war, he was convinced that the emergency situation of 1793 required severe measures, including death for those, such as the Girondins, who opposed the committee's policies.

Robespierre defended the people's right to democratic government, while in practice he supported many emergency measures that restricted their liberties. He personally favored a free-market economy, as did almost all middle-class deputies, but in this time of crisis he was willing to enact price controls and requisitioning. In an effort to stabilize prices, the National Convention established the General Maximum on September 29, 1793, which set limits on the prices of thirty-nine essential commodities and on wages. In a speech to the Convention, Robespierre explained the necessity of government by terror: "The first maxim of your policies must be to lead the people by reason and the people's enemies by terror. . . . Without virtue, terror is deadly; without terror, virtue is impotent." *Terror* was not an idle term; it seemed to imply that the goal of democracy justified what we now call totalitarian means, that is, the suppression of all dissent.

Through a series of desperate measures, the Committee of Public Safety set the machinery of the Terror in motion. It sent deputies out "on mission" to purge unreliable officials and organize the war effort. Revolutionary tribunals tried political suspects. In October 1793, the Revolutionary Tribunal in Paris convicted Marie-Antoinette of treason and sent her to the guillotine. The Girondin leaders and Jeanne Roland were also guillotined, as was Olympe de Gouges.

The new republic won its greatest success on the battlefield. As of April 1793, France faced war with Austria, Prussia, Great Britain, Spain, Sardinia, and the Dutch Republic—all fearful of the impact of revolutionary ideals on their own populations. The execution of Louis XVI, in particular, galvanized European governments; according to William Pitt, the British prime minister, it was "the foulest and most atrocious act the world has ever seen." To face this daunting coalition of forces, the French republic ordered the first universal draft of men in history. Every unmarried man and childless widower between the ages of eighteen and twenty-five was declared eligible for conscription. The government also tapped a new and potent source of power—nationalist pride.

Forges were set up in the parks and gardens of Paris to produce thousands of guns, and citizens everywhere helped collect saltpeter to make gunpowder. By the end of 1793, the French nation in arms had stopped the advance of the allied powers, and in the summer of 1794 it invaded the Austrian Netherlands and crossed the Rhine River. The army was ready to carry the gospel of revolution and republicanism to the rest of Europe.

The Republic of Virtue, 1793–1794

The program of the Terror went beyond pragmatic measures to fight the war and internal enemies to include efforts to "republicanize everything"—in other words, to effect a cultural revolution. The republic left no stone unturned in its endeavor to get its message across. Songs—especially the new national anthem, "La Marseillaise"—and placards, posters, pamphlets, books, engravings, paintings, sculpture, even everyday crockery, chamber pots, and playing cards conveyed revolutionary slogans and symbols. Foremost among the symbols was the figure of Liberty, which appeared on coins and bills, on letterheads and seals, and as statues in festivals. Hundreds of new plays were produced and old classics revised. To encourage the production of patriotic and republican works, the government sponsored state competitions for artists.

At the center of this elaborate cultural campaign were the revolutionary festivals modeled on Rousseau's plans for a civic religion. The Festival of Federation on July 14, 1790, marked the first anniversary of the fall of the Bastille. Under the National Convention, the well-known painter Jacques-Louis David (1748–1825), who was a deputy and an associate of Robespierre, took over festival planning. David aimed to destroy the mystique of monarchy and to make the republic sacred. His Festival of Unity on August 10, 1793, for example, celebrated the first anniversary of the overthrow of the monarchy. In front of the statue of Liberty built for the occasion, a bonfire consumed crowns and scepters symbolizing royalty while a cloud of three thousand white doves rose into the sky. This was all part of preaching the "moral order of the Republic ... that will make us a people of brothers, a people of philosophers."

Some revolutionaries hoped the festival system would replace the Catholic church altogether. They initiated a campaign of **de-Christianization** that included closing churches (Protestant as well as Catholic), selling many church buildings to the highest bidder, and trying to force even those clergy who had taken the oath of loyalty to abandon their clerical vocations and marry. Great churches became store-houses for arms or grain, or their stones were sold off to contractors. The medieval statues of kings on the facade of Notre Dame cathedral were beheaded. Church bells were dismantled and church treasures melted down for government use.

In the ultimate step in de-Christianization, extremists tried to establish what they called the Cult of Reason to supplant Christianity. In Paris in the fall of 1793, a goddess of Liberty, played by an actress, presided over the Festival of Reason in Notre Dame cathedral. Robespierre objected to the de-Christianization campaign's atheism; he favored a Rousseau-inspired deistic religion without the supposedly superstitious trappings of Catholicism. The Committee of Public Safety halted the de-Christianization campaign, and Robespierre, with David's help, tried to institute an alternative, the Cult of the Supreme Being, in June 1794. Neither the Cult of Reason nor the Cult of the Supreme Being attracted many followers, but both show the depth of the commitment to overturning the old order and all its traditional institutions.

In principle, the best way to ensure the future of the republic was through the education of the young. The deputy Georges-Jacques Danton (1759–1794), Robespierre's main competitor, maintained that "after bread, the first need of the people is education." The National Convention voted to make primary schooling free and compulsory for both boys and girls. It took control of education away from the Catholic church and tried to set up a system of state schools at both the primary and secondary levels, but it lacked trained teachers to replace those the Catholic religious orders had provided. As a result, opportunities for learning how to read and write may have diminished. In 1799, only one-fifth as many boys were enrolled in the state secondary schools as had studied in church schools ten years earlier.

Although many of the ambitious republican programs failed, colors, clothing, and daily speech were all politicized. The tricolor—the combination of red, white, and blue that was to become the flag of France—was devised in July 1789, and by 1793 everyone had to wear a tricolor cockade (a badge made of ribbons). Using the formal forms of speech—*vous* for "you" or the title *monsieur* or *madame*—might identify someone as an aristocrat; true patriots used the informal *tu* and *citoyen* or *citoyenne* ("citizen") instead. Some people changed their names or gave their children new kinds of names. Biblical and saints' names such as John, Peter, Joseph, and Mary gave way to names recalling heroes of the ancient Roman republic (Brutus, Gracchus, Cornelia), revolutionary heroes, or flowers and plants. Such changes symbolized adherence to the republic and to Enlightenment ideals rather than to Catholicism.

Even the measures of time and space were revolutionized. In October 1793, the National Convention introduced a new calendar to replace the Christian one. Its bases were reason and republican principles. Year I dated from the beginning of the republic on September 22, 1792. Twelve months of exactly thirty days each received new names derived from nature—for example, Pluviôse (roughly equivalent to February) recalled the rain (*la pluie*) of late winter. Instead of seven-day weeks, ten-day *décades* provided only one day of rest every ten days and pointedly eliminated the Sunday of the Christian calendar. The calendar remained in force for twelve years despite continuing resistance to it. More enduring was the new metric system based on units of ten that was invented to replace the hundreds of local variations in weights and measures. Other countries in Europe and throughout the world eventually adopted the metric system.

Revolutionary laws also changed the rules of family life. The state took responsibility for all family matters away from the Catholic church: people now registered births, deaths, and marriages at city hall, not the parish church. Marriage became a civil contract and as such could be broken and thereby nullified. The new divorce law of September 1792 was the most far-reaching in Europe: a couple could divorce by mutual consent or for reasons such as insanity, abandonment, battering, or criminal conviction. Thousands of men and women took advantage of the law to dissolve unhappy marriages, even though the pope had condemned the measure. (In 1816, the government revoked the right to divorce, and not until the 1970s did French divorce laws return to the principles of the 1792 legislation.) In one of its most influential actions, the National Convention passed a series of laws that created equal inheritance among all children in the family, including girls. The father's right to favor one child, especially the oldest male, was considered aristocratic and hence antirepublican.

Resisting the Revolution

By intruding into religion, culture, and daily life, the republic inevitably provoked resistance. Shouting curses against the republic, uprooting liberty trees, carrying statues of the Virgin Mary in procession, hiding a priest who would not take the oath, singing a royalist song—all these expressed dissent with the new symbols, rituals, and policies. Long bread lines in the cities exhausted the patience of women, and their constant grumbling occasionally turned into spontaneous demonstrations or riots over high prices or food shortages.

Other forms of resistance were more individual. One young woman, Charlotte Corday, assassinated the outspoken deputy Jean-Paul Marat in July 1793. Corday fervently supported the Girondins, and she considered it her patriotic duty to kill the deputy who, in the columns of his paper, had constantly demanded more heads and more blood. Marat was immediately eulogized as a great martyr, and Corday went to the guillotine vilified as a monster but confident that she had "avenged many innocent victims."

Organized resistance against the republic broke out in many parts of France. The arrest of the Girondin deputies in June 1793 sparked insurrections in several departments. After the government retook the city of Lyon, one of the centers of the revolt, the deputy on mission ordered sixteen hundred houses demolished and the name of the city changed to Liberated City. Special courts sentenced almost two thousand people to death.

In the Vendée region of western France, resistance turned into a bloody and prolonged civil war. Between March and December 1793, peasants, artisans, and weavers joined under noble leadership to form a "Catholic and Royal Army." One rebel group explained its motives: "They [the republicans] have killed our king, chased away our priests, sold the goods of our church, eaten everything we have and now they want to take our bodies [in the draft]." The rebels stormed the largest towns in the region. Both sides committed horrible atrocities. At the small town of Machecoul, for example, the rebels massacred five hundred republicans, including administrators and National Guard members; many were tied together, shoved into freshly dug graves, and shot. By the fall, however, republican soldiers had turned back the rebels. Military courts ordered thousands executed, and republican soldiers massacred thousands of others. In one especially gruesome incident, the deputy Jean-Baptiste Carrier supervised the drowning of some two thousand Vendée rebels, including a number of priests. Barges loaded with prisoners were floated into the Loire River near Nantes and then sunk. Controversy still rages about the rebellion's death toll because no accurate count could be taken. Estimates of rebel deaths alone range from about 20,000 to higher than 250,000. Many thousands of republican soldiers and civilians also lost their lives in fighting that continued on and off for years. Even the low estimates reveal the carnage of this catastrophic confrontation between the republic and its opponents.

The Fall of Robespierre and the End of the Terror

In the atmosphere of fear of conspiracy that the outbreaks of rebellion fueled, Robespierre tried simultaneously to exert the National Convention's control over popular political activities and to weed out opposition among the deputies. As a result, the Terror intensified until July 1794, when a group of deputies joined within the Convention to order the arrest and execution of Robespierre and his followers. The Convention then ordered elections and drew up a new republican constitution that gave executive power to five directors. This "Directory government" maintained power during four years of seesaw battles between royalists and former Jacobins.

In the fall of 1793, the National Convention cracked down on popular clubs and societies. First to be suppressed were women's political clubs. Founded in early 1793, the Society of Revolutionary Republican Women urged harsher measures against the republic's enemies and insisted that women have a voice in politics even if they did not have the vote. Women had set up their own clubs in many provincial towns and also attended the meetings of local men's organizations. Using traditional arguments about women's inherent unsuitability for politics, the deputies abolished women's political clubs. The closing of women's clubs marked an important turning point in the Revolution. From then on, the sans-culottes and their political organizations came increasingly under the thumb of the Jacobin deputies in the National Convention.

In the spring of 1794, the Committee of Public Safety moved against its critics among leaders in Paris and deputies in the National Convention itself. First, a handful of "ultrarevolutionaries"—a collection of local Parisian politicians—were arrested and executed. Next came the other side, the "indulgents," so called because they favored a moderation of the Terror. Included among them was the deputy Danton, himself once a member of the Committee of Public Safety and a friend of Robespierre. Danton was the Revolution's most flamboyant orator and, unlike Robespierre, a high-living, high-spending politician. At every critical turning point in national politics, his booming voice had swayed opinion. Now, under pressure from the Committee of Public Safety, the Revolutionary Tribunal convicted him and his friends of treason and sentenced them to death.

"The Revolution," as one of the Girondin victims of 1793 had remarked, "was devouring its own children." Even after the major threats to the Committee of Public Safety's power had been eliminated, the Terror not only continued but worsened. A law passed in June 1794 denied the accused the right of legal counsel, reduced the number of jurors necessary for conviction, and allowed only two judgments: acquittal or death. The category of political crimes expanded to include "slandering patriotism" and "seeking to inspire discouragement." Ordinary people risked the guillotine if they expressed any discontent. The rate of executions in Paris rose from five a day in the spring of 1794 to twenty-six a day in the summer. The political atmosphere darkened even though the military situation improved. At the end of June, the French armies decisively defeated the main Austrian army and advanced through the Austrian Netherlands to Brussels and Antwerp. The emergency measures for fighting the war were working, yet Robespierre and his inner circle had made so many enemies that they could not afford to loosen the grip of the Terror.

The Terror hardly touched many parts of France, but overall the experience was undeniably traumatic. Across the country, the official Terror cost the lives of at least 40,000 French people, most of them living in the regions of major insurrections or near the borders with foreign enemies, where suspicion of collaboration ran high. As many as 300,000 French people—1 out of every 50—went to prison as suspects between March 1793 and August 1794. The toll for the aristocracy and the clergy was especially high. Many leading nobles perished under the guillotine, and thousands emigrated. Thirty thousand to forty thousand clergy who refused the oath left the country, at least two thousand (including many nuns) were executed, and thousands were imprisoned. The clergy were singled out in particular in the civil war zones: 135 priests were massacred at Lyon in November 1793, and 83 were shot in one day during the Vendée revolt. Yet many victims of the Terror were peasants or sans-culottes.

The final crisis of the Terror came as conflicts within the Committee of Public Safety and the National Convention left Robespierre isolated. On July 27, 1794 (the ninth of Thermidor, Year II, according to the revolutionary calendar), Robespierre appeared before the Convention with yet another list of deputies to be arrested. Many feared they would be named, and they shouted him down and ordered him arrested along with the president of the Revolutionary Tribunal in Paris and the commander of the Parisian National Guard. An armed uprising led by the Paris city government failed to save Robespierre when most of the National Guard took the side of the Convention. Robespierre tried to kill himself with a pistol but only broke his jaw. The next day he and scores of followers went to the guillotine.

The men who led the July 27 attack on Robespierre did not intend to reverse all his policies, but that happened nonetheless because of a violent backlash known as the **Thermidorian Reaction**. The new government released hundreds of suspects and arranged a temporary truce in the Vendée. It purged Jacobins from local bodies and replaced them with their opponents. It arrested some of the most notorious "terrorists" in the National Convention, such as Carrier, and put them to death. Within the year, the new leaders abolished the Revolutionary Tribunal and closed the Jacobin Club in Paris. Popular demonstrations met severe repression. In southeastern France, in particular, the "White Terror" replaced the Jacobins' "Red Terror." Former officials and local Jacobin leaders were harassed, beaten, and often murdered by paramilitary bands that had tacit support from the new authorities. Those who remained in the National Convention prepared yet another constitution in 1795, setting up a two-house legislature and an executive body—the Directory, headed by five directors.

The Directory regime tenuously held on to power for four years, all the while trying to fend off challenges from the remaining Jacobins and the resurgent royalists. The puritanical atmosphere of the Terror gave way to the pursuit of pleasure— low-cut dresses of transparent materials, the reappearance of prostitutes in the streets, and "victims' balls" where guests wore red ribbons around their necks as reminders of the guillotine. Bands of young men dressed in knee breeches and rich fabrics picked fights with known Jacobins and disrupted theater performances with loud antirevolutionary songs. All over France, people petitioned to reopen churches closed during the Terror. If necessary, they broke into a church to hold services with a priest who had been in hiding or a lay schoolteacher who was willing to say Mass.

Although the Terror had ended, the Revolution had not. Both the most democratic and the most repressive phases of the Revolution had ended at once in July 1794. Between 1795 and 1799, the republic endured in France, but it directed a war effort abroad that would ultimately bring to power the man who would dismantle the republic itself.

> **REVIEW** What factors can explain the Terror? To what extent was it simply a response to a national emergency or a reflection of deeper problems within the French Revolution?

Revolution on the March

War raged almost constantly from 1792 to 1815. At one time or another, and sometimes all at once, France faced every principal power in Europe. The French republic—and later the French Empire under its supreme commander, Emperor Napoleon Bonaparte—proved an even more formidable opponent than the France of Louis XIV. New means of mobilizing and organizing soldiers enabled the French to dominate Europe for a generation. The influence of the French Revolution as a political model and the threat of French military conquest combined to challenge the traditional order in Europe and offer new prospects to the rest of the world as well.

Arms and Conquests

The powers allied against France squandered their best chance to triumph in early 1793, when the French armies verged on chaos because of the emigration of noble army officers and the problems of integrating new draftees. By the end of 1793, the French had a huge and powerful fighting force of 700,000 men. But the army still faced many problems in the field. As many as a third of the recent draftees deserted before or during battle. Generals might pay with their lives if they lost a key battle and their loyalty to the Revolution came under suspicion. Although France had built up a relatively large navy, the dominance of Great Britain on the seas meant that France had to seek victory on the land.

France nevertheless had one overwhelming advantage: those soldiers who agreed to serve fought for a revolution that they and their brothers and sisters had helped make. The republic was their government, and the army was in large measure theirs, too; many officers had risen through the ranks by skill and talent rather than by inheriting or purchasing their positions. One young peasant boy wrote to his parents, "Either you will see me return bathed in glory, or you will have a son who is a worthy citizen of France who knows how to die for the defense of his country."

When the French armies invaded the Austrian Netherlands and crossed the Rhine in the summer of 1794, they proclaimed a war of liberation (Map 19.2). In the Austrian Netherlands, Mainz, Savoy, and Nice, French officers organized Jacobin Clubs that attracted locals. The clubs petitioned for annexation to France, and French legislation was then introduced, including the abolition of seigneurial dues. As the French annexed more and more territory, however, "liberated" people in many places began to view them as an army of occupation. Despite resistance, especially in the Austrian Netherlands, these areas remained part of France until 1815, and the legal changes were permanent.

The Directory government that came to power in 1795 launched an even more aggressive policy of creating semi-independent "sister republics" wherever the armies succeeded. When Prussia declared neutrality in 1795, the French armies swarmed into the Dutch Republic, abolished the stadholderate, and—with the revolutionary penchant for renaming—created the new Batavian Republic, a satellite of France. The brilliant young general Napoleon Bonaparte gained a reputation by defeating the Austrian armies in northern Italy in 1797 and then created the Cisalpine Republic. Next he overwhelmed Venice and then handed it over to the Austrians in exchange for a peace agreement that lasted less than two years. After the French attacked the Swiss cantons in 1798, they set up the Helvetic Republic and curtailed many of the Catholic church's privileges. They conquered the Papal States in 1798 and installed a Roman Republic, forcing the pope to flee to Siena.

The revolutionary wars had an immediate impact on European life at all levels of society. Thousands of men died in every country involved, with perhaps as many

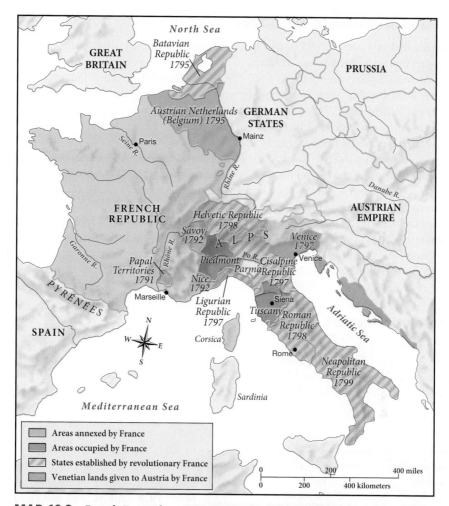

MAP 19.2   French Expansion, 1791–1799   The influence of the French Revolution on neighboring territories is dramatically evident in this map. The French directly annexed the papal territories in southern France in 1791, Nice and Savoy in 1792, and the Austrian Netherlands in 1795. They set up a series of sister republics in the former Dutch Republic and in various Italian states. Local people did not always welcome these changes. For example, the French made the Dutch pay a huge war indemnity, support a French occupying army of 25,000 soldiers, and give up some southern territories. The sister republics faced a future of subordination to French national interests.

as 200,000 casualties in the French armies alone in 1794 and 1795. More soldiers died in hospitals as a result of their wounds than on the battlefields. Constant warfare hampered world commerce and especially disrupted French overseas shipping. Times were now hard almost everywhere, because the dislocations of internal and external commerce provoked constant shortages.

Poland Extinguished, 1793–1795

France had survived in 1793 in part because its enemies were busy elsewhere. Fearing French influence, Prussia joined Russia in dividing up generous new slices of territory in the second partition of Poland (Map 19.3). As might be expected, Poland's reform movement became even more pro-French. Some leaders fled abroad, including Tadeusz Kościuszko (1746–1817), an officer who had been a foreign volunteer in the War of American Independence and who now escaped to Paris. In the spring of 1794, Kościuszko returned from France to lead a nationalist revolt.

The uprising failed. Kościuszko won a few victories, but when the Russian empress Catherine the Great's forces regrouped, they routed the Poles and Lithuanians. Kościuszko and other Polish Patriot leaders languished for years in Russian and Austrian prisons. Taking no further chances, Russia, Prussia, and Austria wiped Poland completely from the map in the third partition (1795). "The Polish question" would plague international relations for more than a century as Polish rebels flocked to any international upheaval that might undo the partitions. Beyond all this maneuvering lay the unsolved problem of Polish serfdom, which isolated the nation's gentry and townspeople from the rural masses.

Revolution in the Colonies

The revolution that produced so much upheaval in continental Europe transformed life in France's Caribbean colonies, too. These colonies were crucial to the French economy. Twice the size in land area of the neighboring British colonies, they also produced nearly twice as much revenue in exports. The slave population had doubled

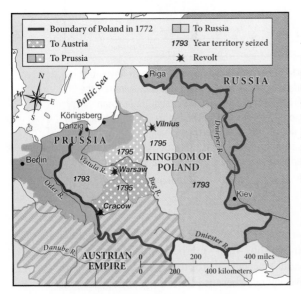

MAP 19.3   The Second and Third Partitions of Poland, 1793 and 1795   In 1793, Prussia took over territory that included 1.1 million Poles while Russia gained 3 million new inhabitants. Austria gave up any claims to Poland in exchange for help from Russia and Prussia in acquiring Bavaria. In the final division of 1795, Prussia absorbed an additional 900,000 Polish subjects, including those in Warsaw; Austria incorporated 1 million Poles and the city of Cracow; Russia gained another 2 million Poles. The three powers determined never to use the term *Kingdom of Poland* again. How had Poland become such a prey to the other powers?

in the French colonies in the twenty years before 1789. St. Domingue (present-day Haiti) was the most important French colony. Occupying the western half of the island of Hispaniola, it was inhabited not only by 465,000 slaves and 30,000 whites but also by 28,000 free people of color, whose primary job was to apprehend runaway slaves and ensure plantation security.

Despite the efforts of a Paris club called the Friends of Blacks, most French revolutionaries did not consider slavery a pressing problem. In August 1791, however, the slaves in northern St. Domingue organized a large-scale revolt. To restore authority over the slaves, the deputies in Paris granted civil and political rights to the free blacks. This action infuriated white planters and merchants, who in 1793 signed an agreement with Great Britain, now France's enemy in war, declaring British sovereignty over St. Domingue. To complicate matters further, Spain, which controlled the rest of the island and had entered on Great Britain's side in the war with France, offered freedom to individual slave rebels who joined the Spanish armies as long as they agreed to maintain the slave regime for the other blacks.

The few thousand French republican troops on St. Domingue were outnumbered, and to prevent complete military disaster, the French commissioner freed all the slaves in his jurisdiction in August 1793 without permission from the government in Paris. In February 1794, the National Convention formally abolished slavery and granted full rights to all black men in the colonies. These actions had the desired effect. One of the ablest black generals allied with the Spanish, the ex-slave François Dominique Toussaint L'Ouverture (1743–1803), changed sides and committed his troops to the French. Toussaint remained in charge until 1802, when Napoleon sent French armies to regain control of the island. They arrested Toussaint and transported him to France, where he died in prison. Toussaint

Toussaint L'Ouverture The leader of the St. Domingue slave uprising appears on horseback, in his general's uniform, sword in hand. His depiction in this print from the early nineteenth century makes him seem much like other military heroes from the time, including Napoleon Bonaparte. (Bibliothèque nationale, Paris, France/Archives Charmet/Bridgeman Images.)

became a hero to abolitionists everywhere, a potent symbol of black struggles to win freedom. Napoleon attempted to restore slavery, as he had in the other French Caribbean colonies of Guadeloupe and Martinique, but the remaining black generals defeated his armies and in 1804 proclaimed the Republic of Haiti.

Worldwide Reactions to Revolutionary Change

As the example of the colonies shows, the French Revolution inflamed politics and social relations far beyond Europe. It soon became one of the most divisive political issues in the United States. Thomas Jefferson wrote in January 1793 that "the liberty of the whole earth" depended on the Revolution's success; John Adams, in contrast, believed that the French Revolution had set back human progress hundreds of years. In India, the ruler of the southern kingdom of Mysore, Tipu Sultan, planted a liberty tree and set up a Jacobin Club in the futile hope of gaining French allies against the British.

Many had greeted the events of 1789 with unabashed enthusiasm. The English Unitarian minister Richard Price had exulted, "Behold, the light . . . after setting AMERICA free, reflected to FRANCE, and there kindled into a blaze that lays despotism in ashes, and warms and illuminates EUROPE." Democrats and reformers from many countries flooded to Paris to witness events firsthand. Supporters of the French Revolution in Great Britain joined constitutional and reform societies that sprang up in many cities. Pro-French feeling ran even stronger in Ireland. Catholics and Presbyterians, both excluded from the vote, came together in 1791 in the Society of United Irishmen, which eventually pressed for secession from England.

European elites became alarmed when the French abolished monarchy and nobility and encouraged popular participation in politics. The British government, for example, quickly suppressed the corresponding societies, charging that their contacts with the French were seditious. When the Society of United Irishmen timed a rebellion to coincide with an attempted French invasion in 1798, the British mercilessly repressed them, killing thirty thousand rebels.

Many leading intellectuals in the German states, including the philosopher Immanuel Kant, initially supported the revolutionary cause, but after 1793 most of them turned against the popular violence and military aggressiveness of the Revolution. The German states, still run by many separate rulers, experienced a profound artistic and intellectual revival, which eventually stimulated anti-French nationalism. This renaissance included a resurgence of intellectual life in the universities, a thriving press (1,225 journals were launched in the 1780s alone), and the multiplication of Masonic lodges and literary clubs.

Despite the turn in opinion, European rulers still dreaded the mere mention of revolution. Spain's royal government simply suppressed all news from France, fearing that it might ignite the spirit of revolt. Despite similar government controls on news in Russia, 278 outbreaks of peasant unrest occurred there between 1796 and 1798. When Naples revolted under French influence in 1799, 100 republicans, including leading intellectuals, were executed when the royalists returned to power.

Conclusion

Growing out of aspirations for freedom that also inspired the Dutch, Belgians, and Poles, the revolution that shook France permanently altered the political landscape of the Western world. Between 1789 and 1799, monarchy as a form of government gave way in France to a republic whose leaders were elected. Aristocracy based on rank and birth was undermined in favor of civil equality and the promotion of merit. Thousands of men held elective office for the first time. A revolutionary government tried to teach new values with a refashioned calendar, state festivals, and a civic religion. Its example inspired would-be revolutionaries everywhere.

But the French Revolution also had its darker side. The divisions created by the Revolution within France endured in many cases until after World War II. Even now, when asked by public-opinion surveys if it was right to execute the king in 1793, most French respondents say they believe that Louis XVI was guilty of treason but should not have been executed. The revolutionaries proclaimed human rights and democratic government as universal goals, but they also explicitly excluded women, even though they admitted Protestant, Jewish, and eventually black men. They used the new spirit of national pride to inspire armies and then used those armies to conquer other peoples. Their ideals of universal education, religious toleration, and democratic participation could not prevent the institution of new forms of government terror to persecute, imprison, and kill dissidents. These paradoxes created an opening for Napoleon Bonaparte, who rushed in with his remarkable military and political skills to push France—and with it all of Europe—in new directions.

REVIEW   Why did some groups outside of France embrace the French Revolution while others resisted it?

MAPPING THE WEST   Europe in 1799   France's expansion during the revolutionary wars threatened to upset the balance of power in Europe. A century earlier, the English and Dutch had allied and formed a Europe-wide coalition to check the territorial ambitions of Louis XIV. Thwarting French ambitions after 1799 would prove to be even more of a challenge to the other European powers. The Dutch had been reduced to satellite status, as had most of the Italian states. Even Austria and Prussia would suffer devastating losses to the French on the battlefield. Only a new coalition of European powers could stop France in the future.

Chapter Review

KEY TERMS AND PEOPLE

Be sure that you can identify the term or person and explain its historical significance.

Louis XVI (p. 554)

Marie-Antoinette (p. 554)

Estates General (p. 555)

Great Fear (p. 558)

Declaration of the Rights of Man and Citizen (p. 559)

Jacobin Club (p. 562)

Maximilien Robespierre (p. 563)

Terror (p. 563)

de-Christianization (p. 565)

Thermidorian Reaction (p. 569)

REVIEW QUESTIONS

1. How did the beginning of the French Revolution resemble the other revolutions of 1787–1789?

2. Why did the French Revolution turn in an increasingly radical direction after 1789?

3. What factors can explain the Terror? To what extent was it simply a response to a national emergency or a reflection of deeper problems within the French Revolution?

4. Why did some groups outside of France embrace the French Revolution while others resisted it?

MAKING CONNECTIONS

1. Should the French Revolution be viewed as the origin of democracy or the origin of totalitarianism (a government in which no dissent is allowed)? Explain.

2. Why did other European rulers find the French Revolution so threatening?

3. What made the French revolutionary armies so powerful in this period?

4. How was the French Revolution related to the Enlightenment that preceded it?

IMPORTANT EVENTS

1787	• Dutch Patriot revolt is stifled by Prussian invasion
1788	• Beginning of Austrian Netherlands resistance against reforms of Joseph II; opening of reform parliament in Poland
1789	• French Revolution begins
1790	• Internal divisions lead to collapse of resistance in Austrian Netherlands
1791	• Beginning of slave revolt in St. Domingue (Haiti)
1792	• Beginning of war between France and rest of Europe; second revolution of August 10 overthrows monarchy
1793	• Second partition of Poland by Austria and Russia; Louis XVI of France is executed for treason
1794	• Abolition of slavery in French colonies; Robespierre's government by terror falls
1795	• Third (final) partition of Poland; France annexes Austrian Netherlands
1797–1798	• Creation of "sister republics" in Italian states and Switzerland

20

Napoleon and the Revolutionary Legacy

1800–1830

CHAPTER FOCUS

How did Napoleon Bonaparte's actions force other European rulers to change their policies?

IN HER NOVEL *FRANKENSTEIN* (1818), the prototype for modern thrillers, Mary Shelley tells the story of a Swiss inventor, Dr. Frankenstein, who creates a humanlike monster. The monster terrifies all who encounter him and ends by destroying Frankenstein's own loved ones. Despite desperate chases across deserts and frozen landscapes, Frankenstein never manages to trap the monster, who is last seen hunched over his creator's deathbed.

Those who witnessed Napoleon Bonaparte's stunning rise to European dominance might have cast him as either Frankenstein or his monster. Like the scientist Frankenstein, Bonaparte created something dramatically new: the French Empire with himself as emperor. Like the former kings of France, he ruled under his first name. This Corsican artillery officer who spoke French with an Italian accent ended the French Revolution even while maintaining some of its most important innovations.

Bonaparte continued the revolutionary policy of conquest and annexation until it reached grotesque dimensions. His foreign policies made many see him as a monster hungry for dominion; he turned the sister republics of the revolutionary era into kingdoms personally ruled by his relatives, and he exacted tribute wherever he triumphed. Eventually, resistance to the French armies and the ever-mounting costs of military glory toppled Napoleon. The powers allied against him met and agreed to restore the monarchical governments that had been overthrown by the French, shrink France back to its prerevolutionary boundaries, and maintain this settlement against future demands for change.

Although the people of Europe longed for peace and stability in the aftermath of the Napoleonic whirlwind, they lived in a deeply unsettled world. Profoundly affected by French military occupation, many groups of people organized to demand ethnic and cultural autonomy, first from Napoleon and then from the restored governments after 1815. In 1830, a new round of revolutions broke out in France, Belgium, Poland, and some of the Italian states. The revolutionary legacy was far from exhausted.

The Rise of Napoleon Bonaparte

In 1799, a charismatic young general took over the French republic and set France on a new course. Within a year, **Napoleon Bonaparte** (1769–1821) had effectively ended the French Revolution and steered France toward an authoritarian state. As emperor after 1804, Bonaparte dreamed of European integration in the tradition of Augustus and Charlemagne. To achieve his goals, he compromised with the Catholic church and with exiled aristocrats willing to return to France. His most enduring accomplishment, the new Civil Code, tempered the principles of the Enlightenment and the Revolution with an insistence on the powers of fathers over children, husbands over wives, and employers over workers. His influence spread into many spheres as he personally patronized scientific inquiry and encouraged artistic styles in line with his vision of imperial greatness.

A General Takes Over

It would have seemed astonishing in 1795 that the twenty-six-year-old son of a noble family from the island of Corsica off the Italian coast would within four years become the supreme ruler of France and one of the greatest military leaders in world history. That year, Bonaparte was a penniless artillery officer, only recently released from prison as a presumed Robespierrist. Thanks to some early military successes and links to Parisian politicians, however, he was named commander of the French army in Italy in 1796.

Bonaparte's astounding success in the Italian campaigns of 1796–1797 launched his meteoric career. With an army of fewer than fifty thousand men, he defeated the Piedmontese and the Austrians. In quick order, he established client republics dependent on his own authority, negotiated with the Austrians himself, and molded the army into his personal force by paying the soldiers in cash taken as tribute from the newly conquered territories. He pleased the Directory government by sending home wagonloads of Italian masterpieces of art, which were added to Parisian museum collections (most are still there) after being paraded in victory festivals.

In 1798, the Directory set aside its plans to invade England, gave Bonaparte command of the army raised for that purpose, and sent him across the Mediterranean Sea to Egypt. The Directory government hoped that French occupation of Egypt would strike a blow at British trade by cutting the route to India. Although the French defeated a much larger Egyptian army, the British admiral Lord Horatio Nelson destroyed the French fleet while it was anchored in Aboukir Bay, cutting the French off from home. Bonaparte insisted that he aimed to liberate the Egyptians from the Ottoman Turks, but though he proclaimed his respect for Islam, he also forced through Enlightenment-inspired legal reforms such as equality before the law and religious toleration. In the face of determined resistance and an outbreak of the bubonic plague, the French armies retreated from a further expedition in Syria.

Even the failures of the Egyptian campaign did not dull Bonaparte's luster. Bonaparte had taken France's leading scientists with him on the expedition, and his soldiers had discovered a slab of black basalt dating from 196 B.C.E. written in both hieroglyphic and Greek. Called the Rosetta stone after a nearby town, it enabled scholars to finally decipher the hieroglyphs used by the ancient Egyptians.

With his army pinned down by Nelson's victory at sea, Bonaparte slipped out of Egypt and made his way secretly to southern France in October 1799. He arrived home at just the right moment: the war in Europe was going badly. The territories of the former Austrian Netherlands had revolted against French conscription laws, and deserters swelled the ranks of rebels in western France. Disillusioned members of the government saw in Bonaparte's return an occasion to overturn the constitution of 1795. They got their wish on November 9, 1799, when troops guarding the legislature ejected those who opposed Bonaparte and left the remaining ones to vote to abolish the Directory and establish a new three-man executive called the consulate.

Bonaparte became **First Consul**, a title revived from the ancient Roman republic. A new constitution—with no declaration of rights—was submitted to the voters. Millions abstained from voting, and the government falsified the results to give an appearance of even greater support to the new regime.

From Republic to Empire

When the constitution of 1799 made Napoleon the First Consul (of three), it gave him the right to pick the Council of State, which drew up all laws. The French government was no longer representative in any real sense: the new constitution eliminated direct elections for deputies and granted no independent powers to the three houses of the legislature. Napoleon and his advisers chose the legislature's members out of a small pool of "notables." Almost all men over twenty-one could vote in the plebiscite (referendum) to approve the constitution, but their only option was to choose *yes* or *no*.

Napoleon's most urgent task was to reconcile to his regime Catholics who had been alienated by revolutionary policies. Although nominally Catholic, Napoleon held no deep religious convictions. "How can there be order in the state without religion?"

he asked cynically. "When a man is dying of hunger beside another who is stuffing himself, he cannot accept this difference if there is not an authority who tells him: 'God wishes it so.'" In 1801, a concordat with Pope Pius VII (r. 1800–1823) ended a decade of church-state conflict in France. The pope validated all sales of church lands, and the government agreed to pay the salaries of bishops and priests who would swear loyalty to the state. Catholicism was officially recognized as the religion of "the great majority of French citizens." (The state also paid Protestant pastors' salaries.)

Napoleon continued the centralization of state power that had begun under the absolutist monarchy of Louis XIV. As First Consul, he appointed prefects who directly supervised local affairs in every department in the country. He created the Bank of France to facilitate government borrowing and relied on gold and silver coinage rather than paper money. He improved tax collection but balanced the budget only by exacting tribute from the territories he conquered.

Napoleon never relied on mass executions to maintain control, but he refused to allow those who opposed him to meet in clubs, influence elections, or publish newspapers. A decree reduced the number of newspapers in Paris from seventy-three to thirteen (and then finally to four). Government censors had to approve all operas and plays, and they banned "offensive" artistic works even more frequently than their royal predecessors had. The minister of police, Joseph Fouché, once a leading figure in the Terror of 1793–1794, imposed house arrest, arbitrary imprisonment, and surveillance of political dissidents. Political contest and debate shriveled to almost nothing. When a bomb attack on Napoleon's carriage failed in 1800, Fouché suppressed the evidence of a royalist plot and instead arrested hundreds of former Jacobins.

When it suited him, Napoleon also struck against royalist conspirators. In 1804, he ordered his police to kidnap the duke d'Enghien from his residence in Germany. Napoleon had intelligence, which proved to be false, that d'Enghien had joined a plot in Paris against him. Even when he learned the truth, he insisted that a military tribunal try d'Enghien, a close relative of the dead king Louis XVI. After a summary trial, d'Enghien was shot on the spot.

By then, Napoleon's political intentions had become clear. He had named himself First Consul for life in 1802, and in 1804, with the pope's blessing, he crowned himself emperor. Once again, plebiscites approved his decisions but only yes/no alternatives were offered.

Napoleon's face and name soon adorned coins, engravings, histories, paintings, and public monuments. His favorite painters embellished his legend by depicting him as a warrior-hero of mythic proportions even though he was short and physically unimpressive in person. He embarked on ostentatious building projects, including the Arc de Triomphe and the Stock Exchange.

Napoleon worked hard at establishing his reputation as an efficient administrator with broad intellectual interests. When not on military campaigns, he worked on state affairs, usually until 10:00 p.m., taking only a few minutes for each meal. To establish his authority, Napoleon relied on men who had served with him in the army. His bureaucracy was based on a patron-client relationship, with Napoleon as the ultimate patron.

Napoleon's Coronation as Emperor   In this detail from *The Coronation of Napoleon and Josephine* (1805–1807), Jacques-Louis David shows Napoleon crowning his wife at the ceremony of 1804. Napoleon orchestrated the entire event and took the only active role in it: Pope Pius VII gave his blessing to the ceremony (he can be seen seated behind Napoleon), but Napoleon crowned himself. What is the significance of Napoleon crowning himself? (Louvre, Paris, France / Bridgeman Images.)

Combining aristocratic and revolutionary values in a new social hierarchy that rewarded merit and talent, Napoleon personally chose as senators the nation's most illustrious men, among them former nobles. Intending to replace both the old nobility of birth and the republic's strict emphasis on equality, in 1802 he took the first step toward creating a new nobility by founding the Legion of Honor. (Members of the legion received lifetime pensions along with their titles.) In 1808, Napoleon introduced a complete hierarchy of noble titles, ranging from princes down to barons and chevaliers. To go along with their new titles, Napoleon gave his favorite generals huge fortunes, often in the form of estates in the conquered territories.

Napoleon's own family reaped the greatest benefits. He made his older brother, Joseph, ruler of the newly established kingdom of Naples in 1806, the same year he installed his younger brother Louis as king of Holland. He proclaimed his twenty-three-year-old stepson, Eugène de Beauharnais, viceroy of Italy in 1805 and established his sister Caroline and brother-in-law General Joachim Murat as king and queen of Naples in 1808 when he moved Joseph to the throne of Spain. Napoleon wanted to establish an imperial succession, but he lacked an heir. In thirteen years of marriage, his wife, Josephine, had borne no children, so in 1809 he divorced her and in 1810 married the eighteen-year-old princess Marie-Louise of Austria. The next year Marie-Louise gave birth to a son, to whom Napoleon immediately gave the title king of Rome.

The New Paternalism: The Civil Code

As part of his restoration of order, Napoleon brought a paternalistic model of power to his state. He successfully established a new **Civil Code**, completed in 1804. Called the Napoleonic Code as a way of further exalting the emperor's image, it reasserted the Old Regime's patriarchal system of male domination over women and insisted on a father's control over his children, which revolutionary legislation had limited. For example, a child under age sixteen who refused to follow his or her father's commands could be sent to prison for up to a month with no hearing of any sort. Still, the Civil Code protected many of the gains of the French Revolution by defining and ensuring property rights, guaranteeing religious liberty, and establishing a uniform system of law that provided equal treatment for all adult males and affirmed the right of men to choose their professions.

Although the code maintained the equal division of family property between all children, both male and female, it sharply curtailed women's rights in other respects. Napoleon wanted to restrict women to the private sphere of the home. The law obligated a husband to support his wife, but the husband alone controlled any property held in common; a wife could not sue in court, sell or mortgage her own property, or contract a debt without her husband's consent. Divorce was severely restricted. A wife could petition for divorce only if her husband brought his mistress to live in the family home. In contrast, a wife convicted of adultery could be imprisoned for up to two years. The code's framers saw these discrepancies as a way to reinforce the family and make women responsible for private virtue, while leaving public decisions to men. Not until 1965 did French wives gain legal status equal to that of their husbands.

Napoleon took little interest in girls' education, believing that girls should spend most of their time at home learning religion, manners, and such "female occupations" as sewing and music. For boys, by contrast, the government set up a new system of lycées, state-run secondary schools in which students wore military uniforms and drumrolls signaled the beginning and end of classes. The lycées offered wider access to education and thus helped achieve Napoleon's goal of opening careers to those with talent, regardless of their social origins. (The lycées have dropped the military trappings and are now coeducational, but they are still the heart of the French educational system.)

The new paternalism extended to relations between employers and employees. The state required all workers to carry a work card attesting to their good conduct, and it prohibited all workers' organizations. After 1806, arbitration boards settled labor disputes, but they took employers at their word while treating workers as minors, demanding that foremen and shop superintendents represent them. The limitations on workers' rights won Napoleon the support of French business.

Patronage of Science and Intellectual Life

An impressive outpouring of new theoretical and practical scientific work rewarded Napoleon's efforts to promote science. Experiments with balloons led to the discovery of laws about the expansion of gases, and research on fossil shells prepared the way for new theories of evolutionary change later in the nineteenth century. The surgeon Dominique-Jean Larrey developed new techniques of battlefield amputation and medical care during Napoleon's wars, winning an appointment as an officer in the Legion of Honor and becoming a baron with a pension.

Napoleon aimed to modernize French society through science, but he could not tolerate criticism. Napoleon considered most writers useless or dangerous. Among those forced into exile was Anne-Louise-Germaine de Staël (1766–1817), the daughter of Louis XVI's finance minister, Jacques Necker. When explaining his desire to banish her, Napoleon exclaimed, "She is a machine in motion who stirs up the salons." While exiled in the German states, de Staël wrote *Corinne* (1807), a novel whose heroine is a brilliant woman thwarted by a patriarchal system, and *On Germany* (1810), an account of the important new literary currents east of the Rhine. Her books were banned in France.

Although Napoleon restored the strong authority of state and religion in France, many royalists and Catholics still criticized him as an impious usurper. François-René de Chateaubriand (1768–1848) admired Napoleon as "the strong man who has saved us from the abyss," but he preferred a restored Bourbon monarchy. In his view, Napoleon

Germaine de Staël   One of the most fascinating intellectuals of her time, Anne-Louise-Germaine de Staël seemed to irritate Napoleon more than any other person did. Daughter of Louis XVI's Swiss Protestant finance minister, Jacques Necker, and wife of a Swedish diplomat, Madame de Staël frequently criticized Napoleon's policies. She published best-selling novels and influential literary criticism, and whenever allowed to reside in Paris she encouraged the intellectual and political dissidents from Napoleon's regime. In this painting from 1809, Élisabeth Vigée-Lebrun depicts her as Corinne, the heroine of one of her novels. (Musée d'Art et d'Histoire, Geneva, Switzerland/ Bridgeman Images.)

had not properly understood the need to defend Christian values against the Enlightenment's excessive reliance on reason. Chateaubriand wrote his *Genius of Christianity* (1802) to draw attention to the power and mystery of faith. His book appeared during a rare lull in wars that soon engulfed much of Europe.

REVIEW   In what ways did Napoleon continue the French Revolution, and in what ways did he break with it?

"Europe Was at My Feet": Napoleon's Conquests

Napoleon revolutionized the art of war with tactics and strategies based on a highly mobile army. By 1812, he was ruling a European empire more extensive than any since ancient Rome (Map 20.1). Yet that empire had already begun to crumble, and with it went Napoleon's power at home. Napoleon's empire failed because it was based on a contradiction: Napoleon tried to reduce virtually all nations of Europe to the status of colonial dependents when Europe had long consisted of independent states. The result, inevitably, was a great upsurge in nationalist feeling that has dominated European politics to the present.

The Grand Army and Its Victories, 1800–1807

Napoleon attributed his military success "three-quarters to morale" and the rest to leadership and superiority of numbers at the point of attack. Conscription provided the large numbers: 1.3 million men ages twenty to twenty-four were drafted between 1800 and 1812, another 1 million in 1813–1814. Military service was a means of social mobility. The men who rose through the ranks to become officers were young, ambitious, and accustomed to the new ways of war. Consequently, the French army had higher morale than the armies of other powers, most of which rejected conscription as too democratic and continued to restrict their officer corps to the nobility.

To end squabbling among his generals, Napoleon united all the French armies into one—the Grand Army—under his personal command. By 1812, he was commanding 700,000 troops; while 250,000 soldiers fought in Spain, others remained garrisoned in France. In any given battle, between 70,000 and 180,000 men, not all of them French, fought for France. Napoleon inspired almost fanatical loyalty. He fought alongside his soldiers in some sixty battles and had nineteen horses shot from under him. One opponent said that Napoleon's presence alone was worth fifty thousand men.

A brilliant strategist who carefully studied the demands of war, Napoleon outmaneuvered virtually all his opponents. He went directly for the main body of the opposing army and tried to crush it in a lightning campaign. He gathered the largest possible army for one great and decisive battle and then followed with a relentless pursuit to break enemy morale altogether. His military command, like his rule within France, was personal and highly centralized. He essentially served as his own

MAP 20.1 Napoleon's Empire at Its Height, 1812 In 1812, Napoleon had at least nominal control of almost all of western Europe. Even before he made his fatal mistake of invading Russia, however, his authority had been undermined in Spain and seriously weakened in the Italian and German states. Still earlier, he had given up his dreams of a worldwide empire. French armies withdrew from Egypt in 1801 and from St. Domingue (Haiti) in 1802. In 1803, Napoleon sold the Louisiana Territory to the United States.

operations officer. This style worked as long as Napoleon could be on the battlefield, but he failed to train independent subordinates to take over in his absence. He also faced constant difficulties in supplying a rapidly moving army, which, because of its size, could not always live off the land.

One of Napoleon's greatest advantages was the lack of coordination among his enemies. Britain dominated the seas but did not want to field huge land armies. On the continent, the French republic had already set up satellites in the Nether-lands and Italy, which served as a buffer against the big powers to the east—Austria, Prussia, and Russia. By maneuvering diplomatically and militarily, Napoleon could usually take these on one by one. He won striking victories against the Austrians at Marengo and Hohenlinden in 1800, forcing them to agree to peace terms. Once the Austrians had withdrawn, Britain agreed to the Treaty of Amiens in 1802, effectively ending hostilities on the continent. Napoleon considered the peace with Great Britain merely a truce, however, and it lasted only until 1803.

Napoleon used the breathing space not only to consolidate his position before taking up arms again but also to send an expeditionary force to the Caribbean colony of St. Domingue to regain control of the island. Continuing resistance among the black population and an epidemic of yellow fever forced Napoleon to withdraw his troops from St. Domingue and abandon his plans to extend his empire to the Western Hemisphere. As part of his retreat, he sold the Louisiana Territory to the United States in 1803.

When war resumed in Europe, the British navy once more proved its superiority by blocking an attempted French invasion and by defeating the French and their Spanish allies in a huge naval battle at Trafalgar in 1805. France lost many ships; the British lost no vessels, but their renowned admiral Lord Horatio Nelson died in the battle.

On land, Napoleon remained invincible. In 1805, Austria took up arms again when Napoleon demanded that it declare neutrality in the conflict with Britain. Napoleon promptly captured twenty-five thousand Austrian soldiers at Ulm, in Bavaria, in 1805. After marching on to Vienna, he again trounced the Austrians, who had been joined by their new ally, Russia. The battle of Austerlitz, often con-sidered Napoleon's greatest victory, was fought on December 2, 1805, the first anniversary of his coronation.

After maintaining neutrality for a decade, Prussia now declared war on France. In 1806, the French routed the Prussian army at Jena and Auerstädt. In 1807, Napoleon defeated the Russians at Friedland. Personal negotiations between Napo-leon and the young tsar Alexander I (r. 1801–1825) resulted in a humiliating settlement imposed on Prussia, which paid the price for temporary reconciliation between France and Russia; the Treaties of Tilsit turned Prussian lands west of the Elbe River into the kingdom of Westphalia under Napoleon's brother Jerome, and Prussia's Polish provinces became the duchy of Warsaw.

The Impact of French Victories

By annexing some territories and setting up others as satellite kingdoms with much-reduced autonomy, Napoleon attempted to colonize large parts of Europe (see Map 20.1, page 587). He brought the disparate German and Italian states together so that he could rule them more effectively and exploit their resources for his own ends. In July 1806, he established the Confederation of the Rhine, which soon included almost all the German states except Austria and Prussia. The Holy Roman Emperor gave up his title, held since the thirteenth century, and became simply the emperor of Austria. Napoleon established three units in Italy: the territories directly annexed to France and the satellite kingdoms of Italy and Naples. Italy had not been so unified since the Roman Empire.

Napoleon forced French-style reforms on both the annexed territories, which were ruled directly from France, and the satellite kingdoms, which were usually ruled by one or another of Napoleon's relatives but with a certain autonomy. French-style reforms included abolishing serfdom, eliminating seigneurial dues, introducing the Napoleonic Code, suppressing monasteries, and subordinating church to state, as well as extending civil rights to Jews and other religious minorities. Yet almost everyone had some cause for complaint. Republicans regretted Napoleon's conversion of the sister republics into kingdoms. Tax increases and ever-rising conscription quotas fomented discontent as well. The annexed territories and satellite kingdoms paid half the cost of Napoleon's wars.

Almost everywhere, conflicts arose between Napoleon's desire for a standardized, centralized government and local insistence on maintaining customs and traditions. Sometimes his own relatives sided with the countries they ruled. Napoleon's brother Louis, for instance, would not allow conscription in the Netherlands because the Dutch had never had compulsory military service. When Napoleon tried to introduce an economic policy banning trade with Great Britain, Louis's lax enforcement infuriated the emperor, and Napoleon annexed the satellite kingdom in 1810.

Napoleon's victories forced defeated rulers to rethink their political and cultural assumptions. After the crushing defeat of Prussia in 1806 left his country greatly reduced in territory, Frederick William III (r. 1797–1840) abolished serfdom and allowed non-nobles to buy and enclose land. Peasants gained their personal independence from their noble landlords, who could no longer sell them to pay gambling debts, for example, or refuse them permission to marry. Yet the lives of the former serfs remained bleak; they were left without land, and their landlords no longer had to care for them in hard times. The king's advisers also overhauled the army to make the high command more efficient and to open the way to the appointment of middle-class officers. Prussia instituted these reforms to try to compete with the French, not to promote democracy. As one reformer wrote to Frederick William, "We must do from above what the French have done from below."

Reform received lip service in Russia. Tsar Alexander I had gained his throne after an aristocratic coup deposed and killed his autocratic and capricious father, Paul (r. 1796–1801), and in the early years of his reign the remorseful young ruler created Western-style ministries, lifted restrictions on importing foreign books, and founded six new universities. In addition, reform commissions studied abuses, nobles were encouraged to free their serfs voluntarily (a few actually did so), and there was even talk of drafting a constitution. But none of these efforts reached beneath the surface of Russian life, and by the second decade of his reign Alexander began to reject the Enlightenment spirit that his grandmother Catherine the Great had instilled in him.

The one power always standing between Napoleon and total dominance of Europe was Great Britain. The British ruled the seas and financed anyone who would oppose Napoleon. In an effort to bankrupt this "nation of shopkeepers" by choking its trade, Napoleon inaugurated the **Continental System** in 1806. It prohibited all commerce between Great Britain and France or France's dependent states and allies. At first, the system worked: in 1807–1808, British exports dropped by 20 percent and manufacturing by 10 percent. The British retaliated by confiscating merchandise from ships that sailed into or out of the prohibited ports—they even took merchandise from powers that were neutral in the wars.

In the midst of continuing wars, moreover, the Continental System proved impossible to enforce, and widespread smuggling brought British goods into the European market. British growth continued, despite some setbacks; calico-printing works, for example, quadrupled their production, and imports of raw cotton increased by 40 percent. At the same time, French and other continental industries benefited from the temporary protection from British competition.

Smuggling British goods was only one way of opposing the French. Almost everywhere in Europe, resistance began as local opposition to French demands for money or draftees but eventually prompted a more nationalistic patriotic defense. Italians formed a network of secret societies called the *carbonari* ("charcoal burners"), which got its name from the practice of marking each new member's forehead with a charcoal mark. Throughout the nineteenth century, the carbonari played a leading role in Italian nationalism. In the German states, intellectuals wrote passionate defenses of the virtues of the German nation and of the superiority of German literature.

No nations bucked under Napoleon's reins more than Spain and Portugal. In 1807, Napoleon sent 100,000 troops through Spain to invade Portugal, Great Britain's ally. The royal family fled to the Portuguese colony of Brazil, but fighting continued, aided by a British army. When Napoleon got his brother Joseph named king of Spain in place of the senile Charles IV (r. 1788–1808), the Spanish clergy and nobles raised bands of peasants to fight the French occupiers. Even Napoleon's taking personal command of the French forces failed to quell the Spanish, who for six years fought a war of national independence that pinned down thousands of French soldiers. Germaine de Staël commented that Napoleon "never understood that a war might be a crusade. . . . He never reckoned with the one power that no arms could overcome—the enthusiasm of a whole people."

Spanish peasants hated French requisitioning of their food supplies and sought to defend their priests against French anticlericalism. Spanish nobles feared revolutionary reforms and were willing to defend the old monarchy in the person of the young Ferdinand VII, heir to Charles IV, even while Ferdinand himself was congratulating Napoleon on his victories. The Spanish Catholic church spread anti-French propaganda that equated Napoleon with heresy. As the former archbishop of Seville wrote to the archbishop of Granada in 1808, "You realize that we must not recognize as king a Freemason, heretic, Lutheran, as are all the Bonapartes and the French nation." The Spanish peasant rebels, assisted by the British, countered every French massacre with atrocities of their own. They tortured their French prisoners (boiling one general alive) and lynched collaborators.

From Russian Winter to Final Defeat, 1812–1815

Despite opposition, Napoleon ruled over an extensive empire by 1812. Only two major European states remained fully independent—Great Britain and Russia—but once allied they would successfully challenge his dominion and draw many other states to their side. Britain sent aid to the Portuguese and Spanish rebels, while Russia once again prepared for war. Tsar Alexander I made peace with the Ottoman Turks and allied himself with Great Britain and Sweden. In 1812, Napoleon invaded Russia with 250,000 horses and 680,000 men, including contingents of Italians, Poles, Swiss, Dutch, and Germans. This daring move proved to be his undoing.

Napoleon followed his usual strategy of trying to strike quickly, but the Russian generals avoided confrontation and retreated eastward, destroying anything that might be useful to the invaders. In September, on the road to Moscow, Napoleon finally engaged the main Russian force in the gigantic battle of Borodino (see Map 20.1, page 587). In just that one day the French casualties numbered 30,000 men; the Russians lost 45,000. Once again the Russians retreated, leaving Moscow undefended. When Napoleon approached, the departing Russians set the wooden city on fire. Within a week, three-fourths of it had burned to the ground. Still Alexander refused to negotiate, and French morale plunged with worsening problems of supply. Weeks of constant marching in the dirt and heat had worn down the foot soldiers, who were dying of disease or deserting in large numbers.

In October, Napoleon began his retreat; in November came the cold. A German soldier in the Grand Army described trying to cook fistfuls of raw bran with snow to make something like bread. Within a week the Grand Army lost 30,000 horses and had to abandon most of its artillery and food supplies. Russian forces harassed the retreating army, now more pathetic than grand. By December only 100,000 troops remained, less than one-sixth the original number, and the retreat had turned into a rout: the Russians had captured 200,000 soldiers, including 3,000 officers.

Napoleon had made a classic military mistake that would be repeated by Adolf Hitler in World War II: fighting a war on two distant fronts simultaneously. The Spanish war tied down 250,000 French troops and forced Napoleon to bully Prussia and Austria into supplying soldiers of dubious loyalty for the Moscow campaign; those soldiers deserted at the first opportunity. The fighting in Spain and Portugal also exacerbated the already substantial logistical and communications problems involved in marching to Moscow.

Napoleon's humiliation might have been temporary if the British and Russians had not successfully organized a coalition to complete the job. By the spring of 1813, Napoleon had replenished his army with another 250,000 men. With British financial support, Russian, Austrian, Prussian, and Swedish armies met the French outside Leipzig in October 1813 and defeated Napoleon in the Battle of the Nations. One by one, Napoleon's German allies deserted him to join the German nationalist "war of liberation." The Confederation of the Rhine dissolved, and the Dutch revolted and restored the prince of Orange. Joseph Bonaparte fled Spain, and a combined Spanish-Portuguese army under British command invaded France. In only a few months, the allied powers crossed the Rhine and marched toward

Paris. In March 1814, the French Senate deposed Napoleon, who abdicated when his remaining generals refused to fight. Napoleon went into exile on the island of Elba off the Italian coast. His wife, Marie-Louise, refused to accompany him. The allies restored to the throne Louis XVIII (r. 1814–1824), the brother of Louis XVI, beheaded during the Revolution. (Louis XVI's son was known as Louis XVII even though he died in prison in 1795 without ever ruling.)

Napoleon had one last chance to regain power. Louis XVIII was caught between nobles returning from exile, who demanded a complete restoration of their lands and powers, and the vast majority of ordinary people, who had supported either the republic or Napoleon during the previous twenty-five years. Sensing an opportunity, Napoleon escaped from Elba in early 1815 and, landing in southern France, made swift progress to Paris. Although he had left in ignominy, now crowds cheered him and former soldiers volunteered to serve him. The period eventually known as the Hundred Days (the length of time between Napoleon's escape and his final defeat) had begun. Louis XVIII fled across the border, waiting for help from the powers allied against Napoleon.

Napoleon quickly moved his reconstituted army of 74,000 men into present-day Belgium. At first, it seemed that he might succeed in separately fighting the two armies arrayed against him—a Prussian army of some 60,000 men and a joint force of 68,000 Belgian, Dutch, German, and British troops led by British general Sir Arthur Wellesley (1769–1852), duke of Wellington. The decisive **battle of Waterloo** took place on June 18, 1815, less than ten miles from Brussels. Napoleon's forces attacked but failed to dislodge their opponents. Late in the afternoon, the Prussians arrived and completed the rout. Napoleon had no choice but to abdicate again. This time the victorious allies banished him permanently to the remote island of St. Helena, far off the coast of West Africa, where he died in 1821 at the age of fifty-two.

The cost of Napoleon's rule was high: 750,000 French soldiers and 400,000 others from annexed and satellite states died between 1800 and 1815. Yet his impact on world history was undeniable. Napoleon's plans for a united Europe, his insistence on spreading the legal reforms of the French Revolution, his social welfare programs, and even his inadvertent awakening of national sentiment set the agenda for European history in the modern era.

> **REVIEW**   Why was Napoleon able to gain control over so much of Europe's territory?

The "Restoration" of Europe

Even while Napoleon was making his last desperate bid for power, his enemies were meeting in the Congress of Vienna (1814–1815) to decide the fate of postrevolutionary, post-Napoleonic Europe. Although interrupted by the Hundred Days, the

Congress of Vienna settled the boundaries of European states, determined who would rule each nation, and established a new framework for international relations based on periodic meetings, or congresses, between the major powers. The doctrine of conservatism that emerged in reaction to the events of the French Revolution bolstered this post-Napoleonic order and in some places went hand in hand with a revival of religion.

The Congress of Vienna, 1814–1815

In addition to determining the boundaries of France, the congress had to decide the fate of Napoleon's duchy of Warsaw, the German province of Saxony, the Netherlands, the states once part of the Confederation of the Rhine, and various Italian territories. All had either changed hands or been created during the wars. These issues were resolved by face-to-face negotiations among representatives of the five major powers: Austria, Russia, Prussia, Britain, and France. With its aim to establish a long-lasting, negotiated peace endorsed by all parties, both winners and losers, the Congress of Vienna provided a model for the twentieth-century League of Nations and United Nations. The congress system, or "concert of Europe," helped prevent another major war until the 1850s, and no conflict comparable to the Napoleonic wars would occur again until 1914.

Austria's chief negotiator, Prince **Klemens von Metternich** (1773–1859), took the lead in devising the settlement and shaping the post-Napoleonic order. A well-educated nobleman who spoke five languages, Metternich served as a minister in the Austrian cabinet from 1809 to 1848. He aimed to return as much as possible to the pre-1789 political order, but to do so he also needed to maintain France's great-power status as a counter to Russia and Prussia. He therefore worked with the British prime minister Robert Castlereagh (1769–1822) to ensure a moderate agreement. Metternich and Castlereagh believed that French aggression must be contained, because it had threatened the European peace since the days of Louis XIV, but at the same time that France must remain a major player to prevent any one European power from dominating the others. Castlereagh hoped to make Britain the arbiter of European affairs, but he knew this could be accomplished only through adroit diplomacy because the British constitutional monarchy had little in common with most of its more absolutist continental counterparts.

The task of ensuring France's status at the Congress of Vienna fell to Prince Charles Maurice de Talleyrand (1754–1838), an aristocrat and former bishop who had embraced the French Revolution, served as Napoleon's foreign minister, and ended as foreign minister to Louis XVIII after helping arrange the emperor's overthrow. When the French army failed to oppose Napoleon's return to power in the Hundred Days, the allies took away all territory conquered since 1790, levied an indemnity against France, and required it to support an army of occupation until it had paid.

The goal of the Congress of Vienna was to achieve postwar stability by establishing secure states with guaranteed borders (Map 20.2). Because the congress aimed to "restore" as many regimes as possible to their former rulers, this epoch is

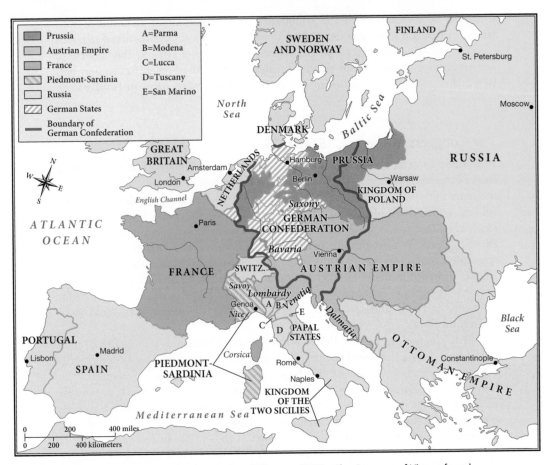

MAP 20.2 Europe after the Congress of Vienna, 1815   The Congress of Vienna forced France to return to its 1789 borders. The Austrian Netherlands and the Dutch Republic were united in a new kingdom of the Netherlands, the German states were joined in a German Confederation that built on Napoleon's Confederation of the Rhine, and Napoleon's duchy of Warsaw became the kingdom of Poland with the tsar of Russia as king. To compensate for its losses in Poland, Prussia gained territory in Saxony and on the left bank of the Rhine. Austria reclaimed the Italian provinces of Lombardy and Venetia and the Dalmatian coast.

sometimes labeled the **restoration**. But simple restoration was not always feasible. The congress turned the duchy of Warsaw, for example, into a new Polish kingdom but made the tsar of Russia its king. (Poland would not regain its independence until 1918.) The former Dutch Republic and the Austrian Netherlands, both annexed to France, were now united as the new kingdom of the Netherlands under the restored stadholder. Austria took charge of the German Confederation, which replaced the defunct Holy Roman Empire and also included Prussia.

The Congress of Vienna also resolved various international trade issues. Great Britain, which had abolished its slave trade in 1807, urged the congress to condemn that trade for other nations. The congress agreed in principle; in reality, however, the slave trade continued in many places until 1850. Nearly three million Africans were sold into slavery between 1800 and 1850, and most were transported on either Portuguese or Brazilian slave ships.

To impart spiritual substance to this very calculated settlement of political affairs, Tsar Alexander proposed the Holy Alliance, which called on divine assistance in upholding religion, peace, and justice. Prussia and Austria signed the agreement, but Great Britain refused to accede to what Castlereagh called "a piece of sublime mysticism and nonsense." Despite the reassertion of traditional religious principles, the congress had in fact given birth to a new diplomatic order: in the future, the legitimacy of states depended on the treaty system, not on "divine right."

The Emergence of Conservatism

The French Revolution and Napoleonic domination of Europe had shown contemporaries that government could be changed overnight, that the old hierarchies could be overthrown in the name of reason, and that even Christianity could be written off or at least profoundly altered with the stroke of a pen. After the French Revolution and the Napoleonic domination of Europe, the old order no longer commanded automatic obedience. It was now merely *old*, no longer "natural" and "timeless." It had been ousted once and therefore might fall again. People needed reasons to believe in their restored governments. The political doctrine that justified the restoration was **conservatism**.

Conservatives benefited from the disillusionment that permeated Europe after 1815. They saw a logical progression in recent history: the Enlightenment, based on reason, led to the French Revolution, with its bloody guillotine and horrifying Terror, which in turn spawned the authoritarian and militaristic Napoleon. Therefore, those who espoused conservatism rejected both the Enlightenment and the French Revolution. They favored monarchies over republics, tradition over revolution, and established religion over Enlightenment skepticism.

The original British critic of the French Revolution, Edmund Burke (1729–1799), inspired many of the conservatives who followed. He had argued that the revolutionaries erred in thinking they could construct an entirely new government based on reason. Government, Burke said, had to be rooted in long experience, which evolved over generations. All change must be gradual and must respect national and historical traditions. Like Burke, later conservatives believed that religious and other major traditions were an essential foundation for any society. Most of them took their resistance to change even further, however, and tried to restore the pre-1789 social order.

Conservatives blamed the French Revolution's attack on religion on the skepticism and anticlericalism of such Enlightenment thinkers as Voltaire, and they defended both hereditary monarchy and the authority of the church, whether Catholic or Protestant. Louis de Bonald, an official under the restored French monarchy, insisted that "the revolution began with the declaration of the rights of man and will only finish when the rights of God are declared." In this view, an enduring social order could be constructed only on the foundations provided by the church, the state, and the patriarchal family. Faith, sentiment, history, and tradition must fill the vacuum left by the failures of reason and excessive belief in individual rights. Across Europe, these views were taken up and elaborated by government advisers, professors, and writers.

The restored French monarchy provided a major test for conservatism because the returning Bourbons had to confront the legacy of twenty-five years of upheaval. Louis XVIII tried to ensure a measure of continuity by maintaining Napoleon's Civil Code. He also guaranteed the rights of ownership to church lands sold during the revolutionary period and created a parliament composed of the Chamber of Peers, nominated by the king, and the Chamber of Deputies, elected by very restricted suffrage (fewer than 100,000 voters in a population of 30 million). In making these concessions, the king tried to follow a moderate course of compromise, but the Ultras (ultraroyalists) pushed for complete repudiation of the revolutionary past. When Louis returned to power after Napoleon's final defeat, armed royalist bands attacked and murdered hundreds of Bonapartists and former revolutionaries. In 1816, the Ultras insisted on abolishing divorce and set up special courts to punish opponents of the regime. When an assassin killed Louis XVIII's nephew in 1820, the Ultras successfully demanded even more extreme measures.

The Revival of Religion

The experience of revolutionary upheaval and nearly constant warfare prompted many to renew their religious faith once peace returned. In France, the Catholic church sent missionaries to hold open-air "ceremonies of reparation" to express repentance for the outrages of revolution. In Rome, the papacy reestablished the Jesuit order, which had been disbanded during the Enlightenment.

In parts of Protestant Germany and Britain, religious revival had begun in the eighteenth century with the rise of Pietism and Methodism, movements that stressed individual religious experience. The English Methodists followed John Wesley (1703–1791), who had preached an emotional, morally austere, and very personal "method" of gaining salvation. The Methodists, or Wesleyans, gradually separated from the Church of England and in the early decades of the nineteenth century attracted thousands of members in huge revival meetings that lasted for days. Shopkeepers, artisans, agricultural laborers, miners, and workers in cottage industries, both male and female, flocked to the new denomination. In their hostility to elaborate ritual and their encouragement of popular preaching, the Methodists in England fostered a sense of democratic community and even a rudimentary sexual equality. From the beginning, women preachers traveled on horseback to preach in barns, town halls, and textile dye houses. The Methodist Sunday schools that taught thousands of poor children to read and write eventually helped create greater demands for working-class political participation.

The religious revival was not limited to Europe. In the United States, the second Great Awakening began around 1790 with huge camp meetings that brought together thousands of worshippers and scores of evangelical preachers, many of them Methodist. (The original Great Awakening had taken place in the 1730s and 1740s, sparked by the preaching of George Whitefield, a young English evangelist and follower of John Wesley—see the illustration on page 531.) Men and women danced to exhaustion, fell into trances, and spoke in tongues. During this period, Protestant sects began systematic missionary activity in other parts of the world. In the British colony of India, for example, Protestant missionaries pushed the British administration to abolish the Hindu custom of *sati*—the burning of widows on the funeral pyres of their husbands—in 1829. The missionaries hoped such actions would make Indians more likely to embrace Christianity. Missionary activity by Protestants and Catholics would become one of the arms of European imperialism and cultural influence in the nineteenth century.

REVIEW   To what extent did the Congress of Vienna restore the old order?

Challenges to the Conservative Order

Conservatives hoped to clamp a lid on European affairs, but the lid kept threatening to fly off. Drawing on the turmoil in society and politics was romanticism, the burgeoning international movement in the arts and literature that dominated artistic expression in the first half of the nineteenth century. Although romantics shared with conservatives a distrust of the Enlightenment's emphasis on reason, romanticism did not translate into a unified political position. Isolated revolts threatened the hold of some conservative governments in the 1820s, but most of these rebellions were quickly bottled up. Then, in 1830, successive uprisings briefly overwhelmed the established order. Across Europe, angry protesters sought constitutional guarantees of individual liberties and national unity and autonomy. The revolutionary legacy came back to life again.

Romanticism

As an artistic movement, romanticism encompassed poetry, music, painting, history, and literature. (See page 530 on the origins of romanticism.) It glorified nature, emotion, genius, and imagination as antidotes to the Enlightenment and to classicism in the arts, challenging the reliance on reason, symmetry, and cool geometric spaces. Classicism idealized models from Roman history; romanticism turned to folklore and medieval legends. Classicism celebrated orderly, crisp lines; romantics sought out all that was wild, fevered, and disorderly. Romantics might take any political position, but they exerted the most political influence when they expressed nationalist feelings.

Romantic poetry celebrated overwhelming emotion and creative imagination. George Gordon, Lord Byron (1788–1824), explained his aims in writing poetry:

> For what is Poesy but to create
> From overfeeling, Good and Ill, and aim
> At an external life beyond our fate,
> And be the new Prometheus of new man.

Prometheus was the mythological figure who brought fire from the Greek gods to human beings. Byron did not seek the new Prometheus among political leaders or military men; he sought him within his own "overfeeling," his own intense emotions. Byron became a romantic hero himself when he rushed off to act on his emotions by fighting and dying in the Greek war for independence from the Turks.

Romantic poetry elevated the wonders of nature almost to the supernatural. In a poem that became one of the most beloved exemplars of romanticism, "Tintern Abbey" (1798), the English poet William Wordsworth (1770–1850) compared himself to a deer even while making nature seem filled with human emotions. Wordsworth had greeted the French Revolution with joy but had gradually become disenchanted and celebrated British nationalism instead.

Their emphasis on authentic self-expression at times drew romantics to exotic, mystical, or even reckless experiences. Some romantics depicted the artist as possessed by demons and obsessed with hallucinations. This more nightmarish side was captured, and perhaps criticized, by Mary Shelley in *Frankenstein*. In his old age, German poet Johann Wolfgang von Goethe (1749–1832) likewise denounced the extremes of romanticism, calling it "everything that is sick."

Romanticism in painting similarly idealized nature and the individual of deep feelings. The German romantic painter Caspar David Friedrich (1774–1840) depicted scenes—often far away in the mountains—that captured the romantic fascination with the sublime power of nature. His melancholy individual figures looked lost in the vastness of an overpowering nature. Friedrich hated the modern world. His landscapes often had religious meaning as well, as in his controversial painting *The Cross in the Mountains* (1808), which showed a Christian cross standing alone in a mountain scene. It symbolized the steadfastness of faith but seemed to separate religion from the churches and attach it to mystical experience.

The English painter Joseph M. W. Turner (1775–1851) depicted his vision of nature in mysterious, misty seascapes, anticipating later artists by blurring the outlines of objects. The French painter Eugène Delacroix (1798–1863) chose contemporary as well as medieval scenes of great turbulence to emphasize light and color and break away from what he saw as "the servile copies repeated *ad nauseum* in academies of art." Critics denounced his techniques as "painting with a drunken broom." To broaden his experience of light and color, Delacroix traveled in the 1830s to North Africa and painted many exotic scenes in Morocco and Algeria.

The towering presence of the German composer **Ludwig van Beethoven** (1770–1827) in early-nineteenth-century music helped establish the direction for musical romanticism. His music, according to one leading German romantic, "sets in motion

Caspar David Friedrich, *The Cross in the Mountains* (1808) Caspar David Friedrich's first major oil painting captures one of the most important characteristics of romanticism: the glorification of nature, which in this case becomes a kind of altar for Christ crucified on the cross. The German artist painted it as an altarpiece on commission from an aristocratic woman, but it broke with most religious conventions, and many reviewers criticized it. In his other paintings, Friedrich often focused on a solitary individual overwhelmed by the majesty of nature. (Oil on canvas by Caspar David Friedrich [1774–1840] / Galerie Neue Meister, Dresden, Germany / © Staaliche Kunstsammlungen Dresden / Bridgeman Images.)

the lever of fear, of awe, of horror, of suffering, and awakens just that infinite longing which is the essence of Romanticism." Beethoven transformed the symphony into a connected work with recurring and evolving musical themes. Some of his work was explicitly political; his Ninth Symphony (1824) employed a chorus to sing the German poet Friedrich Schiller's verses in praise of universal human solidarity. Beethoven had admired Napoleon and even dedicated his Third Symphony, the *Eroica* (1804), to him, but when he learned of Napoleon's decision to name himself emperor, the composer tore up the dedication in disgust.

If romantics had any common political thread, it was the support of nationalist aspirations, especially through the search for the historical origins of national identity. Romantic poets and writers collected old legends and folktales that expressed a shared cultural and linguistic heritage stretching back to the Middle Ages. These collections showed that Germany, for example, had always existed even if it did not currently take the form of a single unified state. Italian nationalists took *The Betrothed* (1825–1827), a novel by Alessandro Manzoni (1785–1873), as a kind of bible. Manzoni, the grandson of the Italian Enlightenment hero Cesare Beccaria, set his novel in the seventeenth century, when Spain controlled Italy's destiny, but his readers understood that he intended to attack the Austrians who ruled northern Italy in his own day.

Manzoni had been inspired to write his novel by the most influential of all historical novelists, **Sir Walter Scott** (1771–1832). While working as a lawyer and then judge in Scotland, Scott first collected and published traditional Scottish ballads that he had heard as a child. After achieving immediate success with his own poetry, especially *The Lady of the Lake* (1810), he switched to historical novels. His novels are almost all renditions of historical events, from *Rob Roy* (1817), with its account of Scottish resistance to the English in the early eighteenth century, to *Ivanhoe* (1819), with its tales of medieval England. Readers snatched them up the minute they appeared; the first printing of *Rob Roy* sold out in two weeks. Very much a man of his time, Scott also published a successful biography of Napoleon only five years after the emperor's death.

Political Revolts in the 1820s

The restoration of regimes after Napoleon's fall disappointed those who dreamed of constitutional freedoms and national independence. Membership grew in secret societies such as the carbonari, attracting tens of thousands of members. Revolts broke out in the 1820s in Spain, Italy, Russia, and Greece (Map 20.3), as well as across the Atlantic in the Spanish and Portuguese colonies of Latin America (see page 602).

When Ferdinand VII regained the Spanish crown in 1814, he ordered foreign books and newspapers to be confiscated at the frontier and allowed the publication of only two newspapers. Many army officers who had encountered French ideas responded by joining secret societies. In 1820, disgruntled soldiers demanded that Ferdinand proclaim his adherence to the constitution of 1812, which he had abolished in 1814. Ferdinand bided his time, and in 1823 a French army invaded and restored him to absolute power. The French acted with the consent of the other great powers. The restored Spanish government tortured and executed hundreds of rebels; thousands were imprisoned or forced into exile.

Hearing of the Spanish uprising, rebellious soldiers in the kingdom of Naples joined forces with the carbonari and demanded a constitution. The promise of reform

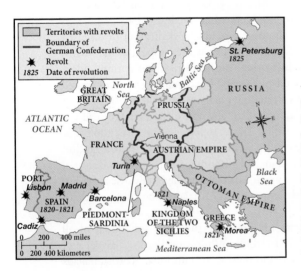

MAP 20.3   Revolutionary Movements of the 1820s   The revolts of the 1820s took place on the periphery of Europe, in Spain, Italy, Greece, Russia, and in the Spanish and Portuguese colonies of Latin America. Rebels in Spain and Russia wanted constitutional reforms. Although the Italian revolts failed, as did the uprisings in Spain and Russia, the Greek and Latin American independence movements eventually succeeded.

sparked rebellion in the northern Italian kingdom of Piedmont-Sardinia, where rebels urged Charles Albert, the young heir to the Piedmont throne, to fight the Austrians for Italian unification. After the rulers of Austria, Prussia, and Russia met and agreed on intervention in 1821, the Austrians defeated the rebels in Naples and Piedmont. Although Great Britain condemned the indiscriminate suppression of revolutionary movements, Metternich convinced the other powers to agree to his silencing the Italian opposition to Austrian rule.

Metternich acted quickly to suppress any sign of dissent closer to home. University students had formed nationalist student societies called *Burschenschaften*, and in 1817 they held a mass rally at which they burned books they did not like, including Napoleon's Civil Code. Metternich was convinced — incorrectly — that the Burschenschaften in the German states and the carbonari in Italy were linked in an international conspiracy. In 1819, when a student assassinated the playwright August Kotzebue because he had ridiculed the student movement, Metternich convinced the leaders of the biggest German states to pass the Carlsbad Decrees, dissolving the student societies and more strictly censoring the press. Professors who criticized their rulers were immediately fired.

Aspirations for constitutional government surfaced in Russia when Alexander I died suddenly in 1825. In December, when the troops assembled in St. Petersburg to take an oath of loyalty to Alexander's brother Nicholas as the new tsar, rebel officers insisted that the crown belonged to another brother, Constantine, whom they hoped would be more favorable to constitutional reform. Constantine, though next in the line of succession after Alexander, had refused the crown. Soldiers loyal to Nicholas easily suppressed the Decembrist Revolt (so called after the month of the uprising). The subsequent trial, however, made the rebels into legendary heroes. For the next thirty years, Nicholas I (r. 1825–1855) used a new political police, the Third Section, to spy on potential opponents and stamp out rebelliousness.

The Ottoman Turks faced growing nationalist challenges in the Balkans. The Serbs revolted against Turkish rule and won virtual independence by 1817. A Greek general in the Russian army, Prince Alexander Ypsilanti, tried to lead a revolt against the Turks in 1820 but failed when the tsar, urged on by Metternich, disavowed him. Metternich feared rebellion even by Christians against their Turkish rulers. A second revolt, this time by Greek peasants, sparked a wave of atrocities in 1821 and 1822. The Greeks killed every Turk who did not escape; in retaliation, the Turks hanged the Greek patriarch of Constantinople and, in the areas they still controlled, pillaged churches, massacred thousands of men, and sold the women into slavery.

Western opinion turned against the Turks; Greece, after all, was the birthplace of Western civilization. While the great powers negotiated, Greeks and pro-Greece committees around the world sent food and military supplies; like the English poet Byron, a few enthusiastic European and American volunteers joined the Greeks. The Greeks held on until the great powers were willing to intervene. In 1827, a combined force of British, French, and Russian ships destroyed the Turkish fleet at Navarino Bay; and in 1828, Russia declared war on Turkey and advanced close to Constantinople. The Treaty of Adrianople of 1829 gave Russia a protectorate over

Simón Bolívar   This watercolor by Fernandez Luis Cancino celebrates Bolívar's promise to abolish slavery in territories he freed from Spanish rule. Although Bolívar liberated his own slaves in 1820, he was unable to persuade the legislators of the newly independent countries to act immediately. They insisted on gradual emancipation. (Watercolor on paper by Fernandez Luis Cancino [19th century], Casa-Museo 20 de Julio de 1810, Bogotá, Colombia/Giraudon/Bridgeman Images.)

the Danubian principalities in the Balkans and provided for a conference among representatives of Britain, Russia, and France, all of whom had broken with Austria in support of the Greeks. In 1830, Greece was declared an independent kingdom under the guarantee of the three powers; in 1833, the second son of King Ludwig of Bavaria became Otto I of Greece. Greek independence, supported by European public opinion, showed that Metternich's systematic suppression of nationalism was reaching its limits.

Across the Atlantic, national revolts also succeeded after a series of bloody wars of independence. Taking advantage of the upheavals in Spain and Portugal that began under Napoleon, restive colonists from Mexico to Argentina rebelled. One leader who stood out was **Simón Bolívar** (1783–1830), born in Caracas (present-day Venezuela) to an aristocratic slave-owning family of Spanish descent. He was educated in Europe on the works of Voltaire and Rousseau. Although Bolívar fancied himself a Latin American Napoleon, he had to acquiesce to the formation of a series of independent republics between 1821 and 1823, even in Bolivia, which is named after him.

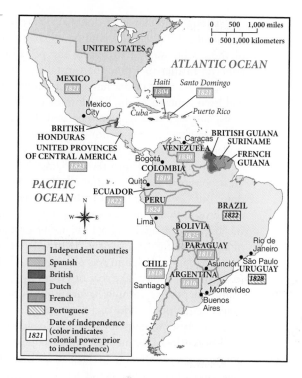

MAP 20.4 Latin American Independence, 1804–1830 Napoleon's occupation of Spain and Portugal seriously weakened those countries' hold on their Latin American colonies. Despite the restoration of the Spanish and Portuguese rulers in 1814, most of their colonies successfully broke away in a wave of rebellions between 1811 and 1830.

By 1825, Portugal had lost all its American colonies, including Brazil, and Spain was left with only Cuba and Puerto Rico (Map 20.4). Brazil declared its independence under the banner of the Portuguese king's own son and therefore maintained a monarchical form of government along with slavery. In contrast, the new republics freed those slaves who fought on their side, abolished the slave trade, and gradually eliminated slavery. The United States and Great Britain recognized the new states, and in 1823 U.S. president James Monroe announced his Monroe Doctrine, closing the Americas to European intervention—a prohibition that depended on British naval power and British willingness to declare neutrality.

Revolution and Reform, 1830–1832

In 1830, a new wave of liberal and nationalist revolts broke out. The revolts of the 1820s had served as warning shots but had been largely confined to the peripheries of Europe. Now revolution once again threatened the established order in western Europe.

French king Louis XVIII's younger brother and successor, Charles X (r. 1824–1830), brought about his own downfall by steering the monarchy in an increasingly repressive direction. In 1825, he agreed to compensate nobles who had emigrated during the French Revolution for the loss of their estates and imposed the death penalty for such offenses as stealing religious objects from churches. He further enraged liberals when he dissolved the legislature and imposed strict censorship. On July 26, 1830, spontaneous demonstrations in Paris turned into street battles that, over three days, left 500 citizens and 150 soldiers dead. A group of moderate liberal leaders, fearing the reestablishment of a republic, offered the crown to Charles X's cousin Louis-Philippe, duke of Orléans, and sent Charles into exile in England.

Though the new king doubled it, the number of men eligible to vote was still minuscule: 170,000 in a country of 30 million. Revolution had broken the hold of those who wanted to restore the pre-1789 monarchy and nobility, but it had gone no further this time than installing a more liberal, constitutional monarchy.

Even so, news of the July revolution in Paris ignited the Belgians, whose country had been annexed to the kingdom of the Netherlands in 1815. Differences in traditions, language, and religion separated the largely Catholic Belgians from the Dutch. An opera about a seventeenth-century insurrection in Naples provided the spark, and students in Brussels rioted, shouting "Down with the Dutch!"

The riot turned into revolt. King William of the Netherlands appealed to the great powers to intervene; after all, the Congress of Vienna had established his kingdom. But Great Britain and France opposed intervention and invited Russia, Austria, and Prussia to a conference that guaranteed Belgium independence in exchange for its neutrality in international affairs. Belgian neutrality would remain a cornerstone of European diplomacy for a century. After much maneuvering, the crown of the new kingdom of Belgium was offered to a German prince, Leopold of Saxe-Coburg, in 1831. The choice, like that of Otto I of Greece, ensured the influence of the great European powers without favoring any one of them in particular. Belgium, like France and Britain, now had a constitutional monarchy.

The Austrian emperor and the Russian tsar would have supported intervention in Belgium had they not been preoccupied with their own revolts. While the carbonari inspired a revolt in Naples in favor of a constitution and an uprising in Palermo demanded independence for Sicily (both were part of the Kingdom of the Two Sicilies), in the north, rebels in Piedmont fought for an Italy independent of Austria. Metternich sent Austrian armies to quell the unrest.

The Polish revolt was more serious. In 1830, in response to news of revolution in France, students raised the banner of rebellion. Polish aristocrats formed a provisional government, but it was defeated by the Russian army. In reprisal, Tsar Nicholas abolished the Polish constitution that his brother Alexander had granted in 1815 and ordered thousands of Poles executed or banished. The independence movements in Poland and Italy went underground only to reemerge later.

Reform of Parliament rather than revolution preoccupied the British. In August 1819, sixty thousand people attended an illegal political meeting held in St. Peter's Fields in Manchester to demand reform of parliamentary elections, which had long been controlled by aristocratic landowners. When the local authorities sent the cavalry to arrest the speaker, panic resulted; eleven people were killed and many hundreds injured. Punsters called it the battle of Peterloo or the Peterloo massacre. An alarmed government passed the Six Acts, which forbade large political meetings and restricted press criticism.

In the 1820s, however, new men came into government. Sir Robert Peel (1788–1850), the secretary for home affairs, revised the criminal code to reduce the number of crimes punishable by death and introduced a municipal police force in London, called the Bobbies after him. In 1824, the laws prohibiting labor unions were repealed, and though restrictions on strikes remained, workers could now organize themselves legally to confront their employers collectively. In 1828, the appointment of the duke of Wellington, the hero of Waterloo, as prime minister kept the Tories in power. Wellington's government pushed through a bill in 1829 allowing Catholics to sit in Parliament and hold most public offices.

When in 1830, and again in 1831, the Whigs in Parliament proposed an extension of the right to vote, Tory diehards, principally in the House of Lords, dug in their heels and predicted that even the most modest proposals would doom civilization itself. Even though the proposed law would grant only limited, not universal, male suffrage, mass demonstrations in favor of it took place in many cities. In this "state of diseased and feverish excitement" (according to its opponents), the **Reform Bill of 1832** passed, after the king threatened to create enough new peers to obtain its passage in the House of Lords.

Although the Reform Bill altered Britain's political structure in significant ways, the gains were not revolutionary. One of the bill's foremost backers, historian and member of Parliament Thomas Macaulay, explained, "I am opposed to Universal Suffrage, because I think that it would produce a destructive revolution. I support this plan, because I am sure that it is our best security against a revolution." Although the number of male voters nearly doubled, only 8 percent of the population qualified to vote. Nevertheless, the bill set a precedent for widening suffrage further. Those disappointed with the outcome would organize with renewed vigor in the 1830s and 1840s.

> **REVIEW**   Why were independence movements thwarted in Italy and Poland in this era, but not in Greece, Belgium, and Latin America?

Conclusion

The agitations and uprisings of the 1820s and early 1830s showed that the revolutionary legacy still smoldered and might erupt into flames again at any moment. Napoleon Bonaparte transformed the legacy but also kept it alive. He reshaped French institutions and left a lasting imprint in many European countries. Moreover, like Frankenstein's monster, he bounced back from numerous reversals; between the French retreat from Moscow in 1812 and his final defeat at Waterloo in 1815, Napoleon lost many battles yet managed to raise an army again and again.

The powers that eventually defeated Napoleon tried to maintain the European peace by shoring up monarchical governments and damping down aspirations for constitutional freedoms and national autonomy. Nevertheless, Belgium separated from the Netherlands, Greece achieved independence from the Turks, Latin American countries shook off the rule of Spain and Portugal, and the French installed a more liberal monarchy than the one envisioned by the Congress of Vienna. Metternich's vision of a conservative Europe still held, but in the next two decades dramatic social changes would prompt a new and much more deadly round of revolutions.

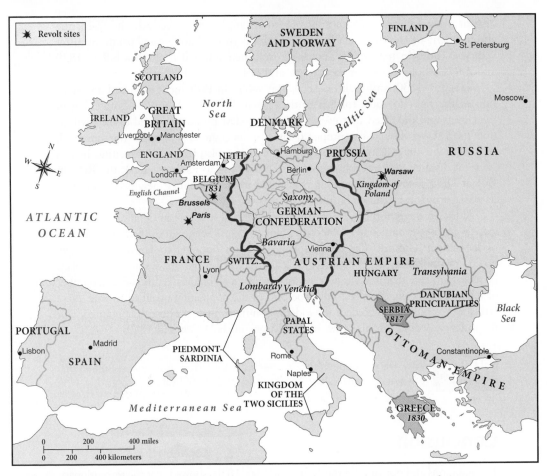

MAPPING THE WEST Europe in 1830   By 1830, the fragilities of the Congress of Vienna settlement had become apparent. Rebellion in Poland failed, but Belgium won its independence from the kingdom of the Netherlands, and a French revolution in July chased out the Bourbon ruler and installed Louis-Philippe, who promised constitutional reform. Most European rulers held on to their positions in this period of ferment, but they had to accommodate new desires for constitutional guarantees of rights and growing nationalist sentiment.

Chapter Review

KEY TERMS AND PEOPLE

Be sure that you can identify the term or person and explain its historical significance.

Napoleon Bonaparte (p. 580)
First Consul (p. 581)
Civil Code (p. 584)
Continental System (p. 590)
battle of Waterloo (p. 592)
Congress of Vienna (p. 593)
Klemens von Metternich (p. 593)

restoration (p. 594)
conservatism (p. 595)
Ludwig van Beethoven
  (p. 598)
Sir Walter Scott (p. 599)
Simón Bolívar (p. 602)
Reform Bill of 1832 (p. 605)

REVIEW QUESTIONS

1. In what ways did Napoleon continue the French Revolution, and in what ways did he break with it?
2. Why was Napoleon able to gain control over so much of Europe's territory?
3. To what extent did the Congress of Vienna restore the old order?
4. Why were independence movements thwarted in Italy and Poland in this era, but not in Greece, Belgium, and Latin America?

MAKING CONNECTIONS

1. What was the long-term significance of Napoleon for Europe?
2. What best explains Napoleon's fall from power: apathy at home, resistance to his rule, or military defeat?
3. In what ways did Metternich succeed in holding back the revolutionary legacy? In what ways did he fail?
4. How did the revolts and rebellions of the 1820s reflect the revolutionary legacy? In what ways did they move in new directions?

IMPORTANT EVENTS

1799	• Coup against Directory government in France; Napoleon Bonaparte is named First Consul
1801	• Napoleon signs concordat with the pope
1804	• Napoleon is crowned emperor of France, issues new Civil Code
1805	• British naval forces defeat French at the battle of Trafalgar; Napoleon wins his greatest victory at the battle of Austerlitz
1807–1814	• French invade and occupy Spain and Portugal
1812	• Napoleon invades Russia
1814–1815	• Congress of Vienna
1815	• Napoleon is defeated at Waterloo and exiled to island of St. Helena, where he dies in 1821
1818	• Mary Shelley, *Frankenstein*
1820	• Revolt of liberal army officers against Spanish crown
1824	• Ludwig van Beethoven, Ninth Symphony
1825	• Russian army officers demand constitutional reform in Decembrist Revolt
1830	• Greece gains its independence from Ottoman Turks; rebels overthrow Charles X of France and install Louis-Philippe; rebellion in Poland against Russia fails
1832	• English Parliament passes Reform Bill

21

Industrialization and Social Ferment

1830–1850

CHAPTER FOCUS

How did the Industrial Revolution create new social and political conflicts?

IN 1830, THE LIVERPOOL AND MANCHESTER Railway Line opened to the cheers of crowds and the congratulations of government officials, including the duke of Wellington, the hero of Waterloo who had been named British prime minister. In the excitement, some of the dignitaries gathered on a parallel track. Another engine, George Stephenson's *Rocket*, approached at high speed—the engine could go as fast as twenty-seven miles per hour. Most of the gentlemen scattered to safety, but former cabinet minister William Huskisson fell and was hit. A few hours later he died, the first official casualty of the newfangled railroad.

Dramatic and expensive, railroads were the most striking symbol of the new industrial age. Industrialization and its by-product of rapid urban growth fundamentally changed political conflicts, social relations, cultural concerns, and even the landscape. So great were the changes that they are collectively labeled the Industrial Revolution. Although this revolution did not take place in a single decade like the French Revolution, the introduction of steam-driven machinery, large factories, and a new working class transformed life in the Western world.

The shock of industrial and urban growth generated an outpouring of commentary on the need for social reforms. Many who wrote on social issues expected middle-class women to organize their homes as a domestic haven from the heartless process of upheaval. Yet despite the emphasis on domesticity, middle-class women participated in public issues, too: they set up reform societies that fought prostitution and helped poor mothers, they agitated for temperance (abstention from alcohol), and they joined the campaigns to abolish slavery.

Social ferment set the ideological pots to a boil. A word coined during the French Revolution, **ideology** refers to a coherent set of beliefs about the way the social and political order should be organized. The dual impact of the French Revolution and the Industrial Revolution prompted the development of a whole spectrum of ideologies to explain the meaning of the changes taking place. Nationalists, liberals, socialists, and communists offered competing visions of the social order they desired: they all agreed that change was necessary, but they disagreed about both the means and the ends of change. Their contest came to a head in 1848 when the rapid transformation of European society led to a new set of revolutionary outbreaks, more consuming than any since 1789.

The Industrial Revolution

French and English writers of the 1820s invented the term **Industrial Revolution** to capture the drama of contemporary change and to draw a parallel with the French Revolution. The chief components of the Industrial Revolution, industrialization and urbanization, are long-term processes that have continued to the present. The Industrial Revolution began in England in the 1770s and 1780s in textile manufacturing and spread from there across the continent. In the 1830s and 1840s, industrialization and urbanization both accelerated quite suddenly, as governments across Europe encouraged railroad construction and the mechanization of manufacturing. Many officials, preachers, and intellectuals worried that unchecked growth would destroy traditional social relationships and create disorder.

Roots of Industrialization

British inventors had been steadily perfecting steam engines for five decades before George Stephenson built his *Rocket*. A key breakthrough took place in 1776 when Scottish engineer James Watt developed an efficient steam engine that could be used to pump water from coal mines or drive machinery in textile factories. Since coal fired the steam engines that drove new textile machinery, innovations tended to reinforce one another. This kind of synergy built on previous changes in the textile industry. In 1733, the Englishman John Kay had patented the flying shuttle, which enabled weavers to "throw" yarn across the loom rather than draw it back and forth by hand. Weavers began producing cloth more quickly than spinners could produce the thread. The resulting shortage of spun thread propelled the invention of the spinning jenny, a spinning wheel that enabled one worker to run eight spools at once. The increased output of yarn then stimulated the mechanization of weaving. Using the engines produced by James Watt and his partner Matthew Boulton, Edmund Cartwright designed a mechanized loom in the 1780s that, when perfected, could be run by a small boy and yet yield fifteen times the output of a skilled adult working a handloom. By the end of the century, manufacturers were assembling new power machinery in large factories that hired semiskilled men, women, and children to replace skilled weavers.

Several factors interacted to make England the first site of the Industrial Revolution. England had a good supply of private investment capital from overseas trade and commercial profits, ready access to raw cotton from the plantations of its Caribbean colonies and the southern United States, and the necessary natural resources at home such as coal and iron. Good opportunities for social mobility provided an environment that fostered the pragmatism of the English and Scottish inventors who designed the machinery. The agricultural revolution of the eighteenth century had enabled England to produce food more efficiently, freeing some agricultural workers to move to the new sites of manufacturing. Cotton textile production skyrocketed.

Elsewhere in Europe, textile manufacturing—long a linchpin in the European economy—expanded even without the introduction of new machines and factories because of the spread of the "putting-out," or "domestic," system. Under the putting-out system, manufacturers supplied the raw materials, such as woolen or cotton fibers, to families working at home. The mother and her children washed, carded, and combed the fibers. Then the mother and oldest daughters spun them into thread. The father, assisted by the children, wove the cloth. The cloth was then finished (bleached, dyed, smoothed, and so on) under the supervision of the manufacturer in a large workshop, located either in town or in the countryside. This system had existed in the textile industry for hundreds of years, but it grew dramatically in the eighteenth century, and the manufacture of other products—such as glassware, baskets, nails, and guns—followed suit. The spread of the putting-out system of manufacturing is sometimes called proto-industrialization to signify that the process helped pave the way for the full-scale Industrial Revolution. Because of the increase in textile production, ordinary people began to wear underclothes and nightclothes, both rare in the past. White, red, blue, yellow, green, and even pastel shades of cotton now replaced the black, gray, or brown of traditional wool.

Workers in the textile industry enjoyed few protections against fluctuations in the market. Hundreds of thousands of families might be reduced to bankruptcy in periods of overproduction. Handloom weavers sometimes violently resisted the establishment of the factory power looms that would force them out of work. In England in 1811 and 1812, for example, bands of handloom weavers wrecked factory machinery and burned mills in the Midlands, Yorkshire, and Lancashire. To restore order and protect industry, the government sent in an army of twelve thousand regular soldiers and made machine wrecking punishable by death. The rioters were called Luddites after the fictitious figure Ned Ludd, whose signature appeared on their manifestos. (The term is still used to describe those who resist new technology.)

Engines of Change

Steam-driven engines took on a dramatic new form in the 1820s when the English engineer George Stephenson perfected an engine to pull wagons along rail tracks. The idea of a railroad was not new: iron tracks had been used since the seventeenth century to haul coal from mines in wagons pulled by horses. A railroad system as a mode of human transport, however, developed only after Stephenson's invention of a steam-powered locomotive. Placed on the new tracks, steam-driven carriages could transport people and goods to the cities and link coal and iron deposits to the new factories. In the 1840s alone, railroad track mileage more than doubled in Great Britain, and British investment in railways jumped tenfold. The British also began to build railroads in India. Private investment that had been going into the building of thousands of miles of canals now went into railroads. Britain's success with rail transportation led other countries to develop their own projects. Railroads grew spectacularly in the United States in the 1830s and 1840s, reaching 9,000 miles of track by midcentury. In 1835, Belgium (newly independent in 1830) opened the first continental European railroad with state bonds backed by British capital. By 1850, the world had 23,500 miles of track, most of it in western Europe.

Railroad building spurred both industrial development and state power (Map 21.1). Governments everywhere participated in the construction of railroads, which depended on both private and state funds to pay for the massive amounts of iron, coal, heavy machinery, and human labor required to build and run them. Demand for iron products accelerated industrial development. Until the 1840s, cotton had led industrial production; between 1816 and 1840, cotton output more than quadrupled in Great Britain. But from 1830 to 1850, Britain's output of iron and coal doubled. Similarly, Austrian output of iron doubled between the 1820s and the 1840s. One-third of all investment in the German states in the 1840s went into railroads.

Steam-powered engines made Britain the world leader in manufacturing. By midcentury, more than half of Britain's national income came from manufacturing and trade. The number of steamboats in Great Britain rose from two in 1812 to six hundred in 1840. Between 1840 and 1850, steam-engine power doubled in Great Britain and increased even more rapidly elsewhere in Europe, as those adopting British inventions strove to catch up. The power applied in German manufacturing, for example, grew sixfold during the 1840s but still amounted to only a little more than a quarter of the British figure.

Although Great Britain consciously strove to protect its industrial supremacy, thousands of British engineers defied laws against the export of machinery or the emigration of artisans. Only slowly, thanks to the pirating of British methods and to new technical schools, did most continental countries begin closing the gap. Belgium became the fastest-growing industrial power on the continent: between 1830 and 1844, the number of steam engines in Belgium quadrupled, and Belgians exported seven times as many steam engines as they imported.

MAP 21.1 Industrialization in Europe, c. 1850   Industrialization (mainly mechanized textile production) first spread in a band across northern Europe that included Great Britain, northern France, Belgium, the northern German states, the region around Milan in northern Italy, and Bohemia. Although railroads were not the only factor in promoting industrialization, the map makes clear the interrelationship between railroad building and the development of new industrial sites of coal mining and textile production.

Industrialization spread slowly east from key areas in Prussia (near Berlin), Saxony, and Bohemia. Cotton production in the Austrian Empire tripled between 1831 and 1845, and coal production increased fourfold from 1827 to 1847. Even so, by 1850, continental Europe still lagged almost twenty years behind Great Britain in industrial development.

The advance of industrialization in eastern Europe was slow, in large part because serfdom still survived there, hindering labor mobility and tying up investment capital: as long as peasants were legally tied to the land as serfs, they could not migrate to the new factory towns and landlords felt little incentive to invest their income in manufacturing. The problem was worst in Russia, where industrialization would not take off until the end of the nineteenth century.

Despite the spread of industrialization, factory workers remained a minority everywhere. In the 1840s, factories in England employed only 5 percent of the workers; in France, 3 percent; in Prussia, 2 percent. The putting-out system remained strong, employing two-thirds of the manufacturing workers in Prussia and Saxony, for example, in the 1840s. Many peasants kept their options open by combining factory work or putting-out work with agricultural labor. From Switzerland to Russia, people worked in agriculture during the spring and summer and in manufacturing in the fall and winter.

Even though factories employed only a small percentage of the population, they attracted much attention. Already by 1830, more than a million people in Britain depended on the cotton industry for employment, and cotton cloth constituted 50 percent of the country's exports. Factories sprang up in urban areas, where the growing population provided a ready source of labor. The rapid expansion of the British textile industry had a colonial corollary: the destruction of the hand manufacture of textiles in India. The British put high import duties on Indian cloth entering Britain and kept such duties very low for British cloth entering India. The effects were catastrophic for Indian manufacturing: in 1813, the Indian city of Calcutta exported to England £2 million worth of cotton cloth; by 1830, Calcutta was importing from England £2 million worth of the product. When Britain abolished slavery in its Caribbean colonies in 1833, British manufacturers began to buy raw cotton in the southern United States, where slavery still flourished.

Factories drew workers from the urban population surge, which had begun in the eighteenth century and now accelerated. The number of agricultural laborers also increased during industrialization in Britain, suggesting that a growing birthrate created a larger population and fed workers into the new factory system. Factory employment resembled labor on family farms or in the putting-out system: entire families came to toil for a single wage, although family members performed different tasks. Workdays of twelve to seventeen hours were typical, even for children, and the work was grueling.

As urban factories grew, their workers gradually came to constitute a new socioeconomic class with a distinctive culture and traditions. The term *working class*, like *middle class*, came into use for the first time in the early nineteenth century. It referred to the laborers in the new factories. In the past, urban workers had labored in isolated trades: water and wood carrying, gardening, laundry, and building. In contrast, factories brought working people together with machines, under close supervision by their employers. Soon developing a sense of common interests, they organized societies for mutual help and political reform. From these would come the first labor unions.

Industry returned unheard-of riches to factory owners and managers even as it caused pollution and created new forms of poverty for exhausted workers. "From this foul drain the greatest stream of human industry flows out to fertilize the whole world," wrote the French aristocrat Alexis de Tocqueville after visiting the new English industrial city of Manchester in the 1830s. "From this filthy sewer pure gold flows." Studies by physicians set the life expectancy of workers in Manchester at just seventeen years (partly because of high rates of infant mortality), whereas the average life expectancy in England was forty years in 1840. In some parts of Europe, city leaders banned factories, hoping to insulate their towns from the effects of industrial growth.

Investigators detailed the pitiful condition of workers. A physician in the town of Mulhouse, in eastern France, described the "pale, emaciated women who walk barefooted through the dirt" to reach the factory. The young children who worked in the factory appeared "clothed in rags which are greasy with the oil from the looms and frames." A report to the city government in Lille, France, in 1832 described the "dark cellars" where the cotton workers lived: "The air is never renewed, it is infected; the walls are plastered with garbage."

Child Labor in Coal Mines The passage of legislation in 1842 against women and girls working underground did nothing to prevent boys from continuing to perform essential tasks in cramped spaces in British coal mines. Lithographs such as this one from 1844 accompanied campaigns against these practices. (akg-images.)

Government inquiries often focused on women and children. In Great Britain, the Factory Act of 1833 outlawed the employment of children under the age of nine in textile mills (except in the lace and silk industries); it also limited the workdays for those ages nine to thirteen to nine hours a day, and those ages thirteen to eighteen to twelve hours. Adults worked even longer hours. Women and young children, sometimes under age six, hauled coal trucks through low, cramped passageways in coal mines. One nine-year-old girl, Margaret Gomley, described her typical day in the mines as beginning at 7:00 a.m. and ending at 6:00 p.m.: "I get my dinner at 12 o'clock, which is a dry muffin, and sometimes butter on, but have no time allowed to stop to eat it, I eat it while I am thrusting the load."

In 1842, the British Parliament prohibited the employment of women and girls underground. In 1847, the Central Short Time Committee, one of Britain's many social reform organizations, successfully pressured Parliament to limit the workday of women and children to ten hours. The continental countries followed the British lead, but since most did not insist on government inspection, enforcement was lax.

Urbanization and Its Consequences

Industrial development spurred urban growth, yet cities with little industry grew as well. **Urbanization** is the growth of towns and cities due to the movement of people from rural to urban areas. Here, too, Great Britain led the way: half the population of England and Wales was living in towns by 1850, while in France and the German states only about a quarter of the total population was urban. Both old and new cities teemed with rising numbers in the 1830s and 1840s; the population of Vienna ballooned by 125,000 between 1827 and 1847, and the new industrial city of Manchester grew by 70,000 just in the 1830s.

Massive emigration from rural areas, rather than births to women already living in cities, accounted for this remarkable increase. City life and new factories beckoned those faced with hunger and poverty, including immigrants from other lands: thousands of Irish emigrated to English cities, Italians went to French cities, and Poles flocked to German cities. Settlements sprang up outside the old city limits but gradually became part of the urban area. Cities incorporated parks, cemeteries, zoos, and greenways—all imitations of the countryside, which itself was being industrialized by railroads and factories.

The rapid influx of people caused serious overcrowding in the cities because the housing stock expanded much more slowly than the population did. In Paris, thirty thousand workers lived in lodging houses, eight or nine to a room, with no separation of the sexes. In 1847, in St. Giles, the Irish quarter of London, 461 people lived in just twelve houses. Men, women, and children with no money for fuel huddled together for warmth on piles of filthy rotting straw or potato peels.

Severe crowding worsened already dire sanitation conditions. Residents dumped refuse into streets or courtyards, and human excrement collected in cesspools under apartment houses. At midcentury, London's approximately 250,000 cesspools were emptied only once or twice a year. Water was scarce and had to be fetched daily from nearby fountains. Parisians, on average, had enough water for only two baths annually per

MAP 21.2   The Spread of Cholera, 1826–1855   Contemporaries did not understand the causes of the cholera epidemics in the 1830s and the 1840s in Europe. Western Europeans knew only that the disease marched progressively from east to west across Europe. Nothing seemed able to stop it. It appeared and died out for reasons that could not be grasped at the time. Nevertheless, the cholera epidemics prompted authorities in most European countries to set up public health agencies to coordinate the response and study sanitation conditions in the cities.

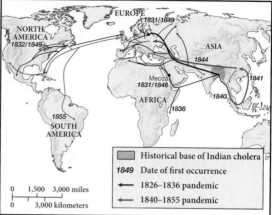

person (the upper classes enjoyed more baths, of course; the lower classes, fewer). In London, private companies that supplied water turned on pumps in the poorer sections for only a few hours three days a week. In rapidly growing British industrial cities such as Manchester, one-third of the houses contained no latrines. Human waste ended up in the rivers that supplied drinking water. The horses that provided transportation inside the cities left droppings everywhere, and city dwellers often kept chickens, ducks, goats, pigs, geese, and even cattle, as well as dogs and cats, in their houses. The result was a "universal atmosphere of filth and stink," as one observer recounted.

Such conditions made cities prime breeding grounds for disease. In 1830 to 1832 and again in 1847 to 1851, devastating outbreaks of cholera swept across Asia and Europe, touching the United States as well in 1849 to 1850 (Map 21.2). Today we know that a waterborne bacterium causes cholera, but at the time no one understood the disease and everyone feared it. The usually fatal illness induced violent vomiting and diarrhea and left the skin blue, eyes sunken and dull, and hands and feet ice cold. While cholera particularly ravaged the crowded, filthy neighborhoods of rapidly growing cities, it also claimed many rural and some well-to-do victims. In Paris, 18,000 people died in the 1832 epidemic and 20,000 in that of 1849; in London, 7,000 died in each epidemic; and in Russia, the epidemic was catastrophic, claiming 250,000 victims in 1831 to 1832 and 1 million in 1847 to 1851.

Epidemics revealed the social tensions lying just beneath the surface of urban life. Middle-class reformers often considered the poor to be morally degenerate. In their view, overcrowding led to sexual promiscuity and illegitimacy. They depicted the lower classes as dangerously lacking in sexual self-control. Officials collected statistics on illegitimacy that seemed to bear out these fears: one-quarter to one-half of the babies born in the big European cities in the 1830s and 1840s were illegitimate, and alarmed medical men wrote about thousands of infanticides. In contrast, only a tiny fraction of rural births were illegitimate. The rising rate of births outside of marriage seemed to go hand in hand with drinking and crime. Beer halls and pubs dotted the urban landscape. By the 1830s, Hungary's twin cities of Buda and

Pest had eight hundred beer and wine houses for the working classes. Police officials estimated that London had seventy thousand thieves and eighty thousand prostitutes. In many cities, nearly half the population lived at the level of bare subsistence, and increasing numbers depended on public welfare, charity, or criminality to make ends meet.

Everywhere reformers warned of a widening separation between rich and poor and a growing sense of hostility between the classes. A Swiss pastor noted: "A new spirit has arisen among the workers. Their hearts seethe with hatred of the well-to-do; their eyes lust for a share of the wealth about them; their mouths speak unblushingly of a coming day of retribution." In 1848, as we will see, it would seem that day of retribution had arrived.

Agricultural Perils and Prosperity

Rising populations created increased demand for food and spurred changes in the countryside, too. Although agricultural yields increased by 30 to 50 percent in the first half of the nineteenth century, population grew by nearly 100 percent. Railroads and canals improved food distribution, but much of Europe—particularly in the east—remained isolated from markets and vulnerable to famines.

Most people still lived on the land, and the upper classes still dominated rural society. In France at midcentury, almost two million economically independent peasants tended their own small properties. But in England, southern Italy, Prussia, and eastern Europe, large landowners, usually noblemen, consolidated and expanded their estates by buying up the land of less successful nobles or peasants. As agricultural prices rose, the big landowners pushed for legislation to allow them to continue converting common land to private property.

Wringing a living from the soil under such conditions put pressure on traditional family life. Men often migrated seasonally to earn cash in factories or as village artisans, while their wives, sisters, and daughters did the traditional "men's work" of tending crops. In the past, population growth had been contained by postponing marriage (leaving fewer years for childbearing) and by high rates of death in childbirth as well as infant mortality. Now, as child mortality declined outside the industrial cities and people without property began marrying earlier, Europeans became more aware of birth control methods. The vulcanization of rubber in the 1840s improved the reliability of condoms. When such methods failed and population increase left no options open at home, people emigrated, often to the United States. Between 1816 and 1850, five million Europeans left their home countries for new lives overseas. When France colonized Algeria in the 1830s and 1840s, officials tried to attract settlers by emphasizing the fertility of the land; they offered the prospect of agricultural prosperity in the colony as an alternative to the rigors of industrialization and urbanization at home.

Rural political power remained in the hands of traditional elites. The biggest property owners controlled the political assemblies and often personally selected local officials. Nowhere did the old rural social order seem more impregnable than in Russia. Most Russian serfs remained tied to the land, and troops easily suppressed serfs' uprisings in 1831 and 1842. Yet in the 1850s railroad construction would begin to transform life in Russia, too, and the railroads would bring with them the same social problems—urbanization, the beginning of industrialization, and a growing awareness of social disparities—that threatened the social and political order in western Europe in the 1830s and 1840s. These new social problems demanded a response. But would that response be reform or revolution?

> **REVIEW**   What dangers did the Industrial Revolution pose to both urban and rural life?

Reforming the Social Order

The experience of dramatic economic and social changes prompted artists and writers to focus on emerging social problems and inspired the creation of new organizations for social reform. Middle-class women often took the lead in establishing charitable organizations that tried to bring religious faith, educational uplift, and the reform of manners to the lower classes. The middle class, both men and women, expected women to soften the rigors of a rapidly changing society, but this expectation led to some confusion about women's proper role: Should they devote themselves to social reform in the world or to their own domestic spaces? Many hoped to apply the same zeal for reform to the colonial peoples living in places administered by Europeans.

Cultural Responses to the Social Question

The *social question*, an expression reflecting the widely shared concern about social changes arising from industrialization and urbanization, pervaded all forms of art and literature. The dominant artistic movement of the time, romanticism, generally took a dim view of industrialization. The English-born American painter Thomas Cole (1801–1848) complained in 1836: "In this age . . . a meager utilitarianism seems ready to absorb every feeling and sentiment, and what is sometimes called improvement in its march makes us fear that the bright and tender flowers of the imagination shall all be crushed beneath its iron tramp." Yet culture itself underwent important changes as the growing capitals of Europe attracted flocks of aspiring painters and playwrights; the 1830s and 1840s witnessed an explosion in culture as the number of would-be artists increased dramatically and new technologies such as photography and lithography brought art to the masses. Many of these new intellectuals would support the revolutions of 1848.

Because romanticism tended to glorify nature and reject industrial and urban growth, romantics often gave vivid expression to the problems created by rapid economic and social transformation. The English poet Elizabeth Barrett Browning, best known for her love poems, denounced child labor in "The Cry of the Children"

(1843). In *Rain, Steam, and Speed: The Great Western Railway* (1844), the leading English romantic painter, Joseph M. W. Turner (1775–1851), portrayed the struggle between the forces of nature and the means of economic growth. Turner was fascinated by steamboats: in *The Fighting "Téméraire" Tugged to Her Last Berth to Be Broken Up* (1838), he featured the victory of steam power over more conventional sailing ships.

Increased literacy, the spread of reading rooms and lending libraries, and serialization in newspapers and journals gave novels a large reading public. Unlike the fiction of the eighteenth century, which had focused on individual personalities, the great novels of the 1830s and 1840s specialized in the portrayal of social life in all its varieties. Manufacturers, financiers, starving students, workers, bureaucrats, prostitutes, underworld figures, thieves, and aristocratic men and women filled the pages of works by popular writers. Hoping to get out of debt, the French writer Honoré de Balzac (1799–1850) pushed himself to exhaustion and a premature death by cranking out ninety-five novels and many short stories. He aimed to catalog the social types that could be found in French society. Many of his characters, like himself, were driven by the desire to climb higher in the social order.

The English fiction writer Charles Dickens (1812–1870) worked with a similar frenetic energy and for much the same reason. When his father was imprisoned for debt in 1824, the young Dickens took a job in a shoe-polish factory. He eventually became a journalist and managed to produce a series of novels that attracted thousands of readers. In them, he paid close attention to the distressing effects of industrialization and urbanization. In *The Old Curiosity Shop* (1841), for example, he depicts the Black Country, the manufacturing region west and northwest of Birmingham, as a "cheerless region," a "mournful place," in which tall chimneys "made foul the melancholy air."

Novels by women often revealed the bleaker side of women's situations. Charlotte Brontë's *Jane Eyre* (1847) describes the difficult life of an orphaned girl who becomes a governess, the only occupation open to most single middle-class women. The French novelist Amandine-Aurore-Lucile Dupin Dudevant (1804–1876), writing under the pen name **George Sand**, took her social criticism a step further. She announced her independence in the 1830s by dressing like a man and smoking cigars. Though she published her work under a male pseudonym, as did many other women writers of the time, she created female characters who prevail in difficult circumstances through romantic love and moral idealism. Her notoriety — she became the lover of the Polish pianist and composer Frédéric Chopin, among others, and threw herself into socialist politics — made the term *George-Sandism* a common expression of disdain toward independent women.

As artists became more interested in society and social relations, ordinary citizens crowded cultural events. Museums opened to the public across Europe. Popular theaters in big cities drew thousands from the lower and middle classes every night; in London, for example, some twenty-four thousand people attended eighty "penny theaters" nightly. The audience for print culture also multiplied. In the German states, for example, the production of new literary works doubled between 1830

George Sand In this lithograph by Alcide Lorentz of 1842, George Sand is shown in one of her notorious male costumes standing on a cloud created by the cigar in her left hand. Sand published numerous works, including novels (*Indiana* is shown at the left of the image), plays, essays, travel writing, and an autobiography. She advocated setting up a Chamber of Mothers to go alongside the Chamber of Deputies (her right arm rests on sheets with those words on them), and she actively participated in the revolution of 1848 in France, writing pamphlets in support of the new republic. Disillusioned by the rise to power of Louis-Napoleon Bonaparte, she withdrew to her country estate and devoted herself exclusively to her writing. (Musée de la Ville de Paris, Musée Carnavalet, Paris, France/Archives Charmet/ Bridgeman Images.)

and 1843, as did the number of periodicals and newspapers and the number of booksellers. Young children and ragpickers sold cheap prints and books door-to-door or in taverns.

The advent of photography in 1839 provided an amazing new medium for artists. The daguerreotype, named after its inventor, French painter Jacques Daguerre (1787–1851), prompted one artist to claim that "from today, painting is dead." Although this prediction was highly exaggerated, photography did open up new ways of portraying reality. It did so only gradually, however, as early photographs required exposure times of twenty to thirty minutes, making it impossible to capture anything or anyone in movement.

Culture expanded its reach in part because the ranks of artists and writers swelled. Estimates suggest that the number of painters and sculptors in France, the undisputed center of European art at the time, grew sixfold between 1789 and 1838. Not everyone could succeed in this hothouse atmosphere, in which writers and artists furiously competed for public attention. Their own troubles made some of them more keenly aware of the hardships faced by the poor. A satirical article in one of the many bitingly critical journals and booklets published in Berlin proclaimed: "In Ipswich in England a mechanical genius has invented a stomach, whose extraordinary efficient construction is remarkable. This artificial stomach is intended for factory workers there and is adjusted so that it is fully satisfied with three lentils or peas; one potato is enough for an entire week."

The Varieties of Social Reform

Lithographs, novels, and even joke booklets helped drive home the need for social reform, but religious conviction also inspired efforts to help the poor. Moral reform societies, Bible groups, Sunday schools, and temperance groups aimed to turn the poor into respectable people. In 1844, for example, 450 different relief organizations operated in London alone.

Religiously motivated reformers first had to overcome the perceived indifference of the working classes. Protestant and Catholic clergy complained that workers had no interest in religion; less than 10 percent of the workers in the cities attended religious services. To combat indifference, British religious groups launched the Sunday school movement, which reached its zenith in the 1840s. By 1851, more than half of all working-class children ages five to fifteen were attending Sunday school, even though very few of their parents regularly went to religious services. The Sunday schools taught children how to read at a time when few working-class children could go to school during the week.

Women took a more prominent role than ever before in charitable work. Catholic religious orders, which by 1850 enrolled many more women than men, ran schools, hospitals, leper colonies, insane asylums, and old-age homes. The Catholic church established new orders, especially for women, and increased missionary activity overseas. Protestant women in Great Britain and the United States established Bible, missionary, and female reform societies by the hundreds. Chief among their concerns was prostitution, and many societies dedicated themselves to reforming "fallen women" and castigating men who visited prostitutes.

Catholics and Protestants alike promoted the temperance movement. The first societies had appeared in the United States as early as 1813, and by 1835 the American Temperance Society claimed 1.5 million members. Temperance advocates viewed drunkenness as a sign of moral weakness and a threat to social order. Yet temperance societies also attracted working-class people who shared the desire for respectability.

Social reformers saw education as one of the main prospects for uplifting the poor and the working class. In 1833, the French government passed an education law that required every town to maintain a primary school, pay a teacher, and provide free education to poor boys. As the law's author, François Guizot, argued, "Ignorance renders the masses turbulent and ferocious." Girls' schools were optional, although hundreds of women taught at the primary level, most of them in private, often religious schools. Despite these efforts, only one out of every thirty children went to school in France, many fewer than in Protestant states such as Prussia, where 75 percent of children were in primary school by 1835. Popular education remained woefully undeveloped in most of eastern Europe. Peasants were specifically excluded from the few primary schools in Russia, where Tsar Nicholas I blamed the Decembrist Revolt of 1825 on education.

Above all else, the elite sought to impose discipline and order on working people. Popular sports, especially blood sports such as cockfighting and bearbaiting, suggested a lack of control, and long-standing efforts in Great Britain to eliminate these recreations now gained momentum through organizations such as the Society for the Prevention of Cruelty to Animals. By the end of the 1830s, bullbaiting had been abandoned in Great Britain. The other blood sports died out more slowly, and efforts in other countries generally lagged behind those of the British.

When private charities failed to meet the needs of the poor, governments often intervened. Great Britain sought to control the costs of public welfare by passing a new poor law in 1834, called by its critics the Starvation Act. The law required that all able-bodied persons receiving relief be housed together in workhouses, with husbands separated from wives and parents from children. Workhouse life was designed to be as unpleasant as possible so that poor people would move on to regions that had better employment prospects. British women from all social classes organized anti–poor law societies to protest the separation of mothers from their children in the workhouses.

Many women viewed charitable work as the extension of their domestic roles: they promoted virtuous behavior and morality in their efforts to improve society. But women's social reform activities concealed a paradox. According to the ideology that historians call **domesticity**, women were to live their lives entirely within the domestic sphere, devoting themselves to their families and the home. The English poet Alfred, Lord Tennyson, captured this view in a popular poem published in 1847: "Man for the field and woman for the hearth; / Man for the sword and for the needle she. / . . . All else confusion."

Most women had little hope of economic independence. The notion that they belonged in a separate, domestic sphere prevented women from pursuing higher education, work in professional careers, or participation in politics through voting or holding office—all activities deemed appropriate only to men. Laws everywhere codified the subordination of women. Many countries followed the model of Napoleon's Civil Code (see page 584), which classified married women as legal incompetents along with children, the insane, and criminals. In some countries, such as France and Austria, unmarried women enjoyed some rights over property, but elsewhere laws explicitly defined them as perpetual minors under paternal control.

Distinctions between men and women were most noticeable in the privileged classes. Whereas boys attended secondary schools, most middle- and upper-class girls still received their education at home or in church schools, where they were taught to be religious, obedient, and accomplished in music and languages. As men's fashions turned practical—long trousers and short jackets of solid, often dark colors; no makeup (previously common for aristocratic men), and simply cut hair—women continued to dress for decorative effect, now with tightly corseted waists that emphasized the differences between female and male bodies. Middle- and upper-class women favored long hair that required hours of brushing and pinning up, and they wore long, cumbersome skirts.

Scientists reinforced stereotypes. Once considered sexually insatiable, women were now described as incapacitated by menstruation and largely uninterested in sex, an attitude that many equated with moral superiority. Thus was born the "Victorian" woman (the epoch gets its name from England's Queen Victoria—see page 656), a figment of the largely male medical imagination. Physicians and scholars considered women mentally inferior. In 1839, Auguste Comte, an influential early French sociologist, wrote, "As for any functions of government, the radical inaptitude of the female sex is there yet more marked . . . and limited to the guidance of the mere family."

Some women denounced the ideology of domesticity and separate spheres; the English writer Ann Lamb, for example, proclaimed that "the duty of a wife *means* the obedience of a Turkish slave." Middle-class women who did not marry, however, had few options for earning a living; they often worked as governesses or ladies' companions for the well-to-do. Most lower-class women worked because of financial necessity; as the wives of peasants, laborers, or shopkeepers, they had to supplement the family's meager income by working on the farm, in a factory, or in a shop. Domesticity might have been an ideal for them, but rarely was it a reality.

Abuses and Reforms Overseas

Like the ideal of domesticity, the ideal of colonialism often conflicted with the reality of economic interests. In the first half of the nineteenth century, those economic interests changed as European colonialism underwent a subtle but momentous transformation. Colonialism became **imperialism**—a word coined only in the mid-nineteenth century—as Europeans turned their interest away from the plantation colonies of the Caribbean and toward new colonies in Asia and Africa. Colonialism had most often led to the establishment of settler colonies, direct rule by Europeans, the introduction of slave labor from Africa, and the wholesale destruction of indigenous peoples. In contrast, imperialism usually meant more indirect forms of economic exploitation and political rule. Europeans still profited from their colonies, but now they also aimed to re-form colonial peoples in their own image—when it did not conflict too much with their economic interests to do so.

Colonialism—as opposed to imperialism—rose and fell with the enslavement of black Africans. British religious groups, especially the Quakers, had taken the lead in forming antislavery societies. They gained a first victory in 1807 when the British House of Lords voted to abolish the slave trade (though not the institution of slavery itself). British reformers finally obtained the abolition of slavery in the British Empire in 1833. Antislavery petitions to Parliament bore 1.5 million signatures, including those of 350,000 women on one petition alone. In France, the new government of Louis-Philippe took strong measures against clandestine slave traffic, virtually ending French participation during the 1830s. Slavery was abolished in the remaining French Caribbean colonies in 1848.

Neither slavery nor the slave trade disappeared immediately just because the British and French had given it up. Because of increased participation by Spanish and Portuguese traders, almost as many slaves were traded in the 1820s as in the 1780s and the overall traffic did not dwindle until the 1850s. Human bondage continued unabated in Brazil, Cuba (still a Spanish colony), and the United States. Some American reformers supported abolition, but they remained a minority. Like serfdom in Russia, slavery in the Americas involved a quagmire of economic, political, and moral problems that worsened as the nineteenth century wore on.

Despite the abolition of slavery, Britain and France had not lost interest in overseas colonies. Using the pretext of an insult to its envoy, France invaded Algeria in 1830 and, after a long military campaign, established political control over most of the country in the next two decades. By 1848, more than seventy thousand French, Italian, and Maltese colonists had settled there with government encouragement, often confiscating the lands of native peoples. In that year, the French government officially incorporated Algeria as part of France. France also imposed a protectorate government over the South Pacific island of Tahiti.

Although the British granted Canada greater self-determination in 1839, they extended their dominion elsewhere by annexing Singapore (1819), an island off the Malay peninsula, and New Zealand (1840). They also increased their control in India through the administration of the East India Company, a private group of merchants chartered by the British crown. The British educated a native elite to take over much of the day-to-day business of administering the country, and they used native soldiers to augment their military control. By 1850, only one in six soldiers serving Britain in India was European.

The East India Company also tried to establish a regular trade with China in opium, long known for its medicinal uses but increasingly bought in China as a recreational drug. The Chinese government forbade Western merchants to venture outside the southern city of Guangzhou (Canton) and banned the import of opium, but these measures failed. By smuggling Indian opium into China and bribing local officials, British traders built up a flourishing market, and by the mid-1830s they were pressuring the British government to force an expanded opium trade on the Chinese. When the Chinese authorities expelled British merchants from southern China in 1839, Britain retaliated by bombarding Chinese coastal cities. The **Opium War** ended in 1842, when Britain dictated to a defeated China the Treaty of Nanking, by which four more Chinese ports were opened to Europeans and the British took sovereignty over the island of Hong Kong, received a substantial war indemnity, and were assured of a continuation of the opium trade. In this case, reform took a backseat to economic interest, despite the complaints of religious groups in Britain.

> **REVIEW** In which areas did reformers trying to address the social problems created by industrialization and urbanization succeed, and in which did they fail?

Ideologies and Political Movements

Although reform organizations grew rapidly in the 1830s and 1840s, many Europeans found them insufficient to answer the questions raised by industrialization and urbanization. How did the new social order differ from the earlier one, which was less urban and less driven by commercial concerns? Who should control this new order? Should governments try to moderate or accelerate the pace of change? New ideologies such as liberalism and socialism offered competing answers to these questions and provided the platform for new political movements. Established governments faced challenges not only from liberals and socialists but also from the most potent of the new doctrines, nationalism. Nationalists looked past social problems to concentrate on achieving political autonomy and self-determination for groups identified by ethnicity rather than by class.

The Spell of Nationalism

According to the doctrine of **nationalism**, all peoples derive their identities from their nations, which are defined by common language, shared cultural traditions, and sometimes religion. When such nations do not coincide with state boundaries, nationalism can produce violence and warfare as different national groups compete for control over territory (Map 21.3).

Nationalist aspirations were especially explosive for the Austrian Empire, which included a variety of peoples united only by their enforced allegiance to the Habsburg emperor. The empire included three main national groups: the Germans, who made up one-fourth of the population; the Magyars of Hungary (which included Transylvania and Croatia); and the Slavs, who together formed the largest group in the population but were divided into different ethnic groups such as Poles, Czechs, Croats, and Serbs. The Austrian Empire also included Italians in Lombardy and Venetia, and Romanians in Transylvania. Efforts to govern such diverse peoples preoccupied Prince Klemens von Metternich, chief minister to the weak Habsburg emperor Francis I (r. 1792–1835). Metternich's domestic policy aimed to restrain nationalist impulses, and it largely succeeded until the 1840s. He set up a secret police organization on the Napoleonic model that opened letters of even the highest officials. Metternich's policies forced the leading Italian nationalist, **Giuseppe Mazzini** (1805–1872), into exile in France in 1831. There Mazzini founded Young Italy, a secret society that attracted thousands with its message that Italy would touch off a European-wide revolutionary movement. The conservative order throughout Europe felt threatened by Mazzini's charismatic leadership and conspiratorial scheming, but he lacked both European allies against Austria and widespread support among the Italian masses.

Austria was deliberately excluded when the German states formed a *Zollverein* ("customs union") in 1834, under Prussian leadership. German nationalists sought a government uniting German-speaking peoples, but they could not agree on its boundaries: Would the unified German state include both Prussia and the Austrian Empire? If it included Austria, what about the non-German territories of the Austrian Empire? And could the powerful, conservative kingdom of Prussia coexist in a unified German state with other, more liberal but smaller states? These questions would vex German history for decades to come.

Polish nationalism revived after the collapse of the revolt in 1830 against Russian domination. It found its most ringing voice in the poet Adam Mickiewicz

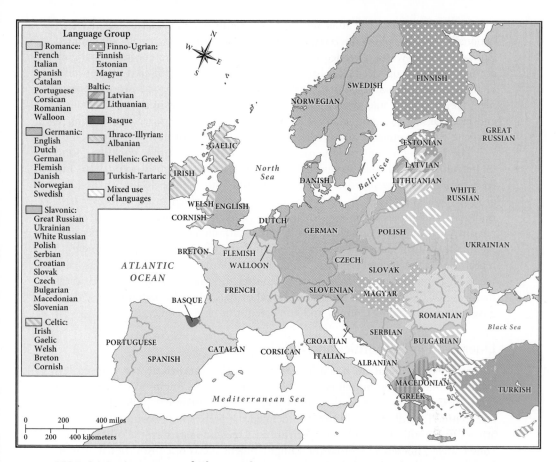

MAP 21.3 Languages of Nineteenth-Century Europe   Even this detailed map of linguistic diversity understates the number of different languages and dialects spoken in Europe. In Italy, for example, few people spoke Italian as their first language. Instead, they spoke local dialects such as Piedmontese or Ligurian, and some who came from the regions bordering France spoke better French than Italian. How does the map underline the inherent contradictions of nationalism in Europe? What were the consequences of linguistic diversity within national borders? Keep in mind that even in Spain, France, and Great Britain, linguistic diversity continued right up to the beginning of the 1900s.

(1798–1855), whose mystical writings portrayed the Polish exiles as martyrs of a crucified nation with an international Christian mission. Mickiewicz formed the Polish Legion to fight for national restoration, but rivalries and divisions prevented united action until 1846, when Polish exiles in Paris tried to launch a coordinated insurrection for Polish independence. Plans for an uprising in the Polish province of Galicia in the Austrian Empire collapsed when peasants instead revolted against their noble Polish masters.

In Russia, nationalism took the form of opposition to Western ideas. Russian nationalists, or Slavophiles (lovers of the Slavs), opposed the Westernizers, who wanted Russia to follow Western models of industrial development and constitutional government. The Slavophiles favored maintaining rural traditions infused by the values of the Russian Orthodox church. Only a return to Russia's basic historical principles, they argued, could protect the country against the corrosion of rationalism and materialism. The conflict between Slavophiles and Westernizers has continued to shape Russian cultural and intellectual life to the present day.

The most significant nationalist movement in western Europe could be found in Ireland. The Irish had struggled for centuries against English occupation, but Irish nationalists developed strong organizations only in the 1840s. In 1842, a group of writers founded the Young Ireland movement, which aimed to recover Irish traditions and preserve the Gaelic language (spoken by at least one-third of the peasantry). Daniel O'Connell (1775–1847), a Catholic lawyer and landowner who sat in the British House of Commons, hoped to force the British Parliament to repeal the Act of Union of 1801, which had made Ireland part of Great Britain. In 1843, London newspapers reported "monster meetings" that drew crowds of as many as 300,000 people in support of repeal of the union. In response, the British government arrested O'Connell and convicted him of conspiracy.

Liberalism in Economics and Politics

As an ideology, **liberalism** had a longer lineage than nationalism but enjoyed less influence among the common people. Liberalism traced its origins to the writings of John Locke in the seventeenth century and the Enlightenment philosophy in the eighteenth. The adherents of liberalism defined themselves in opposition to conservatives on one end of the political spectrum and revolutionaries on the other. Unlike conservatives, liberals supported the Enlightenment ideals of constitutional guarantees of personal liberty and free trade in economics, believing that they would promote social improvement and economic growth. Liberals generally applauded the social and economic changes produced by the Industrial Revolution, while opposing the violence and excessive state power promoted by the French Revolution. The leaders of the expanding middle class composed of manufacturers, merchants, and professionals favored liberalism.

The rapid industrialization and urbanization of Great Britain created a receptive environment for liberalism. Its foremost proponent in the early nineteenth century was the philosopher and jurist Jeremy Bentham (1748–1832). He called his brand of liberalism utilitarianism because he held that the best policy is the one that produces "the greatest good for the greatest number" and is thus the most useful, or utilitarian. Bentham criticized the injustices of the British parliamentary process, the abuses of the prisons and the penal code, and the educational system. In his zeal for social engineering, Bentham proposed model prisons that would emphasize rehabilitation through close supervision rather than corporal punishment.

British liberals wanted government to limit its economic role to maintaining the currency, enforcing contracts, and financing major enterprises like the military and the railroads. They therefore sought to lower or eliminate British tariffs, especially through repeal of the **Corn Laws**, which benefited landowners by preventing the import of cheap foreign grain while keeping the price of food artificially high for the workers. When landholders in the House of Commons thwarted efforts to lower grain tariffs, two Manchester cotton manufacturers set up the Anti–Corn Law League. The league appealed to the middle class against the landlords, who were labeled "a bread-taxing oligarchy" and "blood-sucking vampires," and attracted thousands of workers to its meetings. League members established local branches, published newspapers and the journal *The Economist* (founded in 1843 and now one of the world's most influential periodicals), and campaigned in elections. They finally won the support of the Tory prime minister Sir Robert Peel, whose government repealed the Corn Laws in 1846.

Free trade had less appeal in continental Europe than in England because continental industries needed protection against British industrial dominance. As a consequence, liberals on the continent focused on constitutional reform. French liberals, for example, agitated for greater press freedoms and a broadening of the vote. Louis-Philippe's government thwarted liberals' hopes for reforms by suppressing many political organizations and reestablishing censorship. Repression muted criticism in most other European states as well. Nevertheless, some state bureaucrats, especially university-trained middle-class officials, favored economic liberalism. Hungarian count Stephen Széchenyi (1791–1860) personally campaigned for the introduction of British-style changes. He helped start up steamboat traffic on the Danube, encouraged the importation of machinery and technicians for steam-driven textile factories, and pushed the construction of Hungary's first railway line, from Budapest to Vienna.

In the 1840s, however, Széchenyi's efforts paled before those of the flamboyant Magyar nationalist Lajos Kossuth (1802–1894). After spending four years in prison for sedition, Kossuth grabbed every opportunity to publicize American democracy and British political liberalism, all in a fervent nationalist spirit. In 1844, he founded the Protective Association, whose members bought only Hungarian products; to Kossuth, boycotting Austrian goods was crucial to ending "colonial dependence" on Austria.

Even in Russia, signs of liberal opposition appeared in the 1830s and 1840s. Small circles of young noblemen serving in the army or bureaucracy met in cities, especially Moscow, to discuss the latest Western ideas. Out of these groups came such future revolutionaries as Alexander Herzen (1812–1870), described by the police as "a daring free-thinker, extremely dangerous to society." Tsar Nicholas I (r. 1825–1855) banned Western liberal writings as well as all books about the United States. He sent nearly ten thousand people a year into exile in Siberia as punishment for their political activities.

Socialism and the Early Labor Movement

The newest ideology, **socialism**, took up where liberalism left off: socialists believed that the liberties advocated by liberals benefited only the middle class—the owners of factories and businesses—not the workers. They sought to reorganize society totally rather than to reform it piecemeal through political measures. They envisioned a future society in which workers would share a harmonious, cooperative, and prosperous life.

Early socialists criticized the emerging Industrial Revolution for dividing society into two classes: the new middle class, or capitalists (who owned the wealth), and the working class, their downtrodden and impoverished employees. As their name suggests, the socialists aimed to restore harmony and cooperation through social reorganization. Robert Owen (1771–1858), a successful Welsh-born manufacturer, founded British socialism. In 1800, he bought a cotton mill in New Lanark, Scotland, and began to set up a model factory town, where workers labored only ten hours a day (instead of seventeen, as was common) and children between the ages of five and ten attended school rather than working. Owen moved to the United States in the 1820s and founded a community named New Harmony in Indiana. The experiment collapsed after three years, a victim of internal squabbling. But out of Owen's experiments and writings, such as *The Book of the New Moral World* (1820), would come the movement for producer cooperatives (businesses owned and controlled by their workers), consumers' cooperatives (stores in which consumers owned shares), and a national trade union.

The French socialists Claude Henri de Saint-Simon (1760–1825) and Charles Fourier (1772–1837) shared Owen's alarm about the effects of industrialization on social relations. Saint-Simon—who coined the terms *industrialism* and *industrialist* to define the new economic order and its chief animators—believed that work was the central element in the new society and that it should be controlled not by politicians but by scientists, engineers, artists, and industrialists themselves. To correct the abuses of the new industrial order, Fourier urged the establishment of communities that were part garden city and part agricultural commune; all jobs would be rotated to maximize happiness. Fourier hoped that a network of small, decentralized communities would replace the state.

Women often played key roles in early socialism. In 1832, Saint-Simonian women founded a feminist newspaper, *The Free Woman*, asserting that "with the emancipation of woman will come the emancipation of the worker." In Great Britain, many women joined the Owenites and helped form cooperative societies and unions. They defended women's working-class organizations against the complaints of men in the new societies and trade unions. The French activist Flora Tristan (1801–1844) devoted herself to reconciling the interests of male and female workers. She published a stream of books and pamphlets urging male workers to address women's unequal status, arguing that "the emancipation of male workers is *impossible* so long as women remain in a degraded state."

Even though most male socialists ignored Tristan's plea for women's participation, they did strive to create working-class associations. The French socialist Louis Blanc (1811–1882) explained the importance of working-class associations in his book *Organization of Labor* (1840), which deeply influenced the French labor movement. Similarly, the printer turned journalist Pierre-Joseph Proudhon (1809–1865) urged workers to form producers' associations so that the workers could control the work process and eliminate profits made by capitalists. His 1840 book *What Is Property?* argues that property is theft: labor alone is productive, and rent, interest, and profit unjust.

After 1840, some socialists began to call themselves **communists**, emphasizing their desire to replace private property by communal, collective ownership. The Frenchman Étienne Cabet (1788–1856) was the first to use the word *communist*. In 1840, he published *Travels in Icaria*, a novel describing a communist utopia in which a popularly elected dictatorship efficiently organized work and reduced the workday to seven hours.

Out of the churning of socialist ideas of the 1840s emerged two men whose collaboration would change the definition of socialism and remake it into an ideology that would shake the world for the next 150 years. Karl Marx (1818–1883) had studied philosophy at the University of Berlin, edited a liberal newspaper until the Prussian government suppressed it, and then left for Paris, where he met Friedrich Engels (1820–1895). While working in the offices of his wealthy family's cotton manufacturing interests in Manchester, England, Engels had been shocked into writing *The Condition of the Working Class in England in 1844* (1845), a sympathetic depiction of industrial workers' dismal lives. In Paris, where German and eastern European intellectuals could pursue their political interests more freely than at home, Marx and Engels organized the Communist League, in whose name they published *The Communist Manifesto* in 1848.

It eventually became the touchstone of Marxist and communist revolutions all over the world. Communists, the *Manifesto* declared, must aim for "the downfall of the bourgeoisie [capitalist class] and the ascendancy of the proletariat [working class], the abolition of the old society based on class conflicts and the foundation of a new society without classes and without private property." Marx and Engels embraced industrialization because they believed it would eventually bring on the proletarian revolution and thus lead inevitably to the abolition of exploitation, private property, and class society.

Even when not overtly revolutionary, the upsurge in working-class organizations frightened the middle classes. A newspaper exclaimed in 1834, "The trade unions are, we have no doubt, the most dangerous institutions that were ever permitted to take root." Many British workers joined in **Chartism**, which aimed to transform Britain into a democracy. In 1838, political radicals drew up the People's Charter, which demanded universal manhood suffrage, vote by secret ballot, equal electoral districts, annual elections, and the elimination of property qualifications for and the payment of stipends to members of Parliament. Women took part by founding female political unions, setting up Chartist Sunday schools, organizing boycotts of unsympathetic shopkeepers, and joining Chartist temperance associations. Nevertheless, the People's Charter refrained from calling for woman suffrage because the movement's leaders feared that doing so would alienate potential supporters.

The Chartists organized a massive campaign during 1838 and 1839, with large public meetings, fiery speeches, and torchlight parades. Presented with petitions for the People's Charter signed by more than a million people, the House of Commons refused to act. In response to this rebuff from middle-class liberals, the Chartists allied themselves in the 1840s with working-class strike movements in the manufacturing districts and associated with various European revolutionary movements.

Continental European workers were less well organized because trade unions and strikes were illegal everywhere except Great Britain. Nevertheless, artisans and skilled workers in France formed mutual aid societies that provided insurance, death benefits, and education. In eastern and central Europe, socialism and labor organization—like liberalism—had less impact than in western Europe. Cooperative societies and workers' newspapers did not appear in the German states until 1848. In general, labor organization tended to flourish where urbanization and industrialization were most advanced; even though factory workers rarely organized, skilled artisans did so in order to resist mechanization and wage cuts. When revolutions broke out in 1848, artisans and workers played a prominent—and controversial—role.

REVIEW   Why did ideologies have such a powerful appeal in the 1830s and 1840s?

The Revolutions of 1848

Food shortages, overpopulation, and unemployment helped turn ideological turmoil into revolution. In 1848, demonstrations and uprisings toppled governments, forced rulers and ministers to flee, and offered revolutionaries an opportunity to put liberal, socialist, and nationalist ideals into practice. In the end, the revolutions failed because the various ideological movements quarreled, leaving an opening for rulers and their armies to return to power. Rulers returned, but they now faced populations with greater expectations for political participation, national unification, and government responsiveness to social problems.

The Hungry Forties

Beginning in 1845, crop failures across Europe caused food prices to shoot skyward. In the best of times, urban workers paid 50 to 80 percent of their income for a diet consisting largely of bread; now even bread was beyond their means. Overpopulation hastened famine in some places, especially Ireland, where blight destroyed the staple crop, potatoes, first in 1846 and again in 1848 and 1851. Irish peasants had planted potatoes because a family of four might live off one acre of potatoes but would require at least two acres of grain. By the 1840s, Ireland was especially vulnerable to the potato blight. Out of a population of eight million, as many as one million people died of starvation or disease. Corpses lay unburied on the sides of roads, and whole families were found dead in their cottages, half-eaten by dogs. Hundreds of thousands emigrated to England, the United States, and Canada.

Throughout Europe, famine jeopardized social peace. In age-old fashion, rumors circulated about farmers hoarding grain to drive up prices. Believing that governments should ensure fair prices, crowds took to the streets to protest, often attacking markets or bakeries. Although harvests improved in 1848, by then many people had lost their land or become hopelessly indebted. High food prices also drove down the demand for manufactured goods, resulting in increased unemployment. Industrial workers' wages had been rising, but the cost of living rose even faster.

Another French Revolution

The specter of hunger amplified the voices criticizing established rulers. A Parisian demonstration in favor of reform turned violent on February 23, 1848, when panicky soldiers opened fire on the crowd, killing forty or fifty demonstrators. The next day, faced with fifteen hundred barricades and a furious populace, King Louis-Philippe abdicated and fled to England. A hastily formed provisional government declared France a republic once again.

The new French republican government issued liberal reforms—an end to the death penalty for political crimes, the abolition of slavery in the colonies, and freedom of the press—and agreed to introduce universal adult male suffrage despite misgivings about political participation by peasants and unemployed workers. The government allowed Paris officials to organize a system of "national workshops" to provide the unemployed with construction work. To meet a mounting deficit, the provisional government then levied a 45 percent surtax on property taxes, alienating peasants and landowners.

While peasants grumbled, scores of newspapers and political clubs inspired grass-roots democratic fervor in Paris and other cities. Meeting in concert halls, theaters, and government auditoriums, the clubs became a regular evening attraction for the citizenry. Women also formed clubs, published women's newspapers, and demanded representation in national politics.

This street-corner activism alarmed middle-class liberals and conservatives. Tension between the government and the workers in the national workshops rose. Faced with rising radicalism in Paris and other big cities, the voters elected a largely conservative National Assembly in April 1848; most of the deputies chosen were middle-class professionals or landowners who favored either a restoration of the monarchy or a moderate republic. The Assembly immediately appointed a five-man executive committee to run the government and pointedly excluded known supporters of workers' rights. Suspicious of all demands for rapid change, the deputies dismissed a petition to restore divorce and voted down woman suffrage by 899 to 1. When the numbers enrolled in the national workshops in Paris rocketed from a predicted 10,000 to 110,000, the government ordered the workshops closed to new workers, and on June 21 it directed that those already enrolled move to the provinces or join the army.

The workers exploded in anger. In the June Days, as the following week came to be called, the government forces crushed the workers: more than 10,000 people, most of them workers, were killed or injured; 12,000 were arrested; and 4,000 eventually were convicted and deported to Algeria.

After the National Assembly adopted a new constitution calling for a presidential election in which all adult men could vote, the electorate chose **Louis-Napoleon Bonaparte** (1808–1873), nephew of the dead emperor. Bonaparte got more than 5.5 million votes out of some 7.4 million cast. His election spelled the end of the Second Republic, just as his uncle had dismantled the first one established in 1792. In 1852, on the forty-eighth anniversary of Napoleon I's coronation as emperor, Louis-Napoleon declared himself Emperor Napoleon III, thus inaugurating the Second Empire. (Napoleon I's son died and never became Napoleon II, but Napoleon III wanted to create a sense of legitimacy and so used the Roman numeral III.) Although the revolution of 1848 never had a period of terror like that in 1793–1794, it nonetheless ended in similar fashion, with an authoritarian government that tried to play monarchists and republicans off against each other.

Nationalist Revolution in Italy

In January 1848, a revolt broke out in Palermo, Sicily, against the Bourbon ruler. Then came the electrifying news of the February revolution in Paris. In Milan, a huge nationalist demonstration quickly degenerated into battles between Austrian forces and armed demonstrators. In Venice, an uprising drove out the Austrians. Peasants in the south occupied large landowners' estates. Artisans and workers called for higher wages, restrictions on the use of machinery, and unemployment relief.

But class divisions and regional differences stood in the way of national unity. Property owners, businessmen, and professionals wanted liberal reforms and national unification under a conservative regime; intellectuals, workers, and artisans dreamed of democracy and social reforms. Some nationalists favored a loose federation; others wanted a monarchy under Charles Albert of Piedmont-Sardinia; still others urged rule by the pope; a few shared Giuseppe Mazzini's vision of a republic with a strong central government. Many leaders of national unification spoke standard Italian only as a second language; most Italians spoke regional dialects.

As king of the most powerful Italian state, Charles Albert (r. 1831–1849) inevitably played a central role. After some hesitation caused by fears of French intervention, he led a military campaign against Austria. Although Austrian troops defeated Charles Albert in the north, democratic and nationalist forces prevailed at first in the south. In the fall, the Romans drove the pope from the city and declared Rome a republic. For the next few months, republican leaders, such as Giuseppe Mazzini and Giuseppe Garibaldi (1807–1882), congregated in Rome to organize the new republic. These efforts faltered when foreign powers intervened. The new president of France, Louis-Napoleon Bonaparte, sent an expeditionary force to secure the papal throne for Pius IX. Mazzini and Garibaldi fled. Revolution had been defeated in Italy, but the memory of the Roman Republic and the commitment to unification remained, and they would soon emerge again with new force.

Revolt and Reaction in Central Europe

News of the revolution in Paris also provoked popular demonstrations in central and eastern Europe. When the Prussian army tried to push back a crowd gathered in front of Berlin's royal palace on March 18, 1848, their actions provoked panic and street fighting. The next day the crowd paraded wagons loaded with the dead bodies of demonstrators under the window of the Prussian king Frederick William IV (r. 1840–1860), forcing him to salute the victims killed by his own army. In a state of near collapse, the king promised to call an assembly to draft a constitution.

The goal of German unification soon took precedence over social reform or constitutional changes within the separate states. In March and April, most of the German states agreed to elect delegates to a federal parliament at Frankfurt that would attempt to unite Germany. Local princes and even the more powerful kings of Prussia and Bavaria seemed to totter. Yet the revolutionaries' weaknesses soon became apparent. The eight hundred delegates to the Frankfurt parliament had little practical political experience and no access to an army. Unemployed artisans and workers smashed machines; peasants burned landlords' records and occasionally attacked Jewish moneylenders; women set up clubs and newspapers to demand their emancipation from "perfumed slavery."

The advantage lay with the princes, who bided their time. While the Frankfurt parliament laboriously prepared a liberal constitution for a united Germany—one that denied self-determination to Czechs, Poles, and Danes within its proposed German borders—Frederick William recovered his confidence. First, his army crushed the revolution in Berlin in the fall of 1848. Prussian troops then intervened to help other local rulers put down the last wave of democratic and nationalist insurrections in the spring of 1849. When the Frankfurt parliament finally concluded its work, offering the emperorship of a constitutional, federal Germany to the king of Prussia, Frederick William contemptuously refused this "crown from the gutter."

Events followed a similar course in the Austrian Empire. Just as Italians were driving the Austrians out of their lands in northern Italy and Magyar nationalists were demanding political autonomy for Hungary, a student-led demonstration for political reform on March 13, 1848, in Vienna turned into rioting, looting, and machine breaking. Metternich resigned, escaping to England in disguise. Emperor Ferdinand promised a constitution, an elected parliament, and the end of censorship. The beleaguered authorities in Vienna could not refuse Magyar demands for home rule, and Stephen Széchenyi and Lajos Kossuth (see page 629) both became ministers in the new Hungarian government. The Magyars were the largest ethnic group in Hungary but still did not make up 50 percent of the population, which included Croats, Romanians, Slovaks, and Slovenes, all of whom preferred Austrian rule to domination by local Magyars.

The ethnic divisions in Hungary foreshadowed the many political and social divisions that would doom the revolutionaries. Fears of peasant insurrection prompted the Magyar nationalists around Kossuth to abolish serfdom, thereby alienating the largest noble landowners. The new government infuriated the other nationalities when it imposed the Magyar language on them. In Prague, Czech nationalists convened a Slav congress as a counter to the Germans' Frankfurt parliament and called for a reorganization of the Austrian Empire that would recognize the rights of ethnic minorities.

The Austrian government took advantage of these divisions. To quell peasant discontent, it abolished all remaining peasant obligations to the nobility in March 1848. Rejoicing country folk soon lost interest in the revolution. Military force finally broke up the revolutionary movements. The first blow fell in Prague in June 1848; General Prince Alfred von Windischgrätz, the military governor, bombarded the city into submission when a demonstration led to violence (including the shooting death of his wife, watching from a window). After another uprising in Vienna a few months later, Windischgrätz marched seventy thousand soldiers into the capital and set up direct military rule. In December, the Austrian monarchy came back to life when the eighteen-year-old Francis Joseph (r. 1848–1916), unencumbered by promises extracted by the revolutionaries from his now feeble uncle Ferdinand, assumed the imperial crown after intervention by leading court officials. In the spring of 1849, the Austrian army teamed up with Tsar Nicholas I, who marched into Hungary with more than 300,000 Russian troops. Hungary was put under brutal martial law. Széchenyi went mad, and Kossuth found refuge in the United States.

Aftermath to 1848: Reimposing Authority

Although the revolutionaries of 1848 failed to achieve their goals, their efforts left a profound mark on the political and social landscape. Between 1848 and 1851, the French served a kind of republican apprenticeship that prepared the population for another, more lasting republic after 1870. In Italy, the failure of unification did not stop the spread of nationalist ideas and the rooting of demands for democratic participation. In the German states, the revolutionaries of 1848 turned nationalism from an idea devised by professors and writers into a popular enthusiasm and even a practical reality. The initiation of artisans, workers, and journeymen into democratic clubs increased political awareness in the lower classes and helped prepare them for broader political participation. Almost all the German states had a constitution and a parliament after 1850. The spectacular failures of 1848 thus hid some important underlying successes.

The absence of revolution in 1848 in some regions of the West was just as significant as its presence. No revolution occurred in Great Britain, the Netherlands, or Belgium, the three places where industrialization and urbanization had developed most rapidly. In Great Britain, the Chartist movement mounted several gigantic demonstrations to force Parliament into granting all adult males the vote. But even though Parliament refused, no uprising occurred — in part because the government had already proved its responsiveness: the middle classes in Britain had been co-opted into the established order by the Reform Bill of 1832, and the working classes had won parliamentary regulation of children's and women's work.

The other notable exception to revolution among the great powers was Russia, where Tsar Nicholas I maintained a tight grip through police surveillance and censorship. The Russian schools, limited to the upper classes, taught Nicholas's three most cherished principles: autocracy (the unlimited power of the tsar), orthodoxy (obedience to the church in religion and morality), and nationality (devotion to Russian traditions). These provided no space for political dissent.

Although much had changed, the aristocracy remained the dominant power almost everywhere. As army officers, aristocrats put down revolutionary forces. As landlords, they continued to dominate the rural scene and control parliamentary bodies. They also held many official positions in the state bureaucracies. As conservatives returned to power, all signs of women's political activism disappeared. The French feminist movement, the most advanced in Europe, fell apart when, after the June Days, the increasingly conservative republican government forbade women to form political clubs and arrested and imprisoned two of the most outspoken women leaders for their socialist activities. As rulers reimposed their authority in the years after 1848, many socialists, communists, and nationalists suffered a similar fate: if they did not fall in battle or go to prison, they fled into exile, waiting for another opportunity to voice their demands.

> **REVIEW**   Why did the revolutions of 1848 fail?

Conclusion

In 1851, Europe's most important female monarch presided over a midcentury celebration of peace and industrial growth that helped dampen the still-smoldering fires of revolutionary passion. In the place of revolutionary fervor was a government-sponsored spectacle of what industry, hard work, and technological imagination could produce. Queen Victoria (r. 1837–1901), who herself promoted the notion of domesticity as women's sphere, opened the Great Exhibition of the Works of Industry of All Nations in London on May 1. A huge iron-and-glass building housed the display. Soon people referred to it as the Crystal Palace; its nine hundred tons of glass created an aura of fantasy, and the abundant goods from around the world inspired satisfaction and pride.

Many of the six million people who visited the Crystal Palace display traveled on the new railroads, the foremost symbol of the age of industrial transformation. Along with the railroads, the application of steam engines to textile manufacturing set in motion a host of economic and social changes: cities burgeoned with rapidly growing populations; factories concentrated laborers who formed a new working class; manufacturers now challenged landed elites for political leadership; and social problems galvanized reform organizations and governments alike. The Crystal Palace presented the rosy view of modern, industrial, urban life, but the housing shortages, inadequacy of water supplies, and recurrent epidemic diseases had not disappeared.

The revolutions of 1848 brought to the surface the profound tensions within a European society in transition toward industrialization and urbanization. After them, the Industrial Revolution continued and workers developed more extensive organizations. Confronted with the menace of revolution, conservative elites now

The Crystal Palace, 1851   George Baxter's lithograph (above) shows the exterior of the main building for the Great Exhibition of the Works of Industry of All Nations in London. It was designed by Sir Joseph Paxton to gigantic dimensions: 1,848 feet long by 456 feet wide; 135 feet high; 772,784 square feet of ground-floor area covering no less than 18 acres. The lithograph by Peter Mabuse (left) offers a view of one of the colonial displays at the Great Exhibition. The tented room and carved ivory throne are meant to recall India, Britain's premier colony. (Top: © Maidstone Museum and Art Gallery, Kent, UK/Bridgeman Images. Left: Private Collection/The Stapleton Collection/ Bridgeman Images.)

sought alternatives that would be less threatening to the established order and still permit some change. This search for alternatives became immediately evident in the question of national unification in Germany and Italy. National unification would hereafter depend not on speeches and parliamentary resolutions, but rather on what the Prussian leader Otto von Bismarck would call "iron and blood."

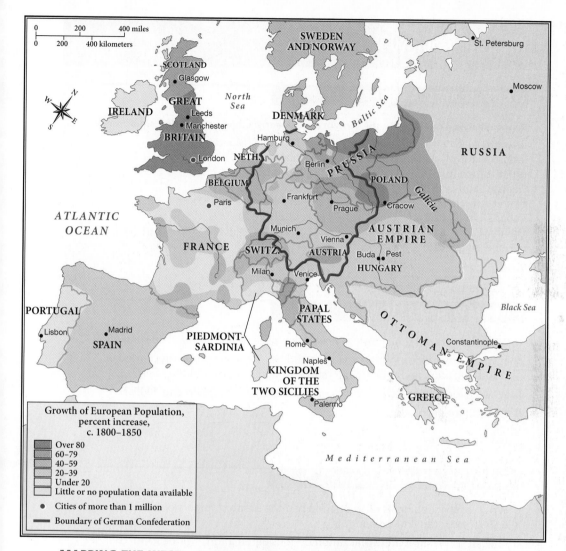

MAPPING THE WEST   Europe in 1850   This map of population growth between 1800 and 1850 reveals important trends that would not otherwise be evident. Although population growth correlated for the most part with industrialization, population also grew in more agricultural regions such as East Prussia, Poland, and Ireland. Ireland's rapid population growth in the early nineteenth century does not appear on this map because the famine of 1846–1851 killed more than 10 percent of the population and forced many others to emigrate.

Chapter Review

KEY TERMS AND PEOPLE

Be sure that you can identify the term or person and explain its historical significance.

ideology (p. 610)
Industrial Revolution (p. 610)
urbanization (p. 616)
George Sand (p. 620)
domesticity (p. 623)
imperialism (p. 624)
Opium War (p. 625)
nationalism (p. 626)

Giuseppe Mazzini (p. 626)
liberalism (p. 628)
Corn Laws (p. 629)
socialism (p. 629)
communists (p. 631)
Chartism (p. 631)
Louis-Napoleon Bonaparte (p. 633)

REVIEW QUESTIONS

1. What dangers did the Industrial Revolution pose to both urban and rural life?

2. In which areas did reformers trying to address the social problems created by industrialization and urbanization succeed, and in which did they fail?

3. Why did ideologies have such a powerful appeal in the 1830s and 1840s?

4. Why did the revolutions of 1848 fail?

MAKING CONNECTIONS

1. Which of the ideologies of this period had the greatest impact on political events? How can you explain this?

2. In what ways might industrialization be considered a force for peaceful change rather than a revolution? (*Hint:* Think about the situation in Great Britain.)

3. In what ways did the revolutions of 1848 repeat elements of the French revolutions in 1789 and 1830, and in what ways did they break with those precedents?

4. Neither Great Britain nor Russia had a revolution in 1848. How is the absence of revolution in those two countries related to their history in the preceding decades?

IMPORTANT EVENTS

1830–1832	• Cholera epidemic sweeps across Europe
1830	• France invades and begins conquest of Algeria
1832	• George Sand, *Indiana*
1833	• Factory Act regulates work of children in Great Britain; abolition of slavery in British Empire
1834	• German *Zollverein* is established under Prussian leadership
1835	• Belgium opens first continental railway built with state funds
1839	• Beginning of Opium War; invention of photography
1841	• Charles Dickens, *The Old Curiosity Shop*
1846	• Famine strikes Ireland; Corn Laws are repealed in England; peasant insurrection in Austrian province of Galicia
1848	• Revolutions of 1848 throughout Europe; last great wave of Chartist demonstrations in Britain; Karl Marx and Friedrich Engels, *The Communist Manifesto*; abolition of slavery in French colonies; end of serfdom in Austrian Empire
1851	• Crystal Palace exhibition in London

22

Politics and Culture of the Nation-State

1850–1870

CHAPTER FOCUS

How did political, international, societal, and cultural developments in individual countries and across Europe in the mid-nineteenth century help create and strengthen nation states?

IN 1859, THE NAME *VERDI* suddenly appeared scrawled on walls across the cities of the Italian peninsula. The graffiti seemed to celebrate the composer Giuseppe Verdi, whose operas thrilled crowds of Europeans. Among Italians, Verdi was a particular hero; his stories of downtrodden groups struggling against tyrannical government seemed to refer specifically to them. As his operatic choruses thundered out calls to rebellion in the name of the nation, Italian audiences were sure that Verdi was telling them to throw off Austrian and papal rule and unite in a newborn Roman Empire. *VERDI* also formed an acronym for *Vittorio Emmanuele Re d'Italia* ("Victor Emmanuel, King of Italy"), and in 1859 it summoned Italians to unite under Victor Emmanuel II, king of Sardinia and Piedmont—the one Italian leader with a nationalist, modernizing profile. The graffiti was good publicity, for the very next year Italy united as a result of warfare and hard bargaining by political realists.

After the failed revolutions of 1848, European statesmen and the politically aware public increasingly rejected idealism in favor of Realpolitik—a politics of tough-minded realism aimed at strengthening the state and tightening social order. Realpolitikers disliked the romanticism of the revolutionaries.

Instead, they put their faith in power politics and even the use of violence to attain their goals. Two particularly skilled practitioners of Realpolitik, the Italian Camillo di Cavour and the Prussian Otto von Bismarck, succeeded in unifying Italy and Germany not by romantic slogans but by war and diplomacy. Most leading figures of the 1850s and 1860s, enmeshed like Verdi's operatic heroes in power politics, strengthened their states by harnessing the forces of nationalism and liberalism that had led to earlier romantic revolts. Their achievements changed the face of Europe.

Making a modern nation-state was a complicated task. Economic development was also crucial, as was using government policy and culture to create a sense of national identity and common purpose. Governments took vigorous steps to improve rapidly growing cities, promote public health, and boost national loyalty. State institutions such as public schools helped establish a common fund of knowledge and political beliefs. Authoritarian leaders like Bismarck and the new French emperor Napoleon III believed that a better quality of life would not only make the state more stable by calming revolutionary impulses of years past but also silence liberal critics.

Culture built a sense of belonging. Reading novels, attending operas and art exhibitions, and visiting the newly fashionable world's fairs gave ordinary people a stronger sense of being French or German or British. Like politicians, artists and writers also came to reject romanticism, featuring instead harsher, more realistic aspects of everyday life. Artists painted nudes in shockingly blunt ways, eliminating romantic hues and dreamy poses. Authors wrote about the bleak life of soldiers in wartime or about ordinary people suffering poverty or turning to crime. Alongside the tough-minded nation-building policies there arose tough-minded art, not just mirroring Realpolitik but encouraging it.

In their quest to build strong nations, Western politicians did not shy away from using violence or causing harm. They sent armies to distant areas to stamp out resistance to their continuing global expansion. At home, governments uprooted neighborhoods to construct public buildings, roads, and parks. The process of nation building was often brutal, bringing foreign wars, arrests, and even civil war—all the centerpieces of many Verdi operas. In 1871, an uprising of Parisians challenged the central government's intrusion into everyday life and its failure to count the costs. Thus, for the most part, the powerful Western nation-state did not arise spontaneously. Instead, its growth and the tighter unification of peoples depended on shrewd policy, deliberate warfare, and new inroads into societies around the world—which together formed the basis of Realpolitik.

The End of the Concert of Europe

The revolutions of 1848 had weakened the concert of Europe and thus allowed the forces of nationalism to flourish. It became more difficult for countries to control their competing ambitions and act together. In addition, the dreaded revival of Bonapartism in the person of Louis-Napoleon Bonaparte (1808–1873), the nephew of Napoleon I, added to European instability as France reasserted itself. One of Louis-Napoleon's targets was Russia, formerly a mainstay of the concert of Europe. To limit Russia's and Austria's grip on power, France helped engineer the Crimean War, which not only changed the distribution of European power but also resulted in the end of serfdom in Russia and the birth of new European nations.

Napoleon III and the Quest for French Glory

Louis-Napoleon Bonaparte, who declared himself Napoleon III in 1852, encouraged the cult of his famous uncle as part of nation building, showing Europe's leaders how to combine economic liberalism and nationalism with authoritarian rule. He claimed to represent people's "families, your property—rich and poor alike," but he closed cafés where men might discuss politics and established a rubber-stamp legislature, the Corps législatif, that made representative government a charade. Napoleon's opulent court dazzled the public, while his wife, Empress Eugénie, followed middle-class norms by playing up her domestic role as devoted mother to her only son and supporting many charities. The authoritarian, apparently old-fashioned order imposed by Napoleon showed that the radicalism of 1848 was under control.

Napoleon III was nonetheless a modernizer. He promoted a strong economy and public works programs that provided jobs. The magnificent rebuilding of Paris made France prosper as Europe recovered from the hard times of the late 1840s. Empress Eugénie wore lavish gowns, encouraging French silk production. The regime also reached a free-trade agreement with Britain and backed the establishment of innovative investment banks. Railway mileage increased fivefold during Napoleon III's reign. During the economic downturn of the late 1850s, he wooed support by allowing working-class organizations to form and introducing features of democratic government.

On the international scene, Napoleon III's main goals were to overcome the containment of France imposed by the Congress of Vienna and to acquire international glory like a true Bonaparte. To reshape European politics in France's favor, Napoleon pitted France first against Russia in the Crimean War and then against Austria in the War of Italian Unification (1860–1861). Napoleon also looked beyond Europe. In Algeria and Southeast Asia, his army struggled to enforce French rule. In Mexico, he attempted to install Maximilian, the brother of Habsburg emperor Francis Joseph, as emperor. In Egypt, he successfully encouraged the construction of the Suez Canal to connect the Mediterranean and the Red Sea. Overall, his foreign policy broke down the international order established at the Congress of Vienna.

The Crimean War, 1853–1856: Turning Point in European Affairs

Napoleon III first flexed his diplomatic muscle in the Crimean War (1853–1856), which began as a conflict between the Russian and Ottoman Empires but ended as a war with long-lasting consequences for much of Europe. While professing to uphold the status quo, Russia had been expanding into Asia and the Middle East. In particular, Tsar Nicholas I wanted territory in the Ottoman Empire, and Napoleon encouraged Nicholas to be even more aggressive in his expansionism—a maneuver that provoked war in October 1853 between the two eastern empires (Map 22.1).

The war drew in other states and upset Europe's balance of power as set in the Congress of Vienna. Napoleon III convinced Austria to remain neutral during the war, thus splitting the conservative Russian-Austrian coalition that had checked French ambitions since 1815. The Austrian government was concerned that the defeat of the Ottomans would bring Russian expansion into the Balkans. To protect its Mediterranean routes to East Asia, Britain prodded the Ottomans to stand up to Russia, but in the fall of 1853, the Russians blasted the Turkish wooden ships to bits at the Ottoman port of Sinope on the Black Sea. The Russians justified their actions as a necessary defense of Christians in the Ottoman Empire. In 1854, France and Great Britain, though enemies in war for more than a century, allied to declare war on Russia and defend the Ottoman Empire.

The Crimean War was spectacularly bloody. British and French troops landed in the Crimea in September 1854 and waged a long siege of the Russian naval base at Sevastopol, which fell only after a year of savage and costly combat. Generals on both sides demonstrated their incompetence, and governments failed to provide combatants with even minimal supplies, sanitation, or medical care. Hospitals had no beds, no dishes, and no water. A million men died, more than two-thirds from disease or starvation.

In the midst of this unfolding catastrophe, **Alexander II** (r. 1855–1881) ascended the Russian throne after the death of Nicholas I, his father. With casualties mounting, the new tsar asked for peace. As a result of the Peace of Paris, signed in March 1856, Russia

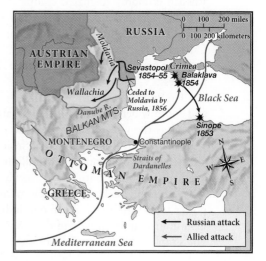

MAP 22.1 The Crimean War, 1853–1856
The most destructive war in Europe between the Napoleonic Wars and World War I, the Crimean War drew attention to the conflicting ambitions around territories of the declining Ottoman Empire. The war fractured the alliance of conservative forces from the Congress of Vienna, allowing Italy and Germany to come into being as unified states.

lost the right to base its navy in the Strait of Dardanelles and the Black Sea, which were declared neutral waters. Moldavia and Wallachia (which soon merged to form Romania) became autonomous Turkish provinces under the victors' protection, drastically reducing Russian influence in that region, too.

The Crimean War was full of consequence. New technologies were introduced into warfare: the railroad, shell-firing cannons, breech-loading rifles, and steam-powered ships. The telegraph and increased press coverage brought news from the Crimean front lines to home audiences more rapidly and in more detail than ever before. Reports of incompetent leadership, poor sanitation, and the huge death toll outraged the public, inspiring some civilians, such as the British nurse **Florence Nightingale**, to head for the front lines to help. Nightingale seized the moment to escape the confines of middle-class domesticity by organizing a battlefield nursing service to care for the British sick and wounded. (See the illustration on page 647.) Through her tough-minded organization of nursing units, she pioneered nursing as a profession and made sanitary conditions for soldiers a new and permanent priority.

More immediately, the war accomplished Napoleon III's goal of severing the alliance between Austria and Russia, the two conservative powers on which the Congress of Vienna peace settlement had rested since 1815. It thus ended Austria's and Russia's grip on European affairs and undermined their ability to contain the forces of liberalism and nationalism.

Reform in Russia

Russia's defeat in the Crimean War also made clear the need for meaningful reform. Hundreds of peasant insurrections had erupted in the decade before the war. "Our own and neighboring households were gripped with fear," one aristocrat reported. The Russian economy stagnated compared with that of western Europe. Old-fashioned farming techniques depleted soil and led to food shortages, and the nobility often ignored the suffering caused by malnutrition and hard labor. When Russia lost the Crimean War, the educated public, including some government officials, found the poor performance of serf armies a disgrace and the system of serf labor a glaring weakness.

Confronted with the need for change, Tsar Alexander II acted. Well educated and more widely traveled than his father, Alexander ushered in what came to be known as the Great Reforms. These granted Russians new rights from above as a way of preventing violent action from below. The most dramatic reform was the emancipation of almost fifty million serfs beginning in 1861. By the terms of emancipation, communities of newly freed serfs, headed by male village elders, received grants of land. The community itself, traditionally called a **mir**, had full power to allocate this land among individuals and to direct their economic activity. Communal landowning and decision making meant that individual peasants could not simply sell their parcel of land and leave their rural communities to work in factories, as laborers had been doing elsewhere in Europe.

Nurse Tending Wounded Man　The Crimean War exposed the backward, and lethal, sanitary conditions of warfare—conditions that became intolerable to nation-states concerned with the well-being of their citizen soldiers. Women's contribution as nurses during both the Crimean War (shown in this photograph) and the U.S. Civil War helped rectify the situation, but voluntary assistance was not enough to prevent horrific death rates from disease and lack of coordinated medical attention. (Private Collection/The Bridgeman Art Library International.)

In Russia peasants were not *given* land along with their personal freedom: they were forced to "redeem" the land they farmed by paying off long-term loans from the government, which in turn compensated the original landowners. The best land remained in the hands of the nobility, and the huge burden of debt and communal regulations slowed Russian agricultural development for decades. Even so, idealistic reformers believed that the emancipation of the serfs, once treated by the nobility virtually as livestock, had produced miraculous results. As one of them put it, "The people are without any exaggeration transfigured from head to foot. . . . The look, the walk, the speech, everything is changed."

The Russian state also reformed local administration, the judiciary, and the military. The government set up zemstvos—regional councils—through which aristocrats could control local affairs such as education, public health, and welfare. Zemstvos became a new political force with the potential for challenging the authoritarian central government. Some aristocrats took advantage of newly relaxed rules on travel to see how the rest of Europe was governed. Their vision broadened as they observed different ways of solving social and economic problems. The principle of equality of all persons before the law, regardless of social rank, was introduced in Russia for the first time as judicial reform gave all Russians access to modern civil courts. Military reform followed in 1874 when the government reduced the twenty-five-year period of service to a six-year term and began focusing on educating troops in an effort to match the efficiency and fitness of soldiers in western Europe.

Alexander's reforms helped landowners be more effective in the market even as they reduced the privileges of the nobility, weakening their authority and sparking family conflict. "An epidemic seemed to seize upon [noble] children . . . an epidemic of fleeing from the parental roof," one observer noted. Rejecting aristocratic leisure, youthful rebels from the upper class valued practical activity and sometimes identified with peasants and workers instead of their own class. Some formed communes in which they hoped to do humble manual labor; others turned to higher education, especially the sciences. Daughters of the nobility opposed their parents, escaping from home through phony marriages so they could study in western European universities. This rejection of traditional society led some to label these young people as nihilists (from the Latin for "nothing") — implying a lack of belief in any values whatsoever. In fact, however, the so-called nihilists represented a defiant spirit percolating not just at the bottom but also at the top of Russian society.

The atmosphere of change also inspired resistance among the more than one hundred Russian-dominated ethnic groups in the Russian Empire. Aristocratic and upper-class nationalist Poles staged an uprising in 1863, demanding full national independence for their country. By 1864, however, Alexander II's army had crushed them. The government then swiftly clamped down on other nationalist uprisings and enforced **Russification**—a tactic meant to reduce the threat of future rebellion by insisting that ethnic minorities within the empire adopt Russian language and culture. Despite these measures, the tsarist regime only partially succeeded in developing the administrative, economic, and civic institutions that made the nation-state strong elsewhere in Europe, allowing few to share in power. In imperial Russia, autocracy and continued abuse of many in the population slowed the development of the sense of common citizenship forming elsewhere in the West, while the urge to revolt grew.

REVIEW   What were the main results of the Crimean War?

War and Nation Building

Dynamic leaders in the German and Italian states used the opportunity provided by the weakened concert of Europe to unify their fragmented countries through warfare. When national disunity threatened, the United States waged a bloody civil war, which opened the way for further expansion and vigorous economic growth. The rise of powerful **nation-states** such as Italy, Germany, and the United States was accompanied by a sense of pride in national identity—or nationalism—among their peoples. This was not an inevitable or universal trend in the West, however. Millions of individuals in the Austrian Empire, Ireland, and elsewhere maintained a regional, local, or distinct ethnic identity even as the nation-state was strengthening and national sentiment was on the rise.

Cavour, Garibaldi, and the Process of Italian Unification

Despite the failure of the revolutions of 1848, hope for national unification remained strong in the Italian states, aided by diplomatic instability across Europe. The pragmatic **Camillo di Cavour** (1810–1861), prime minister of the kingdom of Piedmont-Sardinia from 1852 until his death, had a Realpolitiker's vision of how to unify the Italian states. A rebel in his youth, Cavour in his maturity organized steamship companies, played the stock market, and inhaled the heady air of modernization during his travels to Paris and London. He promoted economic development rather than idealistic uprisings as the means to achieve a united Italy. As a skilled prime minister, Cavour helped King Victor Emmanuel II (r. Piedmont-Sardinia 1849–1861, r. Italy 1861–1878) achieve a strong Piedmontese economy and a modern army as the foundation for Piedmont's claim to lead the unification process (Map 22.2).

To unify Italy, however, Piedmont would have to confront Austria, which governed the northern provinces of Lombardy and Venetia and exerted strong influence over most of the peninsula. Cavour turned for help to Napoleon III, who promised French assistance in exchange for the city of Nice and the region of Savoy. Napoleon III expected that France rather than Austria would then influence the peninsula thereafter. Sure of French help, Cavour provoked the Austrians to invade northern Italy in April 1859. The cause of Piedmont-Sardinia's monarchy now became the cause of nationalist Italians everywhere, even those who had supported romantic republicanism in 1848. The French and Piedmontese armies used the newly built Piedmontese railroad to move troops, thereby achieving rapid victories. Napoleon, suddenly fearing the growth of Piedmont as a potential competing force, independently signed a peace treaty with Austria that gave Lombardy, but not Venetia, to Piedmont. The rest of Italy remained disunited, leaving Cavour's nationalist ambitions still to be realized.

Napoleon III's plan to keep Italy disunited was soon derailed. Support for Piedmont continued to swell among Italians. Giuseppe Garibaldi (1807–1882), a committed republican and veteran of the revolutions of 1848, set sail from Genoa in May 1860 with a thousand red-shirted volunteers (many of them teenage boys) to liberate Sicily. In the autumn of that year, King Victor Emmanuel II's victorious forces descending from the north and Garibaldi's moving up from the south met in Naples. Garibaldi threw his support to the king, and in 1861, the kingdom of Italy was proclaimed with Victor Emmanuel as its ruler.

Exhausted by a decade of overwork, Cavour died within months of leading the unification, leaving lesser men to organize the new Italy. The task ahead was

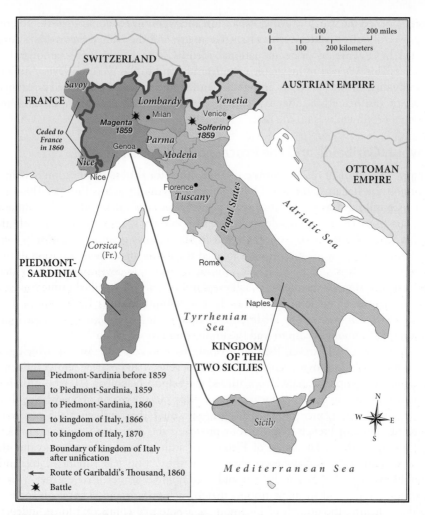

MAP 22.2 Unification of Italy, 1859–1870   The many states of the Italian peninsula had different languages, ways of life, and economic interests. The northern kingdom of Sardinia, which included the commercially advanced state of Piedmont, had much to gain from a unified market and a more extensive pool of labor. Although the armies of King Victor Emmanuel II and Giuseppe Garibaldi brought the Italian states together as a single country, it would take decades to construct a culturally, socially, and economically unified nation.

enormous and complex: there was still no common Italian language; 90 percent of the peninsula's inhabitants spoke local dialects. Moreover, consensus among Italy's elected political leaders was often difficult to reach after the war, and admirers of Cavour, such as Verdi (who had been made a senator), quit the quarrelsome political stage. Politicians from the wealthy commercial north and the impoverished agricultural south disagreed over issues like taxation and development, as they often do even today. Finally, Italian borders did not yet seem complete because Venetia and Rome remained outside them, under Austrian and French control, respectively. Holding the new nation together amid these difficulties was the romanticized retelling of the Italian struggle for freedom from foreign and domestic tyrants under the daring leadership of Garibaldi and his Red Shirts—a legend that papered over Cavour's economic and military Realpolitik.

Bismarck and the Realpolitik of German Unification

The most momentous act of nation building for Europe and the world was the creation of a united Germany in 1871 under Prussian leadership. The architect of the unified Germany was **Otto von Bismarck** (1815–1898). Bismarck came from a traditional Junker (Prussian landed nobility) family on his father's side; his mother's family included high-ranking bureaucrats. At university, the young Bismarck had gambled and womanized. After failing in the civil service, he worked to modernize operations on his landholdings while leading an otherwise decadent life. His marriage to a pious Lutheran woman gave him new seriousness. In the 1850s, his diplomatic service to the Prussian state made him increasingly angry at the Habsburg grip on German affairs. Establishing Prussia as the dominant German power became Bismarck's goal.

In 1862, William I (king of Prussia, r. 1861–1888; German emperor, r. 1871–1888) appointed Bismarck prime minister in hopes that he would crush the growing power of the liberals in the Prussian parliament. The liberals, representing the prosperous professional and business classes, had gained parliamentary strength at the expense of conservative landowners during the decades of industrial expansion. Indeed, the liberals' wealth was crucial to the Prussian state's power, but liberals wanted Prussia to be like other parts of western Europe, with political rights for citizens and increased civilian control of the military. William I, along with members of the traditional Prussian elite such as Bismarck, rejected the western European model. Acting on his conservative beliefs, Bismarck simply rammed through programs to build the army and prevent civilian control. "Germany looks not to Prussia's liberalism, but to its power," he proclaimed. "The great questions of the day will not be settled by speeches and majority decisions—that was the great mistake of 1848 and 1849—but by iron and blood."

After his triumph over the parliament, Bismarck led Prussia into a series of wars: against Denmark in 1864, Austria in 1866, and France in 1870. Using war as a political tactic, he kept the disunited German states from choosing Austrian leadership and instead united them around Prussia. Bismarck drew Austria into the 1864 war over Denmark's proposed incorporation of the provinces of Schleswig and Holstein, with their partially German population. The Prussian-Austrian victory resulted in an agreement that Prussia would administer Schleswig, and Austria, Holstein. That arrangement stretched Austria's geographic interests far from its central European base: "We were very honorable, but very dumb," Emperor Francis Joseph later said of being drawn into the Schleswig-Holstein debacle.

King William I of Prussia and His Generals   Realpolitik politicians used warfare to create new nations like the unified Germany, which led other states in using up-to-date weaponry and transportation. Nonetheless, horses, swords, and flashing helmets such as those worn by King William I and the generals of Prussia were still a major feature of developing modern warfare. (Private Collection / @Look and Learn / Bridgeman Images.)

Austria proved weaker than Prussia, because the Austrian empire lagged in economic development. Bismarck, however, so encouraged Austria's pretensions to grandeur that it disputed the administration of Schleswig and Holstein and in the summer of 1866 confidently declared war on Prussia itself. Within seven weeks, the modernized Prussian army won a decisive victory that allowed Bismarck to drive Austria from the German Confederation and create the North German Confederation, led by Prussia (Map 22.3).

To bring the remaining German states into Prussia's expanding orbit, Bismarck next provoked France into war. The atmosphere became charged when Spain proposed a Prussian prince to fill its vacant royal throne. This candidacy at once threatened France with Prussian rulers on two of its borders and inflated Prussian pride at the possibility of its own princes ruling grand states. To get nationalist sentiments onto the news pages in both countries, Bismarck edited a diplomatic communication to make it look as if the king of Prussia had insulted France over the issue of the vacant throne. Publication of the revised telegram inflamed the French into demanding war. The parliament gladly declared it on July 19, 1870,

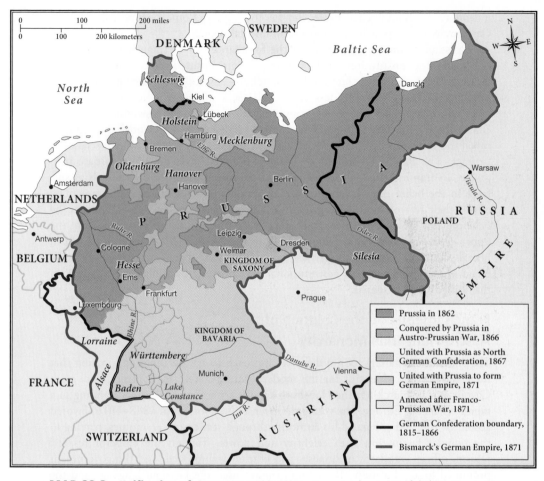

MAP 22.3 Unification of Germany, 1862–1871 In a complex series of diplomatic maneuvers, Prussian leader Otto von Bismarck welded disunited kingdoms and small states into a major continental power independent of the other dominant German dynasty, the Habsburg monarchy. That unity almost immediately unleashed the new nation's economic and industrial potential, but an aristocratic and agrarian elite remained firmly in power.

launching the Franco-Prussian War. The Prussians captured Napoleon III with his army on September 2, 1870, and France's Second Empire fell two days later.

A new French government struggled to carry on, and as Prussian forces besieged Paris, in January 1871 in the Hall of Mirrors at Versailles, King William of Prussia was proclaimed kaiser ("emperor") of the new German Reich ("empire"). The peace terms ending the Franco-Prussian War, signed in May, required France to cede the rich industrial provinces of Alsace and Lorraine to Germany and to pay a multibillion-franc indemnity. Without French protection for the papacy, Rome became part of Italy. Germany was now poised to dominate continental politics.

Prussian military might served as the foundation for German nation building, and a complex constitution for the German Empire ensured the continued political dominance of the aristocracy and monarchy—despite the growing wealth and influence of the liberal business classes. Kaiser William, who remained Prussia's king, controlled the military and appointed Bismarck to the powerful position of chancellor for the Reich. Individual German states were represented in a council called the Bundesrat, while the Reichstag was an assembly elected by universal male suffrage. The Reichstag ratified all budgets but had little power to initiate programs. In framing this political settlement, Bismarck accorded rights such as suffrage in the belief that the masses would uphold conservatism and the monarchy out of their fear of modernizing, exploitative businessmen. Taking no chances, he balanced this move with an electoral system in Prussia in which the votes from the upper classes counted more than those from the lower. He had little to fear from liberals, however. Dizzy with German military success, liberals came to support the blend of economic progress, constitutional government, and militaristic nationalism that Bismarck represented.

Francis Joseph and the Creation of the Austro-Hungarian Monarchy

The Austrian monarchy took a different approach to nation building, proving that there was no one blueprint for the modern nation-state. The confrontations with Cavour and Bismarck left the Habsburg Empire struggling to keep its standing in a rapidly changing Europe. The young monarch Francis Joseph (r. 1848–1916) favored absolutist rule and enhanced his authority through stiff court ceremonies, playing to the popular fascination with celebrity and power. Though the emperor resisted reform, official standards of honesty and efficiency improved, and the government promoted local education. The administration used the German language and the schools taught it, but the government respected the rights of national minorities— Czechs and Poles, for instance—to receive education and communicate with officials in their native tongues. Above all, the government boosted railway construction, attracted foreign capital, and helped trade to flow by abolishing most internal customs barriers. Like Paris, the capital city of Vienna underwent extensive rebuilding, and industrialization progressed, if unevenly.

In the fast-moving nineteenth century, the absolutist Austrian emperor Francis Joseph could not match Bismarck in nation building. Too much of the old regime remained as a roadblock: the Catholic church controlled education and civil institutions such as marriage, prosperous liberals lacked representation in such important policy matters as taxation and finance, and police informers swarmed around them. Wanting truly representative government and free speech, the liberals prevented measures—such as providing funds for modernizing the military—that would have strengthened the reactionary government in Austria. Unlike Bismarck in Prussia, there was no one to override the liberals to bring about change.

After Prussia's 1866 victory over Austria, the vast, wealthy kingdom of Hungary became the key to the Habsburg Empire's existence. The leaders of the Hungarian agrarian elites forced the Austrian emperor to accept a **dual monarchy**—that is, one in which the Magyars had home rule over the Hungarian kingdom within the Habsburg lands. This agreement restored the Hungarian parliament and gave it control of internal policy (including the right to decide how to treat Hungary's ethnic minorities). Although the Habsburg emperor Francis Joseph was king of Hungary and Austro-Hungarian foreign policy was coordinated from Vienna, the Hungarians mostly ruled themselves after 1867, weakening the process of nation building in the empire.

Although designed specifically to address the Hungarian demands, the dual monarchy led to claims by Czechs, Slovaks, and other national groups in the Habsburg Empire for a similar kind of self-rule. Czechs who had helped the empire advance industrially, for example, wanted Hungarian-style liberties. Other leaders of dissatisfied ethnic groups turned to **Pan-Slavism**—that is, the loyalty of all ethnic Slavs across national boundaries. Instead of looking toward Vienna, they turned to the largest Slavic country—Russia—as key to achieving the unity of all Slavs. With so many competing ethnicities, the Austro-Hungarian monarchy remained a dynastic state in which people could show loyalty to the Habsburg dynasty but had difficulty relating to one another as members of a single nation.

Political Stability through Gradual Reform in Great Britain

In contrast to the turmoil on the continent, Great Britain appeared the ideal of liberal progress. By the 1850s, the monarchy symbolized domestic tranquility and propriety. Queen Victoria (r. 1837–1901) and her husband, Prince Albert, portrayed themselves as models of morality, British stability, and middle-class virtues. Britain's parliamentary system steadily brought more men into the political process. Economic prosperity supported peaceful political reform, except that politicians did little to relieve Ireland's continued suffering. A flexible party system helped smooth governmental decision making: the Tories evolved into the Conservatives, who favored a more status-oriented politics but still went along with the emerging liberal consensus around economic development and representative government. The Whigs became the Liberals, so named for their commitment to progress, free trade, and an active role for industrialists as well as the aristocracy. In 1867, the Conservatives, led by Benjamin Disraeli (1804–1881), passed the Second Reform Bill, which extended voting rights to a million more men. Disraeli proposed, like Bismarck somewhat later, that the working classes would choose "the most conservative interests in the country"—not the business ones.

Both political parties supported reforms because citizens had formed pressure groups to influence national policies. Women's groups advocated the Matrimonial Causes Act of 1857, which facilitated divorce, and the Married Women's Property Act of 1870, which allowed married women to own property and keep the wages they earned. The Reform League, another pressure organization, had held mass demonstrations in London to bring about passage of the Second Reform Bill.

Plush royal ceremonies united critics and activists and masked political conflict but, more important, involved all social classes. Queen Victoria and Prince Albert, with their newly devised celebrations of royal marriages, anniversaries, and births, promoted the monarchy so successfully that the term *Victorian* came to symbolize almost the entire nineteenth century. Yet Britain's politicians were as devoted to Realpolitik as those in Germany, Italy, or France. Their policies included the use of violence to expand their overseas empire and, increasingly, to control Ireland, where reform stopped short. This violence occurred beyond the view of most British people, however, allowing them to imagine their nation as peaceful, advanced, and united.

Nation Building in North America

Nation building in the United States involved unprecedented and destructive upheaval at midcentury. The young nation had a more democratic political culture than that of Europe, and nationalism was on the rise. Virtually universal white male suffrage, a rambunctiously independent press, and mass political parties promoted the belief that sovereignty derived from the people. From the beginning, a combative public politics shaped America.

The United States continued to expand westward (Map 22.4). In 1848, victory in the Mexican-American War almost doubled the size of the country: the United States officially annexed Texas, and large portions of California and the Southwest extended U.S. borders into formerly Mexican land. Politicians and citizens alike favored banning native Americans from these western lands and confining them to reservations. There was no agreement, however, on whether slavery would be allowed in the new western territories. The issue polarized the country. In the North, politicians in the new Republican Party ran on a platform of "free soil, free labor, free men."

After Republican Abraham Lincoln (1809–1865) was elected president in 1860, most of the slaveholding states seceded to form the Confederate States of America. Civil war broke out in 1861 when, under Lincoln's leadership, the North fought to preserve the Union. The future of nation building in the United States hung in the balance. Lincoln did not initially aim to abolish slavery, but his Emancipation Proclamation of January 1863 officially freed all slaves in the Confederacy and turned the war into a fight not only for union but also for an end to human bondage. After the summer of 1863, the North's superior industrial strength and military might overpowered and physically destroyed much of the South. By April 1865, the North had prevailed, though a Confederate sympathizer assassinated Lincoln. Constitutional amendments ended slavery and promised full political rights to African American men.

By 1871, northern interest in promoting African American political rights was declining, and whites began regaining control of state politics in the South, often by organized violence and intimidation. The end of northern occupation of the South in 1877 was a setback in obtaining rights for blacks. Nonetheless, in ending

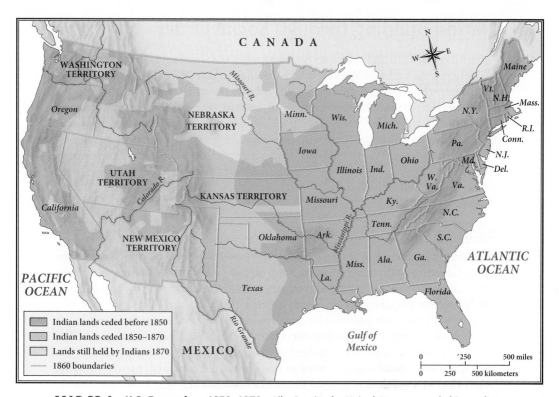

MAP 22.4   U.S. Expansion, 1850–1870   Like Russia, the United States expanded into adjacent regions to create a continental nation-state. In taking over territories, however, the United States differed from Russia by herding native peoples into small confined spaces called reservations so that settlers could acquire thousands of square miles for farming and other enterprises. The U.S. government granted full citizenship for all native Americans only in 1925.

slavery, the Union victory opened the way to stronger national government and to economic advancement no longer tied to the old Atlantic plantation system.

The North's triumph had profound effects elsewhere in North America. The United States also threatened the annexation of Canada to punish Great Britain, whose dependence on cotton had led it to support the Confederacy. To prevent the loss of Britain's largest territory, the British government allowed Canadians to form a united dominion—that is, a self-governing unit of the empire—in 1867. Dominion status answered Canadians' appeal for home rule, weakened the cause of those opposing Britain's control of Canada, and strengthened Canadian national unity.

REVIEW   What role did warfare play in the various nineteenth-century nation-building efforts?

Nation Building through Social Order

Government officials and reformers hoped to offset the violent changes of the nation-building process with new improvements. Population rose and cities grew crowded as the nineteenth century progressed, leading officials across Europe to promote public health and safety. Many liberals wanted a laissez-faire government that left social and economic life largely to private enterprise. In contrast, bureaucrats and reformers took direct action to improve citizens' lives and, along with missionaries and explorers, worked more actively to establish social order and to extend European power to the farthest reaches of the globe. Some of these efforts met violent resistance both within Europe and outside it.

Bringing Order to the Cities

European cities became the backdrop for displays of state power and accomplishment. Governments focused on improving capital cities such as Vienna and Rome with handsome parks, widened streets, stately museums, and massive city halls. In 1857, Austrian emperor Francis Joseph ordered that the old Viennese city walls be replaced with boulevards lined with major public buildings such as the opera house and government offices. These buildings were concrete evidence of national wealth and power, and the broad boulevards allowed crowds to observe royal pageantry. The wide roads were also easier for troops to navigate than the twisted, narrow medieval streets that in 1848 had concealed insurrectionists in cities like Paris and Vienna. Impressive parks and public gardens showed the state's control of nature, ordered people's leisure time, and inspired respect for the nation-state's achievements.

Construction first required destruction: buildings and entire neighborhoods that had intermingled rich and poor disappeared, and thousands of city dwellers were dislocated. Newly built expensive housing was separated from the poor sections of the city. In Paris, the process of urban change was called Haussmannization, named for the prefect Georges-Eugène Haussmann, who implemented a grand design that included eighty-five miles of new streets, many lined with showy dwellings for the wealthy. In London, the many new banks and insurance companies, one architect believed, "help[ed] the impression of stability." There was an expectation that the civic pride resulting from urban rebuilding would replace rebelliousness and disunity.

Amid redevelopment, serious problems menaced the urban population. Repeated epidemics of diseases such as cholera killed alarming numbers of city dwellers and gave the strong impression of social decay, not national power. Poor sanitation allowed typhoid bacteria to spread through sewage and into water supplies, infecting rich and poor alike. In 1861, Britain's Prince Albert—the beloved husband of Queen Victoria—reputedly died of typhoid fever, commonly known as a "filth disease." Heaps of animal excrement in chicken coops, pigsties, and stables; unregulated urban slaughterhouses; and piles of human waste were breeding grounds for disease, making sanitation a top priority.

Scientific research, increasingly undertaken in publicly financed laboratories and hospitals, provided the means to promote public health and control disease. France's Louis Pasteur, three of whose young daughters had also died of typhoid, advanced the germ theory of disease. He suggested that bacteria and parasites might be responsible for human and animal diseases. Pasteur demonstrated that heating foods such as wine and milk to a certain temperature, a process that soon became known as pasteurization, killed these organisms and made food safe. English surgeon Joseph Lister applied Pasteur's germ theory of disease to infection and developed antiseptics for treating wounds and preventing puerperal fever, a condition caused by the dirty hands of physicians and midwives that killed innumerable women after childbirth.

Governments undertook projects to modernize sewer and other sanitary systems and to straighten rivers. Citizens often prized such improvements as signs of national superiority. In Paris, sewage flowed into newly built, watertight underground collectors. In addition, Haussmann piped in water from uncontaminated sources in the countryside to provide each household with a secure supply. To prevent devastating floods and to eliminate disease-ridden marshlands, governments rerouted and straightened rivers such as the Rhine and built canals. Improved sanitation testified to the activist state's ability to bring about progress.

Citizens responded positively to improvements in everyday life. When sanitary public toilets for men became a feature of modern cities, women petitioned governments for similar facilities. More aware of dirt, disease, and smells, the middle classes bathed more regularly, sometimes even once a week. People's concerns for refinement and health mirrored governments' pursuit of order.

Expanding Government Bureaucracy

To build an orderly national community required a more active role for the state, and bureaucracies expanded in these years as government authority reached further into everyday life. Censuses became routine and provided the state with personal details of citizens' lives such as age, occupation, residence, marital status, and number of children. Governments then used these data for everything from setting quotas for military conscription to predicting the need for new prisons. Reformers like Florence Nightingale, who gathered medical, public health, and other statistics to support sanitary reform, believed that such quantitative information would help a government base decisions on facts rather than on influence peddling or ill-informed hunches, and thus reduce corruption and inefficiency.

To bring about their vision of social order, many governments also expanded the regulation of prostitution. Venereal disease, especially syphilis, was common, and like typhoid fever, it infected individuals and whole families. Officials blamed prostitutes, not their clients, for its spread. The police picked up suspect women, examined them for syphilis, and confined infected ones for treatment. As states began monitoring prostitution and other social matters like public health and housing, they had to add departments and agencies. In 1867, Hungary's bureaucracy handled fewer than 250,000 individual cases ranging from health to poverty issues; twenty years later, it handled more than 1 million.

Schooling and Professionalizing Society

Emphasis on empirical knowledge and objective standards changed the professions and raised their status. Growing numbers of middle-class doctors, lawyers, professors, and journalists employed solid information in their work. The middle classes argued that jobs in government should be awarded according to expertise rather than aristocratic birth or political connections. In Britain, a civil service law passed in 1870 required competitive examinations to ensure competency in government posts—a system long used in China. Governments began to allow professionals to determine rules for admission to their fields. Such legislation had both positive and negative effects: groups could set high standards, but otherwise qualified people were sometimes prohibited from working because they lacked the credentials. The medical profession, for example, gained the authority to license physicians, but it tried to block experienced midwives from attending childbirths.

Nation building required the education of all citizens, professional or not. "We have made Italy," one Italian official announced. "Now we have to make Italians." Education was one way of bringing citizens to hold common beliefs and values. Expansion of the electorate and lower-class activism prompted one British aristocrat to say of the common people, whom he feared as they gained influence, "We must now educate our masters!" Governments introduced compulsory schooling to reduce illiteracy rates, which were more than 65 percent in Italy and Spain in the 1870s and even higher in eastern Europe. As ordinary people were allowed to vote, books taught them about the responsibilities of citizenship and provided the practical knowledge necessary for contributing to industrial society.

Educational reform was not easy. At midcentury, religious authorities supervised schools and charged tuition, making primary education an option only for prosperous or religious parents. After the 1850s, critics questioned the relevance of religion in the curricula of modern schools. In 1861, an English commission on education concluded that instead of knowledge of the Bible, "the knowledge most important to a labouring man is that of the causes which regulate the amount of his wages, the hours of his work, the regularity of his employment, and the prices of what he consumes." To feel part of a nation, the young had to learn its language, literature, and history. Replacing religion was a challenge for the secular and increasingly knowledge-based state.

Enforcing school attendance was another challenge. Although the Netherlands, Sweden, and Switzerland had functioning primary-school systems before midcentury, rural parents in these and other countries resisted sending their children to school. Farm families depended on children to perform chores and believed that work in the fields or the household provided the best and most useful education. Urban homemakers from the lower classes needed their children to fetch water, tend younger children, and scavenge for household necessities such as stale bread from bakers or soup from local missions. Yet some of the working poor developed a craze for learning, which made traveling lecturers, reading groups, and debating societies popular.

Secondary education also expanded through the creation of more lycées (high schools) and technical schools, yet it remained even more of a luxury. In authoritarian countries such as Russia, advanced knowledge, including education in science

and technology, was considered suspect because it empowered the young with information and taught them to think for themselves. Reformers pushed for advanced
courses for young women to make them more interesting wives and better mothers
of future citizens. In Britain, the founders of two women's colleges — Girton (1869)
and Newnham (1871) — at Cambridge University believed, and were later proved
right, that exacting standards and a modern curriculum in women's higher education would inspire improvements in the men's colleges of Cambridge and Oxford.

Education also opened professional doors to women, who came to attend
universities — in particular, medical schools — in Zurich and Paris in the 1860s.
Women doctors argued that they could not only bring feminine values to health
care but also get better results because women patients would be more open with
them than with male doctors. The need for educated citizens also offered opportunities for large numbers of women to enter teaching, a field once dominated by
men. Thousands of women founded nursery schools and kindergartens based on
the Enlightenment idea that developmental processes start at an early age. Yet many
men opposed the idea of women studying or teaching. "I shudder at philosophic
women," wrote one critic of female education.

Spreading National Power and Order beyond the West

In an age of nation building, colonies took on new importance because they seemed
to add to the power of the nation-state. This benefit led Great Britain, France, and
Russia to expand their political control of colonies. Sometimes the imperial powers
offered social and cultural services, such as schools. For instance, in the 1850s and
1860s provincial governors and local officials promoted the extension of Russian borders to gain control over nomadic tribes in central and eastern Asia. Russian officials
then instituted common educational and religious policies, such as instruction in the
Russian language and in the principles of the Russian Orthodox church, as a means
to social order.

Great Britain, the era's mightiest imperial power, imposed direct political rule
abroad as part of nation building. Before the 1850s, British liberals desired commercial profits from colonies, but, believing in laissez-faire, they kept political
involvement in colonial affairs minimal. Since the eighteenth century, the East India
Company had been gaining control over various kingdoms' trading and tax collection rights and then began building railroads throughout the Indian countryside.
As commerce with Britain grew, many Indian businessmen became wealthy. Other
local men served in the colonial army, which became one of the largest standing
armies in the world.

In 1857, a contingent of Indian troops, both Muslim and Hindu, violently
rebelled when a rumor spread that Britain would force them to use cartridges of
ammunition greased with cow and pig fat, which violated the Hindu ban on beef
and the Muslim prohibition of pork. This was not their main grievance, however.
The soldiers, more generally angered at widening British control, overran the old
Moghul capital at Delhi and declared the independence of the Indian nation — an
uprising that became known as the Indian Rebellion of 1857.

Simultaneously, local rulers rebelled, condemning "the tyranny and oppression of the infidel and treacherous English." Lakshmibai, the *rani* ("queen") of the state of Jhansi in central India, led a separate military revolt when the East India Company tried to take over her lands after her husband died. Even as the British brutally crushed the rebels, Indian nationalism was born. Victorious, the British government took direct control of India in 1858, and the British Parliament declared Queen Victoria the empress of India in 1876.

A system of rule took shape in which close to half a million South Asians, supervised by a few thousand British men, governed a region that they now called India. Colonial rule meant both outright domination and subtle intervention in everyday life. For example, British taxes on high-quality Indian textiles led many to buy cheaper British cottons. Artisans were directed instead to farm raw materials such as wheat, cotton, and jute to supply Britain's industry and feed its workers. Nevertheless, some of the Indians who benefited from improved sanitation and medicine chose to accept British arguments against Indian customs such as child marriage and *sati*—the self-immolation of a widow on her husband's funeral pyre. Others found Europe's scientific values attractive and came to appreciate that British rule, ironically, brought a kind of unity to India's many separate princedoms, thus laying the foundation for an Indian nation.

French political expansion was similarly complex. The French government pushed to establish its dominion over Cochin China (modern southern Vietnam) in the 1860s. Missionaries in the area, ambitious French naval officers, and even some local peoples—much like Indian merchants and financiers—pulled the French government farther into the region. Like the British, the French brought improvements, but sanitation and public health programs led to a rise in population that strained resources. Furthermore, landowners and French imperialists siphoned off most of the profits from economic improvement. The French also undertook a cultural mission to transform cities like Saigon by adding tree-lined boulevards similar to those of Paris. French literature, theater, and art were popular with both colonial officials and upper-class local people.

In this age of Realpolitik, the Crimean War had shown the great powers the importance of the Mediterranean basin. Napoleon III, remembering his uncle's campaign in Egypt, took an interest in building the Suez Canal, which would connect the Mediterranean with the Red Sea and the Indian Ocean and thus dramatically shorten the route from Europe to Asia. Following the canal's completion in 1869, "canal fever" spread: Verdi composed the opera *Aïda* (set in ancient Egypt), and people across the West applied Egyptian designs to textiles, furniture, art, and even public monuments in cities. The French army had occupied all of Algeria by 1870, when the number of European immigrants to the region reached one-quarter million. French rule in Algeria, as elsewhere, was aided by local people's attraction to European goods and technology and by the opportunity to make money.

Its vastness allowed China to escape complete takeover, but traders and Christian missionaries from Europe made inroads for the Western powers. Defeat in the Opium War caused an economic slump and helped generate the mass movement known as the Taiping ("Heavenly Kingdom"). Headed by a leader who claimed to be the brother of Jesus, the Taiping's millions of adherents wanted an end to the ruling Qing dynasty, the expulsion of foreigners, more equal treatment of women, and land reform. By the mid-1850s, the Taiping controlled half of China. The threatened Qing regime promised the British and French greater influence in exchange for aid in defeating the Taiping. More than 20 million Chinese died in the resulting civil war. When peace finally came in 1864, Western governments controlled much of the Chinese customs service and had virtually unlimited access to the country.

Japan alone in East Asia was able to escape Western domination, because it was keenly aware of the innovations taking place in the West. In 1854, the Japanese agreed to open the country to foreign trade in part to gain Western goods, including the West's superior weaponry. Japanese reformers in 1867 overthrew a government that resisted such change and in 1868 enacted the Meiji Restoration. The word *Meiji* pointed to the "enlightened rule" of the new emperor, whose power reformers had restored. The goal was to combine "Western science and Eastern values" as a way of "making new" — hence, a combination of restoration and innovation. The new regime pushed Japan to become a modern, technologically powerful state free from Western control.

Contesting the Nation-State's Order at Home

Europeans did not simply sit by as the growing nation-state changed and often disrupted their lives. A better-informed urban working class protested the upheavals in everyday life caused when cities were ripped apart for improvements and when the growth of factories destroyed artisans' livelihoods. Increasingly educated by public schools, urban workers frequented cafés and pubs to hear news and discuss economic and political events. After the post-1848 repression of worker organizations, unions gradually started to take shape, sometimes in secret because of continuing opposition from governments.

Many of the most outspoken labor activists were artisans struggling to survive in the new industrializing climate. They were attracted at first by the ideas of former printer Pierre-Joseph Proudhon (1809–1865). In the 1840s, Proudhon proclaimed, "Property is theft," suggesting that property ownership robbed people of their rightful share of the earth's benefits. He opposed the centralized state and proposed that society be organized instead around natural groupings of men in artisans' workshops. (Women, he believed, should work in seclusion at home for their husbands' comfort.) These workshops and a central bank crediting each worker for his labor would replace government.

As the nation-state expanded its power, workers were also drawn to **anarchism**, which maintained that the existence of the state was the root of social injustice. According to Russian nobleman and anarchist leader Mikhail Bakunin (1814–1876), the slightest infringement on freedom, especially by the central state and its laws, was unacceptable. Anarchism thus advocated the destruction of all state power. Its appeal grew as government grew in the second half of the nineteenth century.

Political theorist and labor organizer Karl Marx (1818–1883) opposed both doctrines as lacking the sound, scientific basis of his own theory, subsequently called **Marxism**. Marx's analysis, appearing most notably in *Das Kapital* (*Capital*), adopted the liberal idea, dating back to John Locke in the seventeenth century, that human existence was defined by the necessity to work to fulfill basic needs such as food, clothing, and shelter. Using mathematical calculations of production and profit that would justify Realpolitik for the working classes, Marx held that the fundamental organization of any society derived from the relationships arising from work or production. This idea, known as *materialism*, meant that society rested on class relationships—such as those between serf and medieval lord, slave and master, or worker and capitalist. Marx called the class relationships that developed around work the *mode of production*—for instance, feudalism, slavery, or capitalism. He rejected the liberal focus on individual rights and emphasized instead the unequal class relations caused by those who had taken from workers control of the means of production—that is, the capital, land, tools, or factories that allowed basic human needs to be met.

Marx, like the politicians around him, took a tough-minded and realistic look at the economy, discarding the romantic views of the utopian socialists. He saw struggle, not warmhearted cooperation, as the means for bringing about change. Workers' awareness of their oppression would produce class-consciousness, he argued, leading them to overthrow their exploiters. Society was not basically harmonious; instead social progress could occur only through conflict.

As the Franco-Prussian War ended, revolution and civil war erupted not only in Paris but also in other French cities—catching the attention of Marx as a sign that his predictions were coming true. As the Prussians laid siege to Paris in the winter of 1870–1871, causing many deaths from starvation and bitter cold, Parisians rose up and demanded new republican liberties, new systems of work, and a more balanced distribution of power between the central government and localities. On March 28, 1871, to counter what they saw as the despotism of the centralized government, they declared themselves a self-governing commune. One issue behind the unrest was the nation-state's destruction of city life through urban renovation.

In the Paris Commune's two months of existence, and while trying to maintain "communal" instead of "national" values, Parisians quickly developed a wide array of political clubs, local ceremonies, and self-managed workshops. Women workers, for example, banded together to make National Guard uniforms on a cooperative rather than a for-profit basis. The Commune proposed to liberate the worker and ensure "the absolute equality of women laborers." Thus, a *commune*—in contrast to a *republic*—was meant to bring about social revolution. Communards, however, often disagreed on how to change society. Anticlericalism, feminism, socialism, and anarchism were but a few of the proposed routes to social justice.

In the meantime, the provisional government that succeeded the defeated Napoleon III stamped out similar uprisings in other French cities. In late May, the well-supplied national army crushed the Commune and shot tens of thousands of citizens on the streets. Parisian rebels, one citizen commented, "deserved no better judge than a soldier's bullet." The Communards had promoted a kind of antistate in an age of rising state power. Others saw the Commune as the work of the *pétroleuse* ("woman incendiary")—a case of frenzied women running amok through the streets. While revolutionary men became heroes in the history books, writers were soon blaming the burning of Paris on women—"shameless slatterns, half-naked women, who kindled courage and breathed life into arson."

Defeat in the Franco-Prussian War, the rise of the Paris Commune, and the civil war were all horrendous blows to the French state. Yet in the struggle against the Commune, the nation-state once again showed its strengthening muscle. Executions and deportations by the thousands followed, and fear of workers spread across Europe.

> **REVIEW**   How did Europe's expanding nation-states attempt to impose social order within and beyond Europe, and what resistance did they face?

The Culture of Social Order

Artists and writers of the mid-nineteenth century had complex reactions to the state's expanding reach and the economic growth that sustained it. They saw daily life as filled with commercial values and organized by mindless officials. Ordinary people no longer appeared heroic, as they had during the revolutionary years. "How tired I am of the ignoble workman, the inept bourgeois, the stupid peasant, and the odious priest," wrote the French novelist Gustave Flaubert. Rejecting romanticism, he described ordinary people in a harsh new style called **realism**. Intellectuals of the time proposed scientific theories that also took a cold, hard look at human life in society and challenged both idealism and fervent religious belief. Theirs was a detached point of view similar to that applied by statesmen to politics.

The Arts Confront Social Reality

Culture helped the cause of national unity. A hungry reading public devoured biographies of political leaders, past and present, and credited daring heroes with creating the triumphant nation-state. As schooling spread literacy and a craving for realism— that is, true-to-life portrayals of society without romantic or idealistic overtones— commercially minded publishers produced an age of best sellers. Newspapers published the novels of Charles Dickens in serial form, and each installment attracted buyers eager for the latest plot twist. Drawn from English society, Dickens's characters included starving orphans, grasping lawyers, greedy bankers, and ruthless opportunists. *Hard Times* (1854) depicts the grinding poverty and ill health of workers alongside the heartlessness of businessmen. Novelist **George Eliot** (the pen name of Mary Ann Evans) probed real-life dilemmas in *The Mill on the Floss* (1860) and *Middlemarch* (1871–1872). Describing rural society, Eliot allowed her readers to see one another's predicaments, wherever they lived. She knew the pain of ordinary life from her own experience: despite her fame, she was a social outcast because she lived with a married man. Popular novels that showed a hard reality helped form a shared culture much as state institutions did.

French writers also scorned dreams of utopian, trouble-free societies and ideal beauty. Gustave Flaubert's novel *Madame Bovary* (1857) tells the story of a doctor's wife who longs to escape her provincial surroundings. Filled with romantic fantasies, she has two love affairs to escape her boredom, becomes hopelessly indebted buying gifts for her lovers, and commits suicide by swallowing arsenic. *Madame Bovary* scandalized French society with its frank picture of women's sexuality, but it attracted a wide readership. Poet Charles-Pierre Baudelaire wrote explicitly about sex; in his 1857 collection, *Les Fleurs du mal* (*Flowers of Evil*), he expressed drug- and alcohol-induced passions—some focused on the brown body of his African mistress—and spun out visions that critics condemned as perverse. French authorities brought charges of obscenity against both Flaubert and Baudelaire. At issue was social and artistic order: "Art without rules is no longer art," maintained the prosecutor.

During the era of Alexander II's Great Reforms, Russian writers debated whether western European values were harming Russian culture. Adopting one viewpoint, Ivan Turgenev created a powerful novel of Russian life, *Fathers and Sons* (1862), a story of nihilistic children rejecting both parental authority and their parents' spiritual values in favor of science and facts. Fyodor Dostoevsky, in contrast, portrayed nihilists as dark, ridiculous, and neurotic. The highly intelligent characters in Dostoevsky's *Crime and Punishment* (1866) are personally tormented and condemned to lead absurd, even criminal lives. Dostoevsky used antiheroes to emphasize spirituality and traditional Russian values but added a realistic spin by planting such values in ordinary, often seedy people. The Russian public was drawn together by these debates about Russian identity.

Daumier, *The Burden*   Artists painted stark images of ordinary people as they struggled to survive in an industrializing age. Despite romantic views of a secluded separate sphere for women that was protected from life's realities, the majority of women hardly enjoyed such an existence, as shown by this depiction of a weighted-down working woman and her child. Daumier was one of the artists who captured that reality. (National Gallery, Prague, Czech Republic/photo by Erich Lessing/Art Resource, NY.)

While writers of realism depended on sales to thousands of readers, painters usually depended on government support. Leaders such as Prince Albert of Great Britain actively patronized the arts and purchased works for official collections and for themselves. Having their artwork chosen for display at government-sponsored exhibitions was another way for artists to earn a living. Hundreds of thousands from all social classes attended these exhibitions, though not all could afford to buy the art.

After the revolutions of 1848, artists began rejecting the romantic idealizing of ordinary folk or grand historic events. Instead, painters like Gustave Courbet portrayed groaning laborers at backbreaking work because, as he stated, an artist should "never permit sentiment to overthrow logic." The renovated city, artists found, had become a visual spectacle; its wide new boulevards served as a stage on which urban residents performed. *Universal Exhibition* (1867) by Edouard Manet shows figures from all social classes gazing at the Paris scene and observing one another to learn correct modern behavior. Manet also broke with romantic conventions of the nude. His *Olympia* (1865) depicts a white courtesan lying on her bed, attended by a black woman. This disregard for depicting women in mythical or idealized settings was too much for the critics: "A sort of female gorilla," one wrote of *Olympia* as debate raged over realism.

Unlike most of the visual arts, opera was commercially profitable and an effective means of reaching the nineteenth-century public. Verdi used musical theater to contrast noble ideals with the deadly effects of power and the lure of passion with the need for social order. The German composer Richard Wagner hoped to revolutionize opera by fusing music and drama to arouse the audience's fear and awe. A gigantic cycle of four operas, Wagner's *Ring of the Nibelungen* reshaped ancient German myths into a modern, nightmarish story of a world doomed by its obsessive pursuit of money and power and saved only through unselfish love. His opera *The Mastersingers of Nuremberg* was said to be implicitly anti-Semitic because of its rejection of influences other than German ones in the arts. Wagner's musical innovation made him a major force in philosophy, politics, and the arts across Europe. To his fellow citizens, however, his operas stood for Germany. Artists both implicitly (like George Eliot) and more explicitly (like Richard Wagner) promoted nation building even as they experimented with new forms.

Religion and National Order

The expansion of state power set the stage for clashes over the role of organized religion in the nation-state. In the 1850s, many politicians supported religious institutions and attended public church rituals because they were another source of order. Simultaneously, some nation builders, intellectuals, and economic liberals came to reject the religious worldview of established churches, particularly Roman Catholicism, because it was based in faith, not reason, and slowed the growth of nationalist sentiment.

Bismarck mounted a full-blown **Kulturkampf** ("culture war") against religion. The German government expelled the Jesuits from Germany in 1872, increased state power over the clergy in Prussia in 1873, and introduced a civil ceremony as an obligatory part of marriage in 1875. Bismarck had bragged, "I am the master of Germany in all but name," but he miscalculated his ability to manipulate politics. The pope fought back: "One must obey God more than men," he ordered. German Catholics rebelled, and even conservative Protestants thought Bismarck wrong-headed in attacking religion. Competition between church and state for power and influence heated up in the age of Realpolitik.

The Catholic church felt assaulted. Nation builders had also extended liberal rights to Jews, whom many Christians considered enemies. Attacking changing values, Pope Pius IX issued *The Syllabus of Errors* (1864), which found fault "with progress, with liberalism, and with modern civilization." Becoming pope in 1878, Leo XIII began reconciling the church to modern politics by encouraging up-to-date scholarship in Catholic institutes and universities and by accepting aspects of representative democracy. The Kulturkampf between church and state ended, making it easier for the faithful to be both Catholic and patriotic.

The place of organized religion in society was changing. While many in the upper and middle classes and most of the peasantry remained faithful, church attendance declined among workers and artisans. There was a religious gender gap, too. Women's spiritual beliefs became more intense, with both Roman Catholic and Russian Orthodox women's religious orders increasing in size and number; men, by contrast, were falling away from religious devotion. Many urban Jews abandoned religious practices and assimilated instead to secular, national cultures. Religion no longer included everyone.

In 1854, the pope's announcement of the doctrine of the Immaculate Conception (stating that Mary, alone among all humans, had been born without original sin) was followed by an outburst of popular religious fervor, especially among women. In 1858, a young peasant girl, Bernadette Soubirous, began having visions of the Virgin Mary at Lourdes in southern France. Crowds, mostly of women, flocked to Lourdes, believing that its waters could cure their ailments. In 1867, less than ten years later, a new railroad line to Lourdes enabled millions of pilgrims to visit the shrine on church-organized trips. The Catholic church thus showed that it, too, could use such modern means as railroads, shopping centers, and medical verifications of miraculous cures to make the religious experience more up-to-date. Traditional institutions began making themselves as effective as the nation-state.

At about the time of Soubirous's vision, the English naturalist **Charles Darwin** (1809–1882) published *On the Origin of Species* (1859). In his writings, Darwin argued that life on Earth had taken shape over countless millions of years before humans existed and that human life was the result of this slow development, called evolution. This theory directly challenged the Judeo-Christian dogma that God miraculously brought the universe and all life into being in six days, as described in the Bible. Instead Darwin held that life developed from lower forms through a primal battle for survival and through the sexual selection of mates—a process he called natural selection. For Darwin the Bible gave a "manifestly false history of the world." Darwin's theories also undermined Enlightenment principles that glorified

"Gentlemen, We Are Descended from Monkeys," Spain, Late Nineteenth Century   Darwin's scientific ideas aroused anger, admiration, and even mirth, as shown in this engraving some decades after the publication of his major works. As you consider this image, what message would you say the artist is trying to convey about evolution? (Bibliothèque des Arts Décoratifs Paris/Alfredo Dagli Orti/The Art Archive at Art Resource, NY.)

nature as tranquil and noble, and human beings as essentially rational. The theory of natural selection, in which the fittest survive, suggested a different kind of human society, one composed of warlike individuals and groups constantly fighting one another to triumph over hostile surroundings.

Other innovative biological research placed religious views of reproduction under attack. Working with pea plants in his monastery garden in the 1860s, the Austrian monk Gregor Mendel (1822–1884) discovered the principles of heredity, from which the science of genetics later developed. Investigation into the female reproductive cycle led German scientists to discover the principle of spontaneous ovulation—the automatic release of the egg by the ovary independent of sexual intercourse. Theorists concluded that men had strong sexual drives because reproduction depended on their sexual arousal. In contrast, the automatic release of the egg each month indicated to them that women were passive and lacked sexual feeling.

Many other ideas disturbed the status quo. Even before Darwin, the writer Herbert Spencer (1820–1903) had written that the "unfit" should be allowed to perish in the name of progress. On these grounds Spencer opposed public education and any other attempt to soften the struggle for existence. Darwin continued this line of argument when he claimed that white European men in the nineteenth century were wealthier and better because they were more highly evolved than white women or people of color. A school of thought known as Social Darwinism grew out of Darwin's and Spencer's ideas; it promoted racist, sexist, and other discriminatory policies as a way of strengthening the nation-state.

From the Natural Sciences to Social Science

In an age influenced by Realpolitik, Darwin's revolutionary thought was part of a quest to find alternatives to the idea that the social order was created by God. French thinker Auguste Comte (1798–1857) developed **positivism**—a theory claiming that careful study of facts would generate accurate and useful, or "positive," laws of society. Comte's "sociology" inspired people to believe they could solve the problems resulting from economic and social changes. To accomplish this goal, tough-minded reformers founded study groups and scientifically oriented associations to dig up social facts such as statistics on poverty or the conditions of working-class life. Comte encouraged women's participation in reform because he deemed "womanly" compassion and love as fundamental to social harmony as scientific public policy was. Positivism led not only to women's increased public activism but also to the development of the social sciences in this period. Among them, sociology brought a new realism to the study of human society.

The celebrated English philosopher John Stuart Mill (1806–1873) used Comte's theories to advocate widespread reform and mass education. In his political treatise *On Liberty* (1859), Mill advocated the improvement of society generally, but he also worried that superior people would be brought down by the will of the masses. Influenced by his wife, Harriet Taylor Mill, as well as by Comte, he argued for women's rights and introduced a woman suffrage bill into the House of Commons. The bill's defeat led Mill to publish *The Subjection of Women* (1869), an influential work around the world. *The Subjection of Women* showed the family as a despotic institution, lacking modern values such as rights and freedom. To make a woman appear "not a forced slave, but a willing one," he said, she was trained from childhood not to value her own talent and independence but to welcome her "submission" to men. Mill's progressive thought was soon lost in a flood of Social Darwinist theories. Still, inspired by the social sciences, policymaking came to rely on statistics and fact gathering for building strong, unified nations.

REVIEW How did cultural expression and scientific and social thought help produce the hardheaded and realistic values of the mid-nineteenth century?

Conclusion

Throughout modern history, the development of nation-states has been neither inevitable nor uniform nor peaceful. In the nineteenth century, ambitious politicians, shrewd monarchs, and determined bureaucrats used a variety of methods and policies to transform very different countries into effective nation-states. Nation building was most dramatic in Germany and Italy, where states unified through military force and where people of opposing political opinions ultimately agreed that national unity should be the primary goal. Compelled by military defeat to shake off centuries of tradition, the Austrian and Russian monarchs instituted reforms as a way of keeping their systems in place. The Habsburg Empire became a dual monarchy, an arrangement that gave the Hungarians virtual home rule and raised the level of disunity. Reforms in Russia left the authoritarian monarchy intact and only partially transformed the social order.

After decades of romantic fervor, no-nonsense realism in politics—Realpolitik— became a much touted principle. Realist thinkers such as Darwin and Marx developed theories disturbing to those who maintained an Enlightenment faith in social and political harmony. Realist novels and artworks jarred polite society, and, like the operas of Verdi, portrayed dilemmas of the times. Growing government administrations set policies that were meant to bring order but often brought disorder, including the destruction of entire neighborhoods and violence toward people in far-off lands. In the long term, schooling taught the lower classes to be orderly citizens, and urban renewal ultimately improved cities and public health to complement nation building.

Objections arose to the expanding power of the nation-state. The Indian Rebellion of 1857 against Britain and the Paris Commune of 1871 against the French state were but two examples where violent actions raised difficult questions about nation-building methods. How far should the power of the state extend in both domestic and international affairs? Would nationalism be a force for war or for peace? In the face of state power, would ordinary people have any say in their destiny? As these issues ripened, the next decades saw extraordinary economic advances and an unprecedented surge in Europe's global power—much of it the result of successes in nation building.

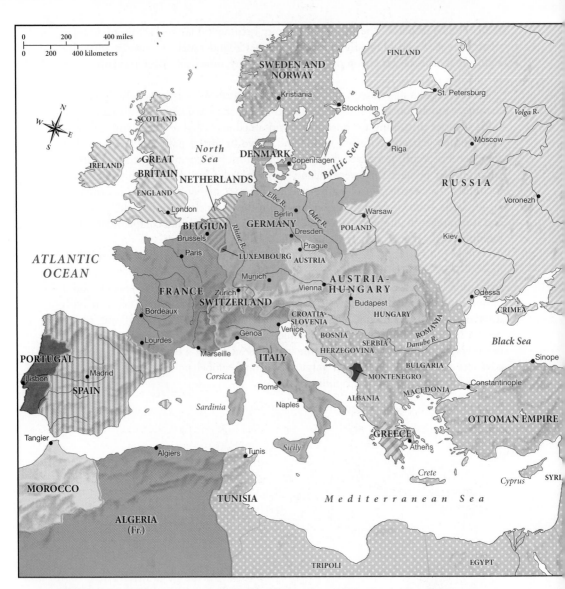

MAPPING THE WEST Europe and the Mediterranean, 1871   European nation-states consolidated their power by building unified state structures and by developing the means for the diverse peoples within their borders to become socially and culturally integrated. Nation-states were also rapidly expanding outside their boundaries, extending their economic and political reach. North Africa and the Middle East—parts of the declining Ottoman Empire—particularly appealed to European governments because of their resources and their potential for further European settlement. They offered a gateway to the rest of the world.

Chapter Review

KEY TERMS AND PEOPLE

Be sure you can identify the term or person and explain its historical significance.

Realpolitik (p. 642)
Alexander II (p. 645)
Florence Nightingale (p. 646)
mir (p. 646)
Russification (p. 648)
nation-state (p. 649)
Camillo di Cavour (p. 649)
Otto von Bismarck (p. 651)
dual monarchy (p. 655)

Pan-Slavism (p. 655)
anarchism (p. 663)
Marxism (p. 664)
realism (p. 665)
George Eliot (p. 665)
Kulturkampf (p. 667)
Charles Darwin (p. 668)
positivism (p. 670)

REVIEW QUESTIONS

1. What were the main results of the Crimean War?
2. What role did warfare play in the various nineteenth-century nation-building efforts?
3. How did Europe's expanding nation-states attempt to impose social order within and beyond Europe, and what resistance did they face?
4. How did cultural expression and scientific and social thought help produce the hardheaded and realistic values of the mid-nineteenth century?

MAKING CONNECTIONS

1. What were the main methods of nation building in the mid-nineteenth century, and how did they differ from those of state building in the early modern period?
2. How did realism in social thought break with Enlightenment values?
3. In what ways did religion emerge as an issue (both within and outside Europe) during the course of nation building?
4. How was the Paris Commune related to earlier revolutions in France? How did it differ from them? How was it related to nation building?

IMPORTANT EVENTS

1850s–1860s	• Positivism, Darwinism become influential
1850s–1870s	• Realism in the arts
1853–1856	• Crimean War
1857	• British-led forces suppress Indian Rebellion
1861	• Victor Emmanuel declared king of a unified Italy; abolition of serfdom in Russia
1861–1865	• U.S. Civil War
1867	• Second Reform Bill in England; Austro-Hungarian monarchy
1868	• Meiji Restoration begins in Japan
1869	• Suez Canal opens
1869–1871	• Women's colleges are founded at Cambridge University
1870–1871	• Franco-Prussian War
1871	• German Empire is proclaimed at Versailles; self-governing Paris Commune is established

23

Empire, Industry, and Everyday Life

1870–1890

CHAPTER FOCUS

How did imperial conquest and industrial advances affect Western society, culture, and politics in the late nineteenth century?

IN THE MID-1880S, Frieda von Bülow, a young German woman of aristocratic birth, joined several activist groups interested in promoting German colonial expansion in Africa. Like other women in these pro-imperial organizations, von Bülow was eager to help German settlers—and even some Africans—in East Africa, which Germany was in the process of colonizing. She also met adventurous men such as Carl Peters, a fanatical nationalist and leading figure in imperialist circles. As Europeans competed to take over the African continent, von Bülow and Peters headed for Zanzibar and other distant cities not only to conquer them but also to carry on a passionate romance. Once in Africa, von Bülow basked in the freedom from her society's restrictions on women and in German superiority over local African peoples. For his part, Peters followed his usual pattern of tricking Africans into giving up their lands and using guns, rape, and other violence to get his way. Peters seduced one African woman and then had her executed because of her relationship with another man. Though Peters's womanizing caused von Bülow to break up with him, she maintained both her racism and her German nationalism, learning to shoot a gun on behalf of colonial conquest, writing

popular novels about empire and white superiority, and setting up a plantation in Southeast Africa.

Von Bülow and Peters were just two of the tens of thousands of Europeans
pursuing imperial adventure as the search for lands to colonize reached a
feverish pitch after the 1870s. Those involved in imperialism had a variety
of motives and, like Peters, were often swaggering and violent. The rapid
expansion of Western takeovers was called the "new imperialism" because
the race for empire now aimed at political rather than mere economic power.

Europeans had been acquiring global territory since the late fifteenth century; the new imperialism intensified this process. In their rush for empire,
Europeans like Frieda von Bülow and Carl Peters worked to control whole
societies instead of dominating coastal trade until, by the beginning of the
twentieth century, Western nations claimed jurisdiction over vast stretches
of the world's surface. Beyond political control, Europeans tried to stamp
other continents with European-style place names, architecture, clothing, languages, and domestic customs. They used culture to secure their empires just
as they used it to forge the nation-state.

Millions of people traveled vast distances in the nineteenth century—a
time of greatly increased mobility and migration, much of which was made
possible by an expansion of industry and colonization. Some migrated temporarily to serve in colonial governments or to find business opportunities.
Others relocated permanently within Europe or outside it. Such migration
uprooted tens of millions of people, disrupted social and family networks,
and often inflicted terrible violence on native peoples dislocated by European
migrants' greed, ambition, or desperation.

The decades from 1870 to 1890 were also an era of expanding industry
in the West. Empire and industry fed on each other as raw materials from
conquered areas supplied Western factories and as innovations in weaponry, transportation, medicine, and communication allowed imperialism to
thrive. Industrialization spread from Britain to central and eastern Europe and
brought a continuous new supply of products to the market. A growing appetite for these products, many of them for household consumption, changed
the fabric of everyday life and built pride in a nation's conquests. Urban
workers began demanding greater participation in the political process. Proud
Europeans brimmed with confidence and hope, while the grimmer aspects of
empire and industrialization played themselves out in distant colonies, urban
slums, and declining rural areas of Europe.

The New Imperialism

Imperialism surged in the last third of the nineteenth century. Industrial demand for raw materials and business rivalry for new markets fueled competition for territory in Africa and Asia, and European nations, the United States, and Japan now aimed to rule sizable portions of the world directly. "Nations are not great except for the activities they undertake," declared a French advocate of imperialism in 1885. Conquering foreign territory and developing wealth through industry appeared to heap glory on the nation-state. Although some missionaries and reformers aimed to spread Western religions and culture as a benefit to colonized peoples, the expansion of the West increased the subjugation of those peoples, inflicted violence on them, and radically altered their lives.

The Scramble for Africa — North and South

European countries had long viewed Africa — North and South — as a vast region for profit through trade and investment. In the late nineteenth century, they aimed for political control as well. Egypt, a convenient and profitable stop on the way to Asia, was an early target. Modernizing rulers had made Cairo into a bustling metropolis with lively commercial and manufacturing enterprises. Production of raw materials, such as cotton for European textile mills, was booming. Europeans invested heavily in the region, first in ventures such as building the Suez Canal in the 1860s, then in laying thousands of miles of railroad track, improving harbors, creating telegraph systems, and finally and most important, loaning money at exorbitant rates of interest.

In 1879, the British and the French took over the Egyptian treasury, allegedly to secure their investments and guarantee the repayment of loans. In 1882, they invaded the country with the excuse of squashing Egyptian nationalists who protested the takeover of the treasury. The British next seized control of the government as a whole and forcibly reshaped the Egyptian economy from a system based on multiple crops that maintained the country's self-sufficiency to one that emphasized the production of a few crops — mainly cotton, raw silk, wheat, and rice — that cheaply fed both European manufacturing and the European working classes. Businessmen from the colonial powers, Egyptian landowners, and local merchants profited from these agricultural changes, while the bulk of the rural population barely eked out an existence.

Alongside the takeover of the Egyptian government, France occupied neighboring Tunisia in 1881. Europeans also turned their attention to sub-Saharan Africa. In the past, contact between Europe and Africa had principally involved the trade of African slaves for a variety of goods, but by this time Europeans had begun to want Africa's raw materials, such as palm oil, cotton, metals, diamonds, cocoa, and rubber. Additionally, Britain needed the southern and eastern coasts of Africa for stopover ports on the route to Asia and its empire in India.

In the 1880s, European military forces conquered one sub-Saharan African territory after another (Map 23.1) to dominate peoples, land, and resources — "the

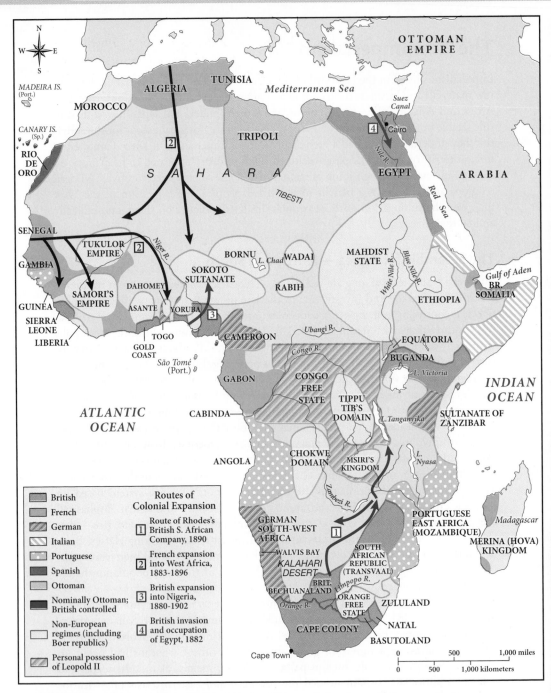

MAP 23.1 Africa, c. 1890 The scramble for Africa entailed a change in European trading practices, which generally had been limited to the coastline. Trying to penetrate economically and rule the interior ultimately resulted in a map of the continent that made sense only to the imperial powers, for it divided ethnic groups and made territorial unities that had nothing to do with Africans' sense of geography or patterns of settlement. This map shows the unfolding of that process and the political and ethnic groupings to be conquered.

magnificent cake of Africa," as King **Leopold II** of Belgium (r. 1865–1909) put it. Insatiable greed drove Leopold to claim the Congo region of central Africa, inflicting on its peoples unparalleled acts of cruelty (see the illustration on page 680). German chancellor Otto von Bismarck, who saw colonies mostly as political bargaining chips, established German control over Cameroon and a section of East Africa, to which Frieda von Bülow and Carl Peters headed. Faced with competition, the British poured millions of pounds into conquering the continent "from Cairo to Cape Town," as the slogan went, and the French cemented their hold on large portions of western Africa.

The scramble for Africa escalated tensions in Europe and prompted Bismarck to call a conference at Berlin. The European nations represented at the conference, held in a series of meetings in 1884 and 1885, decided that control of settlements along the African coast guaranteed rights to interior territory. This agreement led to the strictly linear dissection of the continent—a dissection that cut across boundaries of African culture and ethnic life. The Berlin conference also banned the sale of alcohol and controlled the flow of arms to African peoples. In theory, the meeting was supposed to reduce bloodshed and ambitions for territory in Africa. In reality, the agreement accelerated conquest of the continent and left everyone on edge over the threat of more violence. Newspaper accounts whetted the popular appetite for more takeovers. Music hall audiences rose to their feet and cheered at the sound of popular songs about imperial heroes of the day.

The lust for conquest had perhaps its greatest effect in southern Africa. The Dutch had moved into the area in the seventeenth century, but by 1815 the British had gained control. Thereafter, descendants of the Dutch, called Boers (Dutch for "farmers"), and British immigrants joined together in their fight to wrest farmland and mineral resources from the Xhosa, Zulu, and other African peoples. British businessman and politician Cecil Rhodes, sent to South Africa for his health just as diamonds were being discovered in 1870, cornered the diamond market and claimed a huge amount of African territory hundreds of miles into the interior. His ambition for Britain and for himself was boundless: "I contend that we are the finest race in the world," he explained, "and that the more of the world we inhabit the better it is." Although notions of European racial superiority had been advanced before, Social Darwinism strengthened racism to justify the conquest of African lands.

Wherever necessary to ensure domination, Europeans either destroyed African economic and political systems or transformed them into instruments of their rule. A British governor of the West African region known as the Gold Coast put the matter succinctly in 1886: the British would "rule the country as if there were no inhabitants." Indeed, most Europeans considered Africans barely civilized, despite the wealth local rulers and merchants accumulated in their international trade and despite individual Africans' accomplishments in everything from fabric dyeing to road building and architecture. They felt this justified the confiscation of land from Africans, who were then forced to work for them to pay European-imposed taxes. Agriculture to support families, often performed by women and slaves, declined in favor of mining and farming cash crops. Men were made to leave their homes

The Violence of Colonization King Leopold II, ruler of the Belgian Congo, was so greedy and ruthless that his agents squeezed the last drop of rubber and other resources from local peoples. Missionaries reported and photographed atrocities such as the killing of workers whose quotas were even slightly short or the amputation of hands for the same offense. Belgian agents collected amputated hands and sent them to government officials to show Leopold that they were enforcing his kind of discipline. (Universal History Archive / UIG / Bridgeman Images.)

to work in mines or to build railroads. Family and community networks, though upset by the new arrangements, helped support Africans during this upheaval in everyday life.

Acquiring Territory in Asia

The expansion of imperial power from the 1870s on was occurring around the world, not just in Africa. Much of Asia, with India as the centerpiece, was integrated into Western empires. At the same time, resistance to outside domination was also growing: the educated Indian elite in 1885 founded the Indian National Congress. Some of its members welcomed opportunities for trade, education, and social advancement. Others, however, challenged Britain's right to rule India at all. In the next century, the Indian National Congress would develop into a mass movement.

To the east, British military forces took control of the Malay peninsula in 1874 and of the interior of Burma in 1885. In both areas, political instability often threatened secure trade. The British depended on the region's tin, oil, rice, teak, and rubber as well as on its access to the numerous interior trade routes of China. British troops guaranteed the order necessary to expand railroads for more efficient export of raw materials and the development of Western systems of communication.

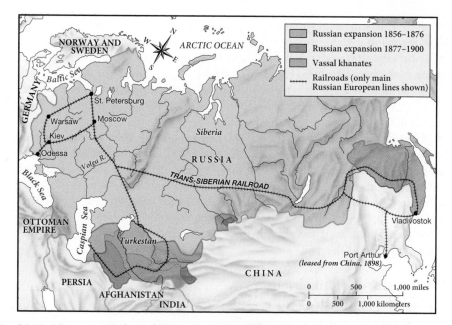

MAP 23.2 Expansion of Russia in Asia, 1865–1895 Russian administrators and military men continued enlarging Russia, bringing in Asians of many different ethnicities, ways of life, and religions. Land-hungry peasants in western Russia followed the path of expansion into Siberia and Muslim territories to the south. In some cases they drove native peoples from their lands, but in others they settled less-populated frontier areas. As in all cases of imperial expansion, local peoples resisted any expropriation of their livelihoods, while the central government tried various policies for integration.

The British added to their holdings in Asia partly to counter Russian and French annexations. For years, Russia had been absorbing the small Muslim states of central Asia, including provinces of Afghanistan (Map 23.2). Besides extending into the Ottoman Empire, Russian tentacles reached Persia, India, and China, often encountering British competition. By the thousands land-hungry Russian peasants moved to these regions, with the Trans-Siberian Railroad (1891–1916) later feeding hundreds of thousands more to Siberia. France meanwhile used the threat of military action to negotiate favorable treaties with Indochinese rulers, creating the Union of Indochina from the ancient states of Cambodia, Tonkin, Annam, and Cochin China in 1887 (the last three now constitute Vietnam). Laos was added to Indochina in 1893.

Japan's Imperial Agenda

Japan escaped European rule by rapidly transforming itself into a modern industrial nation with its own imperial agenda. The Japanese embraced foreign trade and industry. "All classes high and low shall unite in vigorously promoting the economy and welfare of the nation," ran one of the first pronouncements of the Meiji regime that had come to power in 1868. Unlike China, the Japanese government directed the country's turn toward modern industry, and state support led daring innovators like Iwasaki Yataro, founder of the Mitsubishi firm, to develop heavy industries such as mining and shipping. The Japanese sent students, entrepreneurs, and government officials to the West to bring back as much new knowledge as they could.

Change was the order of the day in Japan. Japanese legal scholars, following German models, helped draft a constitution in 1889 that emphasized state power rather than individual rights. Western dress became the rule at the imperial court, and when fire destroyed Tokyo in 1872, a European planner directed the rebuilding in Western architectural style. The Japanese adapted samurai traditions such as spiritual discipline to create a large and technologically modern military. In the 1870s, Japan purchased naval ships from Britain and began conquering adjacent islands, including Okinawa.

The Paradoxes of Imperialism

Imperialism ignited constant, sometimes heated debate because of its many paradoxes. Although it was meant to make European nations more economically secure, imperialism intensified distrust in international politics as countries vied with one another for a share of world influence. In securing India's borders, for example, the British faced Russian expansion in Afghanistan and along the borders of China, raising the costs of empire. Britain thus spent enormous amounts of tax revenue to maintain its empire even as its industrial lead began to slip. Yet for certain businesses, colonies provided crucial markets and large profits: late in the century, French colonies bought 65 percent of France's exports of soap and 41 percent of its metallurgical exports. Imperialism provided huge numbers of jobs to people in European port cities, but taxpayers in all parts of a nation—whether they benefited or not—paid for colonial armies, increasingly costly weaponry, and administrators.

Advocates of imperialism pointed out that whites had a "civilizing mission." The French thus taught some of their colonial subjects French language, literature, and history. In Germany's African colonies, an exam for students in a school run by missionaries asked them to write on "Germany's most important mountains" and "the reign of William I and the wars he waged." The deeds of Africa's great rulers and the accomplishments of its kingdoms disappeared from the curriculum. While Europeans believed in instructing colonial subjects, they did not believe that Africans and Asians were as capable as Europeans of great achievements.

Imperialism's goal of "civilizing" was further conflicted. French advocates argued that their nation "must keep its role as the soldier of civilization." But it was unclear whether imperialism should emphasize soldiering (that is, the conquest and murder of local peoples) or civilizing (the education of local peoples in the European tradition). Western scholars and travelers had long studied Asian and African languages, art, and literature, and had gathered and used botanical and other scientific knowledge. Yet appreciation of foreign cultures was tinged with bias and error. European scholars of Islam characterized Muhammad as an inferior imitation of Jesus, for example, and many Europeans stereotyped Asians and Africans as lying, lazy, self-indulgent, or irrational. One English official pontificated that "accuracy is abhorrent to the Oriental mind." Such beliefs offered still another justification for conquest: that inferior colonized peoples would ultimately be grateful for what Europe had brought them.

European missionaries ventured to newly secured areas of Africa and Asia with attitudes similarly full of contradictions. A woman missionary reflected a common view when she remarked that the Tibetans with whom she worked were "going down, down into hell, and there is no one but me . . . to witness for Jesus amongst them." Many people under colonial rule did accept Christianity, often blending their local religious practices with Christian ones. Christianizing entire populations proved impossible, especially when some imperial adventurers and soldiers became addicted, went mad, or were wantonly murdered. When native people resisted, missionaries often supported brutal military measures against them in the name of upholding Christian values and Western order.

The paradoxes of imperialism are clear in hindsight, but at the time European self-confidence hid many of them. There was the belief that through imperialist ventures "a country exhibits before the world its strength or weakness as a nation," as one French politician announced. Some in government, however, worried that imperialism—because of its expense and the constant possibility of war—might weaken rather than strengthen the nation-state. The most glaring paradox of all was that Western peoples who believed in nation building and national independence invaded the territory of others thousands of miles away and refused them the right to rule themselves.

> **REVIEW** What were the goals of the new imperialism, and how did Europeans accomplish those goals?

The Industry of Empire

Behind the expansion of Western empires lay dramatic developments in economic and technological power. Fed by raw materials from around the world, industry turned out a flood of new products, including the increasingly powerful guns that served imperial conquest, and many workers' wages increased. Beginning in 1873, however, downturns in business threatened both entrepreneurs and the working class. Business-people sought remedies in new technology, managerial techniques, and a revolution-ary marketing institution—the department store. Governments played their part by changing business law and supporting the drive for raw materials and global profits. The steady advance of industry, global trade, and the consumer economy further transformed people's daily lives.

Industrial Innovation

An abundance of industrial, technological, and commercial innovation backed the ambitions of the nation-state and the drive for empire. The last third of the nineteenth century saw new products ranging from the bicycle to the typewriter to the telephone. In 1885, sophisticated German engineer Karl Benz devised a workable gasoline engine; six years later, France's Armand Peugeot constructed a functioning automobile. Electricity became more widely used after 1880, providing power to light everything from private drawing rooms to government office buildings. The Eiffel Tower, constructed in Paris for the Universal Exposition of 1889, stood as a monument to the age's engineering wizardry. Visitors rode to the Eiffel Tower's summit in electric elevators, while to fuel the West's explosive industrial growth, the leading industrial nations mined and produced massive quantities of coal, iron, and steel in the 1870s and 1880s. Manufacturers used the metal to build the more than 100,000 locomotives that pulled trains—trains that transported two billion people a year.

The factory system spread across Europe and around the world, while agriculture continued to be modernized. Historians used to contrast a "second" Industrial Revolution of the late nineteenth century, in which manufacturers concentrated on heavy industrial products like iron and steel, to the "first" one of the eighteenth and early nineteenth centuries, in which innovations in the manufacture of textiles and the use of steam energy predominated. Many historians now believe this distinction mainly applies to Britain, where industrialization did rise in two stages. In countries where industrialization came later, the two developments occurred simultaneously. Numerous and increasingly advanced textile mills were installed on the European continent later than in Britain, for instance, at the same time that blast furnaces were being constructed. Although industrialization led to the decline of traditional crafts like weaving, home industry—or **outwork**, the process of having some aspects of industrial work done outside factories in individual homes (similar to the putting-out system described on page 611)—persisted in garment making, metalwork, and porcelain painting. Industrial production occurring simultaneously in homes, small workshops, and factories has continued to the present day.

Industrial innovations also changed agriculture. Chemical fertilizers boosted crop yields, and reapers and threshers mechanized harvesting. In the 1870s, Sweden produced a cream separator, a first step toward mechanizing dairy farming, while wire fencing and barbed wire replaced wooden fencing and stone walls. Refrigeration, developed during this period, allowed fruits, vegetables, and meat to be transported without spoiling, thus diversifying and increasing the urban food supply. Tin from colonies facilitated large-scale commercial canning, which made many foods available year-round to people in the cities and thus improved their health.

Imperial expansion accelerated because new, more powerful guns, railroads, steamships, and medicines allowed Western penetration of Asia and Africa. Improvements in steamboat technology helped in the conquest of the African interior, but the scientific development of quinine was also crucial. Before the development of medicinal quinine in the 1840s and 1850s, the deadly tropical disease malaria decimated many a European party embarking on exploration or military conquest, giving Africa the nickname "White Man's Grave." The processing of quinine from Andean cinchona bark, long known by local people as preventing or relieving malaria, radically cut deaths from the disease among soldiers, missionaries, adventurers, traders, and bureaucrats.

As Europeans profited from these advances, drought and famine plagued large stretches of both Africa and Asia in these decades, thus weakening local peoples' ability to fight off European attacks. Under those circumstances European weapons did the work of conquest despite stout resistance. Improvements to the breech-loading rifle and the development of the machine gun, or "repeater," between 1862 and the 1880s dramatically increased firepower. Europeans sold outmoded guns to peoples needing protection both from their internal enemies and from the Europeans themselves. In contrast, Europeans crushed African resistance with rapid, accurate, and blazing gunfire: "The whites did not seize their enemy as we do by the body, but thundered from afar," claimed one local African resister. "Death raged everywhere— like the death vomited forth from the tempest."

Despite global expansion, Britain's rate of industrial growth slowed as its entrepreneurs remained wedded to older technologies. Neglecting innovation, Great Britain profited from its investments worldwide and consolidated its global power in the latter nineteenth century. Meanwhile, Germany and the United States began surpassing Britain in research, technical education, and innovation—and ultimately in overall rates of economic growth.

Following the Franco-Prussian War, Germany annexed Alsace and Lorraine, territories with both textile industries and rich iron deposits. Investing heavily in research, German businesses devised new industrial processes and began to mass-produce goods. Germany also spent as much money on education as on its military in the 1870s and 1880s, sending German industrial productivity soaring. The United States began intensive exploitation of its vast natural resources, including coal, metal ores, gold, and oil. Whereas German productivity rested more on state promotion of industrial efforts, U.S. growth often involved innovative entrepreneurs, such as Andrew Carnegie in iron and steel and John D. Rockefeller in oil. Most other countries trailed the three leaders in economic development.

French industry grew steadily, but French businesses remained smaller than those in Germany and the United States. In Spain, Austria-Hungary, and Italy, industrial development was primarily a local phenomenon. Austria-Hungary, for example, had densely industrialized areas around Vienna and in Styria and Bohemia, but the rest of the country remained tied to traditional, nonmechanized agriculture. The Italian government spent more on building Rome into a grand capital than it invested in economic growth. A mere 1.4 percent of Italy's 1872 budget went to education and science, compared with 10.8 percent in Germany. Scandinavian countries eventually made commercial use of electricity to industrialize in the last third of the nineteenth century and became leaders in the use of hydroelectric power.

Russia's road to industrialization was tortuous. The terms of serf emancipation bound many Russian peasants to the mir, or landed community. Some villages sent men and women to industrializing cities, but on the condition that they return for

The Invention of Electric Lighting   By the 1890s, residents of major European cities could see many fresh inventions in a single walk down the newly widened boulevards. In this illustration of Piccadilly in London, electric lighting illuminates the way for modern bicycles and automobiles as well as horse-drawn carriages. By the turn of the century, streets had also become crowded with electric trams. (Mary Evans Picture Library/The Image Works.)

plowing and harvesting. Nevertheless, by the 1890s, Moscow, St. Petersburg, and a few other cities had substantial working-class populations, and the Russian government constructed railroads, including the Trans-Siberian Railroad (1891–1916), which upon completion stretched 5,787 miles from Moscow to Vladivostok. Even as Russia's industrial and military power increased, it exemplified the uneven benefits of industrialization: neither Russian peasants nor underpaid urban workers could afford to buy the goods their country produced.

Facing Economic Crisis

Economic conditions were far from rosy throughout the 1870s and 1880s despite industrial innovation. In 1873, prosperity abruptly gave way to a severe economic depression, followed by almost three decades of economic downturns. People of all classes lost their jobs or businesses and faced long stretches of unemployment or bankruptcy. Because economic ties bound industrialized western Europe to international markets, the downturns affected economies around the world: Australia, South Africa, California, Newfoundland, and the West Indies.

By the 1870s, as industry gained in influence, industrial and financial setbacks—not agricultural ones as in the past—were capable of sending the economy into a long tailspin. Innovation created new or modernized industries on an unprecedented scale, but economic uncertainty accompanied the forward march of Western industrial development, and businesspeople faced real problems. First, the start-up costs of new enterprises skyrocketed. The early textile mills had required relatively small amounts of capital in comparison to the new factories producing steel and iron. **Capital-intensive industry**, which required huge financial investment for the purchase of expensive machinery, replaced labor-intensive production, which relied on the hiring of more workers. Second, the distribution and consumption of goods failed to keep pace with industrial growth, in part because businessmen kept wages so low that workers could afford little besides food. For them, purchasing the new industrial goods was impossible. The series of slumps turned industrialists' attention to finding ways to enhance sales and distribution and to control markets and prices.

Governments took steps to address the economic crisis. New laws spurred the development of the **limited liability corporation**, which protected investors from personal responsibility for a firm's debt and thus encouraged investment. Before limited liability, owners or investors were personally responsible for the debts of a bankrupt business. In one case in England, a former partner who had failed to have his name removed from a legal document after leaving the business remained responsible to creditors when the company went bankrupt. He lost everything he owned except a watch and the equivalent of one hundred dollars. By reducing personal risk, limited liability made investors more confident about financing business ventures, which led to the growth of stock markets. These stock markets raised money from a larger pool of private capital than before and gave businesses the funds to innovate.

Businesses also met the crisis that began in 1873 by banding together in cartels and trusts. Cartels were combinations of industries formed to control prices and competition. A single German coal cartel, founded in the 1880s, eventually dominated more than 95 percent of coal production in Germany and could therefore restrict output and set prices. Trusts—similar to cartels in their power to control prices but different in structure—appeared first in the United States in 1882, when John D. Rockefeller created the Standard Oil Trust by acquiring stock from many different oil companies and placing it under the direction of trustees. The trustees then controlled so much of the companies' stock that they could set prices for the entire industry and even dictate to the railroads the rates for transporting the oil. While expressing their belief in free trade, those who set up cartels and trusts actually restricted the free market to produce soaring profits for themselves.

Much of Europe had adopted free trade after midcentury, but during the downturn of the 1870s and 1880s the resulting huge trade deficits—caused when imports exceeded exports—soured many Europeans on the concept. Countries with trade deficits had less capital available to invest internally, slowing job growth. Farmers in many European countries suffered when improvements in transportation brought in cheap grain from the United States and Ukraine. With broad popular support, governments approved tariffs to make foreign goods, including grain, more expensive.

Revolution in Business Practices

Industrialists also tried to minimize the damage of economic downturns by revolutionizing the everyday conduct of their businesses. Instead of running their firms on their own in the late 1800s, industrialists began to hire managers specializing in a particular aspect of a business—such as sales and distribution, finance, or the purchase of raw materials. A white-collar service sector, composed of workers with mathematical skills and literacy acquired in the new public primary schools, emerged as part of the development of management. Businesses employed armies of secretaries, file clerks, and typists to guide the flow of business information.

Women, responding to the availability of clean, respectable work, formed the bulk of service employees. At the beginning of the nineteenth century, middle-class women still tended businesses with their husbands, but the new ideology of domesticity became so strong that male employers were unwilling to hire married women, and women in the lower-middle and middle classes were themselves ashamed to work outside the home. By the late nineteenth century, the costs of middle-class family life had increased, especially because school-attendance laws meant that children were no longer contributing to family resources by working. Whether to help pay family expenses or to support themselves, both unmarried and married women of the respectable middle class increasingly took jobs despite the ideal of domesticity. Since society had come to believe that women were not meant to work or even not fit to work, businesses made greater profits by consistently paying women in the service sector much less than they would have paid men for doing the same tasks.

The drive to boost consumption led to the development of the department store. Founded after midcentury in the largest cities, department stores such as the Bon Marché in Paris and Wanamaker's in Philadelphia gathered an impressive variety of goods in one place in imitation of the Middle Eastern bazaar. Unlike stores that sold single lines of goods such as dishware or fabrics, department stores were modern shopping palaces built of marble and filled with lights and mirrors. In the department store, luxurious silks and embellished tapestries spilled over railings and counters to stimulate consumer desire. Frenzied shoppers no longer limited their purchases to necessities. Department stores became the domain of women, who came out of their domestic sphere into a new public role. Stores hired attractive salesgirls, another variety of service workers, to inspire customers to buy. Department-store shopping also took place outside of cities: glossy mail order catalogs from the Bon Marché or Sears, Roebuck in Chicago arrived regularly in rural areas, with both necessities and exotic items from the faraway dream world of the city.

Consumerism was shaped by empire. Travelers like Frieda von Bülow and Carl Peters journeyed on speedier ocean liners, carrying quinine, antiseptics, and other medicines as well as cameras, revolvers, and the latest in rubber goods and apparel. Colonial products such as coffee, tea, sugar, tobacco, and cocoa became more widespread for the stimulation they offered hardworking Westerners. Tons of palm oil from Africa were turned into both margarine and soap, allowing even ordinary people in the West to see themselves as cleaner and more civilized than those in other parts of the world, including areas from which those raw materials came. Empire and industry jointly shaped everyday life by exciting the desire for things—whether industrial goods or products from the colonies.

> **REVIEW** What were the major changes in Western industry and business by the end of the nineteenth century?

Imperial Society and Culture

The spread of empire not only made the world an interconnected marketplace but also transformed everyday culture and society. Success in manufacturing and foreign ventures both created millionaires and expanded the professional middle class and the service sector. Many Europeans grew healthier, partly because of improved diet and partly because of government-sponsored programs aimed at promoting the fitness necessary for citizens of imperial powers. At the same time, millions of poor Europeans migrated in search of opportunities around the world—even in the colonies—while artists found new subject matter in the industrial and imperial changes around them.

The "Best Circles" and the Expanding Middle Class

Profits from empire and industrial growth added new members to the upper class, or "best circles," so called at the time because of their members' wealth, education, and social status. People in the best circles often came from the aristocracy, which remained powerful even as aristocrats had to share their social position with new millionaires from the ranks of the upper middle class, or bourgeoisie. Monarchs gratefully bestowed aristocratic titles on wealthy businesspeople, and poorer aristocrats approved marriages between their children and those of the newly rich. Such arrangements brought much-needed money to old, established families and the glamour of an aristocratic title to newly wealthy families. Thus, Jeanette Jerome, daughter of a wealthy New York financier, married England's Lord Randolph Churchill (their son Winston later became Britain's prime minister). To justify their success, the wealthy often quoted Social Darwinist principles, maintaining that their prosperity resulted from their natural superiority over the poor.

Empire reshaped leisure time. Upper-class men bonded over big-game hunting in Asia and Africa, which replaced age-old traditions of fox and bird hunting. European hunters forced native Africans, who had depended on hunting for income, food, and group unity, to work as guides, porters, and domestics on hunts. Collectors brought exotic specimens back to Europe for natural history museums, and wealthy Europeans added empire to their homes with displays of stags' heads, elephant tusks, and animal skins.

People in the best circles saw themselves as an imperial elite, and upper-class women devoted themselves to maintaining its standards of social conduct. Members of the upper class did their best to exclude inferiors by controlling their children's social lives, especially by arranging marriages themselves. Instead of working for pay, upper-class women focused on raising children and directing staffs of servants. They took their role seriously, keeping detailed accounts of their expenditures and monitoring their children's religious and intellectual development. Being active consumers of Oriental carpets, bamboo furniture, Chinese porcelains, and fashionable clothing was also time-consuming for women. In contrast to men's plain garments, upper-class women wore elaborate costumes—featuring constricting corsets, voluminous skirts, bustles, and low-cut necklines for evening wear—that made them symbols of elite leisure. Women offset the grim side of imperial and industrial society with the rigorous practice of art and music. With keys made of ivory from Africa, the piano symbolized the imperial elite's accomplishments and superiority.

Below the best circles, or upper crust, the solid middle class of businesspeople and professionals such as lawyers was expanding, most notably in western and central Europe. In eastern Europe, this expansion did not happen naturally, and the Russian government often sought out foreigners to build its professional and business classes. Although middle-ranked businessmen and professionals occasionally mingled with those at the apex of society, their lives remained more modest. They did, however, employ at least one servant, which might give the appearance of leisure to the middle-class woman in the home even though she did many household chores herself. Professional men working at home did so from a well-appointed, if not lavish, room. Overall, middle-class domesticity celebrated the imperial value of cleanliness.

Working People's Strategies

For centuries, working people had migrated from countryside to city and from country to country to make a living. After the middle of the nineteenth century, empire and industry were powerful factors in migration for a variety of reasons. In parts of Europe, the land simply could not produce enough to support a rapidly expanding population. Because of eroded soil, hundreds of thousands of Sicilians left, often temporarily, to find work in the industrial cities of North and South America. One-third of all European immigrants came from the British Isles, especially Ireland between 1840 and 1920, first because of the potato famine and then because English landlords drove them from their farms to get higher rents by simply changing tenants. Between 1886 and 1900, half a million Swedes out of a population of 4.75 million quit their country. Millions of rural Jews from eastern Europe also fled vicious anti-Semitism. Russian mobs brutally attacked Jewish communities, destroying homes and businesses and even murdering some Jews. These ritualized attacks, called pogroms, were scenes of horror. "People who saw such things never smiled anymore, no matter how long they lived," recalled one Russian Jewish woman who migrated to the United States in the early 1890s.

Commercial and imperial development determined destinations for international migration. Most migrants who left Europe went to North and South America, Australia, and New Zealand as news of opportunity reached Europe. The railroad and steamship made journeys across and out of Europe faster, though most workers traveled in steerage with few comforts. Once established elsewhere, migrants frequently sent money back home; European farm families often received a good deal of their income from husbands or grown sons and daughters who had left. Cash-starved peasants in eastern and central Europe welcomed the arrival of "magic dollars" from their kin. Even though they formed the cheapest pool of labor, often in factories or sweatshops, migrants themselves appreciated the chance to begin anew. One settler in the United States was relieved to escape the meager peasant fare of rye bread and herring: "God save us from . . . all that is Swedish," he wrote home sourly.

More common than international migration was internal migration from rural areas to European cities, accelerating the urbanization of Europe. The most urbanized countries were Great Britain and Belgium, followed by Germany, France, and the Netherlands; established port cities like Riga, Marseille, and Hamburg offered opportunities for work in global trade. Many who moved to the cities were seasonal migrants who worked as masons, cabdrivers, or factory hands to supplement declining income from agriculture. When they returned to the countryside, they provided hands for the harvest. In villages across Europe, independent artisans such as hand-loom weavers often supported their unprofitable livelihoods by sending their wives and daughters to work in industrial cities.

Changes in technology and management practices often made factory work more stressful. Workers complained that new machinery sped up the pace of work to an unrealistic level. For example, employers at a foundry in suburban Paris required workers using new furnaces to turn out 50 percent more metal per day than they had produced using the old furnaces. Despite more physical exertion, workers received no additional pay for their extra efforts. Workers also grumbled about the increased number of managers; many believed that foremen, engineers, and other supervisors interfered with their work. Some women kept their jobs only in return for granting sexual favors to the male manager.

Many in the urban and rural labor force continued to do outwork at home. In Russia, workers made bricks, sieves, shawls, lace, and locks during the slow winter season. Every branch of industry, from metallurgy to toy manufacturing to food processing, also employed urban women at home—and their work was essential to the family economy. Women painted tin soldiers, wrapped chocolate, made cheese boxes, and polished metal. Factory owners liked the system because low piece rates made outworkers willing to work extremely long days. A German seamstress at her new sewing machine reported that she "pedaled at a stretch from six o'clock in the morning until midnight. . . . At four o'clock I got up and did the housework and prepared meals." Owners could lay off women at home during slack times and rehire them whenever needed with little fear of organized protest, as the threat of joblessness meant destitution. By and large, however, urban workers were better informed and more connected to the progress of industry and empire than their rural counterparts were.

National Fitness: Reform, Sports, and Leisure

In an age of Social Darwinist concerns about national fitness in the international struggle to survive, middle- and upper-class reformers founded organizations for social improvement. Settlement houses, clinics, and maternal and child health centers sprang up overnight in cities. Young middle- and upper-class men and women, often from universities, eagerly took up residence in poor neighborhoods to study and help the people there. Believing in the scientific approach to solving social problems, the Fabian Society, a small organization established in London in 1884, undertook studies to devise reforms based on planning rather than socialist revolution. In 1893, the Fabians helped found the Labour Party to make social improvement a political cause. Religious faith also shaped these efforts: the Catholic church in Hungary, for example, ministered to those experiencing rural poverty as agriculture came under the stresses of global competition.

To make the poor more fit in a competitive world, philanthropists and government officials intervened in the lives of working-class families as a way to "quicken evolution." The worry was that the poor, as one reformer put it, "were permanently stranded on lower levels of evolution." Reformers sponsored centers to provide good medical care and food for children and instructed mothers in child-care techniques, including breast-feeding to promote infant health. Some schools distributed free lunches, medicine, and clothing and inspected the health and appearance of their students. Yet the poor were also pressured to follow new standards they could ill afford, such as finding children respectable shoes, and reformers believed they had the right to enter working-class apartments whenever they chose to inspect them.

A few professionals began to distribute birth-control information in the belief that smaller families could better survive the challenges of urban life. In the 1880s, Aletta Jacobs (1851–1929), a Dutch physician, opened the first birth-control clinic, which specialized in promoting the new, German-invented diaphragm. Jacobs wanted to help women in Amsterdam slums who were worn out by numerous pregnancies. Working-class women used these clinics, and knowledge of birth-control techniques spread by word of mouth among workers. The churches adamantly opposed this trend, and even reformers wondered whether birth control would increase sexual exploitation.

Another government reform effort consisted of legislation barring women from night work and from "dangerous" professions such as florist and bartender—allegedly for health reasons. Even though medical statistics demonstrated that women in even the most strenuous jobs became sick less often than men, lawmakers and working-men claimed that women were not producing healthy enough children and were stealing jobs from men. Women who had worked in trades newly defined as dangerous were forced to find other, lower-paying jobs or work at home. The new laws did not prevent women from holding jobs, but they made earning a living harder.

As nations competed for territory and global trade, male athletes created sports teams. Soccer, rugby, and cricket matches drew mass audiences that welded the lower and higher classes into an imperial culture. Competitive sports began to be seen as signs of national strength and spirit, as newspapers reported all sorts of new contests, whether they concerned nations vying for colonies or bicyclists participating in cross-country races such as the Tour de France. "The Battle of Waterloo was won on the playing fields of Eton," ran the wisdom of the day, suggesting that the games played in school could mold the strength of an army—an army that competed with those of other nations in pursuit of empire.

Team sports for men—like civilian military service—helped differentiate male and female spheres and thus promoted a social order based on distinction between the sexes. Reformers introduced exercise classes and gymnastics into schools for girls, often with the idea that these would strengthen them for motherhood and thus help build the nation-state. As knowledge of the world developed, some women began to practice yoga, while wealthy men crossed the empire to challenge themselves with mountain climbing.

Working-class people adopted middle-class habits by joining clubs for such pursuits as bicycling, touring, and hiking. Clubs that sponsored trips often had names like the Patriots or the Nationals, making a clear association between physical fitness and national strength. The emphasis on healthy recreation gave people a greater sense of individual might and promoted an imperial citizenship based less on constitutions and rights than on an individual nation's exercise of raw power. A farmer's son in the 1890s boasted that with a bicycle, "I was king of the road, since I was faster than a horse."

Artistic Responses to Empire and Industry

In the 1870s and 1880s, the arts explored the process of global expansion and economic innovation, often in the same gloomy Darwinistic terms that made reformers anxious. Darwin's theory held out the possibility that strong civilizations, if they failed to adapt to changing conditions, could weaken and collapse. French writer Émile Zola, influenced by fears of social decay, had a dark vision of how industrial society affected individuals. He produced a series of novels set in industrializing France about a family plagued by alcoholism and madness. His characters led violent strikes and in one case even castrated an oppressive grocer. Zola's novel *Women's Paradise* (1883) depicts the upper-class shopper who abandons rational decision making as a consumer for the frenzy of the new department stores. Other fictional heroines were equally upsetting because they violated other long-standing rules. The character Nora in the drama *A Doll's House* (1879), by Norwegian playwright Henrik Ibsen, undermines accepted values regarding the health of society by leaving an unsatisfying marriage.

Some decorative arts of this period featured a countertrend that celebrated a healthy and heroic rural life away from stark realism. Country people used mass-produced textiles to create traditional-looking costumes and developed ceremonies based on a mythical past. Such invented customs, romanticized as old and authentic, brought tourists from the cities to villages. Urban architects and industrial designers copied rustic styles when creating household goods and decorative objects. The influence of empire is apparent in the traditional Persian and Indian motifs used by English designers William Morris (1834–1896) and his daughter May Morris (1862–1938) in their designs of fabrics, wallpaper, and household items based on such natural imagery as the silhouettes of plants. Their work gave birth to the arts and crafts style, whose "traditional" features paradoxically attracted consumers living in the modern industrial age.

Industrial developments directly influenced the work of painters, who by the 1870s felt intense competition from a popular industrial invention—the camera. Photographers could produce cheap copies of paintings and create more realistic portraits than painters could, at affordable prices. In response, painters altered their style, employing new and varying techniques to distinguish their art from the photographic realism of the camera. Claude Monet, for example, was fascinated by the way light transformed an object, and he often portrayed the same place—a bridge or a railroad station—at different times of day.

This daring style of art generally came to be called **impressionism**. It emphasizes the artist's attempt to capture a single moment by focusing on the ever-changing light and color found in ordinary scenes. Using splotches and dots, impressionists moved away from the precise realism of earlier painters. Vincent Van Gogh used vibrant colors in great swirls to capture sunflowers, haystacks, and the starry evening sky. Closely following the impressionists, French painter Georges Seurat depicted with thousands of dots and dabs the Parisian suburbs' newly created parks, with their Sunday bicyclists and office workers in their store-bought clothing, carrying

Mary Cassatt, *The Letter* (c. 1890)   Mary Cassatt, an American artist who spent much of her time in Europe, was one of the many Western artists smitten by Japanese prints. Like many other Western artists of her day, she learned Japanese techniques for printmaking, but she also reshaped her painting style to follow Japanese conventions in composition, perspective, and the use of color. Cassatt is known for her many depictions of Western mothers and children and of individual women. In this painting, the woman herself even looks Japanese. (Worcester Art Museum, Worcester, Massachusetts, USA/Bridgeman Images.)

books or newspapers. Industry contributed to the new styles of painting, as factories produced a range of pigments that allowed artists to use a wider and more intense spectrum of colors than ever before.

An increasingly global vision also influenced painting in the age of empire. In both composition and style, impressionists borrowed heavily from Asian art and architecture. The impressionist goal of portraying the fleetingness of light or human situations came from an ancient Japanese concept—*mono no aware* ("sensitivity to the fleetingness of life"). The color, line, and delicacy of Japanese art (which many impressionists collected) is evident, for example, in Monet's later paintings of water lilies and even his re-creation of a Japanese garden at his home in France as the subject for artistic study. Similarly, the American expatriate Mary Cassatt used the two-dimensionality of Japanese art in *The Letter* (1890–1891) and other paintings. Van Gogh sometimes filled the background of portraits with copies of intensely colored Japanese prints, and in some paintings he imitated classic Japanese wood-cuts. The graphic arts advanced the West's ongoing borrowing from around the globe while responding to the changes brought about by industry.

REVIEW   How did empire and industry influence art and everyday life?

The Birth of Mass Politics

Ordinary people struggled for political voice, especially through the vote, as they watched the wealth and influence of industry and empire increase. By bringing more people into closer contact with one another in cities, the growth of industries helped develop networks of political communication and awareness, leading western European governments to allow more men to vote. Although only men profited from electoral reform in these nations, the era's expanding franchise marked the beginning of mass politics. Women could not vote, but they participated in public life by form-ing auxiliary groups to support political parties. Among the authoritarian monarchies, Germany had male suffrage, but in more autocratic states to the east—for instance, Russia—violence and ethnic conflict shaped political systems. In such places, the harsh rule from above often resembled the control imposed on colonized peoples.

Workers, Politics, and Protest

As the nineteenth century entered its final decades, workers organized formal unions, which attracted the allegiance of millions. Unions reacted to workplace hardships, demanding a say in working conditions and aiming, as one union's rule book put it, "to ensure that wages never suffer illegitimate reductions and that they always follow the rises in the price of basic commodities." Businessmen and governments viewed striking workers as insubordinate, threatening political unrest and destructive vio-lence. Even so, strong unions appealed to some industrialists because a union could make strikes more predictable (or even prevent them) and present worker demands coherently instead of piecemeal by groups of angry workers.

From the 1880s on, the pace of collective action for better pay, lower prices, and better working conditions accelerated. In 1888, for example, hundreds of young women who made matches, the so-called London matchgirls, went on strike to end the fining system, under which they could be penalized an entire day's wage for being a minute or two late to work. The fines, the matchgirls maintained, helped companies reap profits of more than 20 percent. In 1890, sixty thousand workers took to the streets of Budapest to agitate for safer working conditions and the vote; the next year, day laborers on Hungarian farms struck, too. Across Europe between 1888 and 1890, the number of major strikes and demonstrations rose by more than 50 percent, from 188 to 289.

Housewives, who often acted in support of strikers, carried out their own protests against high food prices. They confiscated merchants' goods and sold them at what they considered a fair price. "There should no longer be either rich or poor," argued Italian peasant women. "All should have bread for themselves and for their children." Housewives often hid neighbors' truant children from school officials so that the children could continue to help with work at home. When landlords evicted tenants, women gathered in the streets to return the ousted families' household goods as fast as they were removed. Meeting on doorsteps or at markets, women initiated rural newcomers into urban ways. In doing so, they helped cement the working-class unity created by workers in the factory.

Governments increasingly responded to strikes by calling out troops or armed police, even though most strikes were about working conditions and not about political revolution. Despite government force, unions did not back down or lose their commitment to solidarity. Craft-based unions of skilled artisans, such as carpenters and printers, were the most active and cohesive, but from the mid-1880s on, a movement known as **new unionism** attracted transport workers, miners, matchgirls, and dockworkers. These new unions were nationwide groups with salaried managers who could plan a widespread general strike across the trades, focusing on such common goals as achieving the eight-hour workday but also paralyzing an entire nation through work stoppages. Large unions had the potential for challenging large industries, cartels, and trusts.

Working-class political parties developed from unions. Workingmen helped create the Labour Party in England, the Socialist Party in France, and the Social Democratic Parties of Sweden, Hungary, Austria, and Germany—most of them inspired by Marxist theories. Germany was home to the largest socialist party in Europe after 1890. Socialist parties held out hope that newly enfranchised male working-class voters could become a collective force in national elections, even triumphing over the power of the upper class.

Those who accepted Marx's assertion that "workingmen have no country" also founded an international movement to address workers' common interests across national boundaries. In 1889, some four hundred socialists from across Europe met to form the **Second International**, a federation of working-class organizations and political parties that replaced the First International, founded by Marx before the Paris Commune. The Second International adopted a Marxist revolutionary program, but it also advocated suffrage (in countries where it still did not exist) and better working conditions.

Members of the Second International determined to rid the organization of anarchists, who flourished in the less industrial parts of Europe—Russia, Italy, and Spain—where Marxist theories of worker-controlled factories had less appeal. In an age of tough international competition in agriculture, many rural workers sought a life free from governments that backed the landowners' interests. Thus, many advocated extreme tactics, including physical violence. "We want to overthrow the government . . . with violence since it is by the use of violence that they force us to obey," wrote one Italian anarchist. In the 1880s, anarchists bombed stock exchanges, parliaments, and businesses. Members of the Second International felt that such random violence was counterproductive.

Workingwomen joined unions and workers' political parties, but in much smaller numbers than men. Unable to vote in national elections and usually responsible for housework in addition to their paying jobs, women had little time for party meetings. In addition, their lower wages hardly allowed them to survive, much less pay party or union dues. Many workingmen also opposed women's presence in unions. Contact with women would mean "suffocation," one Russian workingman believed, and end male union members' sense of being "comrades in the revolutionary cause." Unions glorified the heroic struggles of a male proletariat against capitalism. Marxist leaders maintained that capitalism alone caused injustice to women and thus that the creation of a socialist society would automatically end gender inequality. As a result, although the new political organizations wanted women's support, they dismissed women's concerns about lower wages and sexual harassment.

Popular community activities further strengthened worker solidarity. The gymnastics and musical societies that had once united Europeans in nationalistic fervor now served working-class goals. Socialist gymnastics, bicycling, and marching societies promoted physical fitness because it could help workers in the "struggle for existence"—a reflection of the spread of Darwinian thinking to all levels of society. Workers also held festivals and cheerful parades, most notably on May 1—a centuries-old holiday that the Second International now claimed as a labor holiday. Like religious processions of an earlier time, parades fostered unity. As a result, governments frequently banned such public gatherings, calling them a public danger.

Expanding Political Participation in Western Europe

Ordinary people everywhere in the West were becoming aware of politics through newspapers, which, combined with industrial and imperial progress, were important in developing a sense of citizenship in a nation. After 1880, western European countries moved toward mass politics more rapidly than did countries to the east, thanks in part to the rise of mass journalism—itself the product of imperial and industrial development. The invention of automatic typesetting and the production of newsprint from wood pulp lowered the costs of printing, and the telephone allowed reporters to communicate news to their papers almost instantly. Once literary in content, many daily newspapers now emphasized sensational news, using banner headlines, dramatic pictures, and gruesome or lurid details—particularly about murders and sexual scandals—to sell papers. In the hustle and bustle of industrial society, one editor wrote that "you must strike your reader right between the eyes." Stories of imperial adventurers and exaggerated accounts of exploited women workers, some in the white slave trade, drew ordinary people to the mass press.

Journalism created a national community of up-to-date citizens, whether or not they could vote. Unlike the book, the newspaper was meant not for quiet reflection at home or in the upper-class club but for quick reading of attention-grabbing stories on mass transportation and on the streets. Elites complained that the sensationalist press was a sign of social decay, but in western Europe increasing political literacy opened the political process to wider participation.

A change in political campaigning was one example of this widening participation. In the fall of 1879, **William Gladstone** (1809–1898), leader of the British Liberals, whose party was then out of power, took a train trip across Britain to campaign for a seat in the House of Commons. During his campaign, Gladstone addressed thousands of workers, arguing for the people of India and Africa to have more rights and summoning his audiences to "honest, manful, humble effort" in the middle-class tradition of "hard work." Newspapers around the country reported on his trip, and these accounts, along with mass meetings, fueled public interest in politics. Gladstone's campaign was successful, and he took the post of prime minister for the second of the four nonconsecutive terms he served between 1868 and 1894.

Other changes fostered the growth of political participation in Britain. The Ballot Act of 1872 made voting secret, a reform that reduced the ability of landlords and employers to control how their workers voted. The **Reform Act of 1884** doubled the electorate to around 4.5 million men, enfranchising many urban workers and artisans and thus further diminishing traditional aristocratic influence in the countryside. To win the votes of the newly enfranchised, Liberal and Conservative parties alike established national political clubs that competed with small cliques of parliamentary elites for control of party politics. Broadly based interest groups such as unions and national political clubs opened up politics by appealing to many more voters.

British political reforms immediately affected Irish politics by arming poor tenant farmers with the secret ballot. The political climate in Ireland was explosive mainly because of the repressive tactics of absentee landlords, many of them English and Protestant, who drove Irish tenants from their land in order to charge higher rents to newcomers. In 1879, opponents of these landlords formed the Irish National Land League and launched fiery protests. Irish tenants elected a solid bloc of nationalist representatives to the British Parliament, who, voting as a group, had sufficient strength to defeat either the Conservatives or the Liberals. Irish leader **Charles Stewart Parnell** (1846–1891) demanded British support for **home rule**—a system giving Ireland its own parliament—in return for Irish votes. Conservatives called home rule "a conspiracy against the honor of Britain," and when they were in power (1885–1886 and 1886–1892), they cracked down on Irish activism. Scandals reported in the press, some of them totally invented, weakened Parnell's influence. In 1890, the news broke of his affair with a married woman, and he died in disgrace soon after, as the media shaped politics. Still, Irish home rule remained a heated political issue, as did the determination to end Ireland's colonial status.

France's **Third Republic** replaced the Second Empire. The republic was shaky at the start because the monarchist political factions—Bonapartist, Orléanist, and Bourbon—all struggled to destroy it. Their failure to do so led in 1875 to the adoption of a new constitution, which created a ceremonial presidency and a premier (prime minister) dependent on support from the elected Chamber of Deputies. An alliance of businessmen, shopkeepers, professionals, and rural property owners hoped the new system would prevent the kind of strongman politics that had seen previous republics give way to the rule of emperors and the return of monarchs.

Fragile at birth, the Third Republic would remain so until World War II. Economic downturns, widespread corruption, and growing anti-Semitism fueled by a highly partisan and monarchist press kept the Third Republic on shaky ground. Newspaper stories about members of the Chamber of Deputies selling their votes to business interests and about the alleged trickery of Jewish businessmen manipulating the economy added to the instability. As a result, the public also blamed Jews for problems in the republican government and the economy.

In 1889, those disgusted by the messiness of parliamentary politics backed Georges Boulanger, a dashing and highly popular general, in his attempt to take over the government. Boulanger soon lost his nerve, however, thereby saving the French from rule by another strongman. Still, Boulanger's popularity showed that in hard economic times, liberal values based on constitutions, elections, and the rights of citizens could be called into question by someone promising easy solutions.

Republican leaders attempted to strengthen citizen loyalty by instituting compulsory and free public education in the 1880s. In public schools, secular teachers who supported republicanism replaced the Catholic clergy, who usually favored a return to monarchy. A common curriculum—identical in every schoolhouse in the country—featured patriotic reading books and courses in French geography, literature, and history. The government established secular public high schools for young women, seen as the educators of future citizens, while mandatory military service for men inculcated pride in the republic rather than in the monarchy or the church.

Although many western European leaders believed in economic liberalism, constitutions, and efficient government, these ideals did not always translate into universal male suffrage and citizens' rights in the less powerful western European countries. Spain and Belgium abruptly awarded suffrage to all men in 1890 and 1893, respectively, while remaining monarchies. An alliance of conservative landowners and the Catholic church dominated Spain, although there was increasingly lively urban activism in the industrial centers of Barcelona and Bilbao. Reform in the Netherlands increased male suffrage to only 14 percent by the mid-1890s, and an 1887 law in Italy gave the vote to all men who had a primary school education, also 14 percent of the male population. Without receiving the benefits of nation building—education, urban improvements, industrial progress, and the vote—the average Italian in the south felt less loyalty to the new nation than fear of the devastating effects of national taxes and the draft on the family economy.

Power Politics in Central and Eastern Europe

Germany, Austria-Hungary, and Russia diverged from the political paths taken by western European countries in the decades 1870–1890. In all three countries, conservative large landowners remained powerful, often blocking improvements in

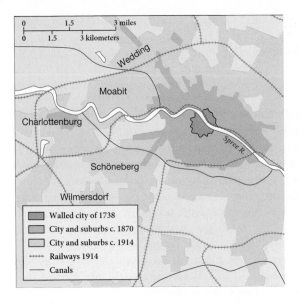

MAP 23.3 Expansion of Berlin to 1914 "A capital city is essential for the state to act as a pivot for its culture," the German historian Heinrich von Treitschke asserted. No other capital city grew as dramatically as Berlin after German unification in 1871. Industrialists and bankers set themselves up in the new capital, while workers migrated there for jobs, swelling the population. The city was newly dotted with military monuments and with museums to show off its culture.

transport, sanitation, and tariff policy that would support a growing urban population. But Bismarck, who had upset the European balance of power by humiliating France in the Franco-Prussian War, created a powerful, unified Germany, with explosive economic growth and rapid development of every aspect of the nation-state, from transport to the thriving capital city of Berlin (Map 23.3).

His goals achieved, Bismarck now desired stability built on diplomacy instead of war. Needing peace to consolidate the new nation, he pronounced Germany "satisfied," meaning that it sought no new territory in Europe. To ensure Germany's long-term security, in 1873 Bismarck forged the Three Emperors' League—an alliance of Germany, Austria-Hungary, and Russia. The three conservative powers shared a commitment to maintaining the political status quo.

At home, Bismarck, who owned land and invested personally in industry, joined with the liberals to create a variety of financial institutions, including a central bank to advance German commerce and industry. After religious leaders defeated his Kulturkampf (see Chapter 22, page 667) against Catholicism, Bismarck turned to attacking socialists and liberals instead of Catholics as enemies of the regime. He outlawed the workers' Social Democratic Party in 1878, and, hoping to lure the working class away from socialism, between 1882 and 1884 he sponsored an accident and disability insurance program—the first of its kind in Europe. In 1879, he put through tariffs protecting German agriculture and industry from foreign competition but also raising the prices of consumer goods, including food for ordinary people. Ending his support for laissez-faire economics, Bismarck broke with political liberals while simultaneously increasing the power of the agrarian conservatives by attacking the interests of Germany's industrial sector.

Like Germany, Austria-Hungary frequently employed liberal economic policies and practices. From the 1860s, liberal businessmen succeeded in industrializing parts of the empire, and the prosperous middle classes erected conspicuously large homes, giving themselves a prominence in urban life that rivaled the aristocracy's. They persuaded the government to enact free-trade provisions in the 1870s and to search out foreign investment to build up infrastructure, such as railroads.

Despite these measures, Austria-Hungary remained monarchist and authoritarian. Liberals in Austria—most of them ethnic Germans—saw their influence weaken under the leadership of Count Edouard von Taaffe, Austrian prime minister from 1879 to 1893. Building a coalition of clergy, conservatives, and Slavic parties, Taaffe used its power to weaken the liberals. In Bohemia, for example, he designated Czech as an official language of the bureaucracy and school system, thus breaking the German speakers' monopoly on office holding. Reforms outraged individuals at whose expense other ethnic groups received benefits, yet those who won concessions, such as the Czechs, clamored for even greater autonomy. By playing nationalities off one another, the government ensured the monarchy's central role in holding together competing interest groups.

Nationalists in the Balkans demanded independence from the declining Ottoman Empire, raising Austro-Hungarian fears and ambitions. In 1876, Slavs in Bulgaria and Bosnia-Herzegovina revolted against Turkish rule, killing Ottoman officials. As the Ottomans slaughtered thousands of Bulgarians in turn, two other small Balkan states, Serbia and Montenegro, rebelled against the sultan, too. Russian Pan-Slavic organizations sent aid to the Balkan rebels and so pressured the tsar's government that Russia declared war on Turkey in 1877 in the name of protecting Orthodox Christians. With help from Romania and Greece, Russia defeated the Ottomans and by the Treaty of San Stefano (1878) created a large, pro-Russian Bulgaria.

The Treaty of San Stefano sparked an international uproar. Austria-Hungary and Britain feared that an enlarged Bulgaria would become a Russian satellite that would enable the tsar to dominate the Balkans. Austrian officials worried about an uprising of their own restless Slavs. British prime minister Benjamin Disraeli moved warships into position against Russia to halt the advance of Russian influence in the eastern Mediterranean, so close to Britain's routes through the Suez Canal. The public was drawn into foreign policy: the music halls and newspapers of England echoed a new jingoism, or political sloganeering, that throbbed with militarism: "We don't want to fight, but by jingo if we do, / We've got the ships, we've got the men, we've got the money too!"

The other great powers, however, did not want a Europe-wide war, and in 1878 they attempted to revive the concert of Europe by meeting at Berlin under the auspices of Bismarck—now a calming presence on the diplomatic scene. The Congress of Berlin rolled back the Russian victory by partitioning the large Bulgarian state carved out of Ottoman territory and denying any part of Bulgaria full independence from the Ottomans (Map 23.4). Austria occupied (but did not annex) Bosnia and Herzegovina as a way of gaining clout in the Balkans; Serbia and

MAP 23.4 The Balkans, c. 1878   After midcentury, the map of the Balkans was almost constantly redrawn. This resulted in part from the weakness of the dominant Ottoman Empire but also from the ambitions of inhabitants themselves and from great-power rivalry. In tune with the growing sense of national identities based on shared culture, history, and ethnicity, various Balkan peoples sought to emphasize local, small-group identities rather than merging around a single dominant group such as the Serbs. Yet there was also a move by some intellectuals to transcend borders and create a southern Slav culture.

Montenegro became fully independent. The Balkans remained a site of ambition for independence and great-power rivalries.

Following the Congress of Berlin, the European powers attempted to guarantee stability through a complex series of alliances and treaties. Anxious about the Balkans, Austria-Hungary forged a defensive alliance with Germany in 1879. The **Dual Alliance**, as it was called, offered protection against Russia and its potential for inciting Slav rebellions. In 1882, Italy joined this partnership (henceforth called the Triple Alliance), largely because of Italy's imperial rivalries with France. Bismarck

Torah Scrolls   After the assassination of Alexander II in 1881, the government unleashed pogroms against the Jews of the Russian Empire. The pogroms involved violent acts such as murder, beatings, and the destruction of property on a grand scale. In this image, Jewish men survey the damage done to the sacred texts of their religion during one such vicious attack.
(© From the Jewish Chronicle Archive/Heritage Images/The Image Works.)

negotiated the Reinsurance Treaty (1887) with Russia guaranteeing neutrality in case of war unless the Habsburgs attacked Russia or Germany attacked France. The intention was to keep the Habsburgs from recklessly starting a war over Pan-Slavism.

Russia itself was beset by domestic problems in the 1870s and 1880s. Young Russians were turning to revolution for solutions to political and social problems. One such group, the Populists, wanted to rouse debt-ridden peasants to revolt. Other people formed terrorist bands to assassinate public officials. The secret police rounded up hundreds of members of one of the largest groups, Land and Liberty, and subjected them to brutal torture and show trials. When in 1877 a young radical, Vera Zasulich, tried unsuccessfully to assassinate the chief of the St. Petersburg police, the people of the capital city applauded her act and acquittal, so great was their outrage at government treatment of young radicals from respectable families.

Writers debated Russia's future, mobilizing public opinion over these issues. Novelists Leo Tolstoy, author of the epic *War and Peace* (1869), and Fyodor Dostoevsky, a former radical, believed that Russia above all required spiritual regeneration — not revolution. Tolstoy's novel *Anna Karenina* (1877) tells the story of an impassioned love affair, but it also weaves in the spiritual quest of Levin, a former "progressive" landowner who, like Tolstoy, idealizes the peasantry's stoic endurance. Dostoevsky satirized Russia's radicals in *The Possessed* (1871), a novel in which a group of revolutionaries murders one of its own members. In Dostoevsky's view, the radicals were simply destructive, offering no solutions whatsoever to Russia's ills.

Despite the influential critiques published by Tolstoy and Dostoevsky, violent action rather than spiritual uplift remained the foundation of radicalism. In 1881, the People's Will, a splinter group of Land and Liberty, killed Tsar Alexander II in a bomb attack. The tsar's death, however, failed to provoke the general uprising the terrorists expected. Alexander III (r. 1881–1894) unleashed a new wave of oppression against religious and ethnic minorities. Popular books and drawings depicted Tatars, Poles, Ukrainians, and others as a horrifying menace to Russian culture. The five million Russian Jews, confined to the eighteenth-century Pale of Settlement (the name for the restricted territory in which they were permitted to live), endured pogroms. Their distinctive language, dress, and isolation in ghettos made them easy targets. Government administrators encouraged these pogroms, blaming Jews for rising living costs that were actually caused by the high taxes levied on peasants to pay for industrialization.

As the tsar inflicted even greater repression across Russia, Bismarck's delicate system of alliances of the three conservative powers was coming apart. A brash but deeply insecure young kaiser, William II (r. 1888–1918), came to the German throne in 1888. William resented Bismarck's power, and his advisers flattered the young man into thinking that his own talent made Bismarck an unnecessary rival. William dismissed Bismarck in 1890 and let the Reinsurance Treaty with Russia lapse in favor of a pro-German relationship with Austria-Hungary. He thus destabilized the diplomatic scene just as imperial rivalries were intensifying among the European powers.

> **REVIEW** What were the major changes in political life from the 1870s to the 1890s, and which areas of Europe did they most affect?

Conclusion

The period from the 1870s to the 1890s has been called the age of empire and industry because Western society pursued both these ends in a way that rapidly transformed Europe and the world. Much of Europe thrived due to industrial innovation, becoming more populous and more urbanized. Using the innovative weapons streaming from Europe's factories, the great powers undertook a new imperialism that established political rule over foreign peoples. As they tightened connections with the rest of the globe, Europeans proudly spread their supposedly superior culture throughout the world and, like Frieda von Bülow and Carl Peters, sought out more power and wealth.

Imperial expansion and industrial change affected all social classes. The upper class attempted to maintain its position of social and political dominance, while an expanding middle class was gaining influence. Working-class people often suffered from the effects of rapid industrial change when their labor was replaced by machinery. Millions relocated to escape poor conditions in the countryside and to find new opportunities. Political reform, especially the expansion of suffrage, gave working-class men a political voice. Workers formed unions and political parties to protect their interests, but governments often responded to workers' activism with repression.

As workers struck for improved wages and conditions and the impoverished migrated to find a better life, the advance of empire and industry was bringing unprecedented tensions to national politics, the international scene, and everyday life. By the 1890s, racism and anti-Semitism were spreading, and many were questioning the costs of empire both to their own nation and to conquered peoples. Politics in the authoritarian countries of central and eastern Europe was taking a more conservative turn, resisting participation and reform. The rising tensions of modern life would soon have grave consequences for the West as a whole.

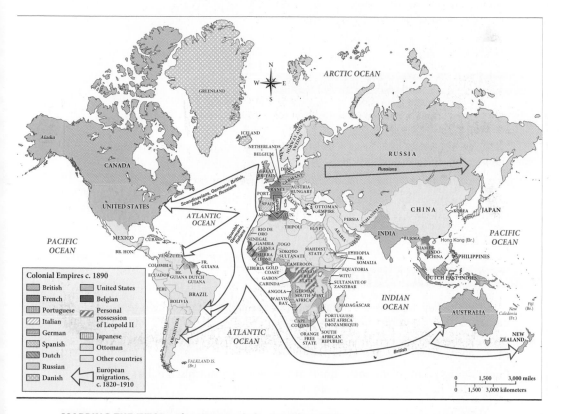

MAPPING THE WEST   The West and the World, c. 1890   In the late nineteenth century, European trade and political reach spanned the globe. Needing markets for the vast quantities of goods that poured from European factories and access to raw materials to produce the goods, governments asserted that the Western way of life should be spread to the rest of the world and that resources would be best used by Europeans. Explorations and scientific discoveries continued both to build the knowledge base of Western nations and to enhance their ability for greater conquest. Simultaneously, millions of Europeans left their homes to find a better life elsewhere.

Chapter Review

KEY TERMS AND PEOPLE

Be sure you can identify the term or person and explain its historical significance.

Leopold II (p. 679)

outwork (p. 684)

capital-intensive industry (p. 687)

limited liability corporation (p. 687)

impressionism (p. 694)

new unionism (p. 696)

Second International (p. 696)

William Gladstone (p. 698)

Reform Act of 1884 (p. 698)

Charles Stewart Parnell (p. 698)

home rule (p. 698)

Third Republic (p. 698)

Dual Alliance (p. 702)

REVIEW QUESTIONS

1. What were the goals of the new imperialism, and how did Europeans accomplish those goals?
2. What were the major changes in Western industry and business by the end of the nineteenth century?
3. How did empire and industry influence art and everyday life?
4. What were the major changes in political life from the 1870s to the 1890s, and which areas of Europe did they most affect?

MAKING CONNECTIONS

1. How did the new imperialism differ from European expansion of two centuries earlier? Of four centuries earlier?
2. Describe the effects of imperialism on European politics and society as a whole from 1870 to 1890.
3. Compare the political and social goals of the newly enfranchised male electorate with those of people from the "best circles."

IMPORTANT EVENTS

1860s–1890s	• Impressionism flourishes in the arts; absorption of Asian influences
1870s–1890s	• Vast emigration from Europe continues; the new imperialism
1871	• Franco-Prussian War ends
1873	• Extended economic recession begins with global impact
1876	• British Parliament declares Victoria empress; invention of telephone
1878	• Treaty of San Stefano
1879	• Dual Alliance is formed between Germany and Austria-Hungary
1881	• Tsar Alexander II is assassinated; France occupies Tunisia
1882	• Triple Alliance is formed between Germany, Austria-Hungary, and Italy; Britain invades Egypt
1882–1884	• Bismarck sponsors social welfare legislation
1884	• British Parliament passes the Reform Act, doubling size of male electorate
1884–1885	• European nations carve up Africa at Berlin conference
1885	• Invention of workable gasoline engine; formation of Indian National Congress
1889	• Japan adopts constitution based on European models; socialists meet in Paris and establish Second International
1891	• Construction of Trans-Siberian Railroad begins

24

Modernity and the Road to War

1890–1914

CHAPTER FOCUS

How did developments in social life, art, intellectual life, and politics at the turn of the twentieth century produce instability and set the backdrop for war?

IN THE FIRST DECADE of the twentieth century, a wealthy young Russian man traveled from one country to another to find relief from a common malady of the time called neurasthenia. Its symptoms included fatigue, lack of interest in life, depression, and sometimes physical illness. In 1910, the young man consulted Sigmund Freud, a Viennese physician whose unconventional treatment—eventually called psychoanalysis—took the form of a conversation about the patient's dreams, sexual experiences, and everyday life. Over the course of four years, Freud uncovered his patient's deeply hidden fear of castration, which was disguised as a fear of wolves—thus the name Wolf-Man, by which he is known to us. Freud worked his cure, as the Wolf-Man himself put it, "by bringing repressed ideas into consciousness" through extensive talking.

In many ways, the Wolf-Man could be said to represent his time. Born into a family that owned vast estates, he reflected Europe's growing prosperity, though on a grander scale than most. Countless individuals were troubled, even mentally disturbed like the Wolf-Man, and suicides were not uncommon. The Wolf-Man's own sister and father died from intentional drug overdoses. As the twentieth century opened, Europeans raised questions about family, gender relationships, empire, religion, and the consequences of technology. Every sign of imperial wealth brought on an apparently irrational sense of Europe's decline. British writer H. G. Wells saw in this prosperous era "the sunset of mankind." Gloom filled the pages of many a book and upset the lives of individuals like the Wolf-Man.

Conflict rattled the world as a growing number of powers, including Japan and the United States, fought their way into even more territories. The nations of Europe had lurched from one diplomatic crisis to another over access to global resources and control of territory—both within Europe and outside it. Competition for empire fueled an arms race that threatened to turn Europe—the most civilized region of the world, according to its leaders— into a savage battleground. In domestic politics, militant nationalism stirred ethnic hatreds and furthered anti-Semitic violence. Women suffragists along with other politically disadvantaged groups such as the Slavs and Irish demanded full citizenship, even as political assassinations and public brutality swept away the liberal values of tolerance and human rights.

These were just some of the conflicts associated with the term *modernity*, often used to describe the rise of mass politics, the spread of technology, and the faster pace of life—all of which were visible in the West from the late nineteenth century on. The word *modern* was also applied to art, music, science, and philosophy of this period. Although many people today admire the brilliant, innovative qualities of modern art, music, and dance, people of the time were offended, even outraged, by the new styles and sounds. Freud's theory that sexual drives exist in even the youngest children shocked people. Every advance in science and the arts simultaneously undermined middle-class faith in the stability of Western civilization.

That faith was further tested when the heir to the Austro-Hungarian throne was assassinated in June 1914. Few gave much thought to the global significance of the event, least of all the Wolf-Man, whose treatment with Freud was just ending. He viewed the fateful day of June 28 simply as the day he "could now leave Vienna a healthy man." Yet the assassination put the spark to the powder keg of international discord that had been building for several decades. The resulting disastrous war, World War I, like the insights of Freud, would transform life in the West.

Public Debate over Private Life

At the beginning of the twentieth century, an increasing number of people could aspire to a comfortable family life because of Europe's improved standard of living. Yet as the twentieth century opened, traditional social norms such as heterosexual marriage and woman's domestic role as wife and mother came under attack by what were seen as the forces of modernity. The falling birthrate, rising divorce rate, and growing activism for marriage reform provoked heated accusations that changes in private life were endangering national health. Discussions about sexual identity became a political issue, and some feared the disappearance of distinct gender roles. Women's visibility in public life prompted one British songster in the late 1890s to write:

> Rock-a-bye baby, for father is near
> Mother is "biking" she never is here!
> Out in the park she's scorching all day
> Or at some meeting is talking away!

Discussions of gender roles and private life contributed to rising social tensions because they challenged so many traditional ideals. Freud and other scientists tried to be dispassionate in their study of such phenomena — sexuality, for example — and to formulate treatments for so-called modern ailments such as those afflicting the Wolf-Man.

Population Pressure

From the 1890s on, European politicians and the public hotly discussed urgent concerns over trends in population, marriage, and sexuality. The European population continued to grow as the twentieth century opened. Germany's population increased from 41 million in 1871 to 64 million in 1910, and tiny Denmark's grew from 1.7 million in 1870 to 2.7 million in 1911. Contributing to the increase were improvements in sanitation and public health, which reduced infant mortality and extended the average human life span. Following the earlier examples of Vienna and Paris, planners tore apart and rebuilt Budapest, Moscow, and Berlin (whose population grew to over 4 million). Less-powerful states also rebuilt cities to absorb population growth: the Balkan capitals of Sofia, Belgrade, and Bucharest gained tree-lined boulevards and improved sanitation facilities.

While the absolute size of the population was rising in the West, the birthrate (measured in births per thousand people) was falling. The birthrate had been decreasing in France since the eighteenth century; other European countries began experiencing the decline late in the nineteenth century. The Swedish birthrate dropped from thirty-five births per thousand people in 1859 to twenty-four per thousand in 1911; Germany went from forty births per thousand in 1875 to twenty-seven per thousand in 1913.

Industrialization and urbanization helped bring about this change. Farm families needed fewer hands because new agricultural machinery was taking the place of human laborers. In cities, individual couples were free to make their own decisions about limiting family size, learning from neighbors or, for those with enough money and education, from pamphlets and advice books about birth-control practices, including coitus interruptus (the withdrawal method of preventing pregnancy). Industrial technology played a further role in curtailing reproduction: condoms, improved after the vulcanization of rubber in the 1840s, proved fairly reliable in preventing conception, as did the diaphragm. Abortions were also common.

The wider use of birth control roused critics who accused middle-class women of holding a "birth strike." Bishops in the Church of England condemned family limitation as "demoralizing to character and hostile to national welfare." Politicians worried that the drop in the birthrate was due to a crisis in masculinity, which would put military strength at risk. The "quality" of those being born troubled activists: If the "best" classes had fewer children, politicians asked, what would society look like if only the "worst" classes grew in number? The decline in fertility, one German nationalist warned, would fill the country with "alien peoples, above all Slavs and probably East European Jews as well." Nationalist groups inflamed the political climate with such racial hatreds. Instead of building consensus to create an inclusive political community, politicians won votes by demonizing ethnic minorities, the poor, and women who limited family size.

Reforming Marriage

Reformers thought that improving conditions within marriage would raise both the quality and quantity of children born. Many educated Europeans believed in eugenics—a set of ideas about producing "superior" people through selective breeding. A famed Italian criminologist declared that "lower" types of people were not humans but "orangutans." Eugenicists wanted increased childbearing for "the fittest" and decreased childbearing—even sterilization—for "degenerates," that is, those deemed inferior. Women of the "better" classes, reformers also believed, would have more children if marriage were made more equal. One step would be to allow married women to keep their wages and to own property, both of which in most legal systems belonged to their husbands. Another step would be to allow women guardianship of their own children.

Reformers worked to improve marriage laws to boost the birthrate, while feminists sought to better the lot of mothers and their children. Sweden made men's and women's control over property equal in marriage and allowed married women to work without their husband's permission. Other countries, among them France (1884), legalized divorce and made it less complicated to obtain. Reformers reasoned that divorce would allow unhappy couples to separate and undertake more loving and thus more fertile marriages. By the early twentieth century, several countries had passed legislation that provided government subsidies for medical care and child support as concerns about population partially laid the foundations for the welfare state—that is, a nation-state whose policies addressed not just military defense, foreign policy, and political processes but also the social and economic well-being of its people.

The conditions of women's lives varied across Europe. For example, a greater number of legal reforms occurred in western versus eastern Europe, but women could get university degrees in Austria-Hungary long before they could at Oxford or Cambridge in England. However, in much of rural eastern Europe, the father's power over the extended family remained almost dictatorial. According to a survey of family life in eastern Europe in the early 1900s, fathers married off their children so young that 25 percent of women in their early forties had been pregnant more than ten times. Yet reform of everyday customs did occur: for instance, among the middle and upper classes of Europe, many grown children were coming to believe that they had a right to select a marriage partner instead of accepting the spouse their parents chose for them.

New Women, New Men, and the Politics of Sexual Identity

Rapid social change set the stage for even bolder behaviors among some middle-class women. Adventurous women traveled the globe on their own to promote Christianity, make money, or learn about other cultures. The increasing availability of white-collar jobs for educated women meant that more of them could adopt an independent way of life. The so-called **new woman** dressed more practically, with fewer petticoats and looser corsets, biked down city streets and country lanes, lived apart from her family, and supported herself. Italian educator Maria Montessori (1870–1952), the first woman in Italy to earn a medical degree and the founder of an educational system that still bears her name, secretly gave birth to an illegitimate child. Other new women lived openly with their lovers. Not surprisingly, there was loud criticism: the new woman, German philosopher Friedrich Nietzsche wrote, had led to the "uglification of Europe."

Sexual identity also fueled debate. A popular book in the new field of "sexology," which studied sex scientifically, was *Sexual Inversion* (1896) by Havelock Ellis. Ellis, a British medical doctor, claimed that there was a new personality type—the homosexual—identifiable by physical affection for members of their own sex. Homosexuals joined the discussion, calling for recognition that they composed a natural "third sex" and were not just people behaving sinfully. Some maintained that, possessing both male and female traits, they marked "a higher order" on the scale of human evolution. The discussion of homosexuality started the trend toward seeing sexuality in general as a basic part of human identity.

The issue became explosive in the spring of 1895, when Irish playwright Oscar Wilde (1854–1900) was convicted of indecency—a charge that referred to his sexual affairs with younger men—and sentenced to two years in prison. "Open the windows! Let in the fresh air!" one newspaper rejoiced at the conviction. Between 1907 and 1909, German newspapers broadcast the courts-martial of military men in Kaiser William II's closest circle who were condemned for homosexuality and transvestitism. The government had to assure the public that William's own family life was "a fine model" for the German nation, as heterosexuality took on patriotic overtones. Despite the harsh judgments against homosexuals, these cases paved the way for growing sexual openness. Yet they also made sexual issues regular weapons in politics.

Sciences of the Modern Self

Scientists and Social Darwinists found cause for alarm not only in the poor condition of the working class but also in modern society's mental complaints such as those of the Wolf-Man. New sciences of the mind such as psychology and psychoanalysis aimed to treat everyone, not just the insane. A number of books in the 1890s presented arguments on causes and cures for modern nervous ailments. *Degeneration* (1892–1893), by Hungarian-born physician Max Nordau, blamed overstimulation for both individual and national deterioration. According to Nordau, nervous complaints and the increasingly bizarre art world reflected a general downturn in the human species. The Social Darwinist remedy for such mental decline was imperial adventure for men and increased childbearing for both sexes because it would restore men's virility and women's femininity.

Sigmund Freud (1856–1939) devised a different approach to treating mental problems — one that challenged the widespread liberal belief in a rational self that consistently acts in its own best interest. Dreams, he explained in *The Interpretation of Dreams* (1900), reveal an unseen and powerful part of one's personality — the "unconscious" — where all sorts of desires are more or less hidden from one's rational understanding. Freud also held that the human psyche is made up of three

Freud's Office and Collection   Sigmund Freud surrounded himself with imperial trophies such as Oriental rugs and African art objects in his study and therapy room in Vienna. Freud was fascinated by cures brought about through shamanism, trances, and other practices of non-Western medicine. Despite his successes, Freud, like other Jews, was a target of anti-Semitism from Nazis and others; he eventually escaped Vienna for exile in London in 1938. (ullstein bild/The Granger Collection, NYC—All rights reserved.)

competing parts: the ego, the part that is most in touch with the need to work and survive—that is, reality; the id (or libido), the part that contains instincts and sexual energies; and the superego, the part that serves as the conscience. Freud's theory of human mental processes and his method for treating their malfunctioning came to be called psychoanalysis.

Freud believed that sexual life should be understood objectively, free from religious or moral judgments. Children, he insisted, have sexual drives from the moment of birth; for the individual to attain maturity and for society to remain civilized, sexual desires—such as impulses toward incest—had to be repressed. Gender identity is more complicated than biology alone, he claimed, adding that girls and women have powerful sexual feelings, an idea that broke sharply with existing beliefs that women were passionless.

The influence of psychoanalysis became pervasive in the twentieth century. For example, Freud's "talking cure," as his method of treatment was quickly labeled, gave rise to a general acceptance of talking out one's problems to a therapist. Terms such as *neurotic* and *unconscious* came into widespread use. Freud attributed girls' complaints about sexual harassment or abuse to fantasy caused by "penis envy," an idea that led members of the new profession of social work to believe that most instances of such abuse had not actually occurred. Like Darwin, Freud rejected optimistic views of the world, believing instead that humans individually and collectively were motivated by irrational drives toward death and destruction.

> **REVIEW**   How did ideas about the self and about personal life change at the beginning of the twentieth century?

Modernity and the Revolt in Ideas

Toward the beginning of the twentieth century, intellectuals and artists so completely rejected long-standing beliefs and traditional artistic forms that they ushered in a new era. In science, the theories of Albert Einstein and other researchers established new truths in physics. Artists and musicians produced shocking works but, like Freud, they were influenced by advances in science and the progress of empire. Their blending of the scientific and the irrational, and of Western and non-Western styles, helped launch the revolution in ideas and creative expression called **modernism**.

The Opposition to Positivism

Late in the nineteenth century, many philosophers and social thinkers rejected the century-old belief that using scientific methods would uncover enduring social laws. This belief, called positivism, had emphasized the verifiable nature of fundamental laws and had motivated attempts to enact legislation based on studies of society. Challenging positivism, some critics declared that because human experience is ever changing, there are no constant social laws. German political theorist Max Weber

(1864–1920) maintained that the sheer number of facts involved in policymaking could make decisive action by bureaucrats impossible. In times of crisis, a charismatic leader might usurp power because of his ability to act simply on intuition. These turn-of-the-century thinkers, called relativists and pragmatists, influenced thinking throughout the twentieth century.

The most radical among the scholars was the German philosopher **Friedrich Nietzsche** (1844–1900), who asserted that "truth" is not certain but rather a human representation of reality. Neither scientists nor other careful observers, he said, can have knowledge of nature that is not filtered through human perception. Nietzsche was convinced that late-nineteenth-century Europe was witnessing the decline of absolute truths such as those found in religion. Thus, he announced, "God is dead, we have killed him." Far from arousing dread, however, the death of God, according to Nietzsche, would give birth to a joyful quest for new "poetries of life" to replace worn-out religious and middle-class rules. Nietzsche believed that an uninhibited, dynamic "superman," free from traditional religious and moral values, would replace the rule-bound middle-class person.

Nietzsche thought that each individual had a vital life energy that he called "the will to power." The idea inspired many people, including his students. As a teacher, Nietzsche was so vibrant—like his superman—that his first students thought they were hearing another Socrates. However, Nietzsche contracted syphilis and was insane in the last eleven years of his life, cared for by his sister. She edited his attacks on middle-class values into attacks on Jews and revised his complicated concepts of the will to power and of superman to appeal to nationalists, anti-Semites, and militarists, all of whom he actually hated.

The Revolution in Science

While Nietzsche and other philosophers questioned the ability of traditional science to provide timeless truths, scientific inquiry itself gained in prestige. Around the turn of the century, however, discoveries by pioneering researchers shook the foundations of scientific certainty. In 1896, French physicist Antoine Becquerel discovered radioactivity. He also suggested the mutability of elements by the rearrangement of their atoms. French chemist Marie Curie and her husband, Pierre Curie, isolated the elements polonium and radium, which are more radioactive than the uranium Becquerel used. From these and other discoveries, scientists concluded that atoms are not solid, as had long been believed, but are composed of subatomic particles moving about a core. In 1900, German physicist Max Planck announced his quantum theory, stating that energy is delivered not in a steady stream but in discrete packets, which he later called quanta.

In this atmosphere of discovery, physicist **Albert Einstein** (1879–1955) proclaimed his special theory of relativity in 1905. According to this theory, space and time are not absolute categories but instead vary according to the vantage point of the observer. Only the speed of light is constant. That same year, Einstein suggested that the solution to problems in Planck's theory lay in considering light both as little packets *and* as waves. Einstein later proposed yet another blurring of two distinct physical properties, mass and energy. He expressed this equivalence in the equation $E = mc^2$, or energy equals mass times the square of the speed of light. In 1916, Einstein published his general theory of relativity, which connected the force, or gravity, of an object with its mass and proposed a fourth mathematical dimension to the universe. Much more lay ahead once Einstein's theories of energy were applied to technology: television, nuclear power, and, within forty years, nuclear bombs.

The findings of Planck, Einstein, and others were not readily accepted, because long-standing scientific truths were at stake. Additionally, Marie Curie faced such sexism from the scientific establishment that even after she became the first person ever to receive a second Nobel Prize (1911), the prestigious French Academy of Science turned down her candidacy for membership. The academy claimed that a woman simply could not have done such outstanding work. Acceptance of these scientists' discoveries gradually came, and Einstein's name became synonymous with *genius*. Scientists of the modern era achieved what historians call a paradigm shift— that is, despite resistance, they transformed the foundations of science as their theories came to replace those of earlier pioneers.

Modern Art

Conflicts between traditional values and new ideas also raged in the arts as artists distanced themselves further from classical Western styles. French painter Paul Cézanne initiated one of the most powerful trends in modern art by using rectangular daubs of paint to portray his geometric vision of dishes, fruit, drapery, and the human body. Cézanne's art accentuated structure—the lines and planes found in nature—instead of presenting nature as it appeared in everyday life. Following in Cézanne's footsteps, Spanish artist Pablo Picasso (1881–1973) developed a style called cubism. Its radical emphasis on planes and surfaces converted his models into bizarre, almost unrecognizable forms. Picasso's painting *Les Demoiselles d'Avignon* (1907), for example, depicted the bodies of the *demoiselles* ("young ladies" or in this case "prostitutes") as fragmented and angular, with their heads modeled on African masks. Picasso's work showed the profound influences of African, Asian, and South American arts, but his use of these features was less decorative and more brutal than that of many other modern artists. Like imperialists who recounted their brutal exploits in speeches and memoirs, Picasso brought knowledge of the empire home in a disturbing style that captured the jarring uncertainties of society and politics in these decades.

Across Europe, artists made stylistic changes in their work that incorporated political criticism and even outrage. "Show the people how hideous is their actual life," anarchists challenged. Picasso, who had spent his youth in working-class Barcelona, a hotbed of anarchist thought, aimed to present the plain truth about industrial society in his art. In 1912, Picasso and French painter Georges Braque devised a new kind of collage that incorporated bits of newspaper stories, string, and various useless objects. The effect was a work of art that appeared to be made of trash. The newspaper clippings Picasso included described battles and murders, suggesting that Western civilization was not as refined as it claimed to be. In eastern and central Europe, artists criticized the boastful nationalism that determined royal purchases of sculpture and painting: "The whole empire is littered with monuments to soldiers and monuments to Kaiser William," one German artist complained.

Scandinavian and eastern European artists produced works expressing the torment many felt at the time. Like the ideas of Freud, their style of portraying inner feelings — called expressionism — broke with middle-class optimism. Norwegian painter Edvard Munch aimed "to make the emotional mood ring out again as happens on a gramophone." His painting *The Scream* (1893) used twisting lines and a tortured skeletal human form to convey the horror of modern life that many artists perceived. The Blue Rider group of artists, led by German painter Gabriele Münter and Russian painter Wassily Kandinsky, used geometric forms and striking colors to express an inner, spiritual truth. Kandinsky is often credited with producing the first fully abstract paintings around 1909; shapes in these paintings no longer bear any resemblance whatsoever to physical objects or reality but are meant to express deep feelings. The work of expressionists and cubists before World War I was a commercial failure in a marketplace run not only by museum curators but by professional dealers — "experts" — like the professionals in medicine and law.

Only one style of this period, **art nouveau** ("new art"), was an immediate, commercial success. Designers manufactured everything from dishes, calendars, and advertising posters to streetlamps and even entire buildings in this new style. As one French official said about the first art nouveau coins issued in 1895, "Soon even the most humble among us will be able to have a masterpiece in his pocket." Adapting elements from Asian design, art nouveau replaced the impersonality of machines with vines and flowers and the softly curving bodies of female nudes intended to soothe the individual viewer. This idea directly contrasted with Picasso's artistic vision. Art nouveau was the notable exception to public rage at innovations in the visual arts.

The Revolt in Music and Dance

"Astonish me!" was the motto of modern dance and music, both of which shocked audiences in the concert halls of Europe. American dancer Isadora Duncan took Europe by storm at the turn of the twentieth century when, draped in a flowing garment, she appeared barefoot in one of the first performances of modern dance. Her sophisticated style was called "primitive" because it no longer followed the steps of classical ballet. Experimentation with forms of bodily expression animated the Russian Ballet's 1913 performance of *The Rite of Spring*, by Igor Stravinsky, the tale of an orgiastic dance to the death performed to ensure a plentiful harvest. The dance troupe struck awkward poses and danced to rhythms intended to sound primitive. At the work's premiere in Paris, one journalist reported that "the audience began shouting its indignation. . . . Fighting actually broke out among some of the spectators."

Composers had been rebelling against Western traditions for several decades, producing music that was disturbing rather than pretty. Having heard Asian musicians at international expositions, French composer Claude Debussy transformed his style to reflect non-European musical patterns and wrote articles in praise of Asian harmonies. Italian composer Giacomo Puccini used non-Western subject matter for his opera *Madame Butterfly*, which debuted in 1904. Listeners were jarred when they heard non-Western tonalities. Like the bizarre representation of reality in cubism, the works of Austrian composer Richard Strauss added to the revolution in music by using several musical keys simultaneously, thus distorting familiar musical patterns. The early orchestral work of Austrian composer Arnold Schoenberg, who also wrote cabaret music to earn a living, shocked even Strauss. Schoenberg proposed eliminating tonality altogether; a decade later, he devised a new twelve-tone scale. "I am aware of having broken through all the barriers of a dated aesthetic ideal," Schoenberg wrote of his music. Audiences, however, found this music unpleasant and incomprehensible. "Anarchist! Nihilist!" they shouted, using political terms to show their distaste for modernist music.

REVIEW   How did modernism transform the arts and the world of ideas?

Growing Tensions in Mass Politics

Alongside disturbances in artistic life, the political atmosphere grew charged. On the one hand, liberal opinions led to political representation for workingmen. Networks of communication, especially the development of journalism, created a common fund of political knowledge that made mass politics possible. On the other hand, many political activists were no longer satisfied with the liberal rights such as the vote sought by earlier reformers. Some militant nationalists, anti-Semites, socialists, suffragists, and others demanded changes that challenged liberal values and individual rights. Traditional elites, resentful of the rising middle classes and urban peoples, aimed to overturn constitutional processes and crush city life. Politics soon threatened national unity.

The Expanding Power of Labor

European leaders worried about the rise of working-class political power late in the nineteenth century. Laboring people's growing confidence came in part from expanding educational opportunities. Workers in England, for example, avidly read works by Shakespeare and took literally his calls for political action in the cause of justice that rang out in plays such as *Julius Caesar*. Unions gained members among factory workers, while the labor and socialist parties won seats in parliaments as men in the lower classes received the vote. In Germany, Kaiser William II had allowed anti-socialist laws to lapse after dismissing Bismarck as chancellor in 1890. Through grassroots organizing at the local level, the German Social Democratic Party became the largest group in the Reichstag by 1912.

Winning elections actually raised problems among socialists. Some felt uncomfortable sitting in parliaments alongside the upper classes—in Marxism, the enemies of working people. Others worried that accepting high public offices would weaken socialists' commitment to the goal of revolution. These issues divided socialist organizations. Between 1900 and 1904, the Second International wrestled with the question of revisionism—that is, whether socialists should work from within governments to improve the daily lives of laborers or push for a violent revolution to overthrow governments. Powerful German Marxists argued that settling for reform would leave the wealthy unchallenged while throwing small crumbs to a few working-class politicians. Police persecution forced some working-class parties to operate in exile. The Russian government, for instance, outlawed political parties, imprisoned activists, and gave the vote to only a limited number of men when it finally introduced a parliament in 1905. Thus, Russian Marxist V. I. Lenin (1870–1924), who would take power during the Russian Revolution of 1917, operated outside the country.

Lenin advanced the theory that a highly disciplined socialist elite—rather than the working class as a whole—would lead a lightly industrialized Russia into socialism. At a 1903 party meeting of Russian Marxists, he maneuvered his opponents into walking out of the proceedings so that his supporters gained control of the party. Thereafter, his faction was known as the Bolsheviks, so named after the Russian word for "majority," which they had temporarily formed. They struggled to suppress the Mensheviks ("minority"), who had been the dominant voice in Russian Marxism until Lenin tricked them. Neither of these factions, however, had as large a constituency within Russia as the Socialist Revolutionaries, whose objective was to politicize peasants, rather than industrial workers, to bring about revolution. All of these groups organized in secret instead of using electoral politics.

During this same period, anarchists, along with some trade union members known as syndicalists, kept Europe in a panic with their terrorist acts. In the 1880s, anarchists had bombed stock exchanges, parliaments, and businesses. By the 1890s, they were assassinating heads of state: the Spanish premier in 1897, the empress of Austria-Hungary in 1898, the king of Italy in 1900, and the president of the United States in 1901, to name a few famous victims. Syndicalists advocated the use of direct action, such as general strikes and sabotage, to paralyze the economy and give labor unions more power. In response, politicians from the old landowning and military elites of eastern and central Europe worked to reverse the trend toward constitutionalism and mass political participation.

Rights for Women and the Battle for Suffrage

Women continued to agitate for the benefits of liberalism such as the right to vote and to own their wages if married. German women focused on widening opportunities for female education. Their activism aimed to achieve the German cultural ideal of *Bildung*—the belief that education can build character and that individual development has public importance. In several countries, women worked to prevent prostitutes from being imprisoned on suspicion of having syphilis when men with syphilis faced no such penalty. Other women took up pacifism—among them Bertha von Suttner, whose popular writing emphasized how war inflicted terror on women and families. (Von Suttner influenced Alfred Nobel to institute a peace prize and then won the prize herself in 1903.)

By the 1890s, many women activists decided to focus their efforts on a single issue—suffrage—as the most effective way to correct the many problems caused by male privilege. Thereafter, suffragists created major organizations involving millions of activists. British suffrage leader Millicent Garrett Fawcett (1847–1929) pressured members of Parliament for women's right to vote. Across the Atlantic, American Susan B. Anthony (1820–1906) traveled the country to speak at mass suffrage rallies, edited a suffragist newspaper, and founded the International Woman Suffrage Alliance in 1904. Its leadership argued that despite men's promises to protect women in exchange for their inequality, the system of male chivalry had led to exploitation and abuse. "So long as the subjection of women endures, and is confirmed by law and custom, . . . women will be victimized," a leading British suffragist claimed. Other activists believed that the characteristics associated with mothering were necessary in shaping a country's policies.

Women's rights activists were predominantly, though not exclusively, from the middle class. Free from the need to earn a living, they simply had more time to organize and to read the works of feminists such as Harriet Taylor and John Stuart Mill. Working-class women also participated in the suffrage movement. Textile

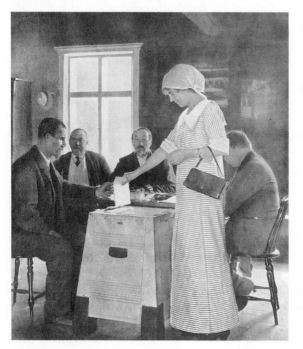

Woman Suffrage in Finland   In 1906, Finnish women became the first in Europe to receive the vote in national elections when the socialist party there—usually opposed to feminism as a middle-class rather than a working-class project—supported woman suffrage. The Finnish vote encouraged activists in the West, now linked together by many international organizations and ties, because it showed that more than a century of lobbying for reform could lead to gains. (© ILN/Mary Evans Picture Library/The Image Works.)

workers of Manchester, England, for example, put together a vigorous movement for the vote, seeing it as essential to improved working conditions. Many of these women, however, distrusted the middle class and believed suffrage to be less crucial than women's pressing economic concerns.

In 1906 in Finland, suffragists achieved their first major victory when the Finnish parliament granted women the vote. The failure of parliaments elsewhere in Europe to enact similar legislation provoked British suffragist **Emmeline Pankhurst** (1858–1928) and her daughters to found the Women's Social and Political Union (WSPU) in 1903. Starting in 1907, members of the WSPU held parades in English cities, and in 1909 they began a campaign of violence, blowing up railroad stations, slashing works of art, and chaining themselves to the gates of Parliament. Disguising themselves as ordinary shoppers, they carried little hammers to smash the plate-glass windows of department stores and shops. Parades and demonstrations made suffrage a public spectacle; some outraged men responded by attacking the marchers. Arrested for disturbing the peace, the marchers went on hunger strikes in prison. Like striking workers, these women were willing to use confrontational tactics to obtain rights.

Liberalism Tested

Governments in western Europe, where liberal institutions were seemingly well entrenched, sought to control turn-of-the-century conflicts with pragmatic policies that often struck at liberalism's very foundations. Political parties in Britain discovered that the recently enfranchised voter wanted solid benefits in exchange for his support. In 1905, the British Liberal Party won a majority in the House of Commons and pushed for social legislation aimed at the working class. "We are keenly in sympathy with the representatives of Labour," one Liberal politician announced. "We have too few of them in the House of Commons." The National Insurance Act of 1911 instituted a program of unemployment assistance funded by new taxes on the wealthy.

The Irish question, however, tested Britain's commitment to such liberal values as autonomy, opportunity, and individual rights. In the 1890s, new groups formed to foster Irish culture as a way of heightening the political challenge to what they saw as Britain's continuing colonization of the country. In 1901, the circle around poet William Butler Yeats and actress Maud Gonne founded the Irish National Theater to present Irish rather than English plays. Gonne took Irish politics into everyday life by opposing British efforts to gain the loyalty of the young. Every time an English monarch visited Ireland, he or she held special receptions for children. Gonne and other Irish volunteers sponsored competing events, handing out candies and other treats for patriotic youngsters. One home rule supporter marveled at "the procession . . . of thirty thousand school children who refused to be bribed into parading before the Queen of England." Promoters of an "Irish way of life" encouraged speaking Irish Gaelic instead of English and supporting Catholicism instead of the Church of England. This cultural agenda gained political force with the founding in 1905 of Sinn Féin ("We Ourselves"), a group that strove for complete Irish independence.

Once committed to economic growth and the rule of law, Italian leaders, now saddled with debt from unification, began to drift away from these liberal values. Instead, corruption plagued Italy's constitutional monarchy, which had not yet developed either the secure parliamentary system of England or the authoritarian monarchy of Germany to guide its growth. To forge national unity in the 1890s, prime ministers used patriotic rhetoric and imperial adventure, notably a second unsuccessful attempt to conquer Ethiopia in 1896. Giovanni Giolitti, who served as prime minister for three terms between 1903 and 1914, adopted a policy known as *trasformismo* (from the word for "transform"), using bribes and public works programs to gain support from deputies in parliament. Political opponents called Giolitti the "Minister of the Underworld" and accused him of preferring to buy the votes of local bosses rather than spending money to develop the Italian economy. In a wave of protest, urban workers in the industrial cities of Turin and Milan and rural laborers in the depressed agrarian south demanded change. Giolitti appeased the protesters by instituting social welfare programs and, in 1912, virtually complete manhood suffrage.

Anti-Semitism, Nationalism, and Zionism in Mass Politics

The real crisis for liberal political values of equal citizenship and tolerance came in the two decades leading up to World War I when politicians used anti-Semitism and militant nationalism to win elections. They told voters that Jews were responsible for the difficulties of everyday life and that anti-Semitism and increased patriotism would fix all problems. Voters from many levels of society responded enthusiastically, agreeing that Jews were villains and the nation-state was the hero in the struggle to survive. In both republics and monarchies, anti-Semitism and militant nationalism provided those on the radical right with a platform to gain working-class votes and thus combat the radical left of social democracy. This new radical right included representatives of the agrarian nobility, aristocrats who controlled the military, and highly placed clergy, and it broke with liberal ideas of the rule of law and the equality of all citizens. Liberals had hoped that voting by the masses would make politics more harmonious as parliamentary debate and compromise smoothed out class and other differences. Instead politics became loud and hateful, a distinct departure from consensus building and rational debate.

A strong tradition of anti-Semitism already existed in Russian politics. Russian tsar **Nicholas II** (r. 1894–1917) believed firmly in Russian orthodox religion, autocratic politics, and anti-Semitic social values. Taught as a child to hate Jews, Nicholas blamed them for any failure in Russian policy. Pogroms became a regular threat to Russian Jews, as Nicholas increasingly limited where Jews could live and how they could earn a living.

Principles of equal citizenship and tolerance were also tested in France. Powerful forces in the aristocracy, the military, and the Catholic church hoped that the Third Republic, like earlier ones, could be overthrown. Economic downturns, widespread corruption, and attempted coups made the republic more vulnerable, and the press attributed failures of almost any kind to Jews. Despite an excellent system of primary education promoting literacy and rational thinking, the public tended to agree, while the clergy and monarchists kept hammering the message that the republic was nothing but a conspiracy of Jews.

Amid rising anti-Semitism, a Jewish captain in the French army, Alfred Dreyfus, was charged with spying for Germany in 1894. The military, whose upper echelons were traditionally aristocratic, Catholic, and monarchist, produced manufactured "evidence" to gain Dreyfus's conviction even though the espionage continued. Then several newspapers received proof that the army had fabricated documents to convict Dreyfus. In 1898, the celebrated French novelist Émile Zola published an article titled "*J'accuse*" (I accuse) on the front page of a Paris daily, exposing the web of perjury that had created the impression of Dreyfus's guilt.

The article, which named the truly guilty parties, led to public riots, quarrels among families and friends, and denunciations of the army. The government finally pardoned Dreyfus in 1899, dismissed the aristocratic and Catholic officers responsible for the false accusations, and ended religious teaching orders to ensure a secular public school system that honored toleration and the rule of law. Still, the Dreyfus Affair made anti-Semitism and official lies standard tools of politics by showing their effectiveness with the public.

The ruling elites in Germany also used anti-Semitism to win support from those who feared the consequences of Germany's sudden and overwhelming industrialization. The agrarian elites, who still controlled the highest reaches of government, lost ground to industry as agriculture (from which they drew their fortunes) declined as a force in Germany's economy. As industrialists grew wealthier and new opportunities drew rural workers to the cities, the agrarian elites came to loathe industry for challenging their traditional authority. A Berlin newspaper noted, "The agrarians' hate for cities . . . blinds them to the simplest needs and the most natural demands of the urban population." To woo the masses, conservatives and a growing radical right claimed that Jews, who made up less than 1 percent of the German population, were responsible for destroying traditional society. They hurled diatribes against Jews, new women, and Social Democrats, whom they branded as internationalist and unpatriotic. This new right invented a modern politics that rejected the liberal value of parliamentary consensus, relying instead on inventing enemies and thus dividing what was supposed to be a unified nation-state.

Politicians in the dual monarchy of Austria-Hungary also used militant nationalism and anti-Semitism to win votes, but here the presence of many ethnic groups meant greater complexity in the politics of hate. Foremost among the nationalists were the Hungarians, who wanted autonomy for themselves while forcibly imposing Hungarian language and culture on all other, supposedly inferior, ethnic groups in Hungary. Their nationalist claims rested on two pieces of evidence: Budapest was a thriving industrial city, and the export of Hungarian grain from the vast estates of the Magyar nobility saved the monarchy's finances. The nationalists disrupted the Hungarian parliament so regularly that it weakened the orderly functioning of the government.

Although capable of causing trouble for the empire, Hungarian nationalists, who mostly represented agrarian wealth, were themselves vulnerable. Hungary's exploited ethnic groups—Slovaks, Romanians, and Ruthenians—resisted Magyarization. Industrial workers struck to protest horrendous labor conditions, and 100,000 activists gathered in the fall of 1905 in front of the Hungarian parliament to demonstrate for the vote. Other nationalities across the Dual Monarchy intensified their demands for rights. Croats, Serbs, and other Slavic groups in the south called for equality with the Hungarians. The central government allowed the Czechs a greater number of Czech officials in the government because of the growing industrial prosperity of their region. But every step favoring the Czechs provoked outrage from the traditionally dominant ethnic Germans. When Austria-Hungary decreed in 1897 that government officials in the Czech region of the empire would have to speak Czech as well as German, the Germans rioted. Discriminatory policies toward these groups and scorn for the imperial government in Vienna created instability throughout Austria-Hungary.

Tensions mounted as German politicians in Vienna linked the growing power of Hungarians and Czechs to Jews. Karl Lueger's newly formed Christian Social Party attracted members from among the aristocracy, Catholics, artisans, shopkeepers, and white-collar workers. Lueger appealed to those for whom modern life meant a loss of privilege and security. His hate-filled speeches helped elect him mayor of Vienna in 1895, but his ethnic nationalism and anti-Semitism threatened the multinationalism on which Austria-Hungary was based. Thereafter a widening group of politicians made anti-Semitism an integral part of their election campaigns, calling Jews the "sucking vampire" of modernity and blaming them for the tumult of migration, the economy, and just about anything else people found disturbing. Politics became a thing not of debate in parliaments but of violent racism in the streets.

Anti-Semites lumped Jewish people into one hated group, but like members of any other religion, Jews were divided by social class and education. Many Jews in western Europe moved out of Jewish neighborhoods, intermarried with Christians, and in some cases converted to Christianity—practices known as assimilation. Many well-educated Jews favored the classical culture of the German Empire because it seemed more rational and liberal than the ritualistic Catholicism of Austria-Hungary. By contrast, less prosperous Jews, such as those in Russia and Romania, were increasingly singled out for persecution, legally disadvantaged, and forced to live in ghettos. Jews from these countries might seek refuge in the nearby cities of central and eastern Europe where they could eke out a living as day laborers or artisans. Jewish migration to the United States and other countries also swelled (Map 24.1). By 1900, some Jews such as Freud were prominent in cultural and economic affairs in cities across the European continent even as far more were discriminated against and victimized elsewhere.

Amid vast migration and continued persecution, a spirit of Jewish nationalism arose. "Why should we be any less worthy than any other . . . people?" one Jewish leader asked. "What about our nation, our language, our land?" In the 1880s, the

MAP 24.1   Jewish Migrations in the Late Nineteenth Century   Pogroms in eastern Europe, increasingly violent anti-Semitism across the continent, and the search for opportunity motivated Jews to migrate to many parts of the world. Between 1890 and 1914, some five million Jews left Russia alone. They moved to European cities, to North and South America, and, as Zionism progressed, to Palestine.

Ukrainian physician Leon Pinsker, seeing the Jews' lack of national territory as fundamental to their persecution, advocated the migration of Jews to found a home-land. In 1896, Theodor Herzl, strongly influenced by Pinsker, called not simply for migration but for the creation of a Jewish nation-state, the goal of a movement known as **Zionism**. A Hungarian-born Jew, Herzl experienced anti-Semitism first-hand as a Viennese journalist and a writer in Paris during the Dreyfus Affair. Backed by eastern European Jews, he organized the first International Zionist Congress (1897). By 1914, some eighty-five thousand Jews had moved into Palestine—the region finally chosen for the Jewish nation.

> **REVIEW** What were the points of tension in European political life at the beginning of the twentieth century?

European Imperialism Challenged

Anti-Semitism was only one sign that the conditions of modern life were deeply troubling and that the rule of law and other liberal values like tolerance were threatened. Militant nationalism across the West made it difficult for nations to calm international tensions. This nationalist atmosphere heated up, and newcomers Italy and Germany now fought for a place at the imperial table, making imperial rivalries among the European powers alarmingly worse. As colonized peoples challenged European control, in 1904–1905, Japanese expansionism came close to toppling the mighty Russian Empire. Chaos dotted the imperial world.

The Trials of Empire

Everyone was quick to violence when it came to empire, and Britain in its pursuit of the **South African War** (or Boer War) of 1899–1902 was no exception. In 1896, Cecil Rhodes, then prime minister of the Cape Colony in southern Africa, directed a raid into the neighboring territory of the Transvaal in hopes of stirring up trouble between the Boers, descendants of early Dutch settlers, and the more recent immigrants from Britain who had come to southern Africa in search of gold and other riches. Rhodes aimed for a British takeover of the Transvaal and the Orange Free State, which the Boers independently controlled. The Boers, however, dealt Britain a bloody defeat.

In 1899, Britain began full-scale operations against the Boers. Foreign correspondents covering the South African War reported on appalling bloodshed, the unfit condition of the average British soldier, and the inhumane treatment of South Africans herded into an unfamiliar institution—the concentration camp, which became the graveyard of tens of thousands, mostly women and children. Britain finally annexed the area after defeating the Boers in 1902, but prominent Britons began to call imperialism not the work of civilization but an act of barbarism (Map 24.2).

Nearly simultaneously with the South African War, the United States defeated Spain in the Spanish-American War in 1898 and took Cuba, Puerto Rico, and the Philippines as its trophies. Experienced in empire, the United States had successfully crushed native Americans and annexed Hawaii in 1898. Both Cuba and the Philippines had begun vigorous efforts to free themselves from Spanish rule before the war. Urged on by the inflammatory daily press, the United States went to war against Spain, but instead of allowing independence the U.S. government annexed

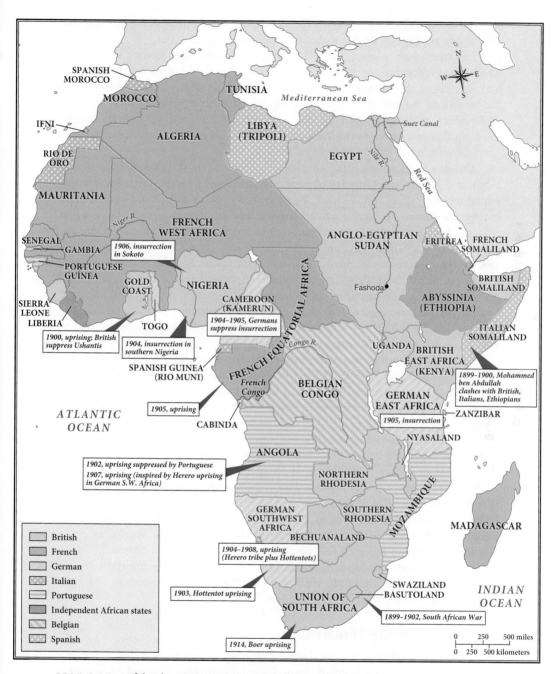

SPANISH MOROCCO

MOROCCO

TUNISIA

Mediterranean Sea

IFNI

ALGERIA

LIBYA (TRIPOLI)

Suez Canal

RIO DE ORO

EGYPT

Nile R.

Red Sea

MAURITANIA

Niger R.

FRENCH WEST AFRICA

ANGLO-EGYPTIAN SUDAN

ERITREA   FRENCH SOMALILAND

SENEGAL

GAMBIA

1906, insurrection in Sokoto

PORTUGUESE GUINEA

GOLD COAST

NIGERIA

CAMEROON (KAMERUN)

1904–1905, Germans suppress insurrection

FRENCH EQUATORIAL AFRICA

Fashoda

BRITISH SOMALILAND

ABYSSINIA (ETHIOPIA)

SIERRA LEONE
LIBERIA

TOGO

1900, uprising; British suppress Ushantis

1904, insurrection in southern Nigeria

SPANISH GUINEA (RIO MUNI)

Congo R.

French Congo

BELGIAN CONGO

UGANDA

BRITISH EAST AFRICA (KENYA)

ITALIAN SOMALILAND

1899–1900, Mohammed ben Abdullah clashes with British, Italians, Ethiopians

GERMAN EAST AFRICA

1905, insurrection

ZANZIBAR

ATLANTIC OCEAN

1905, uprising

CABINDA

NYASALAND

*1902, uprising suppressed by Portuguese
1907, uprising (inspired by Herero uprising in German S.W. Africa)*

ANGOLA

NORTHERN RHODESIA

MOZAMBIQUE

GERMAN SOUTHWEST AFRICA

SOUTHERN RHODESIA

MADAGASCAR

BECHUANALAND

British

French

German

Italian

Portuguese

Independent African states

Belgian

Spanish

1904–1908, uprising (Herero tribe plus Hottentots)

1903, Hottentot uprising

UNION OF SOUTH AFRICA

SWAZILAND
BASUTOLAND

INDIAN OCEAN

1899–1902, South African War

0   250   500 miles

0   250   500 kilometers

1914, Boer uprising

MAP 24.2 Africa in 1914 Uprisings intensified in Africa in the early twentieth century as Europeans tried both to consolidate their rule and to extract more wealth from the Africans. As Europeans were putting down rebellions against their rule, a pan-African movement arose, attempting to unite Africans as one people despite the diversity of cultures and ethnicities.

Puerto Rico and Guam and bought the Philippines from Spain. Cuba was theoretically independent, but the United States monitored its activities.

The triumphant United States then waged a bloody war against the Filipinos, who wanted independence, not another imperial ruler. British poet Rudyard Kipling had encouraged the United States to "take up the white man's burden" by bringing the benefits of Western civilization to those liberated from Spain. However, reports of American brutality in the Philippines, where 200,000 local people were slaughtered, disillusioned some in the Western public, who liked to imagine native peoples joyously welcoming the bearers of civilization.

Almost simultaneously, Italy won a costly victory over the Ottoman Empire in Libya, and Italian hopes rose for imperial grandeur in the future. Germany likewise joined the imperial contest, demanding an end to Britain's and France's domination among the colonial powers. German bankers and businessmen were active across Asia, the Middle East, and Latin America, and by the turn of the century, Germany had colonies in Southwest Africa, the Cameroons, Togoland, and East Africa. Despite these successes, Germany, too, met humiliation and faced constant problems, especially in its dealings not only with Britain and France but also with local peoples in Africa and elsewhere who resisted the German takeover. As Italy and Germany joined the aggressive pursuit of new territory, the confident rule-setting for imperialism at the Berlin Conference a generation earlier was diluted by general anxiety, heated rivalry, and nationalist passion.

Japan's rise as an imperial power further ate into Europeans' confident approach to imperialism. Japan defeated China in 1894 in the Sino-Japanese War, which ended China's domination of Korea. The European powers, alarmed by this victory, forced Japan to relinquish most of its gains, a move that outraged and insulted the Japanese. Japan's insecurity had risen with Russian expansion of the Trans-Siberian Railroad through Manchuria, sending millions of Russian settlers eastward. Angered by the continuing presence of Russian troops in Manchuria, the Japanese attacked the tsar's forces at Port Arthur in 1904 (Map 24.3).

The conservative Russian military proved inept in the ensuing Russo-Japanese War, even though it often had better equipment or strategic advantage. Russia's Baltic Fleet sailed halfway around the globe only to be completely destroyed by Japan in the battle of Tsushima Strait (1905). The Russian defeat opened an era of Japanese domination in East Asian politics. As one English general observed, "I have today seen the most stupendous spectacle it is possible for the mortal brain to conceive—Asia advancing, Europe falling back." Japan annexed Korea in 1910 and began to target other areas for colonization.

The Russian Empire Threatened

Alongside the humiliating loss to Japan, revolution erupted in Russia in 1905, and the empire tottered on the brink of chaos. The mighty Russian Empire had concealed its weaknesses well: state-sponsored industrialization in the 1890s had made the country appear modern to outside observers, and Russification attempted to impose a unified national culture on Russia's diverse population. Burdened by heavy taxes to

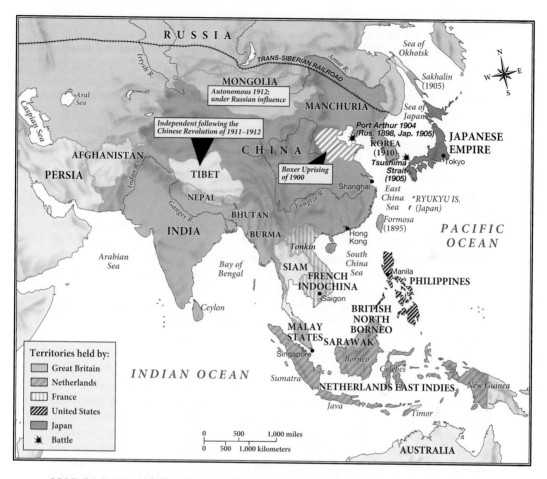

MAP 24.3　Imperialism in Asia, 1894–1914　The established imperialists came to blows in East Asia as they struggled for influence in China and as they met a formidable new rival—Japan. Simultaneously, liberation groups like the Boxers were taking shape, committed to throwing off restraints imposed by foreign powers and eliminating these interlopers altogether. In 1911, revolutionary Sun Yat-sen overthrew the Qing dynasty, which had left China unprepared to resist foreign takeover, and started the country on a different course.

pay for industrialization and by debts owed for the land they acquired during emancipation, peasants revolted in isolated uprisings at the turn of the century. Unrest occurred in the cities, too: in 1903, skilled workers led strikes in Baku; the unity of Armenians and Tatars in these strikes showed how Russification had made political cooperation possible among the various ethnicities. Growing worker activism, along with Japan's victory, challenged the autocratic regime.

On a Sunday in January 1905, a crowd gathered outside the tsar's Winter Palace in St. Petersburg to march in a demonstration to make Nicholas II aware of the brutal working conditions they suffered. Nicholas had often traveled the empire, displaying himself as the divinely ordained "father" of his people; therefore, his "children" thought it natural to appeal to him for aid. Leading the demonstration was a priest who, unknown to the crowd, was a police informant and agitator. Instead of allowing the marchers to pass, troops guarding the palace shot into the trusting crowd, killing hundreds and wounding thousands. Thus began the Revolution of 1905, as news of "Bloody Sunday" moved outraged workers elsewhere to rebel.

In almost a year of turmoil across Russia, urban workers struck over wages, hours, and factory conditions and organized their own councils, called soviets. In June, sailors on the battleship *Potemkin* mutinied; in October, a massive railroad strike brought rail transportation to a halt; and in November, uprisings broke out in Moscow. The tsar's forces kept killing protesters, but their deaths produced an opposition of artisans and industrial workers, peasants, professionals, upper-class reformers, and women, many demanding an end to discriminatory laws such as those firing women teachers who married. Liberals from the zemstvos (local councils) and the intelligentsia (a Russian word for well-educated elites) demanded the creation of a constitutional monarchy and representative legislature. They believed that the reliance on censorship and the secret police, characteristic of Russian imperial rule, marked the empire as backward.

The tsar finally yielded to the violence by creating a representative body called the **Duma**. Although very few Russians could vote for representatives to the Duma, its mere existence, along with the new right of open public debate, liberalized government and allowed people to present their grievances to a responsive body. Political parties committed to parliamentary rather than revolutionary programs also took shape. From 1907 to 1917, the Duma convened, but twice when the tsar disliked its recommendations he simply sent the delegates home. Nicholas had an able administrator in Prime Minister Pyotr Stolypin (1863–1911), who ended the mir system of communal farming and canceled the land redemption payments that had burdened the peasants since their emancipation in 1861. His reforms allowed people to move to the cities in search of jobs and created a larger group of independent peasants.

Stolypin was determined to restore law and order. He clamped down on revolutionary organizations, sentencing so many of their members to death by hanging that nooses were nicknamed "Stolypin neckties." Still rebels continued to assassinate government officials, and Stolypin himself was assassinated in 1911. Stolypin's reforms promoted peasant well-being, which encouraged what one historian has called a "new peasant assertiveness." The industrial workforce also grew, but more strikes broke out, culminating in a general strike in St. Petersburg in 1914. The imperial government's refusal to share power through the Duma left the way open to an even greater upheaval in 1917.

Growing Resistance to Colonial Domination

Japanese military victories over the Qing in China and the Romanovs in Russia upset the status quo in both countries and encouraged nationalist protests across the globe, further setting the West on edge. Uprisings began in China after the 1895 defeat by Japan. Nonhuman factors also affected the Chinese people as drought and famine came to plague the empire. Despairing peasants organized into secret societies to expel the foreigners and restore Chinese dignity and power. One organization was the Society of the Righteous and Harmonious Fists, commonly called the Boxers, whose members maintained that ritual boxing would protect them from a variety of evils, including bullets. Encouraged by the Qing ruler, the dowager empress Tz'u-hsi (Cixi; 1835–1908), the Boxers rebelled in 1900, massacring the missionaries and Chinese Christians to whom they attributed China's troubles. Seven of the colonial powers united to put down the Boxer Uprising and to devastate the areas in which the Boxers operated. Defeated once more, the Chinese had to pay a huge indemnity and allow even greater foreign military occupation.

The Boxer Uprising thoroughly discredited the Qing dynasty, leading a group of revolutionaries to overthrow the dynasty in 1911 and to declare China a republic the next year. Their leader, Sun Yat-sen (1866–1925), who had been educated in Hawaii and Japan, combined Western ideas and Chinese values in his Three Principles of the People: "nationalism, democracy, and socialism." For example, Sun's socialism included the Chinese belief that all people should have enough food, and his Nationalist Party called for revival of the Chinese tradition of correctness in behavior between governors and the governed, modern economic reform, and an end to Western domination of trade. Sun's stirring leadership and the changes brought about by the 1911 revolution helped weaken Western imperialism.

In India, the Japanese victory over Russia and the Revolution of 1905 stimulated politicians to take a more radical course than that offered by the Indian National Congress. The anti-British Hindu leader B. G. Tilak, less moderate than Congress reformers, urged noncooperation: "We shall not give them assistance to collect revenue and keep peace. We shall not assist them in fighting beyond the frontiers or outside India with Indian blood and money." Tilak asserted the distinctiveness of Hindu values from British ways and urged outright rebellion against the British. This brand of nationalism contrasted with that based on assimilating to British culture and promoting gradual change. Trying to stop Tilak, the British sponsored a rival nationalist group, the Muslim League, in a blatant attempt to divide Muslims from Hindus in the Congress. Faced with political activism, Britain conceded to Indians' representation in ruling councils and their right to vote based on property ownership. But discontent also mounted, sometimes silently, as did worries among the most clear-sighted imperialists about the future.

Revolutionary nationalism was simultaneously weakening the Ottoman Empire, which for centuries had controlled much of the Mediterranean. Rebellions plagued Ottoman rule, and this resistance allowed European influence to grow even as

Ottoman reformers aimed to strengthen the government. Sultan Abdul Hamid II (r. 1876–1909) tried to revitalize the multiethnic empire by using Islam to counteract the rising nationalism of the Serbs, Bulgarians, and Macedonians. Instead, he unintentionally provoked Turkish nationalism, which built on the uniqueness of the Turks' culture, history, and language, as many European ethnic groups were also doing. The Japanese defeat of Russia in 1904–1905 electrified these nationalists with the vision of a modern Turkey becoming "the Japan of the Middle East," as they called it. In 1908, a group of nationalists called the Young Turks took control of the government in Constantinople. The Young Turks' triumph motivated other ethnic groups in the Middle East and the Balkans to demand an end to Ottoman domination in their regions. Strong contingents of feminist-nationalists mobilized women to work for independence. However, the Young Turks, often aided by European powers with financial interests in the region, brutally repressed nationalist uprisings in Egypt, Syria, and the Balkans that their own success had encouraged.

The rebellions were part of the turmoil in global relations during the years just before World War I, as empires became the scene of growing opposition in the wake of Japanese, Russian, and Turkish events. In German East Africa, colonial forces responded to native resistance in 1905 with a scorched-earth policy, eventually killing more than 100,000 Africans there. To maintain their grip on Indochina, the French closed the University of Hanoi, executed Indochinese intellectuals, and deported thousands of suspected nationalists. A French general stationed there summed up the fears of many colonial rulers: "The gravest fact of our actual political situation in Indochina is not the recent trouble in Tonkin [or] the plots undertaken against us but in the muted but growing hatred that our subjects show toward us."

> **REVIEW** How and why did events in overseas empires from the 1890s on challenge Western faith in imperialism?

Roads to War

Internationally, competition intensified among the great powers and drove Western nationalists to become more aggressive. In the spring of 1914, U.S. president Woodrow Wilson (1856–1924) sent his trusted adviser Colonel Edward House to Europe to observe the rising tensions there. "It is militarism run stark mad," House reported, adding that he foresaw an "awful cataclysm" ahead. Government spending on what people called the arms race had promoted economic growth while it menaced the future. As early as the mid-1890s, one socialist had called the situation a "cold war" because the hostile atmosphere made war seem a certainty. By 1914, the air was even more charged, with militant nationalism in the Balkan states and politics — both at home and worldwide — propelling Europeans toward mass destruction.

Competing Alliances and Clashing Ambitions

As the twentieth century opened, the Triple Alliance that Bismarck had negotiated among Germany, Austria-Hungary, and Italy confronted an opposing alliance between France and Russia, created in the 1890s. The wild card in the diplomatic scenario was Great Britain, traditional enemy of France, especially in the contest for global power. Britain and France—constant rivals in Africa—edged to the brink of war in 1898 over competing claims to Fashoda, a town in the Sudan. The threat of conflict led France to withdraw, showing both nations as embracing a truce out of mutual self-interest. To prevent another Fashoda, they entered into secret agreements, the first of which (1904) recognized British claims in Egypt and French claims in Morocco. This agreement marked the beginning of the British-French alliance called the **Entente Cordiale**. Still, French statesmen feared that, should war break out, their ally might decide to remain neutral.

Kaiser William II inflamed the diplomatic atmosphere just as France and Britain were developing the Entente Cordiale. After victory in the Franco-Prussian War, Bismarck had proclaimed Germany a "satisfied" nation and worked to avoid further wars. William II, in contrast, was emboldened by Germany's growing industrial might and announced in 1901 that Germany needed greater global power to be achieved by "friendly conquests." His actions, however, were far from friendly, and he used the opportunity presented by the defeat of France's ally Russia in 1904–1905 to contest French advances in Morocco. A boastful, blustery man who was easily prodded to rash actions by his advisers, William landed in Morocco in 1905 to block the French. To resolve what became known as the First Moroccan Crisis, an international conference met in Spain in 1906. There the powers upheld French claims in North Africa. France and Britain, encountering German interference in Morocco, drew closer together.

When the French took over Morocco completely in 1911, Germany triggered the Second Moroccan Crisis by sending a gunboat to the port of Agadir and again demanding concessions from the French. This time no power—not even Austria-Hungary—backed Germany. The British and French now strengthened the Entente Cordiale, and Germany, smarting from its setbacks on the world stage, refocused on its own alliances.

Germany's bold territorial claims unsettled the rest of Europe, particularly the Balkans. German statesmen began envisioning their creation of a **Mitteleuropa**—a term that literally meant "central Europe" but in their minds also included the Balkans and Asia Minor. The Habsburgs, firmly backed by Germany, judged that their own expansion into the Balkans and the resulting addition of even more ethnic groups would weaken the claims of any single ethnic minority in the Dual Monarchy. Russia, however, saw *itself* as the protector of Slavs in the region and wanted to replace the Ottomans as the dominant Balkan power, especially since Japan had crushed Russian hopes for expansion to the east. Austria's swift annexation of Bosnia-Herzegovina during the Young Turks' revolt in 1908 enraged not only the Russians but the Serbs as well, who wanted Bosnia as part of an enlarged Serbia (Map 24.4).

MAP 24.4   The Balkans, 1908–1914   Balkan peoples—mixed in religion, ethnicity, and political views—were successful in asserting their desire for independence, especially in the First Balkan War, which claimed territory from the Ottoman Empire. Their increased autonomy sparked rivalries among them and continued to attract attention from the great powers. Three empires in particular— the Russian, Ottoman, and Austro-Hungarian—simultaneously wanted influence for themselves in the region, which became a powder keg of competing ambitions.

Even without the many greedy eyes cast on the Balkans, the situation would have been extremely volatile. The nineteenth century had seen the rise of national-ism and ethnicity as the basis for the unity of the nation-state, and by late in the century, ethnic loyalty challenged the dynastic rule of the Habsburgs and Ottomans in the region. Greece, Serbia, Bulgaria, Romania, and Montenegro emerged as autonomous states. All of them sought more Ottoman and Habsburg territory to cement a common ethnicity—an impossible desire given the dense intermingling of ethnicities throughout the region. Nonetheless, war for territory was on these nationalists' agenda.

In the First Balkan War, in 1912, Serbia, Bulgaria, Greece, and Montenegro joined forces to gain Macedonia and Albania from the Ottomans. The victors divided up their booty, with Bulgaria gaining the most territory, but in the Second Balkan War, in 1913, Serbia, Greece, and Montenegro contested Bulgarian gains. The quick victory of these allies increased Austria's concern at Serbia's rising power. The region had become perilous: both Austria-Hungary (as ruler of many Slavs) and Russia (as their would-be protector) stationed increasing numbers of troops along the borders. The situation led strategists to think hopefully that a quick war there—something like Bismarck's brief wars—could resolve tension and uncertainty.

The Race to Arms

In the nineteenth century, global rivalries and aspirations for national greatness made constant readiness for war seem increasingly necessary. On the seas and in foreign lands, violence became an everyday occurrence in the drive for empire. Governments began to draft ordinary citizens for periods of two to six years into large standing armies, in contrast to the smaller forces that had served the more limited military goals of the eighteenth century. The per capita expenditure on the military rose in all the major powers between 1890 and 1914; the proportion of national budgets devoted to defense in 1910 was lowest in Austria-Hungary (at 10 percent) and highest in Germany (at 45 percent).

The modernization of weaponry also transformed warfare. Swedish arms manufacturer Alfred Nobel patented dynamite and developed a kind of gunpowder that improved the accuracy of guns and produced a clearer battlefield environment by reducing firearm smoke. By 1914, long-range artillery could fire on targets as far as six miles away. Munitions factories across Europe manufactured ever-growing stockpiles of howitzers, Mauser rifles, and Hotchkiss machine guns. In the Russo-Japanese and South African wars, military leaders had devised new strategies to protect their armies from the heavy firepower and deadly accuracy of the new weapons: in the Russo-Japanese War, trenches and barbed wire blanketed the front around Port Arthur.

Naval construction figured in both the arms race and the rising nationalism in politics. To defend against powerful weaponry, ships built after the mid-nineteenth century were made of metal rather than wood. Launched in 1905, HMS *Dreadnought*, a warship with unprecedented firepower, was the centerpiece of the British navy's plan to construct at least seven battleships per year. Germany also built up its navy and made itself a great land and sea power and planned naval bases as far away as the Pacific. The Germans described their fleet buildup as "a peaceful policy," but, like British naval expansion, it only fed the hostile international climate and intense competition in weapons manufacture.

Public relations campaigns encouraged military buildup. When critics of the arms race suggested a temporary "naval holiday" to stop British and German building, British officials sent out news releases warning that such a cutback "would throw innumerable men on the pavement." Advocates of imperial expansion and nationalist groups lobbied for military spending as boosting national pride, while businessmen promoted large navies as beneficial to international trade and domestic industry. When Germany's Social Democrats questioned the use of taxes and their heavy burden on workers, the press criticized the party for lack of patriotism. The Conservative Party in Great Britain, eager for more battleships, made popular the slogan "We want eight and we won't wait." Public enthusiasm for arms buildups, militant nationalism, and growing international competition set the stage for war. When asked in 1912 about his predictions for war and peace, a French military leader responded enthusiastically, "We shall have war. I will make it. I will win it."

1914: War Erupts

June 28, 1914, began as an ordinary, even happy day not only for Freud's patient the Wolf-Man but also for the Austrian archduke and heir to the Habsburg throne, Francis Ferdinand, and his wife, Sophie, as they ended a state visit to Sarajevo in Bosnia riding in a motorcade. In the crowd was a Serb nationalist, Gavrilo Princip, who had traveled in secret for several weeks to reach this destination, dreaming of reuniting his homeland of Bosnia-Herzegovina with Serbia and smuggling weapons with him to accomplish his end. Princip shot dead the unprotected and unsuspecting Austrian couple.

Some in the Habsburg government saw the assassination as an opportunity to put down the Serbians once and for all. Evidence showed that Princip had received arms and information from Serbian officials, who directed a terrorist organization from within the government. Endorsing a quick defeat of Serbia, German statesmen and military leaders urged the Austrians to be unyielding and promised support in case of war. The Austrians sent an ultimatum to the Serbian government, demanding suppression of terrorist groups and the participation of Austrian officials in an investigation of the crime, among other things. "You are setting Europe ablaze," the Russian foreign minister remarked of the Austrians' humiliating demands made on a sovereign state. Yet the Serbs were conciliatory, accepting all the terms except the presence of Austrian officials in the investigation. Kaiser William was pleased: "All reason for war is gone." His relief proved unfounded. Austria-Hungary, confident of German backing, used the Serbs' resistance to one demand as the pretext for declaring war against them on July 28.

Some statesmen tried desperately to avoid war. Even the tsar and the kaiser sent pleading letters to one another not to start a European war. Still, Germany displayed firm support for Austria in hopes of convincing the French and British to stay out of the war and thus keep Russia from mobilizing. Additionally, German military leaders had become fixed on fighting a short, preemptive war that would provide territorial gains leading toward the goal of a Mitteleuropa. As conservatives, they planned to impose martial law the minute war began, using it as an excuse for arresting the leadership of the German Social Democratic Party, which threatened their rule.

Arrest of the Assassin   Gavrilo Princip belonged to the Young Bosnians, a group devoted to killing Habsburgs in revenge for the Austro-Hungarian monarchy's having sent workers to colonize their homeland. In June 1914, at the age of nineteen, Princip lived out his dream, killing the heir to the Habsburg throne and his wife. Here Princip is shown being apprehended. He spent the rest of his life in prison and was appalled at the carnage of World War I. (© Bettmann / Corbis.)

The European press caught the war fever of nationalist and pro-war organizations, and military leaders, especially in Germany and Austria-Hungary, promoted mobilization rather than diplomacy in the last days of July. The Austrians declared war and then ordered mobilization on July 31 in full confidence of German military aid, because as early as 1909 Germany had promised to defend Austria-Hungary, even if that country took the offensive. Nicholas II ordered the mobilization in defense of the Serbs—Russia's Slavic allies. Encouraging the Austrians to attack Serbia, the German general staff mobilized on August 1. France declared war by virtue of its agreement to aid its ally Russia, and when Germany violated Belgian neutrality on its way to invade France, Britain entered the war on the side of France and Russia.

REVIEW   What were the major factors leading to the outbreak of World War I?

Conclusion

Rulers soon forgot their last-minute hesitations when in some capitals celebration erupted with the declaration of war. "A mighty wonder has taken place," wrote a Viennese actor after watching the troops march off amid public enthusiasm. "We have become *young*." Both sides exulted, as militant nationalism led many Europeans to favor war over peace. There were advantages to war: disturbances in private life and challenges to established truths would disappear, it was believed, in the crucible of war. A short conflict, people maintained, would resolve tensions ranging from the rise of the working class to political problems caused by global imperial competition. German military men saw war as an opportune moment to round up social democrats and reestablish the traditional power of an agrarian aristocracy. Liberal government based on rights and constitutions, some believed, had simply gone too far in allowing new groups full citizenship and political influence.

Modernity helped blaze the path to war. New technology, mass armies, and new techniques of persuasion supported the military buildup. With continuing violence in politics, chaos in the arts, and problems in the industrial order, there was a belief that war would save nations from the modern perils they faced and replace nervous pessimism with patriotism. "Like men longing for a thunderstorm to relieve them of the summer's sultriness," wrote an Austrian official, "so the generation of 1914 believed in the relief that war might bring." Tragically, any hope of relief soon faded. Instead of bringing the refreshment of summer rain, war opened an era of political turmoil, widespread suffering, massive human slaughter, and even greater doses of modernity.

MAPPING THE WEST   Europe at the Outbreak of World War I, August 1914   All the powers
expected a great, swift victory when war broke out. Many saw war as a chance to increase their
territories; as rivals for trade and empire, almost all believed that war would bring them many
advantages. However well prepared and invincible European nations appeared at the start of the war,
relatively few would survive the conflict intact.

Chapter Review

KEY TERMS AND PEOPLE

Be sure you can identify the term or person and explain its historical significance.

new woman (p. 712)
Sigmund Freud (p. 713)
modernism (p. 714)
Friedrich Nietzsche (p. 715)
Albert Einstein (p. 715)
art nouveau (p. 717)
Emmeline Pankhurst (p. 721)

Nicholas II (p. 722)
Zionism (p. 725)
South African War (p. 726)
Duma (p. 730)
Entente Cordiale (p. 733)
Mitteleuropa (p. 733)

REVIEW QUESTIONS

1. How did ideas about the self and about personal life change at the beginning of the twentieth century?
2. How did modernism transform the arts and the world of ideas?
3. What were the points of tension in European political life at the beginning of the twentieth century?
4. How and why did events in overseas empires from the 1890s on challenge Western faith in imperialism?
5. What were the major factors leading to the outbreak of World War I?

MAKING CONNECTIONS

1. How did changes in society at the turn of the twentieth century affect the development of mass politics?
2. How was culture connected to the world of politics in the years 1890–1914?
3. How had nationalism changed since the French Revolution?
4. In what ways were imperial wars from the 1890s to 1914 relevant to the outbreak of World War I?

IMPORTANT EVENTS

1894–1895 • Japan defeats China in Sino-Japanese War

1894–1899 • Dreyfus Affair exposes anti-Semitism in France

1899–1902 • South African War fought between Dutch descendants and British in South African states

1900 • Sigmund Freud publishes *The Interpretation of Dreams*

1901 • Irish National Theater is established by Maud Gonne and William Butler Yeats; death of Queen Victoria

1903 • Emmeline Pankhurst founds Women's Social and Political Union

1904–1905 • Japan defeats Russia in Russo-Japanese War

1905 • Nicholas II establishes the Duma after revolution erupts in Russia; Albert Einstein publishes his special theory of relativity

1906 • Women receive vote in Finland

1907 • Pablo Picasso launches cubist painting with *Les Demoiselles d'Avignon*

1908 • Young Turks revolt against rule by sultan in Ottoman Empire

1911–1912 • Revolutionaries overthrow Qing dynasty and declare China a republic

1914 • Assassination of Austrian archduke Francis Ferdinand and his wife by Serbian nationalist precipitates World War I

World War I and Its Aftermath

1914–1929

CHAPTER FOCUS

What political, social, and economic impact did World War I have during the conflict, immediately after it, and through the 1920s?

JULES AMAR, A FRENCH EXPERT on improving the efficiency of industrial work, changed his career as a result of war. After 1914, as hundreds of thousands of soldiers returned from the battlefront missing body parts, plastic surgery and the construction of masks and other devices to hide deformities developed rapidly. Amar devised artificial limbs that would allow the wounded soldier to return to normal life by "making up for a function lost, or greatly reduced." The artificial arms featured hooks, magnets, and other mechanisms with which veterans could hold a cigarette, play a violin, and, most important, work with tools such as typewriters. Those who had been mangled by the weapons of modern technological warfare would be made whole, it was thought, by technology such as Amar's.

Jules Amar did his part to confront the tragedy of the Great War, so named by contemporaries because of its staggering human toll—forty million wounded or killed in battle. The Great War did not settle problems or restore social order as the European powers hoped it would. Instead, the war produced political chaos, overturning the Russian, German, Ottoman, and Austro-Hungarian Empires. The burden of war crushed the European powers and accelerated the rise of the United States, while colonized peoples who served in the war intensified their demands for independence. In fact, the armistice in 1918 did not truly end conflict: many soldiers remained actively fighting long into what was supposed to be peacetime, and others had been so militarized that they longed for a life that was more like wartime.

World War I transformed society, too. A prewar feeling of doom and decline gave way to postwar cynicism. Many Westerners turned their backs on politics and in the Roaring Twenties embraced life with wild gaiety, shopping for new consumer goods, enjoying once forbidden personal freedoms, and taking pleasure in the entertainment provided by films and radio. Others found reason for hope in the new political systems the war made possible: Soviet communism and Italian fascism. Modern communication technologies such as radio gave politicians the means to promote a utopian mass politics that, ironically, was antidemocratic, militaristic, and violent—like the war itself. A war that was welcomed in some quarters as a remedy for modernity destabilized Europe far into the following decades leaving Europeans, including Jules Amar and those he helped, to deal with its violent aftermath.

The Great War, 1914–1918

When war erupted in August 1914, two months after the assassination of the Austrian archduke and his wife at Sarajevo, there already existed long-standing alliances, well-defined strategies, and a stockpile of military technologies such as heavy artillery, machine guns, and airplanes. Most people felt that this would be a short, decisive conflict similar to Prussia's rapid victories in the 1860s and 1870–1871. In fact, the war lasted for more than four long years. It was what historians call a **total war**, meaning one built on the full mobilization of entire societies—soldiers and civilians— and the industrial capacities of the nations involved. It was the war's unexpected and unprecedented horror that made World War I "great."

Blueprints for War

World War I's two sets of opponents were formed roughly out of the alliances developed during the previous fifty years. On one side stood the Central Powers (Austria-Hungary and Germany), which had evolved from Bismarck's Triple Alliance. On the other side were the Allies (France, Great Britain, and Russia), which had emerged as a bloc from the Entente Cordiale between France and Great Britain and the 1890s treaties between France and Russia. In 1915, Italy, originally part of the Triple Alliance, joined the Allies in hopes of postwar gain. The war soon exploded globally: in late August 1914, Japan, eager to extend its empire into China, went over to the Allies, while in the fall the Ottoman Empire united with the Central Powers against its traditional enemy, Russia (Map 25.1).

MAP 25.1 The Fronts of World War I, 1914–1918   Because the western front remained relatively stationary, devastation of land and resources was intense. All fronts, however, destroyed segments of Europe's hard-won industrial and agricultural capacity, while the immobile trenches increased military casualties whenever heavy artillery fire pounded them. Men long engaged in trench warfare developed an intense camaraderie based on their mutual suffering and deprivation.

Of the Central Powers, Germany wanted a bigger empire, to be gained by annexing Russian territory and incorporating parts of Belgium, France, and Luxembourg. Some German leaders wanted to annex Austria-Hungary as well. Austria-Hungary hoped to keep its great-power status despite the competing nationalisms of ethnic groups within its borders. Among the Allies, Russia wished to reassert its status as a great power and as the protector of the Slavs by adding a reunified Poland to the Russian Empire and by taking formal leadership of other Slavic peoples. The French, too, craved territory, especially the return of Alsace and Lorraine, ceded to Germany after the Franco-Prussian War of 1870–1871. The British wanted to cement their hold on Egypt and the Suez Canal and keep the rest of their world empire secure. By the Treaty of London (1915), France and Britain promised Italy territory in Africa, Asia Minor, the Balkans, and elsewhere in return for joining the Allies.

The colonies participated in the war too, providing massive assistance and serving as battlegrounds. Some one million Africans, one million Indians, and more than a million men from the British commonwealth countries fought on the battlefronts. The imperial powers also conscripted uncounted numbers of colonists as forced laborers: a million Kenyans and Tanzanians alone are estimated to have been conscripted for menial labor in the battle for East Africa. Using Arab, African, and Indian troops, the British waged successful war in the Ottoman lands of the Middle East. In sub-Saharan Africa, the vicious campaign for East Africa cost many lives, including many civilians whose resources were confiscated and whose villages were burned.

Unprecedented use of new machinery determined the course of war. In August 1914, machine guns, fast breech-loading rifles, and military vehicles such as airplanes, battleships, submarines, and motorized transport (cars and trains) were all at the armies' disposal. New technologies such as chlorine gas, tanks, and bombs were developed between 1914 and 1918. The war itself became a lethal testing ground, as both new and old weapons were used, often ineffectively. Many officers on both sides believed in a **cult of the offensive**, which called for spirited attacks against the enemy and high troop morale. Despite the availability of powerful war technology, an old-fashioned, heroic vision of war made many officers unwilling to abandon the more familiar sabers, lances, and bayonets. In the face of massive firepower, the cult of the offensive would cost millions of lives.

The Battlefronts

The first months of the war crushed any hope of a quick victory. The Germans were guided by the **Schlieffen Plan**, named after a former chief of the general staff. The plan outlined a way to combat enemies on two fronts by concentrating on one foe at a time. It called for a concentrated blow to the west against France, which would lead to that nation's defeat in six weeks, accompanied by a light holding action against Russia to the east. The attack on France was to proceed without resistance through neutral Belgium. Once France had fallen, Germany's western armies would move against Russia, which, it was believed, would mobilize far more slowly. None of the great powers expected that war would turn into the prolonged massacre of their nations' youth.

When German troops reached Belgium and Luxembourg at the beginning of August 1914, the Belgians surprisingly mounted a vigorous defense, which slowed the German advance. In September, the British and French armies engaged the Germans along the Marne River in France. Neither side could defeat the other, and in the first three months of war, more than 1.5 million men fell on the western front alone. Guns like the 75-millimeter howitzer, accurate at long range, turned what was supposed to be an offensive war of movement into a stationary standoff along a line that stretched from the North Sea through Belgium and northern France to Switzerland.

On the eastern front, the Russians drove far more quickly than expected into East Prussia in mid-August. The Russians believed that no army could stand up to the massive number of their soldiers, regardless of how badly equipped and poorly trained those soldiers were. Their success was short-lived. The Germans over-whelmed the tsar's army in East Prussia. Victory made heroes of the German military leaders Paul von Hindenburg (1847–1934) and Erich Ludendorff (1865–1937), who demanded more troops for the eastern front, undermining the Schlieffen Plan by removing forces from the west before the western front had been won.

War at sea proved equally indecisive. The Allies blockaded ports to prevent supplies from reaching Germany and Austria-Hungary. Kaiser William and his advisers planned a massive U-boat (*Unterseeboot*, "underwater boat," or submarine) campaign against Allied and neutral shipping. In May 1915, U-boats sank the British passenger ship *Lusitania* and killed 1,198 people, including 124 Americans. Despite U.S. outrage, President Woodrow Wilson (1856–1924) maintained a policy of neutrality; Germany, unwilling to provoke Wilson further, called off unrestricted submarine warfare. In May 1916, the navies of Germany and Britain finally clashed in the North Sea at Jutland. This inconclusive battle demonstrated that the German fleet could not master British seapower.

Ideas of a negotiated peace were discarded: "No peace before England is defeated and

War in the Trenches Men at the front developed close friendships while they lived with daily discomfort, death, and the horrors of modern technological warfare. Some of the complexities of trench warfare appear in this image showing soldiers rescuing their fallen comrades after fighting at Bagatelle in northern France. (Private Collection / Stapleton Collection / Bridgeman Images.)

destroyed," William II stormed against his cousin King George V. French leaders called for a "war to the death." General staffs on both sides continued to prepare fierce attacks several times a year. Campaigns opened with heavy artillery pounding enemy trenches and gun emplacements. Troops then responded to the order to go "over the top" by scrambling out of their trenches and into battle, usually to be mowed down by machine-gun fire from defenders secure in their own trenches. On the western front, the French assaulted the Germans throughout 1915 but accomplished little. On the eastern front, Russian armies captured parts of Galicia in the spring of 1915 and lumbered toward Hungary.

The next year's battles were even more disastrous and futile. To cripple French morale, the Germans launched massive assaults on the fortress at Verdun, firing as many as a million shells in a single day. Combined French and German losses totaled close to a million men. Nonetheless, the French held. The British unleashed an artillery pounding of German trenches in the Somme region in June 1916; 1.25 million men were killed or wounded, but the final result was stalemate. By the end of 1916, the French had suffered more than 3.5 million casualties. To help the Allies engaged at Verdun and the Somme, the Russians struck again, driving into the Carpathian Mountains, recouping territory, and menacing Austria-Hungary. The German army stopped the advance, as the German general staff decided it would take over Austrian military operations.

Had military leaders thoroughly dominated the scene, historians judge, all armies would have been utterly demolished by the end of 1915. Yet ordinary soldiers in this war were not automatons in the face of what seemed to them suicidal orders from their commanders. Informal agreements to avoid battles against each other allowed some battalions to go for long stretches with hardly a casualty. Enemies facing each other across the trenches frequently ate their meals in peace, even though the trenches were within hand-grenade reach. Throughout the war, soldiers on both fronts played an occasional game of soccer or made gestures of agreement not to fight. A British veteran of the trenches explained to a new recruit that the Germans "don't want to fight any more than we do, so there's a kind of understanding between us. Don't fire at us and we'll not fire at you." Many ordinary soldiers came to feel more warmly toward enemies who shared the trench experience than toward civilians back home. This camaraderie relieved some of the misery of trench life and aided survival. In some cases, upper-class officers and working-class recruits became friends in that "wholly masculine way of life uncomplicated by women," as another soldier put it. Soldiers tended one another's blistered feet and came to love one another, sometimes even passionately. This sense of frontline community survived the war and influenced postwar politics.

Troops of colonized soldiers from Asia and Africa often were put in the very front ranks, where the risks were greatest. Yet, like class divisions, racial barriers sometimes fell: a European might give extra blankets and clothing to soldiers from warmer regions. These troops saw their "masters" completely undone and "uncivilized," for when fighting did break out, trenches became a veritable hell of shelling and sniping, flying body parts, blinding gas, and rotting cadavers. Some soldiers became hysterical or shell-shocked through the stress and violence of battle. Those who had gone to war to escape ordinary life in industrial society learned, as one German put it, "that in the modern war . . . the triumph of the machine over the individual is carried to its most extreme form."

The Home Front

Total war demanded the involvement of civilians in manufacturing shells, machine guns, poisonous gases, bombs, airplanes, and eventually tanks — which together formed the backbone of technological warfare. Increased production of coffins, canes, wheel-chairs, and artificial limbs (devised by the likes of Jules Amar) was also required. Because their armies would have utterly failed without them, civilians had to believe in the war and to work overtime and sacrifice for victory. To keep the war machine operating smoothly, governments oversaw factories, transportation systems, and the use of resources. People accepted tight government control as necessary to win the war.

At first, most political parties put aside their differences. Many socialists and working-class people who had formerly criticized the military buildup announced their support for the war. For decades, socialist parties had preached that "the worker has no country" and that nationalism was an ideology meant to keep work-ers disunited and subjected to the will of their employers. In August 1914, however, most socialists became as patriotic as the rest of society. Although many feminists actively opposed the conflict, the British suffrage leader Emmeline Pankhurst and her daughter Christabel were among those who became militant nationalists. In the name of victory, national leaders wanted to end political division of all kinds: "I no longer recognize [political] parties," William II declared on August 4, 1914. "I recognize only Germans." Those who had been at the receiving end of discrimina-tion promoted unity. One rabbi proudly echoed the kaiser: "In the German father-land there are no longer any Christians and Jews, any believers and disbelievers, there are only Germans."

Governments mobilized the home front with varying degrees of success. War ministries set up boards to allocate labor on both the home front and the battlefront and to give industrialists financial incentives to encourage productivity. The Russian bureaucracy, however, only cooperated halfheartedly with industrialists and other groups that could aid the war effort. In several countries, emergency measures allowed the drafting of both men and women for military or industrial service. Municipal governments set up canteens and day-care centers, but rural Russia, Austria-Hungary, Bulgaria, and Serbia, where youths, women, and old men struggled to sustain farms, had no such relief programs.

Governments throughout Europe passed sedition laws that made it a crime to criticize war-related policies and created propaganda agencies, sometimes fabricat-ing atrocities, to advertise the war as a patriotic mission to resist villainous enemies. In Russia, Tsar Nicholas II had changed the German-sounding name of the capital St. Petersburg to the Russian Petrograd as a patriotic move. Maintaining that Arme-nians in the Ottoman Empire were plotting against the Central Powers, the Otto-mans drove those Armenians living in Turkey from their homes, forcing them onto long marches or into concentration camps where they were murdered or simply died. The Allies also caused the deaths of civilians en masse by creating famines, blockading the Syrian provinces of the Ottoman Empire in hopes that the people there would rebel or die of starvation.

Despite widespread popular support for the war, some individuals worked to bring about a negotiated peace. In 1915, activists in the international women's movement met in The Hague to call for an end to the war. "We can no longer endure . . . brute force as the only solution of international disputes," declared Dutch physician Aletta Jacobs. The women had no success, though many brought their cause to individual heads of state. In Austria-Hungary, agitating for ethnic self-determination, the Czechs undertook a vigorous anti-Habsburg campaign, while Croats, Slovenes, and Serbs in the Balkans formed a committee to plan a southern Slavic state independent of Austria-Hungary. The Allies encouraged such independence movements as part of their strategy to defeat Austria-Hungary.

The war upset the social order as well as the political one. In the war's early days, many women lost their jobs when luxury shops, textile factories, and other

A New Workforce in Wartime   With men at the front, women (at right in this French photograph) moved into factory work at jobs from which they had been unofficially barred before the war. In addition, tens of thousands of forced laborers from the colonies were moved to Europe also to replace men sent to the front. The European experience of forced labor and service at the front politicized colonial subjects, fortifying independence movements in the postwar period. (Roger Viollet/Getty Images.)

nonessential businesses closed. As more and more men left for the trenches, women who had lost employment elsewhere joined with low-paid domestic workers to take over higher-paying jobs in munitions and metallurgical industries. In Warsaw women drove trucks, and in London they conducted streetcars. Some young women drove ambulances and nursed the wounded near the front lines.

Women's assumption of men's jobs looked to many like a sign of social disorder. In the words of one metalworker, women were "sending men to the slaughter." Men feared that women would remain in the workforce after the war, robbing men of the breadwinner role. Others criticized young female munitions workers for squandering their pay on ribbons and jewelry. The heated prewar debates over the "new woman" and gender roles returned.

Although soldiers from different backgrounds often felt bonds of solidarity in the trenches, difficult wartime conditions increasingly pitted civilians against one another on the home front. Workers toiled long hours with less to eat, while many in the upper classes bought fancy food and fashionable clothing on the black market (outside the official system of rationing). The cost of living surged and thus contributed to social tensions as shortages of staples like bread, sugar, and meat occurred across Europe and people went hungry. Reviving prewar anti-Semitism, some blamed Jews for the shortages. Colonial populations suffered oppressive conditions as well. The French forcibly transported some 100,000 Vietnamese to work in France for the war effort. Africans also faced grueling forced labor along with skyrocketing taxes and prices. Civilian suffering during the war, whether in the colonies or in Europe, laid the groundwork for ordinary people to take political action.

REVIEW   In what ways was World War I a total war?

Protest, Revolution, and War's End, 1917–1918

By 1917, the situation was becoming desperate for everyone—politicians, the military, and civilians. Discontent on the home front started shaping the course of the war. Neither patriotic slogans before the war nor propaganda during it had prepared people for wartime devastation. Civilians rebelled in cities across Europe. While soldiers in some armies mutinied, nationalist struggles continued to plague Britain and Austria-Hungary. Soon full-fledged revolution was sweeping Europe, toppling the Russian dynasty, and threatening not just war but civil war as well.

War Protest

On February 1, 1917, the German government, hard-pressed by the public clamor over mounting casualties and by the military's growing control, resumed full-scale submarine warfare. The British responded by mining their harbors and the surrounding seas and by developing the convoy system of shipping to drive off German submarines. The Germans' submarine gamble not only failed to defeat the British but also brought the United States into the war in April 1917, after German U-boats sank several American ships.

Political opposition increased in Europe. Irish republicans attacked government buildings in Dublin on Easter Monday 1916 in an effort to gain Ireland's independence from Britain during the crisis. The ill-prepared rebels were easily defeated, and many of them were executed. In the cities of Italy, Russia, Germany, and Austria, women rioted to get food for their families, and factory hands and white-collar workers alike walked off the job. Amid these protests, Austria-Hungary secretly asked the Allies for a negotiated peace; the German Reichstag also made overtures for a "peace of understanding and permanent reconciliation of peoples." In January 1918, President Woodrow Wilson issued his **Fourteen Points**, a blueprint for a nonvindictive peace settlement held out to the war-weary citizens of the Central Powers.

Revolution in Russia

Of all the warring nations, Russia sustained the greatest number of casualties — 7.5 million by 1917. In March,[1] crowds of workingwomen swarmed the streets of Petrograd demanding relief from the harsh conditions. They soon fell in with other protesters commemorating International Women's Day and were then joined by factory workers and other civilians. Instead of remaining loyal to the tsar, many soldiers were embittered by the massive casualties and their leaders' foolhardy tactics. The government's incompetence and Nicholas II's stubborn resistance to change had made the war even worse in Russia than elsewhere. When the riots erupted in March 1917, Nicholas finally realized the situation was hopeless. He abdicated, bringing the three-hundred-year-old Romanov dynasty to a sudden end.

Aristocratic and middle-class politicians from the old Duma formed a new administration called the Provisional Government. At first, hopes were high that under the Provisional Government, as one revolutionary poet put it, "our false, filthy, boring, hideous life should become a just, pure, merry, and beautiful life." To survive, the Provisional Government had to pursue the war successfully, manage internal affairs better, and set the government on a firm constitutional footing, but other political forces had also strengthened during the revolution. Among them, the **soviets** — councils elected from workers and soldiers — competed with the government for political support. Born during the Revolution of 1905, the soviets in 1917 campaigned to end the deference usually given to the wealthy and to military officers, urged respect for workers and the poor, and temporarily gave an air of

---

[1] Until February 1918, Russia observed the Julian calendar, which was thirteen days behind the Gregorian calendar used by the rest of Europe. Hence, the first phase of the revolution occurred in March according to the Gregorian calendar (but February in the Julian calendar), the later phase in November on the Gregorian calendar (October according to the Julian). All dates used in this book follow the Gregorian calendar.

celebration and carnival to the political upheaval. The peasants, also competing for power, began to confiscate landed estates and withhold produce from the market, threatening the Provisional Government.

In hopes of adding to the turmoil in Russia, the Germans in April 1917 provided safe rail transportation for **V. I. Lenin** (1870–1924) and other prominent Bolsheviks to return to Russia through German territory. Lenin had devoted his entire existence to bringing about socialism through the force of his small band of Bolsheviks. Upon his return to Petrograd, he issued the April Theses, a radical document that called for Russia to withdraw from the war, for the soviets to seize power on behalf of workers and poor peasants, and for all private land to be nationalized. As the Bolsheviks aimed to supplant the Provisional Government, they employed such slogans as "All power to the soviets" and "Peace, land, and bread."

New prime minister Aleksandr Kerensky used his commanding oratory to arouse patriotism, but he lacked the political skills needed to create an effective wartime government. The Bolshevik leadership, urged on by Lenin, overthrew the weakened Provisional Government in November 1917, an event called the **Bolshevik Revolution**. In January 1918, elections for a constituent assembly failed to give the Bolsheviks a plurality, so the party used troops to take over the new government completely. The Bolsheviks, observing Marxist doctrine, abolished private property and nationalized factories to stimulate production. The Provisional Government had allowed both men and women to vote in 1917, making Russia the first great power to legalize universal suffrage. This soon became a hollow privilege once the Bolsheviks limited the candidates to chosen members of the Communist Party.

The Bolsheviks asked Germany for peace and agreed to the Treaty of Brest-Litovsk (March 1918), which placed vast regions of the old Russian Empire under German occupation. Because the loss of millions of square miles to the Germans put Petrograd at risk, the Bolsheviks relocated the capital to Moscow and formally adopted the name Communists (taken from Karl Marx's writings) to distinguish themselves from the socialists/social democrats who had voted for the disastrous war in the first place. Lenin called the catastrophic terms of the treaty "obscene." However, he accepted them—not only because he had promised to bring peace to Russia but also because he believed that the rest of Europe would soon rebel against the war and overthrow the capitalist order.

A full-blown civil war now broke out in Russia, with the pro-Bolsheviks (or "Reds") pitted against an array of forces (the "Whites") who wanted to turn back the revolution (Map 25.2). Among the Whites were three distinct groups: the tsarist military leadership, composed mainly of landlords and supporters of aristocratic rule; the liberal educated class, including businessmen whose property had been nationalized; and non-Russian nationalities who saw their chance for independence. In addition, before World War I ended, Russia's former allies—notably the United States, Britain, France, and Japan—landed troops in the country to fight the Bolsheviks. The counterrevolutionary groups lacked a strong leader and unified goals,

MAP 25.2　The Russian Civil War, 1917–1922　Nationalists, aristocrats, middle-class citizens, and property-owning peasants tried to combine their interests to defeat the Bolsheviks, but they failed to create an effective political consensus. As fighting covered the countryside, ordinary people suffered, especially when their grain was confiscated by armies on both sides. The Western powers and Japan also sent in troops to put down this threatening revolution.

however. Pro-tsarist forces, for example, alienated groups seeking independent nation-state status, such as the Ukrainians, Estonians, and Lithuanians, by stressing the goal of restoring the Russian Empire. Even with the presence of Allied troops, the opponents of revolution could not defeat the Bolsheviks without a common purpose.

　　The civil war shaped Russian communism. Leon Trotsky (1879–1940), Bolshevik commissar of war, built the highly disciplined army by ending democratic procedures, such as the election of officers, that had originally attracted soldiers to

Bolshevism. Lenin and Trotsky introduced the policy of war communism — seizing grain from the peasantry to feed the civil war army and workforce. The Cheka (secret police) imprisoned political opponents and black marketers and often shot them without trial. The result was a more authoritarian government — a development that broke Marx's promise that revolution would bring a "withering away" of the state.

As the Bolsheviks clamped down on their opponents during the bloody civil war, they organized their supporters to foster revolutionary Marxism across Europe. In March 1919, they founded the Third International, also known as the Communist International (Comintern), to replace the Second International with a centralized organization dedicated to preaching communism. By mid-1921, the Red Army had defeated the Whites in the Crimea, the Caucasus, and the Muslim borderlands in central Asia. After ousting the Japanese from Siberia in 1922, the Bolsheviks governed a state as multinational as the old Russian Empire had been, and one at odds with socialist promises for a humane and flourishing society.

Ending the War, 1918

In the spring of 1918, the Central Powers made one final attempt to smash through the Allied lines using a new offensive strategy. It consisted of concentrated forces piercing single points of the enemy's defense lines and then wreaking havoc from the rear. Using these tactics, the Central Powers had overwhelmed the Italian army at Caporetto in the fall of 1917, but a similar offensive on the western front in the spring of 1918 ground to a bloody halt within weeks. By then, the British and French had started making limited but effective use of tanks supported by airplanes. The German armies, suffering more than two million casualties between spring and summer, rapidly disintegrated.

By October 1918, the desperate German command helped create a civilian government to take over rule of the home front. As these inexperienced politicians took power, they were also taking blame for the defeat. Shifting the blame from the military, the generals proclaimed themselves fully capable of winning the war. Weak-willed civilians, they announced, had dealt the military a "stab in the back" by forcing a surrender. A sailors' revolt and workers' uprisings led the Social Democratic Party to declare a German republic in an effort to prevent revolution. At the end of October, Czechs and Slovaks declared an independent state, while the Croatian parliament simultaneously announced Croatia's independence. On November 9, 1918, Kaiser William II fled as the Central Powers collapsed on all fronts. Finally, on the morning of November 11, 1918, an armistice was signed and the guns fell silent.

In the course of four years, European civilization had been sorely tested, if not shattered. Conservative figures put the battlefield toll at a minimum of ten million dead and thirty million wounded, incapacitated, or doomed eventually to die of their wounds. In every European combatant country, industrial and agricultural production had plummeted. From 1918 to 1919, a worldwide influenza epidemic left as many as one hundred million more dead. Soldiers returning home in 1918 and 1919 flooded the book market with their memoirs; whereas many had begun by emphasizing heroism and glory, others cynically insisted that the fighting had been absolutely meaningless. Total war had not only drained society of resources and population but also sown the seeds of further catastrophe.

> **REVIEW** Why did people rebel during World War I, and what turned rebellion into outright revolution in Russia?

The Search for Peace in an Era of Revolution

World War I had unforeseen and dramatic consequences. Revolutionary fervor now swept the continent, especially in the former empires of Germany and Austria-Hungary. Many of the newly independent peoples of eastern and central Europe supported socialist principles, and activists on both the left and the right hoped for a political order based on military authority of the kind they had relied on during the war. Diplomats from around the world arrived in Paris in January 1919 to negotiate the terms of peace, though without fully recognizing the fact that the war was still going on not only in city streets, where soldiers were bringing the war home, but also in people's hearts.

Europe in Turmoil

Urban citizens and returning soldiers ignited the protests that swept Europe in 1918 and 1919. In January 1919, the red flag of socialist revolution flew from the city hall in Glasgow, Scotland, while in cities of the collapsing Austro-Hungarian monarchy, workers set up councils to take over factory production and direct politics. Many soldiers did not disband at the armistice but formed volunteer armies, preventing the return to peacetime politics. Germany was especially unstable, partly because of the shock of defeat; German workers and veterans filled the streets, demanding food and back pay. Whereas in 1848, revolutionaries had marched to city hall or the king's residence, the protesters in 1919 took over newspapers and telegraph offices to control the flow of information. One of the most radical socialist factions was the Spartacists, led by cofounders Karl Liebknecht (1871–1919) and Rosa Luxemburg (1870–1919). Unlike Lenin, the two leading Spartacists wanted workers to gain political experience from any uprisings instead of simply following an all-knowing party leadership on a set course.

German conservatives had believed that the war would put an end to Social Democratic influence; instead, it brought German socialists to power. Social Democratic leader Friedrich Ebert, who headed the new German government, rejected revolution and supported the creation of a parliamentary republic to replace the monarchy. He called on the German army and the Freikorps—a roving paramilitary band of students, demobilized soldiers, and others—to suppress the workers' councils and demonstrators. "The enthusiasm is marvelous," wrote one young soldier. "No mercy's shown. We shoot even the wounded." Members of the Freikorps hunted down Luxemburg and Liebknecht, among others, and murdered them.

Violence continued in Europe even as an assembly meeting in the city of Weimar in February 1919 approved a constitution and founded a parliamentary republic called the **Weimar Republic**. This time the right rebelled, for the military leadership dreamed of a restored monarchy: "As I love Germany, so I hate the Republic," wrote one officer. To defeat a military coup by Freikorps officers, Ebert called for a general strike. This action showed the lack of popular support for a military regime. Late in the winter of 1919, leftists proclaimed "soviet republics"— governments led by workers' councils—in Bavaria and Hungary. Volunteer armies and troops soon put the soviets down. The Bolsheviks tried to establish a Marxist regime in Poland, but the Poles resisted and drove the Red Army back in 1920, while the Allied powers rushed supplies and advisers to Warsaw. Though they failed, the various revolts provided further proof that total war had let loose the forces of political chaos. War, it seemed, continued.

The Paris Peace Conference, 1919–1920

As political turmoil engulfed peoples from Berlin to Moscow, the Paris Peace Conference opened in January 1919. Visions of communism spreading westward haunted the deliberations, but the assembled statesmen were also focused on the status of Germany and the reconstruction of a secure Europe. Leaders such as French premier Georges Clemenceau had to satisfy angry citizens: France had lost 1.3 million people—almost an entire generation of young men—and more than a million buildings, six thousand bridges, and thousands of miles of railroad lines and roads. Great Britain's representative, Prime Minister David Lloyd George, caught the mood of the British public by campaigning in 1918 with such slogans as "Hang the kaiser." The Italians arrived on the scene demanding the territory promised to them in the 1915 Treaty of London. Meanwhile, U.S. president Woodrow Wilson, head of the new world power that had helped achieve the Allied victory, had his own agenda. His Fourteen Points, on which the truce had been based, were steeped in the language of freedom and called for open diplomacy, arms reduction, and the right of nationality groups to determine their own government.

The Fourteen Points did not represent the mood of all the victors. Allied propaganda had made the Germans seem like inhuman monsters, and some military experts feared that Germany was using the armistice only to regroup for more warfare. Indeed, Germans widely refused to admit that their army had lost the war. Eager for army support, Ebert had given returning soldiers a rousing welcome: "As you return unconquered from the field of battle, I salute you." Wilson's plan, based on *settlement* as opposed to *surrender*, however, recognized that Germany was still the strongest state on the continent. Economists and other specialists agreed that, harshly dealt with and humiliated, Germany might soon become vengeful and chaotic—a lethal combination.

After six months, the statesmen and their teams of experts produced the **Peace of Paris** (1919–1920), a cluster of individual treaties that shocked the citizens of the countries that had to accept them. The treaties separated Austria from Hungary, reduced Hungary by almost two-thirds of its inhabitants and three-quarters of its territory, broke up the Ottoman Empire, and treated Germany severely. They replaced the Habsburg Empire with a group of small, internally divided, and economically weak states: Czechoslovakia; Poland; and the Kingdom of the Serbs, Croats, and Slovenes (soon renamed Yugoslavia). After a century and a half of partition, Poland was reconstructed from parts of Russia, Germany, and Austria-Hungary—leaving one-third of its population ethnically non-Polish. The statesmen in Paris also created the Polish Corridor, which connected Poland to the Baltic Sea and separated East Prussia from the rest of Germany (Map 25.3). Austria and Hungary were both left reeling at their drastic loss of territory and resources.

MAP 25.3   Europe and the Middle East after the Peace Settlements of 1919–1920
The political landscape of central, east, and east-central Europe changed dramatically as a result of the Russian Revolution and the Peace of Paris. The Ottoman, German, Russian, and Austro-Hungarian Empires were either broken up into multiple small states or territorially reduced. The settlement left resentments among Germans and Hungarians and created a group of weak, struggling nations in the heartland of Europe. The victorious powers took over much of the oil-rich Middle East. Why is it significant that the postwar geopolitical changes were so concentrated in one section of Europe?

The Treaty of Versailles, the centerpiece of the Peace of Paris, specifically dealt with Germany. In it, France recovered Alsace and Lorraine, and the Allies would temporarily occupy the left, or western, bank of the Rhine and the coal-bearing Saar basin. Germany would pay substantial reparations for civilian damage during the war, set in 1921 at the crushing sum of 132 billion gold marks. Germany also had to reduce its army, almost eliminate its navy, stop manufacturing offensive weapons, and deliver a large amount of free coal each year to Belgium and France. Furthermore, it was forbidden to have an air force and had to give up its colonies. Article 231 of the treaty described Germany's "responsibility" for damage caused "by the aggression of Germany and her allies." Outraged Germans interpreted this as a **war guilt clause**, which blamed Germany for the war and allowed the victors to collect reparations from their economically developed country rather than from ruined Austria. War guilt made Germans feel like outcasts in the community of nations.

Besides redrawing the map of Europe, the Peace of Paris set up an organization called the **League of Nations**, whose members had a joint responsibility for maintaining peace—a principle called collective security. It was supposed to replace the divisive secrecy of prewar power politics and arbitrate its members' disputes. The U.S. Senate failed to ratify the peace settlement and refused to join the league. Moreover, Germany and Russia initially were excluded from the league and were thus blocked from working cooperatively with it. The absence of these three important powers weakened the league as a global peacekeeper.

The League of Nations also organized the administration of the former colonies and territories of Germany and the Ottoman Empire—such as Togo, Cameroon, Syria, and Palestine—through systems of political control called mandates. While the victorious powers exercised their mandates, local leaders retained limited authority. The league justified the **mandate system** as providing governance by "advanced nations" over territories "not yet able to stand by themselves under the strenuous conditions of the modern world." The mandate system not only kept imperialism alive at a time when the powers were bankrupt and weak but also, like the Peace of Paris, aroused anger and resistance.

Economic and Diplomatic Consequences of the Peace

The Peace of Paris extended at least two problems into the 1920s and beyond. The first was economic recovery and its relationship to war debts and German reparation payments. The second was ensuring that peace actually came about and lasted. France, hardest hit by wartime destruction and billions of dollars in debt to the United States, estimated that Germany owed it at least $200 billion. Britain, by contrast, had not been physically devastated and was worried instead about maintaining its empire and restoring trade with Germany, not exacting huge reparations to rebuild. Nevertheless, both France and Britain were dependent on some German payments to settle their war debts to the United States.

Germany claimed that the demand for reparations strained its government, already facing political upheaval. In fact, Germany's economic problems had begun long before the Peace of Paris. They had started with the kaiser's policy of not raising taxes — especially on the rich — to pay for the war, leaving the new republic with a staggering debt. Now this republic, an experiment in democracy, needed to win over its citizens, and hiking taxes to pay Germany's debt would only anger them. In 1921, when Germans refused to present a realistic plan for paying reparations, the French occupied several cities in the Ruhr basin until a settlement was reached.

Germany's relations with powers to the west continued to deteriorate. In 1923, after Germany defaulted on coal deliveries, the French (this time joined by the Belgians) again sent troops into the Ruhr basin, planning to seize its output to pay the wartime debt. Urged on by the government, Ruhr citizens shut down industry by staying home from work. The German government printed trillions of marks to support the workers and to pay its own war debts with practically worthless currency. The result was a staggering inflation in Germany: at one point, a single U.S. dollar cost 4.42 trillion marks, and wheelbarrows of money were required to buy a turnip. Negotiations to resolve this economic chaos resulted in the Dawes Plan (1924) and the Young Plan (1929), which reduced reparations and restored the value of German currency. Before that happened, however, inflation had wiped out people's savings and turned many more Germans against their democratic government.

The second burning issue unresolved by the Peace of Paris involved making the peace take hold and last. Statesmen determined that peace needed disarmament, a return of Germany to the community of nations, and security for the new countries of eastern Europe. Hard diplomatic bargaining produced two plans in Germany's favor. At the Washington Conference in 1921, the United States, Great Britain, Japan, France, and Italy agreed to reduce their number of battleships and to stop constructing new ones for ten years. Four years later, in 1925, the League of Nations sponsored a meeting of the great powers, including Germany, at Locarno, Switzerland. The Treaty of Locarno provided Germany with a seat in the league as of 1926. In return, Germany agreed not to violate the borders of France and Belgium and to keep the nearby Rhineland demilitarized — that is, unfortified by troops.

To the east, statesmen feared a German attempt to regain territory lost to Poland, to merge with Austria, or to launch any attack on states spun off from Austria-Hungary. To meet this threat, Czechoslovakia, Yugoslavia, and Romania formed the Little Entente in 1920–1921, a collective security agreement intended to protect them from Germany and Russia. Between 1924 and 1927, France allied itself with the Little Entente and with Poland. In 1928, sixty nations, including the major European powers, Japan, and the United States, signed the Kellogg-Briand Pact, which formally rejected international violence. The pact lacked any mechanism for enforcement and thus resembled, as one critic put it, "an international kiss."

The publicity surrounding the international agreements of the 1920s sharply contrasted with old-style diplomacy, which had been conducted in secret and subject to little public scrutiny. The development of a system of open, collective security suggested a diplomatic revolution that would promote international peace. Yet openness allowed diplomats to feed the press information designed to provoke the masses. For example, the press and opposition parties whipped the German populace into a nationalist fury whenever Germany's diplomats appeared to compromise, even though these compromises worked to undo the Treaty of Versailles. Journalists who hated republican government used international meetings such as the one at Locarno to fire up political hatreds rather than promote peace or rational public discussion.

REVIEW   What were the major outcomes of the postwar peacemaking process?

A Decade of Recovery: Europe in the 1920s

Even after the armistice and the peace treaties, the wartime spirit endured. Towns and villages built their monuments to the fallen, and battlefield tourism sprang up for veterans and their families in search of a relative's final resting place. Words and phrases from the battlefield became part of everyday speech. Before the war the word *lousy* had meant "lice-infested," but English-speaking soldiers returning from the trenches now applied it to anything bad. Raincoats became *trenchcoats*. Maimed, disfigured veterans were present everywhere. While some received prostheses designed by Jules Amar, others without limbs were sometimes carried in baskets—hence the expression *basket case*. Four autocratic governments had collapsed as a result of the war, but whether these states would become workable democracies remained an open question. The Roaring Twenties masked the serious problem of restoring stability and implementing democracy amid the grim legacy of war.

Changes in the Political Landscape

The collapse of autocratic governments and the widespread extension of suffrage to women brought political turmoil as well as the expansion of democracy. Woman suffrage resulted in part from decades of activism, but many men in government claimed that suffrage was a "reward" for women's war efforts. Women were voted into parliaments in the first postwar elections. Yet French men pointedly denied women the vote, threatening that women voters would bring back the rule of kings and priests. (Only at the end of World War II would France and Italy extend suffrage to women.) The welfare state also expanded, with payments being made to veterans and victims of workplace accidents. These benefits stemmed from the belief that more evenly distributed wealth—sometimes called economic democracy—would prevent the outbreak of revolution.

The trend toward economic democracy was not easy to maintain, however, because the cycles of boom and bust that had characterized the late nineteenth century reemerged. A short postwar economic boom prompted by reconstruction and consumer spending was followed by an economic downturn that was most severe between 1920 and 1922. By the mid-1920s, women made up a smaller percentage of the workforce than in 1913, and skyrocketing unemployment produced more discontent with governments. Veterans were especially angered by economic insecurity after years of enduring the war's horrors.

The new republics of eastern Europe in particular were unprepared for hard economic times and poorly equipped to compete in the world market. None but Czechoslovakia had a mature industrial sector, and agricultural techniques were often primitive. Still more pressing problems hampered them. Vast migrations occurred as some 1 million citizens escaped the civil war in Russia and 800,000 soldiers from the defeated Whites searched for safety. Two million people fled Turkey, Greece, and Bulgaria because the postwar settlement called for the new nations to be built along "nationality" lines. Hundreds of thousands landed in new nations: Hungary, for example, had to receive 300,000 people of Magyar ethnicity who were no longer welcome in Romania, Czechoslovakia, or Yugoslavia. Most of these millions of refugees lacked land or jobs. They had nothing to do "but loaf and starve," one English journalist observed of refugees in Bulgaria. The influx of people brought more conflict in various parts of eastern Europe.

Poland exemplified how postwar turmoil could destroy a new nation's parliamentary democracy. One-third of the reunified Poland consisted of Ukrainians, Belorussians, Germans, and other ethnic minorities—many of whom had grievances against the dominant Poles. Varying religious and cultural traditions also divided the Poles, who for 150 years had been split among Austria, Germany, and Russia. Polish reunification occurred without a common currency or political heritage—even the railroad tracks were not a standard size. Despite a new constitution that professed equal rights for all ethnicities and religions, declining crop prices and overpopulation made life in the countryside difficult. The economic downturn brought strikes and violence in 1922–1923. Ultimately, former military leader Jozef Pilsudski took power via a coup in 1926 because of the government's inability to bring about prosperity. In postwar east-central Europe, military solutions to economic hardship demonstrated the endurance of war long after the peace had officially begun.

Germany was a different case. Although its economy picked up and the nation became a center of experimentation in the arts, political life remained unstable because so many people, nostalgic for imperial glory, associated defeat with the new Weimar Republic. Extremist politicians heaped daily abuse on Weimar's democracy. A wealthy newspaper and film tycoon called anyone cooperating with the parliamentary system "a moral cripple." Right-wing parties favored violence rather than consensus building, and nationalist thugs murdered democratic leaders and Jews. Communists were not shy about jumping into street brawls, either.

Support for the far right came from wealthy landowners and businessmen, white-collar workers whose standard of living had dropped during the war, and members of the lower-middle and middle classes hurt by inflation. Bands of disaffected youth and veterans multiplied, among them a group called the Brown Shirts. Their leader was an ex-soldier named Adolf Hitler (1889–1945)—a favorite speaker among antigovernment crowds. In the wake of the Ruhr occupation of 1923, Hitler and German military hero Erich Ludendorff launched a coup d'état—or *putsch* in German—from a beer hall in Munich. Government troops suppressed the Beer Hall Putsch and arrested its leaders, but Ludendorff was acquitted and Hitler spent less than a year in jail. To conservative judges, former aristocrats, and most of the prewar bureaucrats who still staffed the government, such men were national heroes.

In France and Britain, parties on the right were less effective than in Germany because representative institutions were better established and the upper classes were not plotting to restore an authoritarian monarchy. In France, politicians from the conservative right and moderate left successively formed coalitions and rallied general support to rebuild war-torn regions and to force Germany to pay for the reconstruction. Hoping to stimulate population growth after the devastating loss of life, the French parliament made distributing birth-control information illegal and abortion a severely punished crime.

Britain encountered postwar boom-and-bust cycles and continuing conflict in Ireland. Ramsay MacDonald (1866–1937), elected the first Labour prime minister in 1924, represented the political strength of workers. He had to face the unpleasant truth that although Britain had the largest world empire, many of its industries were obsolete or in poor condition. A showdown came in the ailing coal industry. On May 3, 1926, workers launched a nine-day general strike against wage cuts and dangerous conditions in the mines. The strike provoked unprecedented middle-class resistance. University students, homemakers, and businessmen shut down the strike by driving trains, working on docks, and replacing workers in other jobs. Seeing strikers as those who were once again attacking the nation, citizens from many walks of life began working through their wartime traumas with words and deeds, inflicting their violence on conquered lands near and far.

In January 1919, Ireland's republican leaders declared their nation's independence and created a separate parliament. The British government refused to recognize the parliament and sent in the Black and Tans, a volunteer army of demobilized soldiers named for the color of their uniforms. Terror reigned in Ireland, and by 1921, public outrage had forced the British to negotiate a treaty, one that reversed the Irish declaration of independence and made the Irish Free State a self-governing dominion. Northern Ireland, a group of six northern counties containing a majority of Protestants, gained a separate status: it was self-governing but still had representation in the British Parliament. This settlement left bitter discontent.

War had also changed everything in the colonies. European politicians and military recruiters had promised colonized peoples reforms, even independence, in exchange for their support during the war. However, these peoples' political activism — now enhanced by increasing education, trade, and experience with the West — mostly met with a brutal response. British forces massacred protesters at Amritsar, India, in 1919, put down revolts against the mandate system in Egypt and Iran in the early 1920s, and slaughtered women peacefully protesting in Nigeria in 1929. The Dutch jailed political leaders in Indonesia; the French punished Indochinese nationalists. Western governments thus continued warfare in the colonies; the Germans who had lost their holdings brought the war home instead. Maintaining empires abroad was also seen as crucial to ensuring democratic government, for any hint of declining national prestige fed antidemocratic forces.

Despite resistance, the 1920s marked the high tide of imperialism. Britain and France, enjoying new access to Germany's colonies in Africa and the territories of the fallen Ottoman Empire in the Middle East, were at the height of their global power because of the growing profitability that enterprise around the world could bring. Middle Eastern and Indonesian oil, for instance, fueled the West's growing number of automobiles, airplanes, trucks, ships, and buses. Products like chocolate and tropical fruit became regular items in Westerners' diets.

The balance of power among the imperial nations was shifting, however. The most important change was Japan's surging competition for markets, resources, and ultimately colonies. During the war, Japanese output of industrial goods such as metal and ships grew dramatically because the Western powers outsourced their wartime needs for such products. Japan's prosperity skyrocketed, allowing the country to become the dominant power in China. The Japanese government advertised its success as a sign of hope for non-Westerners. Japan's prosperity, the country's politicians claimed, would end the West's domination. Ardently nationalist, the Japanese government was not yet strong enough to challenge the Western powers militarily. Thus, although outraged when the Western powers at Paris refused a nondiscrimination clause in the charter of the League of Nations, Japan cooperated in the Anglo-American-dominated peace.

Reconstructing the Economy

The war had weakened European economies and allowed rivals—Japan, India, the United States, Australia, and Canada—to flourish. At the same time, the war had forced European manufacturing to become more efficient and had expanded the demand for automotive and air transport, electrical products, and synthetic goods. The prewar pattern of mergers and cartels continued after 1918, giving rise to gigantic food-processing firms such as Nestlé in Switzerland and petroleum enterprises such as Royal Dutch Shell. By the late 1920s, Europe was enjoying renewed economic prosperity.

The United States had become the trendsetter in economic modernization: by 1929, Ford Motor Company's Detroit assembly line was producing a Ford automobile every ten seconds. Increased productivity, founder Henry Ford (1863–1947) pointed out, resulted in a lower cost of living and thus increased workers' purchasing power. American efficiency expert Frederick Taylor (1856–1915) had developed methods to streamline workers' tasks for maximum productivity. Industrialists who adopted Taylor's methods were also influenced by European psychologists who emphasized the mental aspects of productivity and thus the need to balance work and leisure activities. In theory, increased productivity not only produced prosperity for all but also united workers and management, avoiding Russian-style worker revolution. For many workers, however, the emphasis on efficiency seemed inhumane; in some businesses restrictions were so severe that workers were allowed to use the bathroom only on a fixed schedule.

The managerial sector in industry had expanded during the war and continued to do so thereafter. Workers' knowledge became devalued, with managers alone seen as creative and innovative. Managers reorganized work procedures and classified workers' skills. They categorized jobs held by women as requiring less skill— whether they did or not—and therefore deserving of lower wages. With male workers' jobs increasingly threatened by labor-saving machinery, unions usually agreed that women should receive lower wages to keep them from competing with men for scarce high-paying jobs. Like the managerial sector, a complex union bureaucracy had ballooned during World War I to help monitor labor's part in the war. Unions could mobilize masses of people, as evidenced by their actions against coups in Weimar Germany and by the general strike in Great Britain in 1926.

Restoring Society

Civilians met the returning millions of brutalized, incapacitated, and shell-shocked veterans with combined joy and apprehension—and that apprehension was often valid. Tens of thousands of German, central European, and Italian soldiers refused to disband; some British veterans vandalized university classrooms and assaulted women streetcar conductors and factory workers. Many veterans were angry that civilians had protested wartime conditions instead of enduring them. Patriotic when the war erupted, civilians, especially women, sometimes felt estranged from the returning warriors who had inflicted so much death and who had lived daily with filth, rats, and decaying human flesh. While women who had served on the front had seen the soldiers' suffering firsthand and could sympathize with them, many British suffragists, for instance, who had fought for equality in men's and women's lives before the war, now embraced separate spheres for men and women, so fearful were they of returning veterans.

For their part, veterans returned to a world that differed from the home they had left. They found that the war had blurred class distinctions, giving rise to expectations that life would be fairer afterward. Despite their expectations, veterans often had few or no jobs open to them, and some found that their wives and sweethearts had abandoned them. Many found, too, that women's roles had gone through other changes: middle-class women did their own housework because former servants could earn more money in factories, and greater numbers of women worked outside the home. Women of all classes cut their hair short, wore sleeker clothes, smoked, and had money of their own because of war work.

Focusing on veterans' needs, governments tried to make civilian life as comfortable as possible to reintegrate men into society and reduce the appeal of communism. Politicians believed in the calming power of family life and supported social programs such as veterans' pensions and housing and benefits for out-of-work men. The new housing—"homes for heroes," as politicians called the program in Vienna, Frankfurt, Berlin, and Stockholm—provided common laundries, day-care centers, and rooms for socializing. Gardens, terraces, and balconies provided a soothing country ambience that offset the hectic nature of industrial life. Inside, they boasted modern kitchens and bathrooms, central heating, and electricity.

Despite government efforts to restore traditional family life, freer relationships and more open discussions of sex characterized the 1920s. Middle-class youths of both sexes visited jazz clubs and attended movies together. Revealing bathing suits, short skirts, and body-hugging clothing emphasized women's sexuality, seeming to invite men and women to join together and replenish the postwar population. British scientist Marie Stopes published the best seller *Married Love* in 1918, and Dutch author Theodor van de Velde produced the wildly successful *Ideal Marriage: Its Physiology and Technique* in 1927. Both authors described sex in glowing terms and offered precise information about birth control and sexual physiology. One Viennese reformer promoted working-class marriage as "an erotic-comradely relationship of equals" rather than the economic partnership of past centuries. Meanwhile, such writers as the Briton D. H. Lawrence and the American Ernest Hemingway glorified men's sexual vigor in, respectively, *Women in Love* (1920) and *The Sun Also Rises* (1926). Mass culture's focus on heterosexuality encouraged the return to normality after the gender disorder that had troubled the prewar and war years.

As images of men and women changed, people paid more attention to bodily improvement. The increasing use of toothbrushes and toothpaste, safety and electric razors, and deodorants reflected new standards for personal hygiene and grooming. A multibillion-dollar cosmetics industry sprang up almost overnight. Women went to beauty parlors regularly to have their short hair cut, dyed, straightened, or curled. They also tweezed their eyebrows, applied makeup, and even submitted to cosmetic surgery. Ordinary women "painted" their faces (something only prostitutes had done formerly) and competed in beauty contests. Instead of wanting to look plump and pale, people aimed to become thin and tan, often through exercise and playing sports. Consumers' new focus on personal health coincided with industry's need for a physically fit workforce.

As prosperity returned in the mid-1920s, people could afford to buy more consumer goods. Middle- and upper-class families snapped up sleek modern furniture, washing machines, and vacuum cleaners. Other modern conveniences such as electric irons and gas stoves appeared in better-off working-class households. Installment buying, popularized from the 1920s on, helped people finance these purchases. Family intimacy increasingly depended on machines of mass communication like radios, phonographs, and even automobiles, which not only transformed private life but also brought changes to the public world of mass culture and mass politics.

REVIEW   What were the major political, social, and economic problems facing postwar Europe, and how did governments attempt to address them?

Mass Culture and the Rise of Modern Dictators

Wartime propaganda had aimed to unite all classes against a common enemy. In the 1920s, new technology made the process of integrating diverse groups into a single Western or mass culture easier. The tools of mass culture — primarily radio, film, and newspapers—expanded their influence in the 1920s. Some intellectuals who wanted to use modern media and art to reach the masses saw their potential for creating an informed citizenry and thus strengthening democracy. At the same time, the media allowed authoritarian rulers and would-be dictators such as Benito Mussolini, Joseph Stalin, and Adolf Hitler to shape uniform political thought and to control citizens' behavior far beyond what previous rulers had been able to do.

Culture for the Masses

The media received a big boost from the war. Bulletins from the battlefront whetted the public's craving for news and real-life stories, and sales of nonfiction books soared. After years of deprivation, people were driven to achieve material success, and they devoured books about how to gain it. A biography of Henry Ford, telling his story of upward mobility and technological accomplishment, became a best seller in Germany. Phonographs, radio programs, and movies also widened the scope of national culture.

In the 1920s, film evolved from an experimental medium to a thriving international business in which large corporations set up theater chains and marketed

The Flapper   This modern workingwoman smoking her cigarette stood for all that had changed—or was said to have changed—in the postwar world. Women worked and had money of their own, they were out in public and could vote in many countries, and they were liberated from old constraints on their sexual and other behavior. (General Photographic Agency/Getty Images.)

movies worldwide. Films of literary classics and political events developed people's sense of a common heritage and were often sponsored by governments. Bolshevik leaders backed the inventive work of director Sergei Eisenstein, whose films *Potemkin* (1925) and *Ten Days That Shook the World* (1927–1928) presented a Bolshevik view of history to Russian and international audiences.

Films incorporated familiar elements from everyday life. The popular comedies of the 1920s made the flapper more visible to the masses, attracting some hundred million weekly viewers, the majority of them women. Films also played to postwar fantasies and fears. In Germany, the influential hit *The Cabinet of Doctor Caligari* (1919) depicted frightening events in an insane asylum as horrifying symbols of state power. Popular detective and cowboy films portrayed heroes who could restore wholeness to the disordered world of murder, crime, and injustice. The plight of gangsters appealed to veterans, who had been exposed to the cheap value of modern life in the trenches. Films featured characters from around the world and were often set in faraway deserts and mountain ranges; newsreels showed athletic, soldier-like bodies in sporting events such as boxing.

Like film, radio evolved from an experimental medium to an instrument of mass culture during the 1920s. Developed from the wireless technology of Italian inventor Guglielmo Marconi, the radio quickly became an affordable consumer item, allowing the public concert or lecture to penetrate the individual's private living space. Specialized programming for men (such as sports reporting) and for women (such as advice on home management) attracted listeners. Through radio, disabled veterans found ways to participate in public events and keep up-to-date. By the 1930s, radio helped politicians to reach the masses wherever they might be—even alone at home.

Cultural Debates over the Future

Cultural leaders in the 1920s either were obsessed with the horrendous experience of war or held high hopes for creating a fresh, utopian future that would have little relation to the past. German artists, especially, produced bleak or violent visions. The sculpture and woodcuts of German artist Käthe Kollwitz, whose son had died in the war, portrayed bereaved parents, starving children, and other heart-wrenching anti-war images. Others thought that Europeans needed to search for answers in far-off cultures. Seeing Europe as decadent, some turned to the spiritual richness of Asian philosophies and religions. An "Asiatic fever" seemed to grip intellectuals, including the British writer Virginia Woolf, who drew on ideas of reincarnation in her novel *Orlando* (1928), and the filmmaker Sergei Eisenstein, who modeled new techniques of film shots (montage) on Japanese calligraphy.

Other artists used satire and contempt to express postwar rage at civilization's wartime failure. George Grosz (1893–1959), stunned by the war's carnage, produced works marked by nonsense and shrieking expressions of alienation. Grosz's paintings and cartoons of maimed soldiers and brutally murdered women reflected his self-proclaimed desire "to bellow back." In the postwar years, the modernist practice of shocking audiences became more savage while portrayals of seedy everyday life flourished in cabarets and theaters in the 1920s and reinforced veterans' beliefs in civilian decadence.

The art world itself became a battlefield, especially in defeated Germany, where it mirrored the Weimar Republic's contentious politics. Popular writers such as veteran Ernst Jünger glorified life in the trenches and called for the militarization of society. In contrast, Erich Maria Remarque, also a veteran, cried out for an end to war in his controversial novel *All Quiet on the Western Front* (1928). This international best seller depicted the shared life of enemies on the battlefield, thus aiming to overcome the national hatred aroused by wartime propaganda. Remarque's novel was part of a flood of popular, and often bitter, literature appearing on the tenth anniversary of the war's end. It coincided with an interest in "Great War tourism" such as visiting battlefields.

The postwar arts produced many a utopian fantasy turned upside down; dystopias of life in a war-traumatized Europe multiplied. In the bizarre stories of Franz Kafka, who worked by day in a large insurance company in Prague, the world is a vast, impersonal machine. His novels *The Trial* (1925) and *The Castle* (1926) show the hopeless condition of individuals caught between the cogs of society's relentlessly turning gears. His themes seemed to capture for civilian life the helplessness that soldiers had felt at the front. As the prewar way of life collapsed in the face of political and technological innovation, other writers depicted the complex, sometimes nightmarish inner life of individuals.

Irish writer James Joyce portrayed this interior self built on memories and sensations, many of them from the war. Joyce's *Ulysses* (1922) illuminates the fast-moving inner lives of its characters in the course of a single day. In one of the most celebrated passages in *Ulysses*, a long interior monologue traces a woman's lifetime of erotic and emotional sensations. The technique of using a character's thoughts to propel a story was called stream of consciousness. Virginia Woolf, too, used this technique in her novel *Mrs. Dalloway* (1925). For Woolf, the war had dissolved the solid society from which absorbing stories and fascinating characters were once fashioned. Her characters experience fragmented conversations and incomplete relationships. Woolf's novel *Orlando* also reflected the postwar attention to women. In the novel, the hero Orlando lives hundreds of years and in the course of his long life is eventually transformed into a woman.

There was another side to the postwar story, however—one based on the promise of technology. Before the war, avant-garde artists had celebrated the new, the futuristic, the utopian. After the war, like Jules Amar crafting prostheses for shattered limbs, many postwar artists were optimistic that technology could make an entire wounded society whole. The aim of art, observed one of them, "is not to decorate our life but to organize it." German artists, calling themselves the Bauhaus (after the idea of a craft association, or *Bauhütte*), created streamlined office buildings and designed functional furniture and utensils, many of them inspired by forms from "untainted" East Asia and Africa. Russian artists, temporarily caught up in the communist experiment, optimistically wrote novels about cement factories and created ballets about steel.

Artists fascinated by technology and machinery were drawn to the most modern of all countries—the United States. Hollywood films, glossy advertisements, and the bustling metropolis of New York tempted careworn Europeans. They loved films about the Wild West or the supposedly carefree "modern girl." They were especially attracted to jazz, the improvisational music developed by African Americans. Performers like Josephine Baker (1906–1975) and Louis Armstrong (1901–1971) became international sensations when they toured Europe's capital cities. Like jazz, the New York skyscraper pointed to the future, not to the grim wartime past.

The Communist Utopia

Communism also promised a shining future and a modern, technological culture. As the Bolsheviks met powerful resistance, however, they became ever more ruthless and authoritarian. In the early 1920s, peasant bands called Green Armies revolted against the Bolshevik policy of war communism that confiscated their crops. Industrial production stood at only 13 percent of prewar levels, and millions of refugees clogged the cities and roamed the countryside. In the early spring of 1921, workers in Petrograd and sailors at the naval base at Kronstadt revolted, protesting the privileged standard of living that Bolshevik supervisors enjoyed. They called for "soviets without Communists"—that is, a worker state without elite leaders.

The Bolsheviks had many of the rebels shot, but the Kronstadt revolt pushed Lenin to institute reform. His New Economic Policy (NEP) returned parts of the economy to capitalist methods that allowed peasants to sell their grain and others to trade consumer goods freely. Although the state still controlled large industries and banking, the NEP encouraged people to produce and even, in the spirited slogan of one official, "get rich." As a result, consumer goods and more food became available; some peasants and merchants prospered. The rise of these wealthy "NEPmen," who bought and furnished splendid homes, broke the Bolshevik promise of a classless utopia.

Further protests erupted within Communist ranks. At the 1921 party congress, a group called the Worker Opposition objected to the party's takeover of economic control from worker organizations and pointed out that the NEP was not a proletarian program for workers. In response, Lenin suppressed the Worker Opposition and set up procedures for purging opponents—a policy that would become a deadly feature of Communist rule. Bolshevik leaders also worked to make the Communist revolution a cultural reality in people's lives and thinking. The Communist Party set up classes to improve the literacy rate—which had been only 40 percent on the eve of World War I. To create social equality between the sexes, which had been part of the Marxist vision of the future, the state made birth control, abortion, and divorce readily available. As commissar for public welfare, **Aleksandra Kollontai** (1872–1952) promoted birth-control education for adults and day care for children of working parents. To encourage literacy, she wrote simply worded novels about love and work in the new socialist state for ordinary readers.

The bureaucracy swelled to promote modern ways, and *hygiene* and *efficiency* became watchwords, as they were in the rest of Europe. Agencies such as the Zhenotdel ("Women's Bureau") taught women about sanitary housekeeping, while efficiency experts aimed to replace backwardness with American-style technological modernity. The short-lived government agency Proletkult tried to develop proletarian culture through such undertakings as workers' universities, a workers' theater, and workers' publishing. Poet Vladimir Mayakovsky wrote verse praising his Communist passport and essays promoting toothbrushing, while composers punctuated their music with the sound of train or factory whistles. As with war communism, many resisted attempts to change everyday life and culture. In Islamic regions of central Asia, incorporated from the old Russian Empire into the new Communist one, Bolsheviks urged Muslim women to remove their veils and generally to become more "modern," but Muslims often attacked both Zhenotdel workers and women who followed their advice.

Lenin suffered a debilitating stroke in the spring of 1922, and amid ongoing cultural experimentation and factional fighting, this architect of the Bolshevik Revolution died in January 1924. The party congress changed the name of Petrograd to Leningrad and elevated the deceased leader into a secular god. Joseph Stalin (1879–1953), who served in the powerful post of general secretary of the Communist Party, was the chief mourner at Lenin's funeral, using the occasion to hand out good jobs. He advertised his role in joining Russian and non-Russian regions into the Union of Soviet Socialist Republics (USSR) in 1923. Concerned with Stalin's influence and ruthlessness, Lenin in his last will and testament had asked that "the comrades find a way to remove Stalin." Stalin, however, prevented Lenin's will from being publicized and discredited his chief rival, Trotsky, as an unpatriotic internationalist. Simultaneously, Stalin organized the Lenin cult, which included the public display of Lenin's embalmed corpse—still on view today. By 1929, Stalin had achieved virtually complete control of the USSR.

Fascism on the March in Italy

In Italy, the rise to power of political journalist **Benito Mussolini** (1883–1945), who had turned from socialism to the radical right, kept the war alive. Italians raged when the Allies at Paris refused to honor the territorial promises of the Treaty of London, and peasants and workers protested their economic plight during the slump of the early 1920s. Many Europeans blamed parliaments and constitutions for their troubles, so Italians backed Mussolini when he gathered veterans and unemployed men into a personal army (the Black Shirts) to overturn parliamentary government. In 1922, his supporters, known as the Fascists, started a march on Rome, forcing King Victor Emmanuel III (r. 1900–1946) to make Mussolini prime minister.

Like the Bolsheviks, Mussolini promised an efficient military utopia and the restoration of men's warrior status. The Black Shirts attracted many young men who felt cheated of wartime glory and many veterans who missed the vigor of military life. The fasces, an ancient Roman symbol depicting a bundle of sticks wrapped around an ax with the blade exposed (representing both unity and force), served as the movement's emblem and provided its name: **fascism**. Unlike Marxism, fascism scoffed at coherent ideology: "Fascism is not a church," Mussolini announced. "It is more like a training ground." The Fascist Party was defined by deeds— specifically its promotion of male violence and its attacks on parliamentary rule.

Mussolini and the Black Shirts, 1922   Mussolini always struck a tough military pose, even when not in uniform, as in this photo taken in 1922 with his Black Shirt supporters, many also without uniforms. Once in power, Mussolini continued the militarization of society that had begun during World War I, instilling a cult of obedience and submission to state authority that he viewed as more important than fancy theories of politics and government. (The Granger Collection, NYC—All rights reserved.)

Mussolini criminalized any criticism of the state and used violence against opponents in parliament. Bands of men from the Fascist Party attacked striking workers, using their favorite tactic of forcing castor oil (which caused diarrhea) down the throats of socialists, and even murdering rivals. Yet the sight of the Black Shirts marching through the streets like disciplined soldiers signaled to many Italians that their country was orderly and modern. Large landowners and businessmen approved the Fascists' attacks on strikers and therefore financed the movement. Their generous funding allowed Mussolini to build a large staff by hiring the unemployed, creating the illusion that the Fascists could rescue the economy when no one else could.

Like a wartime leader, Mussolini used mass propaganda to build support for a kind of military campaign to remake Italy. Peasant men huddled around radios to hear him call for a "battle of wheat" to enhance farm productivity. Peasant women adored him for appearing to value motherhood. In the cities the government launched avant-garde architectural projects and used public relations promoters to advertise its achievements. The modern city became a stage set for Fascist spectacles captured by newsreel cameras and broadcast by radio. Mussolini claimed that he made the trains run on time, and this triumph of modern technology fanned people's hopes that he could restore order, albeit violently.

Mussolini added traditional values and prejudices to his modern order. An atheist himself, he recognized the importance of Catholicism in Italian life. In 1929, the Lateran Agreement between the Italian government and the church made the Vatican an independent state under papal sovereignty. The government recognized the church's right to determine marriage and family policy; in return, the church ended its criticism of Fascist tactics. Mussolini also outlawed labor unions, replacing them with organized groups of employers, workers, and professionals to settle grievances and determine conditions of work. Mussolini drew praise from business leaders and professionals when he announced cuts in women's wages and a ban on women in the professions. Mussolini aimed to confine women to low-paying jobs as part of his scheme for reinvigorating men.

Mussolini's numerous admirers across the West included Adolf Hitler, who throughout the 1920s had been building a paramilitary group of storm troopers alongside a political organization called the National Socialist German Workers' Party (the Nazi Party). During his brief stint in jail for the 1923 Beer Hall Putsch, Hitler wrote *Mein Kampf* (My Struggle); in the book, he expressed both his vicious anti-Semitism and his recipe for manipulating the masses. Hitler was fascinated by Mussolini's legal accession to power and his triumph over all opposition. Late in the 1920s, however, the conditions that had allowed Mussolini to rise to power in 1922 no longer existed in Germany. Although the Nazi Party was becoming a strong political instrument, Weimar democracy was functioning better as the decade wore on.

> **REVIEW**   How did the postwar atmosphere influence cultural life and encourage the trend toward dictatorship?

Conclusion

The year 1929 was to prove just as fateful as 1914 had been. In 1914, World War I began an orgy of death, causing tens of millions of casualties and the destruction of major dynasties. For four years, the war promoted military technology, fierce nationalism, and the control of everyday life by bureaucracy. As dynasties fell, the Peace of Paris treaties of 1919–1920 left Germans bitterly resentful. In eastern and central Europe the creation of new states by the treaties failed to guarantee a peaceful future. Massive migrations produced additional chaos, as refugees fled political upheaval such as that in Russia and as some new nations expelled minority groups.

War furthered the development of mass society. It leveled social classes on the battlefield and in the graveyard, standardized political thinking through wartime propaganda, and extended many political rights to women. Production techniques, improved during wartime, were used in peacetime for manufacturing consumer goods. Technological innovations—from the prostheses built by Jules Amar to air transport, cinema, and radio transmission—became available. Modernity in the arts intensified, probing the nightmarish war that continued to haunt the population.

By the end of the 1920s, the war had so militarized the population that strongmen had come to power in several countries, including the Soviet Union and Italy, with Adolf Hitler waiting in the wings in Germany. These strongmen and their followers kept alive the wartime commitment to violence. Many Westerners were impressed by the tough, modern efficiency of Fascists and Communists who made parliaments and citizen rule seem out of date, even effeminate. When the U.S. stock market crashed in 1929 and economic disaster circled the globe, authoritarian solutions and militarism continued to look appealing. What followed was a series of catastrophes even more devastating than those of World War I.

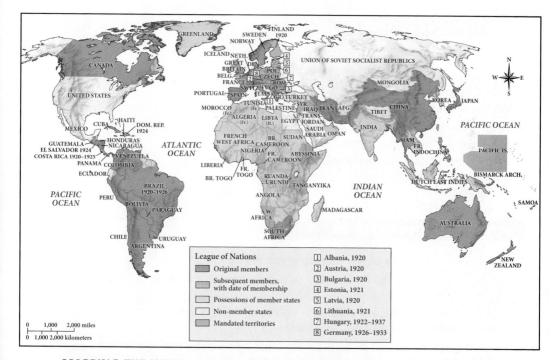

MAPPING THE WEST Europe and the World in 1929 The map reflects the partitions and nations that came into being as a result of war and revolution, while it obscures the increasing movement toward throwing off colonial rule. The high point of empire was still unfolding with the mandate system and the 1930s drive by Germany, Italy, and Japan, all of which searched for land and resources to fuel growth.

Chapter Review

KEY TERMS AND PEOPLE

Be sure you can identify the term or person and explain its historical significance.

total war (p. 743)
cult of the offensive (p. 745)
Schlieffen Plan (p. 745)
Fourteen Points (p. 751)
soviets (p. 751)
V. I. Lenin (p. 752)
Weimar Republic (p. 756)
Peace of Paris (p. 756)

war guilt clause (p. 758)
League of Nations (p. 758)
mandate system (p. 758)
Bolshevik Revolution (p. 759)
Aleksandra Kollontai (p. 769)
Benito Mussolini (p. 770)
fascism (p. 770)

REVIEW QUESTIONS

1. In what ways was World War I a total war?
2. Why did people rebel during World War I, and what turned rebellion into outright revolution in Russia?
3. What were the major outcomes of the postwar peacemaking process?
4. What were the major political, social, and economic problems facing postwar Europe, and how did governments attempt to address them?
5. How did the postwar atmosphere influence cultural expression and encourage the trend toward dictatorship?

MAKING CONNECTIONS

1. How did the experience of war shape postwar mass politics?
2. What social changes from World War I carried over into the postwar years, and why?
3. How did postwar artistic and cultural innovations build on the modern movements that developed between 1890 and 1914?
4. What changes did the war bring to relationships between European countries and their colonies?

IMPORTANT EVENTS

1913–1925   • Suffrage for women expands in much of Europe

1914   • *August:* World War I begins

1916   • Irish nationalists stage Easter Uprising against British rule

1917   • *March:* Revolution in Russia overturns tsarist autocracy

                • *April:* United States enters World War I

                • *November:* Bolshevik Revolution in Russia

1918   • *November:* Armistice ends fighting of World War I; revolutionary turmoil throughout Germany; kaiser abdicates

1918–1922   • Civil war in Russia

1919   • Weimar Republic is established

1919–1920   • Paris Peace Conference redraws map of Europe

1922   • Ireland gains independence; Fascists march on Rome; Mussolini becomes prime minister; Joyce, *Ulysses;* Hitler builds Nazi Party

1924   • Lenin dies; Stalin and Trotsky contend for power

1924–1929   • Period of general economic prosperity and stability

1929   • *October:* Stock market crash in United States

26

The Great Depression and World War II

1929–1945

> **CHAPTER FOCUS**
>
> What were the main economic, social, and political challenges of the years 1929–1945, and how did governments and individuals respond to them?

WHEN ETTY HILLESUM MOVED to Amsterdam from the Dutch provinces in 1932 to attend law school, an economic depression gripped the world. A resourceful young woman, Hillesum pieced together a living as a housekeeper and part-time language teacher so that she could continue her studies. Absorbed in her everyday life, she took little note of Adolf Hitler's spectacular rise to power in Germany, even when he demonized her fellow Jews as responsible for the economic slump and for virtually every other problem Germany faced. In 1939, the outbreak of World War II awakened her to the reality of what was happening. The German conquest of the Netherlands in 1940 led to the persecution of Dutch Jews, bringing Hillesum to note in her diary: "What they are after is our total destruction." The Nazis started relocating Jews to camps in Germany and Poland. Hillesum went to work for Amsterdam's Jewish Council, which was forced to organize the transport of Jews to these death camps. Changing from self-absorbed student to heroine, she did what she could to help other Jews and began carefully recording the deportations. When she and her family were captured and deported in turn, she smuggled out letters from the transit camps along the route to Poland, describing the inhumane conditions and brutal treatment of the Jews. "I wish I could live for a long time so that one day I may know how to explain it," she wrote. Etty Hillesum never got her wish: she died at Auschwitz in November 1943.

The economic recovery of the late 1920s came to a halt with the U.S. stock market crash in 1929, which launched a worldwide economic depression. Economic distress attracted many people to military-style strongmen for solutions to their problems. Among these dictators was Adolf Hitler, who called on the German masses to restore the national glory that had been damaged by defeat in 1918. He urged Germans to scorn democratic rights and root out those he considered to be inferior people: Jews, Slavs, and Sinti and Roma (often called Gypsies), among others. Militaristic and fascist regimes spread to Spain, Poland, Hungary, Japan, and countries of Latin America, crushing representative institutions. In the Soviet Union, Joseph Stalin justified the killing of millions of citizens as necessary for the USSR's industrialization and the survival of communism. For millions of hard-pressed people in the 1930s, dictatorship had great appeal.

Elected leaders in the democracies reacted cautiously to both economic depression and the dictators' aggression. In an age of mass media, leaders following democratic principles appeared timid, while dictators dressed in uniforms looked bold and decisive. Only the German invasion of Poland in 1939 pushed the democracies to strong action, as World War II erupted in Europe. By 1941, the war had spread across the globe with the United States, Great Britain, the Soviet Union, and many other nations united in combat against Germany, Italy, Japan, and their allies. Tens of millions would perish in this war because both technology and ideology had become more deadly than they had been just two decades earlier. More than half the dead were civilians, among them Etty Hillesum, killed for being Jewish.

The Great Depression

The U.S. stock market crash of 1929 and economic developments around the world triggered the Great Depression of the 1930s. Rural and urban folk alike suffered as tens of millions lost their jobs and livelihoods. The whole world felt the depression's impact: commerce and investment in industry fell off, social life and gender roles were upset, and the birthrate plummeted. From peasants in Asia to industrial workers in Germany and the United States, the Great Depression shattered the lives of millions.

Economic Disaster Strikes

In the 1920s, U.S. corporations and banks as well as millions of individual Americans had not only invested their money but also borrowed funds to make these investments in the soaring stock market. They used easy credit to buy shares in popular companies based on electric, automotive, and other new technologies. By the end of the decade, the Federal Reserve Bank—the nation's central bank, which controlled financial policy—tried to slow speculation by limiting credit availability and causing brokers to demand that their clients immediately pay back the money they had borrowed to buy stock. As stocks were sold to raise the necessary cash, the market collapsed. Between early October and mid-November 1929, the value of businesses listed on the U.S. stock exchange dropped from $87 billion to $30 billion. For individuals and for the economy as a whole, it was the beginning of catastrophe.

The crash helped bring on a global depression that unfolded over the course of several years. The United States had financed the international economic growth of the previous five years, so when the suddenly strapped U.S. banks cut back on loans and called in debts, they undermined businesses at home and abroad. Jobs dwindled and a decline in consumer buying slowed the world economy, including the young businesses of eastern Europe.

The Great Depression left no sector of the world economy unscathed, but government actions made the depression worse. To try to spur their economies, governments cut budgets and set high tariffs against foreign goods; these policies discouraged the consumer spending and international trade needed to spark the economy. Officials in charge of the flow of global money that fostered commerce desperately guarded their own supplies of gold. Unemployment soared: Great Britain—with its outdated textile, steel, and coal industries—had close to three million unemployed in 1932. By 1933, almost six million German workers, or about one-third of the workforce, had lost their jobs.

Agricultural prices had been declining for several years because of technological advances and abundant harvests around the world. With their incomes slashed, millions of small farmers had no money to buy the chemical fertilizers and motorized machinery they needed to remain competitive. Now creditors confiscated farms. Eastern and southern European peasants, who had pressed for the redistribution of land after World War I, could not afford to operate their newly acquired farms, and they, too, went under.

Social Effects of the Depression

The Great Depression had complex effects on society. First, life was not uniformly bleak, and despite the slump, modernization continued. Bordering English slums, one traveler in the mid-1930s noticed, were "filling stations and factories that look like exhibition buildings, giant cinemas and dance halls and cafés, bungalows with tiny garages, cocktail bars, Woolworth's [and] swimming pools." Municipal and national governments continued road construction and sanitation projects. New factories manufactured synthetic fabrics, automobiles, and electrical products such as stoves—all of them in demand. With government assistance, eastern European industry developed: Romanian industrial production, for example, increased by 55 percent between 1929 and 1939. Second, the majority of Europeans and Americans had jobs throughout the 1930s, and people with steady employment benefited from a drastic drop in prices. Service workers, managers, and business magnates often prospered. In contrast, towns with heavy industry often saw more than half the population out of work, spreading fear beyond the unemployed.

Economic catastrophe upset gender relations and weakened social ties. Women often found low-paying jobs doing laundry and cleaning house, while unemployed men sometimes stayed home all day and took over housekeeping chores. Some, however, felt that this "women's work" demeaned their masculinity, and as many women became breadwinners, albeit for low wages, men could be seen standing on street corners begging—a change in gender expectations that fed discontent. Young men in cities faced severe unemployment; with nothing to do but loiter in parks, they became ripe for movements like Nazism. Demagogues everywhere attacked democracy's failure to stop the collapse of traditional life, clearing the way for Nazi and Fascist politicians who promised to create jobs and thus restore male dignity.

Politicians drew attention to the declining birthrates. In difficult economic times, people chose to have fewer children than ever before. In addition, compulsory education, enforced more strictly after the war, reduced the income once earned by children, who now cost their families money while they went to school. Family-planning centers opened, receiving many clients, and knowledge of birth control spread across the working and lower middle classes. The situation, leaders believed, would lead to a national collapse in military readiness as "superior" peoples selfishly failed to breed and "inferior" peoples waited to take their place. This racism took a particularly violent form in eastern Europe, where political parties also blamed Jewish bankers for farm foreclosures and Jewish civil servants (of whom there were actually very few) for inadequate relief programs. Thus, population issues along with economic misery produced discord, especially in the form of ethnic hatred and anti-Semitism.

The Great Depression beyond the West

The depression spread discontent in European empires. World War I and postwar investment had produced economic growth, a rising population, and explosive urbanization in Asia, Africa, and Latin America. The depression, however, cut the demand for copper, tin, and other raw materials and for the finished products made in urban factories worldwide. Rising agricultural productivity drove down the price of foodstuffs like rice and coffee, a disaster for colonial peoples who had been forced to grow a single cash crop. Just as in Europe, however, the economic picture in the colonies was uneven. For instance, established Indian industries such as the textile business gained strength, with India no longer needing British cloth.

Economic distress led to anticolonial action. Colonial farmers withheld produce like cocoa from imperial trade, and colonial workers went on strike to protest the wage cuts imposed by imperial landlords. In India, millions of working people,

Gandhi Speaks to Women and Children   Mohandas K. Gandhi, an English-trained lawyer, was central to making the Indian independence movement a mass phenomenon. He made Indians see the superior values in their own culture in contrast to those of the West. The West, he maintained, including the United States, valued only money. Gandhi riveted his audiences, addressing women and children as well as men. (Archiv Peter Rühe / akg-images.)

including hundreds of thousands of veterans, joined with the upper-class Indians, who had organized to gain rights from Britain in the late nineteenth century. Mohandas K. Gandhi (1869–1948), called Mahatma ("great-souled"), emerged as the charismatic leader for Indian independence. Trained in England as a Western-style lawyer, Gandhi preached Hindu self-denial and rejected British love of material wealth. He wore simple clothing made of thread he had spun himself and advocated **civil disobedience**—deliberately but peacefully breaking the law—a tactic he claimed to have taken from the British suffragists and from the teachings of spiritual leaders like Jesus and Buddha. Gandhi aimed to end Indian deference to the British, who jailed him repeatedly and tried to split the Indian independence movement by promoting Hindu-Muslim antagonism. Instead, commitment to independence in India grew.

The end of the Ottoman Empire following World War I led to efforts to build modern, independent nations in the Middle East. Mustafa Kemal (1881–1938), who later took the name Atatürk ("first among Turks"), led the Turks to found an independent republic in 1923 and to craft a capitalist economy. In an effort to Westernize Turkish culture and promote the new Turkish state, Kemal moved the capital from

Constantinople to Ankara in 1923, officially changed the name Constantinople to the Turkish name Istanbul in 1930, mandated Western dress for men and women, introduced the Latin alphabet, and abolished polygamy. In 1936, Turkish women received the vote and were made eligible to serve in the parliament. Persia, which changed its name to Iran in 1935, similarly loosened the European grip on its economy by updating its government and by forcing the renegotiation of oil contracts to keep Western countries from taking the oil for virtually nothing.

Anticolonial activism thrived in French colonies, too, but the government made few concessions. Like all other imperial countries during the depression, France depended increasingly on the profits it could take from its empire; therefore, its trade with its colonies increased as trade with Europe lagged. France also depended on the growing colonial population for sheer numbers. One official estimated what colonial numbers meant for national security: "One hundred and ten million strong, France can stand up to Germany." Ho Chi Minh, founder of the Indochinese Communist Party, rallied his people to protest French imperialism, but in 1930 the French government brutally crushed the peasant uprising he led. Needing their empires, Britain and France increased the number of their troops stationed around the world. As a result, fascism spread largely unchecked in Europe during the 1930s.

> **REVIEW**   How did the Great Depression affect society and politics?

Totalitarian Triumph

Representative government collapsed in many countries under the sheer weight of social and economic crisis. After 1929, Mussolini in Italy, Stalin in the USSR, and Hitler in Germany were able to mobilize vast support for their regimes. Desperate for economic relief, many citizens supported political violence as key to restoring well-being. Scholars have classified the fascist, Nazi, and communist regimes of the 1930s as totalitarian. The term *totalitarianism* refers to highly centralized systems of government that attempt to control society and ensure obedience through a single party and police terror. Born during World War I and gaining support in its aftermath, totalitarian governments broke with liberal principles of freedom and natural rights and came to wage war on their own citizens. Still, important differences existed among totalitarian states, especially between fascist and communist states. Whereas communism denounced private ownership of property and economic inequality, fascism supported them as crucial to national might.

The Rise of Stalinism

In the 1930s, **Joseph Stalin** (1879–1953) led the transformation of the USSR from a rural society into an industrial power. Stalin ended Lenin's New Economic Policy, which had allowed individuals to profit from trade and agriculture, and in 1929 laid out the first of several bold **five-year plans** for industrializing the country. Without an end to economic backwardness, Stalin warned, "the advanced countries . . . will crush us." He thus established economic planning—that is, government direction of the economy used on both sides in World War I and increasingly implemented around the world. Between 1928 and 1940, the number of Soviet workers in industry, construction, and transport grew from 4.6 million to 12.6 million and factory output soared. Stalin's first five-year plan helped make the USSR a leading industrial nation.

A new bureaucratic elite implemented the plans, and despite limited rights to change jobs or even move from place to place, skilled workers benefited from the privileges that went along with their new industrial role. Communist officials received additional rewards such as country homes, good food, and luxurious vacations. New or unskilled workers enjoyed no such benefits, however. Newcomers from the countryside were herded into barracks or tents and subjected to dangerous factory conditions. Despite the hardships, many took pride in their new skills. "We mastered this profession—completely new to us—with great pleasure," a female lathe operator recalled. More often workers fresh from the countryside lacked the technical skills necessary to accomplish goals of the five-year plans, so official lying about productivity became part of the economic system. The attempt to turn an illiterate peasant society into an advanced industrial economy in a single decade brought intense suffering, but people tolerated hardship to achieve a communist society.

Stalin demanded more grain from peasants both to feed the urban workforce and to provide exports whose sale abroad would finance industrialization. Some peasants resisted government demands by withholding produce from the market, prompting Stalin to demand a "liquidation of the kulaks." The word *kulak*, which literally means "fist," was a negative term for prosperous peasants, but in practice it applied to anyone who opposed Stalin's plans to end independent farming. Party workers began searching villages, seizing grain, and forcing villagers to identify the kulaks among them. One Russian remembered believing the kulaks were "bloodsuckers, cattle, swine, loathsome, repulsive: they had no souls; they stank." Denounced as "enemies of the state," whole families were robbed of their possessions, left to starve, or even murdered outright. Confiscated kulak land formed the basis for the new collective farms, or kolkhoz, where the remaining peasants were forced to share facilities. Traditional peasant life was brought to a violent end.

Failure across the economy followed. Factory workers, farmers, and party officials alike were too inexperienced with advanced industrialization to meet quotas. The experiment with collectivization, combined with the murder of farmers, resulted in a drop in the grain harvest from 83 million tons in 1930 to 67 million in 1934. Soviet citizens starved. Blaming failure on "wreckers" deliberately plotting against communism, Stalin instituted **purges**—that is, state violence in the form of widespread arrests, imprisonments in labor camps, and executions—to rid society of these "villains."

The purges touched all segments of society, beginning with engineers who were condemned for causing low productivity. Beginning in 1936, the government next charged prominent Bolshevik leaders with conspiring to overthrow Soviet rule. In a series of "show trials"—trials based on trumped-up charges, fabricated evidence, and coerced confessions—Bolshevik leaders were tortured and forced to confess in court. Most of those found guilty were shot. Some of the top leaders accepted their fate, seeing the purges as good for the future of socialism. Just before his execution, one Bolshevik loyalist and former editor of the party newspaper *Pravda* wrote to Stalin praising the "great and bold political idea behind the general purge."

The spirit of purge swept through society: one woman poet described the scene in towns and cities: "Great concert and lecture halls were turned into public confessionals. . . . Beating their breasts, the 'guilty' would lament that they had 'shown political short-sightedness' and 'lack of vigilance' . . . and were full of 'rotten liberalism.'" In 1937 and 1938, military leaders were arrested and executed without public trials; some ranks were entirely wiped out. Although the massacre of military leaders appeared suicidal at a time when Hitler threatened war, thousands of high military posts became open to new talent. Stalin would not have to worry about an officer corps wedded to old ideas, as had happened in World War I. Simultaneously, the government expanded the system of prison camps, founded under Lenin, into an extensive network stretching several thousand miles from Moscow to Siberia. In the Gulag—an acronym for the government department that ran the camps—some one million died annually as a result of the insufficient food, inadequate housing, and twelve- to sixteen-hour days of crushing physical labor. Regular beatings and murders of prisoners rounded out Gulag life, which became another aspect of totalitarian violence.

In the 1930s, toleration in Soviet social life ended. The birthrate in the USSR, like that in the rest of Europe, declined rapidly. The Soviet Union needed to replace the millions of people lost since 1914. To meet this need, Stalin restricted access to birth-control information and abortion. Lavish wedding ceremonies came back into fashion, divorces became difficult to obtain, and the state made homosexuality a crime. Whereas Bolsheviks had once attacked the family as a capitalist institution, propaganda now referred to the family as a "school for socialism." At the same time, women in rural areas made gains in literacy and received improved health care. Positions in the lower ranks of the party opened to women as the purges continued, and more women were accepted into the professions.

Avant-garde experimentation in the arts also ended under Stalin. He called artists and writers "engineers of the soul" and, thus recognizing their influence, controlled their output through the Union of Soviet Writers. The union not only assigned housing, office space, equipment, and secretarial help but also determined the types of books authors could write. In return, the "comrade artist" adhered to the official style of "socialist realism," derived from the focus on the common worker as hero. Although some writers and artists went underground, others found ways to adjust their talents to the state's demands. The composer Sergei Prokofiev, for example, composed scores both for the delightful *Peter and the Wolf* and for Sergei Eisenstein's 1938 film *Alexander Nevsky*, a work that flatteringly compared Stalin to the medieval rulers of the Russian people. Aided by adaptable artists, workers, and bureaucrats, Stalin stood triumphant as the 1930s drew to a close. He was, as two different workers put it, "our beloved Leader" and "a god on earth."

Hitler's Rise to Power

A different but ultimately no less violent system emerged when **Adolf Hitler** and his followers put an end to democracy in Germany. Since the early 1920s, Hitler had harangued the German masses to destroy the Weimar Republic and drummed at a message of anti-Semitism and the rebirth of the German "race." When the Great Depression struck Germany in 1929, his Nazi Party began to outstrip its rivals in elections, thanks in part to financial support from big business. Film and press tycoon Alfred Hugenberg helped, constantly slamming the Weimar government as responsible for the disastrous economy and for the loss of German pride after World War I. Nazi supporters took to the streets, attacking young Communist groups who agitated just as loudly on behalf of the new Soviet experiment. Hugenberg's newspapers always reported such incidents as the work of Communist thugs who had assaulted blameless Nazis, thus building sympathy for the Nazis among the middle classes.

Parliamentary government practically ground to a halt during the depression, adding to unrest and the sense of disorder. The Reichstag, or German assembly, failed to approve emergency plans to improve the economy, first because its members disagreed over policies and second because Nazi and Communist deputies disrupted its sessions. Its failure to act discredited democracy among the German people. To make parliamentary government look incapable of providing basic law and order, Hitler's followers rampaged unchecked through the streets and attacked Jews, Communists, and Social Democrats. Many thought it was time to replace democratic government with a bold new leader who would take on these enemies military-style, without concern for constitutions, laws, or individual rights. It was time for war at home.

Every age group and class of people supported Hitler, though like Stalin, he especially attracted young people. In 1930, 70 percent of Nazi Party members were under forty and many thought of war as exciting, like the games they played as children during World War I. They believed that a better world was possible under Hitler's command. The largest number of supporters came from the industrial working class, but many white-collar workers and members of the lower middle class also joined the party in percentages out of proportion with their numbers in the population. The inflation that had wiped out savings left them especially bitter and open to Hitler's rhetoric. In the deepening economic crisis, the Nazi Party, which had received little more than 2 percent of the vote in 1928, won almost 20 percent in the Reichstag elections of 1930 and more than twice that in 1932.

Hitler used modern propaganda techniques to build up his following. Nazi Party members passed out thousands of recordings of Hitler's speeches, and teenagers painted their fingernails with swastikas. Nazi rallies were carefully planned displays in which Hitler captivated the crowds, who saw him as their strong, vastly superior *Führer* ("leader"). In actuality, Hitler regarded the masses with contempt, and in *Mein Kampf* he discussed how to deal with them:

> The receptivity of the great masses is very limited, their intelligence is small. In consequence of these facts, all effective propaganda must be limited to a very few points and must harp on those in slogans until the last member of the public understands what you want him to understand.

Hitler's media techniques were so successful that they continue to influence political campaigns today, particularly in the use of simple messages often filled with hate or threats.

In the 1932 elections, both Nazis and Communists did very well, making the leader of one of these two parties the logical choice as chancellor. Influential conservative politicians loathed the Communists for their opposition to private property and favored Hitler as someone they could easily control. When Hitler was invited to become chancellor in January 1933, he accepted.

The Nazification of German Politics

Millions of Germans celebrated Hitler's ascent to power. "My father went down to the cellar and brought up our best bottles of wine. . . . And my mother wept for joy," one German recalled. "Now everything will be all right." Yet instead of being easy to control, Hitler took command brutally, quickly closing down representative government with an ugly show of force. Tens of thousands of his paramilitary supporters—the Stürmabteilung (SA), or "storm troopers"—paraded through the streets with blazing torches. When the Reichstag building was gutted by fire in February 1933, Nazis used the fire as the excuse for suspending civil rights, censoring the press, and prohibiting meetings of other political parties. Hitler had always claimed to hate democracy and diverse political opinions, declaring of parties other than his own: "I have set myself one task, namely to sweep those parties out of Germany."

The storm troopers' violence silenced democratic politicians but also made those who participated in the violence feel part of a glorious whole. At the end of March, intimidated Reichstag delegates let pass the **Enabling Act**, which suspended the constitution for four years and allowed Nazi laws to take effect without parliamentary approval. Solid middle-class Germans approved the Enabling Act as a way to advance the creation of a *Volksgemeinschaft* ("people's community") of like-minded, racially pure Germans—Aryans, the Nazis named them. Heinrich Himmler headed the elite Schutzstaffel (SS), Hitler's "protection squadron," and he commanded the Reich's political police system. These and the Gestapo, the secret police force run by Hermann Goering, had vast powers to arrest people and either execute them or imprison them in concentration camps, the first of which opened at Dachau, near Munich, in March 1933. The Nazis filled it and later camps with political enemies like socialists, and then with Jews, homosexuals, and others said to be enemies of the Volksgemeinschaft.

Hitler deliberately blurred authority in the government and his political party to encourage confusion and competition. He then settled disputes, often with violence. When Ernst Roehm, leader of the SA and Hitler's longtime collaborator, called for a "second revolution" to end the business and military elites' continuing influence on top Nazis, Hitler ordered Roehm's assassination. The bloody Night of the Long Knives (June 30, 1934), during which hundreds of SA leaders and innocent civilians were killed, strengthened the support of the conservative upper classes for the Nazi regime. They saw that Hitler would deal ruthlessly with those favoring a leveling-out of social privilege. Nazism's terrorist politics served as the foundation of Hitler's Third Reich—a German empire grandly advertised as the successor to the First Reich of Charlemagne and the Second Reich of Bismarck and William II.

New economic programs, especially those putting people back to work, were crucial to the survival of Nazism. The Nazi government pursued **pump priming**— that is, stimulating the economy through government spending on tanks and airplanes and on public works programs such as building the Autobahn, or highway system. Unemployment declined from a peak of almost 6 million in 1932 to 1.6 million by 1936. The Nazi Party closed down labor unions, and government managers determined work procedures and set pay levels, rating women's jobs lower than men's regardless of the level of expertise required. Nazi programs produced large budget deficits, but Hitler was already planning to conquer and loot neighboring countries to cover the costs.

Nazi officials devised policies to control everyday life, including gender roles. In June 1933, a bill took effect that encouraged Aryans (those people defined as racially German) to marry and have children. The bill provided for loans to Aryan newlyweds, but only if the wife left the workforce. The loans were forgiven on the birth of the pair's fourth child. The ideal woman gave up her job, gave birth to many children, and completely surrendered her will to that of her husband, allowing him to feel powerful despite military defeat and economic depression. A good wife "joyfully sacrifices and fulfills her fate," as one Nazi leader explained.

The government also controlled culture, destroying the rich creativity of the Weimar years. Although 70 percent of households had radios by 1938, programs were severely censored. Books like Erich Maria Remarque's *All Quiet on the Western Front* were banned, and in May 1933 a huge book-burning ceremony rid libraries of works by Jews, socialists, homosexuals, and modernist writers. In the Hitler Youth, which boys and girls over age ten were required to join, children learned to report those adults they suspected of disloyalty to the Third Reich, even their own parents. People boasted that they could leave their bicycles out at night without fear of robbery, but their world was filled with informers—some 100,000 of them on the Nazi payroll. In general, the improved economy led many to see Hitler working an economic miracle while restoring pride in Germany and strengthening the Aryan community. For hundreds of thousands if not millions of Germans, however, Nazi rule in the 1930s brought anything but harmony and community.

Nazi Racism

The Nazis defined Jews as an inferior "race" dangerous to the superior Aryan "race" and responsible for most of Germany's problems, including defeat in World War I and the economic depression. The reasons for targeting Jews, Hitler declared in a 1938 speech, were "based on the greatest of scientific knowledge." Hitler attacked many ethnic and social groups, but he took anti-Semitism to new and frightening heights. In the rhetoric of Nazism, Jews were "vermin," "abscesses," and "Bolsheviks." They were enemies, biologically weakening the race and plotting Germany's destruction—all of which, given scientific knowledge then and now, was of course utterly false. Thus Hitler's concept of building community also included making some members of the community enemies within. By branding Jews both as evil businessmen and as working-class Bolsheviks, Nazis fashioned an enemy for the population to hate.

Nazis insisted that terms such as *Aryan* and *Jewish* (a religious category) were scientific racial classifications that could be determined by physical characteristics such as the shape of the nose. In 1935, the government enacted the **Nuremberg Laws**, legislation that deprived Jews of citizenship and prohibited marriage between Jews and other Germans. Abortions and birth-control information were readily available to enemy outcast groups, including Jews, Slavs, Sinti and Roma, and mentally or physically disabled people, but were forbidden to women classified as Aryan. In the name of improving the Aryan race, doctors helped organize the T4 project, which used carbon monoxide poisoning and other means to kill large numbers of people—200,000 handicapped and elderly—late in the 1930s. The murder of the disabled aimed to eliminate those whose "racial inferiority" endangered the Aryans. These murders prepared the way for even larger mass exterminations in the future.

Jews were forced into slave labor, evicted from their apartments, and prevented from buying most clothing and food. In 1938, a Jewish teenager, reacting to the harassment inflicted on his parents, killed a German official. In retaliation, Nazis and other Germans attacked some two hundred synagogues, smashed windows of Jewish-owned stores, ransacked apartments of known or suspected Jews, and threw more than twenty thousand Jews into prisons and camps. The night of November 9–10 became known as Kristallnacht, or the Night of Broken Glass. Faced with such relentless persecution, more than half of Germany's 500,000 Jews had emigrated by the outbreak of World War II in 1939. Their enormous emigration fees helped finance Germany's economic recovery, while neighbors and individual Nazis used anti-Semitism to justify stealing Jewish property and taking the jobs Jews were forced to leave.

REVIEW What role did violence play in the Soviet and Nazi regimes?

Democracies on the Defensive

Nazism, communism, and fascism offered bold new approaches to modern politics. These ideologies maintained that democracy was effeminate and that it wasted precious time in building consensus among citizens. Totalitarian leaders' military style made representative government and the democratic values of the United States, France, and Great Britain appear feeble—a sign that these societies were on the decline. Totalitarianism put democracies on the defensive as they aimed to restore prosperity while still upholding individual rights and the rule of law.

Confronting the Economic Crisis

As the depression wore on through the 1930s, some governments experimented with ways to solve social and economic crises in a democratic fashion. In the early days of the economic slump, U.S. president Herbert Hoover (1874–1964) had opposed direct help to the unemployed and even ordered the army to drive away jobless veterans who had marched on Washington, D.C. With unemployment close to fifteen million, Franklin Delano Roosevelt (1882–1945), the wealthy governor of New York, defeated Hoover in the presidential election of 1932 on the promise of relief and recovery. Roosevelt, or FDR as he became known, pushed through a torrent of legislation: relief for businesses, price supports for hard-pressed farmers, and public works programs for the unemployed. The Social Security Act of 1935 set up a fund to which employers and employees contributed. It provided retirement benefits for workers, unemployment insurance, and payments to dependent mothers, their children, and people with disabilities.

Programs such as these in the United States advanced a new kind of state taking shape across the West: the welfare state, in which the government guarantees a certain level of economic well-being for individuals and businesses. Although his "New Deal" angered businesspeople and the wealthy, Roosevelt maintained widespread support. Like other successful politicians of the 1930s, he was an expert at using the new mass media, especially in his broadcasts by radio. Unlike Mussolini and Hitler, however, Roosevelt's public statements promoted rather than attacked democratic rights and government. The participation of First Lady Eleanor Roosevelt sharply contrasted with the antiwoman ideology of Nazis and Fascists, and the Roosevelts insisted that human rights must not be surrendered in difficult times. "We Americans of today . . . are characters in the living book of democracy," FDR told a group of teenagers in 1939. "But we are also its author." Racial violence continued to cause great suffering in the United States, and the economy did not fully recover, yet Americans' faith in democracy was strong.

Sweden also developed a coherent program for solving economic and population problems, assigning the government a central role in promoting social welfare and economic democracy. Sweden devalued its currency to make Swedish exports more attractive on the international market, and addressed the population problem with government programs, but without the racism and coercion of Nazism. Alva Myrdal, a leading member of Sweden's parliament, believed that boosting childbirth depended both on the economy and on individual well-being. It was undemocratic, she maintained, that "the bearing of a child should mean economic distress" to parents. Acting on Myrdal's advice, the government introduced prenatal care, free childbirth in a hospital, a food relief program, and subsidized housing for large families. By the end of the decade, almost 50 percent of all mothers in Sweden received government aid, most effectively in the form of a **family allowance** to help cover the costs of raising children. Because all families — rural and urban, poor or prosperous — received these social benefits, there was widespread approval for developing a welfare state.

The most powerful democracy, the United States, had withdrawn from world leadership by refusing to participate in the League of Nations, leaving Britain and

A Fireside Chat with FDR   President Franklin Delano Roosevelt was a master of words, inspiring Americans during the depression and World War II. Aware of its growing power in making politicians look dynamic, the press never showed that Roosevelt was actually confined to a wheelchair (after being paralyzed by polio). Instead, FDR became a symbol of U.S. resolve and might. Here he addresses the nation over a radio hookup on August 23, 1938, while First Lady Eleanor Roosevelt and the president's mother, Sara, observe—a far different image from that of Hitler and Mussolini. (Keystone/Getty Images.)

France with greater responsibility for international peace and well-being than their postwar resources could sustain. When the Great Depression hit, British prime minister Ramsay MacDonald, though leader of the Labour Party, reduced payments to the unemployed, and Parliament denied unemployment insurance to women even though they had contributed to the unemployment fund. To protect jobs, the government imposed huge tariffs on imported goods, but these only discouraged a revival of international trade and did not relieve British misery. Finally, in 1933, with the economy continuing to worsen, the government began to take effective steps with massive programs of slum clearance, new housing construction, and health insurance for the needy. British leaders rejected pump-priming methods of stimulating the economy as foolish and thus resorted to them only when all else had failed.

Depression struck later in France, but the country endured a decade of public strife in the 1930s. Deputies with opposing solutions to the economic crisis frequently came to blows in the Chamber of Deputies, Parisians took to the streets to protest the government's budget cuts, and Nazi-style paramilitary groups flourished, attracting the unemployed, students, and veterans to the cause of ending representative government. In February 1934, the paramilitary groups joined Communists and other outraged citizens in riots around the parliament building. "Let's string up the deputies," chanted the crowd. "Let's beat in their faces, let's reduce them to a pulp." The right-wing enemies of democratic government, however, lacked both substantial support and a charismatic leader like Hitler or Mussolini.

Shocked into action by fascist violence, French liberals, socialists, and Communists established an antifascist coalition known as the **Popular Front**. Until that time, such a merging of groups had been impossible because Stalin had directed Communists across Europe not to cooperate with other political parties. As fascism attracted followers around the world, however, Stalin allowed Communists to join efforts to protect democracy. For just over a year in 1936–1937 and again briefly in 1938, the French Popular Front led the government, with the socialist leader Léon Blum as premier. Like the American New Dealers and the Swedish reformers, the Popular Front instituted social-welfare programs, including family subsidies. Blum appointed women to his government (though women in France were still not allowed to vote). In June 1936, the French government guaranteed workers two-week paid vacations, a forty-hour workweek, and the right to bargain collectively. Working people would long remember Blum as the man who improved their living standards and provided them with the right to vacations.

During its brief life, the Popular Front offered citizens a youthful but democratic political culture. "In 1936 everyone was twenty years old," one man recalled, evoking the atmosphere of idealism. To express their opposition to fascism, the French celebrated democratic holidays like Bastille Day with new enthusiasm. Not everyone liked the Popular Front, however. Bankers and industrialists sent their money out of the country in protest, leaving France financially strapped. "Better Hitler than Blum" was the slogan of the upper classes. Blum's government lost crucial liberal support for refusing to aid the fight against fascism in Spain because of antiwar sentiment. The collapse of the antifascist Popular Front showed the difficulties that democratic societies had facing the revival of militarism during hard economic times.

Fledgling democracies in central Europe, hit hard by the depression, also struggled for economic survival and representative government, but with little success. In 1932, Engelbert Dollfuss came to power in Austria, dismissing the parliament and ruling briefly as a dictator. Despite his authoritarian stance, Dollfuss would not submit to the Nazis, who stormed his office and assassinated him in 1934 in an unsuccessful coup attempt. In Hungary, where outrage over the Peace of Paris remained intense, a crippled economy allowed right-wing general Gyula Gömbös to take over in 1932. Gömbös reoriented his country's foreign policy toward Mussolini and Hitler. He stirred up anti-Semitism and ethnic hatreds and left considerable pro-Nazi feeling after his death in 1936. In democratic Czechoslovakia, the Slovaks, who were poorer than the urbanized Czechs, built a strong Slovak Fascist Party as the appeal of fascism grew during the Great Depression.

Cultural Visions in Hard Times

Responding to the hard times and political menace, cultural leaders in the democracies captured the spirit of everyday struggle. Some sympathized with the situations of factory workers, homemakers, and shopgirls straining to support themselves and their families; others looked to interpret the lives of an ever-growing number of unemployed. Artists portrayed the inhuman, regimented side of modern life. In 1931, French director René Clair's film *Give Us Liberty* likened the routine of prison to work on a factory assembly line. In the film *Modern Times* (1936), the Little Tramp character created by **Charlie Chaplin** is a factory worker so molded by his monotonous job that he assumes anything he can see, even a coworker's body, needs mechanical adjustment.

Media portrayed women alternately as the cause and as the cure for society's problems. *The Blue Angel* (1930), a German film starring Marlene Dietrich, contrasted a powerfully seductive woman with an impractical, bumbling professor, showing how mixed-up gender roles could destroy men—and civilization. Such films worked to strengthen fascist claims. In comedies and musicals, by comparison, heroines pulled their men out of the depths of despair. In such films as *Keep Smiling* (1938), the British comedienne Gracie Fields portrayed spunky working-class women who remained cheerful despite the challenges of living in hard times. To drive home their antifascist, pacifist, or pro-worker beliefs, writers created realistic studies of human misery and the threat of war that haunted life in the 1930s. The British writer George Orwell described the unemployed in the north of England and published an account of atrocities committed during the Spanish Civil War (1936–1939). German writer Thomas Mann, a Christian, was so outraged at Hitler's ascent to power that he went into voluntary exile. Mann's series of novels based on the Old Testament hero Joseph convey the struggle between humane values and barbarism. One volume praised Joseph's welfare state, in which the granaries were full and the rich paid taxes so that the poor might live decent lives. In *Three Guineas* (1938), one of her last works, English writer Virginia Woolf attacked militarism, poverty, and the oppression of women, claiming they were interconnected parts of a single, devastating ethos undermining Europe in the 1930s.

Scientists in research institutes and universities pointed out limits to human understanding—limits that seemed at odds with the grandiose pronouncements of dictators. Astronomer Edwin Hubble in California determined in the early 1930s that the universe was an expanding entity and thus an unpredictably changing one. Czech mathematician Kurt Gödel maintained that all mathematical systems contain some propositions that are undecidable. The German physicist Werner Heisenberg developed the uncertainty, or indeterminacy, principle in physics. Scientific observation of atomic behavior, according to this theory, itself disturbs the atom and thereby makes precise formulations impossible. Even scientists, Heisenberg asserted, had to settle for statistical probability. Approximation, probability, and limits to understanding were not concepts that military dictators lived by.

Religious leaders helped foster a spirit of resistance to dictatorship among the faithful. Some prominent clergymen hoped for a re-Christianization of ordinary people so that they might choose religious values rather than fascist ones. The Swiss theologian Karl Barth encouraged opposition to the Nazis, teaching that religious people had to take seriously biblical calls for resistance to oppression. In his 1931 address to the world on social issues, Pope Pius XI (r. 1922–1939) condemned the failure of modern societies to provide their citizens with a decent, moral life. To critics, the proclamation seemed an endorsement of the heavy-handed intervention of the fascists. In Germany, nonetheless, German Catholics opposed Hitler, and religious commitment inspired many other individuals to oppose the rising tide of fascism and protect Jews and other fellow citizens whose lives were now threatened.

> **REVIEW** How did the democracies' responses to the twin challenges of economic depression and the rise of fascism differ from those of totalitarian regimes?

The Road to Global War

The economic crash intensified competition among the major powers and made external colonies more important than ever. Governments did not let up on the collection of taxes in the colonies. As Britain, France, and other imperial powers guarded their holdings, Hitler, Mussolini, and Japan's military leaders believed that their nation's destiny was to rule a far larger territory. At first, statesmen in Britain and France hoped that sanctions imposed by the League of Nations would stop these new aggressors. Other people, still traumatized by memories of the past war, wanted to turn a blind eye both to expansionism and to the fascist attack on the Spanish republic.

A Surge in Global Imperialism

The global imperialism of the 1930s ultimately produced a thoroughly global war. The French, Dutch, British, and Belgians increased their control over their colonies, while in Palestine European Jews continued to arrive and claim the area from local peoples especially as Hitler enacted his harsh anti-Jewish policies in 1933. Japan's military and business leaders longed to control more of the Asian continent and saw China, the Soviet Union, and the Western powers as obstacles to the empire's prosperity and the fulfillment of its destiny.

Japan suffered from a weak monarchy in the person of Hirohito, just twenty-five years old when he became emperor in 1926, which led military and other groups to seek control of the government. Nationalists encouraged these leaders to pursue an expanded empire as key to pulling agriculture and small business from the depths of economic depression. A belief in racial superiority and in the right to take the lands of "inferior" peoples led the Japanese army to swing into action. In 1931, Japanese officers blew up a train in the Chinese province of Manchuria, where Japanese businesses had invested heavily. The army made the explosion look like a Chinese plot and used it as an excuse to take over the territory, set up a puppet government, and push farther into China. Amid journalistic calls in Japan for aggressive expansion, Japan continued to attack China from 1931 on, angering the United States, on which Japan depended for natural resources and markets. Advocating Asian conquest as part of Japan's "divine mission," the military solidified its influence in the government. By 1936–1937, Japan was spending 47 percent of its budget on arms.

The situation in East Asia affected international politics. The League of Nations condemned the invasion of Manchuria but imposed no sanctions. The league's condemnation outraged Japanese citizens and goaded the government to ally with Hitler and Mussolini. In 1937, Japan attacked China again, justifying its offensive as a first step toward liberating the region from Western imperialism. Hundreds of thousands of Chinese were massacred in the Rape of Nanjing—an atrocity so named because of the Japanese soldiers' brutality, especially toward girls and women. President Roosevelt immediately announced a U.S. embargo on the exportation of airplane parts to Japan and later drastically cut the flow of the crucial raw materials that supplied Japanese industry. Nonetheless, the Western powers, including the Soviet Union, did not effectively resist Japan's territorial expansion.

Like Japanese leaders, Mussolini and Hitler called their countries "have-nots" and demanded land and resources more in line with the other imperial powers. Mussolini threatened "permanent conflict" to expand Italy's borders. Hitler's agenda included gaining **Lebensraum** ("living space"), to be taken from the "inferior" Slavic peoples and Bolsheviks, who would be moved to Siberia or would serve as slaves. The two dictators portrayed themselves as peace-loving men who resorted to extreme measures only to benefit their country and humanity. Their anticommunism appealed to statesmen across the West, and Hitler's anti-Semitism also had widespread support.

Germany and Italy now moved to plunder other countries openly. In the autumn of 1933, Hitler announced Germany's withdrawal from the League of Nations. In 1935, he loudly rejected the clauses of the Treaty of Versailles that limited German military strength. Germany had been rearming in secret for years, but now it started doing so openly. Mussolini chose in 1935 to invade Ethiopia, one of the few African states not overwhelmed by European imperialism. "The Roman legionnaires are again on the march," one soldier exulted. The poorly equipped Ethiopians resisted, but their capital, Addis Ababa, fell in the spring of 1936. Although the League of Nations voted to impose sanctions against Italy, Britain and France opposed an embargo with teeth in it—that is, one including oil—and thus kept the sanctions from being effective while also suggesting a lack of resolve to fight aggression. In March 1936, Hitler defiantly sent his troops into what was supposed to be a permanently demilitarized zone in the Rhineland bordering France. The inhabitants greeted the arrival with wild enthusiasm, and the French, whose security was most endangered by this action, protested to the League of Nations instead of occupying the region, as they had done in the Ruhr in 1923. The British simply accepted the German military move. The Italian and German dictators thus appeared as powerful heroes, creating, in Mussolini's muscular phrase, a dynamic "Rome–Berlin Axis." Next to them, the politicians of France and Great Britain looked timid and weak.

The Spanish Civil War, 1936–1939

Spain seemed to be headed toward democracy when, in 1931, Spanish republicans overthrew the monarchy and the dictatorship that ruled in its name. For centuries, the Spanish state had backed the domination of large landowners and the Catholic clergy in the countryside. These ruling elites kept an impoverished peasantry in their grip, making Spain a country of economic extremes. People in industrial cities reacted enthusiastically to the end of the dictatorship and began debating the course of change, with constitutionalists, anarchists, Communists, and other splinter groups disagreeing on how to create a democratic nation. For republicans, the air was electric with promise. As one woman recalled: "We saw a backward country suddenly blossoming out into a modern state. We saw peasants living like decent human beings. We saw men allowed freedom of conscience."

With little political experience, however, the republic had a hard time putting in place a political program that would gain support in the countryside. Instead of building popular loyalty by enacting land reform, the various antimonarchist factions struggled among themselves to shape the new government. They wanted political and economic modernization, but they failed to mount a unified effort against their reactionary opponents. In 1936, growing monarchist opposition frightened the pro-republican forces into forming a Popular Front coalition to win elections and prevent the republic from collapsing.

In response to the Popular Front victory, a group of army officers led by General **Francisco Franco** (1892–1975) staged an uprising against the republic in 1936. The rebels, who included monarchist landowners, the clergy, and the fascist Falange Party, soon had the help of fascists in other parts of Europe. Pro-republican citizens — male and female — fought back by forming armed volunteer units. In their minds, citizen armies symbolized republicanism, while professional troops followed the aristocratic rebels against democracy. As civil war gripped the country, the republicans generally held Madrid, Barcelona, and other commercial and industrial areas. The right-wing rebels took the agricultural west and south (Map 26.1).

Spain became a training ground for World War II. Hitler and Mussolini sent military personnel in support of Franco, gaining the opportunity to practice the terror bombing of civilians. In 1937, German planes attacked the town of Guernica, mowing down civilians in the streets. This useless slaughter inspired Pablo Picasso's memorial mural to the dead, *Guernica* (1937), in which the intense suffering is

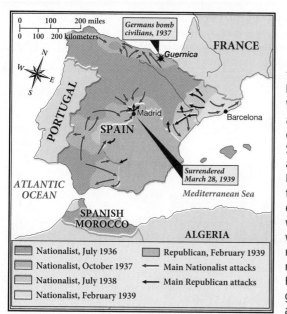

MAP 26.1   The Spanish Civil War, 1936–1939   Republican and antirepublican forces bitterly fought one another to determine whether Spain would be a democracy or an authoritarian state. Germany and Italy sent military assistance to the rebels, notably airplanes to experiment with bombing civilians, while volunteers from around the world arrived to fight for the republic. Defeating the ill-organized republican groups, General Francisco Franco instituted a pro-fascist government that sent many to jail and into exile.

starkly displayed. The Spanish republic appealed everywhere for assistance, but only the Soviet Union answered. Britain and France refused to provide aid despite the outpouring of popular support for the cause of democracy. Instead, a few thousand volunteers from a variety of countries—including many students, journalists, and artists—fought for the republic. "Spain was the place to stop fascism," these volunteers believed. The aid Franco received helped his professional armies defeat the republicans in 1939, strengthening the cause of military authoritarianism in Europe. Tens of thousands fled Franco's brutal revenge; remaining critics found themselves jailed or worse.

Hitler's Conquest of Central Europe, 1938–1939

The next step toward World War II was Germany's annexation of Austria in 1938. Many Austrians had actually wished for a merger, or *Anschluss*, with Germany after the Paris peace settlement stripped them of their empire. So Hitler's troops simply entered Austria, and the joy of Nazi sympathizers there made the Anschluss appear an example of the Wilsonian idea of self-determination by unifying so-called Aryan peoples into one nation. The Nazi seizure of Austria's gold marked an important step in financing German expansion, as Austria was declared a German province. Nazi thugs ruled once-cosmopolitan Vienna; an observer later commented on the scene: "University professors were obliged to scrub the streets with their naked hands, pious white-bearded Jews were dragged into the synagogue by hooting youths and forced to do knee-exercises and to shout 'Heil Hitler' in chorus." Nazis gained additional

MAP 26.2 The Growth of Nazi Germany, 1933–1939 German expansion was rapid and surprising, as Hitler's forces and Nazi diplomacy achieved the annexation of several new states of central and eastern Europe. Although committed to defending the independence of these states through the League of Nations, French and British diplomats were more concerned with satisfying Hitler in the mistaken belief that doing so would prevent his claiming more of Europe. In the process, Hitler acquired the human and material resources of adjacent countries to support his Third Reich. What is the relationship between Germany's expansion during the 1930s and the terms of the Treaty of Versailles after World War I?

support in Austria by attacking the stubborn problem of unemployment—especially among the young and out-of-work rural migrants to the cities. Factories sprang up overnight, and German policies eliminated some of the pain Austrians had suffered when their empire had been reduced to a small country after World War I.

With Austria firmly in his grasp, Hitler turned next to Czechoslovakia and its rich resources. Conquering this democracy looked more difficult, however, because Czechoslovakia had a large army, strong border defenses, and efficient armament factories. The Nazi propaganda machine swung into action, accusing Czechoslovakia of persecuting its German minority. By October 1, 1938, Hitler warned, Czechoslovakia would have to grant autonomy (amounting to Nazi rule) to the German-populated border region, the Sudetenland, or face German invasion.

Hitler gambled correctly that the other Western powers would choose **appeasement**, the prevention of conflict by making concessions for grievances (in this case, the treatment of Germany in the Treaty of Versailles). As the October deadline approached, British prime minister Neville Chamberlain, French premier Edouard Daladier, and Mussolini met with Hitler at Munich and agreed not to oppose Germany's claim to the Sudetenland. Appeasement was widely seen as positive at the time, and the Munich Pact prompted Chamberlain to announce that he had secured "peace in our time." Having portrayed himself as a man of peace, Hitler waited until March 1939 to invade the rest of Czechoslovakia (Map 26.2). Whether the Munich Pact bought Hitler time to build his army and gave him the green light for further aggression or whether it wisely provided France and Britain precious time to beef up their own armies is heatedly debated even today.

Stalin, excluded from the Munich deliberations, saw that the democracies were not going to fight to protect eastern Europe. He took action. To the astonishment of people in the West, on August 23, 1939, Germany and the USSR signed a non-aggression agreement. The **Nazi-Soviet Pact** provided that if one country became embroiled in war, the other country would remain neutral. Moreover, the two dictators secretly agreed to divide Poland and the Baltic states—Latvia, Estonia, and Lithuania—at some future date. The Nazi-Soviet Pact ensured that, should war come, the democracies would be fighting a Germany that feared no attack on its eastern borders. The pact also allowed Stalin extra time to reconstitute his officer corps, which had been wiped out by the purges. In the belief that Great Britain and perhaps even France would continue not to resist, the Nazis now targeted Poland.

> **REVIEW** How did the aggression of Japan, Germany, and Italy create the conditions for global war?

World War II, 1939–1945

World War II opened when Hitler launched an all-out attack on Poland on September 1, 1939. In contrast to 1914, no jubilation in Berlin accompanied the invasion; when Britain and France declared war two days later, the mood in those nations was similarly grim. Although Japan, Italy, and the United States did not join the battle immediately, their eventual participation spread the fighting and mobilized civilians around the world. By the time World War II ended in 1945, millions were starving; countries lay in ruins; and unparalleled atrocities, including genocide, had killed six million Jews and six million Slavs, Sinti and Roma, homosexuals, and other civilian targets of fascism.

The German Onslaught

German forces quickly defeated the ill-equipped Polish troops by launching a **Blitzkrieg** ("lightning war"), in which they concentrated airplanes, tanks, and motorized infantry with overpowering force and speed. Blitzkrieg suggested to Germans at home that the costs of gaining Lebensraum would be low. On September 17, 1939, the Soviets invaded Poland from the east. By the end of the month, the victors had divided the country according to the Nazi-Soviet Pact. Nazi propagandists frightened Germans into supporting the conflict because of the "warlike menace" of world Jewry that supposedly threatened the nation's very existence.

In April 1940, Blitzkrieg crushed Denmark and Norway; the battles of Belgium, the Netherlands, and France followed in May and June. On June 5, Mussolini, eyeing future gains for Italy, invaded France from the southeast. The French defense and its British allies could not withstand the German onslaught. Trapped on the beaches of Dunkirk in northern France, 370,000 French and British soldiers were rescued by an improvised fleet of naval ships, fishing boats, and pleasure craft. The French government surrendered on June 22, 1940, leaving Germany to rule the northern half of the country, including Paris. In the south, named Vichy France after the spa town where the government sat, the aged World War I hero Henri Philippe Pétain was allowed to govern because of his and his administration's pro-Nazi values. Stalin used the diversion in western Europe to annex the Baltic states.

Britain now stood alone, installing as prime minister Winston Churchill (1874–1965), an early campaigner for resistance to Hitler. As Hitler ordered the bombardment of Britain in the summer of 1940, Churchill rallied the nation by radio to protect the ideals of liberty with "blood, toil, tears, and sweat." In the battle of Britain—or Blitz, as the British called it—the German Luftwaffe ("air force") bombed monuments, public buildings, weapons depots, and industry. In response, Britain poured resources into its highly successful code-breaking group called Ultra, further development of radar, and air weaponry, outproducing the Germans by 50 percent.

By the fall of 1940, German air losses compelled Hitler to abandon his plan for a naval invasion of Britain. Forcing Hungary, Romania, and Bulgaria to join the Axis powers, Germany gained access to more food, oil, and other resources. He then made his fatal decision to break the Nazi-Soviet Pact and attack the Soviet Union—the "center of judeobolshevism," he called it. In June 1941, three million German and other troops penetrated Soviet lines along a two-thousand-mile front; by July, they had rolled to within two hundred miles of Moscow. Using a strategy of rapid encirclement, German troops killed, captured, or wounded more than half the 4.5 million Soviet soldiers.

Amid success, Hitler blundered. Considering himself a military genius and the Slavic people inferior, he proposed attacking Leningrad, the Baltic states, and Ukraine simultaneously, even though his generals wanted to concentrate on

Moscow. Driven by Stalin and local party members, the Soviet people fought back. The onset of winter turned Nazi soldiers into frostbitten wretches because Hitler had feared that equipping his army for Russian conditions would suggest to civilians that a long campaign lay ahead. Convinced of a quick victory in the USSR, he switched German production from making tanks and artillery to making battleships and airplanes for war beyond the Soviet Union. Consequently, Germany's poorly supplied armies fell victim not only to the weather but also to a shortage of equipment. As the war became worldwide, Germany still had an inflated view of its own power.

War Expands: The Pacific and Beyond

The militarist Japanese government decided to settle matters once and for all with the United States, which was blocking Japan's access to technology and resources in an attempt to stop its expansionism. On December 7, 1941, it launched an all-out attack on the United States at Pearl Harbor in Hawaii and then decimated a fleet of airplanes in the Philippines. Roosevelt immediately summoned the U.S. Congress to declare war on Japan. By the spring of 1942, the Japanese had conquered Guam, the Philippines, Malaya, Burma, Indonesia, Singapore, and much of the southwestern Pacific. Like Hitler's early conquests, the Japanese victories strengthened the military's confidence: "The era of democracy is finished," the foreign minister announced, marketing Emperor Hirohito as the monarch who would liberate Asians everywhere.

Germany quickly declared war on the United States; Mussolini followed suit. The United States was not prepared for a prolonged struggle at the time, partly because isolationist sentiment remained strong. Its armed forces numbered only 1.6 million, and no plan existed for producing the necessary guns, tanks, and airplanes. In addition, the United States and the Soviet Union mistrusted each other. Yet despite these obstacles to cooperation, Hitler's four enemies came together in the Grand Alliance of Great Britain, the Free French (an exile government in London led by General Charles de Gaulle), the Soviet Union, and the United States along with twenty other countries—known collectively as the Allies. Against the Axis powers—Germany, Italy, and Japan—the Allies had advantages: greater manpower and resources, access to goods from global empires, and Britain's traditional naval strength and its experience in combat on many continents. Allied leaders worked hard to wage effective war against the Axis powers, whose rulers were fanatically committed to global conquest at any price.

The War against Civilians

Far more civilians than soldiers died in World War II. The Axis powers and Allies alike bombed cities to destroy civilian will to resist: the Allied firebombings of Dresden and Tokyo killed tens of thousands of civilians, though Axis attacks were more widespread. The British people, not British soldiers, were the target of the battle of Britain, and in Poland and Ukraine, the Nazi SS murdered hundreds of thousands of Polish citizens. Confiscated Polish land and homes were given to "racially pure"

Aryans from Germany and other central European countries. In the name of collectivization, Soviet forces perpetuated the same violence in the same area of eastern Europe, which has been called the "Bloodlands" for the millions who died in the battle for land and food.

Nazi and Soviet leaders saw literate people in the conquered areas as leading members of the civil society that they wanted to destroy. A ploy of the Nazis was to test captured people's reading skills, suggesting that those who could read would be given clerical jobs while those who could not would be relegated to hard labor. Those who could read, however, were lined up and shot. Because many in the German army initially rebelled at this inhuman mission, special Gestapo forces took up the charge of herding their victims into woods, to ravines, or even against town walls where they would be shot en masse. The Japanese did the same in China, in Southeast Asia, and on the islands in the Pacific. The number of casualties in China alone has been estimated at thirty million, with untold millions murdered elsewhere.

On the eve of war in 1939, Hitler had predicted "the destruction of the Jewish race in Europe." The Nazis' initial plan for reducing the Jewish population included driving Jews into urban ghettos and making them live on minimal rations until they died of starvation or disease. There was also direct murder. Around Soviet towns, the Nazis killed ten thousand or more at a time, often with the help of local anti-Semitic volunteers. In Jedwabne, Poland, some eight hundred citizens on their own initiative beat and burned their Jewish neighbors to death and took their property — evidence that the Holocaust was not simply a Nazi initiative. However, the "Final Solution" — the Nazis' plan to murder all of Europe's Jews systematically — was not yet fully under way.

An organized, technological system for transporting Jews to extermination sites had taken shape by the fall of 1941 and was formalized at a meeting in Wannsee, Germany, in January 1942. Although Hitler did not attend the meeting at Wannsee, his responsibility for the Holocaust is clear: he discussed the Final Solution's progress, issued oral directives for it, and had made violent anti-Semitism a basis for Nazism from the beginning. Scientists, doctors, lawyers, government workers, and Nazi officials took initiative in making the Holocaust work. Six camps in Poland were developed specifically for the purposes of mass murder (Map 26.3). Using techniques developed in the T4 project, which killed disabled and elderly people, the camp at Chelmno initially gassed Christian Poles and Soviet prisoners of war. Specially designed crematoria for the mass burning of corpses started functioning in 1943. By then, Auschwitz had the capacity to burn 1.7 million bodies per year. About 60 percent of new arrivals — particularly children, women, and old people — were selected for immediate murder in the gas chambers; the other 40 percent labored until, utterly used up, they too were gassed.

Victims from all over Europe were sent to extermination camps. In the ghettos of European cities, councils of Jewish leaders, such as the one in Amsterdam where Etty Hillesum worked, often chose those to be sent for "resettlement in the east" — a phrase used to mask the Nazis' true plans. For weakened, poorly armed ghetto

MAP 26.3   Concentration Camps and Extermination Sites in Europe This map shows the major extermination sites and concentration camps in Europe, but the entire continent was dotted with thousands of lesser camps to which the victims of Nazism were transported. Some of these lesser camps were merely way stations on the path to ultimate extermination. In focusing on the major camps, historians often lose sight of the ways in which evidence of deportation and extermination blanketed Europe.

inhabitants, open resistance meant certain death. When Jews bravely rose up against their Nazi captors in Warsaw in 1943, they were mercilessly butchered. The Nazis also took pains to cloak the purpose of the extermination camps. Bands played to greet incoming trainloads of victims, and survivors later noted that the purpose of the camps was so unthinkable that potential victims could not begin to imagine their fate. Those not chosen for immediate murder had their heads shaved and were disinfected. So began life in "a living hell," as one survivor wrote.

The camps were scenes of struggle for life in the face of torture and death. Overworked inmates usually received less than five hundred calories per day, far below the minimum needed to keep an adult in good health. As diseases swept through the camps, doctors performed unbelievably cruel medical experiments with no anesthesia on pregnant women, twins, and other innocent people in the name of advancing "racial science." Despite the harsh conditions, however, some people maintained their spirit: prisoners forged new friendships, and women in particular observed religious holidays and celebrated birthdays. Thanks to those sharing a bread ration, wrote the Auschwitz survivor Primo Levi, "I managed not to forget that I myself was a man." In the end, six million Jews, the vast majority from eastern Europe—along with an estimated five to six million Slavs, Sinti and Roma (often called Gypsies), homosexuals, and countless others—were deliberately murdered in the Nazi genocidal fury. This vast crime perpetrated by apparently civilized people still shocks and outrages the world.

Children in Concentration Camps, c. 1945   When Germany undertook the Holocaust and ethnic cleansing, children of outcast groups were generally automatic victims, unless they seemed useful for medical experiments. Great numbers of children died of starvation in occupied and besieged areas or were killed when the Germans exacted reprisals for acts of resistance. Teenagers were used as slave laborers; the children in this picture may be older than they look because of starvation. (© Fratelli Alinari Museum Collections-Favrod Collection, Florence, Italy/The Image Works.)

Societies at War

Even more than World War I, World War II depended on industrial productivity. The Axis countries remained at a disadvantage throughout the war despite their initial conquests, for the Allies consistently outproduced them. For example, in 1942, Great Britain and Russia produced collectively nearly 50,000 aircraft while Germany produced around 15,000. Even as Germany occupied the Soviet industrial heartland and besieged many of its cities, the USSR increased its production of weapons. Both Japan and Germany made the most of their lower output, especially in the use of Blitzkrieg. The use of vast quantities of stolen resources and of millions of slave laborers also helped, but both Japan's and Germany's belief in their racial superiority prevented them from accurately assessing the capabilities of an enemy they held in contempt.

Allied governments were overwhelmingly successful in mobilizing civilians, especially women. In Germany and Italy, where government policy particularly exalted motherhood and kept women from good jobs, officials began to realize that women were desperately needed in the workforce. Nazis changed their propaganda to emphasize the need for everyone to take a job, but their messages were not effective enough to convince women to take the low-paid work offered them. In contrast, Soviet women constituted more than half their nation's workforce by war's end, and 800,000 volunteered for the military, even serving as pilots. As the Germans invaded, Soviet citizens moved entire factories eastward. In a dramatic about-face, the government encouraged devotion to the Russian Orthodox church as a way of boosting patriotism.

Even more than in World War I, civilians faced propaganda, censorship, and government regulation. People were glued to their radios for war news, but much of it was tightly controlled. The totalitarian powers often withheld news of military defeats and large casualty numbers in order to keep civilian support. Wartime films focused on aviation heroes and infantrymen as well as on the self-sacrificing workingwomen and wives on the home front. In most countries, it was simply taken for granted that civilians would not receive what they needed to survive in good health. Soviet children and old people were at the greatest risk, a high proportion of them among the one million residents who starved to death during the siege of Leningrad. Government specialists regulated the production and distribution of food, clothing, and household products, all of which were rationed and generally of lower quality than before the war. With governments standardizing such items as food, clothing, and entertainment, World War II furthered the development of mass society.

On both sides, propaganda and government policies promoted racial thinking. Since the early 1930s, the German government had published ugly caricatures of Jews and Slavs. Similarly, Allied propaganda during the war depicted Germans as perverts and the "Japs" as insectlike fanatics. The U.S. government forced citizens of Japanese origin into internment camps, while Muslims and minority ethnic groups in the Soviet Union were uprooted and relocated away from the front lines as potential Nazi collaborators. As in World War I, both sides drew colonized peoples into the war through forced labor and conscription into the armies. Some two million Indian men served the Allied cause, as did several hundred thousand Africans. As the Japanese swept through the Pacific and parts of East Asia, they, too, conscripted local men into their army.

From Resistance to Allied Victory

Resistance to fascism began early in the war. Having escaped from France to London in 1940, General Charles de Gaulle directed from a distance the Free French government and its forces—a mixed organization of troops of colonized Asians and Africans, soldiers who had escaped via Dunkirk, and volunteers from other occupied countries. Less well-known than the Free French, resisters in occupied Europe fought in Communist-dominated groups, some of which gathered information to aid the Allied invasion of the continent. Rural groups called partisans not only planned assassinations of traitors and German officers but also bombed bridges, rail lines, and military facilities. Although the Catholic church supported Mussolini in Italy and endorsed the Croatian puppet government's slaughter of a million Serbs, Catholic and Protestant clergy and their parishioners were among those who set up resistance networks, often hiding Jews and fugitives. The Polish resistance attacked imported German settlers; individuals such as Swedish diplomat Raoul Wallenberg saved thousands of Jews.

People also fought back through everyday activities. Homemakers circulated newsletters urging demonstrations at prisons where civilians were detained. In central Europe, hikers smuggled Jews and others over dangerous mountain passes. Danish villagers created vast escape networks, and countless thousands across Europe volunteered to be part of escape routes. Women resisters used stereotypes to good advantage, often carrying weapons to assassination sites in the correct belief that Nazis would rarely suspect or search them. "Naturally the Germans didn't think that a woman could have carried a bomb," explained one Italian resister. Resistance kept alive the liberal ideal of individual action in the face of tyranny.

Both subtle and dramatically visible resistance took place in the fascist countries. Couples in Germany and Italy limited family size in defiance of pro-birth policies. In July 1944, a group of German military officers, fearing their country's military humiliation, tried but failed to assassinate Hitler—one of several such attempts. Wounded and shaken, Hitler mercilessly tortured and killed hundreds of conspirators, innocent friends, and family members. Some ask whether the assassination attempt came too late in the war to count as resistance. However, some five million Germans alone, and millions more of other nationalities, lost their lives in the last nine months of the war. Had Hitler died even as late as the summer of 1944, the relief to humanity would have been considerable.

Amid civilian resistance, Allied forces turned the frontline war against the Axis powers beginning with the battle of Stalingrad in 1942–1943 (Map 26.4). The German army sought Soviet oil through capturing this city. Months of ferocious house-to-house fighting ended when the Soviet army captured the ninety thousand German survivors in February 1943. Meanwhile, the British army in North Africa held against German troops under Erwin Rommel, a skilled practitioner of the new kind of mobile warfare. He aimed to capture the Suez Canal and thus gain access to Middle Eastern oil, but the Allies' code-breaking capacity ultimately helped them block the capture of Egypt and take Morocco and Algeria in the fall of 1942. After driving Rommel out of Africa, the Allies landed in Sicily in July 1943, provoking a German invasion. The slow, bitter fight for the Italian peninsula lasted until April 1945, when Allied forces finally triumphed. After Italy's liberation, partisans shot Mussolini and his mistress and hung their dead bodies for public display.

The victory at Stalingrad marked the beginning of the Soviet drive westward, during which the Soviets bore the brunt of the Nazi war machine. From the air, Britain and the United States bombed German cities, but it was an invasion from the west that Stalin wanted from his allies. Finally, on June 6, 1944, known as D-Day, the combined Allied forces, under the command of U.S. general Dwight

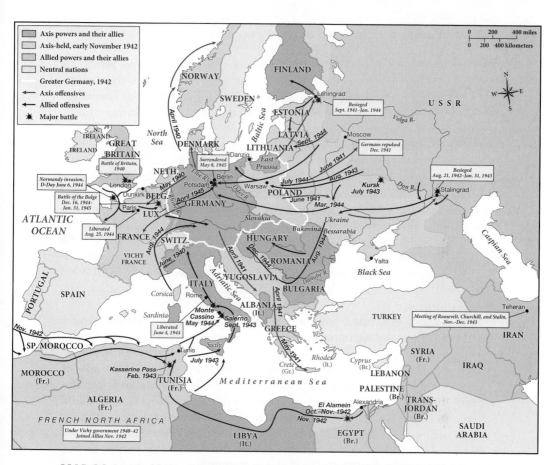

MAP 26.4 World War II in Europe and Africa World War II inflicted massive loss of life and destruction of property on civilians, armies, and all the infrastructure—including factories, equipment, and agriculture—needed to wage total war. Thus, the war swept the European continent as well as areas in Africa colonized by or allied with the major powers. Ultimately the Allies crushed the Axis powers by moving from east, west, and south to inflict a total defeat.

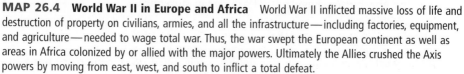

Eisenhower, attacked the heavily fortified French beaches of Normandy and then fought their way through the German-held territory of western France. In late July, Allied forces broke through German defenses and a month later helped liberate Paris. The Soviets meanwhile recaptured the Baltic states and entered Poland, pausing for desperately needed supplies. The Germans took advantage of the pause to put down an uprising of the Polish resistance in August 1944, which gave the Soviets a freer hand in eastern Europe after the war. Facing more than twice as many troops as on the western front, the Soviet army took Bulgaria and Romania at the end of August, then Hungary in 1945. British, Canadian, U.S., and other

Allied forces simultaneously fought their way eastward to join the Soviets in squeezing the Third Reich to its final defeat.

As the Allies advanced, Hitler decided that Germans deserved to perish. He thus refused all negotiations that might have spared them further death and destruction. As the Soviet army took Berlin, Hitler and his wife, Eva Braun, committed suicide. Although many soldiers remained loyal to the Third Reich, Germany finally surrendered on May 8, 1945.

The Allies had followed a "Europe first" strategy in conducting the war. In 1940 and 1941, Japan had ousted the Europeans from many colonial holdings in Asia, but the Allies turned the tide in 1942 by destroying some of Japan's formidable navy in battles at Midway Island and Guadalcanal (Map 26.5). Allied forces stormed one Pacific island after another, gaining bases from which to cut off the importation of supplies and to launch bombers toward Japan itself. Short of men and weapons, the Japanese military resorted to kamikaze tactics, in which pilots deliberately crashed their planes into Allied ships, killing themselves in the process. In response, the Allies stepped up their bombing of major cities, killing more than 100,000 civilians in their spring 1945 firebombing of Tokyo. The Japanese leadership still ruled out surrender.

Meanwhile a U.S.-based international team of more than 100,000 workers, including scientists and technicians, had been working on the Manhattan Project, the code name for a secret project to develop an atomic bomb. The Japanese practice of dying almost to the man rather than surrendering caused Allied military leaders to calculate that defeating Japan might cost the lives of hundreds of thousands of Allied soldiers (and even more Japanese). On August 6 and 9, 1945, the U.S. government therefore unleashed the new atomic weapons on Hiroshima and Nagasaki, killing 140,000 people instantly; tens of thousands later died from burns, wounds, and other afflictions. Hardliners in the Japanese military wanted to continue the war, but on August 14, 1945, Japan surrendered.

An Uneasy Postwar Settlement

Unlike World War I, this war saw neither a celebrated peace conference nor a formal agreement among all the Allies about the final terms for peace. Instead, wartime agreements among members of the Grand Alliance about the future reflected their differences while aiming to guide the postwar years. In 1941, Roosevelt and Churchill crafted the Atlantic Charter, which condemned aggression, endorsed collective security, and supported the right of all people to choose their governments. Not only did the Allies back these ideals, but so did colonized peoples to whom, Churchill said, the charter was not meant to apply. In October 1944, Churchill and Stalin agreed on the postwar distribution of territories. The Soviet Union would control Romania and Bulgaria, Britain would control Greece, and they would jointly oversee Hungary and Yugoslavia. These agreements went against Roosevelt's faith in collective security, self-determination, and open doors in trade. In February 1945, the "Big Three" — Roosevelt, Churchill, and Stalin — met in the Crimean town of Yalta. Roosevelt advocated for the formation of the United

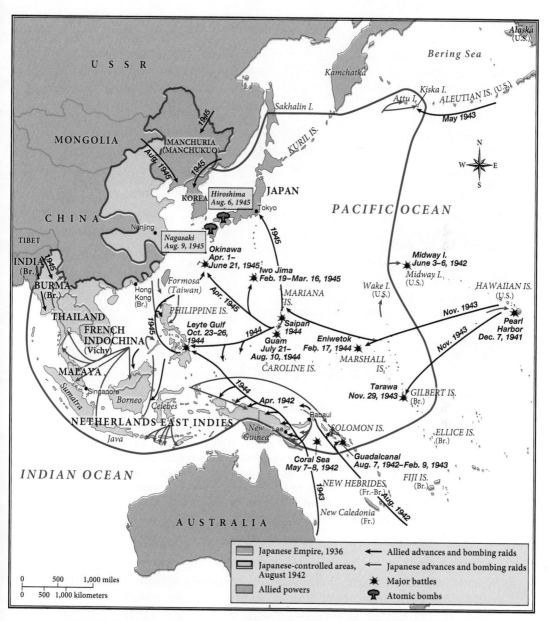

MAP 26.5 World War II in the Pacific   As in Europe, the early days of World War II gave the advantage to the Axis power Japan as it took the offensive in conquering islands in the Pacific and territories in Asia—many of them colonies of European states. Britain countered by mobilizing a vast Indian army, while the United States, after the disastrous losses at Pearl Harbor and in the Philippines, gradually gained the upper hand by costly assaults, island by island. The Japanese strategy of fighting to the last person instead of surrendering when a loss was in sight was one factor in President Truman's decision to drop the atomic bomb in August 1945.

Hiroshima, 1945   This photo captures what little remained of the city of Hiroshima after the United States dropped an atomic bomb on August 6, 1945. Without the bomb, the U.S. military foresaw a long and costly struggle to defeat Japan, given that country's overall strategy of fighting to the last person and in the process inflicting the maximum number of enemy casualties. Some claim that the United States dropped the bomb to menace the Soviet Union, its opponent in the cold war that was just beginning. Others point to the fact that no such bomb was ever dropped on a Caucasian population. (The Everett Collection, Inc.)

Nations to replace the League of Nations as a global peace mechanism, and he supported future Soviet influence in Korea, Manchuria, and the Sakhalin and Kuril Islands. The last meeting of the Allied leaders, with President Harry S. Truman replacing Roosevelt, who had died in April, took place at Potsdam, Germany, in the summer of 1945. At Potsdam, the leaders agreed to give the Soviets control of eastern Poland, to transfer a large stretch of eastern Germany to Poland, and to finalize a temporary four-way occupation of Germany that would include France as one of the supervising powers.

These agreements could hardly undo the war's grim legacy. The Great Depression had inflicted global suffering, while the Second World War left up to 100 million dead, more than 50 million refugees without homes, and one of the most abominable moral legacies in human history. Conscripted into armies or into labor camps for war production, colonial peoples in Vietnam, Algeria, India, and elsewhere were in full rebellion or close to it. The war weakened and even destroyed standards of decency and truth. Democratic Europe had succumbed to continuous wartime values, and it was this Europe that George Orwell captured in his novel *1984* (1949). Orwell had worked for the wartime Ministry of Information (called the Ministry of Truth in the novel) and made up phony war news and threats for civilian audiences. Truth hardly mattered, and words changed meaning during the war to sound better: *battle fatigue* substituted for *insanity*, and *liberating* a country could mean invading it and slaughtering its civilians. Hungry, careworn people walking in ragged clothing along grimy streets characterized both wartime London and Orwell's fictional state of Oceania. Millions cheered the demise of Nazi evil in 1945, but for Orwell, bureaucratic domination depended on continuing conflict. Indeed, as Allied powers competed for territory at the war's end, a new struggle called the cold war was beginning.

REVIEW   How and where was World War II fought, and what were its major consequences?

Conclusion

The Great Depression, which brought fear, hunger, and joblessness to millions, created a setting in which dictators thrived because they promised to restore economic prosperity by destroying democracy and representative government. Desperate people believed the promises of these dynamic new leaders—Mussolini, Stalin, and Hitler—and often embraced the brutality of their regimes. In the USSR, Stalin's program of rapid industrialization cost the lives of millions as he inspired Communist believers to purge enemies—real and imagined. With the democracies preoccupied with economic recovery while preserving the rule of law and still haunted by memories of World War I, Hitler, Mussolini, and their millions of supporters went on to menace Europe unchallenged. At the same time, Japan embarked on a program of conquest aimed at ending Western domination in Asia and taking more of Asia for itself. The coalition of Allies that finally formed to stop the Axis powers of Germany, Italy, and Japan was an uneasy alliance among Britain, Free France, the Soviet Union, and the United States. World War II ended European dominance. Europe's economies were shattered, its colonies were on the verge of independence, and its peoples were starving and homeless.

The costs of a bloody war—one waged against civilians as much as armies—
taught the victorious powers different lessons. The United States, Britain, and
France were convinced that a minimum of citizen well-being was necessary to
prevent a recurrence of fascism. The devastation of the USSR's population and
resources made Stalin increasingly obsessed with national security and compensation
for the damage inflicted by the Nazis. Britain and France faced the end of their
imperial might, underscoring Orwell's insight that the war had utterly transformed
society. The militarization of society and the deliberate murder of millions of innocent citizens like Etty Hillesum were tragedies that permanently injured the West's
claims to being an advanced civilization. Nonetheless, backed by vast supplies of
sophisticated weaponry, the United States and the Soviet Union used their opposing
views on a postwar settlement to justify threatening one another—and the world—
with another horrific war.

Percent of population killed

Over 10%
5–10%
1–5%
Under 1%

■ Military dead
▲ Civilian dead (does not include 12 million death camp victims)
✳ City substantially damaged

NORWAY
■ 4,780

SWEDEN

FINLAND
■ 79,047

Leningrad

ESTONIA

LATVIA

Baltic Sea

GREAT BRITAIN
■ 271,311
▲ 60,595

North Sea

DENMARK
■ 4,339

Königsberg

LITHUANIA

USSR
□ 14,500,000
△ Over 7,000,000

IRELAND

Coventry

London　Rotterdam

NETH.
■ 13,700
▲ 236,300

Hamburg

Bremen

Hanover

Berlin

Warsaw

POLAND
■ 850,000
(169,822 as Allies)
▲ 5,778,000

Kiev

Düsseldorf　✳Dortmund

BELG.
■ 9,561
▲ 75,000

Cologne

GERMANY
■ 2,850,000
▲ 2,300,000

Dresden

Caen

Frankfurt　Würzburg

CZECHOSLOVAKIA
■ 6,683
▲ 310,000

Munich

FRANCE
■ 210,671
▲ 173,260

SWITZ.

AUSTRIA
■ 380,000
▲ 145,000

HUNGARY
■▲ 750,000

ROMANIA
■ 519,822
▲ 465,000　✳ Ploesti

Milan

Genoa

Bologna

YUGOSLAVIA
■△ 1,700,000

Black Sea

SPAIN
■ 4,500 (For Axis)
7,500 (For Allies)
■▲ 10,000
(in concentration camps)

Corsica

ITALY
■ 279,820
▲ 17,400 (as Allies)

BULGARIA
■ 18,500
▲ 1,500

Sardinia

GREECE
■ 16,357
▲ 155,300

0　　200　　400 miles
0　　200　　400 kilometers

MAPPING THE WEST　Europe at War's End, 1945　The damage of World War II left scars that would last for decades. Major German cities were bombed to bits, while the Soviet Union suffered an unimaginable toll of perhaps as many as forty-five million deaths due to the war alone. In addition to the vast civilian and military losses shown on this map, historians estimate that no less than twelve million people were murdered in the Nazi death camps. Everything from politics to family life needed rebuilding, adding to the chaos. (From *The Hammond Atlas of the Twentieth Century* [London: Times Books, 1996], 102.)

Chapter Review

KEY TERMS AND PEOPLE

Be sure you can identify the term or person and explain its historical significance.

civil disobedience (p. 780)
Joseph Stalin (p. 781)
five-year plans (p. 781)
purges (p. 782)
Adolf Hitler (p. 784)
Enabling Act (p. 785)
pump priming (p. 786)
Nuremberg Laws (p. 787)

family allowance (p. 788)
Popular Front (p. 790)
Charlie Chaplin (p. 791)
Lebensraum (p. 793)
Francisco Franco (p. 794)
appeasement (p. 797)
Nazi-Soviet Pact (p. 797)
Blitzkrieg (p. 798)

REVIEW QUESTIONS

1. How did the Great Depression affect society and politics?
2. What role did violence play in the Soviet and Nazi regimes?
3. How did the democracies' responses to the twin challenges of economic depression and the rise of fascism differ from those of totalitarian regimes?
4. How did the aggression of Japan, Germany, and Italy create the conditions for global war?
5. How and where was World War II fought, and what were its major consequences?

MAKING CONNECTIONS

1. Compare fascist ideas of the individual with the idea of individual rights that inspired the American and French Revolutions.
2. What connections can you make between the Great Depression and the coming of World War II?
3. What were the major differences between World War I and World War II?
4. What explains the bleak view of writers like George Orwell after the Allied victory over the Axis powers?

IMPORTANT EVENTS

1929	• U.S. stock market crashes; global depression begins; Soviet leadership initiates "liquidation of the kulaks"; Stalin's first five-year plan officially begins
1931	• Japan invades Manchuria; Spanish republicans overthrow monarchy
1933	• Hitler comes to power in Germany
1935	• German government enacts Nuremberg Laws; Italy invades Ethiopia
1936	• Purges and show trials begin in USSR; Hitler remilitarizes Rhineland; Spanish Civil War begins
1937	• Japan attacks China
1938	• Germany annexes Austria; European leaders meet in Munich to negotiate with Hitler; Kristallnacht in Germany
1939	• Germany invades Czechoslovakia; Spanish Civil War ends; Nazi-Soviet Pact; Germany invades Poland; Britain and France declare war on Germany; World War II begins
1940	• France falls to German army
1940–1941	• British air force fends off German attacks in the battle of Britain
1941	• Germany invades Soviet Union; Japan attacks Pearl Harbor; United States enters war
1941–1945	• The Holocaust
1942–1943	• Siege of Stalingrad
1944	• Allied forces land at Normandy, France
1945	• Berlin falls; United States drops atomic bombs on Hiroshima and Nagasaki; World War II ends

27

The Cold War and the Remaking of Europe

1945–1960s

CHAPTER FOCUS

How did the cold war shape the politics, economy, social life, culture, and international concerns of post–World War II Europe?

LATE IN 1945, WITH THE USSR still reeling from the devastation of World War II, Soviet poet Boris Pasternak began a new project—*Doctor Zhivago*, a novel about a thoughtful medical man caught up in the whirlwind of the Russian Revolution. Like others in the USSR, Pasternak expected the postwar era to usher in, as he put it, "a great renewal of Russian life." So he struggled on with his complex epic even as the cold war tensions between the United States and the USSR unfolded. In 1953, Joseph Stalin's sudden death raised Pasternak's hopes for his masterpiece to receive a warm reception; those hopes were dashed, however, when the Soviets forbade the book's publication.

A determined Pasternak bypassed the Soviet authorities and secretly arranged for *Doctor Zhivago* to be published first in 1957 in Italy—now an anti-Soviet ally of the United States in the cold war. The book became a best seller, showing its readers that the Russian Revolution was far from perfect and so angering the Soviet leadership that Stalin's successor, Nikita Khrushchev, forced Pasternak to decline the Nobel Prize for Literature awarded him in 1958. The cold war, however, allowed *Doctor Zhivago* to live on when the famed Hollywood studio MGM turned it into a blockbuster film (1965), seen by tens of millions. By that time, Pasternak had died—a broken victim of cold war persecutions that haunted the world long after the calamitous years of war and genocide had ended.

Following World War II, people in Europe, Japan, and much of East and Southeast Asia were starving and homeless. Evidence of genocide and other inhumanity was everywhere, and nuclear annihilation menaced the world. The old international order was gone, replaced by the rivalry of the United States and the Soviet Union for control of Europe, whose political, social, and economic order was shattered. The nuclear arsenals of these two superpowers—a term coined in 1947—grew massively in the 1950s, but the enemies did not fight outright. Thus, their terrifying rivalry was called the cold war. The cold war divided the West and led to political persecution in many areas, even in the wealthy and secure United States.

At the same time, the defeat of Nazism inspired cautious optimism and a revival of thoughtful reflection like Pasternak's. Heroic effort had defeated fascism, and that defeat raised hopes that a new age would begin. Atomic science promised advances in medicine, and nuclear energy was seen as a replacement for coal and oil. The creation of the United Nations in 1945 heralded an era of international cooperation. Around the globe, colonial peoples won independence from European masters, while in the United States the civil rights movement grew in strength. The welfare state expanded, and by the end of the 1950s, economic rebirth had made much of Europe more prosperous than ever before. An "economic miracle" had occurred, bringing many Europeans and Americans the highest standard of living they had ever known, including quantities of new consumer goods and simple pleasures such as seeing technicolor films like *Doctor Zhivago*.

The postwar period became one of open redefinition as the experience of total war transformed both society and the international order. New terms arose in the 1950s, dividing the globe into the first world (the West, or capitalist, bloc of countries); the second world (the East, or socialist, bloc); and the third world (countries emerging from imperial domination). This last term, *third world*, was meant as a favorable comparison of emerging nations to the Third Estate—that is, the rising citizens of the French Revolution—but is now considered an insulting term.

As the world's people redefined themselves, the superpowers took the world to the brink of nuclear disaster. From the dropping of the atomic bomb on Japan in 1945 to the Cuban missile crisis of 1962, fear and personal anguish like that suffered by Pasternak gripped much of the world, even in the midst of prosperity and Europe's rebirth.

World Politics Transformed

World War II ended Europe's global leadership. Many countries lay in ruins in the summer of 1945, and conditions would deteriorate before they improved. Though victorious, bombed and bankrupt Britain could not feed its people, and continuing turmoil destroyed the lives of millions in central and eastern Europe. In contrast, the United States, whose territory was virtually untouched in the war, emerged as the world's sole economic giant, while the Soviet Union, despite suffering immense devastation, retained formidable military might. Occupying Europe as part of the victorious alliance against Nazism and fascism, the two superpowers used Germany—at the heart of the continent and its politics—to divide Europe in two. By the late 1940s, the USSR had imposed Communist rule throughout most of eastern Europe as it gained control of the territory that the Nazis had desired for German settlement. Western Europeans found themselves at least partially controlled by the very U.S. economic power that helped them rebuild, especially because the United States maintained air bases and nuclear weapons sites on their soil. The new age of bipolar world politics made Europe its testing ground.

Chaos in Europe

In contrast to the often stationary trench warfare of World War I, armies in World War II had fought a war of movement on the ground and in the air. Massive bombing had leveled thousands of square miles of territory, and whole cities were clogged with rubble. On the Rhine River, almost no bridge remained standing; in the Soviet Union, seventy thousand villages and more than a thousand cities lay in shambles. Everywhere people were suffering. In the Netherlands, the severity of Nazi occupation left the Dutch population close to death, relieved only by a U.S. airlift of food. To control scarce supplies, Italian bakers sold bread by the slice. Allied troops in Germany were almost the sole source of food: "To see the children fighting for food," remarked one British soldier handing out supplies, "was like watching animals being fed in a zoo." There were no mass uprisings as after World War I; until the late 1940s, people were too absorbed by the struggle for bare survival.

The tens of millions of refugees suffered the most, as they wandered a continent where the dangers of assault, robbery, and ethnic violence were great. An estimated thirty million Europeans, many of German ethnicity, were forcibly expelled from Poland, Czechoslovakia, and Hungary (Map 27.1). The USSR lobbied hard for the return of several million Soviet prisoners of war and forced laborers, and the Allies transported millions of Soviet refugees home. The Allies slowed the process when they discovered that Soviet leaders had ordered the execution of many of the returnees for being "contaminated" by Western ideas.

Survivors of the concentration camps discovered that their suffering had not ended with Germany's defeat. Many returned home diseased and disoriented, while others had no home to return to because their property had been confiscated.

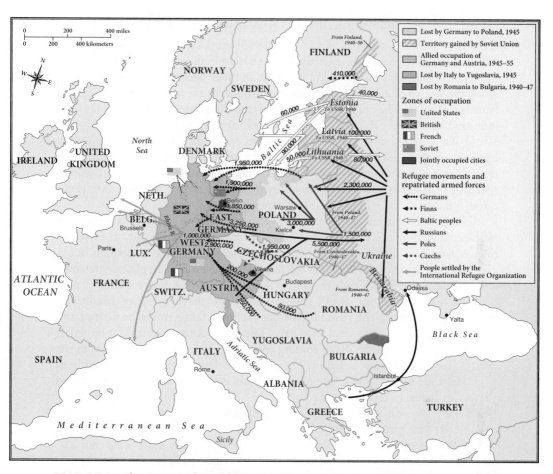

MAP 27.1   The Impact of World War II on Europe   European governments, many of them struggling to provide food and other necessities for their populations, found themselves responsible for hundreds of thousands, if not millions, of new refugees. Simultaneously, millions of prisoners of war, servicemen, and slave laborers were returned to the Soviet Union, many of them by force. This situation unfolded amid political instability and even violence. What does the movement of peoples shown on the map suggest about social conditions in post–World War II Europe?

Anti-Semitism—official policy under the Nazis—lingered in popular attitudes, and people used it to justify their claim to Jewish property and to jobs vacated by Jews. In the summer of 1946, a vicious crowd in Kielce, Poland, assaulted some 250 Jewish survivors, killing at least 40. Survivors fled to the port cities of Italy and other Mediterranean countries, eventually leaving Europe for Palestine, where Zionists had been settling for half a century.

New Superpowers: The United States and the Soviet Union

Only two countries were still powerful in 1945: the United States and the Soviet Union. The United States was now the richest nation in the world. Its industrial output had increased by a remarkable 15 percent annually between 1940 and 1944. By 1947, the United States controlled almost two-thirds of the world's gold bullion and launched more than half of the world's commercial shipping. Continued spending on industrial and military research added to postwar prosperity. In contrast to the post–World War I policy of isolationism, Americans embraced global leadership. Many had learned about the world while tracking the war's progress. Despite widespread fear of nuclear annihilation, a wave of suburban housing development and consumer spending kept the economy buoyant. A baby boom exploded from the late 1940s through the early 1960s in response to prosperity.

The Soviets also emerged from the war with a well-justified sense of accomplishment. Despite horrendous losses—now estimated to be as many as forty-five million lives lost in the war itself—they had resisted the most massive onslaught ever launched against a nation. Indeed many Europeans and Americans gratefully acknowledged the Soviet contribution to Hitler's defeat. Ordinary Soviet citizens believed that the victory would lead to improvement in everyday conditions. Rumors spread among the peasants that the collective farms would be divided and returned to them as individual property. "Life will become pleasant," one writer prophesied. "There will be much coming and going, and a lot of contacts with the West." The Stalinist goals of industrialization and defense against Nazism had been won, and thus many Soviets, among them Boris Pasternak, anticipated an end to decades of hardship and repression.

Stalin took a different view and moved ruthlessly to reassert control. In 1946, his new five-year plan set increased production goals and mandated more stringent collectivization of agriculture. For him, rapid recovery meant more work, not less, and more order, not greater freedom. Stalin also turned his attention to the low birthrate, a result of wartime male casualties and women's long, arduous working days. He introduced an intense propaganda campaign emphasizing that women should hold down jobs and also fulfill their "true nature" by producing many children. A new round of purges began in which people were told that enemies among them were threatening the state. Jews were especially targeted, and in 1953 the government announced that doctors—most of them Jews—had long been assassinating Soviet leaders, murdering newborns and patients in hospitals, and plotting to poison water supplies. Hysteria gripped the nation, and people feared for their lives. "I am a simple worker and not an anti-Semite," one Moscow resident wrote, "but I say . . . it's time to clean these people out." With this rebirth of Stalinism, an atmosphere of fear returned to feed the cold war.

Origins of the Cold War

The cold war between the United States and the Soviet Union, which began in 1945, would afflict the world for more than four decades. No peace treaty officially ended World War II to document what went wrong, as in the Peace of Paris of

1919–1920. Therefore, the origins of the cold war remain a matter of debate, with historians faulting both sides for starting the dangerous rivalry. Some point to consistent U.S., British, and French hostility to the Soviets because of Communists' abolition of private property and Russia's withdrawal from World War I. Others stress Stalin's aggressive policies, notably the 1939 Nazi-Soviet Pact and Soviet expansionism.

Suspicion ran deep among the Allied leadership during the war: Stalin believed that Churchill and Roosevelt were deliberately letting the USSR bear the brunt of Hitler's rampage across the continent as part of their anti-Communist policy. He rightly viewed Churchill in particular as interested primarily in preserving Britain's imperial power, no matter what the cost in Soviet lives. At the time, some Americans believed that dropping the atomic bomb on Japan would also frighten the Soviets and discourage them from making any more land grabs. In addition, the new U.S. president, Harry Truman, cut off aid to the USSR almost the instant the last gun was fired, fueling Stalin's suspicions and leading to the takeover of eastern Europe as a permanent "buffer zone" of dependent European states. Across the Atlantic, members of the U.S. State Department fueled U.S. fears by depicting Stalin as another in a long line of neurotic Asian tyrants thirsting for world domination.

The cold war thus became a series of moves and countermoves in the shared occupation of a rich European heartland that had fallen into chaos. In line with the view of its political needs, the USSR repressed democratic coalition governments of liberals, socialists, Communists, and peasant parties in central and eastern Europe between 1945 and 1949. It imposed Communist rule almost immediately in Bulgaria and Romania. In Romania, Stalin cited citizen violence in 1945 as the excuse to demand an ouster of all non-Communists from the civil service and cabinet. In Poland, the Communists fixed the election results of 1945 and 1946 to create the illusion of approval for communism.

The United States worried that Communist power would spread to western Europe. The Communists' promises of better conditions appealed to hungry workers in Europe, while memories of Communist leadership in the resistance to fascism gave it powerful appeal. In March 1947, Truman reacted by announcing the **Truman Doctrine**—the use of economic and military aid to block communism. The president requested $400 million in military aid for Greece and Turkey, where the Communists were also exerting pressure. Fearing that Americans would balk at backing an undemocratic Greece, the U.S. Congress said it would agree to the program only if, as one congressman put it, Truman would "scare the hell out of the country." Truman thus publicized the expensive aid program as a necessary first step to prevent Soviet conquest of the world. The show of American support made the Communists back off.

In 1947, the United States also devised the **Marshall Plan**—a program of massive economic aid to Europe—to relieve the daily hardships that were making communism attractive to Europeans. "The seeds of totalitarian regimes are nurtured by misery and want," Truman warned. Named after Secretary of State George C. Marshall, who proposed the plan, the program's direct aid would immediately improve everyday life, while its loans and financial credits would restart international trade. The government claimed that the Marshall Plan was not directed "against any country or doctrine but against hunger, poverty, desperation, and chaos." By the early 1950s, the United States had sent Europe more than $12 billion in food, equipment, and services, reducing communism's appeal in the countries of western Europe that received the aid.

Stalin saw the Marshall Plan as a U.S. political trick because the devastated USSR had little aid to offer client countries in eastern and central Europe. He thus clamped down still harder on eastern European governments, preventing them from responding to the U.S. offer of assistance and eliminating the last scraps of democracy in Hungary, Poland, and Czechoslovakia. The populace accepted the change so passively that Communist leaders said the takeover was "like cutting butter with a knife."

The only exception to the Soviet sweep in eastern Europe came in Yugoslavia, under the Communist ruler known as Tito (Josip Broz, 1892–1980). During the war, Tito had led the powerful anti-Nazi Yugoslav "partisans." After the war, he drew on support from Serbs, Croats, and Muslims to mount a Communist revolution, but one explicitly meant to avoid Soviet influence. Eager for Yugoslavia to develop industrially rather than simply serve Soviet needs, Tito remarked, "We study and take as an example the Soviet system, but we are developing socialism in our country in somewhat different forms." Stalin was furious; in his eyes, commitment to communism meant obedience to him. Nonetheless, Yugoslavia emerged from its Communist revolution as a culturally diverse federation of six republics and two independent provinces within Serbia that held together until Tito's death in 1980.

The Division of Germany

The superpower struggle for control of Germany took the cold war to a menacing level. The agreements reached at the Yalta and Potsdam conferences in 1945 provided for Germany's division into four zones, each of which was controlled by one of the four principal victors in World War II — the United States, the Soviet Union, Britain, and France. However, the superpowers disagreed on how to treat Germany. The U.S. occupation forces undertook to reprogram German attitudes by controlling the press and censoring all media in the U.S. zone to ensure that they did not express fascist values. In contrast, believing that Nazism was an extreme form of capitalism, Stalin confiscated the estates of wealthy Germans and redistributed them to ordinary people and supporters.

A second disagreement, concerning the economy, led to Germany's partition. According to the American plan for coordinating the various segments of the German economy, surplus crops from the Soviet-occupied areas would feed urban populations in the western zones; in turn, industrial goods would be sent to the USSR. The Soviets upset this plan. Following the Allied agreement that the USSR would receive reparations from German resources, the Soviets seized German equipment, shipping it all to the Soviet Union. They transported skilled German workers, engineers, and scientists to the USSR to work as forced laborers. The Soviets also manipulated the currency in their zone, enabling the USSR to buy German goods at unfairly low prices. In response, the western Allies agreed to merge their zones into a West German state, and the United States began an economic buildup of the western zone under the Marshall Plan. Notions of a permanently weakened Germany ended as the United States enlisted many former Nazi officials as spies and bureaucrats to jump-start the economy and pursue the cold war.

On July 24, 1948, Stalin retaliated by using Soviet troops to blockade Germany's capital, Berlin. Like Germany as a whole, the city—located more than one hundred miles deep into the Soviet zone and thus cut off from western territory—had been divided into four occupation zones. The Soviets also refused to allow western vehicles to travel through the Soviet zone to reach Berlin. The United States responded decisively with the Berlin airlift—Operation Vittles, as U.S. pilots called it—flying in millions of tons of provisions to some two million isolated citizens (Map 27.2). Given the limited number of available transport planes, pilots kept the plane engines on to achieve a rapid turnaround that would ensure adequate delivery. The Soviets ended their blockade in May 1949, but the cold war rhetoric of good versus evil made the divided capital of Berlin an enduring symbol of the capitalist-communist divide.

The creation of competing military alliances added to cold war tensions (Map 27.3). A few months after the establishment of the West German state in 1948, the USSR formed an East German state. In 1949, the United States, Canada,

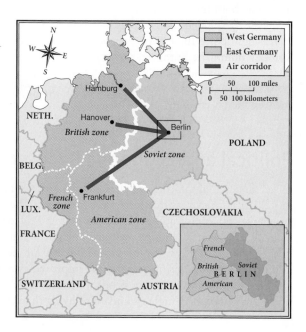

MAP 27.2 Divided Germany and the Berlin Airlift, 1946–1949 Berlin—controlled by the United States, Great Britain, France, and the Soviet Union—was deep in the Soviet zone of occupation and became a major point of contention among the former allies. When the USSR blockaded the western half of the city, the United States responded with a massive airlift. To stop movement between the two zones, the USSR built the Berlin Wall in 1961 and used troops to patrol it.

MAP 27.3 European NATO Members and the Warsaw Pact in the 1950s The two superpowers intensified their rivalry by creating large military alliances: NATO, formed in 1949, included the United States and Canada as well as European states; the Warsaw Pact was formed in 1955 after NATO invited West German membership. International politics revolved around these two alliances, which faced off in the heart of Europe. War games for the two sides often assumed a massive war concentrated in central Europe over control of Germany.

and their allies in western Europe and Scandinavia formed the **North Atlantic Treaty Organization (NATO)**, which provided a unified military force for its member countries. In 1955, after the United States forced France and Britain to invite West Germany to join NATO, the Soviet Union retaliated by establishing with its satellite countries the military organization commonly called the **Warsaw Pact**. By that time, both the United States and the USSR had accelerated arms buildups: the Soviets had exploded their own atomic bomb in 1949, and both nations then tested increasingly powerful nuclear weapons, outstripping the individual might of the formerly dominant European powers.

REVIEW   What were the major events in the development of the cold war?

Political and Economic Recovery in Europe

The clash between the United States and the Soviet Union served as a background to the remarkable recovery that took place in Europe. The first two items on the political agenda were the eradication of the Nazi past and the establishment of stable governments. While western Europe revived its democratic political structures and productivity, eastern Europe was far less prosperous and far more repressive. Even to the east, however, the conditions of everyday life improved as peasant societies were forced to modernize and some consumer goods were restored. By 1960, people across the continent were enjoying a higher standard of living than ever before.

Dealing with Nazism

In May 1945, the goals of feeding civilians, dealing with millions of refugees, purging Nazis, and setting up peacetime governments all needed attention. Governments-in-exile returned to reclaim power, but they often ran up against occupying armies that were a law unto themselves. The Soviets were especially feared for inflicting rape and robbery on Germans—abuses they justified by pointing to the tens of millions of worse atrocities committed by the Nazis. Adding to the sense of disorder was the lively trade in sex for food among starving civilians and well-supplied soldiers in all armies. Employing swift vigilante justice, civilians released pent-up rage and punished collaborators for their participation in genocide and occupation crimes. In France, villagers often shaved the heads of women suspected of associating with Germans and made some of them parade naked through the local streets. Members of the resistance executed tens of thousands of Nazi officers and collaborators without trial.

Allied representatives undertook what they claimed to be a systematic "denazification" that ranged from forcing German civilians to view the death camps to bringing to trial suspected local collaborators. The trials conducted at Nuremberg, Germany, by the victorious Allies in the fall of 1945 used the Nazis' own documents to reveal a horrifying panorama of crimes by Nazi leaders. Although international law lacked any definition of genocide as a crime, the judges at Nuremberg found sufficient cause to impose death sentences on half of the twenty-four defendants, among them Hitler's closest associates, and to give prison terms to the remainder. The Nuremberg trials introduced today's notion of prosecution for crimes against humanity.

Allied prosecution of the Axis leadership was hardly thorough. Some of those most responsible for war crimes were not pursued, leaving many Germans skeptical about Allied intentions. As women in Germany faced violence at the hands of occupying troops, endured starvation, and were forced to do the rough manual labor of clearing rubble (see the image on page 825), Germans came to believe that they themselves were the main victims of the war. Distrust mounted when Allied officials, eager to restore government services and make western Europe more efficient than Soviet-controlled eastern Europe, began to hire former high-ranking Fascists and Nazis. Soon the new West German government proclaimed that the war's real casualties were the German prisoners of war still held in Soviet camps.

Rebirth of the West

Following the immediate postwar chaos, the first civilian governments in western Europe reflected the broad coalitions of the resistance movements and other opposition to the Axis powers. These reform-minded governments conspicuously emphasized democratic values to show their rejection of the totalitarian regimes that had earlier attracted so many Europeans. In France, the leader of the Free French, General Charles de Gaulle, governed briefly as chief of state, and the French approved a constitution in 1946 that established the Fourth Republic and finally granted the vote to

French women. De Gaulle wanted a political system with a strong executive and, failing to achieve that, soon resigned in favor of centrist and left-wing parties. Meanwhile, Italy replaced its constitutional monarchy with a republic that also allowed women the vote for the first time. As in France, a resistance-based government was soon replaced by a coalition headed by the conservative **Christian Democrats**, descended from the traditional Catholic centrist parties of the prewar period. Other countries likewise saw the growing influence of Christian politicians because of their resistance to fascism.

Other voters in western Europe favored communist and labor parties. Symbol of the common citizen, the Soviet soldier was a hero to many western Europeans outside occupied Germany. People also remembered the hardships of the depression of the 1930s. Therefore, in Britain, despite the wartime successes of Winston Churchill's Conservative Party leadership, the government of Labour Party leader Clement Attlee — though not Communist — appeared most likely to fulfill promises to share prosperity better among the classes. The extreme difficulties of the immediate postwar years provided further support for governments that would represent the millions of ordinary citizens who had suffered, fought, and worked incredibly hard during the war.

In West Germany, however, with the Communist takeovers occurring directly to the east and with memories of the millions of German soldiers who had died at the hands of the Red Army, communism and the left in general had little appeal. In 1949, centrist politicians came to power in the new state, officially named the German Federal Republic, whose constitution aimed to prevent the emergence of a dictator and to guarantee individual rights. West Germany's first chancellor was the seventy-three-year-old Catholic anti-Communist Konrad Adenauer, who allied himself with the economist Ludwig Erhard. Erhard stabilized the postwar German currency so that people would have enough confidence in its soundness to resume normal trade and manufacturing, while Adenauer restored the representative government that Hitler had overthrown.

Paradoxically, given its leadership in the fight against fascism, the United States was a country in which individual freedom and democracy were imperiled after the war. Two events in 1949 — the Soviet Union's successful test of an atomic bomb and the Communist revolution in China — brought to the fore Joseph McCarthy, a U.S. senator fearing a reelection defeat. To win the election, McCarthy warned of a great conspiracy to overthrow the U.S. government. As during the Soviet purges, people of all occupations — including government workers, film stars, and union leaders — were called before U.S. congressional panels to confess, testify against friends, and say whether they had ever had Communist sympathies. The atmosphere was electric with confusion, for only five years before, the mass media had run glowing stories about Stalin and the Soviet system. By 1952, however, millions of Americans had been investigated, imprisoned, or fired from their jobs. McCarthy personally oversaw book burnings, and although the Senate finally voted to censure him in the winter of 1954, fearfulness and anticommunism had come to dominate political life.

Women Clearing Berlin   The amount of destruction caused by World War II was staggering, requiring the mobilization of the civilian population in Berlin, where women were conscripted to sort the rubble and clear it away. Scenes like this were ultimately used as propaganda in the cold war to make it seem as if the Germans were the victims rather than the perpetrators of the war. That German soldiers held in Soviet camps were only slowly repatriated added to the image of Soviet rather than German aggression in World War II. (akg-images.)

Given the wartime destruction, the economic rebirth of western Europe was even more surprising than the revival of democracy. In the first weeks and months after the war, the job of rebuilding often involved menial physical labor that mobilized entire populations for such jobs as clearing the massive urban rubble by hand. Initially, governments diverted labor and capital into rebuilding transportation, communications, and industrial capacity instead of producing consumer goods. However, the scarcity of household goods sparked unrest. In the midst of this growing discontent, the Marshall Plan suddenly boosted recovery with American dollars; food and consumer goods became more plentiful; and demand for automobiles, washing machines, and vacuum cleaners accelerated economic growth.

The postwar recovery was helped by the continuation of military spending for the cold war and the adaptation of wartime technology to meet consumer needs. Civilian travel expanded as nations organized their own airlines based on improved airplane technology. Developed to relieve wartime shortages, synthetic goods such as nylon and a vast assortment of plastic products, ranging from pipes to rainwear, enriched civilian life. Governments also ordered bombs, fighter planes, tanks, and missiles and sponsored military research. The outbreak of the Korean War in 1950 (see page 832) increased U.S. orders for manufactured goods to wage that war, further sustaining economic growth in Europe. Ultimately, the cold war prevented a repeat of the 1920s, when reduced military spending threw people out of jobs and fed the growth of fascism.

Large and small European states alike developed and redeveloped modern economies in short order. In the twelve principal countries of western Europe, the annual rate of economic growth had been 1.3 percent per inhabitant between 1870 and 1913. Those countries almost tripled that rate between 1950 and 1973, attaining an annual per capita growth rate of 3.8 percent. Among the larger powers, West Germany surprisingly became the economic leader, achieving by the 1960s a stunning revival called the "economic miracle." The smaller Scandinavian countries also achieved a notable recovery: Sweden succeeded in the development of automobile, truck, and shipbuilding industries. Finland modernized its industry and agriculture, which in turn forced the surplus farm population to seek factory work. Scandinavian women joined the workforce in record numbers, which also boosted economic growth and expanded prosperity. The thirty years after World War II were a golden age of European economic revival.

The creation of the Common Market, which evolved over time to become the European Union, was the final ingredient in the postwar recovery. In 1951, Italy, France, West Germany, Belgium, Luxembourg, and the Netherlands took a major step toward cooperation when they formed the European Coal and Steel Community (ECSC)—an organization to manage the joint production of basic resources. According to the ECSC's principal architect, Robert Schuman, ties created by joint productivity and trade would keep France and Germany from another cataclysmic war. Then in 1957, the six ECSC members signed the Treaty of Rome, which provided for a more general trading partnership called the **European Economic Community (EEC)**, known popularly as the **Common Market**. The EEC reduced tariffs among the six partners, developed common trade policies, and brought under one cooperative economic umbrella more than two hundred million consumers. According to one of its founders, the EEC aimed to "prevent the race of nationalism, which is the true curse of the modern world." Increased cooperation produced great economic rewards for the six members, whose rates of economic growth soared.

Britain pointedly refused to join the partnership at first. Membership would have required it to surrender certain imperial trading rights among its Commonwealth partners such as Australia and Canada and, as one British politician put it, make Britain "just another European country." Even without Britain, the rising prosperity of a new western Europe joined in the Common Market was striking.

Economic planning and coordination by specialists (as developed during wartime) shaped the Common Market. Called technocrats, specialists working for the

Common Market were to base decisions on expertise rather than on personal interest and on the goals of the organization as a whole rather than on the demands of any one nation. The aim was to reduce the potential for irrationality and violence in politics, both domestic and international. Administered by a commission of technocrats based in Brussels, Belgium, the Common Market transcended the borders of the nation-state and thus exceeded the power of many elected politicians.

The Welfare State: Common Ground East and West

On both sides of the cold war divide, governments channeled new resources into state-financed programs such as pensions, disability insurance, and national health care. These social programs taken as a whole became known as the **welfare state**, indicating that states were no longer interested solely in maintaining order and augmenting their power. Veterans' pensions and programs were primary, but the welfare state extended beyond those who had sacrificed in wartime. Because the European population had declined during the war, almost all countries now desperately wanted to boost the birthrate and thus gave couples direct financial aid for having children. Imitating the social security programs initiated under Bismarck in Germany in the 1870s and the more sweeping Swedish programs of the 1930s, nations expanded or created family allowances, health care and medical benefits, and programs for pregnant women and new mothers.

Some welfare-state policies had a strong gender bias against women. Britain's maternity benefits and child allowances favored women who did not work outside the home by providing little coverage for workingwomen. The West German government passed strict legislation that forced employers to give women maternity leave, thus discouraging them from hiring women. It also cut back or eliminated pensions and benefits to married women. In fact, West Germans bragged about removing women from the workforce, claiming that doing so distinguished democratic practices from Communist ones. The refusal to build day-care centers or to allow stores to remain open in the evening so that workingwomen could buy food for their families led West Germany to have among the lowest rates of female employment of any industrial country. Another result of West Germany's discriminatory policies was a high rate of female poverty in old age.

By contrast, in eastern Europe and the Soviet Union, where wartime loss of life had been enormous, women worked nearly full-time and usually outnumbered men in the workforce. As in many western European countries, however, child-care programs, family allowances, and maternity benefits were designed to encourage pregnancies by workingwomen. The scarcity of consumer goods and the lack of household conveniences discouraged workingwomen in Communist countries from having large families no matter what the government wanted. Because women bore the sole burden of domestic duties under such conditions on top of their paying jobs, birthrates in the eastern bloc stagnated.

Across Europe, welfare-state programs aimed to improve people's well-being. State-funded health care systems covered medical needs in most industrial nations except the United States. The combination of better material conditions and state provision of health care dramatically extended life expectancy and lowered rates of infant mortality. Contributing to the overall progress, vaccines greatly reduced the death toll from such diseases as tuberculosis, diphtheria, measles, and polio. In England, schoolchildren stood an inch taller, on average, than children the same age had a decade earlier.

State initiatives in other areas played a role in raising the standard of living. A growing network of government-built atomic power plants brought more thorough electrification of eastern Europe and the Soviet Union. Governments legislated more leisure time for workers; for example, Italian workers received twenty-eight paid holidays annually. To rebuild, postwar governments sponsored new suburbs around the edges of major urban areas in both eastern and western Europe. Many buildings went up slapdash, but they dramatically improved living conditions for postwar refugees, workers, and immigrants.

Recovery in the East

To create a Soviet bloc according to Stalin's vision, Communists revived the harsh methods that had transformed peasant economies earlier in the century. In eastern Europe, Stalin not only continued to collectivize agriculture but also brought about badly needed industrialization through the nationalization of private property. The process was brutal, and people later looked back on the 1950s as dreadful. But some workers in the countryside felt that ultimately their lives and their children's lives had improved. "Before we peasants were dirty and poor, we worked like dogs. . . . Was that a good life? No sir, it wasn't. . . . I was a miserable sharecropper and my son is an engineer," said one Romanian peasant. Despite modernization, government investment in agriculture was never high enough to produce the bumper crops of western Europe, and even the USSR depended on produce from the small plots that enterprising farmers cultivated on the side.

Stalin admired American industrial know-how and prodded the Communist economies to match U.S. productivity. The Soviet Union formed regional organizations like those in the West, instituting the Council for Mutual Economic Assistance (COMECON) in 1949 to coordinate economic relations among the satellite countries of the USSR and Moscow. The terms of the COMECON relationship worked against the satellite states, however, for the USSR was allowed to buy goods from its clients at bargain prices and sell goods to them at exorbitant ones. Nonetheless, these formerly peasant states became oriented toward technology and industrial economies directed by bureaucrats, who touted the virtues of steel plants and modern transport. The Roman Catholic church often protested the imposition of communism, but the government crushed it as much as possible or used agents to infiltrate it.

Culture, along with technology, was a building block of Stalinism in both the USSR and its satellite countries. State-instituted programs aimed to build loyalty to the modernizing regime; thus, citizens were obliged to attend adult education classes, women's groups, and public ceremonies. An intense program of

Propaganda for Collective Farming Dramatic changes were in store for people in eastern Europe who fell under Communist control after World War II. Most objectionable was the policy of collective farming, which stripped farmers of their lands and forced them to farm state property as a group. The poster aims to show Czechs that farming will bring huge benefits, including personal satisfaction. How do you interpret this poster, and why does it show a woman figure so prominently? (German Poster Museum, Essen/Marc Charmet/ The Art Archive at Art Resource, NY.)

OBILÍ JE BOHATSTVÍM VLASTI
ČESTNĚ SPLNÍME VÝKUP

de-Christianization and Russification forced non-Russian students in eastern Europe to read histories of the war that ignored their own country's resistance and gave the Red Army sole credit for fighting the Nazis. Rigid censorship resulted in what even one Communist writer in the USSR characterized as "a dreary torrent of colorless, mediocre literature." Stalin also purged prominent wartime leaders to ensure obedience and conformity. Marshal Zhukov, a popular leader of the Soviet armed forces, was shipped to a distant command, while Anna Akhmatova, a widely admired poet who championed wartime resistance to the Nazis, was confined to a crowded hospital room because she refused to glorify Stalin in her postwar poetry.

In March 1953, amid growing repression, Stalin died, and it soon became clear that the old ways would not hold. Political prisoners in the labor camps rebelled, leading to the release of more than a million people from the Gulag. In June 1953, workers in East German cities, many of them socialists and antifascist activists from before the war, protested the rise of privileged Communists in a series of strikes that spread like wildfire. At the other end of the social order, Soviet officials, despite enjoying luxury goods and plentiful food, had come to distrust Stalinism and now favored change. To calm protests across the Soviet bloc, governments stepped up the production of consumer goods—a policy called goulash communism (after the Hungarian stew) because it resulted in more food for ordinary people.

In 1955, **Nikita Khrushchev** (1894–1971), an illiterate coal miner before the Bolshevik Revolution, outmaneuvered other rivals to become the undisputed leader of the Soviet Union—but he did so without the Stalinist practice of executing his opponents. Khrushchev then made the surprising move of attacking Stalin. At a party congress in 1956, he denounced the "cult of personality" Stalin had built about himself and announced that Stalinism did not equal communism. Khrushchev thus cleverly attributed problems with communism to a single individual. The "secret speech" was a bombshell. Debates broke out in public, and books appeared championing the ordinary worker against the party bureaucracy. The climate of relative tolerance for free expression after Stalin's death was called the thaw.

In early summer 1956, discontented Polish railroad workers struck for better wages, and angry Hungarians rebelled against forced collectivization in October 1956. As in Poland, economic issues (especially announcements of reduced wages) and reports of Stalin's crimes contributed to the outbreak of violence in Hungary. Soon targeting the entire Communist system, tens of thousands of protesters filled the streets of Budapest and returned a popular hero, Imre Nagy, to power. When Nagy announced that Hungary might leave the Warsaw Pact, however, Soviet troops moved in, killing tens of thousands and causing hundreds of thousands more to flee to the West. Nagy was hanged. Despite a rhetoric of democracy, the United States refused to intervene in Hungary, choosing not to risk World War III by challenging the Soviet sphere of influence.

The failure of eastern European uprisings overshadowed the significant changes that had taken place since Stalin's death. While defeating his rivals, Khrushchev ended the Stalinist purges, reformed the courts, and curbed the secret police. "It has become more interesting to visit and see people," Boris Pasternak said of the changes. "It has become easier to work." In 1957, the Soviets successfully launched the first artificial earth satellite, *Sputnik*, and in 1961 they put the first cosmonaut, Yuri Gagarin, in orbit around the earth. The Soviets' edge in space technology shocked the western bloc and motivated the creation of the U.S. National Aeronautics and Space Administration (NASA). For Soviet citizens, such successes indicated that the USSR had achieved Stalin's goal of modernization and might inch further toward freedom.

Khrushchev, however, was inconsistent, showing himself open to changes in Soviet culture at one moment and then bullying honest writers at another. After assaulting Pasternak because of his novel *Doctor Zhivago*, in 1961 he allowed the publication of Aleksandr Solzhenitsyn's *One Day in the Life of Ivan Denisovitch*. This chilling account of life in the Gulag was useful, however, in underscoring Stalin's crimes and excesses. Under the thaw, Khrushchev made several trips to the West and took steps to expand communism's appeal in the new nations of Asia, Africa, and Latin America. Despite the USSR's more relaxed posture, however, the superpowers moved closer to the nuclear brink.

REVIEW   What factors drove recovery in western Europe and in eastern Europe?

Decolonization in a Cold War Climate

After World War II, activists in colonized regions in Asia, Africa, and the Middle East used the postwar chaos and the cold war to achieve their long-held goal of liberation. At war's end, the colonial powers attempted to reimpose their control as if they were still dominant around the world. Yet colonized peoples had been on the front lines defending the West; and as in World War I, they had witnessed the full barbarism of Western warfare. Like African American soldiers in the U.S. army, they experienced discrimination even while saving the West and, returning home, did not receive the rights of citizenship promised them. Moreover, successive wars had allowed local industries in the colonies to develop, while industry in the imperial homelands fell into decline.

The path to independence — a process called **decolonization** — was paved with difficulties. In India, Hindus and Muslims battled one another even though they shared the goal of eliminating the British. In the Middle East and North Africa, pan-Arab and pan-Islamic movements — that is, those wanting to bring together all Arabs or all Muslims as the basis for decolonization — might seem to have been unifying forces. Yet many Muslims were not Arab, not all Arabs were Muslim, and Islam itself encompassed a range of beliefs. Differences among religious beliefs, ethnic groups, and cultural practices — many of them invented or promoted by the colonizers to divide and rule — worked against political unity. Despite these complications, various peoples in what was coming to be called the third world succeeded in overthrowing imperialism, while the United States and the Soviet Union rushed in to co-opt them for the cold war.

The End of Empire in Asia

At the end of World War II, leaders in Asia succeeded in mobilizing mass discontent to drive out foreign rulers. Declining from an imperial power to a small island nation, Britain was the biggest loser. In 1947, it parted with India, whose independence it had promised in the 1930s. Indian business leaders bought out British entrepreneurs short of cash, and armed with an effective military, Indians began to face off with the British in strikes and other protests. Britain quickly faced reality and decreed that two independent countries should emerge from the old colony. The partition of 1947 created India for Hindus and Pakistan (itself later divided into two parts) for Muslims, but political tensions exploded among opposing members of the two religions. Hundreds of thousands of people overall were massacred in the great shift of populations between India and Pakistan. In 1948, a radical Hindu assassinated Gandhi, who though a Hindu himself had continued to champion religious reconciliation. Elsewhere, as some half a billion Asians gained their independence, Britain's sole remaining Asian colony of note was Hong Kong.

In 1949, after prolonged fighting, a Communist takeover in China brought in a government led by Mao Zedong (1893–1976). Chinese communism in the new People's Republic of China emphasized above all that the country was no longer the plaything of the colonial powers as Mao instituted reforms such as civil equality for women and imposed Soviet-style collectivization and brutal repression of the privileged classes.

The United States and the Soviet Union were deeply interested in East Asia — the United States because of the region's economic importance, and the USSR because of its shared borders. The victory of the Chinese Communists spurred both to increase their involvement in Asian politics. The superpowers faced off first in Korea, which had been split at the thirty-eighth parallel after World War II. In 1950, the North Koreans, with the support of the Soviet Union, invaded U.S.-backed South Korea, whose agents had themselves been stirring up tensions with raids across the border. The United States maneuvered the Security Council of the United Nations into approving a "police action" against the North. After two and a half years of a horribly destructive stalemate, the opposing sides finally agreed to a settlement in 1953: Korea would remain split at the thirty-eighth parallel. As a result of the Korean War, the United States increased its military spending from almost $11 billion in 1948 to almost $60 billion in 1953. An Asian counterpart to NATO, the U.S.-backed Southeast Asia Treaty Organization (SEATO), was established in 1954. Another effect of the Korean War was the rapid reindustrialization of Japan to provide the United States with supplies.

The cold war then spread to Indochina (now modern Cambodia, Laos, and Vietnam), where the European-educated Ho Chi Minh (1890–1969) had built a powerful organization, the Viet Minh, to fight colonial rule. He advocated the redistribution of land held by big landowners, who possessed more than 60 percent of the land. In 1954, Viet Minh peasant guerrillas ultimately defeated the technologically superior French army, which was receiving aid from the United States. Later that year, the Geneva Conference carved out an independent Laos and divided Vietnam along the seventeenth parallel into North and South, each free from French control. The Communist-backed Viet Minh, under Ho Chi Minh as president, ruled in the north, while the United States supported the landowner-backed regime in the south. Continued superpower intervention undermined the peace agreement as the superpowers fought the cold war in small foreign nations — conflicts now referred to as proxy wars.

The Struggle for Identity in the Middle East

Independence struggles in the Middle East highlighted the world's growing need for oil and often showed the ability of small countries to maneuver between the superpowers. As in other regions dominated by the West, Middle Eastern peoples resisted attempts to reimpose imperial control after 1945. Weakened by the war, British oil companies wanted to tighten their grip on profits. By playing the Western countries against one another, however, Middle Eastern leaders gained their independence and simultaneously renegotiated higher payments for drilling rights.

The legacy of the Holocaust complicated the Middle Eastern political scene. Since early in the century Western backing for a Jewish settlement in the Middle East had stirred up Arabs' determination not to be pushed out of their ancient homeland. When World War II broke out, 600,000 Jewish settlers and twice as many Arabs lived, tensely, in British-controlled Palestine. In 1947, an exhausted Britain ceded Palestine to the newly created United Nations, which voted to partition Palestine into an Arab region and a Jewish one (Map 27.4). Hostility turned to open war, which Jewish military forces won, and on May 14, 1948, the state of Israel came into being. "The dream had come true," Golda Meir, the future prime minister of Israel, remembered, but "too late to save those who had perished in the Holocaust." Israel opened its gates to immigrants, pitting its expansionist ambitions against its Arab neighbors.

One of those neighbors, Egypt, gained its independence from Britain at the end of the war. Britain, however, still dominated shipping to Asia through its control of the Suez Canal. In 1952, Colonel Gamal Abdel Nasser (1918–1970) became Egypt's president on a platform of economic modernization and true national independence—meaning Egyptian control of the canal. In July 1956, Nasser nationalized the canal: "I am speaking in the name of every Egyptian Arab," he remarked in his speech explaining the takeover, "and in the name of all free countries and of all those who believe in liberty." Nasser became a heroic figure to Arabs in the region, especially when Britain, supported by Israel and France, attacked Egypt while the Hungarian Revolution (see page 830) was in full swing. The British branded Nasser another Hitler, but the United States, fearing that Egypt would turn to the USSR, made the British back down. Nasser's triumph inspired confidence that colonized peoples around the world could gain true independence.

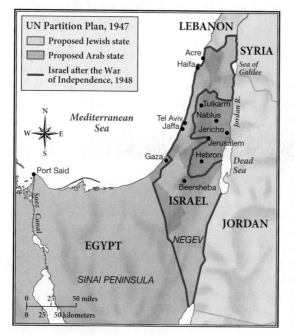

MAP 27.4   The Partition of Palestine and the Creation of Israel, 1947–1948   The creation of the Jewish state of Israel in 1948 against a backdrop of ongoing wars among Jews and indigenous Arab peoples turned the Middle East into a powder keg, a situation that has lasted until the present day. The struggle for resources and for securing the borders of viable nation-states was at the heart of these bitter contests, threatening to pull the superpowers into a third world war.

New Nations in Africa

In sub-Saharan Africa, nationalist leaders roused their people to challenge Europe's increasing demands for resources and labor—demands that resulted in poverty for African peoples. "The European Merchant is my shepherd, and I am in want," went one African version of the Twenty-third Psalm. At the war's end, veterans returned home and protest mounted. Kwame Nkrumah (1909–1972), for example, led the inhabitants of the British-controlled West African Gold Coast in Gandhi-inspired civil disobedience, finally driving the British out and bringing the state of Ghana into being in 1957. Nigeria, the most populous African region, achieved independence in 1960, and many other African states also became free (Map 27.5).

In mixed-race territory with large settler populations, Europeans resisted giving up their control. In British East Africa, where white settlers ruled in splendor and where blacks lacked both land and economic opportunity, fighting erupted in the 1950s. African men formed rebel groups named Mau Mau but called by some the Land and Freedom Army. With women serving as provisioners, messengers, and weapon stealers, Mau Mau bands, composed mostly of war veterans from the Kikuyu ethnic group, tried to recover land from whites. In 1964, Mau Mau resistance helped Kenya gain formal independence, but only after the British had put hundreds of thousands of Kikuyus in concentration camps—called a "living hell" and a "British gulag" by those tortured there. The British slaughtered tens of thousands more.

France followed the British pattern of granting independence with relatively little bloodshed to territories such as Tunisia, Morocco, and West Africa, where there were few white settlers. In Algeria, however, which had one million settlers of European descent, the French fought bitterly to keep control. In the final days of World War II, the French army massacred tens of thousands of Algerian nationalists seeking independence; however, the liberation movement resurfaced with new intensity in 1954 as the Front for National Liberation (FNL). The French dug in and savagely tortured Algerian Arabs; Algerian women, shielded from suspicion by gender stereotypes, planted bombs in European cafés and carried weapons to assassination sites. "The loss of Algeria," warned one statesman, defending French savagery, "would be an unprecedented national disaster," while the FNL, far less powerful and smaller in number, took its case to the court of world opinion. Reports of the French army's barbarous practices against Algeria's Muslim population prompted protests in Paris and around the globe, bringing wartime leader Charles de Gaulle to power in 1958. By 1962, de Gaulle had negotiated independence with the Algerian nationalists, and hundreds of thousands of Europeans in Algeria as well as their Arab supporters fled to France.

Violent resistance to the reimposition of colonial rule also ended the empires of the Dutch and Belgians. As newly independent nations emerged in Asia, Africa, and the Middle East, structures arose to promote international security and worldwide deliberations, including representation from the new states. Foremost among these organizations was the **United Nations (UN)**, convened for the first time in 1945. One notable change ensured the UN a greater chance of success than the League of Nations: both the United States and the Soviet Union were active members from the outset. The UN's charter outlined a collective global authority that would resolve conflicts and provide military protection if any members were

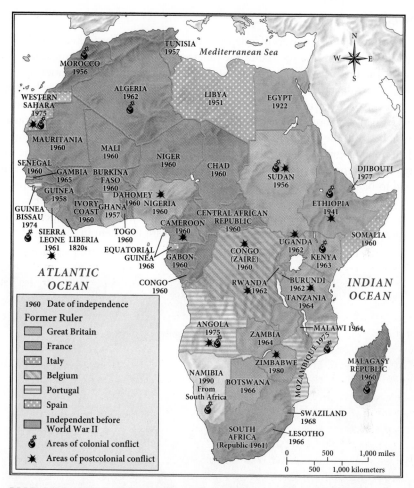

MAP 27.5 The Decolonization of Africa, 1951–1990 The liberation of Africa from European rule was an uneven process, sometimes occurring peacefully and at other times demanding armed struggle to drive out European settlers, governments, and armies. The difficult — and costly — process of nation building following liberation involved setting up state institutions, including educational and other services. Creating national unity out of many ethnicities also took work, except where the struggle against colonialism had already brought people together.

threatened by aggression. In 1955, the Indonesian president Sukarno, who had succeeded in wrenching Indonesian independence from the Dutch, sponsored the Bandung Convention of nonaligned nations to set a common policy for achieving modernization and facing the superpowers. Newly independent countries viewed the future with hope but still had to contend with the high costs of nation building and problems left over from decades of colonial exploitation.

Newcomers Arrive in Europe

Amid the uncertainties of wars of independence, people from the former colonies began migrating to Europe—a reversal of the nineteenth-century trend of migration out of Europe. The first non-Europeans came from Britain's Caribbean territories right after the war. Next, labor shortages in Germany, France, Switzerland, and elsewhere drove governments to negotiate with southern European countries for temporary workers. The German situation was particularly dire; in 1950, the working-age population (people between the ages of fifteen and sixty-four) was composed of 15.5 million men and 18 million women. In an ideological climate that wanted women out of the workforce, the government desperately needed immigrants. Germany and France next turned to North African and then to sub-Saharan countries in the 1960s. Immigrants from around the world flocked to Scandinavia because of reportedly greater opportunity and social programs to integrate newcomers. By the 1980s, some 8 percent of the European population was foreign-born, compared with 6 percent in the United States.

Newcomers to Europe   World War II disrupted everyday life and patterns of trade not only in Europe but also around the globe. Some of the first people to immigrate to Europe in search of postwar opportunity were from the Caribbean (like these men photographed in London in 1956) and South Asia. An expanding welfare state hired some of them to do menial work in hospitals, clinics, and construction, no matter what their qualifications. Governments and businesses in western Europe needed these new laborers to rebuild after World War II, and though some objected, many of these workers—and their wives and children—became not only citizens but political, economic, and cultural leaders as well. (© Hulton-Deutsch Collection/Corbis.)

According to negotiated agreements, immigrant workers would have only temporary resident status, with a regular process of return to their homeland. Turks and Algerians would arrive in Germany or France, for example, to work for a set period of time, return home temporarily to see their families, then head back to Europe for another period as guest workers. They were welcomed because they took few social services, not even needing education because they came as adults. For businesspeople, temporary workers made good economic sense; often their menial work was off the books. "As they are young," one French business publication added, "the immigrants often pay more in taxes than they receive in allowances." Most immigrants did jobs that people in the West avoided: they collected garbage, built roads, and cleaned homes. Although men predominated among migrant workers, women performed similar chores for even less pay.

Immigrants came to see Europe as a land of relatively good government, wealth, and opportunity. Living conditions, too, seemed decent to many. The advantages of living in Europe, especially the higher wages, made many decide to stay and soon attracted clandestine workers to countries like Italy that had formerly exported labor. As empires collapsed, European populations became more diverse in terms of race, religion, ethnicity, and social life. Across Europe and North America, many newcomers eventually became citizens and their children achieved good positions in government, business, education, and the professions.

REVIEW   What were the results of decolonization?

Daily Life and Culture in the Shadow of Nuclear War

Both World War II and the cold war shaped postwar culture. People across Europe engaged in heated debates over who was responsible for Nazism and how to achieve ethnic and racial justice. Europeans also discussed the Americanization that seemed to accompany the influx of U.S. dollars, consumer goods, and cultural media. As Europeans examined their war-filled past and their newfound prosperity, the cold war menaced hopes for peace and stability. In 1961, the USSR demanded the construction of a massive wall that physically divided the city of Berlin in half. In October 1962, the world held its breath while the leaders of the Soviet Union and the United States nearly provoked nuclear conflagration over the issue of missiles on the island of Cuba. In hindsight, the existence of extreme nuclear threat in an age of unprecedented prosperity seems utterly bewildering, but for those who lived with the threat of global annihilation, the dangers were all too real.

Restoring "Western" Values

After the depravity of Nazism and fascism, cultural currents in Europe and the United States reemphasized universal values. Responding to what he saw as a crisis in faith caused by affluence and secularism, Pope John XXIII (r. 1958–1963) in 1962 convened the Second Vatican Council. Known as **Vatican II**, this council modernized the liturgy, democratized many church procedures, and at the last session in 1965 renounced church doctrine that condemned the Jewish people as guilty of killing Jesus. Vatican II promoted ecumenism—that is, mutual cooperation among the world's faiths—and outreach to the world without imperial designs.

In the early postwar years, people in the U.S. bloc emphasized the triumph of a Western heritage, a Western civilization, and Western values as they encountered "barbaric" forces, a concept that came to include nomadic tribes, Nazi armies, Communist agents, or national liberation movements in Asia and Africa. Many white Europeans looked back nostalgically on their imperial history and produced exotic films and novels about conquest and its pageantry.

Readers around the world snapped up memoirs of the death camps and tales of the resistance. Rescued from the Third Reich in 1940, Nelly Sachs won the Nobel Prize for Literature in 1966 for her poetry about the Holocaust. Anne Frank's *Diary of a Young Girl* (1947), the moving record of a Jewish teenager hidden with her family in the back of an Amsterdam house, showed the survival of Western values in the face of Nazi persecution. Amid the menacing evils of Nazism, Frank, who died near the end of the war in the Bergen-Belsen camp, wrote that she never stopped believing that "people are really good at heart." Governments erected permanent plaques at spots where resisters had been killed, and organizations of resisters publicly commemorated their role in winning the war, hiding the fact of widespread collaboration. Many a politician with a Nazi past returned easily to the new cultural mainstream even as the stories of resistance took on mythical qualities.

At the end of the 1940s, **existentialism** became the rage among the cultural elites and students in universities. This philosophy explored the meaning of human existence in a world where evil flourished. Two of existentialism's leaders, Albert Camus and Jean-Paul Sartre, confronted the question of "being," given what they perceived as the absence of God and the tragic breakdown of morality. Their answer was that being, or existing, was not the automatic process either of God's creation or of birth into the natural world. One was not born with spiritual goodness in the image of a creator, but instead one created an "authentic" existence through action and choice. Sartre's writings emphasized political activism and resistance under totalitarianism. Even though they had never confronted the enormous problems of making choices while living under fascism, young people in the 1950s found existentialism compelling and made it the most fashionable philosophy of the day.

In 1949, **Simone de Beauvoir**, Sartre's lifetime companion, published the twentieth century's most important work on the condition of women, *The Second Sex*. Beauvoir believed that most women had failed to take the kind of action necessary to lead authentic lives. Instead, they lived in the world of biological necessity, devoting themselves exclusively to having children. Failing to create an authentic self through action and accomplishment, they had become its opposite—an object, or "Other." Moreover, instead of struggling to define themselves and assert their freedom, women passively accepted their lives as defined by men. Beauvoir's now classic book was a smash hit, and people wrote her thousands of letters asking for advice. Both Sartre and Beauvoir became celebrities, for the media spread the new commitment to humane values just as it had previously spread support for Nazism or for other political ideas.

People of color in Africa and Asia contributed new theories of humanity by exploring the topics of liberation and racial difference. During the 1950s, Frantz Fanon, a black psychiatrist from the French colony of Martinique, began analyzing liberation movements, gaining his insights from his participation in the Algerian war of liberation and other struggles at the time. He wrote that the mental functioning of the colonized person was "traumatized" by the brutal imposition of an outside culture. Ruled by guns, the colonized person knew only violence and would thus naturally decolonize by means of violence. Translated into many languages, Fanon's *Black Skin, White Masks* (1952) and *The Wretched of the Earth* (1961) posed the question of how to decolonize one's culture and mind.

Simultaneously, the commitment to the cause of civil rights intensified in the 1950s. African Americans had fought in World War II to defeat the Nazi idea of white racial superiority; as civilians, they now hoped to advance that ideal in the United States. With its ruling in *Brown v. Board of Education* (1954), the U.S. Supreme Court declared that segregated education violated the U.S. Constitution. In December 1955, in Montgomery, Alabama, Rosa Parks, a seamstress and part-time secretary for the local branch of the National Association for the Advancement of Colored People (NAACP), boarded a city bus and took the first available seat in the "colored" section. When a white man found himself without a seat, the driver screamed at Parks, "Nigger, move back." She refused to move, and her studied use of civil disobedience led to widespread nonviolent disobedience among African Americans throughout the South. Talented leaders emerged, foremost among them the great orator Martin Luther King Jr. (1929–1968), a Baptist pastor from Georgia who advocated "soulforce" — Gandhi's *satyagraha* ("holding to truth") — to counter aggression. The postwar culture of nonviolence shaped the early years of the U.S. civil rights movement until the influence of Fanon and other third world activists turned some toward more violent activism.

Cold War Consumerism and Shifting Gender Norms

Government spending on Europe's reconstruction and welfare after World War II helped prevent the kind of upheaval that had followed World War I. Meanwhile, the rising birthrate and bustling youth culture led to an upsurge in consumer spending that created jobs for veterans. Nonetheless, the war had affected men's roles and sense of themselves. Young men who had missed World War II adopted the rough, violent style of soldiers, and roaming gangs posed as tough military types. While Soviet youth admired aviator aces, elsewhere groups such as the "teddy boys" in England (named after their Edwardian style of dressing) and the *gamberros* ("hooligans") in Spain took their cues from pop culture in rock-and-roll music and film.

Rock and Roll   Rock and roll, born in the 1950s, swept cities around the world with unprecedented energy and speed. Teen women wore the voluminous skirts that the "new look" had made fashionable in the late 1940s, and young men sported hairdos like that of Elvis Presley. East and west, teens thronged and even rioted to attend rock concerts and would continue to do so despite public criticism and even police action against the movement. (ullstein bild/The Granger Collection, NYC—All rights reserved.)

The leader of rock-and-roll style was the American singer Elvis Presley. Sporting slicked-back hair and an aviator-style jacket, Presley bucked his hips and sang sexual lyrics to screaming and devoted fans. Rock-and-roll concerts and movies galvanized youth across Europe, including the Soviet bloc, where teens demanded the production of blue jeans and leather jackets. In a German nightclub late in the 1950s, members of a British rock group of Elvis fans called the Quarrymen performed, yelling at and fighting with one another as part of their show. They would soon become known as the Beatles. Rebellious young American film stars like James Dean in *Rebel Without a Cause* (1955) created the beginnings of a postwar youth culture in which the ideal was to be a bad boy. The rebellious and rough masculine style appeared also in literature, for example in James Watson's autobiography, *The Double Helix* (1968), in which he described how he and Francis Crick had discovered the structure of the DNA molecule by stealing other people's findings. American "beat" poets and writers vehemently rejected the traditional ideals of the upright male breadwinner, family man, and responsible achiever. The 1953 inaugural issue of the American magazine *Playboy*, and the hundreds of magazines that imitated it across Europe, presented the modern man as sexually aggressive and independent of dull domestic life—just as he had been in the war. The definition of men's citizenship had come to include not just political and economic rights but also sexual freedom outside the restrictions of marriage.

In contrast, Western society promoted a postwar model for women that differed from their wartime roles, adopting instead the fascist notion of women's inferiority. Rather than being essential workers and heads of families in the absence of their men, postwar women were to symbolize the return to normalcy by leading a domestic and submissive life at home. Late in the 1940s, the fashion house of Christian Dior launched a clothing style called the "new look." It featured pinched waists, tightly fitting bodices, and voluminous skirts. This restoration of the nineteenth-century female silhouette invited a renewal of clearly defined gender roles. Women's magazines publicized the new look and urged women to give up ambitions for themselves. Even in the hard-pressed Soviet Union, domesticity flourished; recipes for homemade face creams, for example, passed from woman to woman, and beauty parlors did a brisk business. In the West, household products such as refrigerators and washing machines raised standards for housekeeping by giving women the means to be "perfect" housewives.

However, new-look propaganda did not necessarily mesh with reality or even with all social norms. Dressmaking fabric was still being rationed in the late 1940s; even in the next decade, women could not always get enough of it to make voluminous skirts. In Europe, where people had barely enough to eat, the underwear needed for new-look contours simply did not exist—although for many, unfortunately, the semistarved look was not achieved by choice. Moreover, European women continued to work outside the home after the war; indeed, mature women and mothers were working more than ever before—especially in the Soviet bloc. Across the Soviet sphere consumer goods were always in short supply, but opinion makers stressed to these women the importance of a tasteful and up-to-date domestic interior. East and West, the female workforce was going through a profound revolution as it gradually became populated by wives and mothers who would hold jobs all their lives despite being bombarded with images of nineteenth-century femininity.

The advertising business presided over the creation of these cultural messages as part of both the return of consumerism and the cold war. Guided by marketing experts, western Europeans imitated Americans by drinking Coca-Cola; using American detergents, toothpaste, and soap; and driving some forty million motorized vehicles, including motorbikes, cars, buses, and trucks. While many Europeans embraced American business practices, the cold war was ever present: the Communist Party in France led a successful campaign to ban Coca-Cola for a time in the 1950s, and tastemakers in the Soviet sphere initiated competing products and styles.

Radio remained the most influential medium in the 1950s, carrying much of the postwar consumer advertising and making the connection between cold war and consumerism. Even as the number of radios in homes grew steadily, television loomed on the horizon. In the United States, two-thirds of the population had TV sets in the early 1950s, while in Britain only one-fifth did. Only in the 1960s did television become an important consumer item for most Europeans. In radio and television, though, both East and West tried to exceed the other in advertising their values. Russian programs stressed a uniform Communist culture, often emphasizing the importance of family values and practical, if aesthetically pleasing, household tips for women. The United States, by contrast, promoted debate about current affairs and filled the airwaves with advertising for consumer goods. The cold war was thus a consumer as well as a military phenomenon.

The Culture of Cold War

Films, books, and other cultural productions also promoted the cold war even when they conveyed an antiwar message. Books like George Orwell's *1984* (1949) were claimed by both sides in the cold war as supporting their position. Ray Bradbury's popular *Fahrenheit 451* (1953), whose title refers to the temperature at which books would burn, condemned restrictions on intellectual freedom on both sides of the cold war divide. In the USSR, official writers churned out spy stories, and espionage novels topped best-seller lists in the West. *Casino Royale* (1953), by the British author Ian Fleming, introduced the fictional British intelligence agent James Bond, who tested his wit and physical prowess against Communist and other political villains. So popular were such programs that Soviet pilots would not take off for flights when the work of Yulian Simyonov, the Russian counterpart of Ian Fleming, was playing on radio or television. Reports, fictional and real, of Soviet- and U.S.-bloc characters facing one another down became part of everyday life.

High culture also operated in a cold war climate. Europe's major cities rebuilt their war-ravaged opera houses and museums, and both sides tried to win the cold war by pouring vast sums of money into high culture. As leadership of the art world passed to the United States, art became part of the cold war. Abstract expressionists such as American artist Jackson Pollock produced nonrepresentational works by dripping and spattering paint; they also spoke of the importance of the artist's self-discovery in the process of painting. "If I stretch my arms next to the rest of myself and wonder where my fingers are, that is all the space I need as a painter," commented Dutch-born artist Willem de Kooning on his relationship with his canvas. Said to exemplify Western freedom, such painters were awarded commissions at the secret direction of the U.S. Central Intelligence Agency (CIA).

The USSR more openly promoted an official Communist culture. When a show of abstract art like Pollock's opened in the Soviet Union, Khrushchev yelled that it was "dog shit." Pro-Soviet critics in western Europe saw U.S.-style abstract art as "an infantile sickness" and supported socialist realist art with "human content," showing the condition of the workers and the oppressed races in the United States. The Italian filmmakers Roberto Rossellini, in *Open City* (1945), and Vittorio De Sica, in *The Bicycle Thief* (1948), developed the neorealist technique that challenged lush Hollywood-style sets and costumes by using ordinary characters living in devastated, impoverished cities. By depicting stark conditions, neorealist directors conveyed their distance both from middle-class prosperity and from fascist bombast. "We are in rags? Let's show everyone our rags," said one Italian director. Many of these left-leaning directors associated support for the suffering masses with the Communist cause, while on the pro-American side, the film *Doctor Zhivago* became a hit celebrating individualism and condemning the Communist way of life. Overtly or covertly, the cold war affected virtually all aspects of cultural life.

The Atomic Brink

The 1950s were a time of emotional terror for people at the center of the cold war. Radio bombarded the public with messages about the threat of nuclear annihilation at the hands of the villainous superpower enemy (meaning the United States or the USSR, depending). During the late 1940s and 1950s, the Voice of America, with its main studio in Washington, D.C., broadcast in thirty-eight languages from one hundred transmitters and provided an alternative source of news as well as menacing messages for people in eastern Europe. Its Soviet counterpart broadcast in Russian around the clock but initially spent much of its wattage jamming U.S. programming. The public also heard reports of nuclear buildups and tests of emergency power facilities that sent them scurrying for cover. Children rehearsed at school for nuclear war, while at home families built bomb shelters in their backyards. Fear gripped people's emotions in these decades.

In this upsetting climate of cold war, **John Fitzgerald Kennedy** (1917–1963) became U.S. president in 1960. Kennedy represented American affluence and youth; he also confirmed the power of television. A war hero and an early fan of the fictional cold war spy James Bond, Kennedy participated in the escalating cold war over the nearby island of Cuba, where in 1959 Fidel Castro (1926–) had come to power. After being rebuffed by the United States, Castro aligned his new government with the Soviet Union. In the spring of 1961, Kennedy, assured by the CIA of success, launched an invasion of Cuba at the Bay of Pigs to overthrow Castro. The invasion failed miserably and humiliated the United States.

Cold war tensions increased. In the summer of 1961, the East German government directed workers to stack bales of barbed wire across miles of the city's east–west border. This was the beginning of the Berlin Wall, built to block the escape route by which some three million people had fled to the West. In October 1962, tensions came to a head in the **Cuban missile crisis**, when the CIA reported the installation of silos to house Soviet medium-range missiles in

Cuba. Kennedy acted forcefully, ordering a naval blockade of ships headed for Cuba and demanding removal of the installations. For several days, the world stood on the brink of nuclear war. Then, between October 25 and 27, Khrushchev and Kennedy negotiated an end to the crisis. Kennedy spent the remainder of his short life working to improve nuclear diplomacy; Khrushchev did the same. In the summer of 1963, less than a year after the shock of the Cuban missile crisis, the United States and the Soviet Union signed a test-ban treaty outlawing the explosion of nuclear weapons in the atmosphere and in the seas. The treaty held out hope that the cold war and its culture would give way to something better.

> **REVIEW**   How were everyday culture and social life part of the cold war?

Conclusion

Nikita Khrushchev was ousted in 1964 for his erratic policies and for the Cuban missile crisis. In his forced retirement, he expressed regret at his brutal treatment of Boris Pasternak: "We shouldn't have banned [*Doctor Zhivago*]. There's nothing anti-Soviet in it." But the postwar decades were grim times. Two superpowers — the Soviet Union and the United States — each controlling atomic arsenals, overshadowed European leadership and engaged in a menacing cold war, complete with the threat of nuclear annihilation. The cold war saturated everyday life, giving birth to bomb shelters, spies, purges, and witch hunts — all of them creating a culture of anxiety that kept people in constant fear of war. Cold war diplomacy divided Europe into an eastern bloc dominated by the Soviets and a freer western bloc mostly allied with the United States. In this bleak atmosphere, starving, homeless, and refugee people joined the task of rebuilding a devastated Europe.

Despite the chaos at the end of 1945, both halves of Europe recovered almost miraculously in little more than a decade. Eastern Europe, where wartime devastation and ongoing violence were greatest, experienced less prosperity. In the West, wartime technology served as the basis for new consumer goods and welfare-state planning improved health. Spurred on by aid from the United States, western Europe formed the successful Common Market, which became the foundation for greater European unity in the future. As a result of World War II and the cold war, Germany recovered as two countries, not one. The war so weakened the European powers that they lost their colonies to thriving independence movements. Newly independent nations emerged in Asia and Africa, but they were often caught in the cold war and faced the additional problems of creating stable political structures and a sound economic future. As the West as a whole grew in prosperity, its cultural life focused paradoxically on reviving Western values while enjoying the new phenomenon of mass consumerism. Above all, the West — and the rest of the world — had to survive the atomic rivalry of the superpowers.

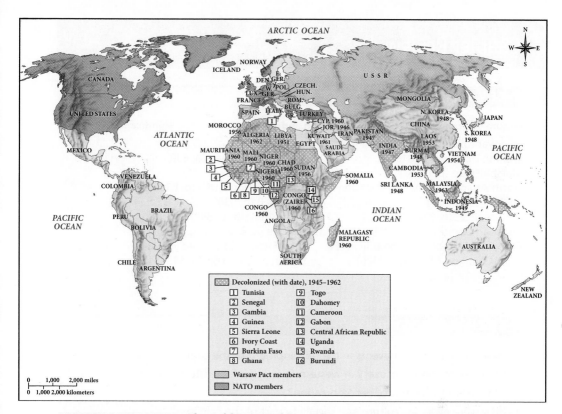

MAPPING THE WEST   The Cold War World, c. 1960   Superpower rivalry between the United States and the Soviet Union resulted in the division of much of the industrial world into cold war alliances. Simultaneously, the superpowers vied for the allegiance of the newly decolonized countries of Asia and Africa by providing military, economic, and technological assistance. Wars such as those in Vietnam and Korea were also products of the cold war. How might this map be said to convey the idea that a first world, a second world, and a third world existed? How does this map differ from the map on page 705?

Chapter Review

KEY TERMS AND PEOPLE

Be sure you can identify the term or person and explain its historical significance.

cold war (p. 815)

Truman Doctrine (p. 819)

Marshall Plan (p. 819)

North Atlantic Treaty Organization
(NATO) (p. 822)

Warsaw Pact (p. 822)

Christian Democrats (p. 824)

European Economic Community (EEC
or Common Market) (p. 826)

welfare state (p. 827)

Nikita Khrushchev (p. 830)

decolonization (p. 831)

United Nations (UN) (p. 834)

Vatican II (p. 838)

existentialism (p. 838)

Simone de Beauvoir (p. 838)

John Fitzgerald Kennedy (p. 843)

Cuban missile crisis (p. 843)

REVIEW QUESTIONS

1. What were the major events in the development of the cold war?
2. What factors drove recovery in western Europe and in eastern Europe?
3. What were the results of decolonization?
4. How were everyday culture and social life part of the cold war?

MAKING CONNECTIONS

1. What was the political climate after World War II, and how did it differ
   from the political climate after World War I?
2. What were the relative strengths of the two European blocs in the cold
   war?
3. What were the main developments of postwar cultural life?
4. Why did decolonization follow World War II so immediately?

IMPORTANT EVENTS

1945   • Cold war begins

1947   • India and Pakistan win independence from Britain

1948   • State of Israel is established

1949   • Mao Zedong leads Communist revolution in China; Simone de Beauvoir publishes *The Second Sex*

1950   • Korean War begins

1953   • Stalin dies; Korean War ends

1954   • *Brown v. Board of Education* prohibits segregated schools in the United States; Vietnamese forces defeat French at Dien Bien Phu

1956   • General Abdel Nasser nationalizes Suez Canal; uprising in Hungary against USSR

1957   • Boris Pasternak publishes *Doctor Zhivago*; USSR launches *Sputnik*; Treaty of Rome establishes European Economic Community (Common Market)

1958   • Fifth Republic begins in France

1962   • United States and USSR face off in the Cuban missile crisis

28

Postindustrial Society and the End of the Cold War Order

1960s–1989

CHAPTER FOCUS

How did technological, economic, and social change contribute to increased activism, and what were the political results of that activism?

IN JANUARY 1969, JAN PALACH, a twenty-one-year-old philosophy student, drove to a main square in Prague, doused his body with gasoline, and set himself ablaze. Before that, he had put aside his coat with a message in it demanding an end to Communist repression in Czechoslovakia. It promised more such suicides unless the government lifted state censorship. The manifesto was signed "Torch No. 1." Jan Palach's suicide stunned his nation. Black flags hung from windows, and close to a million people flocked to his funeral. In the next months, more Czech youth followed Palach's grim example and became torches for freedom.

Before his self-immolation, Jan Palach was an ordinary, well-educated citizen of an increasingly technological society. Having recovered from World War II, the West shifted from a manufacturing economy based on heavy industry to a service economy that depended on technical knowledge in such fields as engineering, health care, and finance. This new service economy has been labeled "postindustrial." To staff it, institutions of higher education sprang up at a dizzying rate and attracted more students than ever before. Young men like Jan Palach—along with women, minorities, and many other activists in the 1960s and 1970s—far from being satisfied with their rising status, struck out against war and cold war, inequality and repression, and even against technology itself. From Czechoslovakia to the United States and around the world, protesters warned that postindustrial nations in general and the superpowers in particular were becoming technological and political monsters. Before long, countries in both the Soviet and U.S. blocs were on the verge of political revolution.

The challenges posed by young reformers came at a bad time for the superpowers and other leading European states. An agonizing war in Vietnam weakened the United States, and China confronted the Soviet Union on its borders. In a dramatic turn of events, the oil-producing states of the Middle East reduced the export of oil to the leading Western nations in the 1970s, bringing on a recession. Despite their wealth and military might, the superpowers could not guarantee that they would emerge victorious in this age of increasingly global competition. As the USSR experienced decay in a climate of postindustrial innovation across the West, a reform-minded leader—Mikhail Gorbachev—initiated new policies of economic and political freedom. It was too late: in 1989, the Soviet bloc collapsed, an event brought about in part by countless acts of protest, not least of them the individual heroism of Jan Palach and his fellow human torches.

The Revolution in Technology

The protests of the 1960s began in the midst of astonishing technological advances in all areas of life. These advances steadily boosted prosperity and changed daily life in the West, where people awoke to instantaneous radio and television news, worked with computers, and used new forms of contraceptives to control reproduction. Satellites orbiting the earth relayed telephone signals and collected military intelligence, while around the world nuclear energy powered economies. Smaller gadgets— electric popcorn poppers, portable radios and tape players, automatic garage door openers—made life more pleasant. The increased use of machines led one philosopher to insist that people were no longer self-sufficient individuals, but rather cyborgs—that is, humans who needed machines to sustain ordinary life processes.

The Information Age: Television and Computers

Information technology powered change in the postindustrial period that began in the 1960s, just as innovations in textile making and the spread of railroads had in the nineteenth century. This technology's ability to transmit knowledge, culture, and political information globally competed with mass journalism, film, and radio via television, computers, and telecommunications. Once-remote villages were linked to urban capitals on the other side of the world thanks to videocassettes, satellite television, and telecommunications. Because of technology, protests became media events worldwide.

Americans embraced television in the 1950s; between the mid-1950s and the mid-1970s, Europeans rapidly adopted television as a major entertainment and communications medium. In 1954, just 1 percent of French households had television; by 1974, almost 80 percent did. With the average viewer tuning in about four and a half hours a day, the audience for newspapers and theater declined. "We devote more . . . hours per year to television than [to] any other single artifact," one sociologist commented in 1969. As with radio, European governments funded television broadcasting with tax dollars and controlled TV programming to avoid what they perceived as the substandard fare offered by American commercial TV; instead they featured drama, ballet, concerts, variety shows, and news. The welfare state, in Europe at least, thereby gained more power to shape daily life.

The emergence of communications satellites and video recorders in the 1960s brought competition to state-sponsored television. Worldwide audiences enjoyed broadcasts from throughout the West as satellite technology allowed for the global transmission of sports broadcasts and other programming. Soap operas, game shows, and situation comedies (sitcoms) from the United States arrived dubbed in native languages. Feature films on videotape first became readily available to television stations; then, in 1969, competition increased when the Sony Corporation introduced the first affordable color videocassette recorder to the consumer market.

East and west, television exercised a powerful political and cultural influence. Even in a rural area of the Soviet Union, more than 70 percent of the inhabitants watched television regularly in the late 1970s. Educational programming united the far-flung population of the USSR by broadcasting shows designed to advance Soviet culture. At the same time, with travel impossible or forbidden to many in the Soviet world, shows about foreign lands were among the most popular. Heads of state could usually bump regular programming. In the 1960s, French president Charles de Gaulle appeared frequently on television, using the grandiose gestures of an imperial ruler to stir patriotism. Increasingly, politicians needed media experts as much as they did policy experts.

Just as revolutionary as television, the computer reshaped work in science, defense, and ultimately industry. Computers had evolved dramatically since the first electronic ones, like the Colossus used by the British in 1943 to decode Nazi military and diplomatic messages. From the 1940s to the 1980s, computing machines shrank from the size of a gymnasium to that of an attaché case. They also became both far less expensive and fantastically more powerful, thanks to the development of increasingly sophisticated digital electronic circuitry implanted on tiny silicon chips, which replaced clumsy radio tubes. Within a few decades, the computer could perform hundreds of millions of operations per second and the price of the integrated circuit at the heart of computer technology would fall to less than a dollar.

Computers changed the pace and patterns of work not only by speeding up tasks but also by performing many operations that workers had once done themselves. Soon, like other outworkers, people could work for large industries at home, connected to a central mainframe. In 1981, the French phone company launched a public computer network, the Minitel (a forerunner of the World Wide Web), through which individuals could make travel reservations, perform stock transactions, and obtain information. Many observers believed that computers would profoundly expand mental capacity, providing, in the words of one scientist, "boundless opportunities . . . to resolve the puzzles of cosmology, of life, and of the society of man." Others countered that computers programmed people, reducing human initiative and the ability to solve problems. Regardless of observers' opinions, positive or negative, the information revolution was under way.

The Space Age

The "space race" between the United States and the Soviet Union, also made possible by computers, began when the Soviets launched the satellite *Sputnik* in 1957. The competition led to increasingly complex space flights that tested humans' ability to survive the process of space exploration, including weightlessness. Astronauts walked in space, endured weeks (and later months) in orbit, docked with other craft, fixed satellites, and carried out experiments for the military and private industry. In addition, a series of unmanned rockets launched weather, television, intelligence, and other

Valentina Tereshkova, Russian Cosmonaut People sent into space became heroes, representing modern values of courage, strength, and well-honed skills. Insofar as the space age was part of the cold war race for superpower superiority, the USSR held the lead during the first decade. The Soviets trained both women and men, and the 1963 flight of Valentina Tereshkova — the first woman in space — supported Soviet claims of gender equality in contrast to the all-male superstar image of the early U.S. space program. (Central Press / Getty Images.)

communications satellites into orbit around the earth. In July 1969, a worldwide television audience watched as U.S. astronauts Neil Armstrong and Edwin "Buzz" Aldrin walked on the moon's surface—the climactic moment in the space race.

The space race also influenced Western culture. Astronauts and cosmonauts were perhaps the era's most admired heroes: Yuri Gagarin, John Glenn, and Valentina Tereshkova—the first woman in space—topped the list. A whole new fantasy world developed. Children's toys and games revolved increasingly around space. Films such as *2001: A Space Odyssey* (1968) portrayed space explorers answering questions about life that were formerly the domain of church leaders. Polish author Stanislaw Lem's popular novel *Solaris* (1961), later made into a film, described space-age individuals engaged in personal quests that drew readers and ultimately viewers into a futuristic fantasy.

The space age grew out of cold war concerns, and advances in rocket technology not only launched vehicles into space but also powered destructive missiles. At the same time, the space age promoted and even depended on global cooperation. From the 1960s on, U.S. spaceflights often involved the participation of other countries. In 1965, an international consortium headed by the United States launched the first commercial communications satellite, *Intelsat I*—a feat envisioned since early in the postwar period. By the 1970s, some 150 countries were working together at more than four hundred stations worldwide to maintain global satellite communications. Although some 50 percent of satellites were for spying purposes, the rest promoted international communication and transnational collaboration.

Pure science flourished amid the space race. Astronomers used mineral samples from the moon to calculate the age of the solar system with unprecedented precision. Unmanned spacecraft provided data on cosmic radiation, magnetic fields, and infrared sources. Although the media depicted the space age as one of warrior astronauts conquering space, breakthroughs depended on the products of technology, including the radio telescope, which depicted space by receiving, measuring, and calculating nonvisible rays. These findings reinforced the so-called big bang theory of the origin of the universe, first outlined in the 1930s by American astronomer Edwin Hubble and given crucial support in the 1950s by the discovery of low-level radiation permeating the universe in all directions. The big bang theory proposes that the universe originated from the explosion of superdense, superhot matter some ten to twenty billion years ago.

The Nuclear Age

Scientists, government officials, and engineers put the force of the atom to economic use, especially in the form of nuclear power, and the dramatic boost in available energy helped continue postwar economic expansion into the 1960s and beyond. The USSR built the world's first civilian nuclear power station, in the town of Obninsk, in 1954; Britain and the United States soon followed suit. During the 1960s and 1970s, nuclear power for industrial and household use multiplied a hundredfold—a growth that did not include nuclear-powered submarines and aircraft carriers, which also multiplied during this period.

Because of the vast costs and complex procedures involved in building, supplying, running, and safeguarding nuclear reactors, governments provided substantial aid and even financed nuclear power plants almost entirely. "A state does not count," announced French president Charles de Gaulle, "if it does not . . . contribute to the technological progress of the world." The watchword for all governments building nuclear reactors was technological development—a new function for the modern state. The USSR sponsored plants throughout the Soviet bloc as part of the drive to modernize, but it was not alone—Western nations, too, funded nuclear power. In 2006, France produced some 80 percent of its energy, and the United States 20 percent, via nuclear power plants. More than thirty countries had substantial nuclear installations in the twenty-first century, with new ones under construction.

Revolutions in Biology and Reproductive Technology

A revolution in the life sciences brought about dramatic health benefits and ultimately changed reproduction itself. In 1952, scientists Francis Crick, an Englishman, and James Watson, an American, discovered the structure of deoxyribonucleic acid (**DNA**), the material in a cell's chromosomes that carries hereditary information. Simultaneously, other scientists were working on "the pill"—an oral contraceptive for women that capped more than a century of scientific work in the field of birth control. Still other breakthroughs in biology lay ahead, including ones that revolutionized conception and made possible the scientific duplication of species (cloning).

Crick and Watson solved the mystery of biological inheritance when they demonstrated the structure of DNA. They showed how the double helix of the DNA molecule splits in cellular reproduction to form the basis of each new cell. This genetic material, biologists concluded, provides a chemical pattern for an individual organism's life. Beginning in the 1960s, genetics and the new field of molecular biology not only increased knowledge about viruses and bacteria but also effectively ended in the West such diseases as polio, mumps, measles, and tetanus through the development of new vaccines.

Other scientists used their understanding of DNA to alter the makeup of plants (for instance, to control agricultural pests) and to bypass natural animal reproduction in a process called cloning—obtaining the cells of an organism and dividing or reproducing them in an exact copy in a laboratory. In 1967, Dr. Christiaan Barnard of South Africa performed the first successful heart transplant. Other researchers later developed both immunosuppressants (to prevent rejection of the transplant) and an artificial heart. As major advances like these occurred, commentators began to ask whether the enormous cost of new medical technology to save a few people would be better spent on helping the many who lacked even basic medical care.

Technology also influenced the most intimate areas of human relations—sexuality and procreation. Matching family size to agricultural productivity no longer shaped sexual behavior in the industrialized and urbanized West. With reliable birth-control devices more readily available, young people began sexual relations earlier, with less risk of pregnancy. These trends accelerated in the 1960s when the birth-control pill, the result of research around the world, was first marketed in the United States. The pill was initially tested on American medical students in Puerto Rico and then on a larger scale among Puerto Rican nurses, many of whom were eager for reliable contraception. By 1970, the pill's use was spreading around the world. New techniques brought abortion, traditionally performed by amateurs, into the hands of medical professionals, making it a safe procedure for the first time.

Conception and childbirth were similarly transformed. Whereas only a small minority of Western births took place in hospitals in 1920, more than 90 percent did by 1970. Obstetricians now performed much of the work midwives had once done. As pregnancy and birth became medicalized, the number of medical interventions such as cesarean births rose. In 1978, the first "test-tube baby," Louise Brown, was born to an English couple. She had been conceived when her mother's eggs were fertilized with her father's sperm in a laboratory dish and then implanted in her mother's uterus—a complex process called **in vitro fertilization**. In reproductive technology, as in other areas, the revolution in biology was dramatically changing human life, improving health, and even making new life possible.

> **REVIEW**   What were the technological and scientific advances of the 1960s and 1970s, and how did they change human life and society?

Postindustrial Society and Culture

Soaring investments in science and the spread of technology put Western countries on what has been labeled a postindustrial course. Instead of being centered on manufacturing and heavy industry, a postindustrial economy emphasized the distribution of services such as health care and education. This meant that intellectual work, as well as industrial work, was central to creating jobs and profits. Moreover, all parts of society and industry interlocked, forming a system constantly in need of complex analysis, as in the nuclear industry. These characteristics of postindustrial society and culture would carry over into the twenty-first century.

Multinational Corporations

A major development of the postindustrial era was the growth of the **multinational corporation**. Multinationals produced goods and services for a global market and conducted business worldwide, but unlike older kinds of international firms, they established major factories and managerial centers in countries other than their home base. For example, of the five hundred largest businesses in the United States in 1970, more than one hundred did over a quarter of their business abroad, with business machine manufacturer IBM operating in more than one hundred countries. Although U.S.-based corporations led the way, European and Japanese multinationals like Volkswagen, Shell, Nestlé, and Sony also had a broad global reach.

Some multinational corporations burst the bounds of the nation-state as they set up shop in whatever part of the world offered cheap labor. In the first years after World War II, multinationals preferred European employees, who constituted a highly educated labor pool and had well-developed consumer habits. Then, beginning in the 1960s, multinationals moved more of their operations to the emerging economies of formerly colonized states to reduce labor costs and avoid taxes. Although multinational corporations provided jobs in developing areas, profits usually went out of those areas to enrich foreign stockholders. Multinational corporations lacked the interest in the well-being of localities or nations that earlier industrialists had often shown. Thus, this system of business looked to some like imperialism in a new form.

Managers believed that their firms could stay competitive only by expanding, merging with other companies, or partnering with governments. They also increased their companies' investment in research and used international cooperation to produce major new products. Beginning with its first commercial flight in 1976, the British-French Concorde supersonic aircraft flew from London to New York in less than four hours. Another venture was the Airbus, a more practical series of passenger jets inaugurated in 1972 by a consortium of European firms. Both projects grew from the strong relationships among government, business, and science as well as from the international cooperation in manufacturing among members of the Common Market. Such relationships allowed European businesses to compete successfully with U.S.-based and other multinational giants.

The New Worker

In the early years of industry, workers often labored to exhaustion and lived in poor conditions. This situation changed fundamentally in postwar Europe with the reduction of the blue-collar workforce and increased automation of industrial work. Manufacturing was simply cleaner and less dangerous than ever before. Meanwhile, a new working class of white-collar service personnel emerged. Its rise undermined economic distinctions based on the way a person worked, for those who performed service work or had managerial titles were not necessarily better paid than blue-collar laborers. The ranks of service workers swelled with researchers, planners, health care and medical staff, and government functionaries. As emphasis on service grew, entire categories of employees such as flight attendants devoted much of their skill to the psychological well-being of customers. By 1969, the percentage of service-sector employees had surpassed that of manufacturing workers in several industrial countries: 61.1 percent versus 33.7 percent in the United States, and 48.8 percent versus 41.1 percent in Sweden.

Postindustrial work life differed somewhat in the Soviet bloc. There, the percentage of farmers remained higher than in western Europe. A huge difference between professional occupations and those involving physical work also remained in socialist countries because of declining investment in advanced machinery and cleaner work processes. Men in both the U.S. and Soviet blocs generally earned higher pay and had better jobs than women. Uniquely in the Soviet bloc, however, women's badly paying jobs included street cleaning, garbage collection, heavy labor on farms, general medicine, and dentistry. Somewhere between 80 and 95 percent of women in socialist countries worked, mostly under difficult conditions.

Farming changed as well, consolidating and becoming more scientific. Small landowners sold family plots to corporations engaged in agribusiness—that is, vast acreage devoted to commercial rather than peasant farming. Governments, farmers' cooperatives, and planning agencies shaped the decision making of the individual farmer, while genetic research that yielded pest-resistant seeds and the skyrocketing use of pesticides, fertilizers, and machinery contributed to economic growth. For example, in the 1970s, a woman named Fernande Pelletier ran a hundred-acre farm in southwestern France, using the advice of a government expert to produce whatever foods might sell competitively in the Common Market and joining with other farmers in her region to buy heavy machinery. Agricultural prosperity required as much managerial and technical know-how as did success in other parts of the economy.

The Boom in Education and Research

Education and research were key to running postindustrial society and had now become the means by which nations maintained their economic and military might. In the West, common sense, hard work, and creative intuition had launched the earliest successes of the Industrial Revolution. By the late twentieth century, a wide variety of expertise and ever-growing staffs of researchers fueled military and industrial leadership. The United States funneled more than 20 percent of its gross national product (a measure of the total value of goods and services a nation produced in a year) into research in the 1960s, attracting many of Europe's leading intellectuals and technicians to move to the United States in a so-called brain drain. Scientists and bureaucrats frequently made more crucial decisions than did elected politicians in the realm of space programs, weapons development, and economic policy. Here East–West differences became important: Soviet-bloc nations proved less adept at linking their considerable achievements in science to real-life applications because of bureaucratic red tape. In the 1960s, some 40 percent of scientific findings in the Soviet bloc became obsolete before the government approved them for application to technology. An invisible backsliding from superpower effectiveness and leadership had begun in the USSR—much of it due to the lack of systems coordination and cooperation.

The centrality of sophisticated knowledge to success in postindustrial society led to unprecedented growth in education, especially in universities and scientific institutes. The number of university students in Sweden rose by about 580 percent and in West Germany by 250 percent between 1950 and 1969. Great Britain established a network of technical universities to encourage the practical research that traditional elite universities often scorned. France set up schools to train future high-level experts in administration. The scientific establishment in the Soviet Union grew rapidly, and some institutions of higher learning added courses in business management, information technology, and systems analysis designed for the new pool of postindustrial workers.

Changing Family Life and the Generation Gap

Just as education changed to meet the needs of postindustrial society, family structures and parent–child relationships shifted from what they had been a century earlier. Households became more varied: cohabiting couples, single-parent families, blended families, families headed by same-sex partners, and childless marriages all became more common. At the end of the 1970s, the marriage rate in the West had fallen by 30 percent from its 1960s level, and after almost two decades of baby boom, the birthrate dropped significantly. Belgian women, for example, bore 2.6 children on average in 1960 but only 1.8 by the end of the 1970s. In the Soviet bloc, the birthrate was even lower.

Daily life within the family also changed. Technological consumer items filled the home, with radio and television often forming the basis of the household's common social life. Appliances such as dishwashers, washing machines, and clothes dryers became more widespread, especially in the western bloc. More women worked outside the home during these years to pay for the prolonged economic dependence of children, and, in contrast with the past, the modern family seemed to have a primarily psychological mission, providing emotional nurturance for children who acquired their intellectual skills in school. Parents turned to psychologists, social workers, other experts, and the media for models of how to deal with life in postindustrial society.

Postindustrial society changed teenagers' lives most dramatically, creating strong differences between adolescents and adults. A century earlier, teens had been full-time wage earners like their parents; now, in the new knowledge-based society, most were students and some were financially dependent on their parents into their twenties. Despite teenagers' longer financial childhood, sexual activity began at an ever younger age, prompting the idea of a "sexual revolution." Youth simultaneously gained new roles as consumers, wooed with items associated with rock music—records, portable radios, and stereos. Rock music celebrated youthful rebellion against adult culture in scornful, critical, and often explicitly sexual lyrics. Sex roles for the young did not change, however: promoters focused on groups of male musicians, whom they depicted as heroic, surrounded by worshipping female "groupies." New models for youth such as the Beatles were themselves the products of advanced technology, marketing for mass consumption, and a unique youth culture separating the young from their parents—the so-called generation gap.

Art, Ideas, and Religion in a Technocratic Society

Cultural trends developed alongside the march of consumer society and technological breakthroughs. A new style in the visual arts was called **pop art**. It featured images from everyday life and employed the glossy techniques and products of what these artists called admass, or mass advertising. Like advertising itself, art leadership passed from Europe to the United States. U.S. pop artist Robert Rauschenberg, for example, made collages from comic strips, magazine clippings, and fabric to fulfill his vision

Pop Art   Claes Oldenburg excelled in highlighting objects of everyday life, such as this hamburger (*Floor Burger*, 1962). He also modeled vacuum cleaners, shuttlecocks, telephones, and many other much-used things—a feature of pop art, which often contained humor in addition. Can you spot the humor in this creation? (Claes Oldenburg, *Floor Burger*, 1962. Canvas filled with foam rubber and cardboard boxes, painted with latex and Liquitex, 4 ft. 4 in. [1.32 m] high; 7 ft. [2.13 m] diameter. Collection Art Gallery of Ontario, Toronto, Canada, Purchase 1967. Photo courtesy the Oldenburg van Bruggen Studio. Copyright © 1962 Claes Oldenburg. Photo provided by The Bridgeman Art Library International.)

that "a picture is more like the real world when it's made out of the real world." Maverick American artists such as Andy Warhol made pop art a financial success with their parodies of modern commercialism. Through images of actress Marilyn Monroe and former first lady Jacqueline Kennedy, Warhol showed, for example, how depictions of women were used to sell everything mass culture had to offer in the 1960s and 1970s. He portrayed Campbell's soup cans as they appeared in advertisements and sold these works as elite artistic creations.

Swedish-born artist Claes Oldenburg portrayed the grotesque aspects of ordinary consumer products in *Floor Burger* (1962) and *Lipstick Ascending on Caterpillar Tractor* (1967). Capturing this mocking world of art, German artist Sigmar Polke did cartoon-like drawings of products and of those who craved them. The Swiss sculptor Jean Tinguely used rusted parts of old machines—the junk of industrial society—to make fountains that could move. His partner Niki de Saint Phalle then decorated them with huge, gaudy figures—many of them inspired by the folk traditions of the Caribbean and Africa. Their colorful, mobile fountains adorned main squares in Stockholm, Paris, and other cities.

The American composer John Cage worked in a similar vein when he added to his musical scores sounds produced by such everyday items as combs, pieces of wood, and radio noise. Buddhist influence led Cage to incorporate silence in music and to compose by randomly tossing coins and then choosing notes by the corresponding numbers in the ancient Chinese *I Ching* (Book of Changes). These techniques continued the trend away from classical melody that had begun with modernism. Other composers, called minimalists, simplified music by featuring repetition and sustained notes instead of producing the lush melodies of nineteenth-century symphonies and piano music. Estonian composer Arvo Pärt wrote minimalist pieces in the 1970s using only three or four notes in total; he called this style "starvation" music to emphasize the lack of both freedom and goods in the Soviet bloc. Improved recording technology and mass marketing brought music of all varieties to a wider home audience than ever before.

The social sciences reached the peak of their prestige in the postindustrial era, often because of the increasing use of statistical models made possible by advanced electronic computations. Anthropology was among the most exciting of the social sciences, for it brought young university students information about societies that seemed untouched by modern technology and industry. Colorful ethnographic films revealed different lifestyles and seemingly exotic practices. While studying people who came to be called "the other," students had their sense of freedom reinforced by the vision of going back to nature. Whatever their discipline, social scientists announced that, like technicians and engineers, their specialized methods and factual knowledge were key to managing the complexities of postindustrial society and setting policy for developing nations.

At the same time, the social sciences undermined Enlightenment beliefs that individuals had true freedom. French anthropologist Claude Lévi-Strauss (1908–2009) developed a theory called structuralism, which insisted that all societies function within controlling structures—kinship, for example. While challenging existentialism's claim that humans could create a free existence, structuralism also attacked the social sciences' faith in rationality. Lévi-Strauss's book *The Savage Mind* (1966) demonstrated that people outside the West, even though they did not use scientific methods, had their own effective systems of problem solving. In the 1960s and 1970s, the findings of some social scientists additionally echoed concerns that technology and highly managed bureaucratic systems were creating a society in which people lacked individuality and freedom.

Religious leaders and parishioners responded to the changing times in a variety of ways. Pope Paul VI (r. 1963–1978) opposed artificial birth control as it became more prevalent, while also becoming the first pontiff to carry out the global vision of Vatican II by visiting Africa, Asia, and South America. In some places, grassroots religious fervor surged in the face of advancing science. Growing numbers of U.S. Protestants, for example, joined sects that denied the validity of scientific discoveries such as the age of the universe and the evolution of the species. In western Europe, however, Christian churchgoing remained at a low ebb. In the 1970s, for example, only 10 percent of the British population went to religious services—about the same number that attended live soccer matches. Most striking was the changing composition of the Western religious public, with immigration of people from former colonies and other parts of the world. Mosques, Buddhist temples, and shrines to other creeds appeared in a greater number of cities and towns.

REVIEW   How did Western society and culture change in the postindustrial age?

Protesting Cold War Conditions

The United States and the Soviet Union reached new heights in the 1960s, but trouble was brewing for the superpowers. By 1965, the six-nation Common Market had temporarily replaced the United States as the leader in worldwide trade, and its members often acted in their own self-interest, not in the interests of the superpowers. In 1973, Britain's membership in the Common Market, followed by Ireland's and Denmark's, boosted the market's exports to almost three times those of the United States. The USSR faced challenges, too. Communist China, along with countries in eastern Europe, contested Soviet leadership, and by the mid-1960s, the United States was waging a devastating war in Vietnam to block the Communist independence movement there. Rising citizen discontent, sometimes expressed in dramatic acts of protest like that of Jan Palach, presented another serious challenge to the cold war order. From the 1960s until 1989, people rose up against technology-driven dehumanization, lack of fundamental rights, and the potential for nuclear holocaust.

Cracks in the Cold War Order

Across the social and political spectrum came calls to reduce cold war tensions in this age of unprecedented technological advance. In the Soviet Union, the new middle class of bureaucrats and managers demanded a better standard of living and a reduction in the cold war hostility that made everyday life so menacing. In Germany, Social Democratic politicians had enough influence to shift money from cold war defense spending to domestic programs. Willy Brandt (1913–1992), the Socialist mayor of West Berlin, became foreign minister in 1966 and worked to improve frigid relations with Communist East Germany to open up trade. This anti–cold war policy, known as **Ostpolitik**, gave West German business leaders what they wanted: "the depoliticization of Germany's foreign trade," as one industrialist put it, and an opening of consumerism in the Soviet bloc. West German trade with eastern Europe grew rapidly, but it left the relatively poorer countries of the Soviet bloc strapped with mounting debt. Nonetheless, commerce began building bridges across the U.S.–Soviet cold war divide.

To break the superpowers' stranglehold on international politics, French president Charles de Gaulle poured huge sums into French nuclear development, withdrew French forces from NATO, and signed trade treaties with the Soviet bloc. However, de Gaulle protected France's good relations with Germany to prevent further encroachments from the Soviet bloc. At home, de Gaulle's government sponsored the construction of modern housing and ordered the exterior cleaning of all Parisian buildings—a massive project taking years—to wipe away more than a century of industrial grime and to demonstrate community, not cold war, values. With his haughty pursuit of French grandeur, de Gaulle offered the European public an alternative to obeying the superpowers.

Brandt's Ostpolitik and de Gaulle's independence had their echoes in Soviet-bloc reforms. After the ouster of Soviet premier Nikita Khrushchev in 1964, the new leadership of Leonid Brezhnev (1909–1982) and Alexei Kosygin (1904–1980) initially continued attempts at reform, encouraging plant managers to turn a profit and using consumer goods to alleviate the discontent of an increasingly educated and informed citizenry. The government also allowed more cultural and scientific meetings with Westerners, another move that relaxed the cold war atmosphere in the mid-1960s. Like the French, the Soviets set up "technopoles"—new cities devoted to research and technological innovation. The Soviet satellites in eastern Europe seized the economic opportunity presented by Moscow's relaxed posture. For example, Hungarian leader János Kádár introduced elements of a market system into the national economy by encouraging small businesses and trade to develop outside the Communist-controlled state network.

Soviet-bloc writers sought to break the hold of socialist realism on the arts and reduce their praise for the Soviet past. Some dissident artists' paintings rejected brightly colored scenes and heroic figures of the socialist realist style and instead depicted Soviet citizens as worn and tired in grays and other monochromatic color schemes. East Berlin writer Christa Wolf challenged the celebratory nature of socialist art when she showed a couple tragically separated by the Berlin Wall in her novel *Divided Heaven* (1965). Repression of artistic expression returned in the later 1960s and 1970s, as the Soviet government took to bulldozing outdoor art shows. For their part, writers relied on **samizdat** culture, a form of protest activity in which individuals reproduced government-suppressed publications by hand and passed them from reader to reader, thus building a foundation for the successful resistance of the 1980s.

Other issues challenged U.S. leadership of the western bloc during the cold war. The assassination of President John F. Kennedy in November 1963 shocked the nation and the world, but only momentarily did it halt the escalating demands for civil rights for African Americans and other minorities. White segregationists murdered and brutalized those attempting to integrate lunch counters, register black voters, or simply march on behalf of freedom. In response to the murders and destruction, Kennedy had introduced civil rights legislation and forced the desegregation of schools and universities. Lyndon B. Johnson (1908–1973), Kennedy's successor, steered the Civil Rights Act through Congress in 1964. This legislation forbade racial segregation in public facilities and created the Equal Employment Opportunity Commission (EEOC) to fight job discrimination based on "race, color, national origin, religion, and sex." Southern conservatives had tacked on the provision outlawing discrimination against women in the vain hope that it would doom the bill. Modeling himself on his hero Franklin Roosevelt, Johnson envisioned what he called the Great Society, in which new government programs would improve the lot of the forty million Americans living in poverty. Johnson's many reform programs included Project Head Start for educating disadvantaged preschool children and the Job Corps for training youth. Black novelist Ralph Ellison called Johnson "the greatest American president for the poor and the Negroes."

Still, the cold war did not go away, and the United States became increasingly embroiled in Vietnam (Map 28.1). After the Geneva Conference of 1954, which

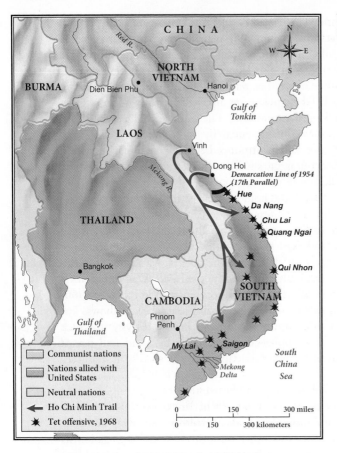

MAP 28.1   The Vietnam War, 1954–1975   The local peoples of Southeast Asia had long resisted incursions by their neighbors. The Vietnamese beat the French colonizers in the battle of Dien Bien Phu in 1954. The Americans soon became involved, trying to stem what they saw as the tide of Communist influence behind the Vietnamese liberation movement. The ensuing war in Vietnam in the 1960s and 1970s spread into neighboring countries, making the region the scene of vast destruction.

divided Vietnam into North and South, the United States increased its support for the corrupt leaders of non-Communist South Vietnam. North Vietnam, China, and the Soviet Union backed the rebel Vietcong, or South Vietnamese Communists. By 1966, the United States had more than half a million soldiers in South Vietnam, yet the strength of the Vietcong seemed to grow daily. Despite massive bombings by the United States, the insurgents, who had struggled against colonialism for decades, rejected a negotiated peace.

The Growth of Citizen Activism

In the midst of cold war conflict and technological advance, a new activism emerged. Prosperity and the rising benefits of a postindustrial, service-oriented economy made people ever more eager for peace and justice. The U.S. civil rights movement broadened as other minorities joined African Americans in demanding fair treatment. In 1965, César Chávez (1927–1993) led Mexican American migrant workers in the California grape agribusiness to strike for better wages and working conditions.

Meanwhile, beginning that same year, urban riots erupted across the United States out of African Americans' frustration in their struggle for equal rights. Some chose to celebrate their race under the banner "black is beautiful," and some urged a push for "black power" to reclaim rights forcefully instead of "begging" for them nonviolently. Separatism, not integration, became the goal of others. Small cadres of militants like the Black Panthers took up arms, believing that, like decolonizing peoples elsewhere, they needed to protect themselves against the violent whites around them.

From the 1950s on, homosexuals had also lobbied for the decriminalization of their sexual lives and practices. Some anti-gay propaganda equated male homosexuality with a lack of militaristic manliness needed to protect the nation-state on either side of the cold war divide. In June 1969, gay men in the Stonewall area of Greenwich Village, New York, rioted against the police and more general persecution, as had African Americans, both to assert their civil rights and to affirm their identity. The gay liberation movement born in that time came to span the globe and to include not only men but gay women, too.

As a result of the new turn in black efforts for change, white American university students who had participated in the early stages of the civil rights movement found themselves excluded from leadership positions in favor of an exclusively black leadership. Many white students soon joined the swelling protests against technological change, consumerism, and the Vietnam War. European youth were also feverish for reform. In 1966, Prague students, chanting "The only good Communist is a dead one," held carnival-like processions to commemorate the tenth anniversary of the 1956 Hungarian uprisings. The "situationists" in France used shocking graffiti and street theater to call on students to wake up from the slumbering pace of consumer society.

Throughout the 1960s, students criticized the traditional university curriculum and flaunted their own countercultural values. They questioned how studying Plato or Dante would help them after graduation. "How to Train Stuffed Geese" was French students' satirical version of the teaching methods inflicted on them. Long hair, communal living, scorn for personal cleanliness, and ridicule for sexual chastity were part of students' rejection of middle-class values. Widespread use of the pill and open promiscuity made the sexual revolution explicit and public. Marijuana use became common among students, who had their own rituals, music, and gathering places. Hated by students, big business nonetheless made billions of dollars by selling everything from blue jeans to natural foods as well as by managing the rock stars of the counterculture.

Women's activism erupted, too. Working for reproductive rights, women in France helped end the nation's ban on birth control in 1965. Middle-class women eagerly responded to the international best seller *The Feminine Mystique* (1963), by American journalist Betty Friedan. Pointing to the stagnating talents of many housewives, Friedan helped organize the National Organization for Women (NOW) in 1966 "to bring women into full participation in the mainstream of American society now." NOW advocated equal pay for equal work and a variety of other legal and economic reforms. In Sweden, women lobbied to make tasks both at home and in the workplace less gender-segregated.

Second-Wave Feminists on the March   Like turn-of-the-century feminists, women in the 1960s and 1970s took to the streets to protest their condition. This march in Paris features signs showing a clock fixed at 7:30 and a list of chores including "breakfast for husband," "wake the children," and "hurry." For many citizens, the sight of "unladylike" women demonstrating in public was a shock—which was the point for many activists. (© Rue des Archives/AGIP/The Granger Collection, NYC—All rights reserved.)

Women who engaged in the civil rights and student movements soon realized that many protest organizations devalued women just as society at large did. Male activists adopted the leather-jacketed machismo style of their film and rock heroes, but women in the movements were often judged by the status of their male protester lovers. "A woman was to 'inspire' her man," African American activist Angela Davis complained, adding that women seeking equality were accused of wanting "to rob [male activists] of their manhood." West German women students tossed tomatoes at male protest leaders in defiance of male domination of the movement and of standards set by society for ladylike behavior.

1968: Year of Crisis

Calls for reform finally boiled over in 1968. In January, on the first day of Tet, the Vietnamese New Year, the Vietcong and the North Vietnamese attacked more than one hundred South Vietnamese towns and American bases, inflicting heavy casualties and fueling the antiwar movement around the world. On April 4, 1968, a white racist assassinated civil rights leader Martin Luther King Jr. Riots erupted in more than a hundred cities in the United States as African Americans vented their anguish and rage. Rejecting King's policy of nonviolence, rioters rampaged through grim inner cities, chanting "Burn, baby, burn." On U.S. campuses, bitter clashes over the intertwined issues of war, technology, racism, and sexism closed down classes.

Similar student unrest erupted across the globe, most dramatically in France. In January, students at the university in Nanterre, outside of Paris, had gone on strike, invading administration offices to protest what they saw as a second-rate education. They called themselves a proletariat—an exploited working class—as worker activists had done for more than a century. They did not embrace Soviet communism but rather considered themselves part of the New Left, not the old Communist or Socialist left.

When students at the prestigious Sorbonne in Paris also took to the streets in protest, police assaulted them. French workers joined in the protest. Some nine million went on strike, occupying factories and calling not only for higher wages but also for participation in everyday decision making. The combined revolt of youth and workers looked as if it might spiral into another French revolution. President Charles de Gaulle sent tanks into Paris, and in June he announced a raise for workers. Many citizens, having grown tired of the street violence, the destruction of so much private property, and the breakdown of services such as garbage collection, began to sympathize with the government instead of the students. The revolutionary moment passed.

By contrast, the 1968 revolt in Prague began within the Czechoslovak Communist Party itself. At a party congress in the autumn of 1967, Alexander Dubček, head of the Slovak branch of the party, had called for more social and political openness, striking a chord among frustrated party officials, technocrats, and intellectuals. Czech citizens began to dream of creating a new society—one based on "socialism with a human face." Reform-minded party delegates elevated Dubček to the top position, and he quickly changed the Communist style of government by ending censorship, instituting the secret ballot for party elections, and allowing competing political groups to form. "Look!" one little girl in the street remarked as the new government took power. "Everyone's smiling today." The Prague Spring had begun as people bought uncensored publications, packed uncensored theater productions, and engaged in nonstop political debate.

Dubček faced the enormous problem of negotiating policies acceptable to both the USSR and reform-minded citizens. Fearing change, the Polish, East German, and Soviet regimes threatened the reform government daily. When Dubček failed to attend a meeting of Warsaw Pact leaders, Soviet threats intensified until finally, in August 1968, Soviet tanks rolled into Prague in a massive show of force. Citizens tried to halt the return to Communist orthodoxy through sabotage: they removed street signs to confuse invading troops, and merchants refused to sell food or other commodities to Soviet troops. The determined Soviet leadership gradually removed reformers from power, however. Jan Palach and other university students immolated themselves the following January, as governments around the world worked to stamp out criticism of the cold war order.

The protests of 1968 challenged the political direction of Western societies, but little turned out the way reformers hoped as governments adopted conservative solutions. In November 1968, the Soviets announced the Brezhnev Doctrine, which stated that reform movements, as a "common problem" of all socialist countries, would face swift repression. In the early 1970s, the hard-liner Brezhnev clamped down on critics, shattering the morale of dissidents in the USSR. "The shock of our tanks crushing the Prague Spring . . . convinced us that the Soviet colossus was invincible," explained one pessimistic liberal. In 1974, Brezhnev expelled author Aleksandr Solzhenitsyn from the USSR after the publication of the first volume of *The Gulag Archipelago* (1973–1976) in the U.S.-led bloc. Solzhenitsyn documented the story of the Gulag (the Soviet system of internment and forced-labor camps) with firsthand reports about the deadly conditions prisoners endured. More than any other single work, *The Gulag Archipelago* disillusioned loyal Communists around the world.

The USSR and other Communist countries used both persecution of ordinary citizens and the "soft" power of the new medium of television to reestablish order. Soviet psychologists, working with the government, certified the "mental illness" of people who did not play by the rules; thus, dissidents wound up as virtual prisoners in mental institutions. In a revival of tsarist Russia's anti-Semitism, Jews faced educational restrictions (especially in university admissions) and severe job discrimination. Soviet officials commonly accused Jews of being "unreliable." In Czechoslovakia, where by 1970 some 80 percent of households had TV, government writers created a new batch of soap operas featuring heroines who taught their families to replace activism in the public sphere with the contentment of private life. Heroes selflessly traveled to the West for their jobs, only to return disillusioned by its faults.

Despite these efforts, the brain drain of eastern European intellectuals to the West increased into the 1970s and beyond. The modernist composer György Ligeti had left Hungary in 1956, after which his work was celebrated in concert halls and in such classic films as *2001: A Space Odyssey*. From exile in Paris, Czech writer Milan Kundera enthralled audiences with *The Book of Laughter and Forgetting* (1979) and *The Unbearable Lightness of Being* (1984). Kundera claimed that the Soviet regime in Czechoslovakia depended on making people forget. The memory of fallen leaders was ruthlessly erased from history books, for instance, and individuals tried to block out grim reality by engaging in lots of sexual activity. Like the migrants from fascist Germany and Italy in the 1930s, newcomers—from noted intellectuals to skilled craftspeople and dancers—enriched the culture of those countries that welcomed them.

In the United States, the reaction against activists was different, though restoring order ultimately succeeded there, too. Elected in 1968, President **Richard Nixon** (1913–1994) promised to bring peace to Southeast Asia, but in 1970 he ordered U.S. troops to invade Cambodia, the site of North Vietnamese bases. Campuses erupted again in protest, and on May 4 the National Guard killed four students and wounded eleven others at a demonstration at Kent State University in Ohio. Nixon called the victims "bums," and a growing reaction against the counterculture led many Americans to agree with one citizen who declared that the guardsmen "should have fired sooner and longer." In 1975, a determined North Vietnamese offensive defeated South Vietnam and its U.S. allies and forcibly reunified the country. A strong current of public opinion turned against activists, born of the sense that somehow they—not the war, government corruption, or the huge war debt—had brought down the United States. Both superpowers were being tested, almost to the limits.

> **REVIEW**   What were the main issues for protesters in the 1960s, and how did governments address them?

The Testing of Superpower Domination and the End of the Cold War

Protesters like Jan Palach left a lasting legacy that continued to motivate those seeking political change, particularly in the Soviet bloc. As order was restored, some disillusioned reformers in the West turned to open terrorism, and like every other political occurrence in these days, television broadcast the events. New forces also emerged from beyond Europe and the United States to challenge superpower dominance. Internal corruption, competition from the oil-producing states, and the pursuit of warfare beyond their borders all threw the superpowers and their allies off balance, allowing reform-minded heads of state to come to the fore. The two most famous innovators were Margaret Thatcher in Britain and Mikhail Gorbachev in the USSR, both of whom introduced drastic new policies in the 1980s to keep their economies moving forward. In the Soviet bloc, however, refining the old system actually contributed to its collapse and thus to the end of the cold war in 1989.

A Changing Balance of World Power

Tested by protest at home, the superpowers found themselves facing a changing balance in world power. In the midst of turmoil, Henry Kissinger, Nixon's secretary of state and a believer—like Otto von Bismarck—in Realpolitik, decided to take advantage of the ongoing rivalry between the USSR and China. After the Communist Revolution in 1949, Mao Zedong, China's new leader, undertook foolish experiments in both manufacturing and agriculture that caused famine and massive suffering. As internal problems grew in both the Soviet Union and China, the two Communist giants skirmished along their shared borders and in diplomatic arenas. In 1972, President Nixon visited China, linking two very different great nations both facing disorder at home. Within China, Nixon's visit helped slow the brutality and excesses of Mao's regime. It also advanced the careers of Chinese pragmatists who were interested in technology and relations with the West and who laid the groundwork for China's boom later in the century.

The diplomatic success of the visit led the Soviets to make their own overtures to the U.S.-led bloc, beginning a process known as détente (a relaxation of tensions). In 1972, the superpowers signed the first Strategic Arms Limitation Treaty (SALT I), which set a cap on the number of antimissile defenses each country could have. In 1975, in the Helsinki accords on human rights, the western bloc officially acknowledged Soviet territorial gains in World War II in exchange for the Soviet bloc's guarantee of basic human rights.

Despite these successes, the war in Vietnam left the United States billions of dollars in debt to other countries and the international currency system in collapse. In the face of the resulting global economic chaos, Common Market countries united to force the United States to relinquish its single-handed direction of Western economic strategy. Another blow to U.S. leadership followed when it was revealed that Nixon's office had threatened the U.S. system of free elections by authorizing the burglary and wiretapping of Democratic Party headquarters at Washington's Watergate building during the 1972 presidential campaign. The Watergate scandal forced Nixon to resign in disgrace in the summer of 1974—one more weak spot in U.S. superpower status in the 1960s and 1970s.

The Middle East's oil-producing nations dealt Western dominance still another major blow. Tensions between Israel and the Arab world provided the catalyst. In 1967, Israeli forces, responding to Palestinian guerrilla attacks, quickly seized Gaza and the Sinai peninsula from Egypt, the Golan Heights from Syria, and the West Bank from Jordan. Israel's stunning victory in this action, which came to be called the Six-Day War, was followed in 1973 by a joint Egyptian and Syrian attack on Israel on Yom Kippur, the most holy day in the Jewish calendar. Israel, with material assistance from the United States, stopped the assault.

Having failed militarily, Arab nations in the **Organization of Petroleum Exporting Countries (OPEC)**, a relatively loose consortium before the Yom Kippur War, combined to quadruple the price of their oil and impose an embargo, cutting off all exports of oil to the United States and its allies because they backed Israel. For the first time since imperialism's heyday, the producers of raw materials—not the industrial powers—controlled the flow of commodities and set prices to their own advantage (Figure 28.1). As a result, unemployment rose by more than 50 percent in Europe and the United States and inflation soared. By the end of 1973, the inflation rate jumped to over 12 percent in France and 20 percent in Portugal. Eastern-bloc countries, dependent on Soviet oil, fared little better because the West could no longer afford their products and the Soviets boosted the price of their own oil. Skyrocketing interest rates discouraged both industrial investment and consumer buying. Prices, unemployment, and interest rates all rising created an unusual combination of economic conditions called **stagflation**. Western Europe drastically cut back on its oil dependence by undertaking conservation, enhancing public transportation, and raising the price of gasoline to encourage the development of fuel-efficient cars.

The U.S. bloc took further blows. In the late 1970s, students, clerics, shopkeepers, and unemployed men in Iran began an uprising that brought to power the Islamic ayatollah (a Shi'ite religious leader) Ruhollah Khomeini (1902–1989). Using

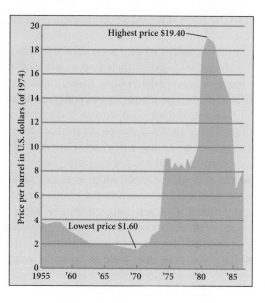

FIGURE 28.1 Fluctuating Oil Prices, 1955–1985 Colonization allowed the Western imperial powers to obtain raw materials at advantageous prices or even without paying at all. OPEC's oil embargo and price hikes of the 1970s were signs of change, which included the exercise of decolonized countries' control over their own resources. OPEC's action led to a decade of painful economic downturn, but it also encouraged some European governments to improve public transportation, support the production of fuel-efficient cars, and make individual consumers cut back their dependence on oil.

the new medium of audiocassette recordings to spread his message, Khomeini called for a transformation of Iran into a truly Islamic society, which meant the renunciation of the Western ways advocated by the American-backed shah, who was overthrown. In the autumn of 1979, supporters of Khomeini took hostages at the U.S. embassy in Teheran even as images of the captives' stricken faces were sent around the globe via satellites. The United States was essentially paralyzed in the face of Islamic militancy, further OPEC price hikes, and a downwardly spiraling economy.

The Western Bloc Meets Challenges with Reform

As the 1980s opened, governments in the West had to put their economic houses in order and confront the growing phenomenon of terrorism—a trend that had actually begun in the West. In the 1970s, terrorist bands of young people in Europe responded to the suppression of activism and the worsening economic conditions with kidnappings, bank robberies, bombings, and assassinations. In West Germany, the Red Army Faction—eager to bring down the Social Democratic coalition that had led the country through the 1970s—assassinated prominent businessmen and public officials. Practiced in random shootings of pedestrians, Italy's Red Brigades kidnapped and then murdered the head of the dominant Christian Democrats in 1978. Advocates of independence for the Basque nation in northern Spain assassinated Spanish politicians and police officers.

In the 1970s, Catholics in Northern Ireland protested job discrimination and a lack of civil rights. With protest escalating, the British government sent in troops who on January 30, 1972 (which became known as Bloody Sunday), fired at demonstrators and killed thirteen, setting off a cycle of violence that left five hundred dead in that year alone. Protestants fearful of losing their dominant position combated a reinvigorated Irish Republican Army (IRA), which carried out bombings and assassinations to put an end to the oppression of Catholics.

Terrorists failed in their goal of overturning the existing democracies, and, battered as it was, parliamentary government scored a few important successes in the 1970s. Spain and Portugal, suffering under dictatorships since the 1930s, set out on a course of political openness and greater prosperity. The death of Spain's Francisco Franco in 1975 ended more than three decades of dictatorial rule. Franco's handpicked successor, King Juan Carlos, surprisingly steered his nation to Western-style constitutional monarchy, facing down threatened military coups. Portugal and Greece also ousted right-wing dictators, thus paving the way for their countries' integration into western Europe. Despite these democratic advances, economic crisis and political terrorism weighed on the West.

More than anyone else, **Margaret Thatcher** (1925–2013), the leader of Britain's Conservative Party and prime minister from 1979 to 1990, reshaped the West's political and economic ideas to meet the crisis. Coming to power amid continuing

On the World Stage: Margaret Thatcher and Mohammed Anwar al-Sadat   Margaret Thatcher, Great Britain's conservative prime minister, and Egyptian president Mohammed Anwar al-Sadat met in London in August 1981, just two months before Sadat was assassinated for participating in the Egyptian-Israeli peace accord. Thatcher's term in office was as memorable as Sadat's: she went on to launch a new conservatism in politics and economics that would sweep the world in the 1980s and 1990s. (© Mary Evans Picture Library/ Marx Memorial Library/The Image Works.)

economic decline, revolt in Northern Ireland, and labor unrest, the combative prime minister rejected the politics of consensus building. She believed that only business could revive the sluggish British economy, so she lashed out at union leaders, Labour Party politicians, and people who received welfare-state benefits, calling them enemies of British prosperity. In her view, business leaders were the key members of society. She characterized immigrants, whose low wages contributed greatly to business profits, as inferior. Under Thatcher, even workers blamed labor leaders or newcomers for Britain's troubles.

The policies of "Thatcherism" were based on monetarist, or supply-side, economic theory. According to monetarist theory, inflation results when government pumps money into the economy at a rate higher than the nation's economic growth rate. Monetarists believe that the government should keep a tight rein on the money supply to prevent prices from rising rapidly. Supply-side economists maintain that the economy as a whole flourishes when businesses grow and their prosperity "trickles down" throughout society. To implement these theories, the British government cut income taxes on the wealthy as a way of encouraging investment and increased sales taxes to compensate for the lost revenue. The result was a greater burden on working people, who bore the brunt of the higher sales tax. Thatcher also refused to prop up "outmoded" industries such as coal mining and slashed education and health programs. Her package of economic policies came to be known as **neoliberalism**.

In the first years of Thatcher's government, the British economy did not respond well to her shock treatment. The quality of universities, public transportation, highways, and hospitals deteriorated, and social unity fragmented as she pitted the lower classes against one another. In 1981, blacks and Asians rioted in major cities. Thatcher revived her sagging popularity with a nationalist war against Argentina in 1982 over ownership of the Falkland Islands off the Argentinian coast. Stagflation ultimately dissipated, and Thatcher's program became the standard for those facing the challenge of stagflation and economic decline. Britain had been one of the pioneers of the welfare state, and now it pioneered in changing course.

In the United States, Ronald Reagan (1911–2004), who served as president between 1981 and 1989, followed a similar road to combat the economic crisis there. Dividing U.S. citizens into the good and the bad, Reagan vowed to promote the values of the "moral majority," which included commitment to Bible-based religion and unquestioned patriotism. He blasted so-called spendthrift and immoral "liberals" when introducing "Reaganomics"—a program of whopping income tax cuts for the wealthy combined with massive reductions in federal spending for student loans, school lunch programs, and mass transit. Funding social programs, he felt, only encouraged bad Americans to be lazy. In foreign policy, Reagan rolled back détente and demanded huge military budgets to counter the Soviets. The combination of tax cuts and military expansion had pushed the federal budget deficit to $200 billion by 1986. As in Britain, inflation was brought under control and business picked up.

Other western European leaders also limited welfare-state benefits in the face of stagflation, though without Thatcher's and Reagan's socially divisive rhetoric. West German leader Helmut Kohl, who took power in 1982, reduced welfare spending, froze government wages, and cut corporate taxes. Unlike Thatcher, Kohl did not fan the flames of class and racial hatreds. Such a strategy would have been particularly unwise in Germany, where terrorism on the left and on the right continued to flourish. Moreover, the legacy of Nazism loomed menacingly: for example, an unemployed German youth said of immigrant Turkish workers, "Let's gas 'em."

By 1981, stagflation had put more than 1.5 million people out of work in France, but the French took a different political path to deal with the economic crisis. They elected a Socialist president, François Mitterrand, who nationalized banks and certain industries and increased wages and social spending to stimulate the economy—the opposite of Thatcherism. New public buildings like museums and libraries arose along with new subway lines and improved public transport. When conservative Jacques Chirac succeeded Mitterrand as president in 1995, he adopted neoliberal policies. Socially divisive politics that had unfolded during hard economic times grew in appeal. From the 1980s on, the racist National Front Party won 10 percent and often more of the French vote with promises to deport African and Middle Eastern immigrants.

At the same time, smaller European states without heavy defense commitments began to thrive, some of them by slashing welfare programs. Spain joined the Common Market in 1986 and used Common Market investment and tourist dollars to help rebuild its sagging infrastructure, as in the southern cities of Granada and Córdoba. In Ireland, new investment in education for high-tech jobs combined with low wage rates attracted business to the country in the 1990s. Prosperity, along with the rising death toll from decades of violence, led to a political rapprochement between Ireland and Northern Ireland in 1999. Austria prospered, too, in part by reducing government pensions and aid to business.

Almost alone, Sweden maintained a full array of social programs. The government offered each immigrant a choice of subsidized housing in neighborhoods inhabited primarily by Swedes or primarily by people from the immigrant's native land. Such programs were expensive, and Sweden dropped from fourth to fourteenth place among nations in per capita income by 1998. The Swedish welfare state came to seem extreme to many citizens, and, as elsewhere, immigrants were cast as the source of the country's problems—past, present, and future: "How long will it be before our Swedish children will have to turn their faces toward Mecca?" ran one politician's campaign speech in 1993.

Collapse of Communism in the Soviet Bloc

Beginning in 1985, reform came to the Soviet Union as well, but instead of fortifying the economy, it helped bring about the collapse of the Soviet bloc. The need for reform was evident. In 1979, the USSR became embroiled against Islam in Afghanistan when it supported a coup by a Communist faction against the government: casualties were 800,000 for the Soviets alone and 3 million for the Afghans. Further, global communications technology showed Soviet citizens that another way of life was possible. Citizens could see that the Soviet system of corrupt economic management produced a deteriorating standard of living. Shortages necessitated the three-generation household, in which grandparents took over tedious homemaking tasks from their working children and grandchildren, including waiting in long lines for basic commodities. "There is no special skill to this," a seventy-three-year-old grandmother and former garbage collector remarked. "You just stand in line and wait." One cheap and readily available product—vodka—pushed alcoholism to crisis levels, diminishing productivity and straining the nation's morale.

In 1985, a new leader, **Mikhail Gorbachev** (1931–), opened an era of change. The son of peasants, Gorbachev had risen through Communist Party ranks as an agricultural specialist and had traveled abroad to observe life in the West. At home, he saw the consequences of economic stagnation: in much of the USSR, ordinary people decided not to have children. The Soviet Union was forced to import massive amounts of grain because 20 to 30 percent of the grain produced in the USSR rotted before it could be harvested or shipped to market, so great was the inefficiency of the state-directed economy. Industrial pollution had reached scandalous proportions because state-run enterprises cared only about meeting production quotas. A massive and privileged party bureaucracy feared innovation and failed to achieve socialism's professed goal of a decent standard of living for working people. To match U.S. military growth, the Soviet Union diverted 15 to 20 percent of its gross national product (more than double the U.S. proportion) to armaments, further crippling the economy's chances of raising living standards.

Gorbachev knew from experience and from his travels to western Europe that the Soviet system was completely inadequate, and he quickly proposed several unusual programs. A crucial economic reform, **perestroika** ("restructuring"), aimed to reinvigorate the Soviet economy by improving productivity, increasing investment, encouraging the use of up-to-date technology, and gradually introducing such market features as prices and profits. The complement to economic change was the policy of **glasnost** (usually translated as "openness" or "publicity"), which called for "wide, prompt, and frank information" and for allowing Soviet citizens new measures of free speech. When officials complained that glasnost threatened their status, Gorbachev replaced more than a third of the Communist Party's leadership. The pressing need for glasnost became most evident after the Chernobyl catastrophe in 1986, when a nuclear reactor exploded and spewed radioactive dust into the atmosphere. Bureaucratic cover-ups delayed the spread of information about the accident, with lethal consequences for people living near the plant.

After Chernobyl, Communist Party meetings suddenly included complaints about the highest leaders and their policies. Television shows adopted the outspoken methods of American investigative reporting, and instead of publishing made-up letters praising the great Soviet state, newspapers were flooded with real ones complaining of shortages and abuse. One outraged "mother of two" protested that the cost-cutting policy of reusing syringes in hospitals was a source of AIDS, the deadly disease that had recently begun to spread worldwide. "Why should little kids have to pay for the criminal actions of our Ministry of Health?" she asked. Debate and factions arose across the political spectrum. In the fall of 1987, one of Gorbachev's allies, Boris Yeltsin, quit the government after denouncing perestroika as insufficient to produce real reform. Yeltsin's political daring inspired others to organize in opposition to crumbling Communist rule. In the spring of 1989, in a remarkably free balloting in Moscow's local elections, not a single Communist was chosen.

Recognizing how severely the cold war arms race was draining Soviet resources, Gorbachev began scaling back missile production. His unilateral actions gradually won over Ronald Reagan. In 1985, the two leaders initiated a personal relationship and began defusing the cold war. "I bet the hard-liners in both our countries are bleeding when we shake hands," said Reagan at the conclusion of one meeting. In early 1989, Gorbachev withdrew the last of his country's forces from the debilitating war in Afghanistan, and the United States started to cut back its own vast military buildup.

As Gorbachev's reforms in the USSR started spiraling out of his control, dissent was rising across the Soviet bloc. In the summer of 1980, Poles had gone on strike to protest government-increased food prices; workers at the Gdańsk shipyards, led by electrician Lech Walesa and crane operator Anna Walentynowicz, created an independent labor movement called **Solidarity**. The organization soon embraced much of the adult population, including a million members of the Communist Party. Both intellectuals and the Catholic church, long in the forefront of opposition to antireligious communism, supported Solidarity workers as they occupied factories in protest against the deteriorating conditions of everyday life. The members of Solidarity waved Polish flags and paraded giant portraits of the Virgin Mary and Pope John Paul II—a Polish native.

Global media coverage encouraged Solidarity leaders. As food became scarce and prices rose, tens of thousands of women joined in with marches, crying "We're hungry!" They also protested working conditions, but as both workers and the only caretakers of home life, it was the scarcity of food that sent them into the streets. The Communist Party teetered on the edge of collapse, until the police and the army, with Soviet support, imposed a military government and in the winter of 1981 outlawed Solidarity. Using world communications networks, dissidents kept Solidarity alive and workers kept meeting, creating a new culture outside the official Soviet arts and newscasts. Poets read dissident verse to overflow crowds, and university professors lectured on such forbidden topics as Polish resistance in World War II. Activism in Poland and the news about it set the stage for communism's downfall across the Soviet bloc.

The year 1989 saw uprisings around the world—in Chile, the Philippines, Haiti, South Africa, and China, for example. The global Cable News Network (CNN), established in 1980, linked many individual movements for democratic change through its twenty-four-hour coverage of world events. The most widely covered of these was the attack on the Communist state in China. Inspired by Gorbachev's visit to Beijing, in the spring of 1989 thousands of Chinese students massed in the city's Tiananmen Square, the world's largest public square, to demand democracy. They used telex machines and e-mail to rush their messages to the international community, and they conveyed their goals through the cameras that Western television, broadcasting via satellite, trained on them. As workers began joining the pro-democracy forces, the government crushed the movement and executed as many as a thousand rebels.

News of the protests in Tiananmen Square was galvanizing to those in eastern Europe who were inspired in their long-standing tradition of resistance. In June

1989, the Polish government, weakened by its own bungling of the economy and lacking Soviet support for further repression, held free parliamentary elections. Solidarity candidates overwhelmingly defeated the Communists, and Walesa became president in early 1990. Gorbachev openly reversed the Brezhnev Doctrine, refusing to interfere in the political course of another nation. When it became clear that the Soviet Union would not intervene in Poland, the fall of communism repeated itself across the Soviet bloc.

Communism had collapsed in Poland; it then collapsed in Hungary, in part because Hungarians, too, had experimented with "market socialism" since the 1960s. Hungarian citizens were already protesting the government, lobbying, for example, against ecologically unsound projects like the construction of a new dam. They encouraged boycotts of Communist holidays, and on March 15, 1989, they boldly commemorated the anniversary of the Hungarian uprising. These popular demands for liberalization led the parliament in the fall of 1989 to dismiss the Communist Party as the official ruling institution.

The most potent symbol of a divided Europe was the Berlin Wall, and East Germans had attempted to escape over it for decades. In the summer of 1989, crowds of East Germans flooded the borders to escape the crumbling Soviet bloc, and hundreds of thousands of protesters rallied throughout the fall against the regime. Satellite television brought them visions of postindustrial prosperity and of free and open public debate in West Germany. Crowds of demonstrators greeted Gorbachev, taken as a hero by many, when he visited the country in October. On November 9, guards at the Berlin Wall allowed free passage to the west, turning protest into a festive holiday. As they strolled freely in the streets, East Berliners saw firsthand the goods available in a successful postindustrial society. Soon thereafter, citizens—east and west—released years of frustration by assaulting the Berlin Wall with sledgehammers.

In Czechoslovakia people also watched televised news of glasnost expectantly. Persecuted dissidents had maintained their critique of Communist rule. In an open letter to the Czechoslovak Communist Party leadership, playwright Václav Havel accused Marxist-Leninist rule of making people materialistic and indifferent to public life. In 1977, Havel, along with a group of fellow intellectuals and workers, signed Charter 77, a public protest against the regime that resulted in the arrest of the signers. In the mid-1980s, they and the wider population heard Gorbachev on television calling for free speech. Protesters clamored for democracy, but the government turned the police on them, arresting activists in January 1989 for commemorating the death of Jan Palach. The turning point came in November 1989 when, in response to police beatings of students, Alexander Dubček, leader of the Prague Spring of 1968, addressed the crowds in Prague's Wenceslas Square with a call to oust the Stalinists from the government. Almost immediately, the Communist leadership resigned. Capping what became known as the "velvet revolution" for its lack of bloodshed, the formerly Communist-dominated parliament elevated Havel to the presidency.

From the mid-1960s on, Nicolae Ceaușescu had ruled Romania as the harshest dictator in Communist Europe since Stalin. In the name of modernization, he destroyed whole villages; to build up the population, he outlawed contraceptives

November 1989: East Germany Meets West Germany   The fall of the Berlin Wall and the "iron curtain" separating the Soviet from the western bloc was a joyous occasion across Europe, but nowhere more so than in Germany. Divided from one another into two countries after World War II, Germans would later find that reunification was a problem, bringing unemployment and social dislocation. In November 1989, however, West Germans lined up to welcome their fellow citizens traveling from the east to see what life was like beyond the Soviet sphere. (ullstein bild/Bildarchiv/The Granger Collection, NYC—All rights reserved.)

and abortions, a restriction that led to the abandonment of tens of thousands of children. He preached the virtues of a very slim body so that he could cut rations and use the savings for buying private castles and building himself an enormous palace in Bucharest. To this end, he tore down entire neighborhoods and dozens of historical buildings and crushed opponents of the gaudy project to make it appear popular. Yet in early December 1989, workers demonstrated against the dictatorial government, and the army turned on Ceaușescu loyalists. On Christmas Day, viewers watched on television as the dictator and his wife were tried by a military court and then executed. For many, the death of Ceaușescu meant that the very worst of communism was over.

REVIEW   How and why did the balance of world power change during the 1980s?

Conclusion

The collapse of communism in the Soviet satellites surprised the world, for U.S.-bloc analysts had reported throughout the 1980s that the Soviet empire was in dangerously robust health. Yet no one should have been unaware of dissent or economic discontent. Since the 1960s, rebellious youth, ethnic and racial minorities, and women had all been condemning conditions across the West, along with criticizing the threat posed by the cold war. By the early 1980s, wars in Vietnam and Afghanistan, protests against scarcity in the Soviet bloc, the power of oil-producing states, and the growing political force of Islam had cost the superpowers their resources and reputations. Margaret Thatcher in Britain and Ronald Reagan in the United States tried to put their postindustrial and cold war houses in order. Mikhail Gorbachev's policies of glasnost and perestroika in the Soviet Union—aimed at political and economic improvements—brought on collapse.

Glasnost and perestroika were supposed to bring about the high levels of prosperity enjoyed outside the Soviet bloc. Across the West, including the USSR, an unprecedented set of technological developments had transformed businesses, space exploration, and the functioning of government. Technological advances also had an enormous impact on everyday life. Work changed as society reached a stage called postindustrial, in which the service sector predominated. New patterns of family life, new relationships among the generations, and revised standards for sexual behavior also characterized these years. It was only in the United States and western Europe, however, that the full consumer benefits of postindustrialization reached ordinary people. The attainment of a thoroughgoing consumer, service, and high-tech society demanded levels of efficiency, coordination, and cooperation unknown in the Soviet bloc.

Many complained, nonetheless, about the dramatic changes resulting from postindustrial development. The protesters of the late 1960s addressed postindustrial society's concentrations of bureaucratic and industrial power (often enabled by technology), social inequality, and environmental degradation. In the Soviet sphere, protests were continuous but were little heeded until the collapse of Soviet domination of eastern Europe in 1989. Soon communism would be overturned in the USSR itself. However, the triumph of democracy in the former Soviet Empire opened an era of painful adjustment for hundreds of millions of people. Amid this rapid change was the growing awareness—via technology's instantaneous coverage of events across the globe—that the world's peoples were more tightly connected than ever before.

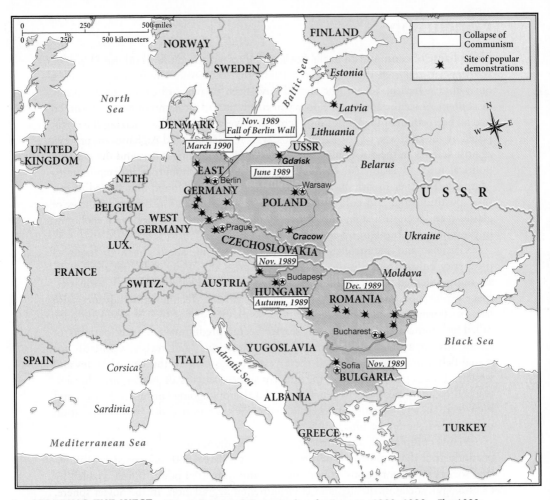

MAPPING THE WEST **The Collapse of Communism in Europe, 1989–1990**   The 1989 overthrow of the Communist Party in the USSR satellite countries of eastern Europe occurred with surprising rapidity. The transformation began when Polish voters tossed out Communist Party leaders in June 1989, and then accelerated in September when thousands of East Germans fled to Hungary, Poland, and Czechoslovakia. Between October and December, Communist regimes were replaced in East Germany, Czechoslovakia, Bulgaria, and Romania. Within three years, the Baltic states would declare their independence, the USSR itself would dissolve, and the breakup of Yugoslavia would lead to war in the Balkans.

Chapter Review

KEY TERMS AND PEOPLE

Be sure you can identify the term or person and explain its historical significance.

DNA (p. 853)
in vitro fertilization (p. 854)
multinational corporation (p. 854)
pop art (p. 857)
Ostpolitik (p. 860)
samizdat (p. 861)
Richard Nixon (p. 866)
Organization of Petroleum Exporting
    Countries (OPEC) (p. 868)

stagflation (p. 868)
Margaret Thatcher (p. 870)
neoliberalism (p. 871)
Mikhail Gorbachev (p. 873)
perestroika (p. 873)
glasnost (p. 873)
Solidarity (p. 874)

REVIEW QUESTIONS

1. What were the technological and scientific advances of the 1960s and 1970s, and how did they change human life and society?
2. How did Western society and culture change in the postindustrial age?
3. What were the main issues for protesters in the 1960s, and how did governments address them?
4. How and why did the balance of world power change during the 1980s?

MAKING CONNECTIONS

1. What were the differences between industrial society of the late nineteenth century and postindustrial society of the late twentieth century?
2. Why were there so many protests, acts of terrorism, and uprisings across the West in the decades between 1960 and 1990?
3. What have been the long-term consequences of Communist rule in the Soviet bloc between 1917 and 1989?
4. How did technology shape politics over the course of the twentieth century?

IMPORTANT EVENTS

1963	• Betty Friedan publishes *The Feminine Mystique*
1966	• Willy Brandt becomes West German foreign minister and develops Ostpolitik
1967	• First successful human heart transplant
1968	• Revolution in Czechoslovakia; student uprisings throughout Europe and the United States
1969	• U.S. astronauts walk on the moon's surface
1972	• SALT I between the United States and Soviet Union
1973	• End of Vietnam War; OPEC raises price of oil and imposes oil embargo on the West
1973–1976	• Aleksandr Solzhenitsyn publishes *The Gulag Archipelago*
1978	• The first test-tube baby is born in England
1978–1979	• Islamic revolution in Iran; hostages are taken at U.S. embassy in Teheran
1980	• Solidarity organizes resistance to Polish communism; British prime minister Margaret Thatcher begins dismantling the welfare state
1981	• Ronald Reagan becomes U.S. president
1985	• Mikhail Gorbachev becomes Soviet premier
1986	• Explosion at Chernobyl nuclear plant; Spain joins the Common Market
1989	• Chinese students revolt in Tiananmen Square; Communist governments are ousted in eastern Europe; Berlin Wall is demolished

29

A New Globalism

1989 to the Present

CHAPTER FOCUS

How has globalization been both a unifying and a divisive influence on the West in the twenty-first century?

THÉRÈSE IS A CONGOLESE IMMIGRANT to France who arrived in Paris in the late 1970s with the help of a brother who worked for an airline. Thérèse had been well-known in Africa as the teenage girlfriend of pop singer Bozi Boziana, who wrote a hit song about her. Congo's political instability had made her search for safety in Paris, however. Once there, Thérèse remained famous among African immigrants because she ran *nganda*, or informal bars, for them. Like Thérèse, the immigrants who frequent her nganda are often Congolese and other Africans who have settled in Paris, many of them illegally. They flock to her nganda because they like her stylish dress, the African food she cooks, the African music she plays, and the African products she sells. Many of Thérèse's small bars and eateries have flourished, only to be closed down by landlords who want more of her handsome profits or who object to her running an unlicensed café. Despite such obstacles, Thérèse keeps business going by moving her faithful clientele around her Paris neighborhood from basement to shop front to spare room. Thérèse is a new global citizen, counting on networks back home for supplies, constantly on the move because she lives on the margins of legality, and always striving to make a good living.

Thérèse's story is just one example of the ways in which people in the post–cold war world crossed national boundaries while maintaining crucial ties around the globe. The end of the cold war rivalry between the superpowers paved the way for a more intimately connected world. In the 1990s, globalization advanced further with the dramatic collapse of communism in Yugoslavia and then of the Soviet Union itself. The world was no longer divided in two by heavily guarded borders and hostile cold war propaganda, allowing nations and individuals more opportunity to trade and interact freely. The Common Market transformed itself into the European Union, which from 2004 on admitted many states from the former Soviet bloc. The telecommunication systems put in place in the 1960s advanced **globalization**, binding peoples and cultures together in an ever more complicated social and economic web. The World Wide Web and its offspring social networking even united them to enact stunning social and political change.

The global age brought the vast national and international migration of tens of millions of people, an expanding global marketplace, and rapid cultural exchange of popular music, books, films, and television shows. On the negative side, the new globalization also brought lethal disasters such as epidemic diseases, environmental deterioration, genocide, and terrorism. Nations in the West faced competition from the rising economic power of Asia and Latin America. International business mergers accelerated in the 1990s, advancing efficiencies but often threatening jobs. Millions of workers in this interlinked economy discovered that the global age was one of both opportunities and insecurities.

The end of superpower rivalry resulted in the dominance of a single power, the United States, in world affairs. When the United States sought to exercise global power through warfare, however, European states would often resist, just as the Soviet satellites had pulled away from the USSR. New forces, including the economic power of non-Western countries and the cultural might of Islam, created new centers of influence. Some observers predicted a huge "clash of civilizations" because of sharp differences between Western civilization and cultures beyond the West. Others, however, saw a different clash—one between a Europe reborn after decades of disastrous wars as a peace-seeking group of nations confronting an imperial United States that, like Europe in the nineteenth century, was frequently at war around the world. Globalization in either of these scenarios could bring global splintering or even catastrophic warfare.

More immediately, globalization brought economic struggles for many. Beginning in 2007, the global economy collapsed, resulting in widespread hardship. U.S. recovery came first, but as Europe and the rest of the world flagged, it became apparent that a reenergizing of economic capacities was needed. Illegal immigrants continued to move into Europe because of its safety and high standard of living, and to the United States because of the promise of opportunity. The fate of Thérèse amid this uncertainty we do not know.

Collapse of the Soviet Union and Its Aftermath

Following the fall of communist regimes in eastern Europe, rejection of communism spread in the 1990s, turning events in unpredictable, even violent directions. Yugoslavia and then the Soviet Union itself fell apart as ethnic groups began to demand independence. The USSR had held together more than one hundred ethnicities, and the five republics of Soviet Central Asia were home to fifty million Muslims. For more than a century, successive governments had attempted to instill Russian and Soviet culture, but the policy of Russification failed to build any heartfelt allegiance, leading to a swift collapse of the USSR. In Yugoslavia, communist rulers had also enforced unity among religious and ethnic groups, and intermarriage among them occurred regularly. Beginning in the unstable years of the early 1990s, however, ambitious politicians seeking to build a following whipped up ethnic hatreds, making it unclear whether peaceful, democratic nations would emerge.

The Breakup of Yugoslavia

In Yugoslavia, tensions erupted in 1990 after Serbia's president **Slobodan Milosevic** began to promote control of the entire Yugoslav federation by ethnic Serbs as a replacement for communism. Other ethnic groups in Yugoslavia resisted Milosevic's militant pro-Serb nationalism and called for secession. "Slovenians . . . have one more reason to say they are in favor of independence," warned one of them in the face of rising Serb claims to dominate the small republics that comprised Yugoslavia (Map 29.1). In the summer of 1991, two of these republics, Slovenia and Croatia, seceded. Croatia, however, lost almost a quarter of its territory when the Yugoslav army, eager to enforce Serbian supremacy, invaded. A devastating civil war broke out in Bosnia-Herzegovina when the republic's Muslim majority tried to create a multicultural and multiethnic state. With the covert military support of Milosevic's government, Bosnian Serb men formed a guerrilla army and gained the upper hand. A United Nations (UN) arms embargo prevented the Bosnian Muslims from equipping their forces even though the Serbs at the time were massacring them.

Relentless violence in the Balkans was inflicted on neighbors in the name of creating "ethnically pure" states in a region where ethnic mixture, not ethnic purity,

MAP 29.1   The Former Yugoslavia, c. 2000   After a decade of destructive civil war, UN forces and UN-brokered agreements attempted to protect the civilians of the former Yugoslavia from the brutal consequences of post-Communist rule. Ambitious politicians, most notably Slobodan Milosevic, used the twentieth-century Western strategy of fostering ethnic and religious hatred as a powerful tool to build support for themselves while making those favoring peace look softhearted and unfit to rule. What issues of national identity does the breakup of Yugoslavia indicate?

was the norm. During the 1990s, civilians died by the tens of thousands as Serbs under Milosevic's leadership pursued a policy they called **ethnic cleansing**—that is, genocide—against non-Serb ethnicities. Serb men raped women to leave them pregnant with Serb babies as another form of conquest. In 1995, Croatian forces murdered Serbs who had helped seize land from Croatia. That same year, the Serbs retaliated by slaughtering eight thousand Muslim boys and men in the town of Srebrenica: "Kill the lot," the commander of the Serb forces ordered. Military units on all sides destroyed libraries and museums, architectural treasures like the Mostar Bridge, and cities rich with history such as Dubrovnik. Many in the West explained violence in the Balkans as part of "age-old" blood feuds typical of a backward, "almost Asian" society. Others saw using genocide to achieve national power as simply a modern political practice that had been employed by the imperial powers and by other politicians, including Adolf Hitler.

Peacekeepers were put in place, but they turned their backs on such atrocities as the Srebrenica massacre and let them proceed to their horrific end. Late in the 1990s, Serb forces moved to attack Muslims of Albanian ethnicity living in the Yugoslav province of Kosovo. From 1997 to 1999, crowds of Albanian Kosovars fled their homes as Serb militias and the Yugoslav army slaughtered the civilian population. North Atlantic Treaty Organization (NATO) pilots bombed the region to drive back both the army and militias, but people throughout the world felt that this intervention came far too late. After a new regime in Serbia emerged alongside the independent republics of Bosnia and Croatia, Milosevic was turned over to the International Court of Justice, or World Court, in the Netherlands to be tried for crimes against humanity. Across a fragmenting eastern Europe, hateful racial, ethnic, and religious rhetoric influenced political agendas in the post-communist states.

The Soviet Union Comes Apart

Less than three years after the overthrow of communism in its eastern European satellites, the once powerful Soviet Union itself fell apart. Perestroika had failed to revitalize the Soviet economy; people confronted corruption and soaring prices, and Mikhail Gorbachev's planned "transition to the market [economy]" satisfied no one. In 1991, the Russian parliament elected Boris Yeltsin over a Communist candidate as president of the Russian Republic—the last straw for a group of eight antireform hard-liners, including the powerful head of the Soviet secret police, or KGB, who attempted a coup. As coup leaders held Gorbachev under house arrest, Yeltsin defiantly stood atop a tank outside the Russian parliament building and called for mass resistance. Residents of Moscow and Leningrad filled the streets, and units of the army defected. People used fax machines and computers to coordinate internal resistance and alert the world. Citizen action defeated the coup and prevented a return to the Communist past.

After the failed coup, the Soviet Union disintegrated. People tore down statues of Soviet heroes; Yeltsin outlawed the Communist Party newspaper, *Pravda*, and sealed the KGB's files. At the end of August 1991, the Soviet parliament suspended operations of the Communist Party itself. The Baltic states of Estonia, Latvia, and Lithuania declared their independence in September; other republics within the USSR followed their lead. Bloody ethnic conflicts and anti-Semitism revived as political tools. On December 31, 1991, the final agreements dissolved the USSR, and twelve of the fifteen former Soviet republics banded together to form the Commonwealth of Independent States (CIS) (Map 29.2).

Weakened by the coup attempt, Gorbachev abandoned politics. Yeltsin stepped in and accelerated the change to a market economy, bringing on an ever-deepening

MAP 29.2   Countries of the Former Soviet Union, c. 2000   Following an agreement of December 1991, twelve of the countries of the former Soviet Union formed the Commonwealth of Independent States (CIS). Dominated by Russia and with Ukraine often disputing this domination, the CIS worked to bring about common economic and military policies. As nation-states dissolved rapidly in the late twentieth century, regional alliances and coordination were necessary to meet the political and economic challenges of the global age.

crisis. Yeltsin's political allies, the military, and bureaucrats bought up or simply confiscated national resources. A new class of superwealthy Russians (including Yeltsin's own family) called oligarchs arose by stealing the wealth in natural resources and factories once seen as belonging to all the people. Meanwhile social disorder prevailed as organized criminals interfered in the distribution of goods and services and assassinated legitimate entrepreneurs, legislators, and anyone who criticized them. Amid these scandals, Yeltsin resigned on December 31, 1999. He appointed a new protégé, **Vladimir Putin**, as interim president.

Putin was a little-known functionary in Russia's new security apparatus, which had evolved from the old KGB. In the presidential elections of spring 2000, Putin surprised everyone when the electorate voted him in. Though associated with the Yeltsin family corruption, he declared himself committed to legality. "Democracy," he announced, "is the dictatorship of law." With a solid mandate, Putin proceeded to drive from power the biggest figures in regional and central government, usually the henchmen of the oligarchs. Putin's popularity rose even higher when the government arrested the billionaire head of the Yukos Oil Company in 2003. The pillaging of the country—the source of ordinary citizens' recent suffering—was finally being punished. According to critics, however, Putin was merely transferring Russia's natural resources and other assets to himself and his own cronies.

Toward a Market Economy

Developing free markets and republican governments initially brought misery to Russia and the rest of eastern Europe. The conditions of everyday life grew increasingly dire as salaries went unpaid, food remained in short supply, and essential services disintegrated. In 1994, inflation soared at a rate of 14 percent a month in Russia, while industrial production dropped by 15 percent. Hotel lobbies became clogged with prostitutes because women were the first people fired as governments privatized industry and cut service jobs. Unpaid soldiers sold their services to the Russian Mafia. Ordinary citizens lined the sidewalks of major cities selling their household possessions. "Anything and everything is for sale," one critic noted at the time.

The new system of government was not without pluses. People with enough money were able to travel freely for the first time, and the media were initially more open than ever before. Some workers, many of them young and highly educated, emigrated to more prosperous parts of the world, further depleting the human resources of the former Communist states. At the same time, as the different republics that had once composed the Soviet Union became independent, the hundreds of thousands of ethnic Russians who had earlier been sent by the state to colonize these regions returned to Russia as hated refugees, putting further demands on the chaotic Russian economy.

Amid chaos, the former Soviet Union itself became, in the words of one critic, a vast "kleptocracy" as the country's resources continued to be stolen for individual gain. An economist described the new scene as "piratization" rather than privatization. In this regard, one Polish adviser noted, democracy and a successful economic transition went hand in hand, for without a powerful representative government, former officials would simply operate as criminals. Corruption fed on the Soviet system of off-the-books dealing, tax evasion, bribery, favoritism, and outright theft. Additionally, because industry had not benefited from technological change or competition, free trade often meant closing factories and firing all the workers.

For many in the former Soviet bloc, the first priority was getting their economies running again on new terms. Given the spiraling misery, however, many opposed the introduction of new market-oriented measures. With the collective farms up for sale, most farmers on them faced landlessness and starvation. The countries that experienced the most success were those in which farmers already sold their produce on the open market or in which independent entrepreneurs or even government factories dealt in international trade. Hungary and Poland thus emerged from the transition with less strain, because both had adopted some free-market practices early on. They set up business schools and worked to attract foreign capital, anchoring themselves securely to the world economy.

A region-wide brain drain followed in a rush of migration from eastern Europe to western Europe, often involving those with marketable skills. "I knew in my heart that communism would collapse," said one Romanian ex-dissident, commenting sadly on the exodus of youth from his country, "but it never crossed my mind that the future would look like this." The everyday advantages of living in western Europe included safe water, adequate housing, personal safety, and at least a minimal level of social services. Although western Europe seemed to follow a neoliberal course of reduced spending on welfare-state programs, most benefits had disappeared entirely in former Communist countries. Day-care centers, kindergartens, and homes for the elderly closed their doors, and health care deteriorated. In these circumstances, the benefits of citizenship in western European countries were a powerful attraction.

International Politics and the New Russia

Although Gorbachev had pulled the Soviet Union out of its disastrous war with Afghanistan, his successors opened another war to prevent the secession of oil-rich Chechnya and to provide a nationalist rallying cry during the difficult transition. For decades, Chechens had been integrated into the Soviet bureaucracy and military, but in the fall of 1991, the National Congress of the Chechen People took over the government of the region from the USSR to gain the same kind of independence achieved by other former Soviet states. In June 1992, Chechen rebels got control of massive numbers of Russian weapons.

In December 1994, the Russian government invaded. An official defended the war: "We now need a small victorious war . . . [to] raise the President's [Yeltsin's] rating." Chechnya's capital city of Grozny was pounded to bits. Casualties mounted not only among Chechen civilians but also among Russians. In 2002, Chechen loyalists took hundreds of hostages in a Moscow theater; Chechen suicide bombers blew up airplanes, buses, and apartment buildings as Putin pursued the Chechen war into the twenty-first century.

Assassination in Moscow   In 2009, Russian citizens honored journalist and human rights activist Anna Politkovskaya, assassinated three years earlier in her Moscow apartment building. Politkovskaya relentlessly investigated the atrocities during the war in Chechnya as well as the corruption in the Putin government. Honest journalism in post-Soviet Russia was increasingly dangerous; scores of journalists were murdered in the twenty years following the collapse of communism, and many of Politkovskaya's collaborators were also killed. Several men were arrested, tried, and acquitted in the Politkovskaya case. (AP Photo/Pavel Golovkin.)

Putin expanded Russian influence in Ukraine, Belarus, India, and China as well by taking advantage of the politics of energy. Russia had the commodities—especially oil and gas—needed to sustain the growth of emerging industries around the world. The sale of commodities made Russia once again a real player in global politics—now because of its economic strength. Democratic values, however, were not put into practice. Critics of the government were mercilessly assassinated, and newspapers and broadcast media were closed down. In 2014, when Ukraine made gestures toward the European Union and away from Russia, Putin annexed Crimea, part of Ukraine, and fortified pro-Russian forces in the country. Putin's popularity remained steady as the Russian government used its new wealth to refurbish cities and everyday life grew easier. Putin served as prime minister between 2008 and 2012, and amid claims of dishonest elections, he was returned to the presidency for a third term in 2012.

REVIEW   What were the major issues facing the former Soviet bloc in the 1990s and early 2000s?

The Nation-State in a Global Age

Although the end of the Soviet system fractured one large regional economy, it gave a boost to European unification. In the 1990s and early 2000s, the European Economic Community (Common Market), which renamed itself the European Community in 1993, was healthy and economically robust compared with other regions of the world. The European Community's economic success provoked the formation of the North American Free Trade Agreement (NAFTA), which established a free-trade zone of the United States, Canada, and Mexico. The nationalist function of cities diminished as major urban areas like London and Paris became packed with people from other countries. Organizations for world governance grew in influence alongside large regional economic blocs. There was also resistance to these trends from those who wanted to preserve their own traditions and who felt the loss of a secure, face-to-face, local way of life.

Europe Looks beyond the Nation-State

The Common Market changed dramatically after the demise of European communism. In 1992, the twelve countries of the Common Market ended national distinctions in certain business activities, border controls, and transportation, effectively closing down passport controls at their shared borders. Citizens of the member countries carried a uniform burgundy-colored passport, and governments, whether municipal or national, had to treat all member nations' firms the same. In 1994, by the terms of the **Maastricht Treaty**, the European Community became the **European Union (EU)**, and in 1999 a common currency—the **euro**—came into being, first for transactions among financial institutions and then in 2002 for general use by the public. Common policies governed everything from the number of American soap operas aired on television to pollution controls on automobiles to the health warnings on cigarette packages. The EU parliament convened regularly in Strasbourg, France, and with the adoption of a common currency, an EU central bank guided interest rates and economic policy.

The EU was seen as the key to a peaceful Europe. "People with the same money don't go to war with one another," said a French nuclear scientist about the introduction of the euro. Greece pushed for the admission of its traditional enemy Turkey in 2002 and 2003 despite the warnings of a former president of France that a predominantly Muslim country could never fit in with the Christian traditions of EU members. Both Greece and Turkey stood to benefit by having their disputes adjudicated by the larger body of European members, principally because they would be able to cut that part of their defense budget used for weapons directed against each other. Like the rivalry between Germany and France, that between Turkey and Greece, it was hoped, would dissolve if bound by the strong economic and political ties of the EU. As of 2015, however, Turkey still awaited progress on its application while beginning to edge away from Europe.

There were drawbacks to EU membership. The EU enforced no common regulatory practices, and individual governments did not always observe common economic policies such as limits on budget deficits. Individual governments also, on occasion, set up hurdles and barriers for businesses, for example obstructing transnational mergers they did not like or blocking the acquisition of a company based on its own soil no matter what the advantages to shareholders, the economy, the workforce, or the consumers of unified Europe. Nonetheless, countries of eastern Europe clamored to join, working hard to meet not only the EU's fiscal requirements but also those pertaining to human rights and social policy (Map 29.3).

MAP 29.3 The European Union in 2015 The European Union (EU) appeared to increase the economic health of its members despite the rocky start of its common currency, the euro. The EU helped end the traditional competition between its members and facilitated trade and worker migration by providing common passports and business laws, and open borders. Many critics, however, feared a loss of cultural distinctiveness among peoples in an age of mass communications.

The collapse of the Soviet system advanced privatization of eastern European industry, and governments sold basic services to the highest bidder. Often, companies in the wealthy western countries of the EU snapped up eastern European assets. For example, the Czech Republic in 2001 sold its major energy distributor, Transgaz, and eight other regional distributors for 4.1 billion euros to a German firm. Lower wages and costs of doing business in eastern Europe attracted foreign investment, especially to Poland, the Czech Republic, Hungary, and Slovenia—the most developed state spun off from Yugoslavia. Eastern European countries sought membership to gain further investment, advance modernization, and protect their economies.

In 2004, the EU admitted ten new members—the Czech Republic, Cyprus, Estonia, Hungary, Latvia, Lithuania, Malta, Poland, Slovakia, and Slovenia—and in 2007 it welcomed Bulgaria and Romania. Just before its admission to the EU, Poland's standard of living was 39 percent of EU standards, up from 33 percent in 1995. The Czech Republic and Hungary were at 55 and 50 percent, respectively. In all three cases these figures masked the discrepancy between the ailing countryside and thriving cities. Citizens in eastern Europe were not always happy at joining the EU. A retiree foresaw the cost of beer going up and added, "If I wanted to join anything in the West, I would have defected." Still others felt that having just established an independent national identity, they should not allow themselves to be swallowed up once again. People in older member states were having second thoughts, too: in the spring of 2005, a majority of voters in France and the Netherlands rejected a complex draft constitution that would have strengthened EU ties. Commentators attributed the rejection to popular anger at the EU bureaucracy's failure to consult ordinary people in decision making.

Although still weak by comparison with most of western Europe, the economic life of eastern Europe had in fact picked up considerably by 2000. In contrast to the massive layoffs, soaring inflation, and unpaid salaries of the first post-Communist years, in 2002 residents of Poland, Slovenia, and Estonia had purchasing power some 40 percent higher than in 1989. Outsourcing by international companies began to flourish across the region, increasing opportunities for those with language and commercial skills. Even in countries with the weakest economies—Latvia, Bulgaria, and Romania—a greater number of residents enjoyed such modern conveniences as freezers, computers, and portable telephones. Shopping malls sprang up, mostly around capital cities, and superstores like the furniture giant IKEA and the electronics firm Electroworld became a consumer's paradise to those long starved of goods. "When Electroworld opened in Budapest [April 2002], it provoked a riot. Two hundred thousand people crowded to get in the doors," reported one amazed observer, a sign of U.S.-style "consumania" of materialism and frenzied shopping. For consumers, however, learning to read labels and to compare prices offered by superstores indicated their membership in a free, global community. Many proudly believed they had left communist poverty behind.

Globalizing Cities and Fragmenting Nations

After the collapse of communism, the West experienced the globalization of major cities. These were cities whose institutions, functions, and visions were overwhelmingly global rather than regional or national. They contained stock markets, legal firms, insurance companies, financial service organizations, and other enterprises that operated worldwide and that were linked to similar enterprises in other global cities. Within these cities, high-level decision makers set global economic policy and enacted global business. The presence of high-powered and high-income global businesspeople made urban life extremely costly, driving middle managers and engineers to lower-priced living quarters in the suburbs, which nonetheless provided good schools and other amenities for well-educated white-collar earners. Crowded into the slums of global cities and the poorer suburbs were the lowest-paid workers—the maintenance, domestic, and other laborers whose menial labor was essential to the needs and comfort of those at the top.

Global cities became centers for migration of highly skilled and medial workers alike. Paris, London, Moscow, and New York were global spaces in direct and constant contact with institutions, businesses, and governments around the world. In contrast, citizens of more locally oriented cities took pride in maintaining a distinctive national culture or local sense of community and often denounced global cities as rootless, their citizens lacking patriotic focus on national causes. Global cities were often the base for diasporas of prosperous migrants, such as the estimated ninety thousand Japanese in England in the mid-1990s who staffed Japan's thriving global businesses. Because these migrants did not aim to become citizens, global cities were said to produce a "deterritorialization of identities"—meaning that many city dwellers lacked both a national and a local sense of themselves.

Ironically, as globalization took hold economically and culturally, there came to be more nation-states in Europe in 2000 than there had been in 1945. Claims of ethnic distinctiveness caused individual nation-states to break apart and separatist movements—like that in Chechnya—to grow. Despite two centuries aimed at unification of the Slavs, for example, Slavs separated themselves from one another in the 1990s and early twenty-first century. Yugoslavia came apart into several states, and in 1993, Czechoslovakia split into the Czech Republic and Slovakia (see Map 29.3, page 891). In 2014, after a heated campaign, Scotland's voters, however, rejected separating from the United Kingdom.

Activists also launched movements for regional independence in France, Italy, and Spain. Some Bretons (residents of the historical French province of Brittany) and Corsicans demanded independence from France, the Corsicans violently attacking national officials. Sharp cultural differences threatened to split Belgium in two. Basque nationalists in northern Spain assassinated tourists, police, and other public servants in an effort to gain autonomy, and although in 2005 they publicly renounced terrorism, violence often resurfaced. The push for an independent northern Italy began when politicians saw its attractiveness to voters and loudly demanded secession. As cities globalized and nations fragmented, new combinations of local, national, and global identities took shape. Such changing identities, plus the overall expansion of the EU, called the nation-state into question.

Global Organizations

Supranational organizations, some regulating international politics and others addressing finance and social issues, also challenged the nation-state. The World Bank, the International Monetary Fund (IMF), and the World Trade Organization (WTO) raised money from national governments and dealt, for example, with the terms of trade among countries and the economic well-being of individual peoples. The IMF made loans to developing countries on the condition that those countries restructure their economies according to neoliberal principles. Other supranational organizations were charitable foundations, think tanks, or service-based organizations acting independently of governments, many of them based in Europe and the United States; they were called **nongovernmental organizations (NGOs)**. Because some of these groups—the Rockefeller Foundation, the Ford Foundation, and the Open Society Foundation, for example—controlled so much money, NGOs often had considerable international power. Some charitable and activist NGOs, like the French-based Doctors Without Borders, depended on global contributions and used them to provide medical attention in such places as the former Yugoslavia, where people facing war had no other medical help. Small, locally based NGOs excelled at inspiring grassroots activism, while the larger NGOs were often criticized for directing government policies with no regard for democratic processes.

Not everyone supported or was pleased with the process of globalization; some people formed activist groups to attack globalization or to influence its course. In 1998, the Association for the Taxation of Financial Transactions and Aid to Citizens (ATTAC) worked to block the control of globalization by the forces of high finance, declaring: "Commercial totalitarianism is not free trade." ATTAC had as its major policy goal to tax international financial transactions (just as the purchase of household necessities was taxed) and to create with the tax a fund for people living in poor countries. Some governments began to suggest such a tax themselves with the aim of raising much-needed revenue, not to help the poor. Another globally known opponent, French farmer José Bové, protested the opening of McDonald's chains in France and destroyed stocks of genetically modified seeds: "The only regret I have now," Bové claimed at his trial in 2003, "is that I didn't destroy more of it." Bové went to jail, but he remained a hero to antiglobalism activists who saw him as an enemy of standardization and an honest champion, in his own words, of "good food."

> **REVIEW**   What trends suggest that the nation-state was a declining institution at the beginning of the twenty-first century?

An Interconnected World's New Challenges

The rising tide of globalization ushered in as many challenges as opportunities. First, world health and the environment came under a multipronged attack from nuclear disaster, acid rain, the global circulation of contagious diseases, and surging population. Second, economic prosperity and physical safety continued to elude great masses of people, especially in the southern half of the globe. Third, as supra-state organizations developed, transnational allegiances and religious and ethnic movements vied for power and influence. Finally, a devastating economic crisis that rippled from Wall Street across the globe challenged the prosperity of the United States and Europe even as Asia, the Middle East, and Latin America developed competitive businesses and trade.

The Problems of Pollution

By the early years of the twenty-first century, industrial growth continued to threaten the environment. The 1986 nuclear explosion at Chernobyl had killed thirty-one people instantly (see page 873); in the aftermath, levels of radioactivity rose for hundreds of miles in all directions and some fifteen thousand people perished over time from the effects of radiation. Moreover, as Russia opened up, it became clear that Soviet managers and officials had thrown toxic waste into thousands of square miles of lakes and rivers. Used nuclear fuel had been dumped in neighboring seas, and many nuclear and other tests had left entire regions of Asia unfit for human, animal, and plant life.

Other environmental problems had devastating global effects. Pollutants from fossil fuels such as natural gas, coal, and oil mixed with atmospheric moisture to produce acid rain, a poisonous brew that destroyed forests in industrial areas. In eastern Europe, the unchecked use of fossil fuels turned trees into brown skeletons and inflicted ailments such as chronic bronchial disease on children. In other areas, clearing the world's rain forests to develop the land for cattle grazing or for cultivation of cash crops depleted the global oxygen supply. By the late 1980s, scientists determined that the use of chlorofluorocarbons (CFCs), chemicals found in aerosol and refrigeration products, had blown a hole in the earth's ozone layer, the part of the blanket of atmospheric gases that prevents harmful ultraviolet rays from reaching the planet.

Simultaneously, automobile and industrial emissions of chemicals were infusing that thermal blanket. The buildup of CFCs, carbon dioxide, and other atmospheric pollutants produced what is known as a greenhouse effect that results in **global warming**, an increase in the temperature of the earth's lower atmosphere. Already in the 1990s, the Arctic pack ice was breaking up, and scientists predicted that global ice melting would raise sea levels by more than ten inches by 2100, flooding coastal areas, disturbing fragile ecosystems, and harming the fresh water supply. In 2012, important island nations such as the Maldives were menaced with disappearance because of rising water levels. Other results of the greenhouse effect included climatic extremes such as drought, drenching rain, and increasingly catastrophic weather events such as deadly storms.

Activism against unbridled industrial growth took decades to develop as an effective political force. Rachel Carson's powerful critique *Silent Spring* (1962) advocated the immediate rescue of rivers, forests, and the soil from the ravages of factories and chemical farming in the United States. In West Germany, environmentalism united members of older and younger generations around a political tactic called citizen initiatives, in which groups of people blocked plans for urban growth that menaced forests and farmland. In 1979, the **Green Party** was founded in West Germany; two decades later Green Party candidates across Europe forced other politicians to voice their concern for the environment.

Spurred by successful Green Party campaigns, Europeans attacked environmental problems on local and global levels. Some European cities—Frankfurt, Germany, for example—developed car-free zones, and in Paris, whenever automobile emissions reached dangerous levels, cars were banned from city streets until the emission levels fell. The Smart car, a very small car using reduced amounts of fuel, became fashionable in Europe. European cities also developed bicycle lanes on major city streets, with some U.S. cities following their lead. To reduce dependence on fossil fuels, parts of Europe developed wind power to such an extent that 20 percent of some countries' electricity was generated by wind. Many cities in the West undertook extensive recycling of waste materials. By 1999, some eighty-four countries, including EU members, had signed the Kyoto Protocol, an international treaty whose signatories agreed to reduce their levels of emissions and other pollutants to specified targets. However, the United States, the world's second leading polluter after China, failed to ratify this agreement, suggesting that the West was fragmenting over values.

Population, Health, and Disease

The issue of population was as difficult in the early twenty-first century as it had been in the 1930s. Nations with less-developed economies struggled with the pressing problem of surging population, while Europe experienced more deaths than births after 1995. The less industrially developed countries accounted for 98 percent of worldwide population growth, in part because the spread of Western medicine enabled people there to live much longer than before. By 2015, the Earth's population had reached 7.25 billion, with a doubling forecast for 2045. Yet many European countries were facing problems related to an aging citizenry and a shortage of younger people to bring new ideas and promote change. In fact, Europe as a region had the lowest fertility in the world. The fertility rate in Italy and Spain was only 1.3 children per woman of reproductive age, far below the replacement level of 2.1 needed to maintain a steady population number. As a consequence, fewer young workers paid into the social security system to fund retirees' pensions and health care.

Population problems were especially urgent in Russia, where life expectancy was declining at a catastrophic rate from a peak of seventy years for Russian men in the mid-1970s to fifty-one years at the beginning of the twenty-first century. Heart disease and cancer were the leading causes of male death, and these stark death rates were generally attributed to increased drinking, smoking, drug use, poor diet, and general stress. Between 1992 and 2014, the Russian population declined from 149 to 142 million. Meanwhile, fertility rates throughout the former Soviet bloc were also declining: the lowest levels of fertility in 2003 were in the Czech Republic and Ukraine (1.1 children per woman of reproductive age), and children in eastern Europe lived on average twelve years less than their counterparts in western Europe.

Good health was spread unevenly around the world. Western medicine brought the less-developed world increased use of vaccines and drugs for diseases such as malaria and smallpox. However, half of all Africans lacked the basic requirements of well-being such as safe drinking water. Drought and poverty, along with the corruption of politicians in some cases, spread famine in Sudan, Somalia, Ethiopia, and elsewhere. Around the world, the poor and the unemployed suffered more chronic illnesses than those who were better off, but they received less care. Whereas in many parts of the world people still died from malnutrition and infectious diseases, in the West noncontagious illnesses (heart disease, stroke, cancer, chronic obstructive pulmonary disease, autoimmune diseases, and depression) were more lethal.

Disease, like population and technology, operated on a global terrain. In the early 1980s, both Western values and Western technological expertise were challenged by the spread of a global epidemic disease: acquired immunodeficiency syndrome (AIDS). An incurable, highly virulent killer that effectively shuts down the body's entire immune system, AIDS initially afflicted heterosexuals in central Africa; the disease later turned up in Haitian immigrants to the United States and in homosexual men worldwide. Within a decade, AIDS became a global epidemic. The disease spread especially quickly and widely among the heterosexual populations of Africa and Asia, passed mainly by men to and through women, but in 2010 the U.S. capital, Washington, D.C., had a rate of infection as high as that in Africa. Protease-inhibiting drugs helped alleviate the symptoms, but treatment was often not provided to poor people living in sub-Saharan Africa and the slums of Asian cities. In addition to the AIDS pandemic, the deadly Ebola virus, severe acute respiratory syndrome (SARS), swine flu, and dozens of other viruses smoldered like so many global plagues in the making. Diseases such as Ebola and the global fears they provoked along with environmental dangers underscored the interconnectedness of the world's peoples.

North versus South?

During the 1980s and 1990s, world leaders tried to address the differences between the earth's northern and southern regions. Other than Australians and New Zealanders, southern peoples generally suffered lower living standards and measures of health than northerners. Emerging from colonial rule, environmental destruction, and economic exploitation by northerners, citizens in the southern regions could not yet count on their governments to provide welfare services or education. Although organizations like the World Bank and the IMF provided loans for economic development, the conditions tied to those loans, such as cutting government spending for education, the environment, and health care, led to criticism.

Southern regions of the world experienced other barriers to economic development. Latin American nations grappled with government corruption, multibillion-dollar debt, widespread crime, and grinding poverty, though some countries—prominent among them Brazil—began to strengthen their economies by marketing their oil and other natural resources more effectively and by building administrative expertise among government officials. Africa suffered from drought, famine, and civil war, while in countries such as Rwanda, Somalia, and Sudan, the military rule, factionalism, and ethnic antagonism encouraged under imperialism produced lethal conflict and genocide in the 1990s and early 2000s. Millions of people perished; others were left starving and homeless due to kleptocracies that drained revenues. In the face of these conditions, other African nations began turning away from violence and dictatorship toward constitutional government, economic sustainability, and prosperity. By 2015, these reforms had made many parts of Africa a major target for outside investment.

Radical Islam Meets the West

North–South antagonisms became evident in the rise of radical Islam, which often flourished where democracy and prosperity for the masses were missing. The Iranian hostage crisis that began in 1979 revealed nationalism and a strong anti-Western sentiment among Islamic fundamentalists. The charismatic leaders of the 1980s and 1990s—the ayatollah Ruhollah Khomeini in Iran, Libya's Muammar Qaddafi, Iraq's Saddam Hussein, and **Osama bin Laden**, a Saudi Arabian by birth and leader of the transnational terrorist organization al-Qaeda—variously promoted a pan-Islamic or (outside Iran) pan-Arabic world order that gathered increasing support. Khomeini's program—"Neither East, nor West, only the Islamic Republic"—had wide appeal even after his death in 1989. Renouncing the Westernization that had flourished under the shah, Khomeini began a regime in Iran that required women once again to cover their bodies almost totally in special clothing, restricted their access to divorce, and eliminated a range of other rights for men and women alike. Buoyed by the prosperity that oil had brought and following Khomeini's lead, Islamic revolutionaries across the wider region aimed to restore the pride and Islamic identity that imperialism had stripped from Middle Eastern men.

Power in the Middle East remained fragmented, however, as war plagued the region. In 1980, Saddam Hussein, fearing a rebellion from Shi'ites in Iraq, attacked Iran in hopes of channeling Shi'ite discontent into a patriotic crusade against non-Arab Iranians. The United States provided Iraq with massive aid in the struggle against Iran, but eight years of combat, with extensive loss of life on both sides, ended in stalemate. In 1990, Saddam tested the post–cold war waters by invading neighboring Kuwait in hopes of annexing the oil-rich country to debt-ridden Iraq. A United Nations coalition led by the United States stopped the invasion and defeated the Iraqi army, but discontent mounted in the region (Map 29.4).

To the east, the Taliban—a militant Islamic group initially funded by the United States, China, Saudi Arabia, and Pakistan during the cold war—took over the government of Afghanistan in the late 1990s. Its leaders imposed a regime that forbade girls from attending schools and women from leaving their homes without a male escort and demanded from men strict adherence to its rules for dress.

To the west, conflict between the Israelis and the Palestinians continued. As Israeli settlers took more Palestinian land and homes, Palestinian suicide bombers

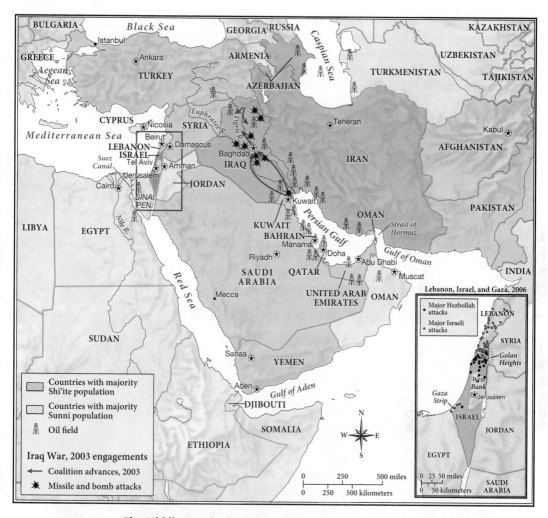

MAP 29.4 The Middle East in the Twenty-First Century   Tensions among states in the Middle East, especially the ongoing conflict between the Palestinians and Israelis and animosities among Shiʿites and Sunnis, became more complicated from the 1990s on. The situation in the Middle East grew more uncertain in 2003 when a U.S.- and British-led invasion of Iraq deteriorated into escalating violence among competing religious and ethnic groups in the country. Additionally, for thirty-four days in the summer of 2006, Israel bombed Lebanon, including its capital city and refugee camps, with fire returned by Hezbollah and Hamas forces in the region.

began murdering Israeli civilians in the late 1990s. The Israeli government retaliated with missiles, machine guns, and tanks, often killing Palestinian civilians in turn. In 2006, the Israelis, responding to the political militia Hezbollah's kidnapping of Israeli soldiers, attacked Lebanon, destroying infrastructure, sending missiles into its capital city of Beirut, and killing hundreds of civilians. Beginning in the 1980s and continuing into the 2000s, terrorists from the Middle East and North Africa planted bombs in European cities, blew airplanes out of the sky, and bombed the Paris subway system. These attacks were said to be punishment for the West's support both for Israel and for Middle Eastern dictatorships.

On September 11, 2001, the ongoing terrorism in Europe and around the world caught the full attention of the United States when Muslim militants hijacked four planes in the United States and flew two of them into the World Trade Center in New York City and one into the Pentagon in Virginia. The fourth plane, en route to the Capitol, crashed in Pennsylvania when passengers forced the hijackers to lose control of the aircraft. The hijackers, most of whom were from Saudi Arabia, were inspired by the wealthy radical leader of al-Qaeda, Osama bin Laden, who sought to end the presence of U.S. forces in Saudi Arabia. They had trained in bin Laden's terrorist camps in Afghanistan and learned to pilot planes in the United States. The loss of more than three thousand lives led the United States to declare

Europeans React to September 11 Terror Attacks   On September 11, 2001, terrorists killed thousands of people from dozens of countries in airplane attacks on the World Trade Center and the Pentagon. Throughout the world, people expressed their shock and sorrow in vigils, and like this British tourist in Rome, they remained glued to the latest news. Terrorism, which had plagued Europeans for several decades, easily traveled the world in the days of more open borders, economic globalization, and cultural exchange. (© Alberto Pizzoli/Corbis-Sygma.)

a "war against terrorism." The administration of U.S. president George W. Bush forged a multinational coalition, which included the vital cooperation of Islamic countries such as Pakistan, with the main goal of driving the ruling Taliban out of Afghanistan.

At first, the September 11 attacks and other lethal terrorist attacks around the world promoted global cooperation. European countries rounded up suspected terrorists and conducted the first successful trials of them in the spring of 2003. Ultimately, however, the West became divided when the United States claimed that Saddam Hussein was concealing weapons of mass destruction in Iraq and suggested ties between him and bin Laden's terrorist group. Great Britain, Spain, and Poland were among those who joined the coalition of invading forces, but some powerful European states—including Germany, Russia, and France—refused, sparking the anger of many Americans, some of whom sported bumper stickers with the demand "First Iraq, Next France" or participated in happy hours devoted to "French bashing."

U.S. war fever mounted with the suggestion that Syria and Iran should also be invaded, while the rest of the world condemned what seemed a sudden American blood lust. Europeans in general, including the British public, accused the United States of becoming a world military dictatorship to preserve its only remaining value—wasteful consumerism. The United States countercharged that the Europeans were too selfishly enjoying their democracy and creature comforts to help fund the military defense of freedom under attack. The Spanish withdrew from the U.S. occupation of Iraq after terrorists linked to al-Qaeda bombed four Madrid commuter trains on March 11, 2004. The British, too, reeled when terrorists exploded bombs in three subway cars and a bus in central London in July 2005. Barack Obama, who was elected the first African American U.S. president in 2008, brought home all the troops from Iraq in 2012, though the United States maintained a presence there of military advisers. As for al-Qaeda, the United States weakened the organization by assassinating top leaders, including Osama bin Laden in 2011.

The Promise and Problems of a World Economy

Amid the violence, an incredible rise in industrial entrepreneurship and technological development took place outside the West. In 1982, the Asian-Pacific nations accounted for 16.4 percent of global gross domestic product, a figure that had doubled since the 1960s. By 1989, East Asia's share of world production had grown to more than 25 percent as that of the West declined. By 2006, China alone was achieving economic growth rates of more than 10 percent per year, and in 2010 it overtook Japan as the second largest national economy after the United States, with Germany falling to fourth place.

South Korea, Taiwan, Singapore, and Hong Kong were popularly called **Pacific tigers** for the ferocity of their growth in the 1980s and 1990s. By the 1990s, China, pursuing a policy of economic modernization and market orientation, had surpassed all the others. Japan, however, led the initial charge of Asian economies with investment in high-tech consumer industries driving the Japanese economy. For example, in 1982, Japan had thirty-two thousand industrial robots in operation; western Europe employed only nine thousand, and the United States had seven thousand. In 1989, the Japanese government and private businesses invested $549 billion to modernize industrial capacity, a full $36 billion more than in the United States. As buyers around the world snapped up automobiles, televisions, videocassette recorders, and computers from Asian-Pacific companies, the United States poured vast sums into its wars and Asian and Middle Eastern governments financed America's ballooning national debt. By 2000, China had become the largest creditor of the United States.

Despite rising national prosperity, individual workers, particularly outside of Japan, often paid dearly for this newly created wealth. For example, safety standards and working conditions in China were abominable, leading to horrendous mining disasters and suicides among workers. Women in the Asia Pacific region and Central America labored in sweatshops to produce clothing for U.S.- and Euroupean-based companies. Using the lure of a low-paid and presumably docile female workforce, governments were able to attract electronics and other industries. At the same time, educational standards rose, along with access to birth control and other medical care for these women, and many valued the escape from rural poverty.

Other emerging economies in the Southern Hemisphere continued to increase their share of the world's gross domestic product over the past four decades, and some achieved political gains as well. In South Africa, native peoples began winning the struggle for political rights when, in 1990, the moderate government of F. W. de Klerk released political leader Nelson Mandela, imprisoned for almost three decades because of his antiapartheid activism. After holding free elections in 1994, which Mandela won, South Africa—like Brazil, Russia, Iran, Saudi Arabia, Nigeria, and Chile—profited from the need for vast quantities of raw materials such as oil and ores to feed global expansion. India made strides in education and women's rights and calmed bitter local rivalries, but the assassination of two successive Indian prime ministers in 1984 and 1991 raised the question of whether India would be able to attract investment and thus continue modernization. India's economy achieved soaring if unsustained growth early in the twenty-first century, taking business from Western firms and making global acquisitions that gave it, for example, the world's largest steel industry.

There was a downside to global economic interconnectedness. Beginning in 1997, when speculators brought down the Thai baht, and continuing with the collapse of the Russian ruble in 1998 and the bursting of the technology bubble in the early 2000s, the global economy suffered a series of shocks. In 2008, the real estate bubble burst in the United States, setting in motion a financial crisis of enormous proportions. For several years, lenders had been making home mortgages available to U.S. consumers who could not afford them. The boom in housing made the economy as a whole look robust. Bankers then sold their bad housing debt around the world to those who hoped to make handsome profits based on rate increases written into the mortgage contracts. When people were unable to make their monthly mortgage payments and pay their credit card debt, a global

Protesting Reform amid Economic Crisis   By 2010 and 2011, global economic crisis and the attempts to repair the damage had led to massive government debt. To remedy the situation, governments cut back on jobs, benefits, and services while giving banks and businesses huge bailouts. Here, on the island of Cyprus, unions and NGOs sponsored this demonstration against the policy of simultaneously heaping money on banks and taking it from ordinary citizens. (EPA/ Katia Christodouloul/Landov.)

credit collapse followed, just as it had in the stock market crash of 1929. Beginning in the United States and continuing around the world, banks and industries became insolvent, forcing governments to set common policies to prop up failing banks with billions of dollars, which in turn added to government debt. Unemployment rose as businesses and consumers alike stopped purchasing goods.

Five years later, the U.S. economy had improved because of unprecedented government intervention even as European nations faced threats of insolvency and unacceptable levels of unemployment—more than 20 percent in Spain. It looked to some as though the EU itself might collapse due to the stubborn downturn. The globalization of economic crises was another of the perils faced by the world's population.

REVIEW   What were the principal challenges facing the West at the beginning of the twenty-first century?

Global Culture and Society in the Twenty-First Century

While warfare, booms, and crises continued, increased migration and growing global communications were changing culture and society, prompting many to ask what would become of national cultures and Western civilization itself. Would the world become a homogeneous mass with everyone wearing the same kind of clothing, eating the same kind of food, watching the same films, and communicating with the same smartphones? Or would there be a global holocaust brought on by a clash of civilizations or a new war of religions? The information revolution and the global sharing of culture argued against the cultural purity of any group, Western or otherwise. "Civilizations," Indian economist and Nobel Prize winner Amartya Sen wrote after the terrorist attacks of September 11, "are hard to partition . . . given the diversities within each society as well as the linkages among different countries and cultures."

Through global communication and migration, some believed that Western society had changed even more rapidly from the 1980s into the twenty-first century than it had hundreds of years earlier when it came into intense contact with the rest of the globe. Culture knew no national boundaries, as East, West, North, and South became saturated with one another's cultural products via satellite television, films, telecommunications, and computer technology. Consequently, some observers labeled the new century an era of denationalization—meaning that national cultures as well as national boundaries were becoming less distinct. There is no denying that even while the West absorbed peoples and cultures, it continued to exercise not only economic but also cultural influence worldwide. Yet the identity of the West was becoming unclear as Westerners themselves absorbed the cultures of other regions.

Redefining the West: The Impact of Global Migration

The global movement of people was massive in the last third of the twentieth century and into the twenty-first. Uneven economic development, political persecution, and warfare (which claimed more than 100 million victims after 1945) sent tens of millions in search of opportunity and safety. By 2010, France had between five and eight million Muslims within its borders, and Europe as a whole had between thirty-five and fifty million. Other parts of the world were as full of migrants as the West. The oil-producing nations of the Middle East employed millions of foreign workers, who generally constituted one-third of the labor force. The Iraq-Iran War and the U.S. invasion of Iraq in 2003 sent millions fleeing, while the rise of the radical Islamic State left 1.7 million more Iraqis homeless. After 2011, more than 2 million Syrians were registered as refugees from the civil war and Islamic State in adjacent nations, bringing the total number of migrants worldwide to more than 200 million in 2015, in part because of escalating conflicts across the Middle East.

Those migrating for work from countries as different as the Yugoslav republics, Egypt, Spain, Mexico, and Pakistan sent money home from abroad that constituted up to 60 percent of national income. Sometimes migration was coerced: many eastern European and Asian prostitutes were held in international sex rings that controlled their passports, wages, and lives. Others came to the West voluntarily, seeking opportunity and a better life: "I do not want to go back to China," said one woman restaurant owner in Hungary in the 1990s. "Some of my relatives there also have restaurants . . . and sometimes they have to bribe somebody. . . . I would not be happy living like that." Like the illegal Congolese café proprietor Thérèse, whose story opens this chapter, many lived on the margins of the law, maintaining global ties with families from a new base in the West.

Foreign workers were often scapegoats for native peoples suffering from economic woes such as unemployment caused by downsizing. On the eve of EU enlargement in 2004, the respected weekly magazine *The Economist* included an article entitled "The Coming Hordes," which warned of Britain's being overrun by Roma (Gypsies) from eastern Europe. The Moscow rock band Corroded Metals campaigned for anti-immigrant politicians with hate-filled songs and chants in English of "Kill, kill, kill, kill the bloody foreigners" running in the background. Even citizens of immigrant descent often had a difficult time being accepted. Thriving anti-immigrant and white supremacist politicians challenged centrist parties, and in Austria and the Netherlands, anti-immigration candidates were elected to head the government. Nonetheless, employers sought out illegal immigrants for the low wages they could be paid.

Headscarf Controversy in Germany

Western countries have long debated the relationship between religion and the nation-state, especially in public education. In an age of global migration, the issue of religion in the schools resurfaced, this time focusing on the headscarves worn by many Muslim women. In 2003, a German court upheld the right of teacher Fereshta Ludin, pictured here, to wear her headscarf while teaching, on the grounds of religious freedom. Note the justices' own different clothing. (© Vincent Kessler / Reuters / Corbis.)

Global Networks and Social Change

Like migration, rapid technological change also weakened traditional political, cultural, and economic borders and to some extent even made borders obsolete. In 1969, the U.S. Department of Defense began to develop a computer network to carry communications in case of nuclear war. This system and others like it in universities, government, and business grew into an unregulated system of more than ten thousand networks worldwide. These came to be known as the Internet—shorthand for *internetworking*. By 1995, users in more than 137 countries were connected to the Internet, creating new "communities" via the World Wide Web that transcended common citizenship in a particular nation-state. By 2015, some three billion people—more than one-third of the world's population—used the Internet, creating an online marketplace that offered goods and services ranging from advanced weaponry to organ transplants, which was itself a booming global business. Critics charged that communications technology favored elites and disadvantaged those without computer skills or the financial resources needed to access computers.

The Internet had brought service jobs to countries that had heretofore suffered unemployment and real poverty. One of the first countries to recognize the possibilities of computing and help-desk services was Ireland, which pushed computer literacy to attract business. In 2003, U.S. firms spent $8.3 billion on outsourcing to Ireland and $7.7 billion on outsourcing to India. In that same year, the United States bought $77.38 billion in services from foreign countries and sold $131.01 billion to them, meaning in fact that more was insourced than outsourced. The Internet allowed for jobs to be apportioned anywhere. Moroccans did help-desk work for French or Spanish speakers, and in the twenty-first century Estonia, Hungary, and the Czech Republic as well as India and the Philippines rebuilt their economies successfully by providing call-center and other business services. The Internet allowed service industries to globalize just as the manufacturing sector had done much earlier through multinational corporations.

Globalization of the economy via the Internet and other technology affected the West in complex ways. Benefiting from the booming global economy of the 1990s, the Irish and eastern Europeans became integrated into the Western consumer economy, and by the 2000s Asians and South Americans were integrated, too. By purchasing automobiles, CD players, and personal computers, non-Westerners may have taken jobs from the West, but they often sent funds back via their new purchasing power. For example, a twenty-one-year-old Indian woman, working for a service provider in Bangalore under the English name Sharon, used her salary to buy Western consumer items such as a cell phone from the Finnish company Nokia. "As a teenager I wished for so many things," she said. "Now I'm my own Santa Claus." Some Western workers often found this global revolution threatening, as it redistributed jobs across the West and worldwide.

On the positive side, digital media enabled widespread information sharing and allowed individuals and organizations to spread awareness of the daunting problems of contemporary life—population explosion, scarce resources, North–South inequities, global pollution, ethnic hatred, and global terrorism—which demand, more than ever, the exercise of humane values and rational thought. Positive social change has occurred, thanks in part to digital media. In 2011, governments were overturned relatively peacefully in Tunisia and Egypt because Facebook, Twitter, and other electronic media brought protesters together with a common purpose, with less public violence than in revolutions a century earlier. Given the dramatic resurgence in conflict in recent years, however, claims that digital communications will ease tensions, advance democracy, and make violence less likely remain unproven.

A New Global Culture?

Despite the sense that national boundaries are weakening, cultural exchange flowing in many directions goes back millennia. In the ancient world, Greek philosophers and traders knew of distant Asian religious beliefs, and Middle Eastern religions such as Judaism and Christianity were influenced by them even as these beliefs spread westward to Europe and the Western Hemisphere. Chinese students in Tiananmen Square in 1989 testified to the global power of the West when in the name of freedom they rallied around their own representation of the Statue of Liberty (which itself was a gift from France to the United States). In Japan, businesspeople wore Western-style clothing and watched soccer, baseball, and other Western sports using English terms, while Europeans and Americans wore flip-flops, carried umbrellas, and practiced yoga—all imports from beyond the West.

Remarkable innovations in communications integrated cultures, possibly giving them a Western flavor. Videotapes and satellite-beamed telecasts transported American television shows to Hong Kong and Bollywood movies to Europe and North America. American rock music sold briskly in Russia and elsewhere in the former Soviet bloc. More than 100,000 Czechoslovakian rock fans, including President Václav Havel, attended a Rolling Stones concert in Prague in 1990, showing that despite half a century of supposed isolation under communism they had been well tuned in to the larger world. Young black immigrants forged transnational culture when they created hip-hop and other pop music styles by combining elements of Africa, the Caribbean, Afro-America, and Europe. Athletes like the Brazilian soccer player Ronaldo and pop icons such as Psy and Beyoncé became better known to countless people than their own national leaders. Even moral titans—the Nobel Peace Prize winners Nelson Mandela, former president of South Africa; the Dalai Lama, the spiritual leader of Tibet; and Aung San Suu Kyi, opposition leader in Burma—have been global figures.

As it had done for centuries, the West continued to devour material from other cultures—whether Hong Kong films, African textiles, Indian music, or Latin American pop culture. One of the most important influences in the West came from what was called the boom in Latin American literature. Latin American authors developed a style known as magical realism, which melded everyday events with Latin American history and geography and with elements of myth, magic, and religion. The novels of Colombian-born Nobel Prize winner Gabriel García Márquez were translated into dozens of languages. His lush fantasies, including *One Hundred Years of Solitude* (1967), *Love in the Time of Cholera* (1988), and many later works, portray people of titanic ambitions and passions who endure war and all manner of personal trials. García Márquez narrated the tradition of dictators in Latin America, but he also paid close attention to the effects of global business. *One Hundred Years of Solitude*, for example, closes with the machine-gunning in 1928 of thousands of workers for the American-owned United Fruit Company because they asked for one day off per week and breaks to use the toilet. Wherever they lived, readers snapped up the book, which sold thirty million copies worldwide. García Márquez's work inspired a host of other outstanding novels in the magical realism tradition, including Laura Esquivel's *Like Water for Chocolate* (1989). In the 1990s, the work was translated into two dozen languages and became a hit film because of its setting in a Mexican kitchen during the revolution of 1910, where cooking, sexuality, and brutality are intertwined. Innumerable authors in the West adopted aspects of this style.

Magical realism influenced a range of Western writers, including those migrating to Europe. British-born Zadie Smith, daughter of a Jamaican mother, became a prize-winning author with her novel *White Teeth* (2000), which describes post-imperial Britain through the lives of often bizarre and larger-than-life characters from many ethnic backgrounds. Odd science fiction technology, deep emotional wounds, and weird but hilarious situations guide a plot full of heartbreak. Equally drawn to aspects of the magical realist style, Indian-born immigrant **Salman Rushdie** published the novel *The Satanic Verses* (1988), which outraged Muslims around the world because it appeared to blaspheme the Prophet Muhammad. From Iran, the ayatollah Khomeini issued a fatwa (decree) promising both a monetary reward and salvation in the afterlife to anyone who would assassinate the writer. Rushdie's Italian and Japanese translators were murdered, while his Norwegian publisher survived an assassination attempt. Soaring above them all in terms of global acceptance was British author J. K. Rowling's series of Harry Potter novels, selling half a billion copies worldwide and being translated into more than seventy languages.

As groups outside the accepted circles engaged in artistic production, battles over culture erupted. U.S. novelist **Toni Morrison** became, in 1993, the first African American woman to win the Nobel Prize for Literature. In works such as *Beloved* (1987), *A Mercy* (2008), and *Home* (2012), Morrison describes the nightmares, daily experiences, achievements, and dreams of those who were brought as slaves to the United States and their descendants. Some parents objected to the inclusion of Morrison's work in school curricula, however. Critics charged that unlike Shakespeare's universal Western truth, the writing of African Americans, native Americans, and women represented only propaganda, not great literature. In both the United States and Europe, politicians on the right saw the presence of multiculturalism as a sign of national decay similar to that brought about by immigration.

In the former Soviet bloc, artists and writers faced unique challenges. After the Soviet Union collapsed, celebrated writers like Mikhail Bulgakov, famous in the West for his novel *The Master and Margarita* (published posthumously in 1966–1967), became known in his homeland. At the same time, the collapse put literary dissidents out of business. In helping bring down the Soviet regime, they had lost their subject matter—the critique of a tyrannical system. Eastern-bloc writers who

Toni Morrison, Recipient of the Nobel Prize   Toni Morrison, shown here receiving the Nobel Prize in Literature in 1993, was the first African American woman to receive the Nobel Prize. Morrison uses her literary talent to depict the condition of blacks under slavery and after emancipation. She also publishes insightful essays on social, racial, and gender issues. (AP Photo.)

formerly found both critical and financial success in the West seemed less heroic, and some were shown to have been part of the Soviet system of reformers. New literature aimed at rethinking the communist experience and eastern Europe's cultural relationship to the West and to its own past. Andrei Makine, an expatriate Russian author, described the attraction of western European culture and the role of the war and the Gulag on the imaginations of eastern-bloc people, including teenagers. Both *Dreams of My Russian Summers* (1995) and *Once Upon the River Love* (1994) describe young people fantasizing about the wealth, sexiness, and material goods of western Europe and the United States. Victor Pelevin wrote more satirically and bitingly in such works as *The Life of Insects* (1993), in which insect-humans buzz around Russia trying to discover who they are in the post-Soviet world. Pelevin, a Buddhist and former engineer, wrote hilarious send-ups of politicians and the almost sacred Soviet space program, depicting it as a media sham run from the depths of the Moscow subway system in which hundreds of cosmonaut-celebrities are killed to prevent the truth from getting out. For him, "any politician is a TV program," as he showed in his novel *Homo Zapiens* (1999), in which politicians are all "virtual"—that is, produced by technical effects, clothing, and scriptwriters.

In music and the other arts, much energy was spent on recovering and absorbing all the underground works that had been hidden since 1917. For example, music lovers were astonished as the work of first-rate composers emerged. Those composers had written their classical works in private for fear that they might contain phrasings, sounds, and rhythms that would be called subversive. Meanwhile, they had often earned a living writing for films, as did Giya Kancheli, who wrote immensely popular music for more than forty films but was in addition a gifted composer of classical music. Alongside great artists, ordinary people in eastern Europe rethought the past, creating ceremonies honoring victims of the Gulag and of Stalin's purges, with some trying to sort out what the legacy of communism, anti-Semitism, and massive slaughter of fellow citizens had meant to their lives and to history. By 2015, Vladimir Putin had slowed such free reflection on the Soviet past.

Simultaneously, the United States' success in marketing its culture, along with the legacy of British imperialism, helped make English the dominant international language by the end of the twentieth century. Such English words as *stop, shopping, parking, okay, weekend,* and *rock* infiltrated dozens of non-English vocabularies. Across Europe, English served as the main language of higher education, science, and tourism. Already in the 1960s, French president Charles de Gaulle, fearing the corruption of the French language, had banned such new words as *computer* in government documents, and succeeding administrations followed his path. The ban did not stop the influx of English into daily life, even though the EU's parliament and national cultural ministries regulated the amount of American programming on television and in cinemas.

American influence in film was dominant: films such as *The Matrix Reloaded* (2003) and *Avatar* (2009) earned hundreds of millions of dollars from global audiences. Simultaneously, however, the United States itself welcomed films such as the British *Slumdog Millionaire* (2009) from around the world. "Bollywood" films—happy, lavish films from the Indian movie industry—had a huge following in all Western countries, even influencing the plots of some American productions. The fastest-growing television market in the United States in the twenty-first century was Spanish-language programming, just one more indication that even in the United States culture was based on mixture and global exchange.

Some have called the global culture of the late twentieth and early twenty-first centuries **postmodernism**, defined in part as intense stylistic mixing in the arts without following an elite set of standards. Striking examples of postmodern art abound in Western society, including the AT&T Building (now known as the Sony Building) in New York City, which looks sleek and modern. Its entryway, however, is a Roman arch, and its cloud-piercing top suggests eighteenth-century Chippendale furniture. The Guggenheim Museum in Bilbao, Spain, designed by American Frank Gehry and considered bizarre by classical or even modern standards, includes forms, materials, and perspectives that, by rules of earlier decades, do not belong together.

Architects working in a variety of hybrid styles completed the postunification rebuilding of the Reichstag in Berlin, whose traditional facade was given a modern dome of glass and steel, along with solar panels. To add to the changing reality, all of these postmodern buildings could be visited virtually on the World Wide Web.

Some intellectuals defined postmodernism in political terms as part of the decline of the eighteenth-century Enlightenment ideals of human rights, individualism, and personal freedom, which were seen as modern. This political postmodernism included the decline of the Western nation-state. A structure like the Bilbao Guggenheim was simply an international tourist attraction rather than an institution reflecting Spanish traditions or national purpose. It embodied consumption, global technology, mass communications, and international migration rather than citizenship, nationalism, and rights. These qualities made it a rootless structure, unlike the Louvre in Paris, for example, which was built by the French monarchy to serve its own purposes. Critics saw the Bilbao Guggenheim as drifting, more like the nomadic businesswoman Thérèse, who moved between nations and cultures with no set identity. Cities and nations alike were losing their function as places providing social roots, personal identity, or human rights. For postmodernists of a political bent, computers had replaced the autonomous, free self and bureaucracy had rendered representative government obsolete.

REVIEW   What social and cultural questions has globalization raised?

Conclusion

Postmodernist thinking has not eclipsed humane values in the global age. The urge to find practical solutions to the daunting problems of contemporary life — population explosion, scarce resources, pollution, global warming, ethnic hatred, North–South inequities, and terrorism — through the careful assessment of facts still guides public policy. Some of these global problems were briefly overshadowed by the collapse of the Soviet empire, which initially produced human misery, rising criminality, and the flight of population during the 1990s and even into the 2000s. Reformers who sought improved conditions of life by bringing down Soviet and Yugoslav communism saw unexpected bloodshed and even genocide. What appeared to be an economic boom resulting from globalization and the collapse of communism itself had disadvantages, as a series of crises beginning in Thailand in 1997 and finally exploding in the more sustained crisis from 2007 on cost jobs and harmed human well-being.

Yet the past twenty-five years have also seen great improvements. Events in South Africa, the Middle East, and Latin America, for example, suggested some progress toward democracy, even as gains at times appeared fragile. Human health gradually improved even as scientists sought to cure the victims of global pandemics and even to prevent such ravages altogether. The global age ushered in by the Soviet collapse unexpectedly brought denationalization to many regions of the world, leading to weakening of borders and cooperation among former enemies. The expansion of the European Union and the tightening of relationships within it are the best example of this development even as they too dealt with challenges in the face of economic adversity.

Some consequences of increasing globalization are still being determined. The Internet and migration suggest that people's empathy for one another grew worldwide. One commentator claimed that there was little bloodshed in the collapse of the Soviet Empire because fax machines and television circulated images of events globally, muting the violence often associated with political revolution. At the same time, militants from Saudi Arabia, Egypt, Indonesia, the Philippines, North Africa, Britain, France, and elsewhere unleashed terrorism on the world in an attempt to push back global forces. Each incident was shocking, including the planned murder of seventeen French journalists, Jews, and police in the winter of 2015. Nor did powerful countries hesitate to wage wars against Ukraine, Chechnya, Kuwait, Iraq, Afghanistan, and Lebanon—or against their own people, as in Libya and Syria. On a different level, even as globalization raised standards of living and education in many parts of the world, in other areas—such as poorer regions in Africa and Asia—people faced disease and the dramatic social and economic crises specifically associated with the global age. In contrast, the most hopeful developments in recent globalization were communication in the arts and in culture more generally and the cooperation that nations undertook with one another in the realm of health, economics, and politics. Social media via the World Wide Web offered people in families, localities, nations, and the world a new way of communicating. Thus, both opportunities and challenges lie ahead for citizens of the West and of the world as they make the transition to what some are calling the Digital Age.

The challenge to the making of the West today involves the inventive human spirit. Over the past five hundred years, the West has benefited from its scientific and technological advances and perhaps never more so than in the Digital Age. Although communication and information technology have brought people closer to one another than ever before, the use of technology has made the period from 1900 to the present one of the bloodiest eras in human history—and one during which the use of technology has threatened, and still threatens, the future of the earth as a home for the human race. While technology has enhanced daily life, it has also facilitated war, genocide, terrorism, and environmental deterioration, all of which pose great challenges to the West and to the world; the use of digital media to promote violent causes, inflame others, and network with and recruit new followers has made some of these challenges even more significant. How will the human race adapt to the creativity the Digital Age has unleashed? How will the West and the world manage both the promises and the challenges of Digital Age technology to protect the human race in the years ahead?

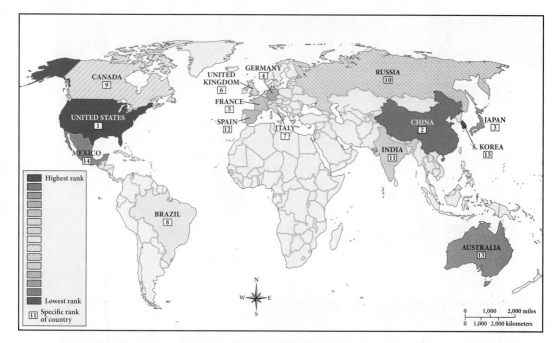

MAPPING THE WEST   The World's Top Fifteen Economies as of 2015   From the nineteenth to the twenty-first centuries, the comparative economic strength of individual nations changed considerably. In the nineteenth century, India and China had the largest economies; they were eclipsed by the European powers as the Industrial Revolution progressed. The European powers in turn were eventually overtaken by the United States. By the end of the twentieth century, the reemergence of non-Western economic powerhouses marked another transformation. How would you describe economic dynamism in the twenty-first century as shown in the map?

Chapter Review

KEY TERMS AND PEOPLE

Be sure you can identify the term or person and explain its historical significance.

globalization (p. 882)

Slobodan Milosevic (p. 883)

ethnic cleansing (p. 884)

Vladimir Putin (p. 887)

Maastricht Treaty (p. 890)

European Union (EU) (p. 890)

euro (p. 890)

nongovernmental organizations (NGOs)
(p. 894)

global warming (p. 895)

Green Party (p. 896)

Osama bin Laden (p. 898)

Pacific tigers (p. 901)

Salman Rushdie (p. 908)

Toni Morrison (p. 908)

postmodernism (p. 910)

REVIEW QUESTIONS

1. What were the major issues facing the former Soviet bloc in the 1990s and early 2000s?

2. What trends suggest that the nation-state was a declining institution at the beginning of the twenty-first century?

3. What were the principal challenges facing the West at the beginning of the twenty-first century?

4. What social and cultural questions has globalization raised?

MAKING CONNECTIONS

1. In what ways were the global connections at the beginning of the twenty-first century different from the global connections at the beginning of the twentieth century?

2. How did the Western nation-state of the early twenty-first century differ from the Western nation-state at the opening of the twentieth century?

3. Migration has been a major factor across the human past. How has it affected the West differently in the twenty-first century?

4. Economic crises caused by climate change, the spread of disease, and trade and financial disturbances have been constants throughout history. How does the economic crisis that began in 2007 compare to earlier crises?

IMPORTANT EVENTS

1990s   • Internet revolution

1990–1991   • War in Persian Gulf

1991   • Civil war erupts in former Yugoslavia; failed coup by Communist hard-liners in Soviet Union

1992   • Soviet Union is dissolved

1993   • Toni Morrison wins Nobel Prize for Literature; Czechoslovakia splits into Czech Republic and Slovakia

1994   • Nelson Mandela is elected president of South Africa; Russian troops invade Chechnya; European Union is officially formed

1999   • European Union introduces the euro; world population reaches six billion

2000   • Vladimir Putin becomes president of Russia

2001   • September 11 terrorist attacks; United States declares "war against terrorism," attacks Afghanistan

2003   • United States invades Iraq; the West divides on this policy

2004   • Ten countries join European Union

2005   • Emissions reductions of Kyoto Protocol go into effect

2007   • Bulgaria and Romania are admitted to European Union; world economic crisis begins

2009   • Barack Obama becomes the first African American president of the United States

2010   • China overtakes Japan to become world's second largest economy

2014   • Russia annexes Crimea and sends military assistance to anti-Ukraine forces

Glossary of Key Terms and People

This glossary contains definitions of terms and people that are central to your understanding of the material covered in this textbook. Each term or person in the glossary is in **boldface** in the text when it is first defined. We have also included the page number on which the full discussion of the term or person appears so that you can easily locate the complete explanation to strengthen your historical vocabulary.

For words or names not defined here, two additional resources may be useful: the index, which will direct you to many more topics discussed in the text, and a good dictionary.

abolitionists (527): Advocates of the abolition of the slave trade and of slavery.

absolutism (457): A system of government in which the ruler claims sole and uncontestable power.

agricultural revolution (499): Increasingly aggressive attitudes toward investment in and management of land that increased production of food in the 1700s.

Alexander II (645): Russian tsar (r. 1855–1881) who initiated the age of Great Reforms and emancipated the serfs in 1861.

Anabaptists (411): Sixteenth-century Protestants who believed that only adults could truly have faith and accept baptism.

anarchism (663): The belief that people should not have government; it was popular among some peasants and workers in the last half of the nineteenth century and the first decades of the twentieth.

appeasement (797): Making concessions in the face of grievances as a way of preventing conflict.

art nouveau (717): An early-twentieth-century artistic style in graphics, fashion, and household design that featured flowing, sinuous lines, borrowed in large part from Asian art.

Atlantic system (490): The network of trade established in the 1700s that bound together western Europe, Africa, and the Americas. Europeans sold slaves from western Africa and bought commodities that were produced by the new colonial plantations in North and South America and the Caribbean.

baroque (buh ROHK) (451): An artistic style of the seventeenth century that featured curves, exaggerated lighting, intense emotions, release from restraint, and even a kind of artistic sensationalism.

battle of Waterloo (592): The final battle lost by Napoleon; it took place near Brussels on June 18, 1815, and led to the deposed emperor's final exile.

Beauvoir, Simone de (see MAWN duh bohv WAHR) (838): Author of *The Second Sex* (1949), a globally influential work that created an interpretation of women's age-old inferior status from existentialist philosophy.

Beethoven, Ludwig van (598): The German composer (1770–1827) who helped set the direction of musical romanticism; his music used recurring and evolving themes to convey the impression of natural growth.

bin Laden, Osama (898): Wealthy leader of the militant Islamic group al-Qaeda, which executed terrorist plots, including the September 11, 2001, attacks on the United States, to end the presence of U.S. forces in his home country, Saudi Arabia.

Bismarck, Otto von (651): 1815–1898. Leading Prussian politician and German prime minister who waged war in order to create a united German Empire, which was established in 1871.

Blitzkrieg (798): Literally, "lightning war"; a strategy for the conduct of war (used by the Germans in World War II) in which motorized firepower quickly and over-whelmingly attacks the enemy, leaving it unable to resist psychologically or militarily.

Bolívar, Simón (602): The Venezuelan-born, European-educated aristocrat (1783–1830) who became one of the leaders of the Latin American independence movement in the 1820s. Bolivia is named after him.

Bolshevik Revolution (759): The overthrow of Russia's Provisional Government in the fall of 1917 by V. I. Lenin and his Bolshevik forces.

Bonaparte, Louis-Napoleon (633): Nephew of Napoleon I (1808–1873); he was elected president of France in 1848, declared himself Emperor Napoleon III in 1852, and ruled until 1870.

Bonaparte, Napoleon (580): 1769–1821. The French general who became First Consul in 1799 and emperor (Napoleon I) in 1804; after losing the battle of Waterloo in 1815, he was exiled to the island of St. Helena.

buccaneers (496): Pirates of the Caribbean who governed themselves and preyed on international shipping.

bureaucracy (462): A network of state officials carrying out orders according to a regular and routine line of authority.

Calvin, John (408): French-born Christian humanist (1509–1564) and founder of Calvinism, one of the major branches of the Protestant Reformation; he led the reform movement in Geneva, Switzerland, from 1541 to 1564.

capital-intensive industry (687): A mid- to late-nineteenth-century development in industry that required great investments of money for machinery and infrastructure to make a profit.

Cavour, Camillo di (649): Prime minister (1852–1861) of the kingdom of Piedmont-Sardinia and architect of a united Italy.

Chaplin, Charlie (791): Major entertainment leader, whose sympathetic portrayals of the common man and satires of Hitler helped preserve democratic values in the 1930s and 1940s.

Charles V (407): Holy Roman Emperor (r. 1519–1556) and the most powerful ruler in sixteenth-century Europe; he reigned over the Low Countries, Spain, Spain's Italian and New World dominions, and the Austrian Habsburg lands.

Chartism (631): The British movement of supporters of the People's Charter (1838), which demanded universal manhood suffrage, vote by secret ballot, equal electoral districts, and other reforms.

Christian Democrats (824): Powerful center to center-right political parties that evolved in the late 1940s from former Catholic parties of the pre–World War II period.

Christian humanism (404): A general intellectual trend in the sixteenth century that coupled love of classical learning, as in Renaissance humanism, with an emphasis on Christian piety.

Civil Code (584): The French legal code formulated by Napoleon in 1804; it ensured equal treatment under the law to all men and guaranteed religious liberty, but it curtailed many rights of women.

civil disobedience (780): The act of deliberately but peacefully breaking the law, a tactic used by Mohandas Gandhi in India and earlier by British suffragists to protest oppression and obtain political change.

classicism (481): A seventeenth-century style of painting and architecture that reflected the ideals of the art of antiquity; in classicism, geometric shapes, order, and harmony of lines took precedence over the sensuous, exuberant, and emotional forms of the baroque.

cold war (815): The rivalry between the United States and the Soviet Union from 1945 to 1989 that led to massive growth in nuclear weapons on both sides.

Columbus, Christopher (400): An Italian sailor (1451–1506) who opened up the New World by sailing west across the Atlantic in search of a route to Asia.

communists (631): Those socialists who after 1840 (when the word was first used) advocated the abolition of private property in favor of communal, collective ownership.

Congress of Vienna (593): Face-to-face negotiations (1814–1815) between the great powers to settle the boundaries of European states and determine who would rule each nation after the defeat of Napoleon.

conservatism (595): A political doctrine that emerged after 1789 and took hold after 1815; it rejected much of the Enlightenment and the French Revolution, preferring monarchies over republics, tradition over revolution, and established religion over Enlightenment skepticism.

constitutionalism (458): A system of government in which rulers share power with parliaments made up of elected representatives.

consumer revolution (497): The rapid increase in consumption of new staples produced in the Atlantic system as well as of other items of daily life that were previously unavailable or beyond the reach of ordinary people.

Continental System (590): The boycott of British goods in France and its satellites ordered by Napoleon in 1806; it had success but was later undermined by smuggling.

Corn Laws (629): Tariffs on grain in Great Britain that benefited landowners by preventing the import of cheap foreign grain; they were repealed by the British government in 1846.

Cortés, Hernán (401): The Spanish explorer (1485–1547) who captured the Aztec capital, Tenochtitlán (present-day Mexico City), in 1519.

Council of Trent (414): A general council of the Catholic church that met at Trent between 1545 and 1563 to set Catholic doctrine, reform church practices, and defend the church against the Protestant challenge.

Cuban missile crisis (843): The confrontation in 1962 between the United States and the USSR over Soviet installation of missile sites off the U.S. coast in Cuba.

cult (50): In ancient Greece, a set of official, publicly funded religious activities for a deity overseen by priests and priestesses.

cult of the offensive (745): A military strategy of constantly attacking the enemy that was believed to be the key to winning World War I but that brought great loss of life while failing to bring decisive victory.

Darwin, Charles (668): The English naturalist (1809–1882) who popularized the theory of evolution by means of natural selection and thereby challenged the biblical story of creation.

de-Christianization (565): During the French Revolution, the campaign of extremist republicans against organized churches and in favor of a belief system based on reason.

Declaration of the Rights of Man and Citizen (559): The preamble to the French constitution drafted in August 1789; it established the sovereignty of the nation and equal rights for citizens.

decolonization (831): The process — whether violent or peaceful — by which colonies gained their independence from the imperial powers after World War II.

deists (526): Those who believe in God but give him no active role in human affairs. Deists of the Enlightenment believed that God had designed the universe and set it in motion but no longer intervened in its functioning.

DNA (853): The genetic material that forms the basis of each cell; the discovery of its structure in 1952 revolutionized genetics, molecular biology, and other scientific and medical fields.

domesticity (623): An ideology prevailing in the nineteenth century that women should devote themselves to their families and the home.

Dual Alliance (702): A defensive alliance between Germany and Austria-Hungary created in 1879 as part of Bismarck's system of alliances to prevent or limit war. It was joined by Italy in 1882 as a third partner and then called the Triple Alliance.

dual monarchy (655): The shared power arrangement between the Habsburg Empire and Hungary after the Prussian defeat of the Austrian Empire in 1866–1867.

Duma (730): The Russian parliament set up in the aftermath of the outbreak of the Revolution of 1905.

Edict of Nantes (428): The decree issued by French king Henry IV in 1598 that granted the Huguenots a large measure of religious toleration.

Einstein, Albert (715): Scientist (1879–1955) whose theory of relativity (1905) revolutionized modern physics and other fields of thought.

Eliot, George (665): The pen name of English novelist Mary Ann Evans (1819–1880), who described the harsh reality of many ordinary people's lives in her works.

Elizabeth I (432): English queen (r. 1558–1603) who oversaw the return of the Protestant Church of England and, in 1588, the successful defense of the realm against the Spanish Armada.

Enabling Act (785): The legislation passed in 1933 suspending constitutional government for four years in order to meet the crisis in the German economy.

enlightened despots (538): Rulers—such as Catherine the Great of Russia, Frederick the Great of Prussia, and Joseph II of Austria—who tried to promote Enlightenment reforms without giving up their own supreme political power; also called enlightened absolutists.

Enlightenment (514): The eighteenth-century intellectual movement whose proponents believed that human beings could apply a critical, reasoning spirit to every problem.

Entente Cordiale (733): An alliance between Britain and France that began with an agreement in 1904 to honor colonial holdings.

Estates General (555): A body of deputies from the three estates, or orders, of France: the clergy (First Estate), the nobility (Second Estate), and everyone else (Third Estate).

ethnic cleansing (884): The mass murder—genocide—of people according to ethnicity or nationality; it can also include eliminating all traces of the murdered people's past. Examples include the post–World War I elimination of minorities in eastern and central Europe and the rape and murders that resulted from the breakup of Yugoslavia in the 1990s.

euro (890): The common currency in seventeen member states of the European Union (EU) and of EU institutions. It went into effect gradually, used first in business transactions in 1999 and entering public circulation in 2002.

European Economic Community (EEC or Common Market) (826): A consortium of six European countries established in 1957 to promote free trade and economic cooperation among its members; its membership and activities expanded over the years, and it later evolved into the European Union (EU).

European Union (EU) (890): Formerly the European Economic Community (EEC, or Common Market), and then the European Community (EC); formed in 1994 by the terms of the Maastricht Treaty. Its members have political ties through the European parliament as well as long-standing common economic, legal, and business mechanisms.

existentialism (838): A philosophy prominent after World War II developed primarily by Jean-Paul Sartre to stress the importance of action in the creation of an authentic self.

family allowance (788): Government funds given to families with children to boost the birthrate in democratic countries (e.g., Sweden during the Great Depression) and totalitarian ones alike.

fascism (770): A doctrine that emphasizes violence and glorifies the state over the people and their individual or civil rights; in Italy, the Fascist Party took hold in the 1920s as Mussolini consolidated power.

First Consul (581): The most important of the three consuls established by the French Constitution of 1800; the title, given to Napoleon Bonaparte, was taken from ancient Rome.

five-year plans (781): Centralized programs for economic development begun in 1929 by Joseph Stalin and copied by Adolf Hitler; these plans set production priorities and gave production targets for individual industries and agriculture.

Fourteen Points (751): U.S. president Woodrow Wilson's World War I peace proposal; based on settlement rather than on conquest, it encouraged the surrender of the Central Powers.

Franco, Francisco (794): 1892–1975. Right-wing general who in 1936 successfully overthrew the democratic republic in Spain and instituted a repressive dictatorship.

Frederick William of Hohenzollern (477): The Great Elector of Brandenburg-Prussia (r. 1640–1688) who brought his nation through the end of the Thirty Years' War and then succeeded in welding his scattered lands into an absolutist state.

Freemasons (534): Members of Masonic lodges, where nobles and middle-class professionals (and even some artisans) shared interest in the Enlightenment and reform.

Freud, Sigmund (713): Viennese medical doctor (1856–1939) and founder, in the late nineteenth century, of psychoanalysis, a theory of mental processes and problems and a method of treating them.

Gladstone, William (698): 1809–1898. Liberal politician and prime minister of Great Britain who innovated popular campaigning and who criticized British imperialism.

glasnost (873): Literally "openness" or "publicity"; a policy instituted in the 1980s by Soviet premier Mikhail Gorbachev calling for greater openness in speech and in thinking, which translated to the reduction of censorship in publishing, radio, television, and other media.

globalization (882): The interconnection of labor, capital, ideas, services, and goods around the world. Although globalization has existed for hundreds of years, the late twentieth and early twenty-first centuries are seen as more global because of the speed with which people, goods, and ideas travel the world.

global warming (895): An increase in the temperature of Earth's lower atmosphere resulting from a buildup of chemical emissions.

Glorious Revolution (470): The events of 1688 when Tories and Whigs replaced England's monarch James II with his Protestant daughter, Mary, and her husband, Dutch ruler William of Orange; William and Mary agreed to a Bill of Rights that guaranteed rights to Parliament.

Gorbachev, Mikhail (873): 1931–. Leader of the Soviet Union (1985–1991) who instituted reforms such as glasnost and perestroika, thereby contributing to the collapse of Communist rule in the Soviet bloc and the USSR.

Great Fear (558): The term used by historians to describe the French rural panic of 1789, which led to peasant attacks on aristocrats or on seigneurial records of peasants' dues.

Green Party (896): A political party first formed in West Germany in 1979 to bring about environmentally sound policies. It spread across Europe and around the world thereafter.

heliocentrism (446): The view articulated by Polish clergyman Nicolaus Copernicus that the earth and other planets revolve around the sun.

Henry VIII (409): The English king (r. 1509–1547) who first opposed the Protestant Reformation and then broke with the Catholic church, naming himself head of the Church of England in the Act of Supremacy of 1534.

Hitler, Adolf (784): 1889–1945. Chancellor of Germany (1933–1945) who, with considerable backing, overturned democratic government, created the Third Reich, persecuted millions, and ultimately led Germany and the world into World War II.

home rule (698): The right to an independent parliament demanded by the Irish and resisted by the British from the second half of the nineteenth century on.

ideology (610): A word coined during the French Revolution to refer to a coherent set of beliefs about the way the social and political order should be organized.

imperialism (624): European dominance of the non-West through economic exploitation and political rule; the word (as distinct from *colonialism,* which usually implied establishment of settler colonies, often with slavery) was coined in the mid-nineteenth century.

impressionism (694): A mid- to late-nineteenth-century artistic style that captured the sensation of light in images, derived from Japanese influences and in opposition to the realism of photographs.

Industrial Revolution (610): The transformation of life in the Western world over several decades in the late eighteenth and early nineteenth centuries as a result of the introduction of steam-driven machinery, large factories, and a new working class.

in vitro fertilization (854): A process developed in the 1970s by which human eggs are fertilized with sperm outside the body and then implanted in a woman's uterus.

Jacobin Club (562): A French political club formed in 1789 that inspired the formation of a national network whose members dominated the revolutionary government during the Terror.

Jesuits (415): Members of the Society of Jesus, a Catholic religious order founded by Ignatius of Loyola (1491–1556) and approved by the pope in 1540. Jesuits served as missionaries and educators all over the world.

Kennedy, John Fitzgerald (843): 1917–1963. U.S. president (1961–1963) who faced off with Soviet leader Nikita Khrushchev in the Cuban missile crisis.

Khrushchev, Nikita (nyih KEE tuh kroosh CHAWF) (830): 1894–1971. Leader of the USSR from c. 1955 until his dismissal in 1964; known for his speech denouncing Stalin, creation of the "thaw," and participation in the Cuban missile crisis.

Koine (koy NAY) (118): The "common" or "shared" form of the Greek language that became the international language in the Hellenistic period.

Kollontai, Aleksandra (769): A Russian activist (1872–1952) and minister of public welfare in the Bolshevik government who promoted social programs such as birth control and day care for children of working parents.

Kulturkampf (667): Literally, "culture war"; a term used in the 1870s by German chancellor Otto von Bismarck to describe his fight to weaken the power of the Catholic church.

laissez-faire (LEH say FEHR) (528): French for "leave alone"; an economic doctrine developed by Adam Smith that advocated freeing the economy from government intervention and control.

League of Nations (758): The international organization set up following World War I to maintain peace by arbitrating disputes and promoting collective security.

Lebensraum (793): Literally, "living space"; the land that Hitler proposed to conquer so that the people he defined as true Aryans might have sufficient space to live their noble lives.

Lenin, V. I. (752): 1870–1924. Bolshevik leader who executed the Bolshevik Revolution in the fall of 1917, took Russia out of World War I, and imposed communism in Russia.

Leopold II (679): King of Belgium (r. 1865–1909) who sponsored the takeover of the Congo in Africa, which he ran with great violence against native peoples.

Lepanto (429): A site off the Greek coast where, in 1571, the allied Catholic forces of Spain's king Philip II, Venice, and the papacy defeated the Ottoman Turks in a great sea battle; the victory gave the Christian powers control of the Mediterranean.

Levellers (467): Disgruntled soldiers in Oliver Cromwell's New Model Army who in 1647 wanted to "level" social differences and extend political participation to all male property owners.

liberalism (628): An economic and political ideology that—tracing its roots to John Locke in the seventeenth century and Enlightenment philosophers in the eighteenth—emphasized free trade and the constitutional guarantees of individual rights such as freedom of speech and religion; its adherents stood between conservatives on the right and revolutionaries on the left in the nineteenth century.

limited liability corporation (687): A legal entity, such as a factory or other enterprise, developed in the second half of the nineteenth century whose owners were liable for only restricted (limited) amounts of money owed to creditors in the case of financial failure.

Louis XIV (458): French king (r. 1643–1715) who in theory personified absolutism but in practice had to gain the cooperation of nobles, local officials, and even the ordinary subjects who manned his armies and paid his taxes.

Louis XVI (554): French king (r. 1774–1792) who was tried for treason during the French Revolution; he was executed on January 21, 1793.

Luther, Martin (406): A German monk (1483–1546) who started the Protestant Reformation in 1517 by challenging the practices and doctrines of the Catholic church and advocating salvation through faith alone.

Maastricht Treaty (890): The agreement among the members of the European Community to have a closer alliance, including the use of common passports and eventually the development of a common currency; by the terms of this treaty, the European Community became the European Union (EU) in 1994.

mandate system (758): The political control over the former colonies and territories of the German and Ottoman Empires granted to the victors of World War I by the League of Nations.

Marie-Antoinette (554): Wife of Louis XVI and queen of France who was tried for treason during the French Revolution and executed in October 1793.

Marshall Plan (819): A post–World War II program funded by the United States to get Europe back on its feet economically and thereby reduce the appeal of communism. It played an important role in the rebirth of European prosperity in the 1950s.

Marxism (664): A body of thought about the organization of production, social inequality, and the processes of revolutionary change as devised by the philosopher and economist Karl Marx.

Mazzini, Giuseppe (626): An Italian nationalist (1805–1872) who founded Young Italy, a secret society to promote Italian unity. He believed that a popular uprising would create a unified Italy.

Médicis, Catherine de (428): Italian-born mother of French king Charles IX (r. 1560–1574); she served as regent and tried but failed to prevent religious warfare between Calvinists and Catholics.

mercantilism (462): The economic doctrine that governments must intervene to increase national wealth by whatever means possible.

mestizo (496): A person born to a Spanish father and a native American mother.

Methodism (532): A religious movement founded by John Wesley (1703–1791) that broke with the Church of England and insisted on strict self-discipline and a "methodical" approach to religious study and observance.

Metternich, Klemens von (KLAY mehnts fawn MEH tur nihk) (593): An Austrian prince (1773–1859) who took the lead in devising the post-Napoleonic settlement arranged by the Congress of Vienna (1814–1815).

Milosevic, Slobodan (883): President of Serbia (1989–1997) who pushed for Serb control of post-Communist Yugoslavia; in 2002, he was tried for crimes against humanity in the ethnic cleansing that accompanied the dissolution of the Yugoslav state.

mir (mihr) (646): A Russian farm community that provided for holding land in common and regulating the movements of any individual by the group.

Mitteleuropa (miht el oy ROH pah) (733): Literally, "central Europe," but used by military leaders in Germany before World War I to refer to land in both central and eastern Europe that they hoped to acquire.

modernism (714): Artistic styles around the turn of the twentieth century that featured a break with realism in art and literature and with lyricism in music.

Morrison, Toni (908): The first African American woman to win the Nobel Prize for Literature; her works include *Beloved* (1987), *Jazz* (1992), and *A Mercy* (2008).

multinational corporation (854): A business that operates in many foreign countries by sending large segments of its manufacturing, finance, sales, and other business components abroad.

Mussolini, Benito (770): 1883–1945. Leader of Italian fascist movement and, after the March on Rome in 1922, dictator of Italy.

nationalism (626): An ideology that arose in the nineteenth century and that holds that all peoples derive their identities from their nations, which are defined by common language, shared cultural traditions, and sometimes religion.

nation-state (649): An independent political unit of modern times based on representing a united people.

Nazi-Soviet Pact (797): The agreement reached in 1939 by Germany and the Soviet Union in which both agreed not to attack the other in case of war and to divide any conquered territories.

neoliberalism (871): A theory first promoted by British prime minister Margaret Thatcher, calling for a return to liberal principles of the nineteenth century, including the reduction of welfare-state programs and the cutting of taxes for the wealthy to promote economic growth.

new unionism (696): A nineteenth-century development in labor organizing that replaced local craft-based unions with those that extended membership to all kinds of workers.

new woman (712): A woman who, from the 1880s on, dressed practically, moved about freely, and often supported herself.

Nicholas II (722): Tsar of Russia (r. 1894–1917) who promoted anti-Semitism and resisted reform in the empire.

Nietzsche, Friedrich (715): Late-nineteenth-century German philosopher (1844–1900) who called for a new morality in the face of God's death at the hands of science and whose theories were reworked by his sister to emphasize militarism and anti-Semitism.

Nightingale, Florence (646): The Englishwoman who in the nineteenth century pioneered the professionalization of nursing and the use of statistics in the study of public health and the well-being of the military.

Nixon, Richard (866): 1913–1994. U.S. president (1969–1974) who escalated the Vietnam War, worked for accommodation with China, and resigned from the presidency after trying to block free elections.

nongovernmental organizations (NGOs) (894): Charitable foundations and activist groups such as Doctors Without Borders that work outside of governments, often on political, economic, and relief issues; also, philanthropic organizations such as the Rockefeller, Ford, and Open Society Foundations that shape economic and social policy and the course of political reform.

North Atlantic Treaty Organization (NATO) (822): The security alliance formed in 1949 to provide a unified military force for the United States, Canada, and their allies in western Europe and Scandinavia.

Nuremberg Laws (787): Legislation enacted by the Nazis in 1935 that deprived Jewish Germans of their citizenship and imposed many other hardships on them.

Opium War (625): War between China and Great Britain (1839–1842) that resulted in the opening of four Chinese ports to Europeans and British sovereignty over Hong Kong.

Organization of Petroleum Exporting Countries (OPEC) (868): A consortium that regulated the supply and export of oil and that acted with more unanimity after the United States supported Israel against the Arabs in the wars of the late 1960s and early 1970s.

Ostpolitik (860): A policy initiated by West German foreign minister Willy Brandt in the late 1960s in which West Germany sought better economic relations with the Communist countries of eastern Europe.

outwork (684): The nineteenth-century process of having some aspects of industrial work done outside factories in individual homes.

Pacific tigers (901): Countries of East Asia so named because of their massive economic growth, much of it from the 1980s on; foremost among these were Japan and China.

Pankhurst, Emmeline (721): 1858–1928. Organizer of a militant branch of the British suffrage movement, working actively for women's right to vote.

Pan-Slavism (655): The nineteenth-century movement calling for the unity of all Slavs across national and regional boundaries.

Parnell, Charles Stewart (698): Irish politician (1846–1891) whose advocacy of home rule was a thorn in the side of the British establishment.

partition of Poland (540): Division of one-third of Poland-Lithuania's territory between Prussia, Russia, and Austria in 1772.

Peace of Augsburg (421): The treaty of 1555 that settled disputes between Holy Roman Emperor Charles V and his Protestant princes. It recognized the Lutheran church and established the principle that all Catholic or Lutheran princes enjoyed the sole right to determine the religion of their lands and subjects.

Peace of Paris (756): The series of peace treaties (1919–1920) that provided the settlement of World War I. The Treaty of Versailles with Germany was the centerpiece of the Peace of Paris.

Peace of Westphalia (436): The settlement (1648) of the Thirty Years' War; it established enduring religious divisions in the Holy Roman Empire by which Lutheranism would dominate in the north, Calvinism in the area of the Rhine River, and Catholicism in the south.

perestroika (873): Literally, "restructuring"; an economic policy instituted in the 1980s by Soviet premier Mikhail Gorbachev calling for the introduction of market mechanisms and the achievement of greater efficiency in manufacturing, agriculture, and services.

Peter the Great (508): Russian tsar Peter I (r. 1689–1725), who undertook the Westernization of Russia and built a new capital city named after himself, St. Petersburg.

Philip II (429): King of Spain (r. 1556–1598) and the most powerful ruler in Europe; he reigned over the western Habsburg lands and all the Spanish colonies recently settled in the New World.

philosophes (fee luh SAWF) (523): French for "philosophers"; public intellectuals of the Enlightenment who wrote on subjects ranging from current affairs to art criticism with the goal of furthering reform in society.

Pietism (503): A Protestant revivalist movement of the early eighteenth century that emphasized deeply emotional individual religious experience.

plantation (492): A large tract of land that produced staple crops such as sugar, coffee, and tobacco; was farmed by slave labor; and was owned by a colonial settler.

politiques (poh lih TEEK) (428): Political advisers during the sixteenth-century French Wars of Religion who argued that compromise in matters of religion would strengthen the monarchy.

pop art (857): A style in the visual arts that mimicked advertising and consumerism and that used ordinary objects as a part of paintings and other compositions.

Popular Front (790): An alliance of political parties (initially led by Léon Blum in France) in the 1930s to resist fascism despite philosophical differences.

positivism (670): A theory developed in the mid-nineteenth century that the study of facts would generate accurate, or "positive," laws of society and that these laws could, in turn, help in the formulation of policies and legislation.

postmodernism (910): A term applied in the late twentieth century to both an intense stylistic mixture in the arts without a central unifying theme or elite set of standards and a critique of Enlightenment and scientific beliefs in rationality and the possibility of certain knowledge.

predestination (409): John Calvin's doctrine that God preordained salvation or damnation for each person before creation; those chosen for salvation were considered the "elect."

Pugachev (poo guh CHAWF) **rebellion** (544): A massive revolt of Russian Cossacks and serfs in 1773 against local nobles and the armies of Catherine the Great; its leader, Emelian Pugachev, was eventually captured and executed.

pump priming (786): An economic policy used by governments, including the Nazis in Germany, to stimulate the economy through public works programs and other infusions of public funds.

purges (782): The series of attacks on citizens of the USSR accused of being "wreckers," or saboteurs of communism, in the 1930s and later.

Puritans (432): Strict Calvinists who in the sixteenth and seventeenth centuries opposed all vestiges of Catholic ritual in the Church of England.

Putin, Vladimir (887): President of Russia from 2000 to 2008; prime minister 2008–present. He has worked to reestablish Russia as a world power through control of the country's resources and military capabilities.

raison d'état (ray ZOHN day TAH) (438): French for "reason of state," the political doctrine, first proposed by Cardinal Richelieu of France, which held that the state's interests should prevail over those of religion.

Razin, Stenka (479): 1630–1671. Leader of the 1667 rebellion that promised Russian peasants liberation from noble landowners and officials; he was captured by the tsar's army in 1671 and publicly executed in Moscow.

realism (665): An artistic style that arose in the mid-nineteenth century and was dedicated to depicting society realistically without romantic or idealistic overtones.

Realpolitik (ray AHL poh lih teek) (642): Policies developed after the revolutions of 1848 and initially associated with nation building; they were based on realism rather than on the romantic notions of earlier nationalists. The term has come to mean any policy based on considerations of power alone.

Reform Act of 1884 (698): British legislation that granted the right to vote to a mass male citizenry.

Reform Bill of 1832 (605): A measure passed by the British Parliament to increase the number of male voters by about 50 percent and give representation to new cities in the north; it set a precedent for widening suffrage.

restoration (594): The epoch after the fall of Napoleon, in which the Congress of Vienna aimed to "restore" as many regimes as possible to their former rulers.

revocation of the Edict of Nantes (462): French king Louis XIV's 1685 decision to eliminate the rights of Calvinists granted in the edict of 1598; Louis banned all Calvinist public activities and forced those who refused to embrace the state religion to flee.

Robespierre, Maximilien (roh behs PYEHR) (563): A lawyer (1758–1794) from northern France who, as leader of the Committee of Public Safety, laid out the principles of a republic of virtue and of the Terror; his arrest and execution in July 1794 brought an end to the Terror.

rococo (502): A style of painting that emphasized irregularity and asymmetry, movement and curvature, but on a smaller, more intimate scale than the baroque.

romanticism (530): An artistic movement of the late eighteenth and early nineteenth centuries that glorified nature, emotion, genius, and imagination.

Rousseau, Jean-Jacques (zhahn zhahk roo SOH) (528): One of the most important philosophes (1712–1778); he argued that only a government based on a social contract among the citizens could make people truly moral and free.

Rushdie, Salman (908): Immigrant British author whose novel *The Satanic Verses* (1988) led the ayatollah Ruhollah Khomeini of Iran to issue a fatwa calling for Rushdie's murder.

Russification (648): A program for the integration of Russia's many nationality groups that involved the forced learning of the Russian language and the practice of Russian Orthodox religion as well as the settlement of ethnic Russians among other nationality groups.

salon (483): An informal gathering held regularly in a private home and presided over by a socially eminent woman; salons spread from France in the seventeenth century to other countries in the eighteenth century.

samizdat (861): A key form of dissident activity across the Soviet bloc in which individuals reproduced government-suppressed publications by hand and passed them from reader to reader, thus building a foundation for the successful resistance of the 1980s.

Sand, George (620): The pen name of French novelist Amandine-Aurore-Lucile Dupin Dudevant (1804–1876), who showed her independence in the 1830s by dressing like a man and smoking cigars. The term *George-Sandism* became an expression of disdain for independent women.

Schlieffen Plan (745): The Germans' strategy in World War I that called for attacks on two fronts—concentrating first on France to the west and then turning east to attack Russia.

scientific method (445): The combination of experimental observation and mathematical deduction used to determine the laws of nature; first developed in the seventeenth century, it became the secular standard of truth.

Scott, Sir Walter (599): A prolific author (1771–1832) of popular historical novels; he also collected and published traditional Scottish ballads and wrote poetry.

Second International (696): A transnational organization of workers established in 1889, mostly committed to Marxian socialism.

secularization (445): The long-term trend toward separating state power and science from religious faith, making the latter a private domain; begun in the seventeenth century, it prompted a search for nonreligious explanations for political authority and natural phenomena.

Seven Years' War (539): A worldwide series of battles (1756–1763) between Austria, France, Russia, and Sweden on one side and Prussia and Great Britain on the other.

social contract (471): The doctrine, originated by Hugo Grotius and argued by both Thomas Hobbes and John Locke, that all political authority derives not from divine right but from an implicit contract between citizens and their rulers.

socialism (629): A social and political ideology, originating in the early nineteenth century, that advocated the reorganization of society to overcome the new tensions created by industrialization and restore social harmony through communities based on cooperation.

Solidarity (874): A Polish labor union founded in 1980 by Lech Walesa and Anna Walentynowicz that contested Communist Party programs and eventually succeeded in ousting the party from the Polish government.

South African War (726): The war (1899–1902) between Britain and the Boer (originally Dutch) inhabitants of South Africa for control of the region; also called the Boer War.

soviets (751): Councils of workers and soldiers first formed in Russia in the Revolution of 1905; they were revived to represent the people in the early days of the 1917 Russian Revolution.

stagflation (868): The combination of a stagnant economy and soaring inflation; a period of stagflation occurred in the West in the 1970s as a result of an OPEC embargo on oil.

Stalin, Joseph (781): 1879–1953. Leader of the USSR who, with considerable backing, formed a brutal dictatorship in the 1930s and forcefully converted the country into an industrial power.

Suleiman the Magnificent (419): Sultan of the Ottoman Empire (r. 1520–1566) at the time of its greatest power.

Terror (563): The policy established under the direction of the Committee of Public Safety during the French Revolution to arrest dissidents and execute opponents in order to protect the republic from its enemies.

Thatcher, Margaret (870): 1925–2013. Prime minister of Britain (1979–1990) who set a new tone for British politics by promoting neoliberal economic policies and criticizing poor people, union members, and racial minorities as worthless, even harmful citizens.

Thermidorian Reaction (569): The violent backlash against the rule of Robespierre that dismantled the Terror and punished Jacobins and their supporters.

Third Republic (698): The French government that succeeded Napoleon III's Second Empire after its defeat in the Franco-Prussian War of 1870–1871. It lasted until France's defeat by Germany in 1940.

total war (743): A war built on the full mobilization of soldiers, civilians, and technology of the nations involved. The term also refers to a highly destructive war of ideologies.

Truman Doctrine (819): The policy devised by U.S. president Harry Truman to limit communism after World War II by countering political crises with economic and military aid.

United Nations (UN) (834): An organization set up in 1945 for collective security and for the resolution of international conflicts through both deliberation and the use of force.

urbanization (616): The growth of towns and cities due to the movement of people from rural to urban areas, a trend that was encouraged by the development of factories and railroads.

Vatican II (838): A Catholic Council held between 1962 and 1965 to modernize some aspects of church teachings (such as condemnation of Jews), to update the liturgy, and to promote cooperation among the faiths (i.e., ecumenism).

Voltaire (515): The pen name of François-Marie Arouet (1694–1778), who was the most influential writer of the early Enlightenment.

Walpole, Robert (507): The first, or "prime," minister (1721–1742) of the House of Commons of Great Britain's Parliament. Although appointed initially by the king, through his long period of leadership he effectively established the modern pattern of parliamentary government.

war guilt clause (758): The part of the Treaty of Versailles that assigned blame for World War I to Germany.

War of the Austrian Succession (512): The war (1740–1748) over the succession to the Habsburg throne that pitted France and Prussia against Austria and Britain and provoked continuing hostilities between French and British settlers in the North American colonies.

Warsaw Pact (822): A security alliance of the Soviet Union and its allies formed in 1955, in retaliation for NATO's admittance of West Germany.

Weimar Republic (756): The parliamentary republic established in 1919 in Germany to replace the monarchy.

welfare state (827): A system (developed on both sides during the cold war) comprising government-sponsored social programs to provide health care, family allowances, disability insurance, and pensions for veterans and retired workers.

Westernization (508): The effort, especially in Peter the Great's Russia, to make society and social customs resemble counterparts in western Europe, especially France, Britain, and the Dutch Republic.

William, prince of Orange (470): Dutch ruler (r. 1689–1702) who, with his Protestant wife, Mary (daughter of James II), ruled England after the Glorious Revolution of 1688.

Zionism (725): A movement that began in the late nineteenth century among European Jews to found a Jewish state.

Index

A note about the index: Names of individuals appear in boldface. Letters in parenthesis following pages refer to: *(i)* illustrations, including photographs and artifacts; *(f)* figures, including charts and graphs; and *(m)* maps.

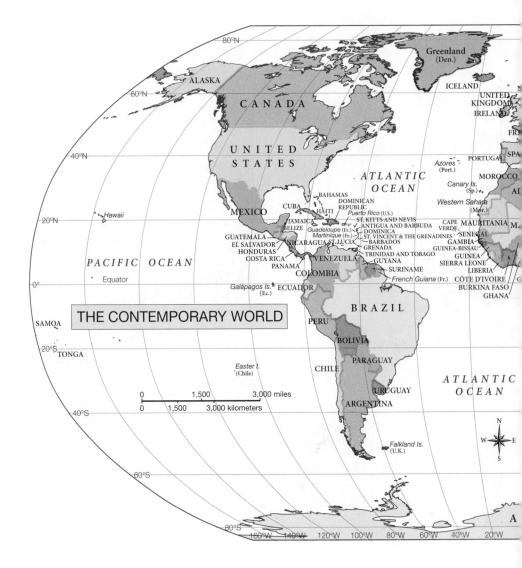

THE CONTEMPORARY WORLD

RCTIC OCEAN

RUSSIAN FEDERATION

SWEDEN
AY FINLAND
DER ESTONIA
H LATVIA
LITHUANIA
POLAND BELARUS
GERMANY UKRAINE
SLK.
AUS.HUNG. MOLDOVA
CR. ROMANIA
ITALY B.H. BULGARIA GEORGIA
KO BMA ARMENIA
GREECE TURKEY
SYRIA AZERBAIJAN
CYPRUS LEBANON IRAQ
ISRAEL IRAN AFGHANISTAN
TUNISIA MALTA JORDAN KUWAIT
Gaza Strip
West Bank BAHRAIN PAKISTAN
LIBYA EGYPT QATAR NEPAL
SAUDI OMAN INDIA
ARABIA
NIGER CHAD SUDAN UNITED ARAB
ERITREA YEMEN EMIRATES
DJIBOUTI
NIGERIA CENTRAL
BENIN AFRICAN SOUTH MALDIVES
TOGO REP. SUDAN ETHIOPIA SRI
CAMEROON UGANDA LANKA
GABON RWANDA KENYA
DEM. REP.
TOME OF THE TANZANIA SEYCHELLES
RINCIPE CONGO
BURUNDI COMOROS
ANGOLA
ZAMBIA MALAWI
NAMIBIA ZIMBABWE MADAGASCAR
BOTSWANA MAURITIUS
MOZAMBIQUE
SOUTH SWAZILAND
AFRICA LESOTHO

KAZAKHSTAN

MONGOLIA

UZBEKISTAN KYRGYZSTAN
TURKMENISTAN TAJIKISTAN

CHINA

N.KOREA
S. KOREA JAPAN

BHUTAN
BANGLADESH MYANMAR
(BURMA)
LAOS
THAILAND
CAMBODIA VIETNAM
BRUNEI
MALAYSIA

SINGAPORE

INDONESIA

TAIWAN

PACIFIC OCEAN

Mariana Is.
(U.S.)

Guam
(U.S.)

PHILIPPINES

PALAU

MARSHALL
IS.

FEDERATED STATES
OF MICRONESIA

NAURU

KIRIBATI

INDIAN OCEAN

TIMOR
LESTE

PAPUA
NEW
GUINEA

SOLOMON
IS.

TUVALU

VANUATU FIJI

AUSTRALIA

New Caledonia
(Fr.)

NEW
ZEALAND

Tasmania
(AUST.)

ABBREVIATIONS	
ALB.	ALBANIA
AUS.	AUSTRIA
BEL.	BELGIUM
B.H.	BOSNIA AND HERZEGOVINA
CR.	CROATIA
CZ.	CZECH REPUBLIC
DEN.	DENMARK
HUNG.	HUNGARY
KO.	KOSOVO
LUX.	LUXEMBOURG
MAC.	MACEDONIA
MO.	MONTENEGRO
NETH.	NETHERLANDS
SE.	SERBIA
SLK.	SLOVAKIA
SLN.	SLOVENIA
SWITZ.	SWITZERLAND

TARCTICA

20°E   40°E   60°E   80°E   100°E   120°E   140°E   160°E

ABOUT THE AUTHORS

Lynn Hunt (PhD, Stanford University) is Eugen Weber Professor of Modern European History at University of California, Los Angeles. She is the author or editor of several books, including most recently *Inventing Human Rights*, *Measuring Time, Making History*, and *The Book that Changed Europe*.

Thomas R. Martin (PhD, Harvard University) is Jeremiah O'Connor Professor in Classics at the College of the Holy Cross. He is the author of *Ancient Greece* and *Ancient Rome*, and was one of the originators of *Perseus: Interactive Sources and Studies on Ancient Greece* (www.perseus.tufts.edu/hopper/).

Barbara H. Rosenwein (PhD, University of Chicago) is professor emerita of history at Loyola University Chicago and has been visiting professor at the Universities of Utrecht (Netherlands), Gothenburg (Sweden), and Oxford (Trinity College, England). She is the author or editor of many books, including *A Short History of the Middle Ages* and the very recent *Generations of Feeling: A History of Emotion, 600–1700*.

Bonnie G. Smith (PhD, University of Rochester) is Board of Governors Professor of History at Rutgers University. She is author or editor of several books including *Ladies of the Leisure Class*; *The Gender of History: Men, Women and Historical Practice*; and *The Oxford Encyclopedia of Women in World History*. Currently she is studying the globalization of European culture and society since the seventeenth century.